Communications in Computer and Information Science 1836

Rationale

The CCIS series is devoted to the publication of proceedings of computer science conferences. Its aim is to efficiently disseminate original research results in informatics in printed and electronic form. While the focus is on publication of peer-reviewed full papers presenting mature work, inclusion of reviewed short papers reporting on work in progress is welcome, too. Besides globally relevant meetings with internationally representative program committees guaranteeing a strict peer-reviewing and paper selection process, conferences run by societies or of high regional or national relevance are also considered for publication.

Topics

The topical scope of CCIS spans the entire spectrum of informatics ranging from foundational topics in the theory of computing to information and communications science and technology and a broad variety of interdisciplinary application fields.

Information for Volume Editors and Authors

Publication in CCIS is free of charge. No royalties are paid, however, we offer registered conference participants temporary free access to the online version of the conference proceedings on SpringerLink (http://link.springer.com) by means of an http referrer from the conference website and/or a number of complimentary printed copies, as specified in the official acceptance email of the event.

CCIS proceedings can be published in time for distribution at conferences or as post-proceedings, and delivered in the form of printed books and/or electronically as USBs and/or e-content licenses for accessing proceedings at SpringerLink. Furthermore, CCIS proceedings are included in the CCIS electronic book series hosted in the SpringerLink digital library at http://link.springer.com/bookseries/7899. Conferences publishing in CCIS are allowed to use Online Conference Service (OCS) for managing the whole proceedings lifecycle (from submission and reviewing to preparing for publication) free of charge.

Publication process

The language of publication is exclusively English. Authors publishing in CCIS have to sign the Springer CCIS copyright transfer form, however, they are free to use their material published in CCIS for substantially changed, more elaborate subsequent publications elsewhere. For the preparation of the camera-ready papers/files, authors have to strictly adhere to the Springer CCIS Authors' Instructions and are strongly encouraged to use the CCIS LaTeX style files or templates.

Abstracting/Indexing

CCIS is abstracted/indexed in DBLP, Google Scholar, EI-Compendex, Mathematical Reviews, SCImago, Scopus. CCIS volumes are also submitted for the inclusion in ISI Proceedings.

How to start

To start the evaluation of your proposal for inclusion in the CCIS series, please send an e-mail to ccis@springer.com.

Constantine Stephanidis · Margherita Antona ·
Stavroula Ntoa · Gavriel Salvendy
Editors

HCI International 2023 Posters

25th International Conference on Human-Computer Interaction, HCII 2023 Copenhagen, Denmark, July 23–28, 2023 Proceedings, Part V

Editors
Constantine Stephanidis
University of Crete and Foundation for Research and Technology - Hellas (FORTH)
Heraklion, Crete, Greece

Margherita Antona
Foundation for Research and Technology - Hellas (FORTH)
Heraklion, Crete, Greece

Stavroula Ntoa
Foundation for Research and Technology - Hellas (FORTH)
Heraklion, Crete, Greece

Gavriel Salvendy
University of Central Florida
Orlando, FL, USA

ISSN 1865-0929 ISSN 1865-0937 (electronic)
Communications in Computer and Information Science
ISBN 978-3-031-36003-9 ISBN 978-3-031-36004-6 (eBook)
https://doi.org/10.1007/978-3-031-36004-6

This Springer imprint is published by the registered company Springer Nature Switzerland AG
The registered company address is: Gewerbestrasse 11, 6330 Cham, Switzerland

Foreword

Human-computer interaction (HCI) is acquiring an ever-increasing scientific and industrial importance, as well as having more impact on people's everyday lives, as an ever-growing number of human activities are progressively moving from the physical to the digital world. This process, which has been ongoing for some time now, was further accelerated during the acute period of the COVID-19 pandemic. The HCI International (HCII) conference series, held annually, aims to respond to the compelling need to advance the exchange of knowledge and research and development efforts on the human aspects of design and use of computing systems.

The 25th International Conference on Human-Computer Interaction, HCI International 2023 (HCII 2023), was held in the emerging post-pandemic era as a 'hybrid' event at the AC Bella Sky Hotel and Bella Center, Copenhagen, Denmark, during July 23–28, 2023. It incorporated the 21 thematic areas and affiliated conferences listed below.

A total of 7472 individuals from academia, research institutes, industry, and government agencies from 85 countries submitted contributions, and 1578 papers and 396 posters were included in the volumes of the proceedings that were published just before the start of the conference, these are listed below. The contributions thoroughly cover the entire field of human-computer interaction, addressing major advances in knowledge and effective use of computers in a variety of application areas. These papers provide academics, researchers, engineers, scientists, practitioners and students with state-of-the-art information on the most recent advances in HCI.

The HCI International (HCII) conference also offers the option of presenting 'Late Breaking Work', and this applies both for papers and posters, with corresponding volumes of proceedings that will be published after the conference. Full papers will be included in the 'HCII 2023 - Late Breaking Work - Papers' volumes of the proceedings to be published in the Springer LNCS series, while 'Poster Extended Abstracts' will be included as short research papers in the 'HCII 2023 - Late Breaking Work - Posters' volumes to be published in the Springer CCIS series.

I would like to thank the Program Board Chairs and the members of the Program Boards of all thematic areas and affiliated conferences for their contribution towards the high scientific quality and overall success of the HCI International 2023 conference. Their manifold support in terms of paper reviewing (single-blind review process, with a minimum of two reviews per submission), session organization and their willingness to act as goodwill ambassadors for the conference is most highly appreciated.

This conference would not have been possible without the continuous and unwavering support and advice of Gavriel Salvendy, founder, General Chair Emeritus, and Scientific Advisor. For his outstanding efforts, I would like to express my sincere appreciation to Abbas Moallem, Communications Chair and Editor of HCI International News.

July 2023 Constantine Stephanidis

HCI International 2023 Thematic Areas and Affiliated Conferences

Thematic Areas

- HCI: Human-Computer Interaction
- HIMI: Human Interface and the Management of Information

Affiliated Conferences

- EPCE: 20th International Conference on Engineering Psychology and Cognitive Ergonomics
- AC: 17th International Conference on Augmented Cognition
- UAHCI: 17th International Conference on Universal Access in Human-Computer Interaction
- CCD: 15th International Conference on Cross-Cultural Design
- SCSM: 15th International Conference on Social Computing and Social Media
- VAMR: 15th International Conference on Virtual, Augmented and Mixed Reality
- DHM: 14th International Conference on Digital Human Modeling and Applications in Health, Safety, Ergonomics and Risk Management
- DUXU: 12th International Conference on Design, User Experience and Usability
- C&C: 11th International Conference on Culture and Computing
- DAPI: 11th International Conference on Distributed, Ambient and Pervasive Interactions
- HCIBGO: 10th International Conference on HCI in Business, Government and Organizations
- LCT: 10th International Conference on Learning and Collaboration Technologies
- ITAP: 9th International Conference on Human Aspects of IT for the Aged Population
- AIS: 5th International Conference on Adaptive Instructional Systems
- HCI-CPT: 5th International Conference on HCI for Cybersecurity, Privacy and Trust
- HCI-Games: 5th International Conference on HCI in Games
- MobiTAS: 5th International Conference on HCI in Mobility, Transport and Automotive Systems
- AI-HCI: 4th International Conference on Artificial Intelligence in HCI
- MOBILE: 4th International Conference on Design, Operation and Evaluation of Mobile Communications

List of Conference Proceedings Volumes Appearing Before the Conference

1. LNCS 14011, Human-Computer Interaction: Part I, edited by Masaaki Kurosu and Ayako Hashizume
2. LNCS 14012, Human-Computer Interaction: Part II, edited by Masaaki Kurosu and Ayako Hashizume
3. LNCS 14013, Human-Computer Interaction: Part III, edited by Masaaki Kurosu and Ayako Hashizume
4. LNCS 14014, Human-Computer Interaction: Part IV, edited by Masaaki Kurosu and Ayako Hashizume
5. LNCS 14015, Human Interface and the Management of Information: Part I, edited by Hirohiko Mori and Yumi Asahi
6. LNCS 14016, Human Interface and the Management of Information: Part II, edited by Hirohiko Mori and Yumi Asahi
7. LNAI 14017, Engineering Psychology and Cognitive Ergonomics: Part I, edited by Don Harris and Wen-Chin Li
8. LNAI 14018, Engineering Psychology and Cognitive Ergonomics: Part II, edited by Don Harris and Wen-Chin Li
9. LNAI 14019, Augmented Cognition, edited by Dylan D. Schmorrow and Cali M. Fidopiastis
10. LNCS 14020, Universal Access in Human-Computer Interaction: Part I, edited by Margherita Antona and Constantine Stephanidis
11. LNCS 14021, Universal Access in Human-Computer Interaction: Part II, edited by Margherita Antona and Constantine Stephanidis
12. LNCS 14022, Cross-Cultural Design: Part I, edited by Pei-Luen Patrick Rau
13. LNCS 14023, Cross-Cultural Design: Part II, edited by Pei-Luen Patrick Rau
14. LNCS 14024, Cross-Cultural Design: Part III, edited by Pei-Luen Patrick Rau
15. LNCS 14025, Social Computing and Social Media: Part I, edited by Adela Coman and Simona Vasilache
16. LNCS 14026, Social Computing and Social Media: Part II, edited by Adela Coman and Simona Vasilache
17. LNCS 14027, Virtual, Augmented and Mixed Reality, edited by Jessie Y. C. Chen and Gino Fragomeni
18. LNCS 14028, Digital Human Modeling and Applications in Health, Safety, Ergonomics and Risk Management: Part I, edited by Vincent G. Duffy
19. LNCS 14029, Digital Human Modeling and Applications in Health, Safety, Ergonomics and Risk Management: Part II, edited by Vincent G. Duffy
20. LNCS 14030, Design, User Experience, and Usability: Part I, edited by Aaron Marcus, Elizabeth Rosenzweig and Marcelo Soares
21. LNCS 14031, Design, User Experience, and Usability: Part II, edited by Aaron Marcus, Elizabeth Rosenzweig and Marcelo Soares

22. LNCS 14032, Design, User Experience, and Usability: Part III, edited by Aaron Marcus, Elizabeth Rosenzweig and Marcelo Soares
23. LNCS 14033, Design, User Experience, and Usability: Part IV, edited by Aaron Marcus, Elizabeth Rosenzweig and Marcelo Soares
24. LNCS 14034, Design, User Experience, and Usability: Part V, edited by Aaron Marcus, Elizabeth Rosenzweig and Marcelo Soares
25. LNCS 14035, Culture and Computing, edited by Matthias Rauterberg
26. LNCS 14036, Distributed, Ambient and Pervasive Interactions: Part I, edited by Norbert Streitz and Shin'ichi Konomi
27. LNCS 14037, Distributed, Ambient and Pervasive Interactions: Part II, edited by Norbert Streitz and Shin'ichi Konomi
28. LNCS 14038, HCI in Business, Government and Organizations: Part I, edited by Fiona Fui-Hoon Nah and Keng Siau
29. LNCS 14039, HCI in Business, Government and Organizations: Part II, edited by Fiona Fui-Hoon Nah and Keng Siau
30. LNCS 14040, Learning and Collaboration Technologies: Part I, edited by Panayiotis Zaphiris and Andri Ioannou
31. LNCS 14041, Learning and Collaboration Technologies: Part II, edited by Panayiotis Zaphiris and Andri Ioannou
32. LNCS 14042, Human Aspects of IT for the Aged Population: Part I, edited by Qin Gao and Jia Zhou
33. LNCS 14043, Human Aspects of IT for the Aged Population: Part II, edited by Qin Gao and Jia Zhou
34. LNCS 14044, Adaptive Instructional Systems, edited by Robert A. Sottilare and Jessica Schwarz
35. LNCS 14045, HCI for Cybersecurity, Privacy and Trust, edited by Abbas Moallem
36. LNCS 14046, HCI in Games: Part I, edited by Xiaowen Fang
37. LNCS 14047, HCI in Games: Part II, edited by Xiaowen Fang
38. LNCS 14048, HCI in Mobility, Transport and Automotive Systems: Part I, edited by Heidi Krömker
39. LNCS 14049, HCI in Mobility, Transport and Automotive Systems: Part II, edited by Heidi Krömker
40. LNAI 14050, Artificial Intelligence in HCI: Part I, edited by Helmut Degen and Stavroula Ntoa
41. LNAI 14051, Artificial Intelligence in HCI: Part II, edited by Helmut Degen and Stavroula Ntoa
42. LNCS 14052, Design, Operation and Evaluation of Mobile Communications, edited by Gavriel Salvendy and June Wei
43. CCIS 1832, HCI International 2023 Posters - Part I, edited by Constantine Stephanidis, Margherita Antona, Stavroula Ntoa and Gavriel Salvendy
44. CCIS 1833, HCI International 2023 Posters - Part II, edited by Constantine Stephanidis, Margherita Antona, Stavroula Ntoa and Gavriel Salvendy
45. CCIS 1834, HCI International 2023 Posters - Part III, edited by Constantine Stephanidis, Margherita Antona, Stavroula Ntoa and Gavriel Salvendy
46. CCIS 1835, HCI International 2023 Posters - Part IV, edited by Constantine Stephanidis, Margherita Antona, Stavroula Ntoa and Gavriel Salvendy

47. CCIS 1836, HCI International 2023 Posters - Part V, edited by Constantine Stephanidis, Margherita Antona, Stavroula Ntoa and Gavriel Salvendy

https://2023.hci.international/proceedings

Preface

Preliminary scientific results, professional news, or work in progress, described in the form of short research papers (4–8 pages long), constitute a popular submission type among the International Conference on Human-Computer Interaction (HCII) participants. Extended abstracts are particularly suited for reporting ongoing work, which can benefit from a visual presentation, and are presented during the conference in the form of posters. The latter allow a focus on novel ideas and are appropriate for presenting project results in a simple, concise, and visually appealing manner. At the same time, they are also suitable for attracting feedback from an international community of HCI academics, researchers, and practitioners. Poster submissions span the wide range of topics of all HCII thematic areas and affiliated conferences.

Five volumes of the HCII 2023 proceedings are dedicated to this year's poster extended abstracts, in the form of short research papers, focusing on the following topics:

- Volume I: HCI Design - Theoretical Approaches, Methods and Case Studies; Multimodality and Novel Interaction Techniques and Devices; Perception and Cognition in Interaction; Ethics, Transparency and Trust in HCI; User Experience and Technology Acceptance Studies
- Volume II: Supporting Health, Psychological Wellbeing, and Fitness; Design for All, Accessibility and Rehabilitation Technologies; Interactive Technologies for the Aging Population
- Volume III: Interacting with Data, Information and Knowledge; Learning and Training Technologies; Interacting with Cultural Heritage and Art
- Volume IV: Social Media - Design, User Experiences and Content Analysis; Advances in eGovernment Services; eCommerce, Mobile Commerce and Digital Marketing - Design and Customer Behavior; Designing and Developing Intelligent Green Environments; (Smart) Product Design
- Volume V: Driving Support and Experiences in Automated Vehicles; eXtended Reality - Design, Interaction Techniques, User Experience and Novel Applications; Applications of AI Technologies in HCI

Poster extended abstracts are included for publication in these volumes following a minimum of two single-blind reviews from the members of the HCII 2023 international Program Boards. We would like to thank all of them for their invaluable contribution, support, and efforts.

July 2023

Constantine Stephanidis
Margherita Antona
Stavroula Ntoa
Gavriel Salvendy

25th International Conference on Human-Computer Interaction (HCII 2023)

The full list with the Program Board Chairs and the members of the Program Boards of all thematic areas and affiliated conferences of HCII2023 is available online at:

http://www.hci.international/board-members-2023.php

HCI International 2024 Conference

The 26th International Conference on Human-Computer Interaction, HCI International 2024, will be held jointly with the affiliated conferences at the Washington Hilton Hotel, Washington, DC, USA, June 29 – July 4, 2024. It will cover a broad spectrum of themes related to Human-Computer Interaction, including theoretical issues, methods, tools, processes, and case studies in HCI design, as well as novel interaction techniques, interfaces, and applications. The proceedings will be published by Springer. More information will be made available on the conference website: http://2024.hci.international/.

General Chair
Prof. Constantine Stephanidis
University of Crete and ICS-FORTH
Heraklion, Crete, Greece
Email: general_chair@hcii2024.org

https://2024.hci.international/

Contents – Part V

Driving Support and Experiences in Automated Vehicles

Applications of AI Technologies in HCI

Driving Support and Experiences in Automated Vehicles

Research on How Community Building Interface Can Become an Intermedium to Support the Application of Unmanned Distribution in the Post-epidemic Era

Yanni Cai(✉) and Hongtao Zhou

Tongji University, Shanghai 200092, China
cyn0904@163.com

Abstract. The research aims to investigate how to promote the rapid adoption of unmanned logistics in the future through community design. The trend of contactless logistics after COVID-19 has gradually accelerated the popularity of unmanned logistics. However, the current unmanned logistics has encountered many problems at the practical application level. The current community space cannot accommodate the existence of such new facilities. Through the futurology research method, this research deduces the method of rapid promotion and application of future community unmanned logistics from different aspects such as trend, analogy prediction, extrapolation and vision. The study proposes to use the building interface space of the community as the intermediate space of the unmanned logistics system, so as to promote the rapid integration of the unmanned logistics system and the community space system, and provide more social services for the community. The study provides a community space-level application strategy for the rapid diffusion of unmanned logistics in the future.

Keywords: community building interface · unmanned distribution · public health crisis

1 Introduction

The containment and isolation of cities have made the concept of contactless delivery popular [1], which also lead to the application of unmanned delivery during the pandemic [2]. However, the application of unmanned equipment is still limited by a variety of factors such as technology, venue, and personnel. Research shows that community space is one of the main reasons why unmanned logistics cannot be used on a large scale [3]. Backward community designs are unable to meet the delivery needs of new logistics technologies. Community infrastructure is still stuck at the traditional human delivery stage, such as mailboxes [4]. Current research on unmanned delivery has focused on delivery technology but lacks consideration of community space. In the future, driven by contactless logistics, the residential community has the potential to evolve new types of space adapted to unmanned delivery.

C. Stephanidis et al. (Eds.): HCII 2023, CCIS 1836, pp. 3–6, 2023.
https://doi.org/10.1007/978-3-031-36004-6_1

This study aims to support the rapid implementation of unmanned logistics through the adaptation of the community space, to improve the community's ability to respond to public health crises. The research question is how to promote the rapid application of unmanned distribution systems through community architecture space renovation to respond to the future public health crisis. This paper will use the methodology of Futurology research to propose a community building space update strategy adapted to unmanned delivery.

2 Methodology

The methodological model of this study is Futurology research.

(1) **Trends.** Based on the current use of unmanned logistics and literature research, the study summarises the current trends in unmanned distribution and forecasts the possible development of unmanned logistics in social and technological terms. The outbreak of the pandemic will promote the gradual acceptance of unmanned logistics and its practical application.
(2) **Forecasting by analogy.** In analogy to the changes in community spaces brought about by past delivery technologies, the era of intelligent delivery by drones and unmanned vehicles will drive the expansion of a new form of docking nodes combined with architectural spaces.
(3) **Extrapolation.** Extrapolation of how unmanned vehicles will be integrated into community space in the future. The delivery of mail has promoted the emergence of letterbox space in the architectural interface. Building interface space will derive docking facilities that combine with future unmanned vehicles and unmanned aerial vehicles.
(4) **Scenarios.** Create a scenario and ideal vision for the future integration of unmanned logistics into community life. Unmanned logistics can be better combined with residential building space to provide corresponding community services.
(5) **Expert survey.** Further clarify the feasibility of the research questions and development vision through expert interviews and questionnaires.
(6) **Sequence of scenario development.** Construct a blueprint for the application of future unmanned logistics and propose a phased development strategy for the integration of future unmanned logistics into the community.

3 Strategies for Community Building Interface as a Spatial Carrier to Support the Application of Unmanned Distribution

3.1 Modular Interface Docking Facilities

From the facility level, the combination of new docking material equipment and interface space will be realized by setting up modules of different scales to achieve docking with unmanned vehicles and drones (Fig. 1). For example, the balcony of each household is equipped with intelligent express boxes and small apron devices for docking with UAV delivery. The original messenger box facility on the first floor of the unit building has been replaced by a box that can dock with unmanned vehicles (Fig. 2).

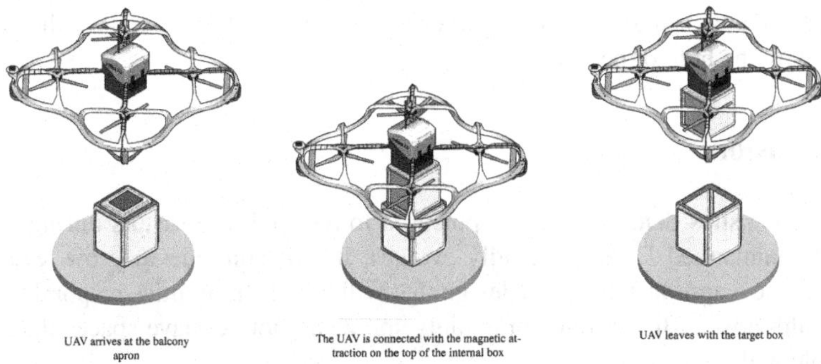

UAV arrives at the balcony apron
The UAV is connected with the magnetic attraction on the top of the internal box
UAV leaves with the target box

Fig. 1. Docking node between building interface and UAV.

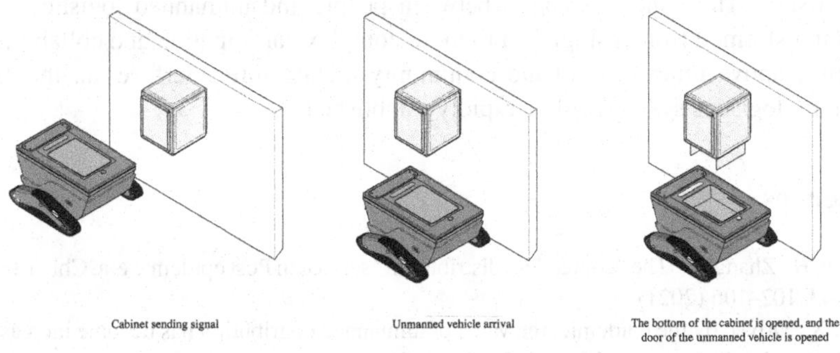

Fig. 2. Docking node between building interface and unmanned vehicle.

3.2 Flexible Allocation Function for Multi-scene Applications

From the spatial level, the building interface of the community will serve as a space node for unmanned logistics docking, thus allowing the unused public space to serve as a flexible distribution space. The architectural interface space connecting with unmanned vehicles and unmanned aerial vehicles will bring more active social activities and social services, making the outer space of the residential building interface be fully utilized. With the establishment of the community interface system, the docking device of unmanned logistics will be combined with the building interface, thus promoting the combination of unmanned logistics and residential space, and achieving rapid application to a certain extent.

3.3 Multi-stakeholder Distribution Collaboration Network

From the system level, with the help of the community architecture interface space, a collaborative distribution network can be established to make use of potential collaborators around residential buildings such as the idle resident labor force, mobile vendors, to integrate them into the collaborative distribution network, enabling unmanned logistics to cooperate with collaborators in different communities. For example, the express cabinet device attached to the building interface can successfully complete the docking of nodes with the help of people.

4 Conclusion

Unmanned logistics demonstrated its potential to respond to disasters during the epidemic. As unmanned logistics rapidly evolves, it will continue to grow, eventually becoming a new approach to space design that will help communities respond to future public health crises. But current community spaces do not yet have spaces that can be compatible with this.

This study proposes to gradually transform the community interface space for last-mile delivery from a single facility to a multifunctional place with social and landscape characteristics. Thus, the interaction between people and unmanned logistics equipment is transformed from a single act to more complex participation and collaboration. Through adaptive innovation of the community architecture interface, an intelligent community logistics system will be rapidly established.

References

1. Zhang, H., Zhang, L.: The "contactless distribution" service in Post epidemic era. China Transp. Rev. **43**, 102–106 (2021)
2. Wen, X.: Driven by the epidemic, the value of unmanned distribution has become increasingly prominent. Intell. Connected Veh. **1**, 26–29 (2021)
3. Tang, Y.: Feasibility study on contactless logistics robotic delivery for civilian use in both normal and epidemic communities. Archit. Tech. **3**, 108–110 (2020)
4. Zhang, X.: Research on intelligent transformation of traditional postal mail box. Stud. Posts **38**(02), 24–27 (2022)

Research on Human-Machine Interface Interaction Preferences Under the Situation of New Energy Vehicles Based on Driving Scenarios

Wei Ding, Mengdie Wang(✉), and Xuenan Li

East China University of Science and Technology, Shanghai, China
303062891@qq.com

Abstract. In recent years, the focus of the development of the world's automobile industry is shifting towards new energy vehicles, and a human-computer interface is an important tool for automobile information transmission. As the display carrier of automobile functions, it is the most intimate contact with the driver, which directly affects the driver's user experience. The purpose of this experiment is to study the user's preference for 2D and 3D design styles, Dashboard, and HUD display methods, to obtain the result of which design style and display method are more likely to be liked by people. This paper uses a comparative research method and questionnaire survey method to compare user preferences through two groups of comparison samples, namely 2D-Dashboard and 2D-HUD, 2D-Dashboard, and 3D-Dashboard, to find out which method is easier to obtain User Preferences. The experiment results show that among 2D and 3D design styles, users prefer 2D design style; among Dashboard and HUD display methods, users prefer Dashboard display form; among the four cases, users prefer 2D-Dashboard, the main reason is because of "simple and clear". And in daily driving, the elements that users prefer and pay more attention to our navigation and road condition information, as well as speed information. The research conclusions can provide theoretical support for HMI design, and in future HMI designs, designers can consider using the 2D-Dashboard method, and focus on speed information and navigation road condition information in driving scenarios.

Keywords: User preferences · HMI · Dashboard and HUD · 2D and 3D · Driving experience

1 Introduction

1.1 Background

In recent years, the center of the development of the world's automobile industry is shifting towards new energy vehicles, and under the guidance of government policies of various countries, the new energy vehicle industry has already had a relatively large scale and market. With the advancement of technology, people continue to bring the

C. Stephanidis et al. (Eds.): HCII 2023, CCIS 1836, pp. 7–15, 2023.
https://doi.org/10.1007/978-3-031-36004-6_2

experience of using other intelligent products into the use of cars, and the requirements for the interactive experience of cars are getting higher and higher. At the same time, with the rapid development of the economy, user needs are gradually changing from material needs to spiritual needs, and products are also changing from functional and appearance designs to experience designs to meet user needs [1]. As a personal means of transportation, a car meets the basic functions of people's travel requirements. The human-computer interface in the car, as the display carrier of the car's functions, is the most intimate part of the driver [2], and its quality will directly affect the driving experience. With the continuous changes in the form of interaction in the car, from the traditional instrument panel to the current HUD, etc., it is still unclear which form of interaction is more likely to win the favor of users.

1.2 Dashboard and HUD

As one of the important elements of the car interior, a dashboard is an important tool for car information transmission. It always reflects the state of the car and guides the driver's driving operation. It is the state display part of the car and the interface of human-computer interaction [3]. However, starting from the simple instruments in the 1950s, the driver's visual information output is almost completely concentrated on the traditional instrument panel; The function is gradually enhanced to an interactive multi-functional information panel. At the same time, additional visual and cognitive pressure problems will be generated, and its complexity becomes the main problem [4, 5]. The dashboard will also directly have adverse effects, line of sight and frequent observation for a long time will lead to cognitive distraction [1]; in response to such problems, the head-up display device HUD came into being, and its application in automobiles has been proven to have many advantages, such as the driver's ability to control the driving speed hold is better, pay more attention to road traffic, don't have to move the camera to the car dashboard, etc. [6]. Based on NHTSA's conclusions from previous studies [7], HUDs may also be used to provide drivers with critical information while minimizing the time the driver takes their eyes off the lane ahead of the driver, which can improve driving by reducing driver eye movement and visual tracking. The speed at which employees acquire information and the time to focus. But at the same time, the design of the HUD will directly affect the driving, which may cause the driver's separation and narrow vision channel, and some studies have shown that the accuracy of information is reduced when augmented reality (AR) is implemented on the HUD. In the application of AR-HUD designers should consider the display timing of information and the optimal design of HUD, etc. [8].

1.3 Graphics Design

Graphics play an important role in modern interfaces and therefore recent empirical research has focused on enhancing graphics processing. The 2D (flat) vs. 3D (three-dimensional) design debate is inconclusive in automotive HMI design, partly due to a lack of empirical evidence to support one or the other graphic style from a functional and aesthetic standpoint. You F et al. compared the three colors of red, green, and blue under the HMI, as well as the five levels of daytime and nighttime contrast, to make the color design of the vehicle center console a reference; Pfannmller L et al. proposed information display timing and The optimal design of the HUD has a significant impact on the driving experience; Ng, A.W.Y., et al. proposed that the visual complexity is related to the number of visual elements displayed in detail in the graphics, thus requiring more attention and time from the user to recognize [9]. So, the vehicle HMI's design case should be measured and considered from multiple perspectives such as the number of visual elements, graphic colors, and presentation forms.

In this study, the HMI experiment plan is divided into two groups of 2D and 3D, Dashboard and HUD for comparison, to explore the user preferences of the Dashboard and HUD display methods under 2D and 3D, and to explore the visual experience through questionnaires and in-depth interviews The user preference scheme under the dimension, and the design strategy is given to provide a practical reference for the information display design in the driving state.

2 Experiment

Since more than 80% of the driver's information comes from visual information when driving [10], and visual reminders are more timely and effective than auditory reminders in emergencies, maximizing visual resources is conducive to allowing drivers to focus on Safe Driving. The experiment compares the user's preferences for the four schemes of 2D-Dashboard, 3D-Dashboard, 2D-HUD, and 3D-HUD by making statistics on the information elements in the driving process and redesigning them, and tries to give design strategies and conclusions.

2.1 Comparative Research Method

The comparative research method is a method of researching and judging the degree of difference between objects. In this experiment, two groups of comparison samples, namely 2D-Dashboard and 2D-HUD; 2D-Dashboard, and 3D-Dashboard are used to compare user preferences, to find out which method is easier to obtain user preferences.

2.2 Statistics of New Energy Vehicle Instrument Display Elements

In the preparatory stage of this experiment, ten new energy vehicles were randomly selected, and the information displayed on the instruments during their normal driving was counted. The information displayed was speed, navigation, and road condition information, cruising range (battery), lights or seat belts and other reminders, and auxiliary information such as time and temperature, total mileage, and media (see Table 1). Since the information that changes during the driving process is mainly focused on speed, navigation, and vehicle battery, the display methods of the three types of information were redesigned during the experimental preparation stage. The styles are flat and three-dimensional, and the carriers are dashboard and HUD respectively. Four ways to display information. Reminders and auxiliary information appear in the design plan as the background, and non-essential total mileage and media do not appear in the plan as design objects.

Table 1. Display element statistics

Elements	Speed	Navigation and road condition information	Cruising range (battery)	Lights or seat belts and other reminders	Auxiliary information	Total mileage	Media
Frequency	10	10	10	10	9	8	8

2.3 Case Design

In the scheme design, to simulate the realism of information display in the driving scene, the dashboard of any model in the market was randomly selected as the background to simulate the dashboard information, and the blurred traffic background was randomly selected to simulate the HUD display background. 2D (referring to the flat effect) mainly uses lines to form information, and 3D (referring to the three-dimensional effect) uses real road condition information, speed mirror processing, and navigation light effects to increase the three-dimensional sense. The final four design schemes are shown in Table 2.

Case 1: 2D-Dashboard. The left side of the 2D-Dashboard is the speed and battery life information, and the right side is the navigation information. Below the speed information, the power battery life is displayed in the form of horizontal lines, surrounded by lights, gears, seat belts, speed limits, time, and temperature information; the navigation on the right is mainly based on the information of the three lanes overlooking and other vehicle information, supplemented up and down Take lane selection and navigation information.

Case 2: 3D-dashboard. The 3D-Dashboard also uses speed and battery life information on the left, and navigation information on the right. The difference from the 2D-Dashboard is that the speed and battery life information uses light effects and mirror effects to increase the three-dimensional effect, and the navigation information on the right corresponds to the physical lane and road conditions, which are more realistic and three-dimensional.

Case 3: 2D-HUD. The information presented on the HUD is more concise. Other information in the background is removed, and only the speed information, battery life information, navigation and road condition information are retained. In addition, only the upper right corner of the speed is added. Speed limit value. The visual effects of speed information, battery life information, navigation and traffic information are the same as the 2D-Dashboard.

Case 4: 3D-HUD. It is the same as 2D-HUD, only the speed, battery life, and navigation information are kept, and only the speed limit value is added in the upper right corner of the speed, and the visual effect of the three information is the same as that of the 3D-dashboard.

Table 2. The 4 case designs

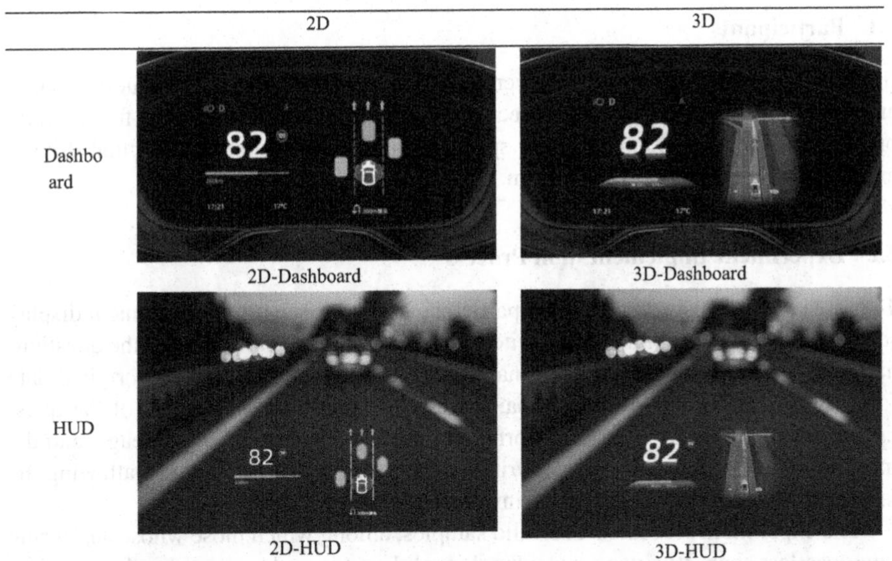

	2D	3D
Dashboard	2D-Dashboard	3D-Dashboard
HUD	2D-HUD	3D-HUD

2.4 Questionnaires Design

In the preparatory stage of the experiment, to explore the user's preference for visual display differences between 2D and 3D; Dashboard and HUD, and which of the four cases is the user's most preferred visual presentation scheme, the questionnaire was edited and set according to the preferences of the four schemes. After removing the basic information of the user, the questionnaire includes four multiple-choice questions:

1. For the cases 2D-dashboard and 3D-dashboard, which one do you prefer?
2. For the cases 2D-dashboard and 2D-HUD, which one do you prefer?
3. Among the four cases, which one do you prefer?
4. Which design element do you like in this (answer to question 3)?

The questionnaire was set up for four questions, and the user's personal information was added for statistics, including the user's gender, age, and driving age. The questionnaire is produced by the third-party questionnaire platform Questionnaire Star and published on the network platform.

2.5 Experimental Hypothesis

Hypothesis 1: For designs in 2D and 3D dimensions, users prefer 3D designs.
Hypothesis 2: For the display forms of the Dashboard and HUD, users prefer the display form of the HUD.
Hypothesis 3: The user's most preferred case is the 3D-HUD solution, which is related to the user's driving experience.
Hypothesis 4: In daily driving, users will prefer and pay attention to navigation and traffic information, and speed information.

3 Experiment

3.1 Participants

In the experiment, 130 participants were randomly invited to answer the questionnaire, and 130 valid questionnaires were recovered. Among them, the male-to-female ratio of the participants is 60:56, the age span is 18–45 years old, and the actual driving experience spans from 0 to 50,000 km.

3.2 Experiment Implementation Process

To more comprehensively obtain the participants' preference for the instrument display scheme, the experiment randomly invited 130 participants to participate in the questionnaire survey. Download the questionnaire data on the platform to get the original data form. Before answering, the participants were informed that the content of the questionnaire would involve personal information such as age and driving mileage, and the information was collected with the written permission of the participants, allowing the information to be used for academic investigation in this study.

The experiment recovered 116 valid samples, among which those whose answering time was less than 30 s were considered invalid samples, the sample collection time lasted 72 h, and the returned questionnaire data was stored in the form of excel.

4 Results

4.1 Result 1

For question 1: "Which one do you prefer, 2D-dashboard or 3D-Dashboard?", 100 people chose the 2D-dashboard and 16 people chose the 3D-Dashboard (see Table 3).

Result 1 shows that among 2D and 3D design styles, 86% of users will prefer the 2D design style. When the screen uses two-dimensional graphics, that is, lines and geometric figures to indicate specific road conditions and other information, users will prefer; Analyzing experimental result 1, it is concluded that compared with 2D and 3D, the 2D dashboard design is more likely to be liked by people, which is contrary to hypothesis 1, indicating that in the subsequent design, the 2D design can be used to win users love and attention.

Table 3. Preference between 2D-dashboard and 3D-Dashboard

	the number of people	The proportion
2D-Dashboard	100	86%
3D-Dashboard	16	14%
Total	116	100%

4.2 Result 2

For question 2: "For case 2D-Dashboard and case 3D-HUD, which one is your preference?", 86 people chose 2D-Dashboard, 30 people chose 2D-HUD, and the proportions were 74% and 26% (Table 4).

Table 4. Preference between 2D-dashboard and 2D-HUD

	the number of people	The proportion
2D-Dashboard	86	74%
2D-HUD	30	26%
Total	116	100%

Result 2 shows that among the design styles of Dashboard and HUD, 74% of users prefer the Dashboard design style. When the information content is the same, the presentation form based on Dashboard will be more likely to be liked by users. Analyzing experimental result 2, it is concluded that compared with the HUD, the presentation form of the Dashboard is more likely to be liked by people, which is contrary to hypothesis 2, but the specific reason for the preference is not clear.

4.3 Result 3

Table 5. Preference between 2D-dashboard, 3D-dashboard, 2D- HUD and case 3D-HUD

	the number of people	The proportion
2D-Dashboard	45	38.8%
3D-Dashboard	39	33.6%
2D-HUD	24	20.7%
3D-HUD	8	6.9%
Total	116	100%

For question 3: "For case 2D-dashboard, 3D-dashboard, 2D-HUD and case 3D-HUD, which one is your preference?", 45 people chose 2D-dashboard, 39 people chose 3D-dashboard, 24 people chose 2D-HUD, 8 people chose 3D-HUD, the proportions were 38.8%, 33.6%, 20.7%, 6.9% (Table 5).

After obtaining the questionnaire data, 20 people were randomly selected for interviews and asked what the specific reasons were when the users chose their most preferred solution. The statistical table obtained is shown in Table 6, which can be summarized into five types of reasons, namely simple, clear, good-looking, harmonious, and relatively easy to find information, among which more people choose the reason because of simplicity and clarity, which can show to a certain extent that when the design is simple and clear, it may be easier to be loved by users.

Table 6. Preference between 2D-dashboard and 3D-Dashboard

Key words	Number of people
Simple	7
Clear	6
Good looking	3
Harmonious	1
Easy to find information	1

4.4 Result 4

For question 4: "Which design element do you like in this product (the answer to question 3)?", 89 people mentioned navigation information, 87 people mentioned speed, and 4 people mentioned battery life display. No one mentioned other information such as time, lighting, etc. (see Table 6).

Table 7. Reasons about why people like the case

Different Part	the number of people	The proportion
navigation and road condition	89	76.7%
Speed	87	75%
cruising range (battery)	4	3.4%
Others	0	0%
Total	116	100%

According to the selected ratio, navigation and road condition information, and speed information are the two elements that users pay the most attention to. The difference between the selection ratio is only 1.7%, which is negligible, and the number of people who choose these two elements is much higher than battery life information and other information, which are negligible. This is in line with Hypothesis 4 of this paper, indicating that users pay more attention to navigation and road condition information, as well as speed information in actual driving. Therefore, in the HMI design of the car, more design research can be done on navigation and road condition information, as well as speed information (Table 7).

5 Discussion

Through statistics on the preferences of the dashboard and HUD display information of 130 users, we concluded that among the 2D and 3D design styles, users prefer the 2D design style; among the presentation methods of dashboard and HUD, users prefer the presentation form of the Dashboard; among the four preferences, the 2D-dashboard design is the most preferred style by users, which is consistent with the selection trend of the aforementioned users. When discussing the reasons for preference with users, users indicated that the most favorite design is a simple and clear design, which indicates that in the subsequent HMI design, we should focus on using simple elements, such as simple geometry in 2D, and avoid using overly complex designs element. In addition, in the comparison between HUD and Dashboard, the user prefers the Dashboard form. It is speculated that this may be related to the user's driving experience, but this has not been verified by the data.

References

1. Ma, X., Jia, M., Hong, Z., Kwok, A.P.K., Yan, M.: Does augmented-reality head-up display help? A preliminary study on driving performance through a VR-simulated eye movement analysis. IEEE Access **9**, 129951–129964 (2021)
2. Zhang, P.: Advanced Industrial Control Technology. William Andrew (2010)
3. Schmidt, A., Dey, A.K., Kun, A.L., Spiessl, W.: Automotive user interfaces: human-computer interaction in the car. In: CHI 2010 Extended Abstracts on Human Factors in Computing Systems, pp. 3177–3180 (2010)
4. Knoll, P.M., Kosmowski, B.: Liquid crystal display unit for reconfigurable instrument for automotive applications. Opto-Electron. Rev. **10**, 75–78 (2002)
5. Wang, W., You, F., Li, Y., Feuerstack, S., Wang, J.: The influence of spatio-temporal based human-machine interface design on driver workload-a case study of adaptive cruise control using in cutting-in scenarios. In: 2022 IEEE/SICE International Symposium on System Integration (SII), pp. 155–160. IEEE (2022)
6. Lee, J., Koo, J., Park, J., Lee, M.C.: Vehicle augmented reality head-up display information visualization enhancement algorithm and system. In: 2021 International Conference on Information and Communication Technology Convergence (ICTC), pp. 701–7060. IEEE (2021)
7. Campbell, J.L., et al.: Human factors design guidance for driver-vehicle interfaces. Report No. DOT HS, 812(360), 252 (2016)
8. Pfannmüller, L., Kramer, M., Senner, B., Bengler, K.: A comparison of display concepts for a navigation system in an automotive contact analog head-up display. Procedia Manuf. **3**, 2722–2729 (2015)
9. Ng, A.W., Chan, A.H.: The effects of driver factors and sign design features on the comprehensibility of traffic signs. J. Saf. Res. **39**(3), 321–328 (2008)
10. Cohen, A.S.: Feed Forward Programming of Car Drivers' Eye Movement Behavior. A System Theoretical Approach, vol. 1. Eidgnoessische technische hochschule Zurich (switzerland) inst for behavioral sciences (1980)
11. Schmidt, G.J., Rittger, L.: Guiding driver visual attention with LEDs. In: Proceedings of the 9th International Conference on Automotive User Interfaces and Interactive Vehicular Applications, pp. 279–286 (2017)

A Study on Mode Awareness of Multi-level Automated Vehicles

Hwisoo Eom[1], Yupeng Zhong[2], Xintong Hou[2], and Sang Hun Lee[2](✉)

[1] Siemens Industry Software, Seoul 06292, Republic of Korea
[2] Kookmin University, Seoul 02707, Republic of Korea
shlee@kookmin.ac.kr

Abstract. Automated vehicles have multiple operating modes, and drivers may be unaware of the mode in which they are driving, leading to mode confusion and potential traffic accidents. To solve this problem, this paper proposes two user interfaces for automated vehicles that are expected to accurately describe vehicle states to reduce mode confusion. Driver-in-the-loop experiments were conducted to examine the possibility of mode confusion in the user interfaces while driving in different automation levels. Results suggest that reducing mode confusion requires a precise and concise user mental model, as well as a user interface designed for simplicity of driver-vehicle interaction, intuitiveness of operation, and consistency.

Keywords: Multi-level Automation · Automated Vehicles · Autonomous Vehicles · Mode Confusion · Situation Awareness · User Interface

1 Introduction

Automated vehicles have the potential to enhance road safety by supporting or supplementing the driver in various situations. Such vehicles are equipped with advanced driver assistance systems (ADAS) and an intelligent co-pilot system to provide appropriate support in all traffic situations, from normal to safety-critical emergency situations. Typically, automated vehicles have several different levels of automation ranging from manual to partially and fully automatic. Although automated systems promise increased safety and reduced human error, a number of substantive human factor challenges must be addressed before these types of automated systems can become a practical reality. These challenges include the potential for negative adaptations occurring due to misunderstanding, misuse, or overreliance on the system or change in attention and distraction from the driving task. In particular, as the driver's role shifts from active vehicle control to passive monitoring of the automated system and environment, the driver's situational awareness in detecting system state changes or perceiving critical environmental factors becomes very important.

Regarding mode confusion in vehicle automation, early studies have focused on adaptive cruise control (ACC) systems [1–5]. Recently, there has been researching on mode confusion in highly automated vehicles [6–11]. Heymann and Degani [6] described a hierarchy of automated driving aids and their functionalities, focusing on ACC and lane

C. Stephanidis et al. (Eds.): HCII 2023, CCIS 1836, pp. 16–21, 2023.
https://doi.org/10.1007/978-3-031-36004-6_3

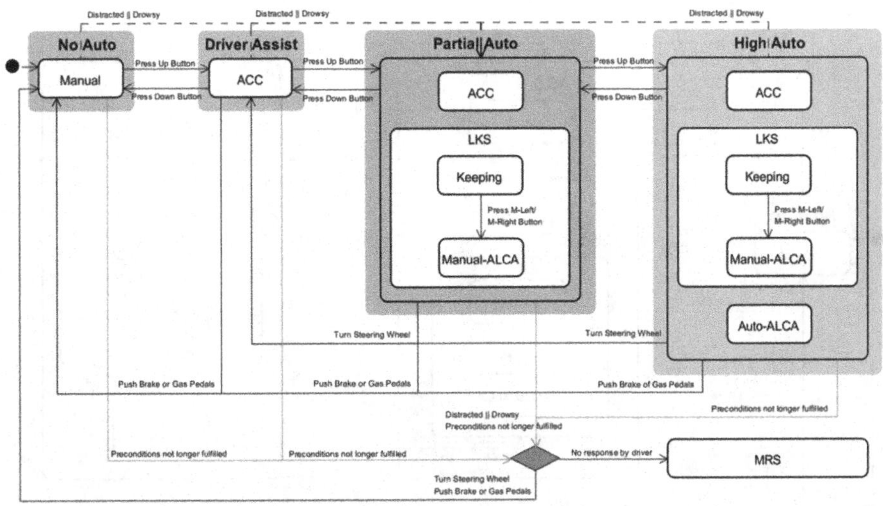

Fig. 1. The stepwise interface model created by grouping of the states of the corresponding machine model.

centering. In the intelligent transport (HAVEit) project [7], the researchers developed and verified a survey of users' cognitive modes and mode transition of the system. Lau et al. [8] investigated the impact of simple and advanced interface designs on driver behavior in a level 3 automated driving system. Miller et al. [9] evaluated four different automation conditions. Özkanet et al. [10] reviewed a state-of-the-art mode awareness from the related domains of automated driving, aviation, and human–robot interaction.

In this study, we designed two user interfaces for automated vehicles operated in modes corresponding to the SAE automation levels 0 to 3. The first is a stepwise interface that allows the driver to increase or decrease the automation level step-by-step. The second is an independence interface with independent driving controls in the longitudinal and lateral directions. We implemented prototypes for the two interfaces and conducted driver-in-the-loop experiments on a driving simulator to verify their effectiveness in the driver's mode awareness. For events on the road, the participants took actions to control the vehicle, which might cause mode changes, and answered the modes they believed. The experimental results show that the mode confusion rate of the stepwise interface is twice higher as that of the independent interface. Also, visual feedback can reduce the mode confusion rate dramatically. The results show that an independent user interface combined with adequate visual and auditory feedback is essential to improve driver's mode awareness when driving an automated vehicle.

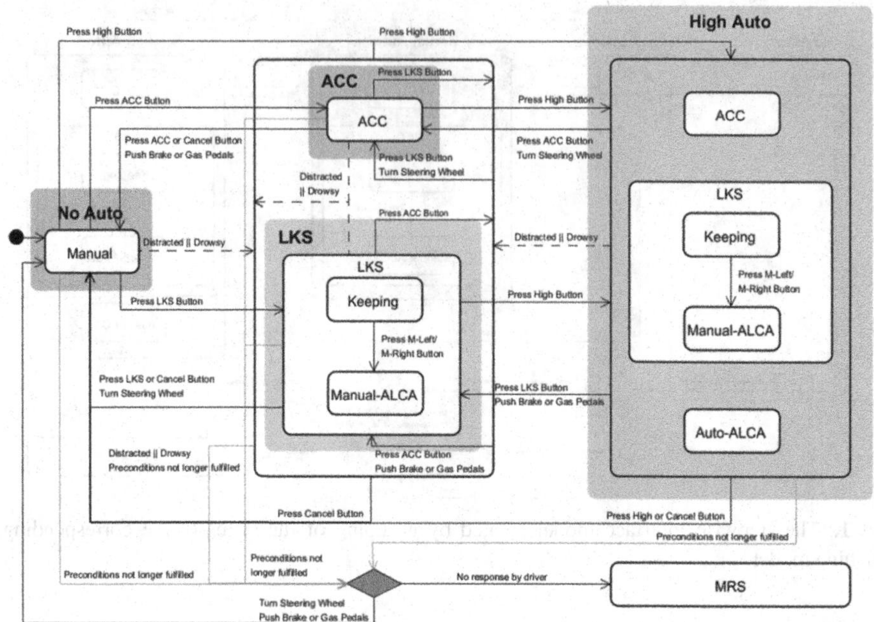

Fig. 2. Independent interface model created by grouping of the states of the corresponding machine model.

2 Machine and Interface Models of Autonomous Vehicles with Multiple Levels of Automation

We designed two different user interfaces, stepwise and independent, to enable the user to perform driving operations correctly and quickly. The stepwise interface model was developed based on that of the HAVEit project [7]. The names of the modes follow SAE's terminologies. "No-Auto' represents the mode in which the driver operates the vehicle manually, 'Driver Assist' refers to the mode in which the ACC system is solely active, 'Partial–Auto' is the mode in which both the ACC and lane keeping (LK) systems are active, and 'High–Auto' represents the mode in which not only the ACC and LK system but also the automatic active lane-change assist (Auto–ALCA) system are active. The combination of the machine and interface model is shown in Fig. 1.

For the independent interface, the mode names were given according to the states of the independent machine model. The state in which a driver operates manually is called 'No-Auto,' the state in which the ACC system is solely active is named 'ACC,' the state in which the LK system is active exclusively is called 'LKS,' and 'High–Auto' represents the state in which the ACC, LK, and Auto–ALCA systems are all active. The combination of the machine and interface model is shown in Fig. 2.

We investigated whether there were any incompatible mode transitions in the interface models using the state and mode transition table that was proposed by Lee et al. [4, 5]. The conclusion was that there were no incompatible transitions in both the stepwise and independent interfaces.

3 Driver-in-the-Loop Experiments

3.1 Participants

The 12 participants consisted of four females and eight males aged between 23 and 31 years (mean = 26.58, SD = 2.23) and students of Kookmin University. Information was obtained from the participants using a basic questionnaire. All the respondents had a valid driver's license and one or more years of driving experience. They had normal or corrected to normal vision.

3.2 Apparatus

The experiments were conducted in a fixed-base driving simulator using the TNO PreScan software. In the driving simulator, we implemented automated systems and the graphical user interface using Simulink and MATLAB. In addition, we modeled a road with three lanes using PreScan, imitating the Detroit Street Circuit of the USA Grand Prix. Ten events were designed to occur in specific regions in the proposed scenario. The host vehicle started to travel in the middle of three lanes. As the host vehicle approached a particular location, one or more surrounding vehicles exhibited predetermined behaviors, such as sudden accelerating or braking.

3.3 Procedure

We conducted experiments with stepwise and independent interfaces for different participants in different orders to eliminate any learning effect. In each experiment, the participant pressed the up/down buttons or turned on individual ADASs such as ACC and LK systems. Depending on the design scenario, a specific event occurred after the host vehicle arrived at a particular location. In response to each event, the participant tried to control the car by pressing the buttons, pushing the brake or gas pedal, and turning the steering wheel. The experimenter observed the participant's actions and the resulting mode changes in the systems. After completing each event, the experimenter covered the interface on the gauge cluster and interrupted the driving simulation to ask the participant about the mode change and the reason for the answer given. The experimenter then uncovered the interface and asked the participant the same question. The experimenter noted the answers given during the experiment. The participants were expected to use several ADASs while driving, and they were given no clues about the correct answers. When the driving experiments were finished, the participants were asked whether and why they felt any mode confusion. Each experimental session lasted 40 min from start to finish.

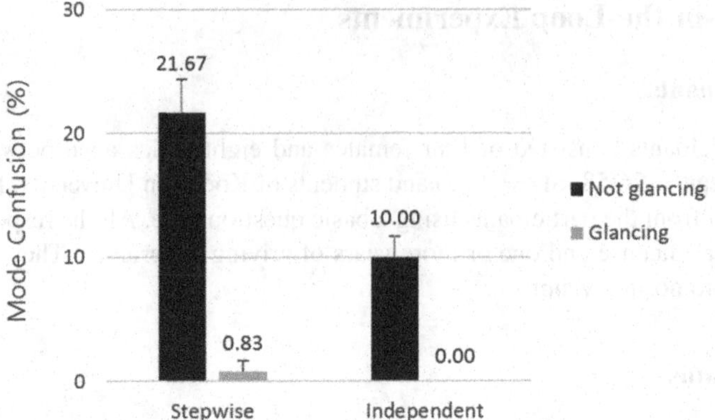

Fig. 3. Mode confusion rates obtained using the two user interfaces for users glancing and not glancing at the display.

4 Results

We examined the mode-confusion rates for two independent variables: the type of interface models and whether the participant glanced at the display. We considered two levels for the type of user interface (i.e., stepwise and independent models) and two levels for glancing at the display (i.e., glancing and not glancing). The mode confusion rates for the participants are shown in Fig. 3. To assess the significance of the two factors, we analyzed the variance (ANOVA) of the measurements using SPSS software.

5 Discussion

The experimental results showed that the independent interface was more effective than the stepwise interface in reducing mode confusion. The total rates of mode confusion with the stepwise and independent interface were 10% and 4%, respectively. As described in Sect. 2, we designed and verified newly proposed user interfaces for automated systems, i.e., designing the stepwise interface, which gradually increases the levels with the combined systems, designing the independent interface, which increases the levels with each system, and testing the compatibility between the modes.

The experimental results showed very little mode confusion after glancing at the display. This means that the interface indicates each mode. We expected that the mode confusion in the stepwise interface was less because the stepwise interface model is systematic and transparent. However, considerable mode confusion occurred before glancing at the display. This means that the actual mode of the systems was different from the user's expectation.

Based on the experimental results, we confirmed that the independent interface was more user-friendly than the stepwise one considering the driver's comfort and safety and that the position of a symbol and the terms of a mode should be moderately used when developing the interfaces.

6 Conclusions

In this paper, we developed and tested two different interface models. Using the proposed formal analysis, we reviewed the compatibility between the machine and interface models. The results of the driver-in-the-loop experiments support the hypothesis that the independent interface was a more compact and easy-to-understand user interface than the stepwise interface. In the future, we plan to conduct research on different user interfaces for drivers [12] and the application of deep learning techniques [13].

Acknowledgement. This work was supported by the National Research Foundation of Korea (NRF) grant funded by the Korea government (MSIT) (No. 2020R1A2C1102767). This is a conference paper presenting preliminary research results, and its extended and revised version will be published in the Journal of Computational Design and Engineering [11].

References

1. Horiguchi, Y., Fukuju, R., Sawaragi, T.: An estimation method of possible mode confusion in human work with automated control systems. In: SICE-ICASE International Joint Conference, pp. 943–948 (2006)
2. Horiguchi, Y., Fukuju, R., Sawaragi, T.: Differentiation of input-output relations to facilitate user's correct awareness of operating mode of automated control system. In: IEEE International Conference on Systems, Man and Cybernetics, pp. 2570–2575 (2007)
3. Furukawa, H., Inagaki, T., Shiraishi, Y.: Mode awareness of a dual-mode adaptive cruise control system. In: IEEE International Conference on Systems, Man and Cybernetics, pp. 832–837 (2003)
4. Lee, S.H., Ahn, D.R.: Design and verification of driver interfaces for adaptive cruise control systems. J. Mech. Sci. Technol. **29**(6), 2451–2460 (2015). https://doi.org/10.1007/s12206-015-0536-9
5. Eom, H.S., Lee, S.H.: Human-automation interaction design for adaptive cruise control systems of ground vehicles. Sensors **15**(6), 13916–13944 (2015)
6. Heymann, M., Degani, A.: Automated driving aids: modeling, analysis, and interface design considerations. In: International Conference on Automotive User Interfaces and Interactive Vehicular Applications, pp. 142–149 (2013)
7. Hoeger, R., et al.: HAVEit (Highly automated vehicles for intelligent transport) Project, Deliverable D61.1 - Final Report (2011)
8. Lau, C.P., Harbluk, J.L., Burns, P.C., El-Hage, Y.: The influence of interface design on driver behaviour in automated driving. In: CARSP: The Canadian Association of Road Safety Professionals (2018)
9. Miller, D., Sun, A., Ju, W.: Situation awareness with different levels of automation. In: IEEE International Conference on Systems, Man, and Cybernetics (SMC), pp. 688–693 (2014)
10. Dönmez Özkan, Y., Mirnig, A.G., Meschtscherjakov, A., Demir, C., Tscheligi, M.: Mode awareness interfaces in automated vehicles, robotics, and aviation: a literature review. In: International Conference on Automotive User Interfaces and Interactive Vehicular Applications, pp. 147–158 (2021)
11. Eom, H., Lee, S.H.: Mode confusion of human–machine interfaces for automated vehicles. J. Comput. Des. Eng. **9**(5), 1995–2009 (2022)
12. Lee, S.H., Yoon, S.-O.: User interface for in-vehicle systems with on-wheel finger spreading gestures and head-up displays. J. Comput. Des. Eng. **7**(6), 700–721 (2019)
13. Lee, S., Woo, T., Lee, S.H.: Multi-attention-based soft partition network for vehicle re-identification. J. Comput. Des. Eng. **10**(2), 488–502 (2023)

How are Different Vehicle Interior Concepts Affecting Social Interaction During Automated Driving?

Patricia Haar(✉), Michaela Teicht, Dominique Stimm, and Arnd Engeln

Hochschule der Medien, Nobelstr. 10, 70569 Stuttgart, Germany
{haar,teicht,stimm,engeln}@hdm-stuttgart.de

Abstract. The goal of the research project RUMBA, funded by the German Federal Ministry for Economic Affairs and Climate Action, is to redesign the user experience for occupants during a highly automated drive (SAE Level 4 [1]) by developing innovative interior and interaction concepts. As part of the second iteration of the user-centered, iterative development process, a field study is conducted. It aims to evaluate a prototype of an innovative vehicle interior concept to support social interaction during automated driving as well as to identify design suggestions for its further development. The vehicle interior concept to be evaluated is compared to a classic vehicle interior in a field-experimental research setting. The participants experience each vehicle interior for 30 min during a simulated automated drive in real traffic (Wizard of Oz). During the drive, participants play a digital board game together: In one condition, the participants are seated in driving direction and play on their respective tablets. In the other condition, they sit facing each other and play on a shared tablet. Besides others, user behavior is observed, and questionnaires are used to assess user experience, system trust and subjective road safety. The data collection for the study is completed by the end of April 2023.Therefore, this short paper focuses on the method, results are not yet included. The conference poster in July depicts both the methodology and the results of the evaluation study.

Keywords: Automated Driving · Vehicle Interior · User Experience · Interaction

1 Introduction

Since this paper is related to the same research project (RUMBA) as [2], the introductions of both papers are identical and their structures are similar. However, they are two different short papers reporting different studies with independent results. This short paper reports on a field study in a real vehicle on the topic of social interaction during automated driving, while [2] reports on a laboratory study in a driving simulator on work and entertainment during automated driving.

C. Stephanidis et al. (Eds.): HCII 2023, CCIS 1836, pp. 22–29, 2023.
https://doi.org/10.1007/978-3-031-36004-6_4

1.1 Research Project RUMBA and User-Centered Development

This contribution results from the publicly funded joint research project RUMBA (German acronym for "Achieving a positive user experience through user-friendly design of the vehicle interior for automated driving functions"), which is funded by the German Federal Ministry for Economic Affairs and Climate Action (BMWK) on the basis of a resolution of the German Bundestag (funding code 19A20007D).

The user-centered development process of DIN EN ISO 9241-210:2020-03 [3] (see Fig. 1) pursued in the RUMBA research project by the Stuttgart Media University is explained in detail below.

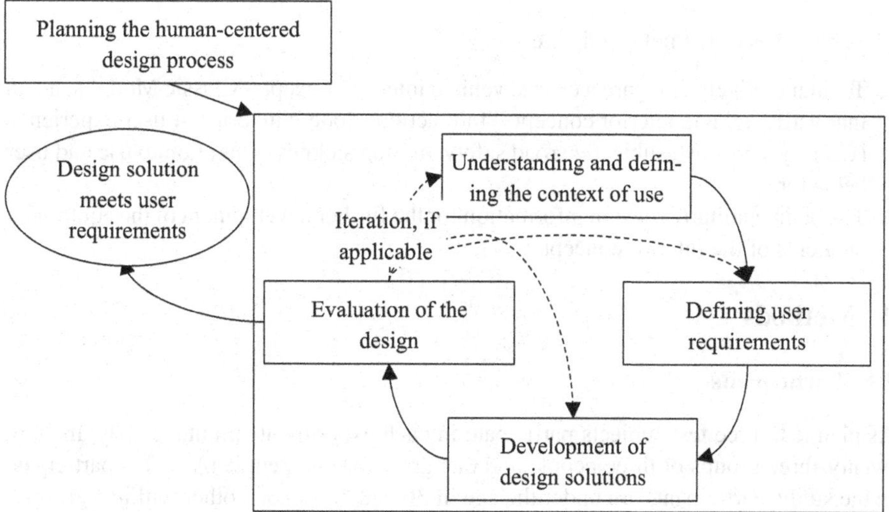

Fig. 1. User-centered development process of DIN EN ISO 9241-210:2020-03 [3]

Based on the planning step ("Planning the human-centered design process"), in which the project goal and approach were conceived, the requirements and needs for SAE Level 4 automated driving were empirically investigated from the user's perspective ("Understanding and defining the context of use"). The authors conducted a simulator and diary study to investigate user requirements for the vehicle interior and for displays and controls in fully automated driving [4, 5]. In the next step ("Defining user requirements"), the research results on user requirements were compiled, key learnings were extracted, and design spaces were derived. This was done in a synthesis workshop. In the subsequent step ("Development of design solutions"), ideas and initial prototypes for the vehicle interior, displays and controls were generated. This was done in a design thinking workshop. There, various alternative concept ideas were generated and concretized in low-fidelity prototypes. On this basis, the authors developed five user narratives [6], which describe the innovative concept ideas integrated there in the form of a usage story. These user narratives were evaluated with users in a first iteration as part of the evaluation step ("Evaluation of the design"). The goal of the evaluation was to gather user feedback on innovation ideas and concept concretization and to identify design cues for their further development.

In the second iteration, based on this initial user feedback, the authors developed the low-fidelity prototypes into mid-fidelity prototypes: With regard to related work [7], a prototype for supporting interaction during an automated drive was created with a Wizard-of-Oz (WoOz) setup in a field setting. This prototype is evaluated in a field study as part of the second evaluation iteration. The prototype and the methodology of this study are described in detail in this short paper. The results of the evaluation study are reported on the HCII poster.

1.2 Objectives

The objectives of the field study are:

1. To quantitatively compare a classic vehicle interior concept ("Classic Mode") and an innovative vehicle interior concept ("Interaction Mode") in terms of user experience (UX), system trust, subjective road safety, motion sickness, intention to use and user behavior.
2. To obtain qualitative design information for the further development of the equipment elements of the interior concept.

2 Methods

2.1 Participants

As planned, three test subjects participate in each experiment simultaneously. In sum, twenty-three groups of three people and one group of two people ($N = 71$) participate in the study. Participants are under the age of 30 and know each other within a group.

2.2 Experimental Design

The study has a field-experimental within-subjects research design in which the two-stage independent variable *vehicle interior concept* (Classic Mode vs. Interaction Mode) is purposefully manipulated. In a group of three, the participants experience the two vehicle interiors in a permuted order in a *WoOz setup* during a simulated automated drive in real traffic.

Vehicle Interior Concept. The *Classic Mode* matches the interior concept of today's vehicles. The innovative interior concept *Interaction Mode* is designed to support passenger interaction during an automated drive. As related work also reveals that participants in a long drive social scenario request a "living room position" with seats rotated between 90° and 180° and a table [7], but the UX of this setting in real traffic has not been tested, the objective of the study reported here is to do so and investigate the setting's impact on variables such as UX and motion sickness. Figure 2 shows the implementation of the two modes in the vehicle and Fig. 3 shows them schematically.

Fig. 2. Interior concept in the test vehicle (interior view): Classic Mode (left), Interaction Mode (right)

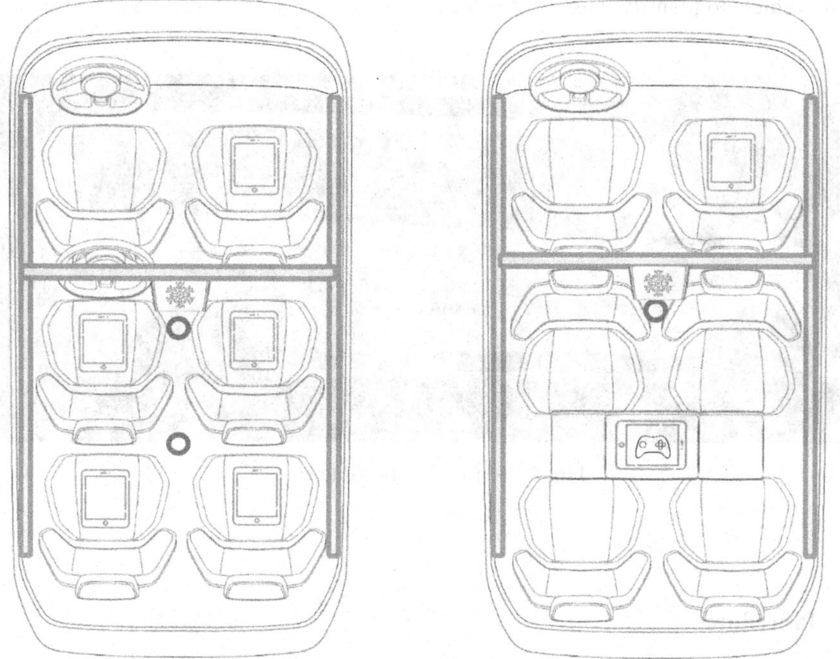

Fig. 3. Schematic representation of the Classic Mode (left) and the Interaction Mode (right)

In the test vehicle, the first row, from where the WoOz driver steers the vehicle, is separated from the rear interior to be tested. The interior to be tested includes the second and the third rows: In the Classic Mode, a mock steering wheel is placed in front of the left front seat. All four participants sit facing the direction of travel. A shared online game can be played via separate tablets. In the Interaction Mode, the steering wheel is removed and the two front seats are reversed. There is a central table between the participants where they can play together on a large tablet (digital board game). In both modes, there is a refrigerator and storage areas as well as mock emergency buttons in the headliner that can theoretically be used to initiate an emergency stop.

WoOz Setup. Participants should believe that the test vehicle (Mercedes Benz V-class) (see Fig. 4) is automated and that the safety driver in the driver's seat in the first row would only intervene in an emergency. In reality, however, the vehicle is being driven manually by the safety driver. To reinforce the impression of an automated vehicle, the view from the rear to the driver's and passenger's seat is blocked. However, in order to support the impression of automated driving but not contribute to motion sickness, a screen is placed in between, showing the front view through the windshield (without the driver) using a webcam (following [13]). In addition, a foiling is applied to the outside of the vehicle to identify it as a test vehicle.

Fig. 4. Test vehicle (outside view)

2.3 Procedure

The study takes place from December 2022 to April 2023 at the Stuttgart Media University. The test procedure includes three parts. These are described below.

Introduction Including Pre-Survey. After the formal introduction (study information and consent forms), participants are accompanied to the test vehicle and are allowed to choose their own seat in the back of the test vehicle. The investigator also takes a seat in the back as a participating observer. The investigator's seat, which is permuted per experimental group, is not allowed to be occupied by the participants. After being seated, participants are asked to explain the reasons for their choice of seat.

Test Drives Including Subsequent Quantitative Surveys. In the vehicle, the participants are instructed about the vehicle, the respective interior and the drive, and subsequently their motion sickness is assessed using an online questionnaire on a tablet. The route is approximately 34 km long, takes about 30 min and runs mostly on the motorway. During the drives, the participants perform several activities: First, they have to open the refrigerator to take out water bottles. Once they reach the motorway, the participants play a digital board game together: In Classic Mode, the participants play on their respective tablets. In Interaction Mode, they play at the central table on a shared tablet. Meanwhile, the investigator observes and notes critical incidents (CIs) [8]. Towards the end of each drive, participants are asked to imagine an emergency situation in which they would like to intervene in the automated drive and press one of the emergency buttons to do so. At the end of each test drive, motion sickness is measured again while the vehicle is stationary. Each drive is followed by a quantitative questionnaire. Table 1 shows the measured variables and their operationalization.

Qualitative Group Interview and Conclusion. As a final part of the study, the participants are interviewed as a group in order to identify the strengths and weaknesses of the vehicle interior concepts. The participants are first interviewed openly and then the observed CIs that have not yet been mentioned are addressed. At the end of the interview, the participants are asked the *WoOz control question* ("How would you rate the degree of automation of the vehicle you just drove?"; 5-point scale, adapted after [13]). The investigator then explains the WoOz design and its reasons. Then the participants provide information about themselves (*technology affinity* (Interactional Technology Affinity Questionnaire (ATI); 9 items; 6-point scale [15]) and *sociodemographic information*). Finally, the investigator notes environmental data of the test drives (weather conditions and traffic density).

3 Results (Preview)

As the data collection is scheduled to end in April 2023, the results cannot be presented in this short paper. At the HCII, initial insights are provided into how vehicle interior concepts influence interaction in automated driving.

4 Discussion

Compared to low-fidelity prototypes, creating a mid-fidelity prototype requires more effort to illustrate concept ideas. However, a simulation prototype in a vehicle allows for greater immersion and interaction of potential users. For example, the surfaces can be touched, the ergonomics of playing with the tablet in one's hand can be directly compared to the ergonomics of playing with the tablet integrated into the table, and the driving experience and its impact on the user is more realistic.

Compared to laboratory research, field research has lower internal validity because not all conditions can be controlled as in a laboratory setting (e.g., changing weather or traffic conditions or the driving behavior of the WoOz-driver). However, the advantages of field research are that authentic subject behavior can be observed while driving, and the results are more likely to be generalizable. In particular, information about driving experience or motion sickness is different from laboratory settings.

The quantitative evaluation and the qualitative user feedback serve to identify the strengths and weaknesses of the concept, thus avoiding a greater development effort to realize a high-fidelity prototype in a potentially unsuitable direction.

Table 1. Variables and their operationalization

Variable	Instrument	Items	References
Motion sickness	Misery Scale (MISC)	single-item; 11-point scale	[9]
Winning the game		single-item; 2-point scale	
User experience	User Experience Questionnaire-Short (UEQ-S)	8 bipolar items; 7-point scale	[10]
	Facets of User Experience	65 bipolar items; 7-point scale	[11]
System trust	Trust in Automation (TiA)	19 items; 5-point scale	[12]
Subjective traffic safety	Single-items on risk and safety	2 items; 5-point scale	[13]
	Subjective safety	12 bipolar items; 7-point scale	*
Accessibility (refrigerator and emergency buttons)		2 items; 6-point scale	
Intention to use		3 items; 5-point scale	Adapted from [14]
Evaluation of equipment elements**	Ranking of equipment elements with regard to ownership preference (scenario: equipment of own vehicle)	7 items; drag ranking	
Acceptance of the interior concepts**	Selection of an interior concept with regard to usage preference (scenario: driving from Stuttgart to Frankfurt)	single-item; 2-point scale	

Note. The variables without a reference are instruments developed by the authors
* The instrument was developed in collaboration with the University of Stuttgart
** These questions are answered only after the second drive

References

1. SAE International: Taxonomy and definitions for terms related to driving automation systems for on-road motor vehicles (2021). https://doi.org/10.4271/J3016_202104
2. Teicht, M., Haar, P., Stimm, D., Engeln, A.: How do different vehicle interior concepts influence work and entertainment experience during automated driving? In: Stephanidis, C., et al. (eds.) HCI International 2023 Posters, CCIS, vol. 1836, pp. 1–9. Springer, Cham (2023). https://doi.org/10.1007/978-3-031-36004-6_15

3. Deutsches Institut für Normung e. V.: DIN EN ISO 9241–210:2020–03, Ergonomie der Mensch-System-Interaktion - Teil 210: Menschzentrierte Gestaltung interaktiver Systeme (ISO 9241-210:2019), Deutsche Fassung EN ISO 9241-210:2019. Beuth, Berlin (2020). https://doi.org/10.31030/3104744
4. Haar, P., Pagenkopf, A., Teicht, M., Engeln, A.: Nutzeranforderungen an die Gestaltung von Fahrzeuginnenräumen beim vollautomatisierten Fahren (2021). https://projekt-rumba.de/wp-content/uploads/2021/09/210908_Nutzeranforderungen-an-die-Gestaltung-von-Fahrzeuginnenraeumen-beim-vollautomatisierten-Fahren-_RUMBA-Website.pdf
5. Haar, P., Pagenkopf, A., Teicht, M., Engeln, A.: Nutzeranforderungen von Pkw-Fahrern an die Gestaltung von Anzeigen und Bedienelementen und Fahrzeuginnenräumen beim automatisierten Fahren in SAE Level 4. In: Kolloquium Future Mobility (2022). ISBN 978-3-943-563-51-1
6. Teicht, M., Haar, P., Pagenkopf, A., Stimm, D., Engeln, A.: Evaluation von Innenraumkonzepten vollautomatisiert fahrender Fahrzeuge. In: Kolloquium Future Mobility (2022). ISBN 978-3-943-563-51-1
7. Jorlöv, S., Bohman, K., Larsson, A.: Seating positions and activities in highly automated cars. A qualitative study of future automated driving scenarios. In: International Research Conference on the Biomechanics of Impact, IRCOBI, pp. 13–22. Association for Computing Machinery, New York (2017). http://www.ircobi.org/wordpress/downloads/irc17/pdf-files/11.pdf
8. Flanagan, J.C.: The critical incident technique. Psychol. Bull. **51**(4), 327–358 (1954). https://doi.org/10.1037/h0061470
9. Bos, J.E., MacKinnon, S.N., Patterson, A.: Motion sickness symptoms in a ship motion simulator: effects of inside, outside, and no view. Aviat. Space Environ. Med. **76**(12), 1111–1118 (2006)
10. Schrepp, M., Hinderks, A., Thomaschewski, J.: Design and evaluation of a short version of the user experience questionnaire (UEQ-S). Int. J. Interact. Multimedia Artif. Intell. **4**(6), 103–108 (2017). https://doi.org/10.9781/ijimai.2017.09.001
11. Engeln, A., Engeln, C.: Customer Experience und kundenzentrierte Angebotsentwicklung. Was gehört dazu? In: Baetzgen, A. (ed.) Brand Experience: An jedem Touchpoint auf den Punkt begeistern, pp. 253–273. Schäffer-Poeschel, Stuttgart (2015)
12. Körber, M.: Theoretical considerations and development of a questionnaire to measure trust in automation. In: Bagnara, S., Tartaglia, R., Albolino, S., Alexander, T., Fujita, Y. (eds.) IEA 2018. AISC, vol. 823, pp. 13–30. Springer, Cham (2019). https://doi.org/10.1007/978-3-319-96074-6_2
13. Flohr, L.A., Valiyaveettil, J.S., Krüger A., Wallach, D.P.: Prototyping autonomous vehicle windshields with AR and real-time object detection visualization: an on-road wizard-of-oz study. In: Designing Interactive Systems Conference (DIS 2023), pp. 1–15. ACM, New York (2023). https://doi.org/10.1145/3563657.3596051
14. Müller, A., Stockinger, C., Walter, J., Heuser, T., Abendroth, B., Bruder, R.: Einflussfaktoren auf die Akzeptanz des automatisierten Fahrens aus der Sicht von Fahrerinnen und Fahrern. In: Winner, H., Bruder, R. (eds.) (Wie) wollen wir automatisiert fahren? 8. Darmstädter Kolloquium, pp. 1–22. Technische Universität Darmstadt, Darmstadt (2017). https://tuprints.ulb.tu-darmstadt.de/5672/1/Mensch%20und%20Fahrzeug%20Tagungsband%202017.pdf
15. Franke, T., Attig, C., Wessel, D.: A personal resource for technology interaction: development and validation of the affinity for technology interaction (ATI) scale. Int. J. Hum.-Comput. Interact. **35**(6), 456–467 (2019). https://doi.org/10.1080/10447318.2018.1456150

Implementation of 34.7 fps Pose and Gaze Estimator for Real-Time Driver-Vehicle Interaction System

Minjoon Kim(✉), Jaehyuk So, and Taemin Hwang

Korea Electronics Technology Institute, Seongnam, South Korea
mjoon@keti.re.kr

Abstract. With the recent rapid development of autonomous driving, many researches on intelligent in-vehicle interaction technologies have been studied. Real-time driver behavior analysis is a key function for various in-vehicle interaction ap-plications. An important performance indicator here is real-time quality because it is directly related to safety. Therefore, in this paper, we design the convolutional neural network (CNN) architecture suited to in-vehicle driver behavior analysis using pose and gaze. First, we define the 11 key points for driver pose and gaze, and modeled a CNN architecture that can detect them quickly. The proposed architecture was re-generated and re-trained with layer reduction for high speed based on the residual CNN model. Furthermore, the hardware implementation result based on FPGA platform to verify the real-time performance are presented. In order to implement real-time interaction, an image processing speed of more than 30 fps and a latency time of less than 100 ms are generally required. We selected and implemented the FPGA platform to meet these requirements. The designed hardware architecture was implemented at the RTL level of the VCU118 FPGA, and simulation results show 34.7 fps and 75.3 ms latency. Finally, we implemented the driver pose and gaze estimator on the FPGA based hardware platform to experiment the driver-vehicle interaction system with the demo application. The detected pose and gaze results were transmitted to the GPU board in real time, reliably supporting 30 fps, and verified application to screen control and driver monitoring applications.

Keywords: Driver-Vehicle Interaction · Driver Behavior Analysis · Autonomous Vehicle · Human Pose Estimation · CNN Accelerator

1 Introduction

Due to the recent introduction of driving assistance systems and autonomous vehicles, driver behavior analysis (DBA) is an essential function to ensure safety through monitoring the driver's condition and behavior in the vehicle [1]. In future automobiles, DBAs will certainly become much more extensive and equipped as a basic feature [2]. In addition, in recent years, DBA are not limited to unilateral understanding of drivers, but are also used to link vehicle functions through driver-vehicle interaction (DVI) as

C. Stephanidis et al. (Eds.): HCII 2023, CCIS 1836, pp. 30–35, 2023.
https://doi.org/10.1007/978-3-031-36004-6_5

shown in as shown in Fig. 1. Vehicle control through driver motion is a representative application example [3]. Therefore, since real-time interaction between the driver and the vehicle must take place, reaction speed and operating speed are very important, and many studies are being conducted [4].

Many studies have been conducted to understand the driver based on the visual characteristics of the driver [5]. In particular, driver posture and gaze estimation is a key function of classifying the driver's condition and behavior and recognizing the situation [6, 7]. With the development of deep-learning based image processing technology that estimates a person's skeleton based on camera images, it is likely to be easily introduced into the driver's environment in the vehicle, but it does not support the 30 fps speed generally required for real-time state analysis [8].

In this paper, we define and design the convolutional neural network (CNN) architecture based 11-keypoints pose and gaze estimation suited to in-vehicle driver environments. Further-more, the hardware design and simulation results are described. Finally, the implementation result based on FPGA platform to verify the real-time performance are presented.

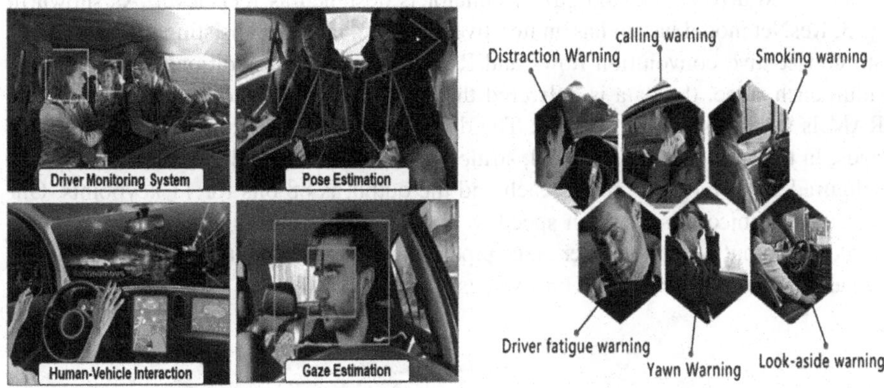

Fig. 1. Concept of driver behavior analysis system based in-vehicle interaction applications.

2 Algorithm Modeling

First, we define the 11 key points for driver pose and gaze, and modeled a CNN architecture that can detect them quickly. Human pose estimation is a general problem of identification and classification of human body by array of keypoints. As shown in Fig. 2, we define the 11 key points, which is reduced from general 18 keypoints according to the COCO [9], one of the representative datasets. Also, we proposed architecture is designed with 16-depth CNN layer which is 4-layer reduced from the existing ResNet-18 model, and computational complexity was decreased by 68.49% [10]. The input image is set to 256 × 192 × 3, and the output data is 64 × 48 × 11 called heatmap including the detected probability. The proposed architecture was re-trained for driver pose and gaze estimation for achieving the detection success within 5% error with the reference model.

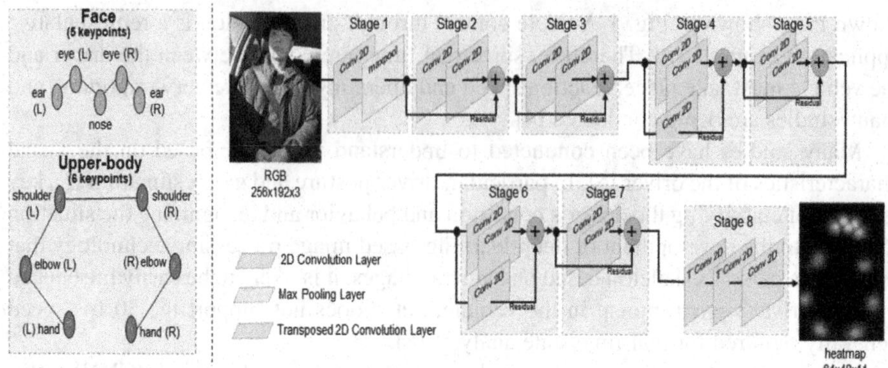

Fig. 2. Proposed 11-keypoints and CNN architecture for the driver pose and gaze estimation.

3 H/W Design and Simulation

The proposed driver pose and gaze estimator is designed as RTL level. As shown in Fig. 3, ResNet model has an has an iterative structure, mainly consisting of CNN stages with consecutive convolution flows and R-CNN stages with additional residual flow. Within each stage, the data is delivered through line buffer, whereas between stages, SRAM is used to separate the data. The designed architecture consists of a total of 8 stages. In the case of ResNet model, stride 2 is mainly used, and therefore the input is configured as 48 bits by 2 pixels each and the output is 88 bits for 11 keypoints. Our performance objectives are high speed & low latency. In each stage, SRAM contains the stage's output to support inter-stage pipelining, and ROM contains CNN parameters such as convolution weight and bias values.

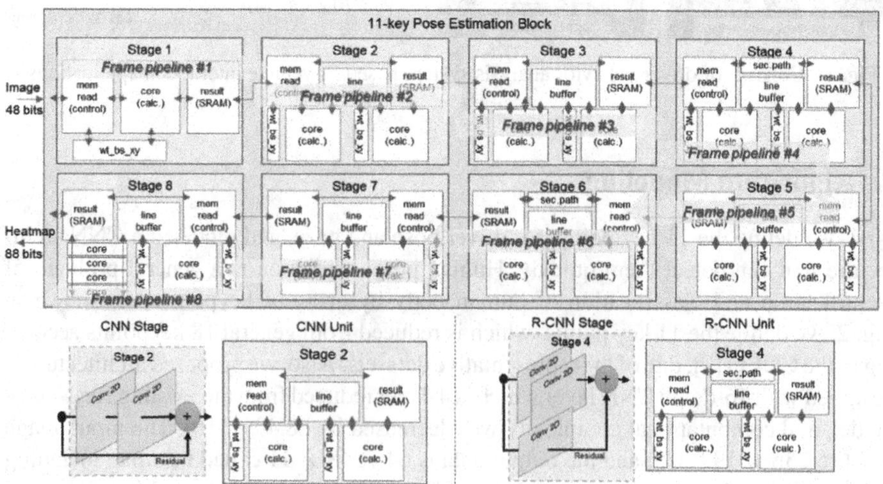

Fig. 3. Hardware block diagram of the designed driver pose and gaze estimator.

In order to implement real-time interaction, an image processing speed of more than 30 fps and a latency time of less than 100 ms are generally required. We selected and implemented the FPGA platform to meet these requirements. The designed hardware architecture was implemented at the RTL level of the Xilinx VCU118 FPGA development kit. The synthesis and implementation results are shown in Fig. 4. We can see the timing and utilization report from synthesis result, and all constraints are met.

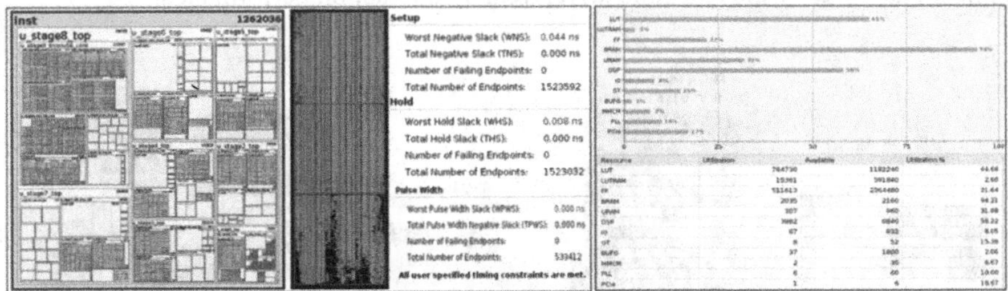

Fig. 4. FPGA synthesis and implementation results at Xilinx VCU118 development kit.

Finally, we simulated the RTL designed to validate the target performance, the processing speed of 30 fps and latency of 100 ms. The functional simulation results is presented in Fig. 5, and for the specific analysis, a timing diagram for each stage in the CNN structure is presented together. It can be seen that continuous image frames operate without problems at intervals of about 28.8 ms, which can be translated into 34.7 fps, and thus it is determined that 30 fps real-time operation is possible. It can also be seen that the output latency time to process one image frame is 75.3 ms, which meets the target performance of 100 ms.

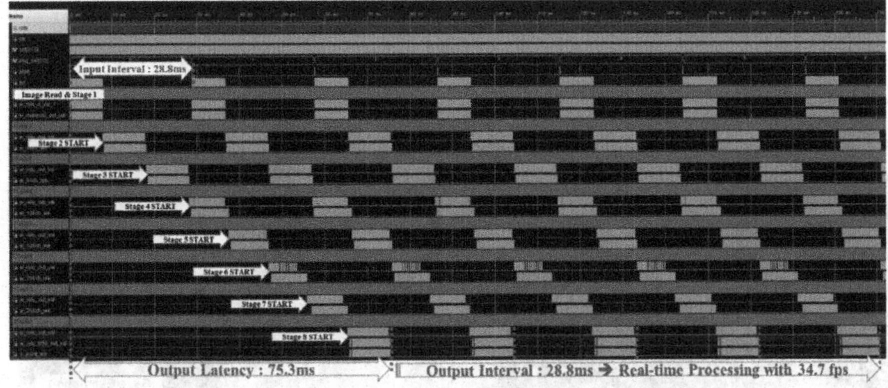

Fig. 5. Functional simulation results and timing diagram for verifying real-time processing.

4 Real-Time Demo Platform

We constructed the hardware platform to implement the driver pose and gaze estimator and to experiment the driver-vehicle interaction system with the demo application. As shown in Fig. 6, 4 cameras are connected to FPGA platform to acquire a real-time image, and a pose estimator is performed. The detected pose and gaze results were transmitted to the GPU board in real time, and applied to the screen control and driver state prediction applications to verify the real-time driver-vehicle interaction performance.

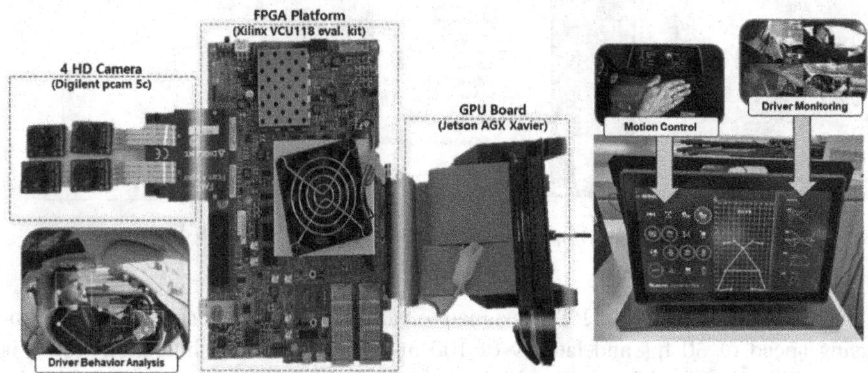

Fig. 6. Demo platform for real-time driver-vehicle interaction system

Finally, the configured demo platform was verified with real people motions as shown in Fig. 7. The developed FPGA system supports images from 30 fps cameras in real time and the results of pose and gaze are output, so that the demo application can be seen to operate smoothly. It was determined that it showed performance suitable for use in motion control or driver monitoring in processing speed and reaction time.

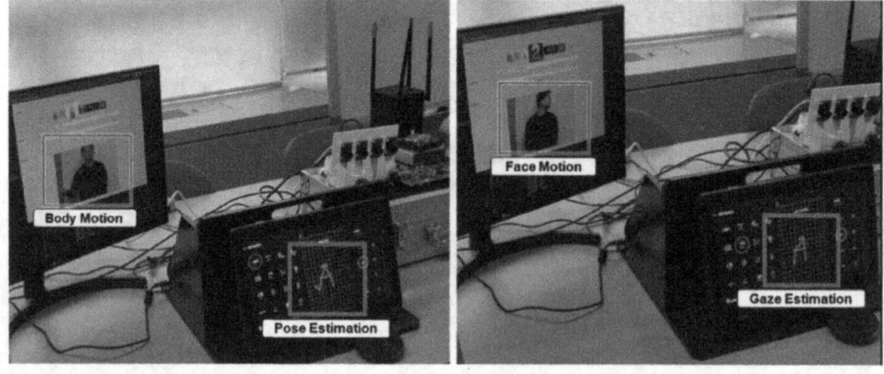

Fig. 7. Demo applications and real-time evaluation results for real people.

5 Conclusion

With the rapid development of autonomous vehicles, DVI technology based on real-time DBA is drawing attention. In this paper, we design and validate a CNN architecture suitable for real-time DBA in vehicles using poses and gaze. An FPGA platform was implemented to verify the image processing speed of more than 30 fps and the latency of less than 100 ms, which is generally required to implement real-time interaction. We experimented with a DVI system with a demo application, resulting in a screen control and driver monitoring application that reliably supports 30 fps.

Acknowledgments. This work was supported by the Technology Innovation Program (20016036, InVehicle Infotainment Integrated AP and Application SW for multi tasking of multi users) funded By the Ministry of Trade, Industry & Energy (MOTIE, Korea).

References

1. Kaplan, S., Guvensan, M.A., Yavuz, A.G., Karalurt, Y.: Driver behavior analysis for safe driving. IEEE Trans. Intell. Transp. Syst. **16**(6), 3017–3032 (2015)
2. Murali, P.K., Dahiya, R.: Intelligent in-vehicle interaction technologies. Adv. Intell. Syst. **4**(2), 1–27 (2022)
3. Das, N., Ohn-Bar, E., Trivedi, M.M.: On performance evaluation of driver hand detection algorithms: challenges, dataset, and metrics. In: Proceedings of IEEE 18th International Conference on Intelligent Transportation Systems (ICITS), Spain (2015)
4. Wijnands, J.S., Thompson, J., Nice, K.A., Aschwanden, G.D.P.A., Stevenson, M.: Real-time monitoring of driver drowsiness on mobile platforms using 3D neural networks. Neural Comput. Appl. **32**(13), 9731–9743 (2019). https://doi.org/10.1007/s00521-019-04506-0
5. Xing, Y., et al.: Identification and analysis of driver postures for in-vehicle driving activities and secondary tasks recognition. IEEE Trans. Comput. Soc. Syst. **5**(1), 95–108 (2018)
6. Borghi, G., Venturelli, M., Vezzani, R., Cucchiara, R.: POSEidon: face-from-depth for driver pose estimation In: Proceedings of IEEE International Conference on Computer Vision and Pattern Recognition (CVPR), Hawaii (2017)
7. Kumar, A., Patra, R.: Driver drowsiness monitoring system using visual behaviour and machine learning In: Proceedings of IEEE Symposium on Computer Applications & Industrial Electronics (ISCAIE), Malaysia (2018)
8. Xiao, B., Wu, H., Wei, Y.: Simple baselines for human pose estimation and tracking. In: Ferrari, V., Hebert, M., Sminchisescu, C., Weiss, Y. (eds.) ECCV 2018. LNCS, vol. 11210, pp. 472–487. Springer, Cham (2018). https://doi.org/10.1007/978-3-030-01231-1_29
9. Lin, T.Y., et al.: Microsoft COCO: Common objects in context. arXiv 2014: arXiv preprint arXiv:1405.0312
10. Kim, M., So, J.: Design of high-speed pose estimator for real-time human-vehicle interaction. In: Proceedings of Asia Pacific International Conference on Information Science and Technology (APIC-IST), South Korea (2021)

Reinforcement Learning Based Power Seat Actuation to Mitigate Carsickness of Autonomous Vehicles

Chang-Gyu Lee(✉) and Ohung Kwon

Korea Institute of Industrial Technology, Gyeonggi-do, South Korea
{cglee,ohung}@kitech.re.kr

Abstract. When autonomous vehicles (AVs) are commercialized, people will be able to engage in various activities in the vehicle, such as reading books and using mobile devices. However, 2/3 of passengers suffer from carsickness when looking at still scene in a moving vehicle. This carsickness is a problem that must be overcome, which eliminates advantages of AV. Therefore, in this paper, a methodology to cancel out the acceleration generated by the AV through the operation of the motor-based power seat was proposed. In addition, a methodology for determining the actuation signal of the power seat through reinforcement learning (RL) was proposed. Then, the effectiveness of the method was verified through a simulation. Consequently, it was confirmed that the proposed method is effective in reducing carsickness. In the future, performance improvement through RL optimization and actual effect verification through human studies are planned.

Keywords: Power seat · Reinforcement learning · Carsickness · Autonomous vehicle

1 Introduction

According to a literature, about 2/3 of passengers suffer from a carsickness [7]. Meanwhile, when autonomous vehicles (AVs) become commercially available, everyone in the AVs becomes a passenger. Therefore, the probability that a passenger suffering from carsickness is in the AV increases. By the way, this carsickness makes passengers uncomfortable and it eliminates the benefits of AVs. Therefore, carsickness is an important problem to be solved.

In previous studies, there was an attempt to install a webcam on a dashboard of a vehicle and use the captured scene as the background of a mobile device (e.g., smartphone or tablet) [5]. And there was an attempt to inform the rotation direction of the vehicle by giving vibration to the haptic devices composed of 7 mini vibration motors installed in both of the passenger's forearm [3]. Also, there was an attempt to inform the vehicle's rotation direction using 32 light-emitting diodes (LEDs) installed around the visual display device [2]. Finally, after setting the border of the smartphone as a visualization area, an attempt was made to

C. Stephanidis et al. (Eds.): HCII 2023, CCIS 1836, pp. 36–41, 2023.
https://doi.org/10.1007/978-3-031-36004-6_6

present a moving bubble in this area according to the vehicle's acceleration direction and magnitude [4]. However, some of them had a limitation that an additional device was necessary (e.g., webcam, haptic device, and LEDs) [2,3,5], and some of them had a limitation that it was effective only when using a mobile device [2,4]. Therefore, in this paper, a method of canceling out the acceleration generated by AVs using a power seat is developed. This does not require an additional device because it uses the power seat already present in the vehicle, and it is applicable not only when using a mobile device but also when reading a book. In the proposed system, depending on which signal is applied to the power seat, carsickness increases or decreases. In this paper, therefore, the actuation signal applied to the power seat was determined through reinforcement learning (RL) that takes best choice by trial-and-error [8].

In order to validate the proposed method, a simulation was performed to compare the otolith response in the following two cases: (i) when vehicle acceleration was not canceled out, (ii) when the vehicle acceleration was canceled out by applying the actuation signal generated by RL to the power seat. As a result, the feasibility of the RL-based power seat actuation for the mitigation of the carsickness was verified.

This paper is organized as follows: Sect. 2 introduces RL and RL for power seat actuation. The next Sect. 3 introduces the simulation condition, measurements, learning environment and hyper parameters for RL, and simulation results. Finally, Sect. 4 closes this paper by presenting the conclusions and future works.

2 Reinforcement Learning

This section briefly introduces RL and the configuration for applying RL to power seat actuation.

2.1 Reinforcement Learning

RL is one of the machine learning methods to achieve performance improvement through trial and error. As shown in Fig. 1, RL consists of two components, agent and environment, and three information of action, state, and reward is transmitted between the two components. During a training, the agent performs various actions in various states and generates various rewards, and as a result, it is possible to know which action generates a higher reward in a given state.

2.2 Reinforcement Learning for Power Seat Actuation

The objective of this paper is to cancel out the acceleration generated by the AV through an actuation of the power seat. In this system, the actuation signal of the power seat is manipulated while observing the vehicle state, the passenger state, and the power seat state. Therefore, the agent of RL is the power seat controller that generates actuation signal, and the environments of RL are vehicle, passenger, and power seat that are observation targets.

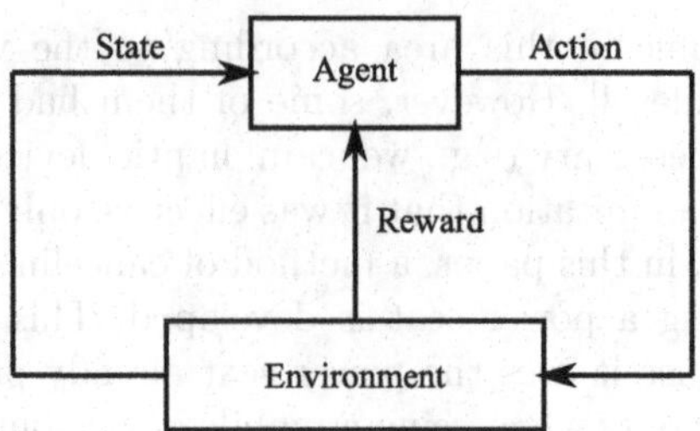

Fig. 1. Structure of the reinforcement learning

Firstly, the agent performs an action that generates a power seat actuation signal in a specific range (between $-1\,\mathrm{m/s^2}$ and $1\,\mathrm{m/s^2}$). Next, the velocity of the power seat was limited to -0.5 m/s and 0.5 m/s. Finally, the workspace of the power seat was limited to 1 m because the AV has space limits.

Secondly, the power seat receiving the actuation signal changes the passenger acceleration (vehicle acceleration minus power seat acceleration), otolith response (perceived vestibular acceleration), and power seat position. Among them, the otolith response can be obtained by a mathematical model [10].

Thirdly, states of vehicle acceleration, passenger acceleration, otolith response of the passenger, and normalized power seat position are provided to the agent.

Finally, the environment generates reward by using otolith response of the passenger as follows:

$$r = \begin{cases} -|\hat{f}_i| + 2, \text{ if } |\hat{f}_i| \leq 2 \\ -|\hat{f}_i| \times 5, \text{ otherwise} \end{cases}. \quad (1)$$

where r and $\hat{f}_i$ are reward and currently perceived force, respectively. If the passenger senses a greater vestibular acceleration, greater motion sickness occurs [6]. Therefore, to make an agent that produces a smaller vestibular acceleration, the reward was generated by multiplying the otolith response by (-1). In the mean time, there is a special phenomenon obtained by the workspace limitation of the power seat. If the power seat reaches the workspace limitation during actuation, the power seat stops with impact (large acceleration). Therefore, the reward must be computed by considering the power seat impact. If there is no impact ($|\hat{f}_i|$ is smaller than 2), an operation was performed to add 2 to maintain the reward as a positive value. On the other hand, when there is an impact, the perceived vestibular acceleration was multiplied by 5 to give a large penalty.

3 Simulation

This section presents the simulation condition, measurement, learning environment and hyper parameters of RL, simulation results, and discussions to find out whether the RL-based power seat actuation method reduces sensory conflict of the AV passenger.

3.1 Simulation Conditions

There are values that must be selected to perform simulation. It includes otolith response related values and acceleration/velocity/position ranges of AV. The values are selected to match the simulation environment and the AV driving environment similarly. Firstly, the vehicle acceleration provided by the environment to the agent is a value randomly selected between -3 m/s^2 and 3 m/s^2. The simulation was performed in an environment in which the AV accelerates and decelerates at random. Secondly, there is no restriction on the position of the vehicle.

To check the feasibility of RL-based power seat actuation, the performance of the general situation in which the power seat does not move and the proposed situation in which the power seat is driven using the RL were compared. This comparison was made on an AV driven for 60 s.

3.2 Measurements

As shown in Fig. 2, if the passenger reads a book or uses a smartphone in AV, the passenger receives fixed visual feedback. That is, perceived visual acceleration is zero. On the other hand, the remainder subtracting the power seat acceleration from the vehicle acceleration is transmitted to the vestibular system. If this remainder acceleration is not zero, the perceived vestibular acceleration of the passenger becomes a non zero value. Carsickness arises from the difference between these two perceived accelerations [6]. And it is intuitively predictable that carsickness will increase as this difference increases [9]. In the meantime, it is assumed that perceived visual acceleration is zero. Therefore, the larger the perceived vestibular acceleration the greater the carsickness, so the magnitude of the perceived vestibular acceleration was used as a measurement for performance comparison.

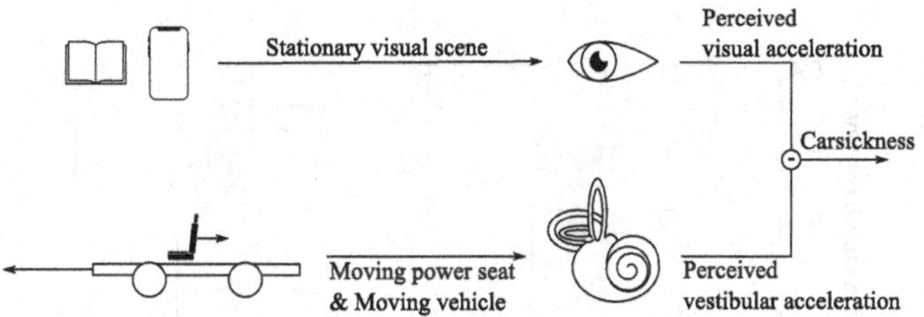

Fig. 2. Carsickness caused by a sensory conflict

Table 1. Hyper parameters

Hyper parameters	Values
batch_size	64
buffer_size	12000
learning_rate	0.003
hidden_units	128
num_layers	2
beta	0.001
epsilon	0.2
lambd	0.99
num_epoch	3

3.3 Learning Environment and Hyper Parameters

The learning environment was configured using the UNITY ml-agents toolkit. For training, a proximal policy optimization (PPO) algorithm [8] that performs better than others and is the most commonly used [1] was used . Also, the hyper parameters used for learning are shown in Table 1. As the learning of 4 million steps progressed, the reward did not increase and the loss did not decrease. After completing the learning, the actuation signal of the power seat was generated using the learned model.

3.4 Simulation Results

Figure 3 shows the mean otolith response when RL based power seat actuation is applied and when the power seat is stationary without motion. As seen in the figure, after applying RL based power seat actuation, the mean otolith response was reduced about 38.44%. A statistical analysis was performed to check whether the difference in mean otolith response between the two conditions was statistically significant. Consequently, there was a statistically significant difference between the mean otolith responses of the two conditions ($F(1, 98) = 481.039$, $p < 0.001$***).

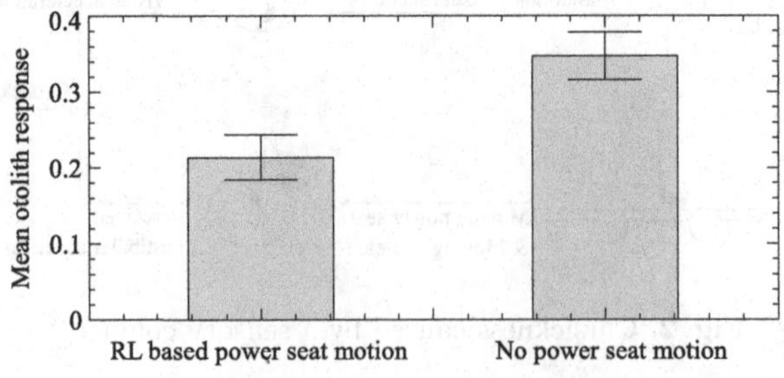

Fig. 3. Mean otolith response for two conditions

4 Conclusions and Futureworks

This paper proposed an RL based power seat actuation method to alleviate the carsickness that AV passengers may experience. And simulation was performed to verify the proposed methodology. As a result, it was confirmed that the otolith response decreased by about 38% when the proposed method was applied. In the future, the authors of this paper will conduct a study to find the optimal reward that minimizes the otolith response, and will verify whether this methodology is actually effective through human studies.

References

1. Andrychowicz, M., et al.: What matters in on-policy reinforcement learning? a large-scale empirical study (2020). arXiv preprint arXiv:2006.05990
2. Karjanto, J., Yusof, N.M., Wang, C., Terken, J., Delbressine, F., Rauterberg, M.: The effect of peripheral visual feedforward system in enhancing situation awareness and mitigating motion sickness in fully automated driving. Transport. Res. F: Traffic Psychol. Behav. **58**, 678–692 (2018)
3. Md. Yusof, N., Karjanto, J., Kapoor, S., Terken, J., Delbressine, F., Rauterberg, M.: Experimental setup of motion sickness and situation awareness in automated vehicle riding experience. In: Proceedings of the 9th International Conference on Automotive User Interfaces and Interactive Vehicular Applications Adjunct, pp. 104–109 (2017)
4. Meschtscherjakov, A., Strumegger, S., Trösterer, S.: Bubble margin: motion sickness prevention while reading on smartphones in vehicles. In: Lamas, D., Loizides, F., Nacke, L., Petrie, H., Winckler, M., Zaphiris, P. (eds.) INTERACT 2019. LNCS, vol. 11747, pp. 660–677. Springer, Cham (2019). https://doi.org/10.1007/978-3-030-29384-0_39
5. Miksch, M., Steiner, M., Miksch, M., Meschtscherjakov, A.: Motion sickness prevention system (MSPS) reading between the lines. In: Adjunct Proceedings of the 8th International Conference on Automotive User Interfaces and Interactive Vehicular Applications, pp. 147–152 (2016)
6. Reason, J.T.: Motion sickness adaptation: a neural mismatch model. J. R. Soc. Med. **71**(11), 819–829 (1978)
7. Schmidt, E.A., Kuiper, O.X., Wolter, S., Diels, C., Bos, J.E.: An international survey on the incidence and modulating factors of carsickness. Transport. Res. F: Traffic Psychol. Behav. **71**, 76–87 (2020)
8. Schulman, J., Wolski, F., Dhariwal, P., Radford, A., Klimov, O.: Proximal policy optimization algorithms. arXiv preprint arXiv:1707.06347 (2017)
9. Stoffregen, T.A., Riccio, G.E.: An ecological critique of the sensory conflict theory of motion sickness. Ecol. Psychol. **3**(3), 159–194 (1991)
10. Young, L.R., Meiry, J.L.: A revised dynamic otolith model. In: Third Symposium on the Role of the Vestibular Organs in Space Exploration, NASA SP-152, pp. 363–368 (1968)

A Study on Communication by Verbal: Focusing on Image Formation of Electric Vehicles

Heng Li(✉) and WonSeok Yang

Shibaura Institute of Technology, 3-9-14 Shibaura Minato-ku, Tokyo 108-8548, Japan
hl40538@gmail.com

Abstract. This study used the laddering method to evaluate "electric car-like" characteristics, and the following findings were obtained. First, we obtained a rough image of the front of a car that is likely to be perceived as an electric car. In addition, the classification of the front design areas and their characteristics revealed areas that influence the judgment of electric car-like structures. Finally, the words used by students in their 20s with no driving experience were identified. These findings can be used as a reference for designing electric vehicles. However, it was pointed out that research is still insufficient on how the characteristics of the modeling are connected to the image, the degree of influence is yet to be confirmed, and that issues remain in the number and diversity of the samples. Further research is required to gain deeper insight. Overall, this study is expected to be valuable in providing electric vehicle designs that are attractive to conservative Japanese consumers.

Keywords: electric car-like · front design · sensitivity

1 Research Background

Globally, the transition from "gasoline and diesel-free" to EVs is underway to achieve a decarbonized world. According to 2020 data, EV sales in the U.S. account for approximately 1.8% of vehicle sales, China for 4.4%, and the U.K. for 5.6%. Norway dominates the rest of the world at 54%. In Japan, however, EVs have not been widely adopted, accounting for just over 20,000 of the approximately 2.4 million new vehicles sold in 2022, or 0.9% of the total [1]. Under these circumstances, it is predicted that the Japanese government will find it difficult to achieve the goal of automobile decarbonization.

Although the Japanese government actively promotes EVs, there are several obstacles. First, major companies are maintaining their existing competitive advantage (PHVs), which delays the development of social infrastructure to accommodate EVs and slows the adoption of EVs. Second, major Japanese manufacturers were ahead of HVs, resulting in a mismatch between the market and the time when they introduced them due to the maturity of the technology, the high cost of social infrastructure development, and the cost of bearing the burden. In addition, while replacement demand is the primary demand in the Japanese market, consumers are price sensitive and have long periods of ownership, which has hindered the generation of sufficient new demand.

C. Stephanidis et al. (Eds.): HCII 2023, CCIS 1836, pp. 42–48, 2023.
https://doi.org/10.1007/978-3-031-36004-6_7

Finally, the conservative nature of Japanese consumers and their inability to distinguish EVs from conventional gasoline-powered vehicles has also contributed to the lack of motivation to purchase EVs [2].

2 Advance Research

Prior research on this theme includes the following studies:

Moriguchi discussed the changing significance and role of automobiles in today's increasingly urbanized society and the growing need for car designs that respond to this change [3]. Matsumura et al. aimed to analyze how car advertisements influence consumer perceptions and attitudes. They investigated the effects of information content and emotional stimuli in advertisements on consumers' perceptions and attitudes and used the results to propose effective methods for creating car advertisements [4]. In a study by Sato, a questionnaire survey was conducted to evaluate consumers' emotional evaluations of automobiles' front grille designs and to determine how subjects felt about those designs [5]. Minamimoto et al. aimed to determine how provocation items (proportions, balance, etc.) influence impressions of the "1.5 box" shape, which is an important element in the design of light cars [6].

These studies indicate the need to change car designs according to changing times and demand to change consumer perceptions and attitudes through advertising. They also suggest that although many studies have been conducted on car design and impression evaluation, research on electric car design is still insufficient.

Because there is a need to reinforce the unique image of electric vehicles to conservative Japanese consumers while distinguishing them from conventional gasoline-powered vehicles, this study attempts to clarify the embodiment of the sensibility of "electric vehicle-ness" in car design and the criteria for judging it in order to promote electric vehicles.

3 Experimental Procedure

3.1 Summary

In this experiment, we used the laddering method to evaluate the impressions of the proposed designs for the front parts of automobiles [7]. Focusing on eco-cars, which have a large consumer base, subjects were selected from cars sold in Japan. Students with different attributes, such as age, gender, design experience, and driving experience, were selected as the subject group, and the proposed designs were presented to them for impression evaluation. In addition, we asked the students about the parts and impressions that influenced their evaluation.

3.2 Experimental Procedure

First, the subjects were interviewed regarding their age, gender, design experience, and driving experience. Next, we sampled 25 design proposals from compact cars produced by Japanese automakers and asked subjects to select the five that they think are the "most electric car-like". The selected samples were placed side by side, and the participants were asked to rank them in order from the most to the least electric car-like. The results were photographed and recorded. Next, the samples were allotted numbers 1 and 2 and asked "Why is number 1 more like an electric car than number 2?" If it is a concrete feature, it ladders up and asks for an abstract image. Conversely, if an image is abstract, the ladder down is used to listen to specific features. All what was heard was recorded and documented. If they were unable to provide a reason, we asked them "why number 2 is not like an electric car." Finally, we asked a few questions about issues or concerns that were not clearly answered during the survey and asked for their opinions. The experimental procedure is illustrated in Fig. 1.

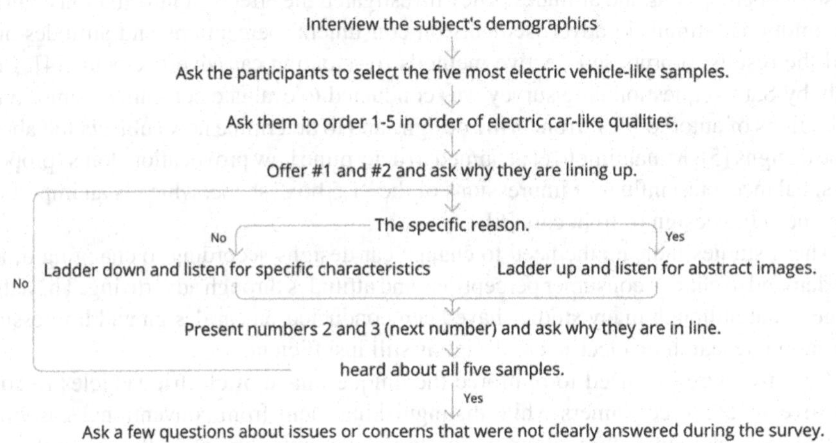

Fig. 1. Experimental procedure

3.3 Sample for Experiment

To evaluate the designs specifically for Japanese consumers, 25 different vehicle designs were selected from Japanese automakers, regardless of the power source, and the front portion of the vehicle was targeted to avoid the influence of body lines. Furthermore, to eliminate the influence of body color and visual size, all design proposals were changed to gray using Photoshop, adjusted for size, and a number was assigned to each, as shown in Fig. 2.

Fig. 2. Experimental sample

3.4 Experimental Results

The experiment was conducted using 32 Shibaura Institute of Technology students (aged 20–24) (male to female ratio 5:5) as subjects to obtain data on samples perceived as electric vehicles, their image of the samples, and the formative characteristics that influence their judgment. The results are presented in Table 1.

Table 1. Summary of experimental results

Number	Name	Gender	Age	Design Experience	driver's license	Drives well	Selected samples, 1st place	2nd	3rd	4th	5th	Sensitivity words mentioned	Mentioned sites
1	わかな	female	21	2	0	0	7	15	14	3	18	Simplicity, everyday appearance, practicality, around town, cute, Japanese loo	Headlight Radiator Krill (top), Size, Aspect Ratio
2	うわじま	man	22	2	1	0	14	2	23	5	11	Simple, modern, cluttered, crisp, compact, ecological	Headlight, Radiator Cril (above), Radiator Cril curve, with/without bumpers, overall shape
3	みうら	man	21	3	0	0	14	15	18	7	11	Simple, unfamiliar, futuristic, stylish, compact	Headlight, Radiator Krill (top), Radiator Krill (bottom), contours
4	たかや	female	20	3	0	0	17	9	7	11	3	Simple, futuristic, technical, outdoor	Contour and Radiator Krill
5	たなべ	female	21	3	0	0	6	2	18	7	9	Cool, cute, sharp, futuristic, familiar	Round shapes, square shapes, lines, lights, radiator acrylic (below)
6	やじま	man	21	2.5	1	0	11	18	14	6	2	Futuristic, stylish	Linear, radiator krill (bottom), front hamburger
7	もりた	man	21	3	0	0	14	15	18	8	7	Futuristic, familiar, simple	Line, streamlined, radiator krill (below)
8	ますこ	female	22	4	1	0	7	18	17	6	13	New, clean, compact.	Line and gloss (rounded corners)
9	ふるはし	man	21	4	1	0	15	14	6	18	24	Friendly, old, newest, cute, cutting edge, compact, cool	form
10	あきば	female	24	6	1	0	17	14	9	7	15	Futuristic, stylish, compact	Luster, size (large or small), cheek, width
11	たにお	female	23	2	0	1	7	11	1	18	14	Compact, storage, familiar, retro	Curves, lines, and luster
12	わたなべ	female	23	5	1	0	15	11	16	17	3	Compact, cutting-edge, futuristic, luxurious, cheap, fashionable	Light, aspect ratio, shape, concave, flat, curved
13	はるか	man	21	3	1	0	11	7	9	2	17	In town, cool	Streamline and light
14	ありま	man	24	6	1	1	14	15	18	11	17	Compact, Simple.	Frill (bottom), line, width
15	ぜん	female	21	4	0	0	7	14	15	18	6	Futuristic, familiar, and technological	Light, Smooth, Lumpy
16	ふくい	female	24	3	1	0	18	2	12	17	3	Clean, boxy, looks like a foreign car, powerful, cute, young, old	Aspect ratio, width, gloss, radiator grille
17	よこもり	man	21	0	1	1	15	14	7	17	2	Simple, up-to-date, vision, old-fashioned, smooth-running, new	Shape, windshield size, radiator grille
18	かわぐち	man	21	0.5	0	0	15	14	18	19	6	Near-future, rugged, cool	Light Radiator Krill (top), delimited
19	まつもと	man	22	4	0	0	18	17	9	2	12	Novelty, freshness, feminine, soft, familiar, old, smart, sophisticated, minimal	Light, aspect ratio, smoothness, roundness
20	かつふじ	man	21	3	1	0	15	14	10	2	9	Near future, apparent, old, cool, new	Straight & Curved (lateral), Rounded
21	なかむら	man	21	0	0	0	14	7	18	11	2	Simple, futuristic, smart, aerodynamic, horsepower, noisy	Roundness, Radiator Krill (bottom), Shape
22	さこ	man	21	0.5	0	0	15	18	14	6	2	Familiar, futuristic, new, multifunctional, convenient	Light, round, cheek, radiator krill (bottom)
23	まつお	man	22	3	1	0	14	15	11	18	2	Girlish, voluminous, simple, new	Light Radiator acrylic, horizontal line
24	いしわだ	female	221	3	1	0	15	17	18	12	19	Simple, new, cute, familiar, and secure	Curved surface, smoothness, shape, expression
25	い	man	24	4	0	0	14	19	19	18	13	Free, recent, smooth, made	Shape, radiator cell, smoothness, hole
26	やまもと	female	21	0	1	1	15	14	8	18	10	Newness, coolness, friendliness, and interior space	Radiator cricles, shape and light
27	ばしょうみや	female	21	4	1	0	14	7	15	18	11	Never seen before, futuristic, simple, square, sharp, cute	Light Radiator Krill (upper and lower), Lines, Cheeks
28	よこやま	female	21	4	1	0	15	6	18	19	9	New, futuristic, energy-saving, lean, glossy	Roundness, line, shape
29	とりゆみ	female	21	3	1	0	8	14	3	21	10	Unstumped, familiar, cutting-edge	Light Radiator acrylic, glossy
30	ごとう	man	22	0.5	0	0	14	15	18	11	6	Familiar, cute, new, clean, cool, familiar	Radiator Krill (below), smooth, size, aspect ratio, light
31	たかだま	female	23	5	0	0	15	14	19	17	10	Volume Kan, Latest, Familiar, and	Lights, light spacing, cheeks
32	あんざい	man	24	5	1	0	15	18	19	13	25	Cute, energy-saving, soft, old	Light spacing, round, radiator cricle, light

4 Discussion of Experimental Results

4.1 Samples Perceived as "Electric Vehicle-Like

As a result of the experiment, the number of times the 32 subjects selected each of the five samples that appeared to be typical of electric cars was determined statistically. Although we did not perform statistics by rank, we considered samples selected more than 10 times as electric car-like. The images of the top eight ranked samples are shown in Fig. 4 (Fig. 3).

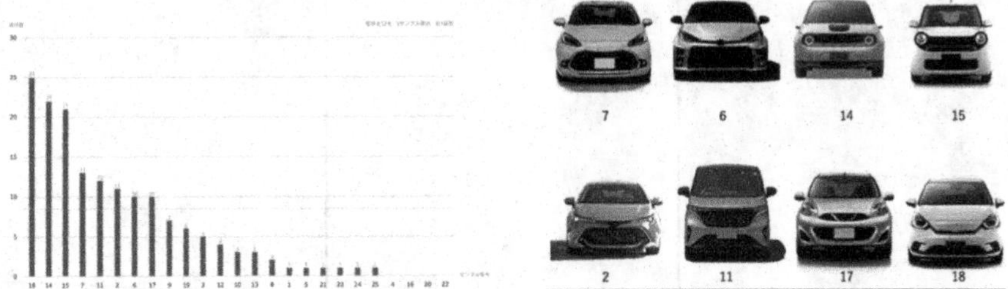

Fig. 3. Number of sample selections. **Fig. 4.** Top 8 selections in the sample.

The results of the experiment confirm that there is a disparity in the number of times the design was chosen among the electric-car-like designs. Samples 14, 15, and 18 were chosen more often than other five samples, suggesting that these shapes provide a more electric car-like impression.

4.2 Formative Features that Influence the Judgment of Electric Vehicle Character

Based on the statistical results of the parts mentioned when judging the electric car-like characteristics, the parts that greatly influence the judgment of electric car-like characteristics can be divided into seven parts: "headlights," "radiator acrylic top,"

"radiator acrylic bottom," "bumper," "foglines," "aspect ratio," and "contour shape," and the smaller parts of "presence or absence of gaps." The seven categories are "Gaps," "Gloss," "Straight and Curved," "Flat and Curved," and "Curvature."

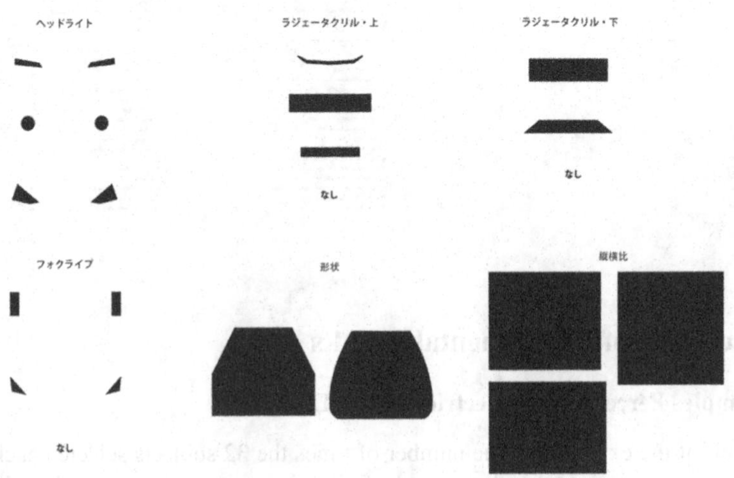

Fig. 5. Results of analysis of characteristics of each part

The top eight sample items that seemed to be typical of electric vehicles were extracted for each characteristic, and the results are shown in Fig. 5. We did not analyze the features of the bumpers because no differences were found among the eight samples. In addition, no analysis was performed on the detailed features because it was difficult to classify them.

From the above results, we identified the important areas and their characteristics that influence the judgment of electric-car-like features. Headlights, radiator grille tops, and radiator grille bottoms can be broadly classified into two categories: square and rectangular. However, it is still not known how the characteristics of each area influence the electric car-like features, and this should be considered in future research.

4.3 Images Related to Electric Vehicle-Like Features

When asked why they judged it to be electric vehicle like, 53 image words were generated. The results are presented in Table 2.

Table 2. Words of Reasons Influencing Decisions

square	refinement	cheap	feminine	cutting-edge	interior space
hard	compactness	cleanliness	wild	latest	downtown
harshness	stylish	cool	freshness	seen on the street	field of vision
rugged	receipts	softness	novelty	cutting-edge	outdoor
crunchy	indecisive	strength	gentle	old-fashioned	energy conservation
voluminous	cute	sense of class	smart	outmoded	noisy
minimal	cool	modern	familiarity	multifunction	Smooth running
feeling of clutter	sharp	technical	velvety	practicality	air resistance
simple	stylish	ecology	sense of the near future		convenient

To further clarify the image, a cluster analysis was performed using 53 words. As these words are a mixture of those used to determine what is and is not electric vehicle-like, the cluster analysis yielded 11 sets of results. The results are shown in the table below (Table 3).

Table 3. 11 pairs of words

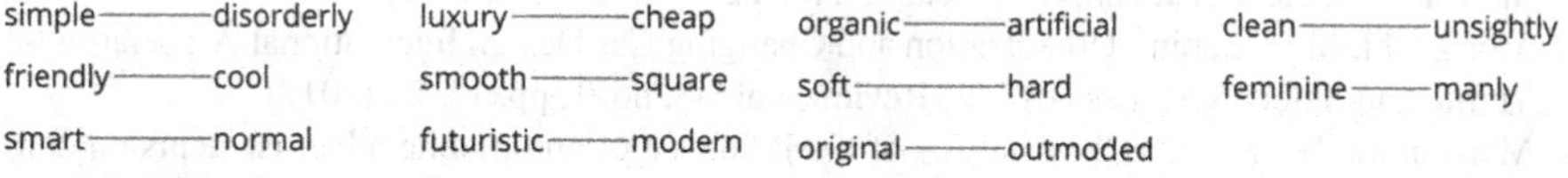

simple——disorderly	luxury——cheap	organic——artificial	clean——unsightly
friendly——cool	smooth——square	soft——hard	feminine——manly
smart——normal	futuristic——modern	original——outmoded	

These results clearly show the impressions that subjects have of electric vehicles compared to gasoline-powered vehicles. We believe that the results can be divided into three types of impressions: "impression by modeling," "impression by experience," and "impression by imagination."

5 Result

This study evaluated the front design using the laddering method to obtain the following findings

- Rough image of the front of a car that is likely to be perceived as an electric car.
- The classification of the front design parts and their characteristics, which influence the judgment that the car is likely to be an electric car, was clarified.
- Words used by students in their 20s with no driving experience to describe the image of an electric car. Based on these findings, we developed automobile design guidelines to reinforce the unique image of electric vehicles.

The results allowed us to study automobile design guidelines to reinforce the unique image of electric vehicles while distinguishing them from conventional gasoline-powered vehicles for conservative Japanese consumers.

6 Conclusion

This study attempted to clarify the embodiment of the sensibility of "electric vehicle-ness" in car design and the criteria for judging it to promote the widespread use of electric vehicles. From the results, it was inferred that there is a common criterion for judging the sensibility of "electric vehicle-ness," and the characteristics of modeling connected with the specific meaning of this sensibility were clarified to some extent. The results of this study can serve as a reference for designing electric vehicles. However, research at this stage is still at its infancy, and the degree of influence and how the characteristics of the modeling are connected to the image have yet to be confirmed. Further research is needed to gain deeper insight on this topic.

References

1. Japan Automobile Dealers Association. http://www.jada.or.jp/data/month/m-fuel-hanbai/. Accessed 6 Nov 2022
2. Goo, S.-H.: Ecosystem restructuring and innovation dynamics in the EV market research and innovation society of Japan. Res. Acad. Plann. **32**(4), 360–379 (2017)
3. Moriguchi, M.: Ongoing Urbanization and Changing Car Design International Association of Traffic and Safety Sciences (IATSS) Review, vol. 43, no. 1, pp. 15–24 (2018)
4. Matsumura, N., Kawata, S.: Analysis of the influence of automobile advertisements on consumer perceptions and attitudes public interest incorporated association. J. Civil Eng. Plann. (25), 663–672 (2008)
5. Sato, H., Kansei: Evaluation for automobile front grille design Japan society of kansei engineering. Trans. Japan Soc. Kansei Eng. 16(1), 51–60 (2017)
6. Sho Minamimoto and Toshinori Harada Clarifying the Relationship between Proportion Items and Impressions in 1.5-Box Mini Car Design Transactions of the Japan Society of Kansei Engineering, Japan 2018, Vol. 17, No. 1, pp. 139–148
7. Katsuo Inoue [Methods for Surveying Consumer Insight] Laddering Method (Evaluation Grid Method). https://www.youtube.com/watch?v=H3rg_URtwL4. Accessed 16 Dec 2022

Analysis of the Geometry Applied in the Steering System of a Formula-Type Single-Seater Vehicle

Humberto Lopez[1(✉)], Leopoldo Laborde[1], Vladimir Pinzón[1], Carlos Barros[1], Alonso Barrera[2], and Vladimir Cudris[1]

[1] Institución Universitaria de Barranquilla, 45 Street #48-31, Barranquilla, Colombia
hlopez@itsa.edu.co

[2] Universidad de La Costa, 58 Street #55 66, Barranquilla, Colombia

Abstract. The ANGUILA F13 is a formula-type vehicle designed and built for the SENA ECO FORMULA competition. The objective of this research is to analyze the geometry applied to the steering system of vehicle ANGUILA F13 in order to know the characteristics and implementation of the system in the car. The method used for the design of the steering system had reference frame geometry, the rules of competition, the battle and track of the vehicle and the angle camber, caster and ackerman. In the results, the steering column to be fragmented into three parts provides greater security to the driver in case of frontal impact, the ackerman angle obtained allows the vehicle to have a smooth shift, total control of the vehicle when cornering and bonding gimbals makes it manageable direction. In conclusion, it was possible to obtain a good system performance and career management evidence taken in preventing the vehicle slipping when cornering.

Keywords: vehicle · mechanics · mechanical engineering · automotive systems · geometry

1 Introduction

The ANGUILA F13 is a formula-type vehicle designed and built for the FORMULA SENA ECO competition by university students and SENA apprentices with SENA instructor guidance [1], The design of the vehicle was carried out taking into account the regulations foreseen by the organizers of the event and the requirements demanded by the optimal performance conditions of the vehicle.

This type of events aimed at students related to the development of prototyping in a competitive way, allows the development of professional skills and abilities for the generation of value of future professionals through practical mechanisms that test the capabilities and creativity of the work team [2, 3]. In this sense, the FORMULA SENA ECO competition is aimed directly at students with the potential to generate innovative proposals to the academic and training environment of robotics.

In the arc of this competition, it is mentioned that the steering system is vital in the race strategy, control and safety of the vehicle, For this reason its proper implementation and configuration is important for the correct functioning of the car on the track, in

C. Stephanidis et al. (Eds.): HCII 2023, CCIS 1836, pp. 49–56, 2023.
https://doi.org/10.1007/978-3-031-36004-6_8

the design many factors that could affect the direction of the vehicle were taken into account, for example the turning force of the wheels, the inclination of the car, the steering column among others. It should also be considered that the vehicle is piloted by a person therefore it must provide a minimum of safety to safeguard the integrity of the driver, taking into account this, The frame and survival cell play an important role in the safety of the pilot, as does the direction that in the event of a frontal collision must broken, thus preventing the rudder from moving in the direction of the pilot.

The objective sought by the article is the design and analysis of the geometry of the steering system considering the factors of safety, vehicle stability, vehicle control, optimize the maneuverability of the single-seater, in addition to characteristics such as weight and aerodynamics for this, the location of the elements, the material to be used and the geometry of the components that comprise the complete system must be taken into account.

2 Material and Method

This article shows an applied and experimental research process, which shows the process of development of the single-seater vehicle. The method used for the design of the steering system had reference frame geometry, the rules of competition, the battle and track of the vehicle and the angle camber, caster and ackerman.

On the track the proper implementation and configuration of the system is important for the correct functioning of the vehicle. In the design process, many factors were taken into account which could affect the direction of the vehicle, from the turning force of the wheels, the inclination among others.

3 Results

3.1 Positioning of the Steering Rack

The steering rack was placed behind the chassis, 110 mm from the front tube of the chassis and, in turn, this will be held by anchors, which are attached to the front tube of the chassis; The positioning of the rack influences the length of the steering arms and the steering of the vehicle. Staples were used to ensure the fixation of the bottle.

3.2 Wheelbase

Figure 1 shows the dimensions of the vehicle as it is the wheelbase of the vehicle, which is the distance between the axle of the front tire and the axle of the rear tire [4], this measurement plays an important role in the stability of the vehicle; Taking this into account a vehicle with a long wheelbase has greater stability than a short wheelbase. For the design of the Anguilla F13 a wheelbase of 2310 mm was used, considering that the regulations of the contest specified the maximum total length that the vehicle could have.

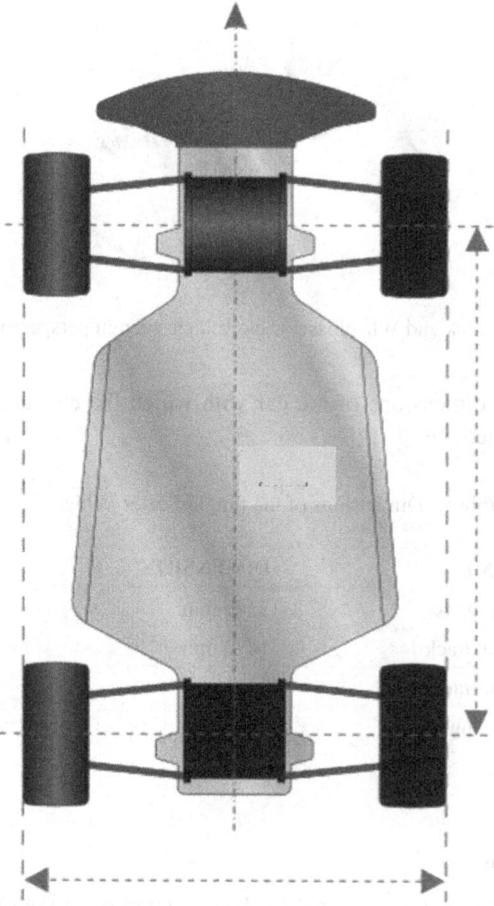

Fig. 1. Track and Wheelbase of a formula vehicle upper view.

3.3 Front Track of the Vehicle

The path of the vehicle is the distance from the center of the tire on one side to the center of the tire on the other side Both the front and rear track width is the distance, The front track does not need to match the rear track, commonly the front track is shorter than the rear track for stability, traction and rotation of the vehicle. In Fig. 2, the perspective view of the vehicle model is shown, allowing us to know from where the measurement of the Track and the Wheelbase are taken [4, 5].

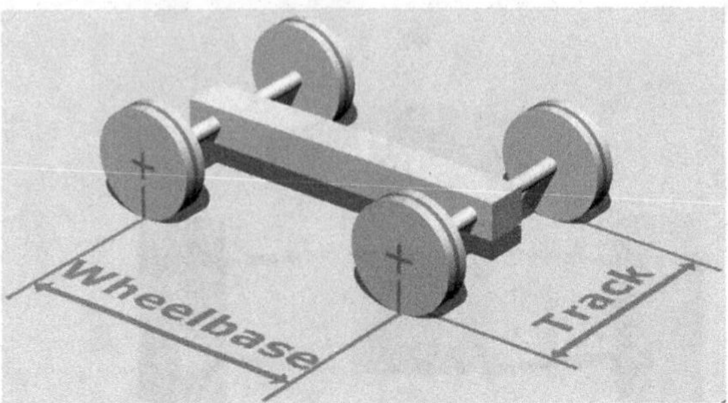

Fig. 2. Track and Wheelbase of the vehicle seen in perspective

Table 1 shows the dimensions of the car with which the calculation of the angle Ackerman will be carried out.

Table 1. Dimensions of the Single-Seater Vehicle.

NAME	DIMENSION
Wheelbase	2310 mm
Front track	1470 mm
Rear track	1471 mm
Steering arms	141 mm

3.4 Steering Column

The steering column is sectioned into 3 parts, because it gives the pilot greater security in the event of a crash. This column was designed based on the positioning of the steering rack. The steering column goes through two bearings for its mobility and has an anchorage at an angle that in the event of an accident, breaks forward of the pilot, preventing said column from causing injuries to the pilot. For the design of the steering column material, the torque in which the column would work was taken into account by applying the following formula:

$$\frac{F_p}{F_v} = \frac{R_v}{R_p} \tag{1}$$

F_p: Force obtained in the drive pinion of the steering box. (N).
F_v: Force applied to the steering wheel. (N).
R_p: Steering box drive pinion radius. (m).
R_v: Steering wheel radius. (m).

$$F_v = \frac{F_p R_p}{R_v} = \frac{\left(\frac{\mu.m.g}{2}\right) \cdot R_p}{R_v} = \frac{(0,8)(500\ kg)(0,4)\left(9,8\frac{m}{s^2}\right)(0,0365\ m)}{2(0,25\ m)} = 114,5N \tag{2}$$

Taking into account that the force exerted was 114.5N on the material. Table 2 shows the characteristics of ASTM A36 Steel, which was selected for being able to withstand said stress.

Table 2. Characteristics of the Material Used

DATA	
Material	ASTM A36 Steel
Elastic limit	250 MPa
Pull limit	400 MPa

3.5 Steering Column Simulation

From the defined load of 114.5N, the simulation of the steering column is carried out in the Solidworks program in its Solidworks Simulation complement, which is shown in Fig. 3, where it shows the fastening point and the effort made, symbolized by colors.

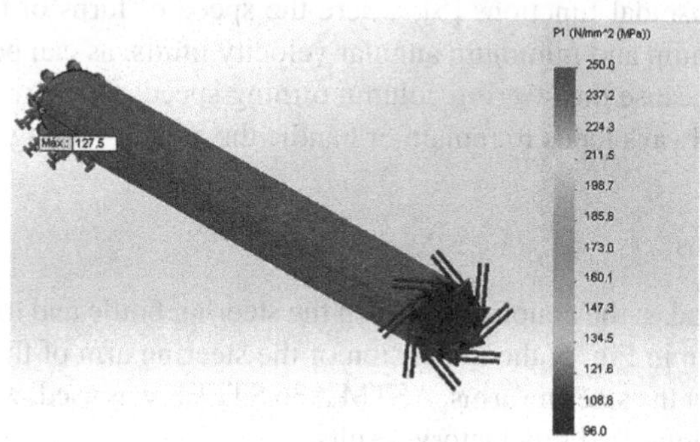

Fig. 3. Steering Column Torque Analysis SOLIDWORK Software.

As can be seen in the simulation, the maximum effort is 127 MPa, this means that the steering column will fully fulfill its function without suffering damage.

3.6 Effect of Universal Joints on the Steering Column

The use of cardan joints have a direct effect on the rotation of the axes, since they add a better mechanical operation to the steering column, the advantage that this type of element has compared to other employees in similar jobs, is to improve performance. When performing a certain turn according to the abrupt conditions of the environment, that is, that the movements that are generated are smooth, a cardan joint adds a response

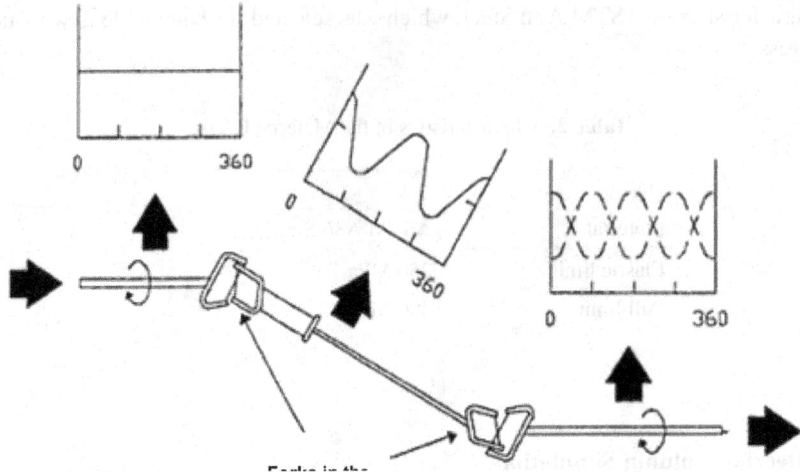

Fig. 4. Cardan jointed steering column.

form based on sinusoidal functions [5], where the speed of turns of the axes is found between the maximum and minimum angular velocity limits, as can be seen in Fig. 4.

Despite this, because the steering column turning speeds are very small, this effect is almost nil, and always tends to remain or handle the actual steering turning speed.

3.7 Steering Arms

The steering arm makes the coupling between the steering bottle and the fastening point on the rim as shown in Fig. 5, the dimension of the steering arm of the F13 eel vehicle was 487.55 mm. For the steering arms, ASTM A36 STEEL was used, which, when faced with stress simulations, had satisfactory results.

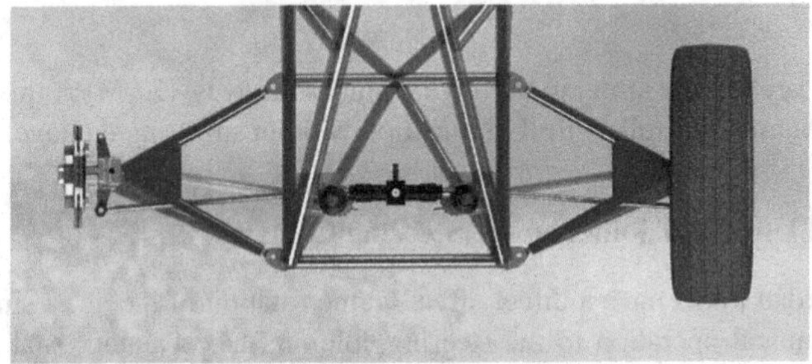

Fig. 5. Steering arm, fork, bottle and tire.

3.8 Ackerman Plates

The Ackerman angle is a method created to solve the problem of the inner and outer wheel when turning a vehicle, creating a circle of different radii. [6, 7]. Because the steering rack only allows a linear movement of the bar is 139 mm, it is necessary to use an Ackerman, with the aim of providing sustainability in closed and open curves, in the case of the ANGUILLA FS-13, the Ackerman It will allow you to spin more than normal. Table 3 describes all rack positions and the resulting external and internal angle of the tires.

Table 3. Ackerman Angle Calculation.

Ackerman Angle								
Bottle Dist (mm)	Ball Joint Dist (mm)	Front Track (mm)	Rear Track (mm)	Track Dif (mm)	Incl. Wheel	Ext Wheel Ang	Int Wheel Ang	Ang Dif
20	33,7	1470,3	1471,2	0,9	46°	30,99	32,9	1,91
40	31,95	1470,2	1471,3	1,13	46°	30,99	33,78	2,79
42,5	31,8	147,1	1741,4	1,28	46°	30,99	33,89	2,9
44	31,67	1470,0	1471,5	1,57	46°	30,99	33,99	3
50	31,4	1470,3	1471,3	1	46°	30,99	34,27	3,28
80	30,9	1469,9	1471,6	1,75	46°	30,99	35,88	4,89
100	31,69	1470,3	1471,2	0,95	46°	30,99	37,07	6,08
90	31,2	1470,1	1471,4	1,25	46°	30,99	36,43	5,44
91	31,25	1470,2	1471,3	1,07	46°	30,99	36,5	5,51

4 Conclusions

The vehicle performed well in cornering, also stability and smooth steering handling. The steering arm did not present problems of rotation, mechanical lock, twisting or breaking due to overexertion. The materials used for the construction of the suspension and steering met the minimum stress requirements. It is recommended to make an ackerman table with different measurements, to adjust the vehicle to a position that gives an optimal behavior of the vehicle in the race.

The process carried out in the present study allows to demonstrate the effectiveness of the formative results of a competence related to the area of robotics; where students can generate effective and functional value propositions within a controlled environment and accompanied by a group of tutors and expert evaluators [8, 9].

Acknowledgments. The authors thank Ministerio de Ciencia, Tecnología e Innovación from Colombia and the Institución Universitaria de Barranquilla for funding this product under the project "FORTALECIMIENTO DE LAS CAPACIDADES DE INVESTIGACIÓN, INNOVACIÓN Y DESARROLLO DE TECNOLOGÍAS EN LA INSTITUCIÓN UNIVERSITARIA ITSA, A TRAVÉS DE LA DOTACIÓN DEL LABORATORIO DE PRODUCTIVIDAD EN EL DEPARTAMENTO DEL ATLÁNTICO" BPIN: 2020000100316.

References

1. Rico, Y., Rendón, W.: Desarrollo de carrocería aerodinámica para monoplaza eléctrico de la escudería ara de la Regional Antioquia en el marco de la formula SENA ECO 2013–2014. Ingenierías USBMed **7**(2), 48–53 (2016)
2. Brancalião, L., Gonçalves, J., Conde, M.Á., Costa, P.: Systematic mapping literature review of mobile robotics competitions. Sensors **22**(6), 2160 (2022)
3. Sullivan, A., Bers, M.U.: VEX robotics competitions: gender differences in student attitudes and experiences. J. Inf. Technol. Educ. **18**, 97–112 (2019)
4. Font, J., Dols, J.: Tratado Sobre Los Automoviles, pp. 550–555. Universidad Politecnica de Valencia, Valencia (2004)
5. Pérez, M.: Circuitos Fluidos Suspensión y Dirección. Paraninfo, Madrid (2011)
6. Burnhill, D.: RCTEK. http://www.rctek.com/technical/handling/ackerman_steering_principle.html. Accessed 21 Nov 2020
7. Crouse, W.: Mecánica del Automóvil I. Barcelona (1993)
8. Canek, R., Chicas, Y., Rodas, O.: Fomenting stem careers through robotics competitions: a work in progress. In: 2019 IEEE Integrated STEM Education Conference (ISEC), pp. 270–273. IEEE (2019)
9. Chiang, F.K., Liu, Y.Q., Feng, X., Zhuang, Y., Sun, Y.: Effects of the world robot Olympiad on the students who participate: a qualitative study. Interact. Learn. Environ. **31**, 1–12 (2020)

Systematic Evaluation of Driver's Behavior: A Multimodal Biometric Study

Michela Minen[1,2], Luisina Gregoret[1(✉)], Divya Seernani[1], and Jessica Wilson[1]

[1] iMotions A/S, Copenhagen, Denmark
Luisina.Gregoret@imotions.com
[2] University of Padua, Padua, Italy

Abstract. Complex traffic areas and high cognitive workload while driving are leading contributors to traffic crashes. Even though cognitive workload and stress have been previously assessed through various neurophysiological responses, they are rarely characterized simultaneously, limiting the triangulation of behavioral metrics (like drivers' visual attention and facial coding) with physiological measures to investigate their interplay. The aim of the present study was to systematically characterize stress and cognitive workload through a multimodal assessment comprising eye-tracking, facial expressions, galvanic skin response (GSR), electromyography (EMG), electrocardiography (ECG) and respiration in three controlled driving simulations of varying complexity: 1. Baseline driving on an open road (Baseline); 2. Navigating between traffic cones (Cones); and 3. Driving in a neighborhood with multiple stressors (Traffic). The selected metrics were eye tracking dwell time, the presence of facial brow furrow, GSR peaks/minute, EMG activity of the upper trapezius muscle, heart rate and heart rate variability (HRV) and respiration cycles/minute. Physiological responses showed significant increases in GSR, heart rate and trapezius EMG activity with Cones and Traffic compared to Baseline. Eye tracking metrics were shown to be indicative of driving behavior in different conditions. There were no significant differences in facial expressions, HRV or respiration. These results are somewhat consistent with previous literature, suggesting that a multimodal approach to physiological signals can characterize affective and cognitive states in driving scenarios.

Keywords: Driving simulator · Cognitive workload · Eye tracking · Physiology

1 Introduction

The interaction between complex driving conditions and high cognitive workload while driving is one of the leading contributing factors to traffic crashes. Recent studies have employed several physiological and behavioral tools to help assess driver behavior in controlled studies. These can include eye tracking, which can reveal information about a driver's visual processing of the road. Other promising biosensors include electromyography (EMG), electrocardiography (ECG), and galvanic skin response (GSR) which measure muscle contraction, heart rate and heart rate variability and eccrine gland activity, respectively [1–3]. EMG can be used to study motor strategies and ergonomics, and

C. Stephanidis et al. (Eds.): HCII 2023, CCIS 1836, pp. 57–64, 2023.
https://doi.org/10.1007/978-3-031-36004-6_9

detect driver fatigue. Heart rate and heart rate variability (HRV), derived from the ECG signal, is one of the most frequently used techniques for assessing driver workload and has been shown to decrease significantly during periods of increased mental workload and stress while driving [4–6]. GSR, by comparison, is a pure reflection of sympathetic nervous system activity [7] and is thus increased in periods of high physiological arousal [8]. Lastly, the use of camera-based facial expression analysis has been to predict unsafe driving behaviors [9].

The combination of a comprehensive biometric assessment with realistic driving simulators can help pinpoint specific instances where drivers may be distracted, overwhelmed cognitively, or dealing with navigation-related issues that could compromise their safety while operating a motor vehicle. The overall aim of the present study, therefore, was to systematically characterize stress and cognitive workload through a multimodal assessment comprising eye-tracking, facial expressions, GSR, EMG, ECG and respiration in three randomized and controlled driving simulations to holistically measure driver performance.

2 Methods

Ten healthy respondents (31.4 ± 7.1 years old; 5 female) were recruited and participated in this evaluation. The inclusion criteria included individuals within an age range of 18–40 years who have a drivers license and no previous experience driving a car simulator, whereas the exclusion criteria included visual and motor disabilities, chronic or current acute pain at the time of the experiment, and cardiorespiratory disorders.

2.1 Experimental Procedure

Respondents were instructed to drive a professional driving simulator (VI-GRADE, Italy) in a 3-screen desktop set-up with dedicated steering wheel and pedals (Logitech G29, Logitech, Switzerland). The simulation software used was "MCity Traffic" (WorldSim, VI-GRADE, Italy). All signals were recorded and analyzed by a biometric software (iMotions 9.3.3, iMotions A/S, Denmark).

The study protocol consisted of:

1. Low-workload Baseline scenario (Baseline): Drive 3 min on an open highway, without traffic.
2. Medium-workload Cones scenario (Cones): Slalom the car between traffic cones and perform a double lane change maneuver as fast as reasonably possible, followed by 1.5 min of straight driving recovery.
3. High-workload city traffic scenario (Traffic): Drive 5 min through a city with random traffic conditions, traffic lights, other vehicles, and pedestrians.

The Baseline scenario was fixed at the start of the study protocol, while Traffic and Cones scenarios were pseudorandomized.

2.2 Data Collection

Eye-Tracking. Eye-tracking was performed with a multicam system of 3 infrared cameras (n = 10, Smart Eye Pro, Smart Eye, Sweden), positioning one infrared camera per simulator screen. Fixations were classified using a velocity-based I-VT filter (iMotions 9.3.3, iMotions A/S, Denmark) set at 30°/s. Dwell time (as a percentage of total task time) and number of revisits were selected as primary variables to evaluate the visual attention of the drivers.

Facial Expression Analysis. Drivers were recorded using a Logitech C920 webcam (n = 10, 640 × 480 resolution, 30 fps) positioned on top of the middle screen of the 3-screen setup. Affectiva's AFFDEX 2.0, embedded in the iMotions software (iMotions 9.3.3, iMotions A/S, Denmark) was used to detect and quantify facial movements. Brow Furrow was selected as a metric because of its affiliation with negative valence as well as workload.

Respiration. Respiration rate was recorded using a stretch belt connected to a respiration amplifier (n = 5, RSP 100 and MP160, Biopac systems Inc, US). Respiration rate (cycles/min) was determined based on the respiration count and the duration of the signal.

EMG. EMG activity was recorded from the right upper trapezius muscle using bipolar surface EMG electrodes connected to either a stationary EMG device (n = 5, Biopac Systems EMG100C and MP160, USA) or a bluetooth wireless EMG device (n = 2, Shimmer EXG, Shimmer Sensing, Ireland). The reference electrode was placed on the right acromion. EMG signals were sampled at 512 Hz and bandpass filtered from 20–500 Hz with a 4th order Butterworth filter, rectified, then smoothed using a zero-phase-shift 4th-order Butterworth filter with a 10-Hz cut-off frequency. The area under the curve (AUC) was calculated from the smoothed EMG signal.

GSR. GSR were registered by a portable device (n = 10, Shimmer3 GSR+, Shimmer Sensing, Ireland), positioning the two electrodes on the volar side of the ring and middle fingers of the non-dominant hand. A threshold of 0.01 uS and 0 uS was established to detect the onset and offset of every GSR peak, respectively. After the labeling of GSR peaks, a peaks/minute metric was computed.

ECG. ECG activity was obtained through a wireless strap (n = 8, Polar Belt H10, Polar, Switzerland) applied on the chest. Heart rate and HRV was calculated from R-R intervals; HRV was expressed using the standard deviation of the N-N intervals (SDNN).

2.3 Statistics

All signal processing was conducted using the iMotions R-Library (iMotions 9.3.3, iMotions A/S, Denmark). Statistical analyses were performed in Matlab using the statistics and machine learning toolbox v12.3 (Mathworks, Massachusetts, US). Threshold for statistical significance was set as $p < 0.05$. All data was assessed for normality by the Shapiro-Wilk test. Friedman tests were applied for all analyses across the three driving conditions, with p-values adjusted by Bonferroni correction for multiple comparisons. Results are reported as median (interquartile ranges) in both text and plots.

3 Results

Driver physiology and behavior across multiple biosensor modalities (eye tracking, GSR, FEA, ECG, EMG and respiration) were compared across three driving conditions of varying complexity (Baseline, Cones and Traffic). A summary of the descriptive statistics is presented in Table 1.

Table 1. Descriptive statistics of multimodal metrics during three driving conditions (Baseline, Cones and Traffic). Values are represented as median (interquartile range). † denotes a significant main effect, $p < 0.05$. †† denotes a significant main effect, $p < 0.01$. *a* denotes significant differences compared to Baseline, $p < 0.05$. *b* denotes significant differences compared to Baseline, $p < 0.01$. *c* denotes significant differences compared to Cones, $p < 0.05$.

Sensor	Metric	Condition		
		Baseline	Cones	Traffic
Eye Tracking	Dwell Time (speedometer)††	26.54 (15.29–35.56)	[a]22.41 (12.78–34.87)	[b]6.65 (4.00–8.61)
Eye Tracking	Dwell Time (left screen)†	0.21 (0.12–0.43)	0.12 (0.07–0.14)	[c]1.02 (0.57–2.40)
Eye Tracking	Dwell Time (center screen)	65.39 (55.4–73.5)	72.38 (69.07–75.61)	70.86 (68.65–75.75)
Eye Tracking	Dwell Time (right screen)†	0.25 (0.22–0.32)	0.15 (0.06–0.16)	[c]1.04 (0.57–1.99)
Facial Coding	% Time Spent Brow Furrow	0.90 (0.15–1.72)	0.0 (0.0–1.89)	1.12 (.12–5.18)
GSR	Peaks/Minute††	3.06 (1.77–4.25)	6.41 (4.64–7.79)	[a]6.05 (4.88–8.30)
EMG	AUC Upper Trapezius (mV*s)††	2.93 (2.35–3.94)	3.66 (2.34–4.61)	[b, c]5.92 (4.58–6.60)
ECG	Heart Rate (beats/minute)†	74.95 (66.67–81.67)	78.81 (71.07–81.99)	[c]74.88 (66.99–80.83)
ECG	Heart Rate Variability (SDNN)	42.33 (41.17–65.60)	55.29 (44.97–81.76)	47.28 (45.3–66.50)
Respiration	Cycles/Minute	13.76 (12.79–14.59)	12.77 (9.76–13.35)	12.23 (11.89–12.34)

There was a significant effect of dwell time on the speedometer across tasks ($F(2) = 14.888$, $p < 0.001$, $N = 10$). Post hoc analyses show higher dwell time % on the speedometer in the Baseline scenario as compared to both the Cones ($p < 0.05$) and Traffic ($p < 0.001$) scenarios. While dwell time on the center screen did not change across conditions, there was a significantly higher dwell time on the left ($F(2) = 8.857$, $p = < 0.02$, post hoc $p = 0.01$, $N = 10$) and right ($F(2) = 6.400$, $p < 0.05$, $N = 10$; post hoc $p < 0.05$) screens in the Traffic scenario compared to the Cones scenario.

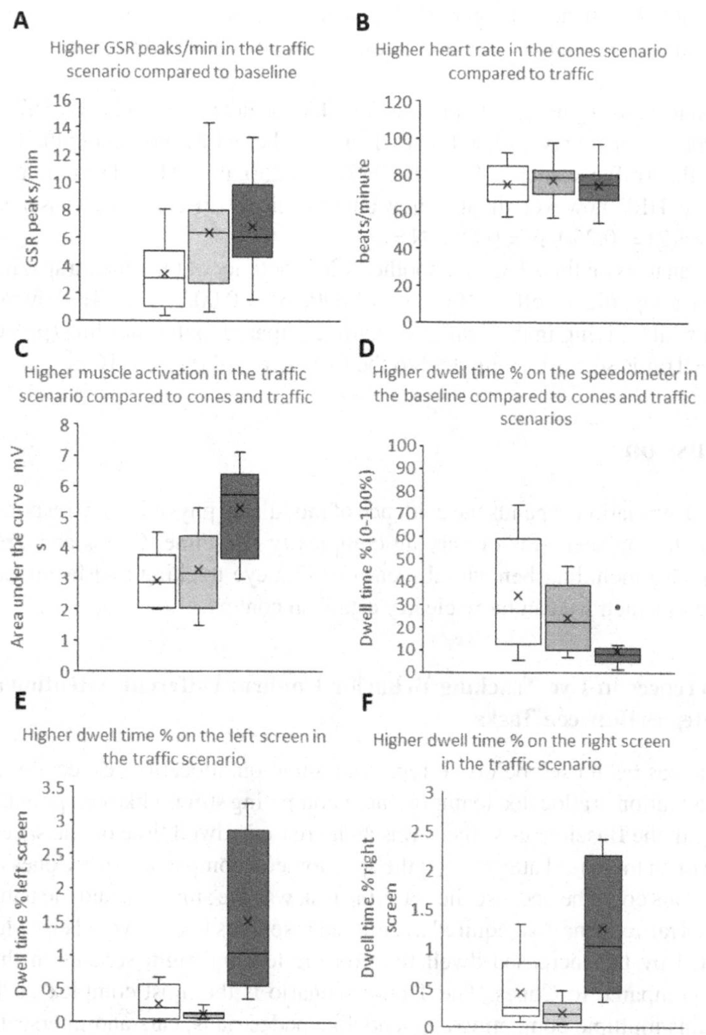

Fig. 1. Box plots of the biometric responses in the Baseline (white), Cones (light gray) and Traffic (dark gray) scenarios showing the mean (cross), the median (horizontal line), quartile ranges and minimum and maximum values. **A)** Higher GSR peaks/min were observed in the Traffic scenario compared to Baseline. **B)** Higher heart rate was observed in the Cones scenario compared to Traffic. **C)** Higher muscle activation was observed in the Traffic scenario compared to Cones and Baseline. **D)** Higher dwell time % over the speedometer occurred in the Baseline compared to Cones and Traffic scenarios. **E** and **F)** Higher dwell time % over the left and right screens were observed in the Traffic scenario, as compared to Cones and Baseline.

There was also a significant effect of task on GSR peaks/minute ($F(2) = 9.750$; $p = 0.008$, $N = 10$). Post hoc analysis showed that drivers exhibited higher GSR peaks/min while driving in the Traffic scenario as compared to the Baseline scenario (adjusted p <

0.01, Fig. 1A). A tendency of higher GSR peaks/min is observed while navigating Cones as compared to the Baseline scenario, but this was not statistically significant (adjusted $p = 0.073$).

Friedman analysis indicated a significant effect on heart rate ($F(2) = 6.867$, $p < 0.05$, $N = 8$). Post hoc analysis revealed that HR was higher while navigating the Cones than driving in the Traffic scenario (Fig. 1B - $F(2) = 1.250$, $p < 0.05$), but not compared to the Baseline. HRV, however, did not show any significant differences across the different scenarios ($F(2) = 0.250$, $p = 0.882$, $N = 8$).

Friedman tests on the AUC of smoothed EMG activity of the upper trapezius muscle resulted in a significant effect ($F(2) = 13.000$; $p = 0.002$, $N = 8$) showing higher activation while driving in the Traffic scenario compared to the Baseline ($p = 0.001$) as well in the Traffic scenario compared to the Cones ($p < 0.05$, Fig. 1C).

4 Discussion

The present evaluation expands the evidence of modulated physiological responses while navigating driving scenarios of varying complexity (Baseline, Cones and Traffic scenarios) by also including behavioral measures like eye tracking and facial expression analysis with which we can more clearly establish context.

4.1 Differences in Eye Tracking Behavior Confirm Different Attentional Strategies Between Tasks

Dwell time has been used before to represent attention allocation, especially in seeing how long attention is allocated to important or competing stimuli like cell phones or sign-posts [10]. In the Baseline task, there was an increase in dwell time on the speedometer, indicative of an increased attention on the speedometer compared to the Cones or Traffic scenarios. This could be because the Baseline task was the simplest, and the nature of the Cones and Traffic scenarios required attentional resources to be devoted elsewhere. This is supported by the increased dwell time on the left and right screens in the Traffic condition compared to Cones. The Traffic scenario is the most complex of the three, as it contains multiple competing elements like pedestrians, cars and intersections that require different attentional strategies [11]. In short, we see differences in eye tracking behavior across the scenarios due to the varying attentional requirements of the driver.

4.2 Modulation of GSR, EMG and HR in Complex Driving Scenarios

The overall hypothesis of the electrophysiological evaluation was that GSR peaks/min, heart rate, muscle activity and respiration rate would be facilitated and heart rate variability would be diminished under the most demanding scenarios (Cones and Traffic). We did find that GSR peaks/min and muscle activity were significantly facilitated in the Traffic scenario as compared to Baseline, possibly in response to increased task loads. This is only partially in agreement with Healey and Picard (2005), who did not see EMG changes, but found that GSR and ECG together correlated the highest with drivers' perceived stress in real-life drives [12].

Respiration and heart rate variability did not show significant differences across tasks. A lack of significant change in HRV was surprising given previous literature but HRV can also be influenced by a multitude of environmental, neurophysiological and lifestyle factors [13]. Studies involving HRV as a variable might benefit most from a multimodal approach.

We did not see a significant change in brow furrow across the tasks, although other head and facial movements have been shown to correlate with driving behaviors [9]. As the technology continues to advance in this arena, it will be interesting to see what combination of head and face movements can be most predictive of a driver's internal state.

5 Conclusion

The application of multiple biosensors in driver research has the potential to advance our comprehension of driving behavior, guide the creation of fresh driver-training initiatives and safety interventions, and eventually aid in lowering the rate of traffic accidents. The results of the present study indicate higher muscle tension (EMG activity), modulated arousal (heart rate and GSR peaks/min) and higher perceptual load (dwell time %) in complex driving scenarios. Most, but not all our findings are consistent with what we have seen in prior literature. The interaction between the driver's cognitive and physiological states and the environment inside and outside the vehicle produce a complex system that can be difficult to model and predict. It is only through repeated studies, with the triangulation of multiple physiological and behavioral measures, that we can gain deeper insights that can be leveraged to protect the driver.

References

1. Yang, X., et al.: The effects of traveling in different transport modes on galvanic skin response (GSR) as a measure of stress: an observational study. Environ. Int. **156**, 106764 (2021). https://doi.org/10.1016/j.envint.2021.106764
2. Mehler B., Reimer, B., Wang, Y.: A comparison of the heart rate and heart rate variability indices in distinguishing single-task driving and driving under secondary cognitive workload. In: Proceedings of the Sixth International Driving Symposium on Human Factors in Driver Assessment, Training and Vehicle Design, pp. 590–597. Lake Tahoe, CA (2011)
3. Brookhuis, K.A., de Waard, D.: Monitoring drivers' mental workload in driving simulators using physiological measures. Accid. Anal. Prev. **42**, 898–903 (2010). https://doi.org/10.1016/j.aap.2009.06.001
4. Lenneman, J.K., Backs, R.W.: Cardiac autonomic control during simulated driving with a concurrent verbal working memory task. Hum. Factors **51**, 404–418 (2009). https://doi.org/10.1177/0018720809337716
5. Lenneman, J.K., Backs, R.W.: Enhancing assessment of in-vehicle technology attention demands with cardiac measures. In: Proceedings of the 2nd International Conference on Automotive User Interfaces and Interactive Vehicular applications, pp. 20–21. ACM, New York (2010)
6. Collet, C., Clarion, A., Morel, M., Chapon, A., Petit, C.: Physiological and behavioral changes associated to the management of secondary tasks while driving. App. Ergon. **40**(6), 1041–1046 (2009). https://doi.org/10.1016/j.apergo.2009.01.007

7. Boucsein, W.: Electrodemal Activity. 2nd edn. Springer, New York (2012). https://doi.org/10.1007/978-1-4614-1126-0
8. Mehler, B., Reimer, B., Coughlin, J.F., Dusek, J.A.: Impact of incremental increases in cognitive workload on physiological arousal and performance in young adult drivers. Transp. Res. Rec. **2138**(1), 6–12 (2009). https://doi.org/10.3141/2138-02
9. Jabon, M., Bailenson, J., Pontikakis, E., Takayama, L., Nass, C.: Facial expression analysis for predicting unsafe driving behavior. IEEE Pervasive Comput. **10**(4), 84–95 (2011). https://doi.org/10.1109/MPRV.2010.46
10. Strayer, D.L., Drews, F.A., Johnston, W.A.: Cell phone-induced failures of visual attention during simulated driving. J. Exp. Psychol. Appl. **9**(1), 23–32 (2003). https://doi.org/10.1037/1076-898x.9.1.23
11. Liang, N., et al.: Using eye-tracking to investigate the effects of pre-takeover visual engagement on situation awareness during automated driving. Accid. Anal. Prev. **157**, 106143 (2021). https://doi.org/10.1016/j.aap.2021.106143
12. Healey, J.A., Picard, R.W.: Detecting stress during real-world driving tasks using physiological sensors. IEEE Trans. Intell. Transp. Syst. **6**(2), 156–166 (2005). https://doi.org/10.1109/TITS.2005.848368
13. Fatisson, J., Oswald, V., Lalonde, F.: Influence diagram of physiological and environmental factors affecting heart rate variability: an extended literature overview. Heart Int. **11**(1), 32–40 (2016). https://doi.org/10.5301/heartint.5000232

Enabling Efficient Emulation of Internet-of-Vehicles on a Single Machine: Practices and Lessons

Xiaoxing Ming, Yicun Duan, Junyu Liu, Zhuoran Bi, Haoxuan Sun, Zilin Song, Xiangjun Peng, and Wangkai Jin(✉)

User-Centric Computing Group, Hangzhou, China
wangkaijin00@gmail.com

Abstract. The rise of Intelligent Vehicles and next-generation networks accelerates the advent of Internet-of-Vehicles (IoV), where each vehicle acts as a node and interconnects with other nodes for data sharing and processing. The primary challenges for evaluating Human-Vehicle Interactions (HVI) designs in the context of IoV are (1) computation on limited on-vehicle hardware resources; and (2) varied network connectivity in different settings. Moreover, existing emulators are highly customized for specific scenarios, which can limit the comprehensiveness of evaluations for IoV. To this end, we present a relatively general and portable emulation platform, that is designed for evaluating a variety of novel HVI designs under different IoV settings. Our emulation platform consists of two key components: 1) an automatic extractor to extract workload patterns in different IoV topologies and 2) configurable network settings to examine different HVI designs in various network conditions. We then characterize two IoV applications to examine the feasibility of our proposed emulation platform.

Keywords: Internet-of-Vehicles · Software Emulation

1 Background & Motivation

The rise of Intelligent Vehicles and next-generation networks accelerates the advent of Internet-of-Vehicles (IoV), where each vehicle acts as a node and interconnects with other nodes for data sharing and processing. Given its distributed nature and high costs to prototype, developers and researchers are prone to evaluate novel Human-Vehicle Interactions (HVI) designs for IoV in emulators.

However, current platforms and software impose limitations on exploring and analyzing IoV systems. To address this issue, several emulation platforms have been proposed for assessing the feasibility of advanced designs in IoV settings. For instance, OMNet++ [14] presents diverse protocols and wired/wireless network simulation models that are useful for discrete event systems. Simulation of Urban Mobility (SUMO) [8] concentrates on traffic simulations to examine traffic management strategies, while Vehicles in Network Simulation (VEINS) [10]

C. Stephanidis et al. (Eds.): HCII 2023, CCIS 1836, pp. 65–72, 2023.
https://doi.org/10.1007/978-3-031-36004-6_10

integrates both the network simulator OMNet++ and the road traffic simulator to evaluate the performance of Inter-Vehicle Communication (IVC) protocols. However, all these approaches focus on a particular application scenario and are highly customized for specific contexts. Therefore, no current platforms offer (A) the flexibility to adapt various application designs to the IoV context, and (B) the flexibility to explore a broad range of scenarios, such as geo-distributed scenarios.

To this end, we propose a relatively general and portable emulation platform that enables the development and evaluation of novel HVI designs in the context of IoV. Specifically, our platform has two main components that support HVI application designs in various scenarios, which are: 1) an automatic extractor to extract the key patterns of HVI workloads deployment on nodes within the IoV and 2) configurable network connections that enable the evaluation of HVI design in varied network conditions. Based on our emulation platform, we then characterize its impacts on two HVI applications in the context of IoV, which consist of a Deep-Neural-Network-based application and its Differentially-private version. We discuss our key takeaways throughout these two characterizations and discuss future works.

2 Design Overview

In this section, we first introduce our platform design in Sect. 2.1. Then, we brief the prototype implementation in Sect. 2.2.

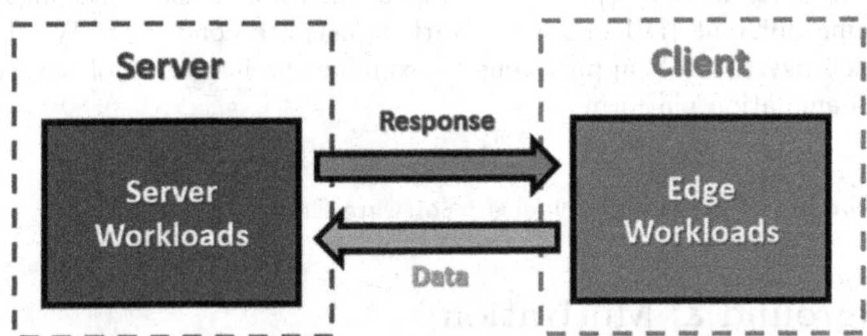

Fig. 1. Overview of workload distribution in the context of Internet-of-Vehicles

2.1 Study Design

Our platform design can be divided into two parts, which are automatic extractor and configurable network connection supports. First, it includes an automatic extractor that identifies and retrieves key patterns from real-world workloads. Second, the platform offers a configurable networking connection that supports the flexible enabling of different studies. Here is a brief explanation of these two components:

The automatic extractor is designed to identify and retrieve workload patterns. It starts to perform a static full-program analysis by identifying key components of data movements, specifically networking transfer/synchronization. The extractor only considers networking movements as networking connections have significantly higher delays than local data transfer. The extractor then organizes all significant data movements into a data sheet, recording all major behaviors and separating them into the server and edge workloads, with a particular focus on networking behaviors.

The configurable networking connection is supported by the platform in two ways. Firstly, the platform receives the generated data sheet from the automatic extractor and models the workloads in a server-client manner. Figure 1 illustrates the organization of the modeled workloads. Secondly, the platform offers a wide range of configurable parameters to support different study purposes. For instance, it can be configured with different numbers of connections (to examine the effects of concurrent services) and different response latencies (to examine the effects of geo-distributed scenarios).

2.2 Prototype Implementation

We build a prototype system using 2,000+ lines of C code, which we rigorously tested on a Linux system. Our prototype supports highly-concurrent emulation through the socket and connection pooling. To make the emulations more realistic and reduce the emulation latency, we leverage multiple parallelism-driven techniques, such as multi-threading, to increase throughput. Additionally, we provide customized support for porting high-level applications to the emulation, such as MySQL and Epoll.

In our emulation platform, we assumed that the server is always ready to be connected by edge vehicles for any type of request or query. It's worth noting that our emulation platform supports the interaction of multiple types of data, ranging from plain text to complex images. We believe such a feature can best reflect real-world scenarios where the communication between servers and clients is based on various data types.

3 Evaluations

We experimentally evaluate two representative IoV applications (i.e., DNN model inference and DNN model training with Differential-Private protection) on our platform. For experimental details, we discuss the workload settings and testing environment in Sect. 3.1, and then showcase our emulation results and takeaways for these two applications in Sect. 3.2.

3.1 Experimental Setup

Workload 1: Face2Multi-Modal. We consider positioning the pipeline of Face2Multi-modal in either (1) on-edge devices or (2) servers during services.

Therefore, there are two configuration settings in our experiments: 1) models are deployed on edge servers, which considers the scenarios that intelligent vehicles process the data in a local region and then synchronize with the corresponding server; 2) models are hosted on the servers, which considers a centralized server to process all the tasks in the server side and send results back to waiting vehicles. For each setting, it takes 20,000 images of 224×224 pixels as input and takes the heart rate and vehicle speed predicted by the model as output. And we also conduct 2000,5000, and 10000 times of concurrent connections for these two settings, to examine the impacts of the above strategies in the IoV context.

Workload 2: Differentially-Private Face2Multi-Modal Training. We also test the privacy-protected DNN training process whose training samples are obtained from the (1) centralized server or the (2) edge vehicles using Differentially-Private (DP) protected queries. For the first case, we conduct Global DP (GDP) queries on a centralized server to get the training data that is protected by the server (i.e., adding random noises). For the second case, the Local DP (LDP) method applies privacy protections locally before we train the per-vehicle DNN model. As for detailed GDP and LDP settings during training, we vary the ϵ value within the range [0.01, 1.2] to comprehensively characterize GDP and LDP for different privacy-protection levels. Face2Multi-modal uses BROOK dataset [4,6,9] for training under Differential Privacy settings.

Hardware Support: Our emulation platform of IoV is deployed on a single laptop, as the end goal of this work is to support the development and evaluation of novel HVI design in the context of IoV using accessible hardware resources. The detailed configurations of our selected laptop are listed as follows: The CPU is Intel(R) Core(TM) i7-8750H and the GPU is NVIDIA GeForce 1060. Ideal, the emulation platform has minimal requirements on the device and can be deployed on any machine.

3.2 Characterization Results

We present the characterization results of afore-mentioned two workloads respectively, and briefly summarize four important takeaways from the results.

Face2Multi-Modal on Edge or Server. Figure 2 reports our emulation results for testing two deployment patterns of Face2Multi-Modal on IoV. From the figure, we draw two key takeaways, which are presented as follows.

Key Takeaway 1: Latency-critical workload should be hosted on edge. As shown in Fig. 2, when the Face2Multi-Modal is deployed on the edge side, the average time consumption achieves the lowest level no matter how many clients are served concurrently. At concurrent numbers 2,000/5,000/10,000, the service time cost for the model deployed on edge is merely about 50%/63%/67% of that for the model on the server. This is because, from the perspective of

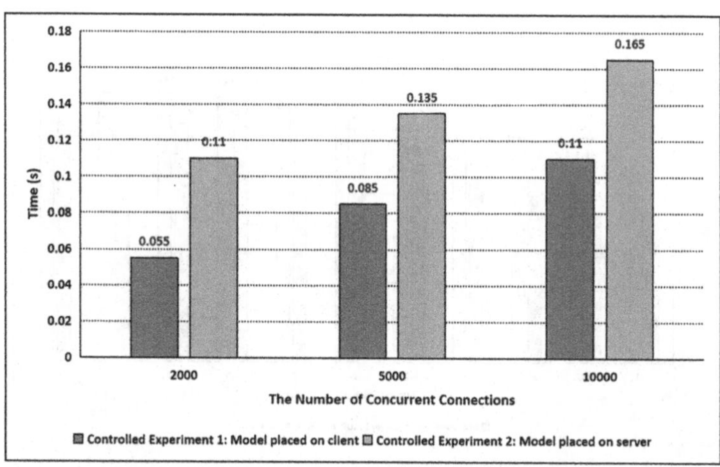

Fig. 2. Characterization results of Face2Multimodal in different client/server deployment settings on our emulation platform

time consumption, transferring data frequently between edge and server is less efficient than computing the DNN inference directly on edge. Therefore, in the context of IoV, it's efficient for us to deploy workload on edge when the latency is the users' primary concern.

Key Takeaway 2: Server should take the throughput-critical workload. Figure 2 demonstrates that the latency of hosting services on the server is less amenable to the increase in the number of concurrent connections. When the number of concurrent connections grows from 2,000 to 5,000, the latency of server-side services increases by approximately 22%, compared to that for services on edge (about 55% increment). Similarly, when the concurrent number reaches 10,000, the time cost for server-side workload suffers a 22% increase (compared to the latency with 5000 connections), while edge devices take about 30% more time to handle the workload. Hence, we should offload the throughput-critical workload to a server in the context of IoV.

DP-Protected Face2Multi-Modal Training. Figure 3 reports the emulation results of Face2Multi-Modal training in different Differential Privacy settings (i.e., GDP and LDP). From the figure, we draw two key takeaways.

Key Takeaway 3: In comparison to GDP, LDP shows its overwhelming advantages in the context of IoV. From Fig. 3, we can see a 1.7× validation accuracy gain when comparing the result of LDP and GDP. This may be because locally trained models fit better to the driver's features, which leads to higher accuracy. In light of this, we should employ LDP rather than GDP for privacy protection on IoV.

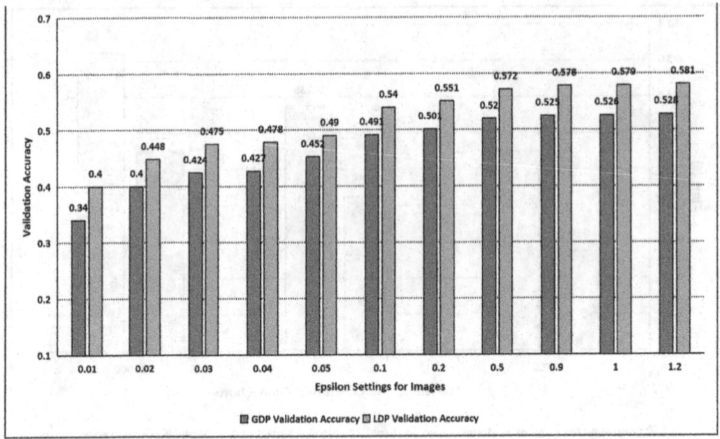

Fig. 3. Charaterization results of Differential-Privacy-enabled Face2Multimodal in different Differential Privacy protection settings on our emulation platform

Key Takeaway 4: An appropriate ϵ value of DP lies in the range [0.03, 0.5], which is expected to bring a reasonable tradeoff between privacy protection and inference accuracy. It's shown in Fig. 3 that the choice of ϵ value from an extremely low margin (i.e., [0.01, 0.03)) will greatly degrade the performance of Face2Multi-Modal. Improving the protection extent (ϵ) slightly from 0.03 to 0.01 takes the large cost of about 8% accuracy degradation. In the other margin (i.e., (0.5, 1.2]), the variance of ϵ brings about an inapparent effect on model accuracy, which means that choosing a ϵ value larger than 0.5 will not significantly benefit the accuracy, but compromises the privacy protection. Hence, we empirically verify that a preferred ϵ value should be located between 0.03 and 0.5.

4 Discussion and Future Work

The characterization results showcase the capability of our emulation platform to examine novel HVI applications in the context of IoV, by observing application behaviors in different server/client settings and evaluating parameter scopes for better tuning. The current takeaways we obtained are potentially applicable to other DNN-based HVI applications (e.g., [1,17]). In the future, we aim to add more functionalities to support the evaluation and characterization of various HVI designs and provide fine-grained emulation controls and detailed performance analysis to increase the usability of our platform. Some example works that can be deployed on our emulation platform to understand its performance in different IOV settings include 1) time-series-based analysis (e.g., driver style classifications [18], facial expressions distributions [15]) and 2) security and privacy protection designs [2,3,7,13]. Also, our emulation platform can be co-worked or integrated with existing IoV-related development toolkits (e.g.,

[11,12,16]), to provide a fast and glueless transition from prototype development to design emulation.

5 Conclusions

In this work, we present our emulation platform that is designed for developing and evaluating novel Human-Vehicle Interaction design in the context of Internet-of-Vehicles. We present the design and implementation details of our emulation platform and conduct two characterization studies to evaluate the feasibility of our platform. We then extract several key takeaways from the characterization studies. We also discuss potentials for future work of our platform.

Acknowledgements. We thank the anonymous reviewers from HCI 2023 and all members from the User-Centric Computing Group for their valuable feedback and comments. An earlier version of this work was positioned at [5] as a work-in-progress.

References

1. Bi, Z., et al.: FIGCONs: exploiting FIne-Grained CONstructs of facial expressions for efficient and accurate estimation of in-vehicle drivers' statistics. In: International Conference on Human-Computer Interaction (2023)
2. Duan, Y., et al.: Characterizing and optimizing differentially-private techniques for high-utility, privacy-preserving internet-of-vehicles. In: International Conference on Human-Computer Interaction (2023)
3. Duan, Y., et al.: Characterizing differentially-private techniques in the era of internet-of-vehicles. In: arXiv (2022)
4. Jin, W., et al.: BROOK Dataset: A Playground for Exploiting Data- Driven Techniques in Human-Vehicle Interactive Designs. Technical report- Feb-01 at User-Centric Computing Group, University of Nottingham Ningbo, China (2022)
5. Jin, W., et al.: Towards emulating internet-of-vehicles on a single machine. In: Automotive UI 2021: 13th International Conference on Automotive User Interfaces and Interactive Vehicular Applications, Leeds, United Kingdom, September 9–14, 2021 - Adjunct Proceedings, pp. 112–114. ACM (2021). https://doi.org/10.1145/3473682.3480275
6. Liu, J., et al.: BROOK dataset: a playground for exploiting data- driven techniques in human-vehicle interactive designs. In: HCII (2023)
7. Liu, J., et al.: HUT: enabling high-utility, batched queries under differential privacy protection for internet-of-vehicles. In: arXiv (2022)
8. Lopez, P.A., et al.: Microscopic Traffic Simulation using SUMO. In: ITSC (2018)
9. Peng, X., Huang, Z., Xu, S.: Building BROOK: a multi- modal and facial video database for human-vehicle interaction research. In: CHI workshop (2020)
10. Sommer, C., German, R., Dressler, F.: Bidirectionally coupled network and road traffic simulation for improved IVC analysis. In: IEEE TMC (2011)
11. Song, Z., et al.: First attempt to build realistic driving scenes using video-to-video synthesis in OpenDS framework. In: AutomotiveUI (2019)
12. Song, Z., et al.: Omniverse-OpenDS: enabling agile developments for complex driving scenarios via reconfigurable abstractions. In: HCII (2022)

13. Xu, S., et al.: Exploring Personalised Autonomous Vehicles to Influence User Trust. In: Cogn. Comput. (2020)
14. Andras Varga. "OMNeT++". In: Modeling and tools for network simulation (2010)
15. Wang, J., et al.: The Importance Distribution of Drivers Facial Expressions Varies over Time! In: AutomotiveUI (2021)
16. Wang, S., et al.: Oneiros-OpenDS: an interactive and extensible toolkit for agile and automated developments of complicated driving scenes. In: HCII (2022)
17. Xiong, Z., et al.: Face2Statistics: user-friendly, low-cost and effective alternative to in-vehicle sensors/monitors for drivers. In: HCII (2022)
18. Zhang, Y., et al.: Demystifying interactions between driving behaviors and styles through self-clustering algorithms. In: HCII (2021)

A Study on the Effects of Intrinsic Motivation from Self-determination on Driving Skill

Yuki Nakagawa[1(✉)], Sayuri Matsuda[1], Takumi Takaku[1], Satoshi Nakamura[1], Takanori Komatsu[1], Takeshi Torii[2], Ryuichi Sumikawa[2], and Hideyuki Takao[2]

[1] Meiji University, Nakano 4-21-1, Nakano-Ku, Tokyo, Japan
nakagawa.yuki55@gmail.com

[2] SUBARU CORPORATION, Ebisu1-20-8, Shibuya-Ku, Tokyo, Japan

Abstract. There are many novice drivers and inexperienced drivers who have difficulty driving a car. In this work, we focused on intrinsic motivation to increase the effectiveness of practice driving and support drivers' skill improvement. We proposed a system in which drivers themselves select what they pay attention to when driving from a list of options before driving. To verify the effectiveness of the proposed method, we compared a case in which the driver selected what to pay attention to when driving from among three options and a case in which the experimenter told the driver what to pay attention to when driving. The experiment results showed that intrinsic motivation was better than extrinsic motivation in preventing drivers from overcorrecting the steering wheel angle. However, there was no difference between the two in the skills of maintaining a constant speed and being aware of the left and right-hand widths because of their difficulty to master.

Keywords: Driving · Intrinsic motivation · Self-determination · Driving skill improvement

1 Introduction

There are many novice drivers and inexperienced drivers. It has been shown that inexperienced young drivers have poor risk perception and are more likely to cause accidents [1–5]. Many training programs have been conducted to improve the driving skills of inexperienced drivers [6–9], and there have been numerous experiments using simulators [10–13].

In this work, we first conducted a questionnaire survey on driving using Yahoo! Crowdsourcing for Japanese drivers with driver's licenses. Then, we received 2,609 responses (1519 males, 1056 females, and 34 others) after removing inauthentic responses. This survey found that 40% of respondents drove a car daily, and 20% drove "less than once every few months" or "rarely." We also found that novice and inexperienced drivers were more likely than other drivers to feel that they were not good at driving (see Fig. 1). In addition, we asked about issues they had difficulty with when driving. Then we found that 29% of novice and 42% of inexperienced drivers indicated

C. Stephanidis et al. (Eds.): HCII 2023, CCIS 1836, pp. 73–81, 2023.
https://doi.org/10.1007/978-3-031-36004-6_11

that they were poor at steering wheel operation. Furthermore, novice and inexperienced drivers were less skilled at changing direction and driving at high speeds compared to other drivers.

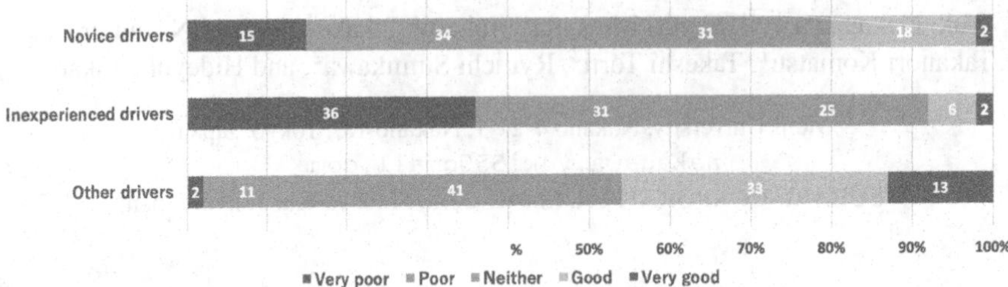

Fig. 1. Level of difficulty in driving a car (Q. Are you a good driver or a poor driver?).

From these results, we can say that a system should be designed to improve the driving skills of those who are not good at driving while motivating them to drive and increasing the effectiveness of their driving practice.

Intrinsic and extrinsic motivations for doing something are well-known [14]. Intrinsic motivation is when there is no external reward, such as money, and the action itself is the goal. Extrinsic motivation is motivated by external stimuli such as money, reward, or coercion. Several studies have clarified that intrinsic motivation is more likely to lead to richer experiences, better problem-solving, and sustained effects [15]. Therefore, if we induce intrinsic motivation in novice or inexperienced drivers for driving practice, their driving skills might improve.

Ryan et al. [16] found that intrinsic motivation is promoted in situations where competitiveness, autonomy, and relatedness are met. Self-determination theory also reveals that autonomy influences motivation and that greater autonomy increases intrinsic motivation. In other words, self-determination plays an essential role in inducing intrinsic motivation. Zuckerman et al. [17] found that the feeling of self-determination in choosing one's tasks enhances intrinsic motivation.

We hypothesize that intrinsically motivated drivers would focus more on driving skills and would improve their driving skills more than extrinsically motivated drivers. We also propose a method that enhances intrinsic motivation by making drivers choose a driving skill to focus on before driving. This method requires drivers to select a target driving skill from three driving skills and to drive while focusing on the selected skill. We also implement a system and verify our hypothesis through experiments using a driving simulator.

2 Experiment

This study aimed to improve driving skills through intrinsic motivation and hypothesized that "intrinsically motivated drivers will focus more on their driving and improve their driving skills more than extrinsically motivated drivers."

We conducted a comparative experiment to verify the proposed method's effectiveness. We divided the experimental participants into two conditions as follows.

- The participants themselves chose what they paid attention to when driving (intrinsic motivation condition).
- The experimenter told the participants what to pay attention to when driving (extrinsic motivation condition).

2.1 Implementation of the Experimental System

For the experiment, we improved an experimental driving simulator [18], which enables the experimenter to set straight lengths, curved lengths, and curve radii. The experimenter could control the road width for each trial.

We also implemented a motivational system. For the intrinsic motivation condition, the system showed three buttons for choices on the screen (see Fig. 2). Once an option was selected, it could not be selected again. For the extrinsic motivation condition, one of the three options was randomly displayed on the screen (see Fig. 3).

The scene of the experiment is shown in Fig. 4. We used the Podium Lenkrad Classic 2 for the steering wheel, Club Sport Wheel Base V2.5 for the steering controller, Club Sport Pedals V3 Inverted for the pedals, Next Level Racing for the seat, the Oculus Quest 2 for the head-mounted display and an iPad for the motivational system.

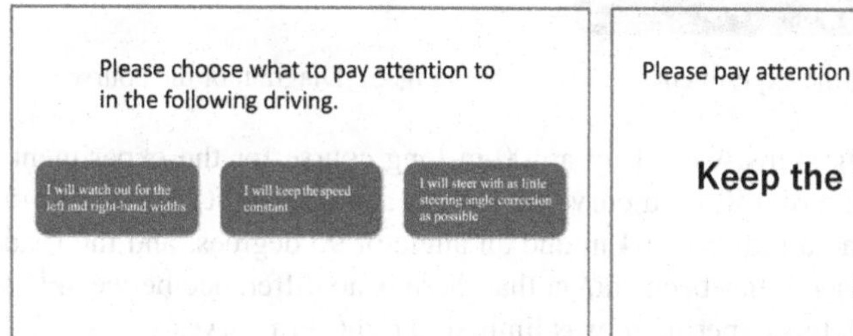

Fig. 2. Intrinsic motivation mode screen.

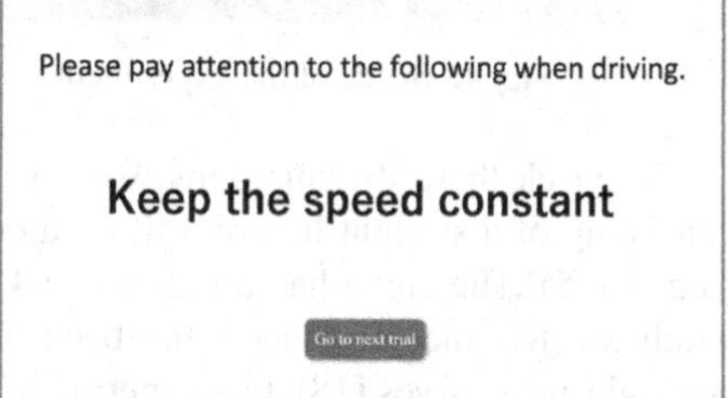

Fig. 3. Extrinsic motivation mode screen.

2.2 Driving Skills Used in the Experiment

To induce intrinsic motivation to drive, participants in the intrinsic motivation condition were presented with a choice of basic driving skills and asked to select one skill that they would pay attention to in their subsequent driving. The participants in the extrinsic motivation condition were given instructions on the basic driving skills to pay attention to in the experiment.

We chose three driving skills for this experiment as follows:

- Watch out for the left and right-hand widths.
- Keep the speed constant.
- Steer with as little steering angle correction as possible.

The reasons for choosing these skills are maintaining a constant speed and having a feel for the vehicle are essential for safe driving. Furthermore, driving with too much turning of the steering wheel decreases vehicle ride comfort and stability. In particular, novice and inexperienced drivers who are not accustomed to driving do not have a sense of the steering angle when driving around curves. They tend to correct the steering more frequently.

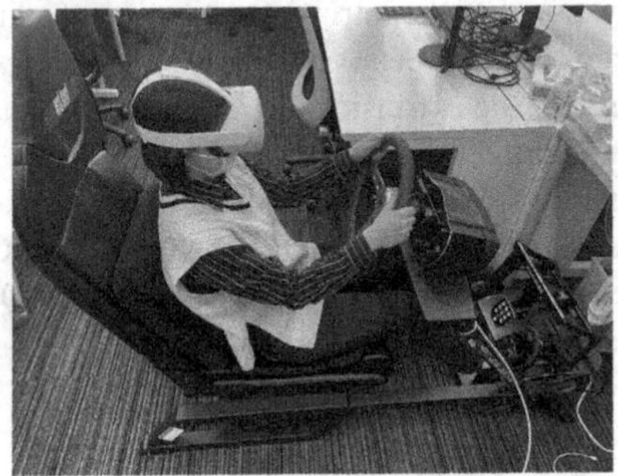

Fig. 4. Scene of the experiment.

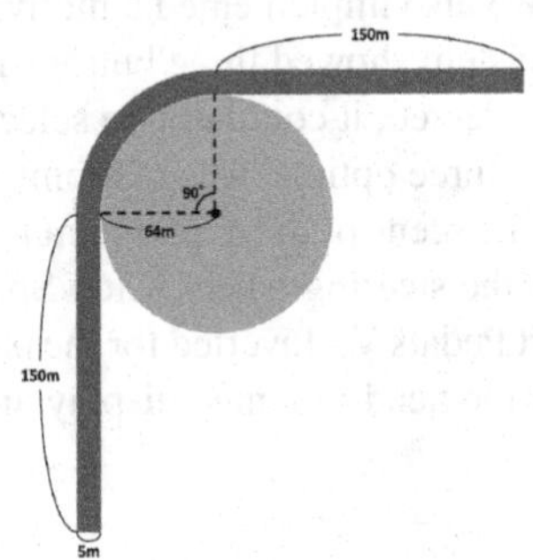

Fig. 5. Diagram of the course.

To check these driving skills, we set up a 400-m-long course for the experiment, consisting of a straight line of 150 m, a curve of 100 m, and a straight line of 150 m (see Fig. 5). The curve had a radius of 64 m and an angle of 90 degrees, and the road width was five meters. Since it has been shown that there is no difference between left and right-turn curves [18], this experiment was limited to right-turn curves.

2.3 Experimental Procedure

The experimental procedure was as follows.

1. We asked the participants to practice driving the course until they were satisfied with it so they could familiarize themselves with the driving simulator. We instructed the participants to drive from 40 km/h to 60 km/h.
2. We presented the motivational system to the participants and asked them to use it. In the intrinsic motivation condition, we asked the participants to choose what they would be careful about when driving. In the extrinsic motivation condition, we asked the participants to read and confirm the driving instructions displayed on the motivational system.
3. We asked the participants to drive the course on the driving simulator ten times.
4. The participants took a five-minute break.
5. Process (2)-(4) was repeated three times.

6. We asked the participants to answer a post-experiment questionnaire (using a five-point Likert scale to indicate how much they were conscious of the skills selected or instructed in each set of driving motivation systems).

Each course began with a countdown. One course ended when the driver had driven to the end of the course. If an accident occurred due to contact with the guardrails, the driving ended there. At the end of the set, the trial that resulted in the error was presented again, and the measurement was retaken.

3 Results

The participants were 14 university and graduate students (13 males and one female) between 18 and 25 years old. They owned a driver's license, drove less than two to three times per month, and had experience with the simulator. There were seven subjects in both the intrinsic and extrinsic motivation conditions.

In this study, we prepared three options and analyzed each of the driving skills as follows:

- When "Watch out for the left and right-hand widths" was selected or instructed, we analyzed it by the degree of deviation from the center of the road. Specifically, the starting point of the course was set as the center of the road, and the deviation from the center was calculated integrally from time to time.
- When "Keep the speed constant" was selected or instructed, we analyzed it by the standard deviation of the speed. Since the driver continues to accelerate until a constant speed is reached in the first 100 m immediately after the start of the course, we set the calculation target for the standard deviation of speed from 100m to 400m (the end of the course).
- When "Steer with as little steering angle correction as possible" was selected or instructed, we analyzed it by finding the number of times the steering was corrected. To assess corrective steering, the number of times the steering wheel angle changed from positive to negative and from negative to positive while driving was counted.

Figures 6, 7 and 8 compare intrinsic and extrinsic motivation in driving skills for each option. The statistical evaluation showed no significant difference between intrinsic and extrinsic motivation in any of the skills. Here, feedback from the post-experiment questionnaire indicated that the participants felt that the vehicle body was shifted to the left. Therefore, it may be possible that the "Watch out for the left and right-hand widths" instruction was not appropriate as an option due to the difficulty of finding the center of the road.

In addition, Fig. 7 compares the standard deviation of driving speed when "Keep the speed constant" was selected or indicated with intrinsic and extrinsic motivation. The results show no difference between intrinsic and extrinsic motivation for "Keep the speed constant."

On the other hand, Fig. 8 compares the number of times the driver corrected the steering wheel for intrinsic and extrinsic motivation when the option selected by the driver or shown by the experimenter was "Steer with as little steering angle correction as possible." The results show that the number of steering corrections tended to be fewer in the intrinsically motivated group than in the extrinsically motivated group.

In the post-experiment questionnaire, we asked the participants, "How conscious were you of the instructions selected or indicated in each set?" We asked participants to rate their level of consciousness on a five-point scale from 1 (not conscious at all) to 5 (very conscious) (see Fig. 9). The subjective evaluation showed that the extrinsic motivation group was more conscious of the skill in both the trial in which they were careful to keep a constant speed and the trial in which they were careful about how they turned the steering wheel.

4 Discussion

Figure 7 shows no difference between intrinsic and extrinsic motivation in "Keep the speed constant." On the other hand, Fig. 8 indicates that the intrinsically motivated group tended to have fewer steering corrections than the extrinsically motivated group in the set in which they were careful to correct the turning of the steering wheel. In other words, motivation through making one's own choices may be more effective for improving skills in steering corrections than when others give instructions.

For the participants in the experiment, "Steer with as little steering angle correction as possible" literally required the participant to focus only on the steering wheel, which was direct manipulation. On the other hand, "Keep the speed constant" was indirect; the participant controlled the speed by stepping on the accelerator pedal. We believe that intrinsic motivation by choosing what to pay attention to when driving may be effective for improving driving skills whose operation is direct and easy to understand. We prepared three options, "Watch out for the left and right-hand widths," "Keep the speed constant," and "Steer with as little steering angle correction as possible" for this experiment. "Steer with as little steering angle correction as possible" was easy to understand from a sensory point of view since the focus was on steering adjustments. In addition, the driver only needed to be aware of direct steering wheel actions.

On the other hand, the skill of keeping the speed constant required a complex combination of the steering wheel and acceleration operations. The complexity of the operations may have prevented the driver from developing motivation. The experimental results showed that intrinsic motivation was effective only for corrective steering, suggesting that intrinsic motivation is more likely to be effective in tasks where the operation is direct and easy to understand. Thus, there is a possibility that effective motivational styles for skill improvement will vary depending on the difficulty and proficiency of the skill, so further study is needed.

In the post-experiment questionnaire, several participants answered, "I felt the car body was shifted to the left" and "the steering wheel felt different from the actual car."

This feedback suggests that the results may have been affected by difficulty in finding the center of the road and the problem of keeping the center of the road in a curved section. It is also possible that some participants did not interpret the "Watch out for the left and right-hand widths" task as keeping to the center of the road. Therefore, we should prepare much more appropriate tasks in the future.

In the subjective evaluation conducted after the experiment, the extrinsically motivated group was more conscious when the instruction was "Keep the speed constant"

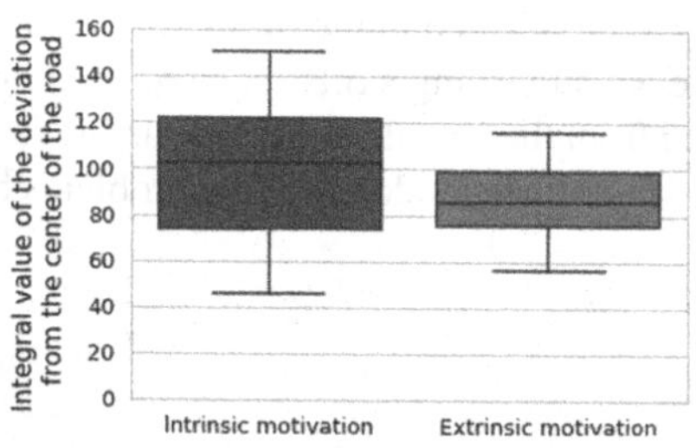

Fig. 6. Comparison of the integral value of the deviation from the center of the road when "Watch out for the left and right-hand widths" was selected or instructed.

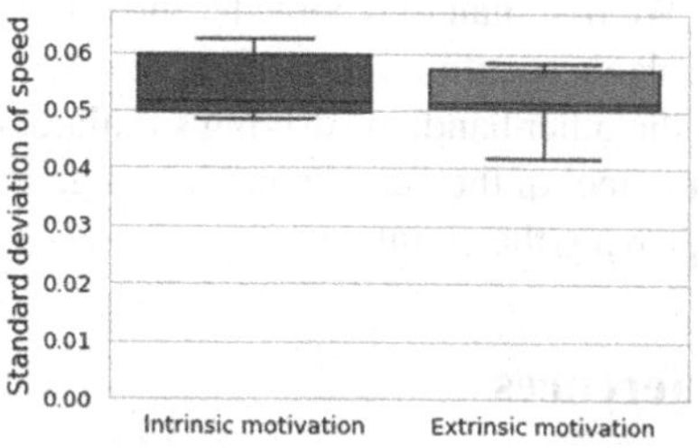

Fig. 7. Comparison of the standard deviation of speed when "Keep the speed constant" was selected or instructed.

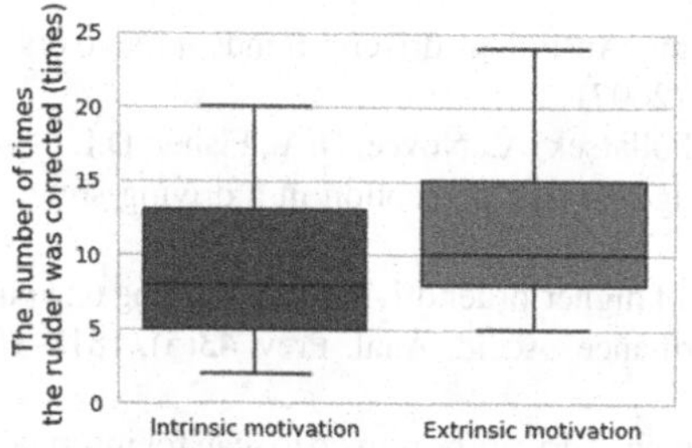

Fig. 8. Comparison of the number of steering corrections when "Steer with as little steering angle correction as possible" was selected or instructed.

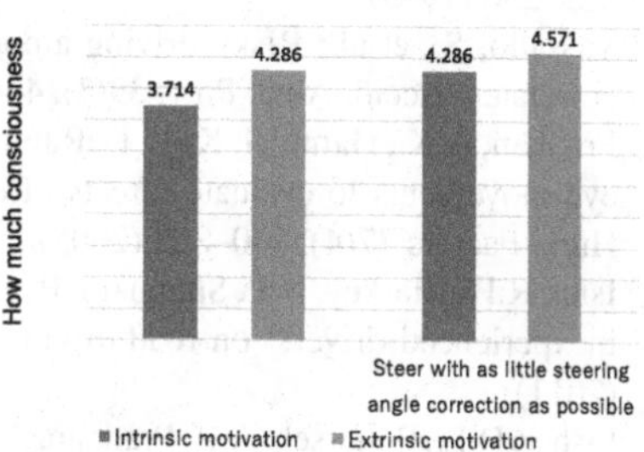

Fig. 9. Subjective evaluation.

and "Steer with as little steering angle correction as possible." On the other hand, the number of steering corrections was fewer in the intrinsically motivated group than in the extrinsically motivated group. This result suggests that extrinsic motivation may be ineffective in improving specific skills just because they are assumed to be conscious.

5 Conclusion

In this study, we proposed a method to support novice and inexperienced drivers by inducing intrinsic motivation to drive by letting the drivers choose the skills they would pay attention to in subsequent driving sessions immediately before driving. We experimented by comparing cases in which the drivers themselves chose what to focus on and cases in which the experimenter told them what to focus on to verify whether the driving skills they chose improved. The results showed that the number of corrective steering maneuvers carried out by directly manipulating the steering wheel was lower in the intrinsically motivated group than in the extrinsically motivated group. The results also suggest that intrinsic motivation may improve direct manipulation skills more effectively than skills requiring complex manipulation.

We first plan to reconsider the driving skills to be selected in the future. In addition, we plan to continue improving and seeking the actual driving skills required by users. On the other hand, the driving simulator differed from the actual car in some areas, such as the feel of the vehicle and braking, and we plan to further address these problems by improving the simulator.

References

1. McKnight, A.J., McKnight, A.S.: Young novice drivers: careless or clueless? Accid. Anal. Prev. **35**(6), 921–925 (2003)
2. Machin, M.A., Sankey, K.S.: Relationships between young drivers' personality characteristics, risk perceptions, and driving behaviour. Accid. Anal. Prev. **40**(2), 541–547 (2008)
3. Deery, H.A.: Hazard and risk perception among young novice drivers. J. Safety Res. **30**(4), 225–236 (1999)
4. Vassallo, S., et al.: Risky driving among young Australian drivers: trends, precursors and correlates. Accid. Anal. Prev. **39**(3), 444–458 (2007)
5. Pradhan, A.K., Hammel, K.R., DeRamus, R., Pollatsek, A., Noyce, D.A., Fisher, D.L.: Using eye movements to evaluate effects of driver age on risk perception in a driving simulator. Hum. Factors **47**(4), 840–852 (2005)
6. Isler, R.B., Starkey, N.J., Sheppard, P.: Effects of higher-order driving skill training on young, inexperienced drivers' on-road driving performance. Accid. Anal. Prev. **43**(5), 1818–1827 (2011)
7. Fisher, D.L., Pollatsek, A.P., Pradhan, A.: Can novice drivers be trained to scan for information that will reduce their likelihood of a crash? Inj. Prev. **12**, i25–i29 (2006)
8. Agrawal, R., Knodler, M., Fisher, D.L., Samuel, S.: Advanced virtual reality based training to improve young drivers' latent hazard anticipation ability. In: Proceedings of the Human Factors and Ergonomics Society Annual Meeting 61(1), pp. 1995–1999. SAGE Publications, Sage CA, Los Angeles (2017)
9. Regan, M. A., Deery, H. A., Triggs, T. J.: Training for attentional control in novice car drivers: A simulator study. In: Proceedings of the Human Factors and Ergonomics Society Annual Meeting, vol. 42(20), pp. 1452–1456. SAGE Publications, Sage CA, Los Angeles (1998)
10. Jamson, S.L., Hibberd, D.L., HamishJamson, A.: Drivers' ability to learn eco-driving skills; effects on fuel efficient and safe driving behaviour. Transp. Res. Part C: Emerg. Technol. **58**, 657–668 (2015). https://doi.org/10.1016/j.trc.2015.02.004
11. Fisher, D.L., et al.: Use of a fixed-base driving simulator to evaluate the effects of experience and PC-based risk awareness training on drivers' decisions. Hum. Factors **44**(2), 287–302 (2002)
12. Roenker, D.L., Cissell, G.M., Ball, K.K., Wadley, V.G., Edwards, J.D.: Speed-of-processing and driving simulator training result in improved driving performance. Hum. Factors **45**(2), 218–233 (2003)
13. Ivancic, K., IV., Hesketh, B.: Learning from errors in a driving simulation: effects on driving skill and self-confidence. Ergonomics **43**(12), 1966–1984 (2000)
14. Ryan, R.M., Deci, E.L.: Intrinsic and extrinsic motivations: classic definitions and new directions. Contemp. Educ. Psychol. **25**(1), 54–67 (2000)
15. Deci, E.L., Flaste, R.: Why we do what we do: the dynamics of personal autonomy. GP Putnam's Sons (1995)
16. Ryan, R.M., Deci, E.L.: Self-determination theory and the facilitation of intrinsic motivation, social development, and well-being. Am. Psychol. **55**(1), 68–78 (2000)

17. Zuckerman, M., Porac, J., Lathin, D., Deci, E.L.: On the importance of self-determination for intrinsically-motivated behavior. Pers. Soc. Psychol. Bull. **4**(3), 443–446 (1978)
18. Funazaki, Y., Seto, N., Ninomiya, K., Hikawa, K., Nakamura, S., Yamanaka, S.: Driving experiment system using HMDs to measure drivers' proficiency and difficulty of various road conditions. In: Krömker, H. (ed.) HCI in Mobility, Transport, and Automotive Systems, HCII 2022, LNCS, vol. 13335, pp. 247–257. Springer, Virtual Event (2022)

Impact of Locus of Control on Dangerous Driving Behavior and Positive Driving Behavior in China

Weina Qu[1,2](✉), Xiaohui Luo[1,3], Jiqing Hou[1], and Yan Ge[1,2]

[1] CAS Key Laboratory of Behavioral Science, Institute of Psychology, Beijing, China
quwn@psych.ac.cn

[2] Department of Psychology, University of Chinese Academy of Sciences, Beijing, China

[3] Faculty of Psychology, Beijing Normal University, Beijing, China

Abstract. Locus of control (LOC) reflects a person's perception of events as within his or her internal control or under the control of external factors. The main purpose of this study was to reconfirm the factor structure and items of the Traffic Locus of Control (T-LOC) scale among Chinese drivers and investigate the influences of drivers' LOC on their dangerous and positive driving behavior. A total of 299 drivers completed the Chinese version of the T-LOC scale, personality scales of sensation seeking, anger and altruism, driver behavior questionnaire (DBQ) and positive driving behavior scale (PDBS). A 17-item four-factor Chinese version of the T-LOC scale was verified to be appropriate in China. More importantly, after controlling the impacts of demographic variables and three personalities, self-attribution positively predicted driving errors. For the external LOC, other drivers negatively predicted positive driving behavior, while vehicle/environment positively predicted positive driving behavior. Additionally, fate attribution was a positive predictor of all kinds of dangerous driving behavior. In conclusion, this study further validated the Chinese version of the T-LOC scale and revealed the impact of drivers' LOC based on a comprehensive consideration of driving behavior, including not only dangerous driving behavior, but also positive driving behavior.

Keywords: Personality · Locus of control · Fate attribution · T-LOC · Dangerous driving behavior · Positive driving behavior

1 Introduction

Locus of control (LOC), a personality concept originally proposed by Rotter (1966), is defined as a generalized enduring expectancy or belief about how responsive and controllable the environment is. In the field of driving, LOC is a critical variable among the psychological factors that are predictive to driving behavior.

C. Stephanidis et al. (Eds.): HCII 2023, CCIS 1836, pp. 82–90, 2023.
https://doi.org/10.1007/978-3-031-36004-6_12

1.1 Measurement of Driver's Locus of Control

Targeted at drivers, Montag and Comrey (1987) first developed the Driving Internality (DI) scale and the Driving Externality (DE) scale. Almost thirty years later, Özkan and Lajunen (2005) considered that the DI and DE scales were too simple to use in the traffic environment; therefore, they developed the 15-item Traffic Locus of Control scale (T-LOC) to focus on traffic conditions as a whole. It is composed of four dimensions: self, which reflects an individual's tendency toward an internal LOC, and vehicle/environment, other drivers and fate, which jointly reflect an individual's tendency toward an external LOC. In a subsequent study (Özkan et al. 2005), an item "shortcomings in my driving skills" was added to the dimension of self, and an item "coincidence" was added to the dimension of fate, which contributed to the 17-item T-LOC scale. According to different cultural backgrounds, further investigations of LOC adapted the T-LOC scale into different language versions, including the Swedish version (Warner et al. 2010), the Romanian version (Măirean et al. 2017) and the Chinese version (Sun et al. 2020). Due to the differences in traffic rules and driving habits among different countries, the factor structure and items of the T-LOC scale varied, with the Swedish version and the Romanian version showing a five-factor structure with 17 and 41 items, respectively, while the Chinese version remained a four-factor structure with 15 items only.

1.2 Impacts of Locus of Control on Driving Behavior

A great number of studies with respect to driver personality focused on LOC. However, the findings on the relationship between drivers' LOC and their driving behavior were inconsistent. Some researchers found that drivers with an external LOC performed more dangerous driving behaviors (Măirean et al. 2017; Sarma et al. 2013). They tend to interpret driving outcomes as the result of uncontrollable influences, which is associated with less caution and failure to take preventive measures to avoid potentially dangerous behavior. However, conflicting results have also been reported. It was shown that drivers with an internal LOC were more likely to be involved in traffic accidents (Sun et al. 2020) and engaged in dangerous driving behavior (Lemarié et al. 2019). These findings may reflect the role of overconfidence and optimism bias: confident drivers believe that the likelihood of having traffic crashes, to a large degree, depends on their own behavior and skills but not on other drivers or environments.

Currently, researchers still have not reached a consensus about whether drivers with internal or external LOC exhibit more dangerous driving behavior. Notably, various LOC measurement scales were used in previous studies, including the general LOC scale for ordinary people and the T-LOC scale specially designed for drivers. In addition, as we mentioned, there were various versions of the LOC scale and T-LOC scale with different factor structures and items. Thus, we argued that the contradictory conclusions may, at least partly, result from various LOC measurement tools. Additionally, they were probably a reflection of cultural differences.

1.3 The Present Study

The main purpose of the current study was to investigate the effect of drivers' LOC on their dangerous driving behavior and positive driving behavior while controlling the influence of other important personality variables. First, to reconfirm the factor structure and items of the Chinese version of the T-LOC scale, we verified its reliability and validity with a Chinese driver sample. More importantly, since inconsistent conclusions of the relationship between LOC and driving behavior were proposed and the majority of these studies only focused on dangerous driving behavior, to comprehensively understand driving behavior and reveal the direct effect of drivers' LOC, this study made a contribution by adding positive driving behavior as a predicted variable and controlling the impacts of drivers' anger, altruism and sensation seeking.

2 Methods

2.1 Participants and Procedure

The participants were recruited from social networks through an online questionnaire link. All participants were told that their answers would be kept strictly confidential and used only for scientific research. After they signed the consent form, the participants completed a series of self-report questionnaires and received 30 RMB ($ 4.63). The final sample included 299 drivers. A total of 298 (99.67%) participants reported their age, which ranged from 20 to 58 years (mean (M) = 35.07 years, standard deviation (SD) = 8.66), and the final sample included 182 males (60.9%) and 117 females (39.1%). The study was approved by the Institutional Review Board of the Institute of Psychology, Chinese Academy of Sciences.

2.2 Instruments

The Traffic Locus of Control (T-LOC) scale. The 17-item T-LOC scale developed by Özkan et al. (2005) was translated into Chinese according to the translation/back-translation procedure suggested by Bentler and Bonett (1980). First, three assistant professors in psychology independently translated the English version of the T-LOC scale into Chinese simultaneously. Then, considering the Chinese driving culture, all the authors jointly developed a draft to ensure its accuracy, fluency and appropriateness. Next, a professional English-Chinese translator back-translated the draft to confirm the correctness and accuracy of the Chinese version. In addition, we invited three drivers to revise the text in accordance with the Chinese language so that each item could be clearly understood by Chinese drivers. Finally, the scale was revised and finalized through group discussion and comprehensive consideration of drivers' opinions. For each item, the drivers were asked to evaluate how possible they would attribute a traffic crash to a certain factor using a five-point scale (1 = not at all possible; 5 = highly possible).

The personality scales. In this study, personality scales from the International Personality Item Pool (IPIP, http://ipip.ori.org, Goldberg et al. 2006) were used to measure three personalities: anger (10 items), altruism (10 items) and sensation seeking (10 items). Each trait was scored by averaging the items on the relevant scale, and each item was evaluated from 1 ("strongly disagree") to 5 ("strongly disagree") on a five-point Likert scale based on the degree of conformity between each item and the participant's own situation.

The DBQ and the PDBS. The Driver Behavior Questionnaire (DBQ) has been widely used to measure aberrant driving behavior (Reason et al. 1990). The Chinese version of the DBQ, adapted by Yang et al. (2013), and the Chinese version of the PDBS, validated by Shen et al. (2018), were used in this study. In both scales, the participants evaluated their driving behavior on a five-point Likert scale (1 = "never", 5 = "always") based on how often they had engaged in each of the 41 behaviors in the past year.

3 Results

3.1 Descriptive Statistics

61.2% of the drivers reported that they had one or more traffic accidents in the past three years, and 46.15% of the drivers reported that they had been punished for traffic violations during the last year. In the entire sample, the α reliabilities of the four T-LOC subscales (self, other drivers, vehicle/environment and fate) were 0.83, 0.83, 0.67, and 0.76, respectively.

3.2 Internal Structure of the T-LOC Scale

The data were analyzed using SPSS (v. 19.0) and AMOS (v. 17.0). Descriptive statistics (means, standard deviations, internal consistencies, etc.) were calculated for each scale. The T-LOC factorial structure was adjusted by confirmatory factor analysis (CFA). Figure 1 shows the results of the estimated model and the standardized path coefficients of the structural relationships among the tested variables.

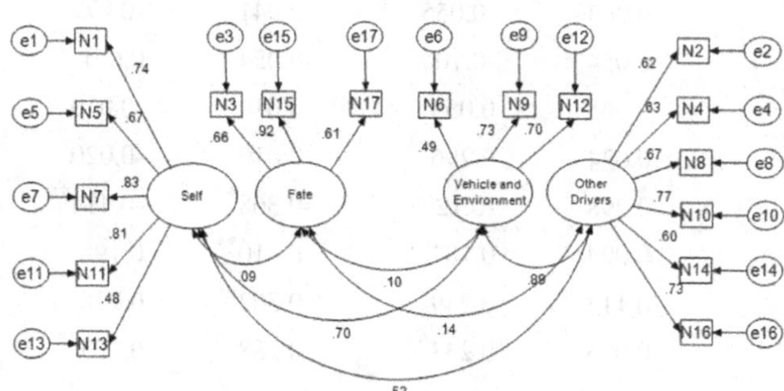

Fig. 1. The measurement model of T-LOC. N_i (i = 1,2,3…17) refers to the score of item i and e_i refers to its residual.

Generally, if the root mean square error of approximation (RMSEA) < 0.08, goodness-of-fit index (GFI) > 0.9, comparative fit index (CFI) > 0.9 and Tucker-Lewis index (TLI) > 0.9, the model is considered to be a good fit. In the present study, the original four-factor model of the indices of the T-LOC scale was acceptable (RMSEA = 0.046 ≤ 0.05; GFI = 0.93 < 0.9; CFI = 0.96 < 0.9; TLI = 0.95 < 0.9). Moreover, the χ2/df value approached one (χ2/df = 1.63, p < .001), which suggested that the 17-item model fit was already very good.

3.3 Hierarchical Multiple Regression Analysis

In each of the regression analyses, age, gender, and driving years were entered into the model in the first step to control their effect. Then, the personalities (anger, sensation seeking, altruism) were entered in the second step. In the third step, the subscales of the T-LOC (self, other drivers, vehicle/environment, fate) were entered. The predicted variables were positive driving behavior and the four dimensions of the DBQ (aggressive violations, general violations, errors, lapses).

Table 1. Hierarchical multiple regression model standardized regression coefficients (β).

	Positive driving behaviors	Aggressive violations	General violations	Errors	Lapses
Step1					
Age	0.031	-0.060	0.006	-0.087	0.019
Gender	0.065	-0.103	-0.072	0.022	0.184**
Driving years	0.042	0.080	0.075	0.039	-0.037
Model R^2	0.007	0.018	0.013	0.005	0.037*
Adjusted R^2	-0.003	0.008	0.003	-0.005	0.027*
Step2					
Age	0.044	-0.055	0.041	-0.072	0.022
Gender	0.054	-0.100	-0.024	0.061	0.208**
Driving years	0.065	0.055	0.019	-0.010	-0.076
Anger	-0.034	0.296**	0.010	-0.020	0.071
Altruism	0.298**	-0.129	-0.368**	-0.414**	-0.358**
Sensation seeking	-0.024	0.187**	0.310**	0.195**	0.147**
Model R^2	0.113**	0.249**	0.302**	0.238**	0.253**
Adjusted R^2	0.095**	0.233**	0.288**	0.223**	0.238**
Step3					

(continued)

Table 1. (*continued*)

	Positive driving behaviors	Aggressive violations	General violations	Errors	Lapses
Age	0.009	-0.079	0.000	-0.078	-0.007
Gender	0.062	-0.108	-0.043	0.055	0.194**
Driving years	0.074	0.073	0.058	-0.011	-0.051
Anger	-0.066	0.282**	0.002	-0.006	0.073
Altruism	0.221**	-0.105	-0.308**	-0.355**	-0.300**
Sensation seeking	-0.020	0.179**	0.308**	0.174**	0.141*
Self	-0.016	0.027	0.043	0.166*	0.081
Other drivers	0.280**	0.057	0.009	-0.110	-0.041
Vehicle/environment	-0.192*	-0.012	-0.069	-0.017	-0.061
Fate	-0.048	0.164**	0.253**	0.115*	0.189**
Model R^2	0.154*	0.281*	0.361**	0.269*	0.289**
Adjusted R^2	0.124*	0.256*	0.339**	0.244*	0.264**

Notes: Gender was a dummy variable, female = 0, male = 1; $^{*}p < 0.05$. $^{**}p < 0.01$

As shown in Table 1, the driver's age and driving experience could not significantly predict any driving behavior, while gender could positively predict lapses, which indicated that males performed more driving lapses than females. For personalities, anger positively predicted aggressive violations; altruism positively predicted positive driving behaviors and negatively predicted general violations, errors and lapses; sensation seeking positively predicted aggressive violations, general violations, errors and lapses. After controlling age, sex, years of driving experience and personalities, self was a significant positive predictor only of errors. For the external T-LOC, other drivers could only negatively predict positive driving behaviors, while vehicle/environment could only positively predict positive driving behaviors. Moreover, fate was a positive predictor of all four kinds of dangerous driving behavior, including aggressive violations, general violations, errors and lapses.

4 Discussion

In the current study, we first verified the reliability and validity of the T-LOC scale in the context of China and confirmed the 17-item four-factor Chinese version of the T-LOC scale, which contributed to dealing with the psychometric problem of LOC and promoted further investigations on LOC in China. More importantly, to obtain an overall understanding of the relationship between drivers' LOC and their driving behavior, both dangerous driving behavior and positive driving behavior were set as predicted variables. The results showed that drivers' various kinds of LOC, including self, other drivers, vehicle/environment and fate, were all significant predictors of driving behavior even after controlling demographic variables and other personalities.

First, it was confirmed that the Chinese version of the T-LOC scale had a stable internal structure. Through CFA analysis, the four-factor model of LOC, including self, other drivers, vehicle/environment and fate, was supported, and it was consistent with the factor structure of the original version (Özkan and Lajunen 2005; Özkan et al. 2005) and the Chinese version of the T-LOC scale developed by Sun et al. (2020).

More importantly, the result of the hierarchical multiple regression analysis showed that four factors of the T-LOC displayed different impacts on positive driving behavior and four types of dangerous driving behavior after controlling demographic variables (i.e., age, sex and driving years) and other personalities (i.e., anger, altruism and sensation seeking). Self, which represented the internal locus of control, could only positively predict driving errors. The dimension of self was used to measure to what extent an individual had an internal attribution orientation about traffic accidents (Ozkan and Lajunen, 2005; Rotter 1966), and drivers with a high score on the dimension of self were sometimes overconfident in their own skills and abilities to reduce the risk of accidents (Özkan and Lajunen 2005; Warner et al. 2010). Some researchers pointed out that driving errors, defined as planned actions that failed to achieve the intended effect, were usually misjudgments and failures of self-observation, which had a strong relationship with drivers themselves (Parker et al. 1998). Therefore, it made sense that self-attributed drivers reported more driving errors since they were too confident in themselves.

Concerning three external factors of LOC, an interesting finding was that other drivers could positively predict positive driving behavior, while vehicle/environment could negatively predict positive driving behavior. Another unexpected finding of the impacts of an external locus of control was that fate seemed to be the most crucial predictor of dangerous driving behavior in this study. The fate subscale was used to measure drivers' tendency to attribute traffic accidents to fate or bad luck. In the current study, even after controlling demographic variables and other personalities, fate could positively predict all types of dangerous driving behavior, including general violations, aggressive violations, errors, and lapses, which, we believed, was a reflection of the fatalism attribution of Chinese people. Under the influence of Buddhist and Taoist philosophies, many Chinese people attached great importance to fate when having causal thinking (Arkush 1984). Empirical studies found that people from Eastern countries were more likely to attribute outcomes of life events to fate (Leung et al. 2002). Since many Chinese people generally believe that various life outcomes are "destined to happen", in other words, they are predetermined and inevitable, they might feel less burden to drive in a risky way, which leads to more unsafe driving behavior. More importantly, this study indicated the importance of fate attribution among Chinese drivers, which might reveal an inadvertently ignored cultural differences of the relationship between driver's LOC and driving behavior. Still, whether certain aspect of LOC would play a critical role under certain cultural background is await future researches.

The study had several limitations. First, although we revealed the impacts of drivers' LOC on both their dangerous driving behavior and positive driving behavior, we still lack an understanding of the mechanism underlying the predictive effect of each dimension of drivers' LOC. Further studies could focus on exploring the root cause that leads to different predicting effects of each dimension. In addition, the measurement of driving behavior and accident involvement was barely based on drivers' self-reports, which might be influenced by social desirability and recall bias. In the future, researchers are recommended to use objective accident records or penalty point information. Moreover, the participants might not be a representative sample of all Chinese drivers, which mitigated the generalizability of our conclusions. Additionally, limited by the sample size, no grouping analysis based on gender, driving mileage or age was allowed. Since the relationship between drivers' LOC and their driving behavior may vary according to drivers' experience and demographic characteristics, a larger sample divided into various groups could be used in further investigation.

References

Arkush, R.D.: "If man works hard the land will not be lazy" entrepreneurial values in North Chinese peasant proverbs. Mod. China **10**(4), 461–479 (1984)

Bentler, P.M., Bonett, D.G.: Significance tests and goodness of fit in the analysis of covariance structures. Psychol. Bull. **88**(3), 588 (1980)

Goldberg, L.R., et al.: The international personality item pool and the future of public-domain personality measures. J. Res. Pers. **40**(1), 84–96 (2006)

Lemarié, L., Bellavance, F., Chebat, J.C.: Regulatory focus, time perspective, locus of control and sensation seeking as predictors of risky driving behaviors. Accid. Anal. Prev. **127**, 19–27 (2019)

Leung, K., et al.: Social axioms: the search for universal dimensions of general beliefs about how the world functions. J. Cross Cult. Psychol. **33**(3), 286–302 (2002)

Măirean, C., Havârneanu, G.M., Popuşoi, S.A., Havarneanu, C.E.: Traffic locus of control scale–Romanian version: psychometric properties and relations to the driver's personality, risk perception, and driving behavior. Transport. Res. F: Traffic Psychol. Behav. **45**, 131–146 (2017)

Montag, I., Comrey, A.L.: Internality and externality as correlates of involvement in fatal driving accidents. J. Appl. Psychol. **72**(3), 339 (1987)

Özkan, T., Lajunen, T.: Multidimensional traffic locus of control scale (T-LOC): factor structure and relationship to risky driving. Personal. Individ. Differ. **38**(3), 533–545 (2005)

Özkan, T., Lajunen, T., Kaistinen, J.: Traffic locus of control, driving skills and attitudes towards in-vehicle technologies (ISA & ACC). In: Proceedings of the 18th international cooperation on theories and concepts in traffic safety (ICTCT) (2005)

Parker, D., Lajunen, T., Stradling, S.: Attitudinal predictors of interpersonally aggressive violations on the road. Transport. Res. F: Traffic Psychol. Behav. **1**(1), 11–24 (1998)

Reason, J., Manstead, A., Stradling, S., Baxter, J., Campbell, K.: Errors and violations on the roads: a real distinction? Ergonomics **33**(10–11), 1315–1332 (1990)

Rotter, J.B.: Generalized expectancies for internal versus external control of reinforcement. Psychol. Monogr. Gen. Appl. **80**(1), 1 (1966)

Sarma, K.M., Carey, R.N., Kervick, A.A., Bimpeh, Y.: Psychological factors associated with indices of risky, reckless and cautious driving in a national sample of drivers in the Republic of Ireland. Accid. Anal. Prev. **50**, 1226–1235 (2013)

Shen, B., Ge, Y., Qu, W., Sun, X., Zhang, K.: The different effects of personality on prosocial and aggressive driving behaviour in a Chinese sample. Transport. Res. F: Traffic Psychol. Behav. **56**, 268–279 (2018)

Sun, L., Ma, Y., Hua, L.: Adaptation and validity of the traffic locus of control scale in Chinese drivers. Personality Individ. Differ. **159**, 109886 (2020)

Warner, H.W., Özkan, T., Lajunen, T.: Can the traffic locus of control (T-LOC) scale be successfully used to predict Swedish drivers' speeding behaviour? Accid. Anal. Prev. **42**(4), 1113–1117 (2010)

Yang, J., Du, F., Qu, W., Gong, Z., Sun, X.: Effects of personality on risky driving behavior and accident involvement for Chinese drivers. Traffic Inj. Prev. **14**(6), 565–571 (2013)

Study of Night Vision Configuration with Augmented Reality in Automotive Context

Neha Singhal[1(✉)], Areen Alsaid[2], Walter Talamonti[1], and Kenneth Mayer[1]

[1] Ford Motor Company, One American Road, Dearborn 48126, USA
{nsinghal,wtalamo1,kmayer9}@ford.com
[2] University of Michigan, 4901 Evergreen Road, Dearborn 48128, USA
alsaid@umich.com

Abstract. Range of recognition of experienced drivers considerably decreases in low light conditions (i.e., night, fog, heavy rain, etc.) and this further impacts their judgement in anticipating road activities. Despite the large body of work on driving in nighttime conditions, like providing night vision cameras to the drivers using white hot configuration or vulnerable road users (VRU) detection systems using white hot configuration, the former carries a risk of drivers driving by the camera whereas the later heavily focuses on VRUs. Moreover, these studies consider only white-hot configuration of the Far Infrared (FIR) technology. Our solution focuses on considering white hot as well as black hot FIR configuration combined with Augmented Reality (AR) technology. Multiple studies suggest that the Far Infrared produces better recognition performance at night than near-infrared (NIR) technology. This paper attempts to take the FIR research a step further by studying it in combination with Augmented Reality (AR) systems. More specifically, we study the effects of FIR configuration (black and white-hot) on drivers' preference and recognition rate in an AR environment. To gather data, interviews with 11 volunteers were conducted. The results indicated that the white-hot configuration had a higher recognition performance in comparison to the black-hot configuration. Nonetheless, participants preferred black hot over white-hot configuration. These results can guide future development of in-vehicle augmented reality and night vision systems.

Keywords: Driver Information and Assistance Systems · In-Vehicle Head-up Displays and Augmented Reality · Usability Tests in Virtual or Augmented Reality · Virtual and Augmented Reality

1 Introduction

1.1 Introduction to Augmented Reality in Automotive Context

Driving is a complex task requiring knowledge-based skills and multiple attentional resources. Advanced Driver Assistance (ADAS) features reduce the complexity of the driving task by reducing workload to free up resources. These driver assist features are often categorized as active (anti-lock brakes, stability control, automated emergency

C. Stephanidis et al. (Eds.): HCII 2023, CCIS 1836, pp. 91–98, 2023.
https://doi.org/10.1007/978-3-031-36004-6_13

braking) or passive (forward collision warning, blind spot indication). One promising use case of Augmented Reality (AR) as a passive driver assist technology is to highlight important elements in the driving environment. The most recent iteration of AR aims to improve drivers' environmental awareness in the vehicle. Objects that reside in the real world are enhanced by computer-generated perceptual information like street names, Points of Interest (POI) and directions. A study compared the AR personal navigation device with a standard map-based personal navigation device and found improved visual attention with the former device versus the later device during daytime. In terms of preference, the participants preferred the former device [7]. At night or in darkness, drivers have a hard time seeing the road, and hence inaccurately judge the environment around them [11, 22]. A study described the use of augmented reality in identifying hazards in high-risk domain like construction [6]. This motivated us to study AR technology in a domain like automotive for environmental awareness purposes during nighttime. A study highlights the use of thermal technology to anticipate potential fire hazards [3]. Satellites like CALIPSO that use Infrared technology, have been proposed in the recognition of fog around the Arctic [24]. Thermal technology was also useful in monitoring wildfires in the California region [4]. This paper studies the combination of the AR and thermal technology to enhance recognition performance in the tested driving environments. Before we elaborate on the study particulars, we would like to discuss the evidence of driving complexity, especially at nighttime. According to the NHTSA's reports, one-third of the fatal pedestrian crashes happen at night [8, 9]. Almost half of the crashes happen during conditions which are dark but partially lighted [16]. Night-time driving is a problem not only in North America but also in other parts of the world. In Europe, pedestrian fatalities are high particularly in winters from late afternoon to early nighttime when it is dark, and visibility is compromised [2]. In India, driving at night is riskier than driving during the day [14]. According to the National Safety Council of America the "shorter days"," fatigue", "compromised night vision", "rush hour" and "impaired drivers" are some of the risks we face when driving at night. These risks become especially pronounced moving into the weekend, with fatal crashes peaking on Saturday nights, according to NSC analysis of NHTSA data [8, 9].Also, their crash data suggests that most of the fatal crashes in North America happen between 8:00 pm to 11:59 pm. The crashes peak in the months of October through March between 4:00 pm to 7:59 pm (dusk through nighttime) [8, 9]. There is 60% less traffic at night but 40% of fatalities happen at night [1]. Cataracts are common in North America effecting adults between 40–50 years of age. Cataracts cause clouding of eye lens. Oncoming headlights along with an impaired night vision can be fatal for a driver driving at night [19]. To address nighttime driving challenges, thermal technology like far-infrared has been widely used.

1.2 Night Vision Enhancement Systems (NVES)

Existing night vision technologies remain only partly effective during night driving. Most automotive manufacturers consider using Night Vision Enhancement Systems (NVES) to improve drivers' nighttime vision. Far-infrared (FIR) and Near-Infrared (NIR) are two of the most effective NVES. FIR technologies have been more popular in the driving domain for its recognition distance advantages and insusceptibility to glare in comparison to NIR [18]. The contrast that the FIR video footage provides helps the users identify the pedestrians as a 'large blob' on the dark background. A highlight on this blob is far more effective than the blob itself [25]. FIR uses heat recognition, wherein, a hot body appears to be brighter than the background. The FIR has two types of configurations: White hot and black hot, the hot bodies appear white (white-hot) or black (black-hot) when the FIR detects heat. Figure 2 shows images from visible camera and thermal camera respectively and the two configurations of the FIR image (Fig. 1).

Fig. 1. Visible RGB image at night (left most image). Thermal image of the same road at night (left image). Examples of White Hot (right image) and Black Hot (right most image)

Fig. 2. White hot with Augmented Reality (AR) (left image) Black Hot with Augmented reality (right image)

The combination of AR and FIR has not been examined. Drivers' awareness may be improved using AR and visibility in nighttime/low-light hours may be improved through a night vision system like FIR. In this paper, we look at, AR elements on top of two different FIR image configurations and study recognition performance in a virtual study. First, we examine the effect of black hot or white-hot FIR image configuration on the participants' recognition performance of AR elements and other objects in the environment. Previous research in thermal imaging used recognition rate or recognition accuracy to determine the accuracy with which the drivers were able to detect targets on the road. One of the most important parameters considered for a system to be robust is its accuracy level [26]. Other measures collected were recognition distances for efficiency and subjective measures for effectiveness. The white-hot configuration is preferred for most of these experiments. We did not find any black hot configuration related research or research that compares both the white hot and black hot configurations of thermal imaging. Previous studies have found correlation between luminance and visual acuity that could negatively affect driving performance [10]. Reduced road illumination has also seen to negatively affect recognition of pedestrians, average speed and recognition of road signs decreased significantly as functions of increased age and reduced illumination. Recognition of pedestrians at night was significantly enhanced by retroreflective markings of limb joints as compared with markings of the torso, and this benefit was greater for middle-aged and older drivers. Lane keeping showed nonlinear effects of lighting, which interacted with task conditions and drivers 'lateral bias, indicating that older drivers drove more cautiously in low light. Different body reflectors affected behavior and recognition (the more the reflectors looked like a human body the better the performance). In this study, we investigate if the thermal image configuration (white-hot/black-hot) affects objects recognition performance, with the hypothesis that the driver's recognition performance in the white-hot image is higher and the second experimental question investigates the drivers' preference for the image configuration (black cold/white hot), with the hypothesis that the white-hot view is preferable.

2 Method

2.1 Experiment Design

Participants. Data was collected from 11 volunteers. All participants were Ford Motor Company employees, who completed this study as part of their workday with no other compensation. Due to Covid-19 restrictions, the study was virtual and was conducted through a web conferencing tool. They all had a valid driving license.

Independent Variables. In this study, we used a counterbalanced 2 X 1, within-subject experimental design. The independent variable was thermal configuration. Black hot: This is a thermal configuration that illuminates considerably hot signatures as black and relatively cooler surrounding areas as shades of grey using grayscale. White hot: This is a thermal configuration that illuminates considerably hot signatures as white and relatively cooler surrounding areas as shades of grey using grayscale.

Dependent Variables. The study consisted of two parts. In the first, participants were asked to detect AR elements and/or pedestrians in the videos of black and white hot. In the second, participants were asked to describe what they like and do not like about each of the configurations. The recognition performance was defined as the number of elements recognized by the participants in each length of time. Therefore, the dependent variables were recognition performance, and preference.

2.2 Apparatus and Scenario

We recorded one video from southeast Michigan, within the city of Ypsilanti, Michigan. The baseline video was recorded using Garmin camera. Thermal white-hot video was recorded using a 50deg FOV FLIR Boson camera mounted on the roof of the vehicle and the baseline video was captured by mounting the camera behind the windshield at the center of the driver view of the vehicle. The black-hot video was post-processed. Both the cameras captured videos from driver view of the vehicle. Both variations involved similar routes. Augmented Reality elements were then overlayed on top of each of the videos. In total we had three videos from the same route, namely, baseline, black hot and white hot. Before showing them the two thermal videos, we showed them a baseline video. During the experiment, participants watched the two videos, and were asked to report any AR elements they see, as soon as they see them. Each of the routes included seven AR elements: three Points of Interest (PoI), at least three street names, and one navigation sign. The two thermal videos had similar placement of AR elements. We randomized the order in which the videos were shown to the users. The routes for each video are shown in (See Fig. 3).

Fig. 3. Black Hot (left), White Hot (middle) and Baseline (right) Route Diagram with POIs

2.3 Procedure

We utilized Wizard of Oz [16] and Think Aloud [6, 14] protocol in this study. Prior to the study, participants signed an informed consent via DocuSign and agreed to have their audio recorded for further data analysis. At the beginning of the study, participants were introduced to the concepts of augmented reality and thermal imaging. Next, participants were shown a practice video, which was a regular RGB video with AR elements, and they were asked to call out any AR elements they see before the experiment started. Once they were comfortable with the task, the experiment started. The participants were shown the baseline, black-hot and white-hot videos in randomized order. While they were watching the videos, they were asked to call out the AR elements and pedestrians that they see in the video. Following this, the participants were asked a few open-ended questions that described their preference of each of the thermal configurations. After the experiment is complete, participants are thanked for their time and the Webex session is immediately closed out. We maintained participant anonymity.

3 Results

3.1 Participants' Feedback

During the semi-structured interviews, participants were asked about what they did and did not like about each of the configurations. A team of two researchers used thematic analysis and classified the comments into seven main themes; image crispiness, level of details, distracting effects, easiness on the eyes, highlighting important content, whether it looks natural or not, and whether it is preferable or not (See Fig. 4). The figure shows the main themes and the number of times it was mentioned during the interviews. Overall, participants seemed to prefer black hot configuration.

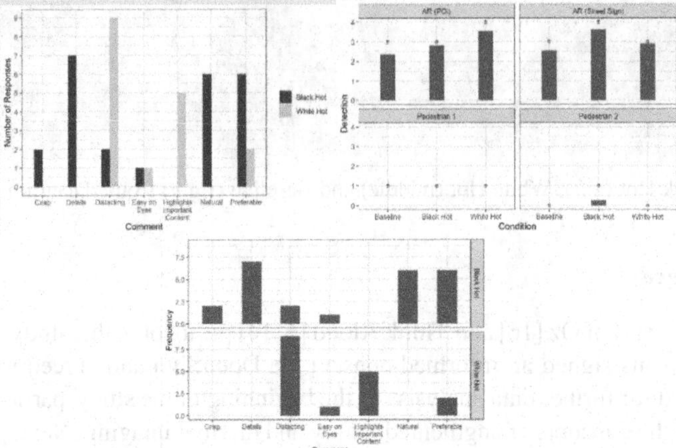

Fig. 4. White hot v/s Black hot comparison chart (left and middle); Recognition performance of white hot and black hot with respect to baseline. The dots indicate the total number of elements considered (right)

3.2 Recognition Performance

In addition to user's feedback, we looked at the recognition performance of users in the black-hot and white-hot configuration as well as the baseline (the practice RGB video.) While participants clearly preferred black hot, there was no significant difference in recognition performance between black and white hot (t = 0.7408, df = 17.639, p-value = 0.4686.) Nonetheless, both black and white hot significantly improved recognition rates in comparison with the RGB baseline video (t = 3.5355, df = 18.349, p-value = 0.002307, t = 3.334, df = 14.706, p-value = 0.004638, respectively.). The results are shown in Figure (See Fig. 5). In the figure, the bar charts on the y-axis shows the average number of recognized objects (AR or pedestrians.).

3.3 Discussion and Conclusion

In this study, we examined users' preference and performance for two different thermally enhanced vision systems configurations. Both configurations seemed to improve recognition performance in comparison to RGB. Research suggests that continuous exposure to a monochromatic blue light is shown to decrease the number of inappropriate line crossings (lateral position of the car from the lateral lane marker of the road Continental Automotiv® video system) and improve driving performance compared to driving with placebo caffeine or caffeine [17]. Monochromatic retinal light exposure is shown to evoke responses that modify brains alertness and cognition [20]. Some more studies found that a" dynamic blinking" cue is used for highlighting to be effective at attracting attention [12]. One other study suggests that visual highlighting can increase the response time of search tasks [21]. Visual cues are inferred to enhance recognition in the aviation space involving search tasks [23]. Based on the results above, the visual cues and the monochromatic light exposure studies, steer us to conclude that, a monochromatic exposure of FIR image configurations, namely, black hot or white hot with AR visual cues has the potential to increase the driver recognition. There are other parameters like angle of viewing, brightness etc. that can affect the driver's recognition performance but those are not studied in this experiment. We have only considered visual cues with monochromatic light. Another limitation of our study is that the pedestrian data in the FIR was not highlighted whereas the other elements used AR visual cues. The results mentioned above is a study to learn the feasibility of an idea. Using these results in actual practice will require a simulator or an in-vehicle study.

References

1. AI Trends: Nighttime Driving and AI Autonomous Cars (2019). https://www.aitrends.com/ai-insider/nighttime-driving-and-ai-autonomous-cars/
2. ERSO: Annual Accident Report 2018. Erso, 86 (2018). https://ec.europa.eu/transport/road_safety/sites/roadsafety/files/pdf/statistics/dacota/asr2018.pdf
3. Ferreira, L.M., Coimbra, A.P., de Almeida, A.T.: Autonomous system for wildfire and forest fire early detection and control. Inventions **5**(3), 1–14 (2020). https://doi.org/10.3390/inventions5030041
4. FLIR: Teledyne FLIR Thermal Security Cameras Help Firefighters Monitor Wildfires in California (2021)
5. Lewis, C., Rieman, J.: Task-Centered User Interface Design: A Practical Introduction. Text, 190 (1993). http://hcibib.org/tcuid/tcuid.pdf
6. Li, X., Yi, W., Chi, H. L., Wang, X., Chan, A.P.C.: A critical review of virtual and augmented reality (VR/AR) applications in construction safety. Autom. Constr. **86**(July 2016), 150–162 (2018). https://doi.org/10.1016/j.autcon.2017.11.003
7. Medenica, Z., Kun, A., Paek, T.: Comparing augmented reality and street view navigation. In: Adjunct Proceedings of the Second International Conference on Automotive User Interfaces and Interactive Vehicular Applications, Automotive UI (2010)
8. National Safety Council. (n.d.-a). National Safety Council Injury Facts. https://injuryfacts.nsc.org/motor-vehicle/overview/crashes-by-time-of-day-and-day-of-week/#_ga=2.181839975.1700599729.1646689738-1591115977.1646689738
9. National Safety Council. (n.d.-b). The most dangerous time to drive. National Safety Council. https://www.nsc.org/road-safety/safety-topics/night-driving#:~:text=While. We do only one quarter of our, car crashes in 2016%2C according to Injury Facts
10. Owens, D.A., Tyrrell, R.A.: Effects of luminance, blur, and age on nighttime visual guidance: a test of the selective degradation hypothesis. J. Exp. Psychol. Appl. **5**(2), 115–128 (1999). https://doi.org/10.1037/1076-898X.5.2.115
11. Owens, D.A., Wood, J.M., Owens, J.M.: Effects of age and illumination on night driving: a road test. Human Factors J. Human Factors Ergon. Soc. **49**(6), 1115–1131 (2007). https://doi.org/10.1518/001872007X249974
12. Pratt, J., Hommel, B.: Symbolic control of visual attention: the role of working memory and attentional control settings. J. Exp. Psychol. Hum. Percept. Perform. **29**(5), 835–845 (2003). https://doi.org/10.1037/0096-1523.29.5.835
13. Simon, H.A., Newell, A.: Human problem solving: the state of the theory in 1970. Am. Psychol. **26**(2), 145–159 (1971). https://doi.org/10.1037/h0030806
14. Singh, S.K.: Road traffic accidents in India: issues and challenges. Transp. Res. Proc. **25**, 4708–4719 (2017). https://doi.org/10.1016/j.trpro.2017.05.484

15. Sukovoy, O., Kuo, C.: An iterative design methodology for user-friendly natural language information applications. Proc. Inst. Mech. Eng.Part M: J. Eng. Maritime Environ. **2**(1), 26–41 (2003)
16. Swanson, E.D., Yanagisawa, M., Najm, W., Foderaro, F., Azeredo, P.: Crash avoidance needs and countermeasure profiles for safety applications based on light-vehicle-to-pedestrian communications. August, 155 (2016)
17. Taillard, J., Capelli, A., Sagaspe, P., Anund, A., Akerstedt, T., Philip, P.: In-car nocturnal blue light exposure improves motorway driving: a randomized controlled trial. PLoS ONE **7**(10), e46750 (2012). https://doi.org/10.1371/journal.pone.0046750
18. Tsimhoni, O., Bärgman, J., Flannagan, M.J.: Pedestrian detection with near and far infrared night vision enhancement. Leukos **4**(2), 113–128 (2007)
19. US News: Blinded By the Night: Coping With Impaired Night Vision While Driving (2018). https://health.usnews.com/health-care/for-better/articles/2018-05-14/blinded-by-the-night-coping-with-impaired-night-vision-while-driving
20. Vandewalle, G., et al.: Brain responses to violet, blue, and green monochromatic light exposures in humans: prominent role of blue light and the brainstem. PLoS ONE **2**(11), 1 (2007). https://doi.org/10.1371/journal.pone.0001247
21. Fisher, D.L., Tan, K.C.: Visual displays: the highlighting paradox. Human Factors J. Human Factors Ergon. Soc. **31**(1), 17–30 (1989). https://doi.org/10.1177/001872088903100102
22. Wood, J.M.: Nighttime driving: visual, lighting and visibility challenges. Ophthalmic Physiol. Opt. **40**(2), 187–201 (2020). https://doi.org/10.1111/opo.12659
23. Yeh, M., Wickens, C.D.: Display signaling in augmented reality: effects of cue reliability and image realism on attention allocation and trust calibration. Hum. Factors **43**(3), 355–365 (2001). https://doi.org/10.1518/001872001775898269
24. Yi, L., Li, K.F., Chen, X., Tung, K.K.: Arctic fog detection using infrared spectral measurements. J. Atmos. Oceanic Tech. **36**(8), 1643–1656 (2019). https://doi.org/10.1175/JTECH-D-18-0100.1
25. Tsimhoni, O., Flannagan, M.: Pedestrian detection with night vision systems enhanced by automatic warnings. Proc. Human Factors Ergon. Soc. Ann. Meet. **50**(22), 2443–2447 (2006). https://doi.org/10.1177/154193120605002220
26. Dr. Knoll, Reppich, P., Andreas: A novel approach for a night vision system", Robert Bosch GmbH, Germany

Trust Repair of Automated Driving System: A New In-Vehicle Communication Strategy of Voice Assistant

Zhe Song(✉), Ye Yang, and Mengying Deng

Banma Network Technology Co., Ltd, Shanghai 210100, China
songzhe.song@alibaba-inc.com

Abstract. Chinese market penetration rate of automated driving systems (ADS) is increasing rapidly. Users are willing to try ADS, but the negative feeling is along with the substantial experience as well. One reason is the gap between users experience and expectation of ADS function, which was formed based on the market information. The other reason is ADS cannot meet different individuals' driving preferences and habits in short term.

As a consequence, users might decrease their trust with ADS, therefore reducing the usage frequency and losing opportunities to rebuild trust. This counteract with the original intention of ADS, which is to improve driving safety.

In the human-machine cooperative ADS, trust repair is necessary for maintaining the trust between the human and the system; in terms of method, anthropomorphic in-vehicle voice communication can enhance the degree of trust. However, there are scarce amounts of studies regarding these two concepts.

Regarding the circumstance, our research proposes a trust repair strategy that is centered on voice communication in ADS. Based on existing ADS technical capabilities, our goal is to improve users' trust and experience with ADS in the early stage of use.

Through market user research, our team systematically summarized the types of scenarios and reasons for the reduction of trust in ADS as the basis of our research. Furthermore, based on the concept of trust repair, a voice-communication-based interaction strategy for ADS is established, and specific dialogues are designed. Finally, a scenario simulated user test (N = 60) was conducted to verify the effectiveness of the strategy: this trust repair approach can significantly improve users' trust in the early use of ADS and their subjective attitudes to use it. Overall, the results provide a new perspective and direct implications for ADS and in-vehicle voice assistant designers.

Keywords: Automated Driving · Trust Repair · Voice Assistant

1 Introduction

The adoption of Automated Driving System (ADS) is steadily increasing, with sales of Level 2 ADS vehicles in the Chinese market reaching 2.88 million in the first half of 2022, up 46.2% year on year.

C. Stephanidis et al. (Eds.): HCII 2023, CCIS 1836, pp. 99–106, 2023.
https://doi.org/10.1007/978-3-031-36004-6_14

ADS aims to reduce driving stress and enhance safety. However, a recent survey of Chinese consumers found that 39% expressed concerns about how to handle ADS malfunctions, indicating uncertainty in the transition from manual to cooperative driving with [1] ADS. User trust is directly related to automation usage, as shown in a study by Lee and See [2]. Lack of trust in autonomous vehicle systems is a frequently cited reason for driver reluctance to use them, according to recent surveys[3, 4]. Supporting appropriate trust is critical in avoiding misuse and disuse of automation [2, 5, 6]. Therefore, trust is a critical factor in the ADS experience.

Trust consists of initial trust and dynamic trust[7]. A common strategy to increase the likelihood of using ADS is to establish initial trust through pre-teaching or providing guidebooks. Dynamic trust, which changes during ADS driving, is the focus of this study. The study considers how users update their level of trust during the learning phase[8] and how the design of the HMI affects users' dynamic trust and human-machine team performance.

Negative interactions are found to have a greater impact on dynamic trust than positive interactions[9]. During the learning phase, a negative experience can cause a decrease in trust or even lead to users abandoning the use of ADS, as researched by Fredrick Ekman[8]. There are two advantages to dynamically repair trust in the vehicle. Firstly, users can continuously understand the capabilities of ADS by receiving timely information and encountering different situations with relevant explanations. Secondly, ADS can receive real-time data, such as user behavior, emotional state, and environmental changes, and provide more precise explanations and caring communications. To effectively repair users' trust and improve their experience, we propose to implement a voice assistant communication strategy in ADS. Therefore, we first ask the following two general research questions.

RQ1: How can trust in ADS be repaired through voice communication?

RQ2: How do users' trust and attitudes towards ADS vary with and without trust repair strategies?

2 Research

2.1 Negative Experience and Reduction of Trust

An in-depth interview was conducted in the early stage of this research with 10 Chinese users. All of them had purchased a new car equipped with an ADS within half a year and had some basic knowledge and experience of the ADS. Based on the interviews, four main factors were identified regarding costly acts and negative experiences:

The Imperfection of Conditional ADS Functionality. In some situations, ADS may suddenly exit, and its performance in complex road conditions is unstable.

Mismatched Driving Style due to Differences in System and Individual Preferences. In a short period of time, automatic driving functions may not be able to match the driving habits and preferences of different individuals. The limited settings offered by manufacturers may not be adaptable to different dynamic scenarios. The resulting tense experience may lead users to take over driving, which can reduce their trust in ADS and decrease the frequency of use [10].

Cognitive Bias and "Disappointment". Users' initial cognitive understanding of new technologies often comes from the media and may lead to high expectations. During the early stage of usage, understanding and summarizing the system logic and boundaries can be challenging and time-consuming due to the complexity of the ADS function. Additionally, some users may not be interested in the underlying logic. Unchecked high expectations can cause frustration, a decrease in trust [11], and disuse, if the system fails to meet users' expectations during actual experiences [12].

Lack of Transparency and Communication Channels. The primary issues are concentrated in the following areas: a lack of understanding of specialized terminology and symbols, unclear identification of the specific reasons for system failures, and an inability to predict system behavior. There are few convenient channels for obtaining accurate information, causing users to rely on community or online searches for help. Furthermore, effectively describing the problems remains a challenging task.

2.2 The Main Factors Affecting Trust Repair in ADS

Beneficial Acts. According to the Transactional Model of Trust Repair by Ewart, beneficial acts can repair trust, which are perceived as positive or pleasant interactions by the human[13]. For ADS, such beneficial acts may include improved performance, recognition of costly acts, empathetic responses, clear explanations for system's behavior, maintaining a positive tone, demonstrating learning capabilities, and making promises for future improvements[13].

Timing. First, humans have learned to trust the system that exhibit expected or predictable behavior[14]. To align users' expectations to a more objective level and reduce feelings of frustration, it can be helpful to inform them of the system's limitations and reasons in advance. Second, when users encounter negative experiences or have inquiries, active communication can be employed to provide timely and accurate responses. Finally, in highly stressful situations, such as sudden takeovers, providing complex explanations may increase safety risks. Therefore, the timing of post-explanation after costly acts is crucial in such situations.

Voice Communication. Anthropomorphization is an approach to trust repair [13]. By explaining complex and technical operations in a more accessible way, users are more likely to trust the system. Through interviews, it was found that some users asked an experienced co-pilot about ADS-related questions during the learning phase. The voice assistant can combine vehicle data to support fuzzy search and provide instant feedback, enabling users to ask questions such as "What was that sound just now?" or "What does that icon mean?" Moreover, considering the multitasking in driving, the speech style used in voice assistance needs to be direct and concise.

2.3 Communication Strategy of Trust Repair in ADS

In conclusion, a communication strategy for an in-vehicle voice assistant was proposed as a mean of repairing trust in ADS (Fig. 1). This strategy was complemented by a specific conversation design tailored to typical ADS scenarios. The objective of this proposal is to enhance users' trust and overall user experience during the initial phase of use effectively, based on the same technical capabilities. The effectiveness of the repair strategy and dialogue design was validated through comparative testing.

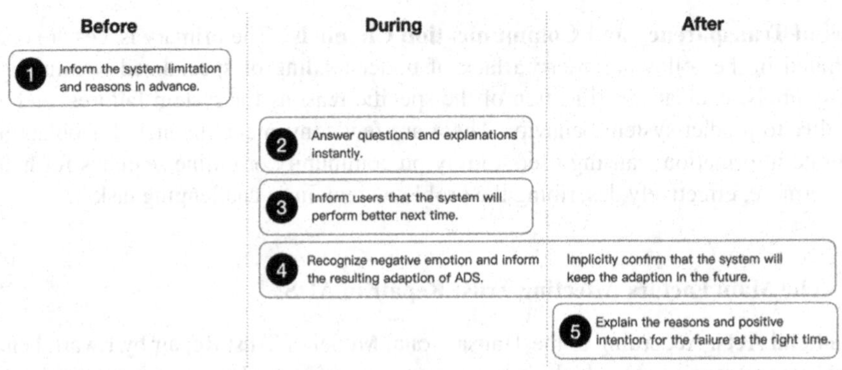

Fig. 1. In-vehicle communication strategy for ADS based on trust repair theory.

3 Method

3.1 Questionnaire

The online survey questionnaire consists of five scenarios, each divided into two groups. One group includes the use of a voice assistant to repair trust (TR), while the other (NTR) does not.

Scenario 1 (S1): Driving home on a rainy night. In the TR, the voice assistant reminds users in advance: "the weather is bad and may affect the performance of the ADS." A message is also displayed on the dashboard when user turns on the ADS. In NTR, there is no voice prompt.

Scenario 2 (S2): An unfamiliar icon appears on the dashboard and the user asks the voice assistant for help. In NTR, the voice assistant will assist in opening the user manual page, while in TR, the assistant will directly explain the meaning of the icon to the user.

Scenario 3 (S3): While driving on an elevated road, if the vehicle system detects that the user is trying to maintain a distance from a large vehicle, the voice assistant in the TR will inform the user that the system has learned about their driving habits and will execute it in the future. On the other hand, the NTR does not have any voice prompts.

Scenario 4 (S4): When the preceding vehicle changes lanes, the automated driving vehicle may quickly accelerate to close the distance, which can cause discomfort for the user due to consecutive acceleration and sudden braking. In both TR and NTR, the system detects the user's discomfort and adjusts the acceleration strategy accordingly. However, in TR, the voice assistant informs the user that it has recognized the discomfort and changed the acceleration mode. After discomfort was reduced, the assistant confirms with user by saying "the same driving mode will be maintained in the future".
Scenario 5 (S5): Due to the inability to accurately recognize unclear lane markings on the elevated road, the ADS exits directly and requires the user to take over the vehicle immediately. Both TR and NTR will display message on the dashboard without any communication (see Fig. 2 a). When the user's cognitive load is reduced or the vehicle comes to a stop, TR's voice assistant provides explanation to user (see Fig. 2 b). NTR does not provide any further communication or explanation.

Fig. 2. Pictures of scenario 5 in the questionnaire.

3.2 Procedure and Measurement

In the questionnaire, the participants were instructed to imagine themselves using a new ADS and experienced both TR and NTR in five different scenarios. The user experience was evaluated by two criteria: "Attitude" and "Trust". The attitude questionnaire was designed based on a 7-point semantic differential scale and divided into 4 dimensions (from 1 to 7 points): "Complicated - Simple", "Obstructive - Supportive", "Foolish - Intelligent" and "Conservative - Creative". The trust scale, adapted from Choi and Ji [15], measured 3 dimensions: TRU1 - "The system is dependable", TRU2 - "The system is reliable" and TRU3 - "Overall, I can trust the system". The questionnaire has distributed a total of 60 copies, with the Cronbach's α coefficient being 0.959, the KMO value being 0.742, and Bartlett's sphere test being $\chi 2=2353.706$, $p < 0.05$, which is indicated to be suitable for analysis.

4 Result

4.1 The Effect of Trust Repair Strategies on Trust

Table 1 demonstrates that the trust repair strategies (TRS) have a significant impact on the trust of the participants ($p = 0.01 < 0.05$), particularly for the participants over 46 years old. The results indicate that the age of the participant had a significant influence on trust repair ($p = 0.03 < 0.05$).

Table 1. Result of Paired Sample T-Test on trust.

	Groups	Mean	SD	Difference	t	p
Pair1	TR-TRU1	5.45	1.59	0.47	2.087	0.041*
	NTR-TRU1	4.98	1.78			
Pair 2	TR-TRU2	5.17	1.66	1.65	4.392	0.000**
	NTR-TRU2	3.52	1.94			
Pair 3	TR-TRU3	5.18	1.63	0.48	2.039	0.046*
	NTR-TRU3	4.7	1.87			

Note. * $p < 0.05$ ** $p < 0.01$

4.2 The Effect of Trust Repair Strategies on Attitude

Over all, the participants in the study found that the communication based on TRS was helpful, and the post-explanation voice had a significant impact on their trust in the system. As shown in Table 2, the TRS had a significant impact on the Participant's attitude in S5. Specifically, when the user was required to take over urgently, the post-explanation voice increased their trust in the system.

Table 2. Results of Paired Sample T-Test on attitude for 5 scenarios.

	S1	S2	S3	S4	S5
Simple	0.78* (4.93–4.15)	0.32 (5.2–4.88)	0.02 (5.25–5.23)	-0.37 (4.8–5.17)	0.7* (4.75–4.05)
Supportive	0 (4.98–4.98)	0.17 (5.48–5.32)	0.37 (5.63–5.27)	0.33 (5.3–4.97)	0.75* (5.12–4.37)
Intelligent	0.25 (5.1–4.85)	-0.08 (5.28–5.37)	0.17 (5.67–5.5)	0.23* (5.3–5.07)	0.6* (5.15–4.55)
Creative	-0.12 (4.55–4.67)	-0.02 (5.17–5.18)	0.25 (5.48–5.23)	0.35 (5.3–4.95)	0.78** (5.03–4.25)

Note. The values are: Difference (TRmean - NTRmean) * $p < 0.05$ ** $p < 0.01$

The strategy of enhancing the transparency of ADS to restore trust is effective in improving users' overall evaluation of the system's supportiveness. The results of S1 indicate that the repair strategy significantly improved users' perception of the interaction as being simpler. However, it did not demonstrate a significant difference in creativity and supportiveness compared to NTR. Based on the results of S4, participants felt significantly simpler, but more complicated in TR.

5 Conclusion and Discussion

5.1 Conclusion

In general, TRS improves users' trust and subjective evaluation in using ADS. Users feel supported in all the scenarios, proving the communication strategy is effective.

The timing of voice assistant communication should take into account the user's real-time emotions and cognitive load, especially in emergency situations such as taking over control (scenario 5). Additionally, it is important to provide explanations for ADS failures, which can help users gain a clear understanding of the system's limits and capabilities.

Directly providing feedback can significantly simplify and enhance the user experience (S1). The voice design strategy should address users' cognitive issues more instinctively to reduce the learning cost. Due to the inability to predict user intents accurately, there was no improvement in the dimensions of intelligence and creativity (S2). S4 made it more complicated for users, possibly because it introduced one more round of dialogue compared to the NTR.

There is also a notable increase in trust and attitude scores towards the ADS, especially among participants aged 46 years old and above.

5.2 Limitation and Future Work

The study has several limitations. Firstly, the survey was conducted through online questionnaires, which may not fully represent real-life scenarios. Participants responded to pictures and scenario descriptions, while voice conversations were represented in text form. Future research should incorporate real vehicle environments and live voice assistant conversations. Secondly, measuring initial trust and trust after negative experiences could provide a better evaluation of the effectiveness of the repair strategy. Thirdly, the appropriate level of user trust was not discussed, and communication between ADS and humans should be restrained to avoid over-trust. Lastly, the study found age differences in the effectiveness of trust repair strategies, but future comparative research could investigate the impact of other demographic characteristics such as gender and driving experience.

References

1. J.D.POWER Webpage article. https://china.jdpower.com/resources/china-self-driving-confidence-index. Accessed 13 May 2021

2. Lee, J.D., See, K.A.: Trust in automation: designing for appropriate reliance. Human Factors J. Human Factors Ergon. Soc. **46**(1), 50–80 (2004). https://doi.org/10.1518/hfes.46.1.50.30392
3. Hillary, A., Lee, C.: Autonomous Vehicles and Alternatives to Driving: Trust, Preferences, and Effects of Age (2017)
4. Zmud, J., Sener, I.N., Wagner, J.: Self-driving vehicles: determinants of adoption and conditions of usage. Transp. Res. Rec. J. Transp. Res. Board **2565**(1), 57–64 (2016). https://doi.org/10.3141/2565-07
5. Parasurman, R., Riley, V.: Humans and automation: use, misuse, disuse, abuse. Human Factors **39**(2), 230–253 (1997)
6. Berman, S.L., Wicks, A.C., Kotha, S., Jones, T.M.: Does stakeholder orientation matter? The relationship between stakeholder management models and firm financial performance. Acad. Manage. J. **42**(5), 488–506 (1999). https://doi.org/10.2307/256972
7. Hoff, K.A., Bashir, M.: Trust in automation: integrating empirical evidence on factors that influence trust. Hum Factors. **57**, 407–434 (2015). https://doi.org/10.1177/0018720814547570
8. Ekman, F., Johansson, M., Sochor, J.: Creating appropriate trust in auto-mated vehicle systems: a framework for HMI design. IEEE Trans. Human-Mach. Syst. **48**, 95–101 (2018). https://doi.org/10.1109/THMS.2017.2776209
9. Roderick, M.K.: Trust and distrust in organizations: emerging perspectives: enduring questions. Ann. Rev. Psychol. **50**, 569–598 (1999)
10. Huysduynen, H. H., Terken. J., Eggen.B.: Why disable the autopilot? In: 10th International ACM Automotive UI (2018) . https://doi.org/10.1145/3239060.3239063
11. Cohen M.S., Parasuraman R., Freeman.T.J.: Trust in Decision Aids: A Model and Its Training Implications (2002)
12. Dzindolet, M.T., Pierce, L.G., et al.: The perceived utility of human and automated aids in a visual detection task. Hum. Factors **44**(1), 79–94 (2002). https://doi.org/10.1518/0018720024494856
13. de Visser, E.J., Pak, R., Shaw, T.H.: From 'automation' to 'autonomy': the importance of trust repair in human–machine interaction. Ergonomics **61**, 1409–1427 (2018). https://doi.org/10.1080/00140139.2018.1457725
14. Haspiel, J., Du, N., Meyerson, J., et al.: Explanations and expectations: trust building in automated vehicles. In: Companion of the 2018 ACM/IEEE International Conference on Human-Robot Interaction (HRI 2018). Association for Computing Machinery, New York, NY, USA, pp. 119–120 (2018). https://doi.org/10.1145/3173386.3177057
15. Choi, J.K., Ji, Y.G.: Investigating the importance of trust on adopting an autonomous vehicle. Int. J. Human-Comput. Interact. **31**(10), 692–702 (2015). https://doi.org/10.1080/10447318.2015.1070549

How Do Different Vehicle Interior Concepts Influence Work and Entertainment Experience During Automated Driving?

Michaela Teicht(✉), Patricia Haar, Dominique Stimm, and Arnd Engeln

Hochschule der Medien, Nobelstr. 10, 70569 Stuttgart, Germany
{teicht,haar,stimm,engeln}@hdm-stuttgart.de

Abstract. The goal of the research project RUMBA, which is funded by the German Federal Ministry for Economic Affairs and Climate Action, is to redesign the user experience for occupants during a highly automated drive (SAE level 4 [1]) by developing innovative interior and interaction concepts. As part of the second iteration of the user-centered, iterative development process, a laboratory study is conducted. It aims to evaluate a simulated prototype of an innovative vehicle interior concept for work and entertainment during automated driving as well as to identify design suggestions for its further development. The vehicle interior concept to be evaluated is compared with a classic vehicle interior in an experimental research setting. Test subjects experience the two vehicle interior prototypes during two simulated automated test drives of approximately 15 min each. In the first ride, one subject performs work tasks while the other watches a movie; in the second ride vice versa. Besides others, user experience, system trust, and subjective road safety of the occupants are measured. Data collection for the study is completed by the end of March 2023. Therefore, this short paper focuses on the method and does not yet include results. The HCII conference poster in July 2023 reports both, the methodology and the results of the evaluation study.

Keywords: Automated Driving · Vehicle Interior · User Experience · Work · Entertainment

1 Introduction

Since this paper is related to the same research project (RUMBA) as [2], the introductions of both papers are identical and their structures are similar. However, they are two different short papers reporting on different studies with independent results. This short paper reports on a laboratory study in a driving simulator on the topic of work and entertainment during automated driving, while [2] reports on a field study in a real vehicle on social interaction during automated driving.

1.1 Research Project RUMBA and User-Centered Development

This contribution results from the publicly funded joint research project RUMBA (German acronym for "Achieving a positive user experience through user-friendly design of

C. Stephanidis et al. (Eds.): HCII 2023, CCIS 1836, pp. 107–115, 2023.
https://doi.org/10.1007/978-3-031-36004-6_15

the vehicle interior for automated driving functions"), which is funded by the German Federal Ministry for Economic Affairs and Climate Action (BMWK) on the basis of a resolution of the German Bundestag (funding code 19A20007D).

The user-centered development process of DIN EN ISO 9241–210:2020–03 [3] (see Fig. 1) pursued in the RUMBA research project by the Stuttgart Media University is explained in detail below.

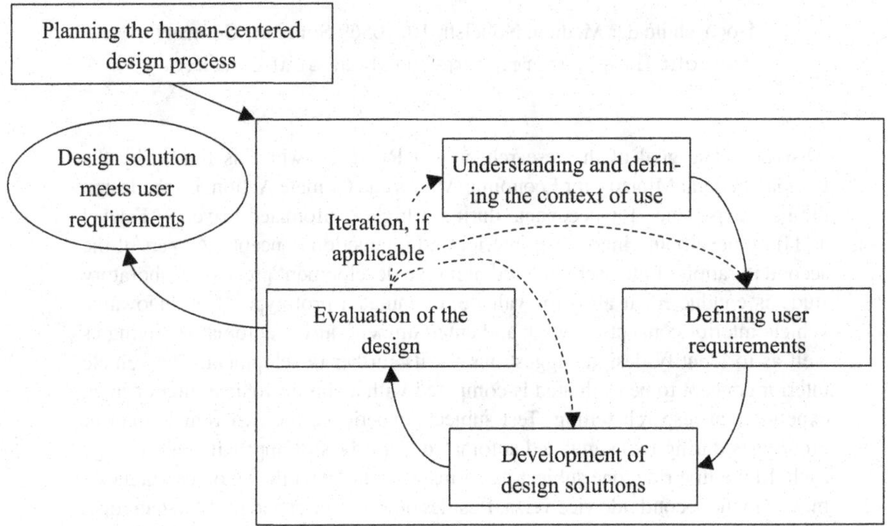

Fig. 1. User-centered development process of DIN EN ISO 9241–210:2020-03 [3]

Based on the planning step ("Planning the human-centered design process"), in which the project goal and approach were conceived, the requirements and needs for SAE Level 4 automated driving were empirically investigated from the user's perspective ("Understanding and defining the context of use"). The authors conducted a simulator and a diary study to investigate user requirements for the vehicle interior and for displays and controls in fully automated driving [4, 5]. In the next step ("Defining user requirements"), the research results on user requirements were compiled, key learnings were extracted, and design spaces were derived. This was done in a synthesis workshop. In the subsequent step ("Development of design solutions"), ideas and initial prototypes for the vehicle interior, displays and controls were generated. This was done in a design thinking workshop. There, various alternative concept ideas were generated and concretized in low-fidelity prototypes. On this basis, the authors developed five user narratives [6], which describe the innovative concept ideas integrated there in the form of a usage story. These user narratives were evaluated with users in a first iteration as part of the evaluation step ("Evaluation of the design"). The goal of the evaluation was to gather user feedback on innovation ideas and concept concretization and to identify design cues for their further development.

In the second iteration, based on this initial user feedback, the authors developed the low-fidelity prototypes into mid-fidelity prototypes: A simulation prototype for working and watching movies during an automated ride was created in a laboratory setting. This prototype was then evaluated in a laboratory study as part of the second evaluation iteration. The prototype and the methodology of this study are described in detail in this short paper. The results of the evaluation study are reported on the HCII poster.

1.2 Objectives

The objectives of the laboratory study were:

1. To quantitatively compare a classic interior concept (Classic Mode) and an innovative interior concept (Individual Occupation Mode) for work and entertainment during automated driving.
2. To obtain qualitative design information for the further development of the equipment elements of the interior concept.

2 Methods

2.1 Participants

Two test subjects participated in each experiment simultaneously. A total of 26 females and 22 males participated in the study. The mean age of the participants was 23.25 years ($SD = 3.68$) and the age range was 18 to 31 years.

2.2 Experimental Design

In the experimental two-factor within-subjects research design, the two-level independent variables *interior concept* (Classic Mode vs. Individual Occupation Mode) and *non-driving activity* (completing work tasks vs. watching a movie) were purposefully manipulated. To avoid sequence effects due to the within-subject design, the experimental conditions were counterbalanced.

Interior Concept. The *Classic Mode* bases on the familiar interior concept of today's vehicles. The *Individual Occupation Mode* is designed to support work and movie watching during automated driving by means of innovative equipment elements. Figure 2 shows the two interior concepts set up in a laboratory driving simulation.

Non-Driving Activity. To simulate the *work tasks*, two comparable task sets were created, each with four task types (text input, addition, proofreading, and creative thinking) [7–9]. The tasks were designed to take a total of 15 min. To simulate the *movie* entertainment, Interstellar was chosen, based on a preliminary study. The first and the subsequent 15 min of the movie were shown during the study.

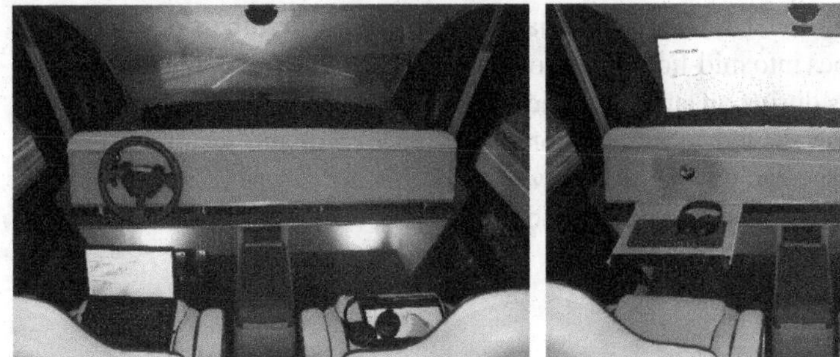

Fig. 2. Interior concept[1] (left: Classic Mode, right: Individual Occupation Mode)

Table 1 below lists the equipment elements per interior concept and non-driving activity.

Table 1. Equipment elements per interior concept and non-driving activity

	Classic Mode	Individual Occupation Mode
Work tasks	– With steering wheel and pedals on driver's side – Laptop – Front view through (transparent) windshield	– Without steering wheel and pedals on driver's side – Extendible screen – Visibility to the front not given due to milky windshield – Extendible table top – Integrated keyboard – Noise-canceling headphones
Movie	– Steering wheel and pedals on driver's side – Tablet – Headphones	– Without steering wheel and pedals on driver's side – VR glasses (simulating a cinema environment) – Noise-canceling headphones – Extendable table top – Controller for the VR glasses

The following additional equipment elements were included in both interior concepts: flexible seats, an emergency button, a refrigerator, and storage compartments.

2.3 Procedure

The study took place from December 2022 to March 2023 at the Stuttgart Media University. The test procedure includes three parts. These are described below.

Introduction and Pre-Questionnaire. The study began with a welcome and an introduction to the study. This was followed by a pre-survey via a questionnaire on personal

[1] Vehicle interior mockup by Fraunhofer IAO.

details (e.g. gender, age, and driving performance) and affinity for technology. The participants were then instructed in the use of the driving simulator.

Four Experimental Test Drives Followed by Interim Questionnaires. Prior to each test drive, participants were instructed on the non-driving activity to be performed and the available equipment elements.

All participants experienced each of the two interior concepts during two simulated, automated drives of approximately 15 min each. This resulted in a total of 4 test drives for each participant. Each subject performed work tasks in each of the two interior concepts once and watched a movie once, while the second subject simultaneously carried out the other non-driving activity during the respective test drives. The subjects always took the same seat in the driving simulator (driver seat or passenger seat) during all four drives. During the test drives, the participants were observed by four cameras installed in the driving simulator.

After each of the four test drives, the participants completed a questionnaire on simulator sickness, user experience, system trust, subjective traffic safety, and intention to use. The participant who had completed work tasks additionally answered questions about flow, subjective work performance, distraction, and subjective work ability. The participant who watched a movie additionally answered a questionnaire about the film immersion experience.

Final Questionnaire, Interview, and Conclusion. After the fourth test drive and interim questionnaire, participants answered questions about system trust, ranked the equipment elements they experienced, and selected their preferred interior concept. This was followed by an interview about their experiences with the interior concepts and the equipment elements included. Finally, the incentives were handed out (3 h of test person time or 30 euros per person).

2.4 Measurement Methods

Table 2 below provides an overview of the measurement instruments used to collect the measurement variables.

Table 2. Measurement variables and instruments

Variable	Instrument	Measuring point in time
Personal information	Closed and open questions	1
Technology affinity	Interactional Technology Affinity Questionnaire (ATI) [10]	1
Objective work performance	Speed and accuracy on four different task types adapted from [7–9]	2a
Simulator sickness	Simulator Sickness Questionnaire (SSQ) [11] (translation from [12])	2b
User experience	User Experience Questionnaire-Short (UEQ-S) [13]	2b
	Facets of user experience [14]	2b
System trust	Trust in Automation (TiA) [15]	2b, 3
Subjective traffic safety	Single-items on risk and safety [16]	2b
Intention to use	Intention to use adapted from [17]	2b
Flow	Flow Short Scale (FSS) [18]	2b
Subjective work performance	Subjective work performance [19, 20] (own translation)	2b
Distraction	Distraction [19] (own translation)	2b
Subjective work ability	Single item on work ability adapted from [7] (own translation)	2b
Film immersion experience	Immersive Experience Questionnaire for Film and TV (Film IEQ) [21] (own translation verified via back translation by state-certified translator)	2b
Evaluation of equipment elements	Ranking of equipment elements with regard to ownership preference (scenario: equipment of own vehicle)	3
Acceptance of the interior concepts	Selection of an interior concept with regard to usage preference (scenario: driving from Stuttgart to Frankfurt)	3
Design information	Open questions about the experience (oral)	3

Note. 1 = Pre-questionnaire, 2a = During test drive, 2b = Interim questionnaire, 3 = Final questionnaire

3 Results (Preview)

As the data collection is scheduled to be completed by end of March 2023, the results cannot be presented in this short paper. At HCII in July 2023, initial insights are provided into how vehicle interior concepts influence the work and entertainment experience of automated driving.

4 Discussion

Compared to low-fidelity prototypes, creating a mid-fidelity prototype requires more effort to illustrate concept ideas. However, a simulation prototype in a driving simulator allows for greater immersion and interaction of users. For example, equipment elements can be directly interacted with and the spatial experience is more realistic. Therefore, more detailed hints for interaction concepts and real behavioral data can be generated.

Compared to field research, laboratory research has lower external validity. However, advantages of laboratory research are that confounding variables can be controlled better and innovations can be tested already, before complex traffic safety solutions have to be developed (e.g. crash safety of equipment elements).

The quantitative evaluation and qualitative user feedback serve to identify the strengths and weaknesses of the concept, thus avoiding greater development effort to realize a high-fidelity prototype in a potentially inappropriate direction.

References

1. SAE International: Taxonomy and definitions for terms related to driving automation systems for on-road motor vehicles (2021).https://doi.org/10.4271/J3016_202104
2. Haar, P., Teicht, M., Stimm, D., Engeln, A.: How are different vehicle interior concepts affecting social interaction during automated driving? In: Stephanidis, C., et al. (eds.) HCI International 2023 Posters, CCIS, vol. 1836, pp. 1–8. Springer, Cham (2023). https://doi.org/10.1007/978-3-031-36004-6_4
3. Deutsches Institut für Normung e. V.: DIN EN ISO 9241–210:2020-03, Ergonomie der Mensch-System-Interaktion - Teil 210: Menschzentrierte Gestaltung interaktiver Systeme (ISO 9241-210:2019), Deutsche Fassung EN ISO 9241-210:2019. Beuth, Berlin (2020). https://doi.org/10.31030/3104744
4. Haar, P., Pagenkopf, A., Teicht, M., Engeln, A.: Nutzeranforderungen an die Gestaltung von Fahrzeuginnenräumen beim vollautomatisierten Fahren (2021). https://projekt-rumba.de/wp-content/uploads/2021/09/210908_Nutzeranforderungen-an-die-Gestaltung-von-Fahrzeuginnenraeumen-beim-vollautomatisierten-Fahren-_RUMBA-Website.pdf
5. Haar, P., Pagenkopf, A., Teicht, M., Engeln, A.: Nutzeranforderungen von Pkw-Fahrern an die Gestaltung von Anzeigen und Bedienelementen und Fahrzeuginnenräumen beim automatisierten Fahren in SAE Level 4. In: Kolloquium Future Mobility, ISBN 978-3-943-563-51-1 (2022)
6. Teicht, M., Haar, P., Pagenkopf, A., Stimm, D., Engeln, A.: Evaluation von Innenraumkonzepten vollautomatisiert fahrender Fahrzeuge. In: Kolloquium Future Mobility, ISBN 978-3-943-563-51-1 (2022)

7. Witterseh, T., Wyon, D.P., Clausen, G.C.: The effects of moderate heat stress and open-plan office noise distraction on SBS symptoms and on the performance of office work. Indoor Air, Supplement **14**(8), 30–40 (2004). https://doi.org/10.1111/j.1600-0668.2004.00305.x
8. Wargocki, P., Wyon, D.P., Sundell, J., Clausen, G., Fanger, P.O.: The effects of outdoor air supply rate in an office on perceived air quality, sick building syndrome (SBS) symptoms and productivity. Indoor Air **10**(4), 222–236 (2000). https://doi.org/10.1034/j.1600-0668.2000.010004222.x
9. Foldbjerg, P., Reimann, G.: Impact of reduced air temperature and increased radiant temperature on perceived air quality, thermal comfort, SBS symptoms and performance. Master thesis, Technical University of Denmark (2001). https://www.researchgate.net/publication/228558936
10. Franke, T., Attig, C., Wessel, D.: A personal resource for technology interaction: development and validation of the affinity for technology interaction (ATI) scale. Int. J. Human-Comput. Interact. **35**(6), 456–467 (2019). https://doi.org/10.1080/10447318.2018.1456150
11. Kennedy, R.S., Lane, N.E., Berbaum, K.S., Lilienthal, M.G.: Simulator sickness questionnaire: an enhanced method for quantifying simulator sickness. Int. J. Aviat. Psychol. **3**(3), 203–220 (1993). https://doi.org/10.1207/s15327108ijap0303_3
12. Hösch, A.: Simulator Sickness in Fahrsimulationsumgebungen: Drei Studien zu Human Factors. Dissertation, Technische Universität Ilmenau (2018). https://nbn-resolving.org/urn:nbn:de:gbv:ilm1-2018000487
13. Schrepp, M., Hinderks, A., Thomaschewski, J.: Design and evaluation of a short version of the user experience questionnaire (UEQ-S). Int. J. Interact. Multimed. Artif. Intell. **4**(6), 103–108 (2017). https://doi.org/10.9781/ijimai.2017.09.001
14. Engeln, A., Engeln, C.: Customer experience und kundenzentrierte Angebotsentwicklung. Was gehört dazu? In: Baetzgen, A. (ed.) Brand Experience: An jedem Touchpoint auf den Punkt begeistern, pp. 253–273. Schäffer-Poeschel, Stuttgart (2015)
15. Körber, M.: Theoretical considerations and development of a questionnaire to measure trust in automation. In: Bagnara, S., Tartaglia, R., Albolino, S., Alexander, T., Fujita, Y. (eds.) Proceedings of the 20th Congress of the International Ergonomics Association (IEA 2018). AISC, vol. 823, pp. 13–30. Springer, Cham (2019). https://doi.org/10.1007/978-3-319-96074-6_2
16. Flohr, L.A., Valiyaveettil, J.S., Krüger A., Wallach, D.P.: Prototyping autonomous vehicle windshields with AR and real-time object detection visualization: an on-road wizard-of-oz study. In: Designing Interactive Systems Conference (DIS 2023), pp. 1–15. ACM, New York (2023). https://doi.org/10.1145/3563657.3596051
17. Müller, A., Stockinger, C., Walter, J., Heuser, T., Abendroth, B., Bruder, R.: Einflussfaktoren auf die Akzeptanz des automatisierten Fahrens aus der Sicht von Fahrerinnen und Fahrern. In: Winner, H., Bruder, R. (eds.) (Wie) wollen wir automatisiert fahren? 8. Darmstädter Kolloquium, pp. 1–22. Technische Universität Darmstadt, Darmstadt (2017). https://tuprints.ulb.tu-darmstadt.de/5672/1/Mensch%20und%20Fahrzeug%20Tagungsband%202017.pdf
18. Rheinberg, F., Vollmeyer, R., Engeser, S.: Die Erfassung des Flow-Erlebens. In: Stiensmeier-Pelste, J., Rheinberg, F. (eds.) Diagnostik von Motivation und Selbstkonzept (Tests und Trends N.F. 2), pp. 261–279. Hogrefe, Göttingen (2003). https://publishup.uni-potsdam.de/opus4-ubp/frontdoor/deliver/index/docId/551/file/Rheinberg_ErfassungFlow_Erleben_mitAnhangFKS.pdf
19. Lee, S.Y., Brand, J.L.: Can personal control over the physical environment ease distractions in office workplaces? Ergonomics **53**(3), 324–335 (2010). https://doi.org/10.1080/00140130903389019

20. Oldham, G.R.: Effects of changes in workspace partitions and spatial density on employee reactions: a quasi-experiment. J. Appl. Psychol. **73**(2), 253–258 (1988). https://doi.org/10.1037/0021-9010.73.2.253
21. Rigby, J.M., Brumby, D.P., Gould, S.J.J., Cox, A.L: Development of a questionnaire to measure immersion in video media: the film IEQ. In: Proceedings of the 2019 ACM International Conference on Interactive Experiences for TV and Online Video (TVX 2019), pp. 35–46. Association for Computing Machinery, New York (2019). https://doi.org/10.1145/3317697.3323361

Haptic Feedback Research of Human-Computer Interaction in Human-Machine Shared Control Context of Smart Cars

Junwen Xiao(✉)

Wuhan University of Technology, 122 Luoshi Road, Wuhan, Hubei, People's Republic of China
460244388@qq.com

Abstract. Since 2007, when the world's first self-driving car was tested on real roads, smart cars have gradually become the main direction of automotive development. Nowadays, with the development of smart car technology, the car driving mode has seen a huge change, and haptic feedback research of human-computer interaction in human-machine shared control and autonomous driving have gradually become the main contexts of future smart cars. The International Society of Automotive Engineering (ISAE) has divided different autonomous vehicle behaviors into six levels from L0 to L5. In the automation level L0-L3 smart cars, people are indispensable in the whole driving process, while the automation level L4-L5 smart cars do not need people to participate in driving tasks at all. However, due to various factors such as automotive technology, laws and regulations, and morality and ethics, humans will remain the participants and dominators of car driving in the foreseeable future. At the same time, the new iterations of smart car in-vehicle devices are leading to the gradual failure of classical car interaction feedback. Among these interactive feedback, haptic is a real physical feedback, which is an important way for humans to receive physical information about objective things. Haptic feedback allows the driver to obtain timely information about the proximal environment and vehicle movement, which can directly affect the driver's next driving behavior. In addition, haptic feedback also has the ability to carry emotion. The haptic feedback of different interaction objects will bring different experiences to the driver.

Keywords: Smart cars · human-machine shared control · haptic feedback

1 Human-Machine Shared Control Context

1.1 From Driver-Led to Human-Machine Shared Control

Smart cars will not be able to achieve fully autonomous driving in the foreseeable future, so humans are still participants in car driving, and this new driving context is called human-machine shared control. The traditional car driving context is centered on people, especially the driver, where the "center" refers to both the center of the user experience and the center of vehicle control, and the driver is the main initiator of driving behavior and interaction. But in the intelligent car driving context, the driver and the vehicle intelligent system are in a "co-driving" state, and the human and intelligent system work together to complete the driving task.

C. Stephanidis et al. (Eds.): HCII 2023, CCIS 1836, pp. 116–121, 2023.
https://doi.org/10.1007/978-3-031-36004-6_16

The task allocation in the intelligent vehicle Human-machine Shared Control Context differs according to the different driving controllers, so here we discuss the task allocation in the Human-machine Shared Control Context with the driver as the driving controller and the in-vehicle intelligent system as the driving controller.

The driver-intelligent system is usually the driver in an ideal road situation, where the car obtains real-time information about the surrounding environment based on pre-programmed algorithms and sensors, and intelligently handles the overall task using the "experience" learned as artificial intelligence. In this case, the driver gradually changes from a user to a supervisor. The driver is the car controller mainly for non-ordinary driving contexts, where the in-vehicle intelligent system uses the above-mentioned technology to guide the driver in driving. This task distribution is similar to that of a driver and a navigator in a car rally. The in-vehicle intelligent system provides information to the driver through real-time monitoring of the environment and the vehicle, and assists the driver in completing the driving task.

1.2 Situational Awareness and Haptic Feedback

According to Walker G.H. et al., people perform more than 1600 tasks in the car,[1] and in the human-vehicle context, people are freed from the main driving task to perform other behaviors, which makes the context of smart cars tend to be diverse and complex. The complexity of the context dictates that the human in the car needs to understand the changes in the context, that is situational awareness. [2] Situational awareness refers to the user's awareness of what is dynamically changing in the environment, and it explains how the user manages the relationship between long-term goals of driving (e.g., reaching a destination) and short-term goals (e.g., accident avoidance, entertainment communication, etc.).

Haptic feedback, as an effective physical information transfer pathway in the smart cockpit, can play an important role in facilitating a shift in the driver's situational awareness. First, the Human-machine Shared Control Context in smart cars requires the driver and the car's intelligent system to be involved simultaneously and to switch the driving state and the dominant player according to the actual situation. Therefore, appropriate haptic feedback can alert the driver during the process of switching between driving state and dominant, trigger the driver's situational awareness, and avoid traffic accidents caused by negligence. Secondly, haptic feedback is more efficient than visual and auditory feedback in conveying simple information. The intelligent car cockpit can replace the less efficient visual and auditory feedback with haptic feedback to improve the efficiency of the driver's processing of changes in the driving situation. Finally, haptic feedback can be combined with other sensory information to form a multimodal and integrated intelligent driving experience.

2 Haptic Feedback in Smart Cars

Various tactile receptors and nerve endings distributed on the human skin transmit external information to the central nervous system to obtain tactile perception. Compared with other senses, haptics is a direct, zero-distance physical contact between the cognizer and the object. Haptics allows the cognizer to recognize the surface features, spatial characteristics, material properties, and other characteristics of an object. And in the process of recognition, tactile sensation can spawn emotional tactile sensations such as surprise, fear, and pleasure. Thus, haptics has both material and mental properties. Accordingly, the current research on tactile sensation is divided into two aspects: the direct sensation based on the actual material and the actual structure of the material surface, and the psychological sensation based on the imagery of the material surface organization. Usually, the two complement each other in haptic experience, and the study of the two is not isolated.[3].

Tactile perception consists of multimodal information about the shape, size, texture, hardness, roughness, material, temperature, weight, and force of an object, and can be divided into the sensation of touch felt by the skin and the sensation of force felt by the joint ligaments. The complete haptic experience is presented by the mutual integration of touch and force sensation. The simulation of haptic feedback is also achieved by computer simulation of haptic feedback and force feedback. Among them, the tactile feedback is through the vibration, texture and temperature of the object surface to identify the object of touch. Force feedback, on the other hand, discriminates the object of contact by factors such as weight, hardness, and friction characteristics.[4].

In smart cars, the environment and driving conditions around the car can be sensed through a wealth of sensors, and haptic feedback can be provided to the driver through interactive smart devices within the smart cockpit. According to the type of haptic feedback can be divided into force feedback, tactile feedback and pseudo-haptic feedback.

2.1 Force Feedback in Smart Cars

Force feedback is widely used in current automobiles, such as steering wheel steering, throttle and brake down resistance, etc. There are also many studies trying to optimize the driving safety and driving experience of smart cars through force feedback. Bosch developed in '16 to add haptic feedback to a prototype gas pedal to communicate with the driver during acceleration. This active pedal system uses an integrated motor set in the pedal to provide feedback. The system generates resistance and vibrations at specific pedal depths to remind the driver to save fuel and be safe, depending on the driving situation. In driving, if the driver presses the gas pedal too deep, then the system will increase the pedal resistance appropriately to remind the driver to pay attention to the fuel consumption, through the experiment shows that this system can reduce the fuel consumption by about 7%. When the vehicle is in a dangerous situation, such as cornering too fast, the pedal will vibrate to remind the driver to improve driving behavior. In addition, the system can be personalized according to the driver's preference to meet the needs of different users. In addition, Bosch has partnered with Ultra Haptics in Bristol, UK, to create a prototype motion gesture function to provide haptic feedback. As the hand floats above the console, the driver makes gestures and ultrasonic waves hit the user's hand and provide feedback, making it feel as if the user is actually touching the physical knob. Similarly, BMW's Holo Active haptic interface uses a haptic gesture control system (sensors "see" the hand, and through the use of ultrasonic technology, the driver can "feel" the controls), so the driver doesn't have to touch the screen. Simply move in the air. Such haptic feedback and interaction not only improves the efficiency of human-vehicle interaction, but also improves the driver's dangerous driving behavior.

2.2 Tactile Feedback in Smart Cars

Haptic perception consists of multimodal information such as the shape, size, texture, hardness, roughness, material, temperature, weight, and force of an object, which can be divided into touch sensation felt by skin and force sensation felt by joint ligaments. [5] The complete haptic experience is presented by the mutual integration of touch and force sensation. The simulation of haptic feedback is also achieved by computer simulation of haptic feedback and force feedback. Among them, tactile feedback is to identify the object to be touched by the vibration, texture and temperature of the object surface.

If force feedback is the in-vehicle intelligent system to provide assistance to the driver's driving behavior according to the driving situation, then tactile feedback is to give the driver a rich experience through different devices in the intelligent cockpit. In particular, the development of intelligent interactive surfaces has brought new possibilities for the haptic experience of smart cars. Smart interactive surfaces break the boundaries between interior decorative surfaces and touch panels, embedding electronic components and smart sensors in textile materials to achieve interactive functions. For example, with a combination of decorative lighting elements, capacitive switching technology and haptic actuation integrated with force sensors embedded under the textile material, users can interact with touch seat gestures to switch on and off seat memory and seat heating. Most recently, BMW also presented an intelligent surface for interior and exterior surfaces, called "Shy Tech". This smart surface contains cameras, radar and many sensors, has digital functions and is self-healing. This textile-mediated smart interactive surface can be used for automotive seat covers, seat belts, roof, door panels and dashboard components. The smart interactive surface combines traditional surface materials with smart components and information technology to provide the driver with a rich tactile experience through technology while retaining the traditional material tactile experience.

3 Multimodal Pseudo-haptic Experiences

Multimodality refers to the integration of multiple senses. Multimodal interaction is the fusion of multiple senses such as human vision, hearing, and touch, and the computer responds to input using multiple communication channels and simulates human interaction. Now it is widely used in the interaction design of various intelligent products. Humans input information through voice, gestures, expressions and other modalities, and the computer responds and gives feedback through computer vision and auditory channels, which is a typical multimodal interaction. Currently, multimodal interaction and related technologies have been commonly used in the interaction design of intelligent vehicles, and multimodal design related to haptic interaction and haptic feedback has also attracted much attention. Research on multimodal haptic feedback is mainly focused on two areas. The first is the combination of existing haptic feedback and other sensory modalities to form a comprehensive haptic feedback. The second is the combination of multimodal sensory feedback to form pseudo-haptic feedback.

3.1 Pseudo-haptic Feedback

With the advancement of interaction technology and the enrichment of interaction methods, more and more attention has been paid to the study of pseudo-haptic feedback. The so-called pseudo-haptic feedback refers to the haptic experience that is different from the traditional physical haptic feedback simulation and does not even require contact with physical objects.[6] It is a technique for presenting tactile perception through cross-sensory information, which is an aid and compensation for the formation of tactile sensation through the experience of other senses using the principle of fluency. The purpose of pseudo-haptic feedback is to generate haptic illusions, i.e., haptic perceptions under the influence of other senses. Pseudo-haptic feedback based on multisensory illusions has been used to simulate various haptic properties, such as the stiffness of a virtual spring, the texture or quality of an object. In the current situation where smart products are generally equipped with touch displays and speakers and other devices are constantly improved and upgraded, pseudo-haptic feedback formed by visual, auditory and other perceptions has a broad application prospect.

3.2 Pseudo-haptic Feedback Formed by Different Senses

First, in the formation of pseudo-haptic feedback, the visual senses can play a significant role. This is because there is a large degree of overlap between tactile and visual senses in terms of the types of information represented and the neural basis on which they rely.[7] It can be said that humans have innate characteristics of visual haptic perception.[8] In the intelligent design of haptic experiences, the construction of visual for haptic information can be done either through sensory substitution, converting visual information into haptic information, or through pseudo-haptic feedback to simulate haptic information as a technical complement to real haptic feedback. At present, it has been possible to form different pseudo-haptic feedback through vision, such as pseudo-haptic simulation by adjusting the speed of visual stimuli to characterize friction, and pseudo-haptic simulation by distorting and deforming video images to characterize wind resistance.

Second, hearing also plays an important role in the formation of pseudo-haptic feedback. The conversion of a specific modality to haptics in pseudo-haptic feedback requires that this sensory modality has the type of data specified by the biophysiological characteristics of haptics. For both hearing and touch, the vibration and sound information generated by touching an object are wave signals, which dictate that hearing and touch share physical properties such as vibration frequency and amplitude, which enables a mapping relationship between the two in terms of properties such as intensity, frequency, velocity, and roughness. [9] Therefore, in the case where the tactile sensation cannot reach a satisfactory state, the auditory modality can be used in an intelligent way to provide tactile illusion.

3.3 Pseudo-haptic Feedback for Smart Cars

Haptic feedback in smart cars never exists in isolation, especially pseudo-haptic feedback, a feedback system that can be formed through other senses. For example, in the cockpit of a smart car, different driving contexts can be simulated through the in-car display, intelligent interactive surfaces, ambient lights, interior aromatherapy and audio devices. When the display and ambience present images and colors related to the ocean and the beach, and the audio device simulates the sound of the sea breeze, it can make the driver feel as if he or she is on the seaside highway, at which time, although the driver is still in the closed cockpit, the pseudo-haptic feedback experience of the sea breeze can be formed through the multi-sensory simulation. At present, there are relatively few pseudo-haptic feedback designs actually used in smart cars, and the related research and technology are in their infancy. However, under the context of human-machine shared control in smart cars, the identity of human gradually changes from driver to supervisor, and the focus of interaction design of smart cars also starts to transition from function to user experience, and the experience and entertainment value of smart cars increases.

4 Conclusion

Different brands of smart cars are constantly appearing in the market, and artificialintelligence and different sensing technologies make smart cars more and more feature-rich. However, it is undeniable that the traditional haptic feedback experience is gradually failing, and the haptic feedback interaction system adapted to new technologies and new driving contexts has not yet been fully formed. Therefore, this paper distinguishes different forms of haptic feedback, describes the three main types of haptic feedback: force feedback, tactile feedback and pseudo-haptic feedback, and discusses the use of different forms of haptic feedback in smart cars in conjunction with smart car Human-machine Shared Control Context s, and proposes design recommendations to further improve the design quality from the perspective of safety and experience.

References

1. Walker, G.H.F., Stanton, N.A.S., Young, M.S.T.: Hierarchical task analysis of driving: a new research tool. Contempor. Ergon. **435**, 40 (2001)
2. Hao, T., Zhang, F., Yingli, S.: Safety-oriented intelligent vehicles information & interaction design research. Zhuangshi **352**(08), 22–27 (2022)
3. Ma, X., Tong, Q., Li, Y.: Research on the construction of intelligent design haptic experience based on multimodal haptic and pseudo-haptic Feedback. Zhuangshi **353**(09), 28–33 (2022)
4. Qi, B., Hu, F., Zhu, F.: Tactile interaction service framework for blind readers and application research. Libr. Inf. Work. **14**, 20–29 (2019)
5. Wang, D., Ohnishi, K., Xu, W.: Multimodal Haptic Display for Virtual Reality: A Survey. IEEE Transactions on Industrial Electronics **67**(1), 610–623 (2020). https://doi.org/10.1109/TIE.2019.2920602
6. Lécuyer A,F., Coquillart, S., Kheddar, A.T.: Pseudo-haptic Feedback: can isometric input devices simulate force Feedback?. Proceedings of the IEEE International Conference on Virtual Reality (2000)
7. Lécuyer, A.: Simulating haptic feedback using vision: a survey of research and applications of pseudo-haptic Feedback. Presence Teleoper. Virtual Environ. **18**(1), 39–53 (2009). https://doi.org/10.1162/pres.18.1.39
8. Yu, W., Liu, Y., Fu, X.: Cognitive mechanisms of haptic two-dimensional image recognition. Adv. Psychol. Sci. **4**, 611–622 (2019)
9. Yang, Z., Li, H., Ma, S., Shu, T.: Applying "Audible" tactile experiences: cues from multi-sensory channel integration. Adv. Psychol. Sci. **3**, 580–590 (2022)

Based on Data-Driven Research on the Emotional Experience of Electric Vehicle Users

Ying Zhang, Jie Zhang(✉), Yue Cui, Chenglin He, and Dashuai Liu

School of Art Design and Media, East China University of Science and Technology, Shanghai 200237, China
zyydyjya@163.com

Abstract. Under the global goal of "dual carbon", rich and diversified new energy vehicle products continue to meet market demand, and new energy vehicles are increasingly recognized by consumers, but the current evaluation research on their user emotions is still insufficient. In order to more accurately understand the relatively real user emotional experience of electric vehicles, this paper proposes a method for collecting, drawing and analyzing these online reviews based on the online comment text of electric vehicle big data, text mining and natural language processing, and combined with the sentiment analysis method of user evaluation. Firstly, taking the typical electric car BYD-Song PLUS as an example, the online short text review about BYD-Song PLUS on the online review website is obtained through the crawler software; Secondly, natural language processing technology is used to preprocess the data to obtain the visual statistics of word frequency related to eight subject words. Then, a user sentiment analysis method is established to obtain sentiment analysis of short text data. Finally, combined with the theory of emotional experience, the application of emotional experience electric vehicles is analyzed from three aspects: instinctual level, behavioral level and reflection level. Compared with the traditional research focusing on individual user evaluation, this study explores the possibility of a user perceptual evaluation research method in the context of big data. This will provide a certain theoretical reference for the research of user perceptual evaluation system, and help people related to new energy vehicles and even more related products to understand the emotional experience of users closer to the truth.

Keywords: Data-driven · Perceptual evaluation · Sentiment analysis methods · Electric vehicle

1 Introduce

In the context of global warming, in response to the goal of carbon neutrality proposed by international organizations, China has vigorously promoted the low-carbon economy, a new form of civilization development, to achieve a win-win situation between the social economy and the ecological environment. China has continuously improved the

C. Stephanidis et al. (Eds.): HCII 2023, CCIS 1836, pp. 122–130, 2023.
https://doi.org/10.1007/978-3-031-36004-6_17

innovation and research and development of new energy vehicles in recent years, but compared with traditional fuel vehicles, the time is relatively short, in addition to the research and development of innovative technologies, consumers' concept changes and emotional needs still need to be studied. The user's experience and emotion are subjective feelings that are difficult to quantify, so it is of great value to analyze the emotional needs of new energy vehicles to provide a basis for designers to design new energy vehicles, thereby strengthening user services and experience. Taking the well-known brand BYD-Song PLUS in the domestic electric vehicle market as the research object, this paper uses big data mining online reviews, quantifies unstructured text, and constructs a relationship model between users' needs and product design elements that are difficult to quantify according to the characteristics of emotional design, so as to obtain users' emotional experience and improve user satisfaction.

2 Data-Driven

Data-driven, as the name implies, is to extract key information from data and use it as the main basis for product development or project conduct, that is, data as the main driving force to promote the project [1]. With the rapid development of artificial intelligence, text analysis technology with the help of computer deep learning has become an emerging research tool. Natural Language Processing (NLP) is an important direction in the field of artificial intelligence, processing human natural language through computers. From the 20th century to the present, natural language processing based on deep learning has been relatively mature and applied to major fields, and as an important part of human-computer interaction. In the field of design, natural language processing is widely used in design activities and academic research, mainly in two aspects: (1) to help designers obtain relevant information. For example, Robert Ireland [2] et al. introduce a computational system for analyzing online product reviews, and use Coleman chair's online review application to let designers analyze the same corpus to verify the accuracy of the model; (2) In addition to obtaining information, there is also simple sentiment analysis, and deep, multi-dimensional information such as hidden needs are mined from comments. Such as Wang Xin [3]. Using the metaphor extraction technology of the cloud platform, the clustering based on the similarity calculation of Synonyms and the improved k-means algorithm, the gestalt logical system method maps implicit requirements to the technical characteristics of the product.

As a direct link between products and users, online reviews imply valuable user feedback information, and how to obtain useful information is currently a hot spot and difficult point in the research of scholars at home and abroad [4]. A data-driven approach captures, analyzes, processes massive amounts of data in a timely manner, and extracts the value contained in it.

3 User Perceptual Evaluation Research

3.1 Kansei Engineering

The term "Kankan Engineering" first came from Mr. Yamamoto Kenichi, the former chairman of Mazda Motor Group in Japan, in his speech "On Automobile Culture" in 1986 [5] "Sensibility" in Japanese means consumers' psychological feelings and image of a new product. This theory emphasizes that users will form a direct psychological image of the product through a series of senses such as vision, hearing, touch, smell, and taste during the process of using the product, and use "luxury", "simple", and "business-like" " and other emotional words are exposed [6] Therefore, Kansei Engineering is a consumer-oriented product development technology, and the goal of Kansei Engineering is to produce new products according to the feelings and needs of consumers [7]. Kansei engineering, as a representative method in emotional design, guides and evaluates design schemes by obtaining users' perceptual images of specific product attributes and connecting them. After Kansei Engineering was proposed at the end of the 20th century, it has been widely used in the design fields of automobiles, home appliances, and clothing. Kansei engineering methods generally have four aspects: Kansei word collection, Kansei word selection, Kansei evaluation and mapping model, so as to obtain the design that meets the needs of users [8].

3.2 Sentiment Analysis Methods

Sentiment analysis is a basic task in the field of natural language processing and belongs to the category of text analysis. Its purpose is to determine and identify arguments from the text, mine and analyze emotional tendencies, and extract the main points of view. The object of sentiment analysis is text, and text can be large or small, which can be a complete document, a sentence, or a word or phrase. According to this characteristic of text, sentiment analysis research can be divided into three levels, namely: document-level sentiment analysis, sentence-level sentiment analysis, and attribute-level sentiment analysis. Don Norman proposed that the three stages of emotion correspond to the three levels of emotional design, the first is the human nature stage, which refers to people's intuitive feelings about things, corresponding to the instinctive layer design; The second is the behavior stage, which refers to people's feelings when using things, corresponding to the behavior layer stage; The third is the thinking stage, in which the comprehensive feelings of people in the first two stages correspond to the reflection layer design.

However, the current emotional design is not perfect enough, design practice cannot meet people's urgent demand for emotional products, emotional analysis has also been valued by many institutions, in technology, a variety of emotional feature extraction methods and classification strategies have been produced; In terms of application, application systems based on sentiment analysis emerge one after another, such as opinion mining systems and public opinion analysis systems. However, due to the diversity of natural language emotion expressions, emotion analysis still faces many difficulties, and in technology, a variety of emotion feature extraction methods and classification strategies have been produced. In terms of application, application systems based on sentiment analysis emerge one after another, such as opinion mining systems and public opinion analysis systems. However, due to the diversity of natural language emotional expressions, sentiment analysis still faces many difficulties.

3.3 User Perceptual Research Methods

The user's perceptual needs are divided into three levels: cognitive needs, emotional needs and behavioral needs, through the research of emotional design of products, a wider range of user groups can have a better experience when using products, and increase the inclusiveness of product design and user satisfaction. At present, there are three types of commonly used perceptual engineering collection methods: the first type is a demand collection method based on physiological feature sensors, that is, the use of measuring instruments to collect physiological responses to obtain data on users' psychological changes, mainly eye tracking methods; The second type is the demand collection method based on interview questionnaire, that is, the method of interview or questionnaire is used to obtain data and analyze and quantify, mainly including semantic difference method and Likert scale; The third category is based on big data user emotional demand collection, that is, accurate acquisition of user comments in Internet big data, mainly crawler software or natural language processing technology.

Among them, the advantage of the product perceptual evaluation method based on text data mining using the third type of perceptual engineering collection method is that the amount of data can be obtained is large and the coverage is wide. It mainly includes the following four steps:(1) The construction of the original corpus of text, which obtains the text data of the network platform through the method of web crawler, has the characteristics of convenience, speed and easy processing; (2) Data preprocessing, the obtained text data through pre-processing such as part-of-speech classification, and the unstructured data such as online text is structured through word vector technology to facilitate subsequent data analysis; (3) Online comment mining, build a polar dictionary in the user's subjective emotional words, and obtain product characteristics in combination with product specifications, so as to obtain the core characteristics of user attention; (4) Perceptual evaluation and analysis, based on the core characteristics of products that users pay attention to, to provide guidance for the adjustment of product design.

4 Data-Driven

Human designers are still in a key position, but they are a major innovation compared to the traditional design development process. Data is a core resource for the new era, and the same is true for design. Reasonable data analysis can make designers closer to user pain points, and the process is more convincing, and the design process is not based on the designer's subjective experience. PCAUTO's user reviews are in the form of short texts that express the user's experience. Through the text analysis of it, you can dig more into the actual user feelings and get specific and real evaluations.

The research methods of this paper are divided into three parts: data acquisition, data processing and data analysis. (1) Data acquisition. Using the PCAUTO platform as the data source, the commentary dataset of BYD-Song PLUS users was obtained through the Octopus collector as the basis for research. (2) Data processing. Firstly, the product review data is extracted, the data preprocessing is performed, and the adjective word frequency analysis of the eight subject words is analyzed. (3) Data analysis. The sentiment analysis of the adjective word frequency table and sentences of the resulting users, combined with the theory of emotional experience, draws validity conclusions.

4.1 Data Collection

Using the Octopus collector, PCAUTO was selected as the target, and the user experience reviews of BYD-Song PLUS were collected, and a total of 4469 comments were collected after collection, and after deduplication of 219 reviews, 4250 reviews were finally summarized for further screening. This paper summarizes and analyzes the user review data collected by the automated crawler system, and through the analysis content, we can initially understand that the website platform sets the problems that general consumers are more concerned about: advantages, disadvantages, appearance, interior, space, configuration, power, fuel consumption, so as to grasp the user's use feelings, and also play a guiding role in subsequent sentiment analysis.

4.2 Data Analysis

KH Coder is a text mining tool. Through KH Coder's information preprocessing of natural language descriptions, including setting stop words and special words, extracting and adjusting feature words, and counting the frequency of keywords in the filtered text, so that Carry out data analysis to pave the way for the analysis of user emotional needs. Compared with traditional questionnaire information, online comment texts are colloquial, fragmented, and unstructured. Therefore, multi-dimensional comprehensive analysis is used to conduct sentiment analysis and multi-dimensional comprehensive analysis of text information through parameters such as stop words, word frequency, correlation, and emotional concentration. Based on sentiment analysis technology combined with word frequency and sentence analysis, the words with high correlation between electric vehicle design and emotional evaluation are summarized. The experimental result terms include emotional keywords, emotional polarity, sentences, etc. Sentiment keywords are highly relevant words obtained by sentiment analysis technology combined with word frequency and sentiment sentences, and combined with positive sentiment words and negative sentiment words to obtain positive sentiment scores and negative sentiment scores respectively. Positive sentiment is defined as sentiment value greater than 0, and sentiment value Less than 0 is defined as negative emotion. Finally, the overall sentiment score of each dimension is comprehensively calculated based on the frequency of strongly related words. The overall sentiment score is greater than 0, indicating positive sentiment, and less than 0, indicating negative sentiment. Positive emotions include excitement, liking, comfort, pleasure, and stability. Negative emotions include nervousness, fear, anger, sadness, and disgust.

4.3 Data Analysis

Using the KH Coder tool, the online review data of BYD-Song PLUS is divided into eight dimensions for part-of-speech tagging, all adjectives are obtained, and the invalid or similar adjectives are eliminated and classified, and then sorted by word frequency, and the top 10 adjectives in each dimension and their word frequency are shown in the table. As shown in the adjective frequency of Tables 1, 2, 3, 4, 5, 6, and 7, the eight dimensions are more positive emotional words, and the overall positive and pleasant emotions caused by the user can be used, but the space and configuration dimensions.

In addition to positive emotions, the space also reflects that the space is crowded and small, and the configuration dimension reflects the configuration low and expensive.

Table 1. The top 10 adjectives and word frequencies in the dynamic dimension.

Adjective	Frequency	Adjective	Frequency
快	1140	平顺	309
不错	745	大	280
好	686	强劲	279
轻松	290	轻松	243
强	406	新	239

Table 2. The top 10 adjectives and word frequencies in the space dimension.

Adjective	Frequency	Adjective	Frequency
大	2277	满意	418
宽敞	1382	高	370
不错	836	小	315
舒服	624	拥挤	312
方便	430	合理	292

Table 3. The top 10 adjectives and word frequencies in the interior dimension.

Adjective	Frequency	Adjective	Frequency
好	1206	简单	355
不错	1105	满意	267
舒服	407	好看	264
科技感	388	丰富	259
大	370	简洁	251

Combining the eight-dimensional word frequency table and analyzing the sentiment values of the sentiment sentences generated by the generated analysis of the sentiment statement, it can be found that the power, interior, exterior and fuel consumption in the word frequency table perform better. According to Norman's theory of emotional levels, eight dimensions can be corresponded to the instinctive layer (interior, appearance, space), behavioral layer (power, fuel consumption, configuration) and reflection layer (advantages, disadvantages), and the comparison of the emotional intensity of the instinct layer shows that the positive emotional intensity of the interior and exterior is

Table 4. The top 10 adjectives and word frequencies in the configuration dimension.

Adjective	Frequency	Adjective	Frequency
不错	1191	高的	232
好	923	丰富	213
低	518	贵	211
满意	462	划算	195
大	302	合适	176

Table 5. The top 10 adjectives and word frequencies in the appearance dimension.

Adjective	Frequency	Adjective	Frequency
不错	853	大	225
好	649	满意	225
流畅	561	强	220
时尚	355	精致	191
帅气	242	饱满	141

Table 6. The top 10 adjectives and word frequencies in the fuel consumption dimension.

Adjective	Frequency	Adjective	Frequency
好	1046	灵敏	318
不错	698	方便	292
精准	431	轻	288
轻松	394	稳	276
大	361	高	265

Table 7. The top 10 adjectives and word frequencies in the disadvantages dimension.

Adjective	Frequency	Adjective	Frequency
满意	802	小	110
好	568	舒服	104
大	490	久	95
不错	225	快	77
高	137	硬	73

Table 8. The top 10 adjectives and word frequencies in the advantages dimension.

Adjective	Frequency	Adjective	Frequency
好	1154	舒服	441
不错	1024	省	377
高	845	多	374
大	792	方便	372
低	583	强	358

significantly better than that of space, which is similar to the analysis results of the word frequency table; The positive emotion intensity configured in the behavior layer is higher than the power and fuel consumption, which is different from the result of the word frequency table. It is normal for the emotional intensity of the strengths to be higher than the emotional intensity of the weaknesses in the reflection layer. The overall sentiment values of advantages, interior, exterior and configuration in the overall attribute sentiment analysis chart are better, and can better show the user's positive pleasure and optimism, relatively speaking, the overall emotional score of power, fuel consumption, space and shortcomings is low, which needs to be improved (Table 8).

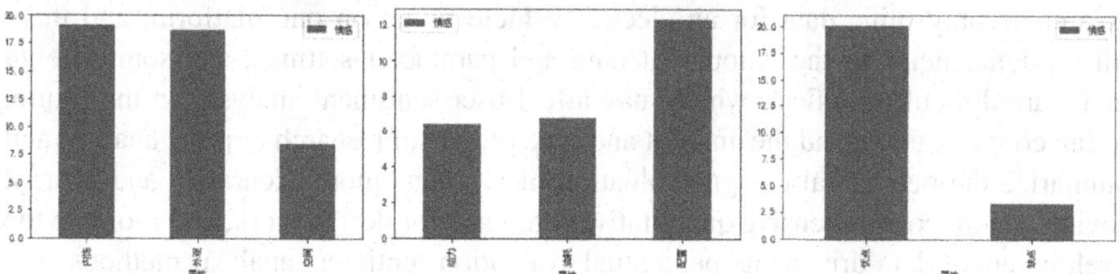

Fig. 1. Instinctive layer, behavioral layer, reflective layer sentiment analysis diagram.

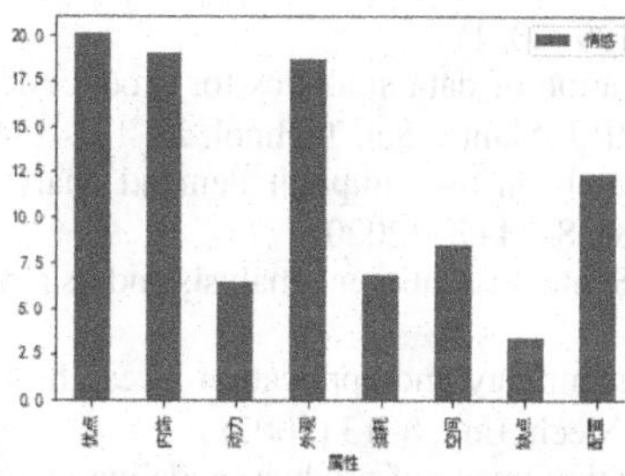

Fig. 2. Sentiment analysis comparison chart for all attributes.

5 Application and Thinking of User Sentimental Evaluation of Typical Electric Vehicles

Consumers' evaluation of electric vehicles mainly starts from eight aspects: advantages, disadvantages, appearance, interior, space, configuration, power, and fuel consumption. When designing and developing an electric vehicle, enterprises should fully consider their market positioning and target group, conduct research on the target group, fully understand the user's demand scenarios for the use of electric vehicles, so as to customize and better improve the attractiveness of the target group (Figs. 1 and 2).

Taking the electric vehicle BYD-Song PLUS as an example, this study innovatively uses the octopus collector, KH Coder mining tool and sentiment analysis method to comprehensively analyze the big data of product review text, preliminarily analyzes the correlation of design features through the keyword word frequency table, and then deeply explores consumers' perceptual cognition of the product, studies the design characteristics of user emotional experience, and preliminarily establishes eight dimensions and user sentiment analysis diagram, and finds the appearance of the electric vehicle. The interior and configuration can cause more positive emotional feedback from users, but the space also has the problem of crowding, and the performance of fuel consumption and power needs to be improved.

Compared with traditional questionnaires, interviews and other research methods, this study can improve efficiency, eliminate subjective factors of research, and apply more widely and conveniently. There are still some limitations in this study, at present, researchers only mine data for an electric vehicle brand on one platform, and there will be deficiencies in the amount of data and parameter settings, and some design details are difficult to reflect, which may affect user sentiment analysis. In the future, we can continue to expand the amount and type of data of research objects, analyze and summarize the perceptual design evaluation of products more accurately and clearly, provide a more comprehensive quantitative reference for design work, and promote the development of data-driven and perceptual evaluation sentiment analysis methods.

References

1. Cao, J., Liu, J., Xu, X.: Research on intelligent acquisition method based on data-driven user needs. Pack. Eng. **42**, 129–139 (2021)
2. Ireland, R., Liu, A.: Application of data analytics for product design: sentiment analysis of online product reviews. CIRP J. Manuf. Sci. Technol. **23**, 128–144 (2018)
3. Wang, X., Qiao, W.: Research on user implicit demand analysis method based on cloud platform. Mech. Des. Res. **36**, 8–11+23 (2020)
4. Li, G., Cheng, Y., Kou, G.: Sentence sentiment analysis and its key issues. Libr. Inf. Work. **54**, 104–107+127 (2010)
5. Luo, S., Pan, Y.: Theory, technology and application research of kansei imagery in product design progress. Chinese J. Mech. Eng. 8–13 (2007)
6. Luo, S., Zhu, S.: The perception image of product modeling by users and designers. Chinese J. Mech. Eng. 28–34 (2005)
7. Nagamachi, M.: Kansei engineering: a new ergonomic consumer-oriented technology for product development. Int. J. Ind. Ergon. **15**, 3–11 (1995)
8. Hartono, M.: The modified Kansei Engineering-based application for sustainable service design. Int. J. Indus. Ergon. **79**, 102985 (2020)

Developing an Interpretable Driver Risk Assessment Model to Increase Driver Awareness Using In-Vehicle Records

Min Zheng[1,2] and Jingyu Zhang[1,2(✉)]

[1] Institute of Psychology, Chinese Academy of Sciences, Beijing 100101, China
zhangjingyu@psych.ac.cn

[2] Department of Psychology, University of Chinese Academy of Sciences, Beijing 100049, China

Abstract. Providing feedback to drivers on their risky driving behaviors is an important method to improve drivers' awareness in reducing future accidents. However, it is hard to identify risk-prone behaviors and explain them to drivers. In the present study, we used driving log from 103370 electric vehicles equipped with L2-assisted driving functions. We used 28 explainable features to establish a binary classification model of accidents and eight features can be used to establish an acceptable model. Further, we developed an easy-to-understand safety score formula using these eight features. Through this accurate and transparent feedback, we may improve drivers' safety awareness without undermining their trust in the L2 and higher level automated vehicles. This will not only reduce accidents but enable them to adapt to the development of automated driving technology in a smoother manner.

Keywords: High-risk Driving Behavior Features · Automated Driving Technology · Logic Regression Model · Big Data Analysis

1 Introduction

Driving safety in the stage of man-machine co-driving is a difficult problem that needs to be solved in the development of automatic driving technology [1]. The purpose of a large number of previous studies is to design the machine to adapt to people on the basis of understanding the features of people [1], and let people match the machine to some extent to fill up the immaturity of technological development.

In-car warning functions such as DMS (Driver Monitoring System), HOD (Hands Off Detection), FCW (Forward Collision Warning), and AEB (Autonomous Emergency Braking) are sent out to remind the driver to adjust their behavior. They are important ways to provide drivers with timely feedback on their just-performed risky driving behaviors to improve their safety. However, an long-term evaluation of drivers' behaviors is also needed to increase drivers' overall awareness of their style and skills.

In order to develop an effective tool for that purpose, several principles should be met. First, such an evaluation must be based on continuous and unintrusive measures, so

C. Stephanidis et al. (Eds.): HCII 2023, CCIS 1836, pp. 131–136, 2023.
https://doi.org/10.1007/978-3-031-36004-6_18

it can be updated quickly as the drivers' behavior changes. Second, such an evaluation must reflect the actual risk of accidents, so the drivers can really trust the evaluation. Third, such an evaluation must be based on an easy-to-understand criterion, so the drivers can grasp their meaning intuitively and are glad to use it.

This study sought to make an initial step in developing such a tool. We used real vehicle records of 103370 electric vehicles equipped with L2-assisted driving functions. We first filtered the features by experts to keep the most explainable ones. Then we used these selected features to establish a model to predict accidents. Finally, we developed a safety evaluation score based on the established prediction model and developed a user-friendly interface for drivers to understand the meaning of that score.

2 Method

2.1 Data Collecting

The data used the real vehicle driving and accident data of a certain automobile enterprise within two months. More than 400 features collected from the in-car detector were used as the source of data, and all accidents were restored as far as possible by collecting data from the following three sources: (1) airbag ejection record; (2) insurance report record; (3) repair work order records.

The number of subjects in a month was 103370, and the number of accidents in the previous month was 1598. The number of accidents in the next month was 1286.

2.2 Extracting Explainable Features Through Expert Evaluation

We asked 10 experts to first choose the dimensions that were important in resulting in an accident and are explainable to ordinary drivers. They were asked to make their own judgment separately and then discuss to reach an agreement. They agreed there were five dimensions including active safety warning, attention state, acceleration and deceleration behavior, sharp turning behavior and car-following behavior. Then 28 features were selected from the five dimensions.

2.3 Using the Explainable Features to Establish an Accident Prediction Model

In order to achieve better robustness, the number of features must be reduced further. We calculated the IV (Importance Value) to choose the more relevant feature [3]. We selected a total of eight features based on the criterion of selecting the feature with the highest IV value in each category. The value of eight features were transformed into WOE (Weight of Evidence) value which were used to build the binary classification model with the same standard of measurement. From the result we got the coefficient of each feature.

The coefficient were important because they were needed for the calculation of safety score. We then validated the model through AUC value. The AUC values for the previous month and the following month were 0.75 and 0.72 respectively which were considered acceptable [4].

2.4 Establishing a User-Friendly Safety Score

"y(x)" was the probability that the sample was predicted to be 1,"1 − y(x)" was the probability that the sample was predicted to be 0. The "odds" or "y(x)/1 − y(x)" was the ratio of accident rate to non-accident rate.

$$\begin{aligned} odds &= \frac{y(x)}{1-y(x)} \\ &= \left(e^{a_1}\right)^{x_1} \times \left(e^{a_2}\right)^{x_2} \times \ldots \left(e^{a_n}\right)^{x_n} \times e^b \end{aligned} \tag{1}$$

x_1, x_2, …, x_n was the value of WOE which was the feature after discretization transformation and a_1~a_n is coefficients. The calculation formula of odds was obtained by substituting the coefficient:

$$\begin{aligned} odds = 1.0089 \times 1.4589^{\text{dec3-2-woe}} \times 1.9338^{\text{acc3-1-woe}} \times \\ 1.4412^{\text{st3-2-woe}} \times 2.2853^{\text{zgc3-woe}} \times 2.7437^{\text{AEB-woe}} \times \\ 2.2526^{\text{HOD-woe}} \times 1.8626^{\text{DMS-woe}} \times 1.5123^{\text{FCW-woe}} \end{aligned} \tag{2}$$

We used a linear regression formula to convert odds into easy-to-understand score:

$$\text{Score} = \text{A} - \text{B} \times \text{odds} \tag{3}$$

"A" and "B" were constants. We got the A and B values according to the needs of the score distribution. Finally, each driver could get two sets of scores, that were total score and different driving behavior scores.

From the eight features we could realize short distance from the vehicle in front, urgent acceleration and deceleration, and sharp turning had strong correlation with accidents, as well as attention status and hands-off the steering wheel. These six behaviors were the key behaviors leading to accidents. The driver's six driving behavior scores were calculated from formula (3) except car-following score. The car-following score was calculated from scores of zgc3, FCW and AEB.

We used a user-centered design approach to develop such a tool. The results were conveyed to the drivers in a way that was easy to understand.

3 Results

3.1 Explainable Features Extracted

Among the on-board features, AEB has the strongest correlation, followed by urgent acceleration, sharp turning, urgent deceleration, FCW, HOD, DMS, and the longitudinal car-following (Table 1).

Table 1. Features sorted based on IV values

Dimension	Category	Feature	IV
Active safety warning	AEB	**AEB**	**0.1904**
Acceleration and deceleration behavior	Acceleration	**acc3-1**	**0.1415**
		acc2-1	0.1361
		acc3-2	0.1353
		acc2	0.1137
		acc3	0.1089
		acc1	0.089
Sharp turning	Sharp turning	**st3-2**	**0.123**
		st2-1	0.1008
		st2	0.0752
		st3	0.0562
		st3-1	0.056
		st3	0.0267
Acceleration and deceleration behavior	Deceleration	**dec3-2**	**0.1198**
		2-Dec	0.1122
		dec2-1	0.0801
		3-Dec	0.0748
		dec3-1	0.0708
		1-Dec	0.0701
Active safety warning	FCW	**FCW**	**0.1182**
Attention status warning	HOD	**HOD**	**0.0985**
	DMS	**DMS**	**0.0696**
Car-following behavior	Car-following	**zgc3**	**0.0097**
		zgc2	0.0057
		zgc1	0.0026
		cgc3	0.0008
		cgc2	0.0007
		cgc1	0.0001

3.2 Accident Prediction Model

A binary classification model was established to quantitatively evaluate the accident risk of each driver and passed the validation (Table 2).

Table 2. Logit Regression Results

Dep. Variable:		label		No. Observations:		142480
Model:		Logit		Df Residuals:		142471
Method:		MLE		Df Model:		8
Date:		Wed, 15 Feb 2023		Pseudo R-squ.:		0.1546
Time:		18:25:29		Log-Likelihood:		−83496
converged:		True		LL-Null:		−98759
Covariance Type:		nonrobust		LLR p-value:		0.000
	coef	std err	z	P > |z|	[0.025	0.975]
const	0.0089	0.006	1.480	0.000	−0.003	0.021
dec3-2	0.3777	0.016	22.924	0.000	0.345	0.410
acc3-1	0.6595	0.013	52.338	0.000	0.635	0.684
st3–2	0.3655	0.016	22.914	0.000	0.334	0.397
zgc3	0.8265	0.042	19.640	0.000	0.744	0.909
AEB	1.0093	0.011	87.814	0.000	0.987	1.032
HOD	0.8121	0.018	44.207	0.000	0.776	0.848
DMS	0.622	0.021	29.138	0.000	0.580	0.664
FCW	0.4136	0.017	24.261	0.000	0.380	0.447

3.3 The Calculation and the Interface of the Safety Score

Scoring rules were obtained by calculating the accident rate odds. Two sets of scores were got. The car could convey it in a way that was easy for drivers to understand through the interface (Table 3).

Table 3. The results conveyed to drivers(example)

Score basis	Shown to driver	
	total score: 70	better than 50% drivers
zgc3, FCW, AEB	car-following score: 65	better than 45% drivers
acc3-1	urgent acceleration score: 77	better than 54% drivers
dec3-2	urgent deceleration score: 80	better than 60% drivers
st3-2	sharp turning score: 60	better than 47% drivers
DMS	attention status score: 68	better than 50% drivers
HOD	hands-off score: 70	better than 50% drivers

4 Discussion

Because the cause of the accident was not only human factors, but also the factors of the vehicle itself, as well as the factors of scene and road conditions, other traffic participants, traffic management, etc. And although there were literatures on human factors showed that gender, age, driving age, cognitive ability, attitude, personality traits, etc. can significantly affect driving behavior [5], it was difficult to collect data on these factors because of the principle of privacy protection and minimizing the disturbance to users. If only human behaviors were taken into account without other factors, the final effect would be limited. Therefore, the next task will be establishing a complete set of assessment system consisting of vehicle safety assessment, road safety assessment, scene safety assessment, etc., to comprehensively consider the safety score. Only after trying to break through the bottleneck in other aspects can the effect of safety score be further improved.

5 Conclusion

In this study, we made an initial step by using real vehicle recording data to establish a safety score that is continuous, explainable and predictive of accidents. We hope the drivers can use this can of feedback to improve their driving awareness.

Acknowledgment. This study was supported by the National Natural Science Foundation of China (Grant No. T2192932).

References

1. Third Global Ministerial Conference on Road Safety. Stockholm Declaration. Stockholm, Sweden (2020)
2. Huang, C., Hang, P., Hu, Z.X., Lv, C.: Collision-probability-aware human-machine cooperative planning for safe automated driving. IEEE Trans. Veh. Technol. **70**, 9752–9763 (2021)
3. Mays, E., Lynas, N.: Credit Scoring for Risk Managers: The Handbook for Lenders. CreateSpace Independent Publishing Platform (2011)
4. Fawcett, T.: An introduction to ROC analysis. Pattern Recogn. Lett. **27**, 861–874 (2006)
5. Wang, X.: Traffic Safety Analysis Shanghai. Tongji University Press (2022)

eXtended Reality: Design, Interaction Techniques, User Experience and Novel Applications

A Hybrid Method Using Gaze and Controller for Targeting Tiny Targets in VR While Lying down

Kouga Abe[1(✉)], Hironori Ishikawa[2], and Hiroyuki Manabe[1]

[1] Shibaura Institute of Technology, Tokyo 135-8548, Japan
ma22009@shibaura-it.ac.jp, manabehiroyuki@acm.org
[2] NTT DOCOMO, Kanagawa 239-8536, Japan
ishikawahiron@nttdocomo.com

Abstract. Virtual reality (VR) head-mounted displays (HMDs) can be used in a variety of body postures, including standing, sitting, and lying down (supine). If VRHMD can be used effectively even from the supine position, it will not only allow bedridden people to comfortably access VR content, but also evolve VRHMDs into familiar devices that can be used in any body position, like smartphones. Though existing interaction methods for VR, such as moving the controller in the air, are assumed to be used while standing or sitting, the gaze input interface is a promising method that is available while supine. However, there are some issues unique to gaze input. It is unsuitable for fine pointing because the estimated gaze position movers continually, even if the user tries to gazes at a particular target. We propose a hybrid method that uses both gaze and the controller to overcome this issue. The proposed method combines controller rotation, a single button, and gaze input from an eye tracker. An experiment is conducted to compare three methods: the proposed method, a method using only gaze, and a method using only the controller. The experiment included the task of clicking tiny buttons that required high pointing resolution. The results show that when the eye tracker works as intended, the proposed method has an input speed almost equal to or faster than the method that uses only the controller, and it is superior to the method that uses only the eye tracker.

Keywords: Virtual Reality · Head-mounted display (HMD) · Eye gaze input · Body posture

1 Introduction

New content for VR and the metaverse is being developed every year. The number of VRHMD owners accessing VR space is also growing, with research[1] showing that one VRHMD product, the Oculus Quest 2, is estimated to have sold 15 million units by June 2022. Users of VR content are also increasing, with RecRoom, a

[1] https://uploadvr.com/quest-2-sold-almost-15-million-idc/.

C. Stephanidis et al. (Eds.): HCII 2023, CCIS 1836, pp. 139–146, 2023.
https://doi.org/10.1007/978-3-031-36004-6_19

game in the genre known as VRSNS, seeing a tenfold increase in users over the past three years[2]. As the number of users of VR content and VRHMDs continues to increase, it is expected that more users will use VRHMDs, in various postures such as sitting and lying down (supine), rather than just the standing position. By allowing VRHMDs to be used in both supine and standing positions, it can become a familiar device that supports any body position, like a smartphone.

Common computer interaction methods include those based on touch screens [10], trackballs, and hand gestures [14]. The typical interaction techniques for VRHMDs are controller tracking, hand tracking, and raycasting from the VRHMD. Most, including ray-casting input from the VRHMD [9], require physical user movement for interaction. While these work well while standing, the users face some difficulties while supine. Since the supine posture limits the user's physical movements, and most interaction techniques depend on physical movements, the posture decreases interface performance. In fact, the authors confirmed that pointing methods using conventional VR controllers incur the problem of reduced input speeds when used while supine [2]. On the other hand, eye gaze input [4] can be used without hand or head movements. It could be suitable as an interface technique especially for supine posture use.

There are models of VRHMDs that have built-in eye-tracking sensors and they could be useful tools for VR use while supine. However, such sensors make it difficult for the user to select small targets. To address this issue, we propose a hybrid interaction method that combines eye tracking and VR controller rotation for VR while supine.

2 Related Work

2.1 Eye Gaze Input

Gaze input incurs the Midas touch problem [4]. The simplest input approach is to use dwell time [15]. However, this approach has a disadvantage that input speed is determined in large part by the set dwell time; short dwell times can easily lead to misjudgments. One approach to avoid the Midas touch problem with eye-tracking alone is to use eye movements, such as saccades, in which the eyes move at high speed to look at a target [13]. As a method to solve the Midas touch problem using only eye gaze without using dwell time, Pallavi et al. proposed the method called DualGaze [11]. This is an interaction method in which a button called a "flag" is displayed next to an interactive object when the user's line of sight touches it, and the user moves his or her line of sight to that button to select the object. The Midas touch problem can be eased by supplementing gaze with other devices. An example is MAGIC [16] proposed by Morimoto et al. This method first realizes coarse pointing by gaze input and then performing fine pointing through use of an input device such as a trackball. Thammathip et al. describe a technique using head rotation to solve the Midas touch problem. Called Nod and Roll [12], it determines pointing by eye gaze and

[2] https://steamcharts.com/app/471710.

nodding movements of the HMD. Strictly speaking head rotation is not eye gaze, but it works similar to eye gaze. Kwon et al. proposed PillowVR [9], a method for manipulating the user interface while supine that uses head movements to control the playback position of VR video.

2.2 User Interaction While Supine

There have been several studies on human-computer interaction while supine. Keskin et al. presented examples of how hand gesture-based techniques can help patients who need to be stationary, such as in hospital or rehabilitation center, to communicate [8]. Kai et al. proposed a method that allows bedridden patients to operate drones using their line of sight [5]. PillowVR [9] mentioned below is also one example. In our previous research [1], we investigated the differences eye trackers made on VRHMD performance when used while supine. The results of the experiment showed that more than half of the subjects showed significant improvements in performance while supine. However, one problem we observed during the experiment was that the subject's gaze was never steady, which made it difficult for the user to select small targets. In addition, the displayed gaze point may be slightly off the actual gaze position, and this could cause problems.

2.3 Combining Eye Gaze with VRHMD

Kakinuma et al. describe an experiment on a pointing method that combined gaze with the angle of the VR controller and touchpad input [6]. The results showed that using the VR controller in combination with eye gaze input reduced fatigue compare to eye-gaze input alone, while pointing speed nearly matched that of the VR controller alone. They also proposed a method that switched the input method from eye-gaze input to VR controller rotation input only while the trigger button was pressed [7]. However, the problem is that moving the controller while holding down the controller's trigger button, or requiring additional controls such as sticks, increases the complexity of operation.

3 Proposed Method

In this paper, we propose a method that captures the user's gaze by the VRHMD's built-in eye tracker, angle data from the VR controller, and a single button input. The basic operation is to alter the tracking beam emitted in the frontal direction of the VRHMD according to the orientation of the controller (see Fig. 1). Four vectors are used to calculate the pointing position. First, the controller difference vector v3 is calculated, which is the controller's current vector v2 minus the controller's reference vector v1. Next, the controller difference vector v3 is multiplied by a sensitivity value. The pointing position is calculated by combining this value with the "pointing reference vector v4," which extends from the HMD in the frontal direction. RayCast is used to determine the hit of a ray on a button. Sensitivity was set to 0.5 in the current setup. The controller

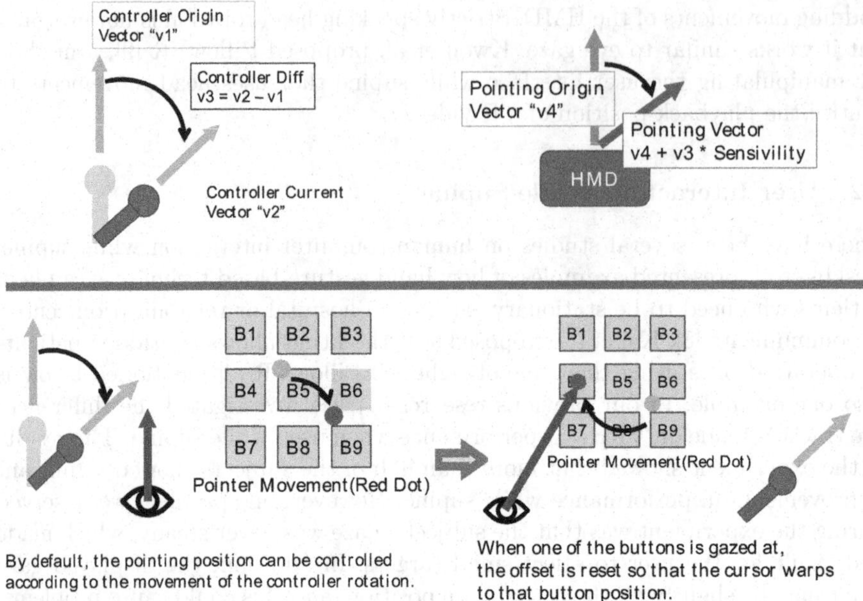

Fig. 1. Diagram showing how the method works. The rotation vector of the controller multiplied by the sensitivity is added to the pointing origin vector and this vector is taken as the pointing target. The offset is also reset when the line of sight comes in contact with the interactive object.

buttons were used to confirm pointing accuracy. From these points, our method seems a combination of head-based pointing, e.g. [9], and fine adjustment by the controller.

The gaze data from the eye tracker is used to automatically reset the pointing position offset as follows; when the gaze point hits a button or other object, the pointing position offset is changed to the button, regardless of the actual direction of the controller. Note that if the gaze is fixed on the object for more than 0.5 s, it is recognized as the gaze hits the object. The fine adjustment by the controller is triggered by the user's intentional button press in the existing method [7]. The advantage of using a switchable pointing technique is that rough pointing can be done by eye tracking with fine pointing done by the controller. However, requiring another operation while pressing a button would be complicated. Compared to existing methods, the proposed method does not require the user's intentional actions to switch pointing methods, which simplifies the operation and could improve input speed. In addition, by using the eye tracker only to reset the pointing position offset, it is possible to suppress the effect of gaze position uncertainty on pointing.

4 User Study

4.1 Setup

In the experiment, we used an experimental application to test how well the proposed method performs when used supine, compared to input using only VR controllers or eye gaze input. The subjects were four university students enrolled at the Shibaura Institute of Technology. VIVE Pro Eye and VIVE Controller were used in the experiment. Unity2019 4.31f1 was used to develop the experimental application. The application displays buttons 1 through 9 and a four-digit number (see Fig. 3). The experiment consisted of the subject pressing the number buttons specified by the numbers displayed to enter the same four-digit number displayed on the screen. The four-digit number and the nine buttons were displayed 1.5 m in front of the HMD, with button spacing of 5 cm. Each button was a 3 cm squares, which is relatively small compared with general buttons used in VR. Interacting anywhere other than the button will not cause an error, but if the wrong button is selected, an error was recorded. The numbers on the screen are normally white, but change to green as each digit is entered, even if the wrong number is selected. This makes it impossible for the subject to explicitly confirm whether or not the number entered was correct or incorrect. After entering four digits, the displayed four-digit number changed to another random number and the entered number was also reset. The experiment examined three cases: the case with only the VR controller, only eye gaze input, and the proposed method. The VR controller-based method was used to manipulate the pointing reference position with six degrees of freedom. The subjects performed the experiment while were lying on their backs. Prior to the experiment, the interpupillary distance was adjusted and the eye tracker was calibrated using the calibration software included with the Vive Pro Eye. The task of inputting the four digit numbers was repeated for one minute of practice and five minutes of evaluation for each method, and data were collected on how often the numbers were entered and whether the user's inputs were correct. The order of the methods used in the experiment was different for each subject to reduce the learning effect. A one-minute rest period was provided for each method to suppress the effect of fatigue.

4.2 Result

Fig. 2 shows the number of inputs in 5 min for each subject. Only Subject A had very low scores for Eye Gaze and the proposed Controller + Eye Gaze method. This is because Subject A encountered significant problems with the eye tracker making normal operation impossible. Other subjects attained almost the same performance with Controller and Controller + Eye Gaze, regardless of Eye Gaze score. They recorded about 150 correct entries in 5 min. The proposed method achieved its highest score with Subject C. In terms of the number of incorrect entries, Subject B and Subject C recorded fewer incorrect entries with the proposed method than with the controller, while the reverse was true for the others.

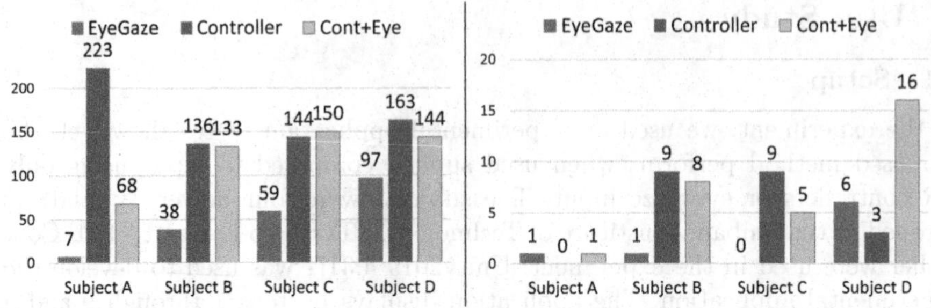

Fig. 2. The number of entries in 5 min for each subject. Left: data for correct entries only, right: data for incorrect entries.

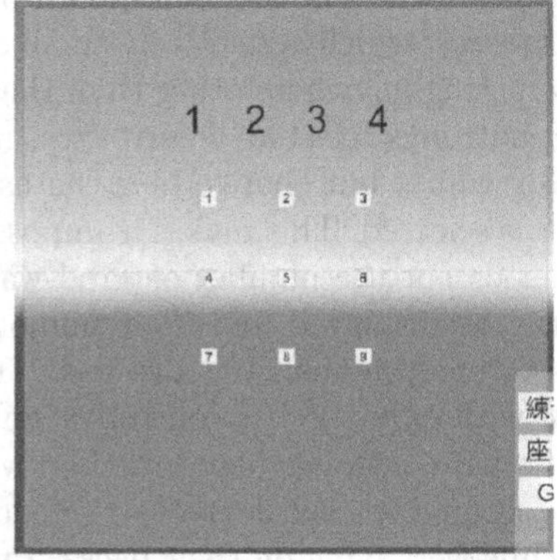

Fig. 3. Screen layout of the experimental application.

5 Discussion

First, we focused on input speed. For almost all subjects, the input speed of the proposed method almost matched that of the controller, while the input speed of the gaze-only method was lower. The proposed method allowed half of the subjects to decrease the number of errors compared to the controller only method. We confirmed the proposed method works appropriately in many cases; moving the cursor roughly by eye gaze, fine adjustment by the controller, and offset resetting by gaze. However, resetting the offset by gaze in the proposed method sometimes shifted the pointing to a target other than the intended target. This may have increased the number of errors for some subjects. It is important to find ways to reduce the number of errors in order to improve the proposed method. However, it should be noted that the present experiment had a small number of subjects and that these results may vary depending on the pointing task and conditions used. Moreover, in this experiment, the target size was set at 3 cm, and further research is needed to determine what target size is optimum when the proposed method is used.

In this experiment, we used a rather widely spaced button layout (see Fig. 3). As a result, we were able to confirm that unintentional resets do not occur° However, there is a possibility that unintentional resets may occur with tighter key layouts, such as a QWERTY keyboard. At the same time, increasing the number of targets may increase the number of incorrect pointing attempts. Therefore, it is necessary to experiment with tighter target layouts. In addition, it is necessary to determine optimum sensitivity values for achieving the best typing speed and number of misses.

While we currently intend to develop the proposed method to suit average people, it has already been shown that providing the VR experience to people who are bedridden is beneficial. For example, Gerber et al. studied the effects of visual stimulation via VRHMD on patients in intensive care units and other facilities who were unable to move their bodies freely [3]. They reported visual stimulation with VRHMD is useful because of its relaxing effect. We believe our method would also support a wide range of people.

6 Conclusion

In this study, we proposed a method suitable for small target selection in VR applications, especially those used while supine. Experiments were conducted to see how well the proposed method performed compared to other methods. As a result, it was confirmed that the proposed method can provide almost the same input speed as the controller, even for small targets, when the eye tracker is working properly. Since there are still some issues, e.g. some subjects had a very high number of errors with the proposed method, further research is needed.

References

1. Abe, K., Ishikawa, H., Manabe, H.: Eye gaze input performance when using VRHMD with eye tracker while lying down (written in Japanese). In: Proceedings of INTERACTION 2023, pp. 497–501 (2023)
2. Abe, K., Manabe, H.: Proposal of a method for comfortable text input while lying down using a VR controller (written in in Japanese). In: Proceedings of INTERACTION 2022. pp. 784–787 (2022)
3. Gerber, S.M., et al.: Visuo-acoustic stimulation that helps you to relax: a virtual reality setup for patients in the intensive care unit. Sci. Rep. **7**(1), 13228 (2017). https://doi.org/10.1038/s41598-017-13153-1
4. Jacob, R.J.K.: What you look at is what you get: eye movement-based interaction techniques. In: Proceedings of the SIGCHI Conference on Human Factors in Computing Systems, pp. 11–18. CHI 1990, Association for Computing Machinery, New York, NY, USA (1990). https://doi.org/10.1145/97243.97246
5. Kai, Y., et al.: Evaluation of a remote-controlled drone system for bedridden patients using their eyes based on clinical experiment. Technologies. **11**(1) (2023). https://doi.org/10.3390/technologies11010015, https://www.mdpi.com/2227-7080/11/1/15

6. Kakinuma, I., Komiyama, S.: A study on 2D pointing method using gaze and a controller device in VR (written in Japanese). The 18th Forum on Information technology(FIT2019) Proceedings 3, pp. 281–286 (2019)
7. Kakinuma, I., Komiyama, S.: The effect of using a controller to adjust gaze pointing in VR space (written in Japanese). Trans. Human Interface. **23**(1), 89–100 (2021). https://doi.org/10.11184/his.23.1_89
8. Keskin, C., Balci, K., Aran, O., Sankur, B., Akarun, L.: A multimodal 3d healthcare communication system. In: 2007 3DTV Conference, pp. 1–4 (May 2007). https://doi.org/10.1109/3DTV.2007.4379488
9. Kwon, D., Choi, H., Jun Cho, H., Lee, J., Kim, G.: PillowVR: virtual reality in bed. In: Proceedings of the 25th ACM Symposium on Virtual Reality Software and Technology. VRST 2019, Association for Computing Machinery, New York, NY, USA (2019). https://doi.org/10.1145/3359996.3365029
10. Lee, S., Zhai, S.: The performance of touch screen soft buttons. In: Proceedings of the SIGCHI Conference on Human Factors in Computing Systems, pp. 309–318. CHI 2009, Association for Computing Machinery, New York, NY, USA (2009). https://doi.org/10.1145/1518701.1518750
11. Mohan, P., Goh, W.B., Fu, C.W., Yeung, S.K.: Dualgaze: addressing the Midas touch problem in gaze mediated VR interaction. In: 2018 IEEE International Symposium on Mixed and Augmented Reality Adjunct (ISMAR-Adjunct), pp. 79–84 (2018). https://doi.org/10.1109/ISMAR-Adjunct.2018.00039
12. Piumsomboon, T., Lee, G., Lindeman, R.W., Billinghurst, M.: Exploring natural eye-gaze-based interaction for immersive virtual reality. In: 2017 IEEE Symposium on 3D User Interfaces (3DUI), pp. 36–39 (2017). https://doi.org/10.1109/3DUI.2017.7893315
13. Rayner, K.: Eye movements in reading and information processing: 20 years of research. Psychol. Bull. **124**(3), 372–422 (1998)
14. Rehg, J., Kanade, T.: Digiteyes: vision-based hand tracking for human-computer interaction. In: Proceedings of 1994 IEEE Workshop on Motion of Non-rigid and Articulated Objects, pp. 16–22, November 1994. https://doi.org/10.1109/MNRAO.1994.346260
15. Sibert, L.E., Jacob, R.J.K.: Evaluation of eye gaze interaction. In: Proceedings of the SIGCHI Conference on Human Factors in Computing Systems, pp. 281–288. CHI 2000, Association for Computing Machinery, New York, NY, USA (2000). https://doi.org/10.1145/332040.332445
16. Zhai, S., Morimoto, C., Ihde, S.: Manual and gaze input cascaded (magic) pointing. In: Proceedings of the SIGCHI Conference on Human Factors in Computing Systems, pp. 246–253. CHI 1999, Association for Computing Machinery, New York, NY, USA (1999). https://doi.org/10.1145/302979.303053

Don't Miss the Fairytale Forest for the Trees: Integrating Location-Based Authoring in Interactive Story Development for Immersive Augmented Reality

Jessica L. Bitter(✉) and Ulrike Spierling

Hochschule RheinMain, Wiesbaden, Germany
{jessicalaura.bitter,ulrike.spierling}@hs-rm.de

Abstract. Authoring in location-based Interactive Storytelling (IS) for Augmented Reality (AR) requires a combination of, at one end, process-intensive development of assets and complex conditional storylines on a desktop computer, and at the other end, the creation of situational aspects in the field. While there are occasional solutions for hand-held AR to support such a distributed workflow, the topic has not yet been explored in depth for immersive AR using a head-mounted display. We therefore propose to combine an existing IS-tool with Unity3D to bridge this gap. We describe our development process and discuss our findings. Early results show that the combination of Ink and Unity3D has the potential to support authors by providing a more integrated development workflow as they alternate between editing phases on the desktop computer and on-site.

Keywords: Location-based Interactive Storytelling · Immersive Augmented Reality · Authoring Tool

1 Introduction

When creating a location-based Interactive Storytelling (IS) experience for Augmented Reality (AR), storytellers are faced with the task to not only create storylines connected to physical places, but also with the creation of content like 3D models and sound. While the development of storylines with potentially complex conditional structures, and the creation of assets, preferably takes place at the office desk [1], situated aspects, including testing, must take place at the final location. The necessary changes between the two work places impedes an integrated workflow [2], and the possibility to change story conditions on-the-fly. In the specific case of head-mounted (HMD)-AR, app development is a time-consuming and processing-intensive procedure, which further constricts quick iterative cycles between development and testing on a target device such

C. Stephanidis et al. (Eds.): HCII 2023, CCIS 1836, pp. 147–154, 2023.
https://doi.org/10.1007/978-3-031-36004-6_20

as the MS HoloLens 2. In existing immersive AR app creation projects, story development was usually completed before asset creation and implementation began, with no iterative evolution of storylines along with other components of the application [1,3]. We hypothesize that this gap between developing on a computer and testing on-site on a HoloLens can be mediated by a combination of already existing tools. The aim of this work is therefore to determine how to combine an Interactive Storytelling authoring tool and an Augmented Reality authoring tool to support creative authors in the making of storylines alongside asset creation, implementation and testing on-site on immersive AR devices. To this end, the method of Design Science Research [4,5] was followed. We built artifacts to learn which functionalities are needed for a tool, because this process allowed us to identify the specifically needed toolkit for our problem.

2 Related Work

When researching authoring for Interactive Storytelling in immersive AR, only few works can be found. A general review of authoring tools for IS including those for handheld (HHD) AR can be found in [6].

The requirements of authoring for locative Interactive Storytelling in immersive AR, however, have been explored to some extent [7,8], as they also partially apply to authoring location-based handheld AR IS applications. The project 'Spirit', for example, focused on the implementation of tools that support location-based IS authoring [2]. With their tools, the story and interactions could be tested on-site on the target device with prototypical assets, which allowed for iterative cycles.

Location-based IS in immersive AR targeting HMDs so far includes research projects that focus foremost on the usability of the new medium, but not on authoring. For example, Jin et al. [1] built an IS application for the MS HoloLens 1. Their authoring process resembled a sequential model with few iterative cycles. Most importantly, they finished the story creation before starting the implementation. Similarly, in the case of Hammady et al. [3], the story development was completed before the implementation began. Both projects used the game engine Unity3D to build their immersive AR apps. AR-able game engines like Unity3D are complex to understand for creative non-programmers. Recent approaches to reduce the complexity of developing immersive AR Unity3D for non-programmers do not focus on storytelling or IS in particular [9].

The combination of a game engine with an IS tool has recently been mostly used to include a dialog system in a video game being developed, for example with Yarnspinner [10]. Similary, Rotach [11] combined Twine with Unity3D to create an immersive VR application. While his approach allows for iterations in general, the storyline is not developed in iterative cycles alongside the VR scenes and assets. However, none of these advances aimed at supporting an authoring process for (immersive) AR.

This shows that there is a gap in tools that support the development of IS in immersive AR. As a result, the story development is mostly finished before the implementation starts. With our work, we offer a first step to close this gap.

3 Concept

3.1 Tool Selection

The Microsoft HoloLens 2 was our target device. Our aim was to create a tool which allows for iterative cycles that span from story concept to testing on-site with the HoloLens and back, as described by Spierling [12], because the effect of the story can only be experienced and evaluated on-site, by means of the target device [8]. Our tool should shorten iterative cycles without limiting the creative work of authors, as was tried by Kampa et al. [2], to make it possible to iterate story conditions while the app is running on the target device. The aim is to let authors create a story while getting to know the targeted experience, instead of writing at a desk remote of the planned location.

There is a plethora of tools accessible for both IS and AR [13]. Shibolet's [13] review of IS-tools served as a starting point to select a tool for our experiment. After an extensive analysis of their listed tools, and one additional tool called YarnSpinner, we found that Ink, Twine and YarnSpinner were applicable, as all three are still maintained, offer extensive documentation and an API for a game engine.

Two of the most popular game engines that support immersive AR development currently are Unreal Engine and Unity3D. In comparison to Unreal Engine, Unity3D has the greater community and is more beginner friendly [14]. As our three chosen IS authoring tools are also compatible with it and we already had previous experience with the tool, we chose Unity3D as our AR game engine.

3.2 Scenario Creation

By means of a sample story, we wanted to determine how certain steps in the authoring process could be simplified. We expected that the story would be fleshed out during the iterations. Therefore, it was the aim to create a placeholder scenario on the basis of which the process of authoring with the combination of Unity3D and each of the three IS-tools could be described and evaluated later on.

For this purpose, we chose the fairy tale Little Red Riding Hood as the base of our story, as it is popular in the community of IS [7,15]. The story was transformed to be interactive by providing a choice, and would be displayed on a virtual canvas in front of the user. It was re-written in the second person singular, placing the player in the role of Little Red Riding Hood. The user could choose between different paths that lead from the defined home to grandmother's hut, and choose whether to pick up virtual flowers located in the physical space. Depending on the action chosen, the wolf may or may not succeed in eating the grandmother and Little Red Riding Hood. Figure 1 shows the final structure of the story after our development iterations.

The short experience is designed to take place in the premises of the university. Opening physical doors to leave or enter the fictional houses aims at creating a connection between the real world and the virtual content. Figure 2 shows the floor plan of the area where the game would be playable.

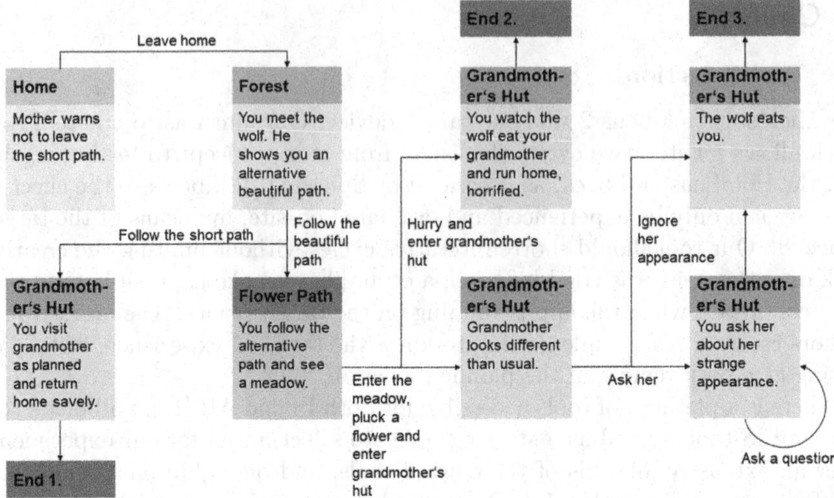

Fig. 1. Story structure of the scenario. Boxes show the locations of the story events, differentiated by color. Arrows show the possible actions and choices by the user and indicate the consequential story events.

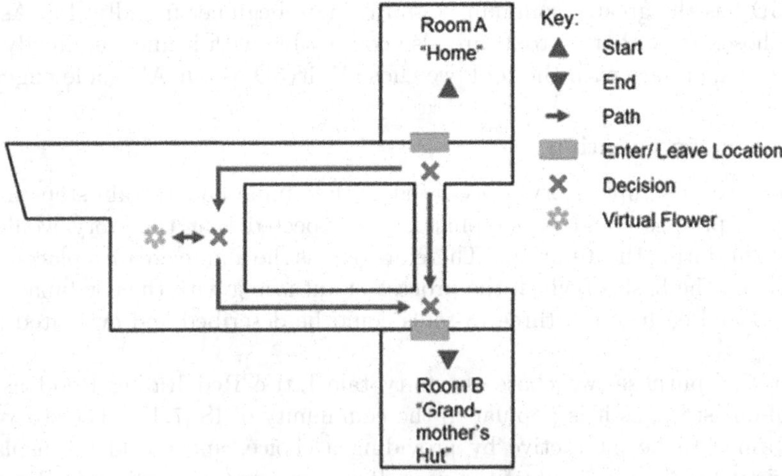

Fig. 2. Location-based story structure. The fictional locations are represented in the physical world. The story starts in room A, from which two different paths can be taken.

4 Development

We implemented three versions, each combining the Unity3D game engine once with Twine, Yarnspinner and Ink. For each of our tool combinations, we wrote the same textual story in the IS-tool and implemented the 3D assets in Unity3D.

We also used Unity3D to build the three applications for the HoloLens, which we then tested on-site. Only during the tests did we find out which functionalities we needed in order to facilitate authoring as much as possible directly on the Hololens.

Tool Interaction: When picking up the virtual flower, the textual story should proceed. For this purpose, a bridge between Unity3D and the IS-tool needs to be set up initially. The flower is only toggled when the user decides to follow the path suggested by the wolf. It will vanish when the user has 'plucked' it, and then a prompt for the necessary interaction to progress the story will be shown.

HoloLens Integration: The usability and experience of an AR app cannot be simulated in Unity3D. Therefore, repeated deployment to the HoloLens during the development is necessary. For example, we tested different 3D objects for the flowers, and incrementally added prompts for the user when to interact with the 3D objects to proceed the story.

Story Flow and Interaction Control: Concerning interactions with the story, we decided to use so-called colliders to register when a user has entered a specific story area, e.g., Grandmother's Hut. For testing the sizes and positions of the colliders, the app again needed to run on the HoloLens. While authoring the positions for the first time on the HoloLens 2, we noticed that accidental collisions with the colliders already change the story state. To prevent that from happening during the authoring phase, an 'authoring mode' must be implemented in which the story progression is deactivated and author-specific tasks are possible, like positioning a collider or exchanging story conditions. By having a dedicated authoring mode and a dedicated story mode for users, we can make sure that users do not accidentally modify story elements.

Storytelling Functions: To prevent deploying the whole application to the HoloLens again every time a word or a story branch was changed, we added a function that enabled to exchange the story text at run-time on the HoloLens. With this function, the textual story elements, including conditions for 3D objects, could be changed in Unity3D and then copied to the HoloLens, where an author could access the changed story in the running application. In the future, a function to directly write text in the running application on the HoloLens via a Bluetooth keyboard could be added.

5 Evaluation and Discussion

5.1 Tool Comparison

The three tools have a different focus each. While YarnSpinner is mainly designed as a dialogue system, Twine focuses on the visual development of branching storylines and Ink tries to bridge the gap between story and dialogue flow in collaboration with a game engine. In Table 1, we have listed their strengths and weaknesses based on the identified functionalities needed for our tool, as described in the previous section.

Table 1. Comparison of the features of Twine, YarnSpinner and Ink.

Category	Twine	YarnSpinner	Ink
Can be used iteratively in concert with Unity3D	Yes	Yes	Yes
Updating the Story in Unity3D	Inconvenient	Easy	Easy
Exchanging values of variables between Unity3D and the IS-tool	**Yes**, usable in any C#-script, simple object referenced call	**Yes**, usable in any C#-script, needs 'using Yarn.Unity' and 4 lines of code	**Yes**, usable in story script, needs getter and setter and extra function, 10+ lines of code
Exchanging text choices with interaction with GameObjects	**No**; Twine needs a named link to call after an interaction with a GameObject	**Yes**, does not require displaying the links as text	**Yes**, does not require displaying the links as text
Changing the story without deploying to the HoloLens	**Limited**; possible without build and deploy, but not on the HoloLens 2	**Limited**; possible without build and deploy, but not on the HoloLens 2	**Yes**, possible without build and deploy and to alter story on the HoloLens 2, but in JSON format

5.2 Discussion

We have seen that all three implemented tools are effective, whereas Ink showed to be the most efficient of the tools. It offers the best suited functionality for this use case, which also can be expanded. The authoring process based on the combination of Ink and Unity3D showed to be modular and iterative (see Fig. 3). It allows to iterate on the story throughout the whole development process. For example, the test of different paths and the length of a story section like the first encounter with the wolf, could be tested and evaluated quickly. Meanwhile, related projects completely implemented planned stories and evaluated the application as a whole at the end, where changes are more time-consuming and expensive. This shows that the demonstrated approach of combining Unity3D with Ink has potential to support the authoring process for Interactive Storytelling in immersive AR, which also meets the tool requirements described in Sect. 3.1.

Still, our toolset relies on development on a computer. While it would be difficult to transfer the whole authoring process including asset creation to the HoloLens, there could be more functionalities developed to broaden the authoring on the target device: For example, the implementation of automated declaration of story variables, as well as a simulation of the physical location in Unity3D could be helpful. A tool to add or change 3D assets on the HoloLens and a list from which the author could choose interactions to reduce coding are also part of future work.

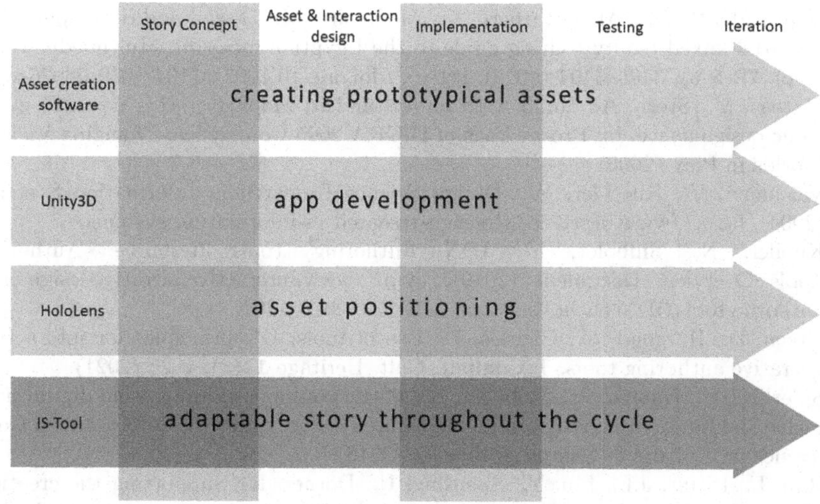

Fig. 3. Story development process based on our tool combination.

6 Conclusion

This work helped to understand current issues in authoring for Interactive Storytelling for Immersive Augmented Reality. Our work contributes results from a reflection on an authoring process for creative authors, where the story can be iterated throughout the whole authoring process. The aim was to create a combination of tools that allow to author a story and its belonging assets on the target device to give authors more possibilities to integrate necessary changes on-site directly. We showed that the combination of Ink and Unity3D has the potential to be such a supporting toolset.

The evaluation of our tools was done by one author. The findings are therefore subjective and serve as formative results. The tools are not yet fully developed to perfectly support authoring IS in immersive AR. In that regard, future work includes a more extensive user study of our tool based on Ink and Unity3D, as well as further work on our tool.

References

1. Jin, Y., Ma, M., Liu, Y.: Interactive narrative in augmented reality: an extended reality of the holocaust. In: Chen, J.Y.C., Fragomeni, G. (eds.) HCII 2020. LNCS, vol. 12191, pp. 249–269. Springer, Cham (2020). https://doi.org/10.1007/978-3-030-49698-2_17
2. Kampa, A., Spierling, U.: Smart authoring for location-based augmented reality storytelling applications. In: Eibl, M., Gaedke, M. (eds.) Lecture Notes in Informatics (LNI), vol. 275, pp. 915–922 (2017)

3. Hammady, R., Ma, M., Strathern, C., Mohamad, M.: Design and development of a spatial mixed reality touring guide to the Egyptian museum. Multimedia Tools Appl. **79**(5–6), 3465–3494 (2020). https://doi.org/10.1007/s11042-019-08026-w
4. Mateas, M., Stern, A.: Build it to understand it: ludology meets narratology in game design space. In: Proceedings of DiGRA 2005 Conference: Changing Views - Worlds in Play (2005)
5. Vaishnavi, V., Kuechler, W.: Design Science Research in Information Systems (2004). http://www.desrist.org/design-research-in-information-systems/
6. Knoller, N., Shibolet, Y.: IDN Authoring Tools Resource: Authoring Tools Overview Document (2019). http://www.interactivenarrativedesign.org/authoringtools/IDN-authoring-tools-DB-12.6.2018.pdf
7. Green, D., Hargood, C., Charles, F.: Use of tools: UX principles for interactive narrative authoring tools. J. Comput. Cult. Heritage **14**(3), 1–25 (2021)
8. Spierling, U., Kampa, A., Stöbener, K.: Magic equipment: integrating digital narrative and interaction design in an augmented reality quest. In: International Conference on Culture & Computer Science (2016)
9. Rau, L., Bitter, J.L., Liu, Y., Spierling, U., Dörner, R.: Supporting the creation of non-linear everyday AR experiences in exhibitions and museums: an authoring process based on self-contained building blocks. Front. Virtual Reality **3**, 955437 (2022)
10. Twin Stick: YarnSpinner for Unity Guide (2020). https://www.youtube.com/watch?v=CJu0ObGDQHY
11. Rotach, S.: Digital futures: Demokratie am Rande der technologischen Singularität: Implementierung eines Szenarios mittels immersiver Virtual Reality. Master's thesis, Züricher Hochschule für Angewandte Wissenschaften (ZHAW), Zürich (2020)
12. Spierling, U.: Authoring interactive narrative meets narrative interaction design. In: Hargood, C., Millard, D.E., Mitchell, A., Spierling, U. (eds.) The Authoring Problem. HCIS, Springer, Cham (2022). https://doi.org/10.1007/978-3-031-05214-9_8
13. Shibolet, Y., Knoller, N., Koenitz, H.: IDN Authoring Tools Resource: Appendix I: Tools Shortlist (2018). http://www.interactivenarrativedesign.org/authoringtools/appendix.pdf
14. Broll, W., Weidner, F., Schwandt, T., Weber, K., Dörner, R.: Authoring of VR/AR applications. In: Dörner, R., Broll, W., Grimm, P., Jung, B. (eds.) Virtual and Augmented Reality (VR/AR): Foundations and Methods of Extended Realities (XR), pp. 370–400 (2022)
15. Spierling, U., Iurgel, I.: Pre-conference demo workshop "little red cap": the authoring process in interactive storytelling. In: Göbel, S., Malkewitz, R., Iurgel, I. (eds.) TIDSE 2006. LNCS, vol. 4326, pp. 193–194. Springer, Heidelberg (2006). https://doi.org/10.1007/11944577_20

MRespond – An Innovative and Flexible MR Training System for First Responders

Elisabeth Broneder[1](✉), Christoph Weiß[1], Helmut Schrom-Feiertag[1], Jaison Puthenkalam[1], Valentin Miu[1], Georg Aumayr[2], Sofia Kirilova[2], and Daniela Weismeier-Sammer[2]

[1] AIT Austrian Institute of Technology GmbH, Vienna, Austria
elisabeth.broneder@ait.ac.at

[2] JOAFG Johanniter Österreich Ausbildung und Forschung gemeinnützige GmbH, Research and Innovation Center, Vienna, Austria
Georg.aumayr@johanniter.at

Abstract. First responders are often lacking opportunities to train for dangerous situations such as big fires or chemical accidents, because these scenarios are often either too dangerous to simulate in real life or associated with high costs or personnel expenditure. The MRespond project addresses this challenge by providing a Mixed Reality (MR) solution that allows first responders such as fire fighters or paramedics to train hazardous situations in a multi-story building. Virtual hazards such as fire or chemical substances can be blended into the real world. The MR system offers free movement of trainees within a multi-story building and an outdoor area. First responders can train with their usual equipment. Objects and equipment such as doors, fire nozzles or emergency manikins are tracked and integrated into the system, so that the trainees can interact with the training scenario as they are used to. Real objects can interact vith virtual objects so that e.g., the fire propagation changes by opening doors and windows. Virtual injuries can be projected onto real emergency manikins so that trainees can train triage scenarios and still have the tactile feedback if they e.g., apply a bandage. Further, an exercise instructor interface provides the possibility to adapt the scenario in real-time by e.g., placing fires or changing the vital parameters of a patient. Thus, MRespond offers a highly adaptable training system.

Keywords: Mixed Reality · Training · First Responders · User Interaction

1 Introduction

Particularly during the last decade [1], virtual and augmented reality has been used for training purposes in various domains and industries, such as medical [2, 3], aerospace [4, 5], workforce (vocational) [1, 6, 7], first responder [8, 10–12], CBRNE [9], and army training [13]. Reasons for the use of virtual or mixed reality simulations over traditional training methods include reduced cost [12, 14], increased safety [12, 15], higher immersion [8, 16], lower complexity [16], higher flexibility of training simulations [3], and lower equipment and human resource requirements [15].

C. Stephanidis et al. (Eds.): HCII 2023, CCIS 1836, pp. 155–162, 2023.
https://doi.org/10.1007/978-3-031-36004-6_21

These benefits are especially evident in the training of first responders, such as firefighters and paramedics. For paramedics, VR/AR training methods often use real manikins as a property for haptic feedback, which is overlaid with a virtual manikin [8, 17–21]. For example, in [8], the manikin is overlaid with a virtual body with wound textures to simulate various injuries. Existing methods either require the manikin to be fixed throughout the exercise after initial calibration [21, 22], use manikin trackers to allow the body to move without changing the limb pose [8, 18, 19], or use real actors [23].

In firefighter training, trainees usually need to navigate a larger area, while avoiding or extinguishing various hazards [16]. VR is often used for this purpose, since it is expensive and dangerous to use real fire for training [12, 14, 16]. Since existing VR-based simulations have a limited physical training area [10–12, 24–26], augmented and mixed reality has more recently been used for first responder training [27, 28], including our work.

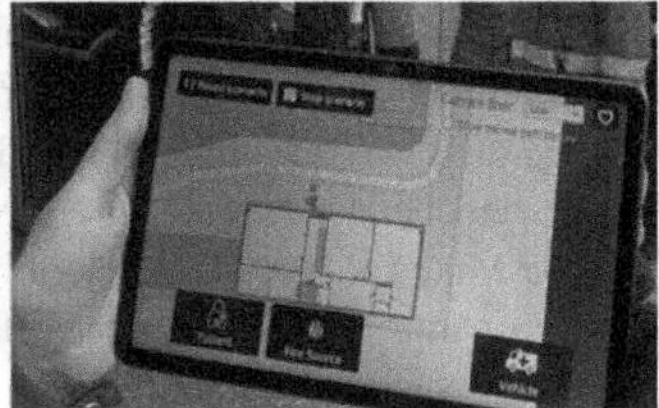

Fig. 1. First responders are testing the MRespond training system

The MRespond mixed reality (MR) system allows for combined training of paramedics and firefighters, with multiple training manikins and virtual fire and smoke at configurable locations in a real building. The use of the Magic Leap One (ML1) MR glasses with inside-out optical tracking allows for a large, theoretically boundless physical training area, which in our case comprises multiple floors of a building. Initial alignment and pose drift correction is done automatically through optical markers at known locations on the building walls.

Virtual manikins are used with configurable appearances, injuries and behaviors, overlaid onto the pose-tracked real manikins. Use of real actors is also supported. Both the fire and virtual manikins can be updated before or during the simulation by multiple training supervisors, who can observe the trainees and simulation in real-time using a tablet, showing a top-down view of the entire simulation area. Together with the large-area mixed reality space comprising multiple building floors, this makes a realistic simulation of the entire first responder process possible (see Fig. 1).

2 The MRespond System

The MRespond MR training system offers the possibility for interorganizational training with fire fighters and paramedics. The training system can be used by a flexible number of users but is only tested with 8 users simultaneously – 2 operational forces from the fire brigade, 2 paramedics, 1 commander on-site per organization, and two trainers. Figure 2 shows an overview of the system. The trainees can freely move within a multistory building and the enclosing outdoor area. Virtual hazards like fires or chemical substances can be blended into the real world. The commander on-site of the fire brigade can assess the situation from outside (A) and deploy the operational forces. The fire fighters can dissolve dangerous situations with their real-life equipment with attached sensors. In our tests virtual fires can be extinguished using a fire hose with a tracked nozzle to regulate the virtual water flow (B). The trainers can see the location of all trainees at all times, can place virtual hazards and control health parameters and virtual injuries during the training (C). For training triage situations, virtual injuries are projected onto emergency manikins so that the paramedics can treat wounds on the manikin as they are used to (D). The training scenario also adapts to the behavior and actions of the trainees – e.g., opening windows and doors influence the spread of fire and smoke.

Fig. 2. Overview of the elements of the MRespond training system. (A) Commander on-site, (B) firefighters inside the building (C) trainer, (D) paramedics on the triage site

The MRespond system consists of an MR application, a server, and an exercise instructor interface.

2.1 Mixed Reality Trainings Application

The trainees are equipped with the Magic Leap One (ML1) MR glasses as well as a GPS antenna and mobile phone for outdoor tracking. The MR application displays the virtual elements within the training scene, handles the localization of the trainees and the detection and tracking of emergency manikins. For the correct positioning of virtual elements in the scene, the trainees need to be tracked with high accuracy indoor and outdoor. For indoor tracking an approach is used that combines the internally used SLAM algorithm from the glasses with a marker tracking approach that uses April tag markers to determine the position and rotation of users within the building. This information is forwarded to the server which distributes it to the exercise instructor interfaces for map updates. To determine the location in relation to the building, the measurements of the building and the location of the markers have to be known. For this a 3D model of the building was generated via a 3D scan. The position of doors and windows in the building is also provided to allow for an accurate simulation of the fire and smoke distribution within the scenario. Outdoor tracking is achieved using a high-precision GNSS system and merging this position data with the marker-based approach, while rotation data needs to be derived by tracking AprilTag markers placed in the outdoor area. To allow interaction with the real environment, algorithms were developed to track the emergency manikins and the fire nozzle. Emergency manikins are tracked using a set of April tag markers on a T-Shirt to get the position and orientation of the manikin's torso. Inertial sensors on upper body, head and limbs are used to get the movements of the body's joints in relation to the torso. Additional sensor data (nozzle valve state, door/window states via home automation) is collected on the server and distributed to the devices of the trainees and instructors.

2.2 Exercise Instructor Interface

The exercise instructor interface enables the trainer to place virtual hazards like fire and chemical substances. Apart from that, health parameters and virtual injuries can be configured for each patient. This can also be changed during the training. Thus, actions of the trainees influence the progression and effects of the injuries. The location and viewing direction of the trainees, the location of detected victims as well as the spread of virtual hazards – in this case fire – can be seen on a map. All changes made in the exercise instructor interface are sent to the server and from there distributed to the other devices.

2.3 Server

The server retrieves the data from the exercise instructor interface and the MR app. The server calculates the state changes of the training scenario over time, which includes the fire propagation and location of manikins and trainees. The server gets data from window and door sensors as well as from the fire nozzle and the inertial sensors of the manikin and distributes the simulation state to all devices. All inputs within the exercise instructor interface are also distributed via the server. The server shows the same UI as the exercise instructor interface – so everything can also be configured directly on the server.

3 Design and Development Methodology

The project follows a user centered design process involving the end-users during the entire design and development cycle. In the first project phase, first responders have generated a set of requirements for the MRespond training system as well as training scenarios and objectives. A focus was put on the cooperation between different first responder organizations (fire fighters, paramedics, armed forces). For testing the training system with first responders, two scenarios have been defined: a large building fire and a chemical accident with hazardous materials. The goal was to provide an integrated exercise for fire fighters and paramedics and to train the handover of casualties and wounded. Identified training objectives for the fire fighters are the detection and identification of threats and training of standard operation procedures (SOPs). The focus for the paramedics is on the triage of victims and interaction with fire fighters as well as advanced life support. The development of the MRespond system and the corresponding training scenarios is accompanied by two scenario tests and three field trials. Within the scenario tests key elements of the system are demonstrated to end-user organizations and future functionalities are drafted based on their feedback. During the field trials the training system is tested by first responders in the defined training scenarios. Data collection in these trials follows the approach of participating observation. The results of the second scenario test are described in Sect. 4.

For the exercise instructor interface, in an initial UX workshop, the processes were discussed with the participants from the perspective of trainers, which were represented using personas. In collaboration with the end users, user stories were defined for the scenario setup, adding hazards, parametrization of victims, training execution and debriefing. For this purpose, the essential interaction steps were defined in chronological order on a digital whiteboard. Furthermore, for each of these interaction steps, suitable interaction modalities were defined based on current expectations, to ensure easy handling and higher user acceptance. Afterwards, an initial mockup of a possible interaction concept was discussed with the end users, in order to guide the design of the system. These concepts were then further refined in iterative online sessions based on end-user feedback (see Fig. 3). Furthermore, a common nomenclature and a set of relevant KPIs (for assessing the trainee performance) were defined.

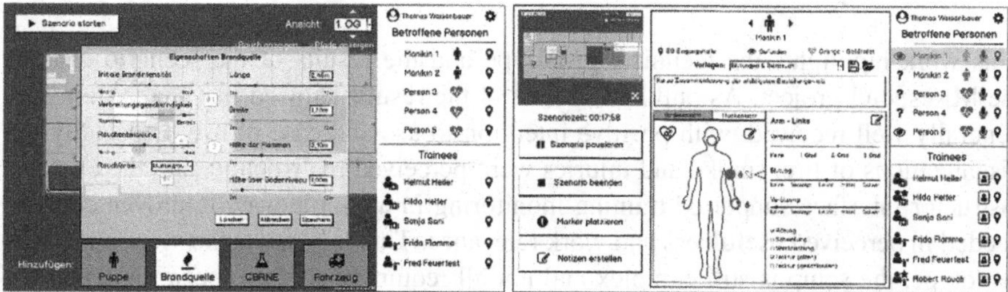

Fig. 3. Second iteration of the exercise instructor interface for firefighters (left) and medical first responders (right).

4 Results

In the second scenario test, a prototype of the MRespond system was set up at the fire brigade in Linz. Two fire fighters and seven paramedics evaluated the system in a fire scenario and provided feedback via observations, questionnaires, and interviews. In this scenario, the fire fighters had to rescue two injured people from a burning building and extinguish the fire, while the paramedics had to examine and treat the injured. The MR training system was evaluated using the Technology Acceptance Model 2 (TAM2) [29] questionnaire, which measures various factors related to technology acceptance. The items were measured on a 7-point Likert scale ranging from 1 (strongly disagree), over 4 (neutral) to 7 (strongly agree). The results indicate that participants had a positive intention to use the technology, with a mean value of 4.7 (standard deviation SD = 1.6). Participants also found the system easy to use, mean value of 4.7 (SD = 1.4). Perceived usefulness had a neutral mean value of 3.7 (SD = 0.9), indicating that participants saw some value in the technology, but not as much as its ease of use. The image of the technology had a mean value of 3.8 (SD = 1.3), indicating that participants had a mixed perception of the system's image. The job relevance of the technology had a neutral mean value of 3.4 (SD = 1.2), indicating that participants saw the technology as somewhat relevant to their job. Output quality had a mean value of 3.8 (SD = 1.3), indicating that participants were generally satisfied with the quality of the system's output. Finally, result demonstrability had a positive mean value of 4.6 (SD = 1.5), indicating that participants saw the results of the system as visible and easy to demonstrate.

Overall, the results suggest that the mixed reality training system was generally well-received by participants, with a positive intention to use and ease of use. However, there is room for improvement in perceived usefulness and job relevance, which were rated as neutral. In summary, the MR visualizations were realistic, and the exercise instructor interface supported the training monitoring well. Weak points were the stability of the MR app and partly inaccurate tracking which made the overlays inaccurate. The evaluation results provided important feedback which will be used for further development and evaluation cycles.

5 Summary and Outlook

This work highlights the technical prototype and the results of the scenario tests of the MRespond project. As outlined in Sect. 4 the results showed that the system was generally well received, with positive intention to use and ease of use. Especially the visualizations of fire, smoke and injuries were perceived realistically, and the exercise instructor interface supported training monitoring in a simple way. Improvements are needed in perceived usefulness and work relevance. This is because the system is a first prototype, the setup is still complex and not all requirements have been implemented yet. The feedback from the scenario tests will be incorporated into the three field trials at the fire brigade in Linz, where first responders from the fire brigade, Red Cross and armed forces will test the system together in the test scenario of a building fire and a chemical accident.

Acknowledgment. The project MRespond is funded by the Austrian security research program KIRAS of the Federal Ministry for Finance.

References

1. Chiang, F.K., Shang, X., Qiao, L.: Augmented reality in vocational training: a systematic review of research and applications. Comput. Hum. Behav. **129**, 107125 (2022)
2. Moglia, A., Ferrari, V., Morelli, L., Ferrari, M., Mosca, F., Cuschieri, A.: A systematic review of virtual reality simulators for robot-assisted surgery. Eur. Urol. **69**(6), 1065–1080 (2016)
3. Ricci, S., Calandrino, A., Borgonovo, G., Chirico, M., Casadio, M.: Viewpoint: virtual and augmented reality in basic and advanced life support training. JMIR Serious Games **10**(1), e28595 (2022)
4. Valentino, K., Christian, K., Joelianto, E.: Virtual reality flight simulator. Internetworking Indones. J. **9**(1), 21–25 (2017)
5. Oberhauser, M., Dreyer, D.: A virtual reality flight simulator for human factors engineering. Cognit. Technol. Work **19**(2–3), 263–277 (2017). https://doi.org/10.1007/s10111-017-0421-7
6. Lee, I.J.: Applying virtual reality for learning woodworking in the vocational training of batch wood furniture production (2020). https://doi.org/10.1080/10494820.2020.1841799
7. Lavrentieva, O., Arkhypov, I., Kuchma, O., Uchitel, A.: Use of simulators together with virtual and augmented reality in the system of welders' vocational training: past, present, and future, February 2020
8. Girau, E., et al.: A mixed reality system for the simulation of emergency and first-aid scenarios. In: Proceedings of the Annual International Conference of the IEEE Engineering in Medicine and Biology Society, EMBS, pp. 5690–5695, July 2019
9. Altan, B., et al.: Developing serious games for CBRN-e training in mixed reality, virtual reality, and computer-based environments. Int. J. Disaster Risk Reduct. **77**, 103022 (2022)
10. Braun, P., Grafelmann, M., Gill, F., Stolz, H., Hinckeldeyn, J., Lange, A.-K.: Virtual reality for immersive multi-user firefighter training scenarios. Virtual Real. Intell. Hardw. **4**(5), 406–417 (2022)
11. Capasso, I., Bassano, C., Bracco, F., Solari, F., Viola, E., Chessa, M.: A VR multiplayer application for fire fighting training simulations. In: De Paolis, L.T., Arpaia, P., Sacco, M. (eds.) Extended Reality. XR Salento 2022. LNCS, vol. 13445, pp. 130–138. Springer, Cham (2022). https://doi.org/10.1007/978-3-031-15546-8_11
12. Tao, R., Ren, H., Zhou, Y.: A ship firefighting training simulator with physics-based smoke. J. Mar. Sci. Eng. **10**(8), 1140 (2022)
13. Mao, C.C., Chen, C.H.: Augmented reality of 3D content application in common operational picture training system for army. Int. J. Hum. Comput. Interact. **37**(20), 1899–1915 (2021)
14. Xie, B., et al.: A review on virtual reality skill training applications. Front. Virtual Real. **2**, 49 (2021)
15. Jamah, A., Alnagrat, A., Ismail, R.C., Zulkarnain, S., Idrus, S.: Virtual transformations in human learning environment: an extended reality approach. J. Hum. Centered Technol. **1**(2), 116–124 (2022)
16. Engelbrecht, H., Lindeman, R.W., Hoermann, S.: A SWOT analysis of the field of virtual reality for firefighter training. Front. Robot. AI **6**, 101 (2019)
17. Vaughan, N., John, N., Rees, N.: ParaVR: paramedic virtual reality training simulator. In: Proceedings - 2019 International Conference on Cyberworlds, CW 2019, pp. 21–24, October 2019
18. Buttussi, F., Chittaro, L., Valent, F.: A virtual reality methodology for cardiopulmonary resuscitation training with and without a physical mannequin. J. Biomed. Inform. **111**, 103590 (2020)
19. Bench, S., Winter, C., Francis, G.: Use of a virtual reality device for basic life support training: prototype testing and an exploration of users' views and experience. Simul. Healthc. **14**(5), 287–292 (2019)

20. Leary, M., et al.: Using an immersive virtual reality system to assess lay provider response to an unannounced simulated sudden cardiac arrest in the out-of-hospital setting. Simul. Healthc. **14**(2), 82–89 (2019)
21. Liyanage, S.U., Jayaratne, L., Wickrarnasinghe, M., Munasinghe, A.: Towards an affordable virtual reality solution for cardiopulmonary resuscitation training. In: 26th IEEE Conference on Virtual Reality and 3D User Interfaces, VR 2019 - Proceedings, pp. 1054–1055, March 2019
22. Vaughan, N., Gabrys, B., Dubey, V.N.: An overview of self-adaptive technologies within virtual reality training. Comput. Sci. Rev. **22**, 65–87 (2016)
23. Help, V.R.: First Aid Course VR - Szkolenie w Wirtualnej Rzeczywistości (2022). https://4helpvr.com/en/oferta/first-aid-course-vr/. Accessed 12 Dec 2022
24. Grabowski, A.: Practical skills training in enclosure fires: an experimental study with cadets and firefighters using CAVE and HMD-based virtual training simulators. Fire Saf. J. **125**, 103440 (2021)
25. Jeon, S., Paik, S., Yang, U., Shih, P.C., Han, K.: The more, the better? Improving VR firefighting training system with realistic firefighter tools as controllers. Sensors **21**(21), 7193 (2021)
26. Lorenzis, F.D., Prattico, F.G., Lamberti, F.: Work-in-progress - blower VR: a virtual reality experience to support the training of forest firefighters. In: Proceedings of 2022 8th International Conference of the Immersive Learning Research Network, iLRN 2022 (2022)
27. Ingrassia, P.L., et al.: Augmented reality learning environment for basic life support and defibrillation training: usability study. J. Med. Internet Res. **22**(5) (2020)
28. Leary, M., McGovern, S.K., Balian, S., Abella, B.S., Blewer, A.L.: A pilot study of CPR quality comparing an augmented reality application vs. a standard audio-visual feedback manikin. Front. Digit. Health **2**, 1 (2020)
29. Venkatesh, V., Davis, F.: A theoretical extension of the technology acceptance model: four longitudinal field studies. Manag. Sci. **46**, 186–204 (2000). https://doi.org/10.1287/mnsc.46.2.186.11926

Multimodal Interactive System for Visualization of Energy Data in Extended Reality (XR) Settings

Margarita Chikobava[1(✉)], Anton Moisieiev[1], Thomas Achim Schmeyer[1], Peter Poller[1], Matthieu Deru[1], Alassane Ndiaye[1], Albert Klimenko[1], Christian Braun[2], Jörg Baus[1], and Boris Brandherm[1]

[1] Department of Cognitive Assistants, German Research Center for Artificial Intelligence, 66123 Saarbrücken, Germany
{margarita.chikobava,Albert.klimenko}@dfki.de
[2] Stadtwerke Saarlouis, 66740 Saarlouis, Germany

Abstract. The municipal utility supervises all aspects of the city's public utilities, e.g., the power grid. For example, power grid maintenance requires the technician to know where underground cables are installed while having their hands free for maintenance work. Using an immersive headset such as HoloLens provides a technician with these capabilities. This contribution presents DENKI (Data, Energy, Network, Knowledge, Interaction). This HoloLens application supports technicians of the municipal utility "Stadtwerke Saarlouis GmbH" with a detailed overview of the equipment, its utilization, and possibilities to investigate malfunctions. We will exemplify some app functions.

Keywords: Mobile HCI · UX (User Experience) · AR · MR · HoloLens · multimodal Interaction · Smart Grid

1 Introduction

The municipal utility supervises all city's public utilities, including water supplies and the power grid. Power grid maintenance requires the technician to know where the underground cables run while having their hands free to perform manual tasks, such as road marking. Using an immersive headset such as HoloLens provides a technician with these capabilities.

This contribution presents DENKI (Data, Energy, Network, Knowledge, Interaction). This HoloLens application provides technicians of the municipal utility "Stadtwerke Saarlouis GmbH" with a detailed overview of the equipment, its utilization, and possibilities to investigate malfunctions. It is achieved by leveraging multiple data sources and incorporating this knowledge into the application as a digital twin of the power grid. It describes all the components and sensors and integrates sensor values, forecasts, and status data [1]. The DENKI app enables interaction with the digital twin via speech, gaze, and gesture [2, 3]. The DENKI app overlays the digital twin in-situ over its real-world

C. Stephanidis et al. (Eds.): HCII 2023, CCIS 1836, pp. 163–168, 2023.
https://doi.org/10.1007/978-3-031-36004-6_22

(and sometimes non-visual) counterparts and simplifies tasks like malfunction detection or infrastructure expansion planning (see Fig. 1).

Besides describing DENKI's architecture and its current implementation state, we also address the challenges when using HoloLens. These include using the indoor-designed HoloLens outdoors. Furthermore, the integration of cardinal directions, geo coordinates, and large-scale visualization is crucial.

Fig. 1. Visualization of the power grid cables in the DENKI app

2 Related Work

The research field of augmented reality's possibilities in visualizing energy systems and other underground public utilities is a promising area of modern research. In recent years, more and more developments and studies have appeared in this research field.

In 1998, [4] proposed using augmented reality and developing "stereo vision systems," imaging technologies, and specialized robotic vehicles for underground inspection and maintenance of pipelines. In the LARA project [5], the researcher developed hardware and software systems and integrated global navigation satellite systems, sensors, and geographic information systems (GIS) to depict underground utilities using augmented reality. The Project "Smart Vidente" [6] proposes a mobile platform built around a tablet computer to visualize, create and modify geospatial data representing real-world artifacts. A similar project [7] suggests using the Google Tango platform.

A recent study [8] examined 50 relevant papers both qualitatively and quantitatively. Most studies (73%) use tablets or smartphones to implement AR. According to the researchers, performance improvement through AR is the main acceptance factor, and non-technical aspects are the main reason for the rejection of AR. A study from 2008 [9] suggested see-through head-mounted displays to efficiently perform the required tasks, as the user can operate the AR system hands-free. However, it also acknowledged that the technical level at the time was insufficient to implement such a project. Among other things, the user had to carry around additional devices in a backpack, which limited the mobility of the system and thus made the work more cumbersome.

The above projects are like the DENKI project regarding the scope of tasks to be solved. But they differ in implementation and equipment. The DENKI project uses

Microsoft HoloLens – a next-generation platform with a see-through head-mounted display for augmented reality, facilitating user mobility. It overcomes performance issues of other systems. We prepared this hardware platform for outdoor use, significantly improving a user's performance issues seen in similar works. Additionally, the DENKI App provides a multimodal interaction via speech, gaze, and gesture, especially a convenient two-handed interaction. These are some innovative features in the field of underground infrastructure visualization.

3 Architecture and Current State of the Implementation

The DENKI applies to various use cases in utility management, engineering, and beyond. In this work, we showcase DENKI's usability through the power grid modeling of the 'Stadtwerke Saarlouis.' The DENKI builds on a multimodal interaction and presentation platform. Its generic platform design enables developers to implement different use cases, adapt the applications to other end devices, and transfer the concepts to other regions. The platform (see Fig. 2) consists of a geospatial data layer, several application-specific GIS layers, a content, data and services layer and a use case layer.

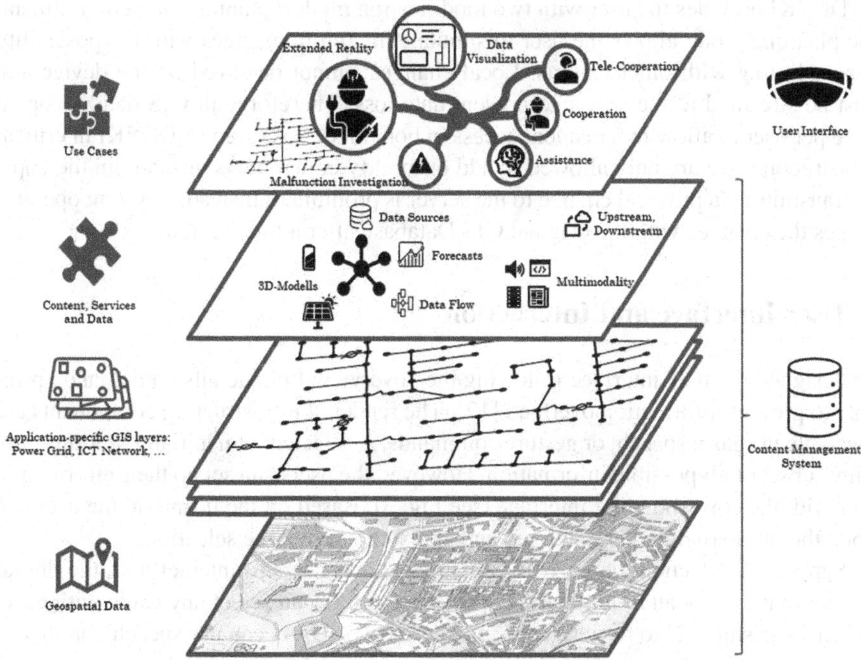

Fig. 2. The platform with geospatial data layer, several application-specific GIS layers, a content, data and services layer and a use case layer

Multimodal databases build the basis of the content management system and hold the relevant content for the respective layers and applications. The application-specific

GIS layers include, for example, a GIS database with the laid power and fiber optic lines and any empty pipes, the topology of the electricity network with information about line lengths and cross-sections, details about transformer stations, charging stations, and switch boxes, as well as the measurement sensors installed in these resources, data sheets and technical data for the assets and their components. The content, services and data layer, e.g., contain annotated 3D models of various assets, descriptions of the components and sensors and integrates sensor data (e.g., smart meter data), forecast data (e.g., day-ahead photovoltaic production forecast), and simulation data (e.g., simulated local grid status) [10]. Forecast and simulation data come from different projects like e.g. [1, 11]. The use case layer contains different uses cases like, e.g., tele-cooperation, data visualization, assistance or extended reality. The DENKI deploys with the HoloLens, e.g., the extended reality with data visualization and assistance.

The geospatial data layer provides data to enable the positioning of digital components relative to the user's position. First, it streams the user's coordinates and transcodes them in the format appropriate for the global coordinate system. Afterward, the system conducts the opposite transcoding: the received digital twin components are translated into the user's coordinate system and visualized. With this global coordinate system, the positioning layer can locate a digital twin infrastructure within a certain radius of the user's position.

DENKI provides the user with two modification modes: planning and commitment. The planning mode allows the user to simulate his future changes with the possibility of cooperating with other experts. Local changes cannot be saved on the device and must be streamed to the server to prevent data loss. Therefore, all GIS data is copied twice per user to allow independent access in both modes. As we use DENKI in critical infrastructure, we are only allowed to add or modify components virtually in the copy, but transmitting a physical change to the server is prohibited. Instead, a system operator merges the changes with the original GIS Database after a final review.

4 User Interface and Interaction

We designed the user interface following the "overview first, details on demand" principle to prevent information overload [12]. The rendered infrastructure components are selectable via gaze, speech, or gesture commands. A selected item initially presents only a tiny subset of all possible information. However, the users can set up their information filter with the corresponding interface (see Fig. 3). Based on the filtration, the user can group the infrastructure parametrized and apply changes to the selection.

Support of selection via gaze and gestures allows users to interact with the digital twin more naturally and intuitively. For instance, users can select any cable with gaze, speech, or gesture [2] to retrieve cable characteristics. Users can use speech commands to investigate/simulate actions before applying them to the power grid.

It also improves efficiency by allowing users to perform tasks faster with fewer errors. For instance, in the planning mode, users can look at cables of the type NAYCWY 3x150/150 and exchange all cables of this type with cables of the type NKBA 3x95 with one speech command. Selecting and manipulating cables based on other parameter selections is also possible, like all cables with a diameter in a specific value range.

Fig. 3. DENKI's UI elements: filtering menu (left) and cable information window (right)

DENKI with the layers, data, services for forecasting and simulation, its interaction capabilities can be seen as a Digital Twin [13].

5 Challenges

The biggest challenge we are facing during the development of DENKI is the integration of data from different sources. For instance, we have three coordinate systems to handle in visualization: geo position of the HoloLens Device – GPS coordinates expressed as the combination of latitude and longitude, GIS description of the power grid in the gaussian coordinate system and the internal coordinate system of the application. The limitation of this approach is the GPS sensor observation error, which can lead to a misplacement of the digital twin.

Using the mixed reality headset HoloLens outdoors presents a further challenge - bright sunlight makes 3D-Objects appear too transparent or even invisible. To see the holograms well, even under strong sunlight, we used sun protection film specially developed for HoloLens 2. We also investigated which colors are best suitable for the visualization of the digital twin under different lighting conditions.

Another challenging task was the visualization of cables with correspondence to their physical characteristics. Since the cables do not just form an angular and rigid network, most of the nodes were interpolated with a planar cubic Bézier curve. More precisely the rendering of the cable is divided into two steps: firstly, based on the measurement points a one-dimensional Bézier path is calculated. Lastly a 3-dimensional mesh is rendered around the Bézier path. The interpolation also helps to represent a more accurate model with less measure points. The main limitation of the current visualization is the missing information about cable intersections. Therefore, it is not possible to investigate which cable lies above which. However, after the deployment of DENKI into praxis, it will be possible to store this information too.

6 Conclusion and Future Work

In this work, we introduced DENKI – the application that is designed to support technicians and engineers of "Stadtwerke Saarlouis GmbH" in utility maintenance activities. We presented DENKI's architecture as well as the current state of the implementation.

By showcasing the various features and functionalities, we demonstrated the power grid maintenance use case and highlighted DENKI's scalability, adaptability, and flexibility, which make it suitable for a wide range of applications. Furthermore, we described the main challenges that arose during the implementation phase. As further research and development are conducted, we will evaluate DENKI with domain experts.

Acknowledgement. This work was supported by the Project "5G-Inno-SLS" funded by the German Federal Ministry for Digital and Transport (BMDV) under grant number 45FGU105 and the Project "GridAnalysis" funded by the German Federal Ministry for Economic Affairs and Climate Action (BMWK) under grant number 03EI6034D.

References

1. Brandherm, B., Deru, M., Ndiaye, A., et al.: Integration of renewable energies—AI-based prediction methods for electricity generation from photovoltaic systems. In: Barton, T., Müller, C. (eds.) Apply Data Science: Introduction, Applications and Projects, pp. 137–158. Springer Fachmedien, Wiesbaden (2023). https://doi.org/10.1007/978-3-658-38798-3_9
2. Poller, P., Chikobava, M., Hodges, J., et al.: Back-end semantics for multimodal dialog on XR devices (2021)
3. Prange, A., Chikobava, M., Poller, P., et al.: A multimodal dialogue system for medical decision support inside virtual reality. In: Proceedings of the 18th Annual SIGdial Meeting on Discourse and Dialogue. pp. 23–26 (2017)
4. Lawson, S.W., Pretlove, J.R.G.: Augmented reality for underground pipe inspection and maintenance. In: Telemanipulator and Telepresence Technologies V. SPIE, pp. 98–104 (1998)
5. Stylianidis, E., et al.: Augmented reality geovisualisation for underground utilities. PFG – J. Photogrammetry Remote Sens. Geoinf. Sci. **88**(2), 173–185 (2020). https://doi.org/10.1007/s41064-020-00108-x
6. Schall, G., Zollmann, S., Reitmayr, G.: Smart Vidente: advances in mobile augmented reality for interactive visualization of underground infrastructure. Pers. Ubiquitous Comput. **17**, 1533–1549 (2013). https://doi.org/10.1007/s00779-012-0599-x
7. Soria, G., Ortega Alvarado, L.M., Feito, F.R.: Augmented and virtual reality for underground facilities management. J. Comput. Inf. Sci. Eng. **18**, 041008 (2018). https://doi.org/10.1115/1.4040460
8. Kolaei, A.Z., Hedayati, E., Khanzadi, M., Amiri, G.G.: Challenges and opportunities of augmented reality during the construction phase. Autom. Constr. **143**, 104586 (2022). https://doi.org/10.1016/j.autcon.2022.104586
9. Schall, G., Mendez, E., Kruijff, E., et al.: Handheld augmented reality for underground infrastructure visualization. Pers. Ubiquitous Comput. **13**, 281–291 (2009). https://doi.org/10.1007/s00779-008-0204-5
10. Deru, M., Ndiaye, A.: Deep learning MIT TensorFlow, Keras und TensorFlow.js. Rheinwerke Computing (2022)
11. Schmeyer, T., Kiefer, G.-L., Brandherm, B., et al.: Assistance system for AI-based monitoring and prediction in smart grids (2023)
12. Shneiderman, B., Plaisant, C., Cohen, M., et al.: Designing the User Interface: Strategies for Effective Human-Computer Interaction, 6th Ed. CCE Fac Books Book Chapters (2016)
13. Botín-Sanabria, D.M., Mihaita, A.-S., Peimbert-García, R.E., et al.: Digital twin technology challenges and applications: a comprehensive review. Remote Sens. **14**, 1335 (2022). https://doi.org/10.3390/rs14061335

Motion as a Determinant of Presence in Immersive Virtual Reality

Andrew Dilanchian(✉), Michael Prevratil, and Walter R. Boot

Florida State University, Tallahassee, FL 32304, USA
dilanchian@psy.fsu.edu

Abstract. Presence, defined as the "sense of being there", is suggested to be the main facilitator of success in immersive virtual reality (IVR) interventions. While system factors (e.g., refresh rate, resolution, degrees of freedom) have been at the forefront of IVR and presence research, less attention is paid to how individual behaviors in an IVR experience may affect the degree of presence achievable. These differences in behavior may influence users' experience, independent of the IVR hardware or software. With that, this study investigated if a user's motion in an IVR experience, specifically user-initiated motion (UIM), could predict their self-reported presence scores. Eighty younger adults (22 male, 57 female, 1 non-binary) completed a 10-min IVR experience in Vesper Peak on the HTC Vive where they were asked to explore the environment. Motion data were collected via the pyopenvr package in which telemetry data of the headset were recorded. UIM was then calculated by first calculating the distance between two of these data points and then averaging the distance across each pair of points for the entire dataset. Presence was collected via the IGroup Presence Questionnaire (Cronbach's α = 0.87). 5 participants' data were removed due to corruption. A regression model was used to analyze UIM and presence scores. The overall model was significant ($R^2 = 0.147$, RSE = 5.561, $F(1,73) = 12.61$, $p < 0.001$), demonstrating that UIM could significantly predict presence. These results suggest that a user's behavior may influence feelings of presence.

Keywords: Virtual reality · Individual differences · Presence

1 Introduction

Immersive virtual reality (IVR) has shown great potential in supporting disseminatable and customizable interventions. In this paper, we define IVR as a head-mounted display system that provides a three-dimensional stereoscopic rendering of an otherwise two-dimensional virtual environment and allows for multiple degrees of freedom (DOF), commonly through motion-tracked sensors on the body. Examples of this technology are the *HTC Vive* and *Meta Quest* headsets. In both cases, users are immersed in a virtual world and are allowed six DOF (pitch, yaw, roll, forward or backward, left or right, and up or down) via tracked headsets and controllers.

C. Stephanidis et al. (Eds.): HCII 2023, CCIS 1836, pp. 169–175, 2023.
https://doi.org/10.1007/978-3-031-36004-6_23

1.1 IVR – Past and Present

While IVR research can be dated back to the early 1990s (Gigante 1993), the scalability of these interventions was concerning. Indeed, cost, comfort, and accessibility all played a role in precluding the technology's mass adoption. Current IVR systems have largely addressed these concerns: PC-bound headsets can provide a much higher fidelity experience than before. Additionally, all-in-one headsets (e.g., Meta Quest, HTC Vive Cosmos) provide a PC-bound IVR experience while staying wireless, reducing the overall cost of the system, and allowing a greater degree of comfort. With that, investigations into this medium for interventions and academic research have grown. Indeed, a wide variety of domains have adopted the use of IVR in their studies. The technology has been looked at for a large range of mental disorders (Freeman et al. 2017; Geraets et al. 2021), pain distraction and rehabilitation (Pittara et al. 2020; Chow et al. 2021). IVR and aging has also been largely investigated (Benham et al. 2019) with focuses on general health outcomes (Dermody et al. 2020), mobility and balance (Neri et al. 2017; Pacheco et al. 2020), and leisure and enrichment (Dilanchian et al. 2021; Kalantari et al. 2022; Baker et al. 2020; Thach et al. 2020). With the breadth of IVR research discussed, it is important to elucidate possible factors that may drive these observed outcomes.

1.2 Presence and IVR

Presence, defined as the "subjective sense of being in a virtual environment" (Schubert 2003), is a defining aspect of IVR. That is, while presence can be formed and maintained in technologies with lower DOF, IVR elicits significantly higher levels of presence (Wu et al. 2019). There is some promise in presence being a strong predictor of social and behavioral outcomes in IVR interventions (Kalantari et al. 2022; Dilanchian et al. 2021; Yang and Zhang 2022). Similarly, presence has been shown to predict the success of IVR-based exposure therapies (Gromer et al. 2019). Furthermore, an association between presence and performance has been shown in a study looking at subsequent task performance following IVR-based training (Grassini et al. 2020). Given the importance of presence in IVR-based activities, research into how presence is formed and maintained, and conversely how it is lost, has been at the forefront of literature. Design-focused research has been conducted looking at how properties of the IVR system (e.g., headset resolution, software fidelity, haptics, sound, etc.) may influence presence (Gibbs et al. 2022; Hvass et al. 2017; Newman et al. 2022; Stefan et al. 2021; Gonçalves et al. 2022; Kreimeir et al. 2019; Seltzer et al. 2019; Melo et al. 2022). Subject-level physiological factors have also been considered. Weech et al. (2019) examine the negative relationship between cybersickness and presence. Specifically, they posit that presence may protect a user from cybersickness in IVR experiences, although the directionality of this relationship cannot be discerned. Anxiety has also been investigated in its effects on presence (Riches et al. 2019; Diemer et al. 2015). While investigating subject-level physiological factors is important, of equal concern are subject-level behavioral factors -- these may elucidate why some users experience higher levels of presence than others (Dilanchian et al. 2021; Mitzner et al. 2021) on a level beyond hardware and physiological elements.

1.3 Motion and Its Influence on Presence

User motion (head, arm, and body movements) has been posited as a potential facilitator of successful IVR interventions (Pallavicini and Pepe 2020). Additionally, Venkatakrishnan et al. (2020) found that affording control over motion in a driving IVR environment resulted in significantly higher presence. Indeed, motion plays a crucial role in IVR methodologies across two aspects: 1.) users' motion in IVR may provide a window into assessing involvement, a known factor of presence (Schubert 2003) and 2.) motion becomes a necessary facet of an IVR experience when users are required to interact with the environment. With this, motion becomes a critical and inseparable aspect of IVR user as well as a factor that requires further investigation.

2 Protocol

The current paper aims to understand how people interact with IVR environments and how those interactions shape presence. That is, we argue that subject-level behavioral differences may have significant implications on the formation and maintenance of presence within IVR. We turn toward motion as this remains a lightly explored and inextricable aspect of IVR that may influence presence. Specifically, we examined user-initiated motion (UIM). We define UIM as visual changes of the environment directly resulting from a user's physical motion (e.g., a user turns their head, their vision turns with them). Our primary hypothesis was that users who had higher measurements of UIM would also report higher levels of presence in that they would be more involved and attentive to the experience. Additionally, we explored the relationship between UIM and cybersickness, a common side effect of IVR that results in a symptomatology like motion sickness (dizziness, nausea, headache, etc.), and presence and cybersickness as the literature suggests a negative relationship between the two (Weech et al. 2019).

2.1 Software and Equipment

An HTC Vive headset was used to administer the IVR experience. Headset location within the physical room was tracked via base stations located in two corners of the room. Location was tracked at a rate of 90Hz. This rate was chosen to match the refresh rate of the headset's displays. For the IVR experience, we chose *The Lab: Vesper Peak* as it has been used in the literature (Dilanchian et al. 2021) and shown to be a comfortable, non-goal oriented experience that provides a variety of interactions (playing with a robot dog, moving around a mountain side, throwing objects).

2.2 Participants

Eighty younger adults were recruited to participate in the study (22 male, 1 non-binary, 57 female). Our sample consisted of undergraduate psychology students at Florida State University enrolled in general and upper-level general psychology courses. Participants were given extra credit for their classes as compensation for participating in the study.

2.3 Methods

Prior to engaging with the IVR experience, participants were given a demographics survey and a virtual reality experience survey (VRET). The VRET gathered data on how familiar participants were with current IVR systems and applications. Participants were then familiarized with IVR using the *SteamVR Home* software. This is a free software that resembles a bedroom connected to an outdoor patio. Participants were familiarized with teleporting (a common locomotion technique in IVR experiences) and interacting with objects (grabbing, throwing, manipulating, etc.). Following this familiarization, participants entered *The Lab: Vesper Peak*. Participants were given ten minutes of free exploration and interaction with the experience. Specifically, participants were told to explore and interact, but there was no area nor object in which we directed them to. During this time, we collected UIM data by tracking headset location within the room. After the ten minutes, participants were asked to complete the IGroup Presence Questionnaire (IPQ, Schubert et al. 2001) and the Simulator Sickness Questionnaire (SSQ, Kennedy et al. 1993). Five participants' data were discarded due to corruption of the data file resulting in a total sample size of 75.

2.4 Analysis

To calculate UIM, we recorded headset location within the physical room at a rate of 90Hz. Then, we found the difference between each pair of coordinates. Finally, these pairwise differences were averaged for each individual participant, resulting in an average distance traveled per cycle, in meters (90 cycles per second). Figure 1 depicts a participant who had low UIM (top) compared to a participant with high UIM (bottom). With this, we conducted a regression analysis with UIM was the predictor and presence as the predictand (collected via the IPQ).

The overall model was significant (R^2 = 0.14, *RSE* = 5.56, $F(1,73 = 12.61$, $p < 0.001$). Additionally, we found the relationship between UIM and presence to be positive in that higher UIM resulted in higher reported presence levels (see Fig. 2). Next, we conducted a similar regression analysis with UIM as the predictor and cybersickness as the predictand (collected via the SSQ). The overall model was non-significant (R^2 = 0.002, *RSE* = 5.71, $F(1,73 = 0.15$, $p = 0.69$). This finding suggests that the degree of motion one may enact in an IVR environment has no bearing on their levels of cybersickness, although cybersickness levels were low overall ($M = 21.1$). Finally, we conducted a correlation analysis on presence and cybersickness as evidence suggests there to be a negative relationship (Weech et al. 2021). Contrary to this, we found no correlation between presence and cybersickness among our sample ($r = 0.09$).

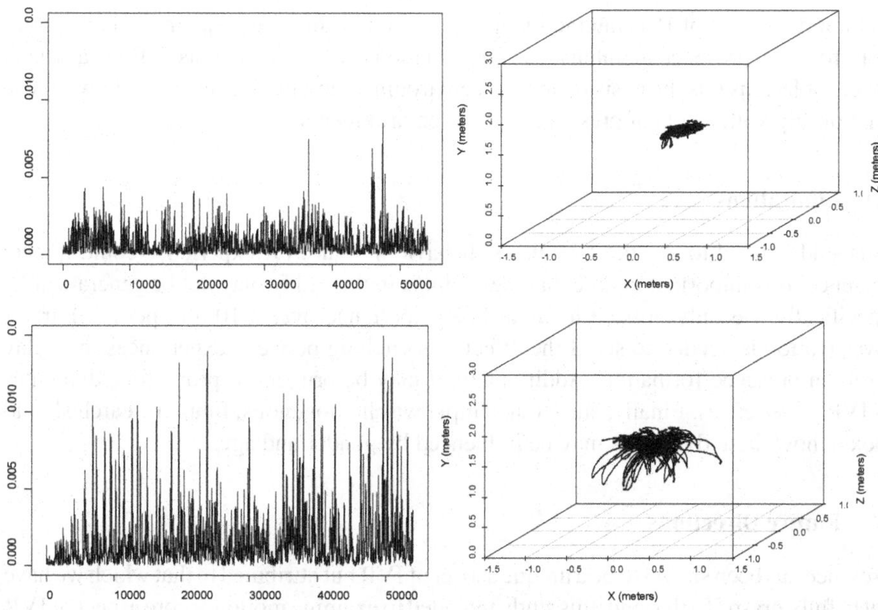

Fig. 1. UIM visualized as difference between two coordinates (left) and in 3D space (right). Top is an example of a high-UIM participant while bottom is an example of a low-UIM participant.

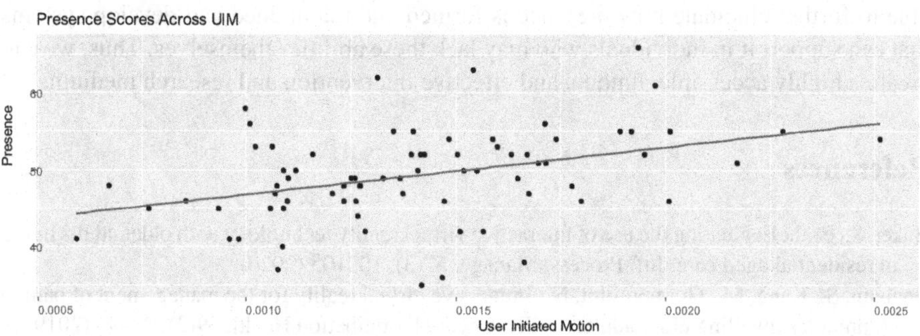

Fig. 2. Regression line of UIM across presence scores.

3 Conclusion

IVR has shown promise across a variety of intervention domains. Indeed, having a technology that can immerse users in a virtual world that provides a great deal of customizability in an easily disseminatable format yields highly novel interventions. A defining factor of IVR, presence has been shown to influence the outcome of various IVR-based measures and interventions. While a large breadth of research has been conducted on the technology's hardware and software aspects, as well as subject-level physiological differences, less attention has been paid to subject-level behavioral differences. This is an important facet of IVR interaction to understand as this may explain the large variations found in presence maintenance and formation across populations. UIM is a crucial aspect of IVR as it is the basis of any IVR environment interaction and may show a close relationship with levels of presence in these environments.

3.1 Limitations

This study aimed to explore how users' behaviors in an IVR experience could impact presence. It is important to note that the findings in this study may not be generalizable. Specifically, we only utilized a single IVR experience over a 10 min period. Further investigation is needed to see if the effect of switching between experiences may play a role in presence formation. Additionally, it may be prudent to probe time dynamics in IVR experiences. Finally, since our sample was homogenous, future research should look at how these dynamics may be influenced by gender and age.

3.2 Future Directions

Presence has been shown to be a unique aspect of IVR but attributed to that which we have yet to fully grasp. To that end, this study intended to examine motion, a core aspect of IVR interaction and, consequently, presence. Along with the limitations mentioned above, it may prove fruitful to continue examining these core facets of IVR interaction such as the factors posited by Schubert (2001). In starting from these base concepts, we may be able to further elucidate how presence is formed and maintained and develop systems that can support it in individuals who may lack these abilities themselves. Thus, we can create a highly accessible, unique, and effective intervention and research medium.

References

Baker, S., et al.: Evaluating the use of interactive virtual reality technology with older adults living in residential aged care. Inf. Process. Manage. **57**(3), 102105 (2020)

Benham, S., Kang, M., Grampurohit, N.: Immersive virtual reality for the management of pain in community-dwelling older adults. OTJR: Occup. Participation Health **39**(2), 90–96 (2019)

Chow, H., Hon, J., Chua, W., Chuan, A.: Effect of virtual reality therapy in reducing pain and anxiety for cancer-related medical procedures: a systematic narrative review. J. Pain Symptom Manage. **61**(2), 384–394 (2021)

Dermody, G., Whitehead, L., Wilson, G., Glass, C.: The role of virtual reality in improving health outcomes for community-dwelling older adults: systematic review. J. Med. Internet Res. **22**(6), e17331 (2020)

Diemer, J., Alpers, G.W., Peperkorn, H.M., Shiban, Y., Mühlberger, A.: The impact of perception and presence on emotional reactions: a review of research in virtual reality. Front. Psychol. **6**, 26 (2015)

Dilanchian, A.T., Andringa, R., Boot, W.R.: A pilot study exploring age differences in presence, workload, and cybersickness in the experience of immersive virtual reality environments. Front. Virtual Reality **2**, 736793 (2021)

Freeman, D., et al.: Virtual reality in the assessment, understanding, and treatment of mental health disorders. Psychol. Med. **47**(14), 2393–2400 (2017)

Geraets, C.N., Van der Stouwe, E.C., Pot-Kolder, R., Veling, W.: Advances in immersive virtual reality interventions for mental disorders: a new reality? Curr. Opin. Psychol. **41**, 40–45 (2021)

Grassini, S., Laumann, K., Rasmussen Skogstad, M.: The use of virtual reality alone does not promote training performance (but sense of presence does). Front. Psychol. **11**, 1743 (2020)

Gromer, D., Reinke, M., Christner, I., Pauli, P.: Causal interactive links between presence and fear in virtual reality height exposure. Front. Psychol. **10**, 141 (2019)

Hvass, J., Larsen, O., Vendelbo, K., Nilsson, N., Nordahl, R., Serafin, S.: Visual realism and presence in a virtual reality game. In: 2017 3DTV Conference: The True Vision-Capture, Transmission and Display of 3D Video (3DTV-CON), pp. 1–4. IEEE (2017)

Kalantari, S., et al.: Using immersive virtual reality to enhance social interaction among older adults: a multi-site study. arXiv preprint arXiv:2210.04954 (2022)

Kennedy, R.S., Lane, N.E., Berbaum, K.S., Lilienthal, M.G.: Simulator sickness questionnaire: an enhanced method for quantifying simulator sickness. Int. J. Aviat. Psychol. **3**(3), 203–220 (1993)

Kreimeier, J., et al.: Evaluation of different types of haptic feedback influencing the task-based presence and performance in virtual reality. In: Proceedings of the 12th ACM International Conference on Pervasive Technologies Related to Assistive Environments, pp. 289–298 (2019)

Melo, M., et al.: Immersive multisensory virtual reality technologies for virtual tourism: a study of the user's sense of presence, satisfaction, emotions, and attitudes. Multimedia Syst. **28**(3), 1027–1037 (2022). https://doi.org/10.1007/s00530-022-00898-7

Neri, S.G., et al.: Do virtual reality games improve mobility skills and balance measurements in community-dwelling older adults? Systematic review and meta-analysis. Clin. Rehabi. **31**(10), 1292–1304 (2017)

Newman, M.A.R.K., Gatersleben, B., Wyles, K.J., Ratcliffe, E.: The use of virtual reality in environment experiences and the importance of realism. J. Environ. Psychol. **79**, 101733 (2022)

Pacheco, T.B.F., de Medeiros, C.S.P., de Oliveira, V.H.B., Vieira, E.R., De Cavalcanti, F.A.C.: Effectiveness of exergames for improving mobility and balance in older adults: a systematic review and meta-analysis. Syst. Rev. **9**, 1–14 (2020). https://doi.org/10.1186/s13643-020-01421-7

Pallavicini, F., Pepe, A.: Virtual reality games and the role of body involvement in enhancing positive emotions and decreasing anxiety: within-subjects pilot study. JMIR Serious Games **8**(2), e15635 (2020)

Pittara, M., Matsangidou, M., Stylianides, K., Petkov, N., Pattichis, C.S.: Virtual reality for pain management in cancer: a comprehensive review. IEEE Access **8**, 225475–225489 (2020)

Riches, S., Elghany, S., Garety, P., Rus-Calafell, M., Valmaggia, L.: Factors affecting sense of presence in a virtual reality social environment: a qualitative study. Cyberpsychol. Behav. Soc. Netw. **22**(4), 288–292 (2019)

Schubert, T.W.: The sense of presence in virtual environments: a three-component scale measuring spatial presence, involvement, and realness. Z. für Medienpsychologie **15**(2), 69–71 (2003)

Schubert, T., Friedmann, F., Regenbrecht, H.: The experience of presence: factor analytic insights. Presence: Teleoper. Virtual Environ. **10**(3), 266–281 (2001)

Thach, K.S., Lederman, R., Waycott, J.: How older adults respond to the use of virtual reality for enrichment: a systematic review. In: Proceedings of the 32nd Australian Conference on Human-Computer Interaction, pp. 303–313 (2020)

Weech, S., Kenny, S., Barnett-Cowan, M.: Presence and cybersickness in virtual reality are negatively related: a review. Front. Psychol. **10**, 158 (2019)

Wu, T.L., Gomes, A., Fernandes, K., Wang, D.: The effect of head tracking on the degree of presence in virtual reality. Int. J. Human-Comput. Interact. **35**(17), 1569–1577 (2019)

Yang, S., Zhang, W.: Presence and flow in the context of virtual reality storytelling: what influences enjoyment in virtual environments? Cyberpsychol. Behav. Soc. Netw. **25**(2), 101–109 (2022)

Virtual Reality and the Interactive Design of Elevated Public Spaces: Cognitive Experience vs VR Experience

Ahmed Ehab(✉), Tim Heath, and Gary Burnett

Human Factors Research Group, University of Nottingham, University Park, Nottingham NG7 2RD, UK
ahmed.abdelsalam@nottingham.ac.uk

Abstract. VR and visualization are visual aids, but can give much more than sight, such as a wider sensation of being in the 3D world. For the past ten years, researchers and organizations have been trying to find ways to get the public more involved in social project design and execution. Technologies such as Visual Simulation (VS) and Virtual Reality (VR) could make it possible to provide final stakeholders and consumers with closer access to the design and implementation processes of social projects. This paper analyzed two recent developments in London, Sky Garden and Crossrail Place. The study investigates how technologies such as VR can enhance the design experience of elevated urban spaces. The main aim of this study is to explore the difference and similarities between human interaction in the real cognitive experience and the virtual world. The method used in this study is walk-long interviews with the visitors of both gardens and a VR exploratory experiment, followed by semi-structured interviews with the participants. This methodology brings the participant as an active element of the project, able to explore the space and propose changes.

The paper discussed (i) the design quality of elevated social spaces such as accessibility, circulation, activities, design concerns and design features, (ii) the participant's experience and behaviour during the study and (iii) the effectiveness of the design used tools. The results showed a positive impact on enhancing user involvement and allowed users to produce and test different design alternatives in real time. The research findings include a study of human activities in the physical and the virtual world, pedestrian modelling for the selected case studies, and an analysis of the potential need for new rules and regulations relating to the use of such spaces. The research also highlighted the limitations and potentials of using these new methods as a co-design approach for designing public and social spaces in the city.

Keywords: Virtual Reality · Computational design · Gamification · Participatory design · Elevated Public Spaces

C. Stephanidis et al. (Eds.): HCII 2023, CCIS 1836, pp. 176–184, 2023.
https://doi.org/10.1007/978-3-031-36004-6_24

1 Introduction

The integration of public participation in decision-making and design policy formation has been a fundamental aspect of urban design and the design of public spaces in democratic societies since the late 20th century [1, 2]. In recent years, digital technologies, such as Virtual Reality (VR) and Visual Simulation (VS), have presented designers with new opportunities to enhance public engagement and involvement in social project design, while also presenting the need to evaluate the validity and legitimacy of these new processes [3, 5]. The use of VR and VS technologies has been gaining momentum as innovative tools for public engagement and stakeholder involvement, with a growing body of literature exploring their potential benefits in various design fields [4, 6].

VR is an emerging field of research that has garnered significant attention in recent years. It holds the potential to revolutionize the way we engage with physical and informational elements. The key challenge in the development of VR technology and applications lies in the creation of innovative methods for designing information, storytelling, and narratives, as the full potential of this medium has yet to be fully realized [7, 8]. This challenge extends beyond the technological domain and encompasses the development of interaction dynamics with users, including gameplay, as well as the potential for applications in novel fields. The application of Virtual Reality (VR) technology in the fields of architectural and urban design has the potential to broaden the definition of what is considered "real", thereby creating opportunities for entirely new simulations and sensory experiences [9]. With this approach, participants in VR-based architectural and urban design projects are not limited to passive observation but instead become active contributors who can preview the space, propose modifications, and have a sense of ownership over the eventual interactive environment [10]. VR technology provides users with the capability to experience changes and actions in real-time, in an immersive manner. While professionals in the Architecture, Engineering, and Construction (AEC) field may be familiar with VR, it remains a novel and challenging technology for the general public [11].

1.1 Research Background

Virtual Reality (VR) is a technology that allows users to experience computer-generated simulations in a 3D environment that can range from being similar to the real world to being entirely different [9]. VR systems typically utilize VR headsets or multi-projected environments to generate realistic visuals and sounds, allowing users to immerse themselves in the virtual environment.

The exploration of the impact of Immersive Virtual Environments (ImVE) on design perception, physiology, and cognition has produced knowledge to support improved design patterns, creativity, and reasoning among multiple users [3, 7]. Research has shown that ImVE can positively impact designers' cognitive processes, including working memory, design data search and access, spatial cognition, and attention allocation. Additionally, ImVE has been found to positively impact users' perception and memory. Studies have indicated that ImVE can lead to improved performance of designers, particularly in problem finding, and can have a positive impact on both the problem and solution spaces [6, 12]. Collaborative design in ImVE has also been found to be effective in increasing inspiration for new approaches to problem-solving among design collaborators.

The use of VR technology in urban design has the potential to greatly enhance the participatory design process by allowing for greater collaboration between designers, stakeholders, and the general public [20]. By integrating VR with Building Information Modelling (BIM), urban design projects can benefit from increased engagement with end-users and a more immersive and interactive design experience [6, 10, 11]. There are several VR plugins, such as Revit Live and Enscape, available to architects and urban designers that enable the integration of VR into their design and collaboration processes [15].

Similarly, game engines, such as Unreal Engine and Unity 3D, have the potential to support public participation in the design process. These game engines, originally developed for gaming development, can be customized by independent developers to meet the specific needs of the architecture and urban design fields [8]. However, it is important to note that while the use of game engines in architecture and urban design has the potential to improve public participation, there are also limitations that must be considered, such as the validity and legitimacy of information obtained through VR simulations and the potential for biases [12, 14].

The use of VR technology in participatory design also raises concerns about user comfort and accessibility, as well as the potential differences between people's behavior and interactions in VR environments compared with their interactions in real-life cognitive experiences [5, 13]. These limitations highlight the need for further research into people's behavior and interactions in VR environments to fully understand the potential and limitations of VR technology in participatory design processes.

1.2 Purpose

The purpose of this research is to investigate the potential of Virtual Reality (VR) technology in enhancing the design experience of elevated urban spaces, through analyzing two recent developments in London, Sky Garden and Crossrail Place. The study aims to explore the differences and similarities between human interaction in the real world and the virtual world, and to examine the impact of VR technology on user involvement, design quality, and participant experience and behavior.

1.3 Case Studies

The research study involved the examination of two diverse elevated urban spaces located in London. The first of these spaces was the Sky Garden, which is situated on the upper three floors of the "Walkie Talkie" skyscraper in the center of London's financial district [16]. The second was the Crossrail Place roof garden, located in North Dock, Canary Wharf, which is an elevated green park covering an area of 10,000 square meters and located above the Elizabeth Line [17].

2 Methodology

The methodology includes **walk-along interviews** with the visitors (n = 33) of both gardens and a **VR exploratory experiment**, followed by semi-structured interviews with the participants (n = 33), which brings the participant as an active element of the project. These methods were selected to provide insights into the effectiveness of VR technology as a co-design approach for designing public and social spaces in the city, and to explore the potential need for new rules and regulations relating to the use of such spaces.

2.1 Walk-Along Interviews

A total of 33 participants were recruited for walk-along interviews in each of the Sky Garden and Crossrail Place in London to understand their physical experience in elevated urban spaces. Participants, all aged 18 years and above, came from different age groups. The 20-min interviews were conducted on-site and analyzed through qualitative data sets. The author employed a theme-based analysis, including content analysis, to examine the impact of physical experience on social interaction and activities. The analysis followed a descriptive approach, guided by a summative approach, to effectively analyze the data [18, 19]. Participants provided informed consent and signed an ethics form before contributing to the study.

2.2 VR Experiment

The purpose of the VR experiment is to compare two different approaches to creating an interactive design model, one using BIM software (Autodesk Revit + Enscape) and the other using a game engine (Unreal Engine). The experiment is followed by qualitative semi-structured interviews with the participants (n = 33) to gather their views on their virtual experience and behavior during the experiment.

2.2.1 VR Experimental Setup and Procedures

The VR laboratory experiment lasted for one hour, and participants had the opportunity to interact with VR models of the Sky Garden and Crossrail Place. The VR model allowed participants to see and interact with changes and actions that could be made to the environment. The experiment was divided into three stages: induction and consent, filling out a survey, and testing the VR models.

Building an interactive design model in VR involved two methods, one for constructing the Sky Garden and the other for constructing the Crossrail Place. The Sky Garden was designed and modelled on 3DS Max and then imported to Unreal Engine for further visual coding. The Crossrail Place was designed using BIM software (Autodesk Revit 2022), with an Enscape plugin for real-time design changes in VR. The study used Oculus Quest 2 and a GoPro 360-degree camera to ensure the safety of participants during the VR experience. The researcher took safety precautions such as good ventilation, anti-nausea wristbands, and a 'guardian' feature to reduce the risk of VR-induced discomfort.

In the Sky Garden experiment, participants were guided to interact with the space design by changing materials, moving objects, and taking virtual photos. In the Crossrail Place experiment, participants were asked to add or remove design features and components and test them in real-time using the light simulation tool and the virtual camera. The semi-structured interviews focused on participants' views on their virtual experience and behavior during the study.

3 Results

The study targeted participants from different age groups and different backgrounds such as architects, urban designers, interior designers, computer engineers, academics, and public users. The interview analysis highlighted four overarching themes which are; space circulation design, design concerns, activities and interactive design,

3.1 Space Circulation Design

The results showed that a significant number of participants (n = 20) preferred the Sky Garden's circulation design, which was described as open, welcoming, linear, and straightforward. 45% (n = 15) of the participants accepted the one-way circulation system due to its necessity for safety and social distancing. The participants who had not visited Sky Garden before (n = 21) appreciated the experience of going up the stairs to different levels and found it to be more adventurous and interactive. However, they also raised concerns about accessibility for wheelchair users. On the other hand, the other group of participants (n = 13) preferred the Crossrail Place circulation design, which was described as an adventure, natural experience, walking and discovering, and exploratory. The participants noted that the curvy pathways in Crossrail Place were narrow and needed to be designed wider for privacy and accessibility (Fig. 1).

Fig. 1. Participants teleporting and testing the space design circulation, source: author.

3.2 Design Concerns

In examining the design aspects of the Sky Garden and Crossrail Place, results from the VR study showed that several limitations and concerns were identified by the participants. A significant number of participants, both those who had previously visited the Sky Garden in real life and those who had not, noted the need for more green spaces and public seating near the plants, as well as the reorganization of seating areas to accommodate for privacy, social distancing, and accessibility. Additionally, there were design concerns raised regarding the restaurant and outdoor viewing platform.

On the other hand, the elevated nature and landscape features of Crossrail Place were favored by a substantial number of participants, who viewed it as a more public space than the Sky Garden. However, they also expressed the need for comfortable and sociable seating areas, wider pathways, and an increase in plants and flowers. Further, a significant number of participants stated that the garden would benefit from additional interactive elements such as public art, statues, an outdoor viewing platform, a water fountain, a pet-friendly area, and an outdoor bar and café.

3.3 Activities

The results of the study revealed that participants had diverse preferences for the activities they would likely engage in if they visited the Sky Garden and Crossrail Place. In the Sky Garden, the most frequently cited activities were appreciating the views of the city, consuming beverages and food, socializing with friends, and capturing memories through photography. In contrast, the participants preferred to relax, immerse themselves in the natural surroundings, engage in reading, have a lunch, and take pictures in Crossrail Place. The participants also reported a high level of enjoyment while exploring the virtual models and saw potential for conducting virtual activities within the spaces. They recommended offering virtual tickets as a means of encouraging more visitors to physically visit the spaces, and a majority of participants who had not previously been to either space expressed interest in visiting after participating in the VR experiment.

The study found that exploring the virtual environment allowed participants to engage in physical and virtual activities that they may not be able to do in real life, such as jumping, flying, dancing, running, and sitting on the floor. Observing these physical motions in the virtual space highlighted the potential benefits of using VR as a social online platform in the event of future pandemics. A number of participants who shared their experience of lockdown in 2020 emphasized the importance of this as a means to support mental health for those living alone during such crises. However, the participants also acknowledged that virtual social interaction cannot completely replace the physical experience.

3.4 Interactive Design

The results of the VR laboratory experiment indicate that the participants viewed the interactive design opportunity as a critical and pleasurable aspect of the experience. All participants concurred that the utilization of advanced tools and features can enhance their understanding of the design quality of both the Sky Garden and Crossrail Place. The usage of these tools in architectural design can significantly engage users to visualize and refine the details of a project, comprehend design limitations, and test the utilization of space based on their requirements and desired activities (Fig. 2). The interactive design simulation included features such as light simulation, material alteration, X-ray visualization, virtual annotations, and a virtual camera. The results indicated that light simulation and material alteration were the most favored simulation tools, while the virtual camera was perceived as an enjoyable and efficient tool for real-time changes and communication with the designer. The X-ray visualization and virtual annotations were also deemed as important interactive design tools for testing diverse design strategies and communication among project team members.

The use of the Revit BIM software with the Enscape plugin in the VR experiment allowed for real-time design changes based on participant requirements. Participants frequently identified design concerns and suggested new design scenarios and activities for Crossrail Place roof garden, such as a water element, exercise area, public art, comfortable seating, more plants, an open plaza for events, gaming areas, an outdoor café, and an outdoor space for animals.

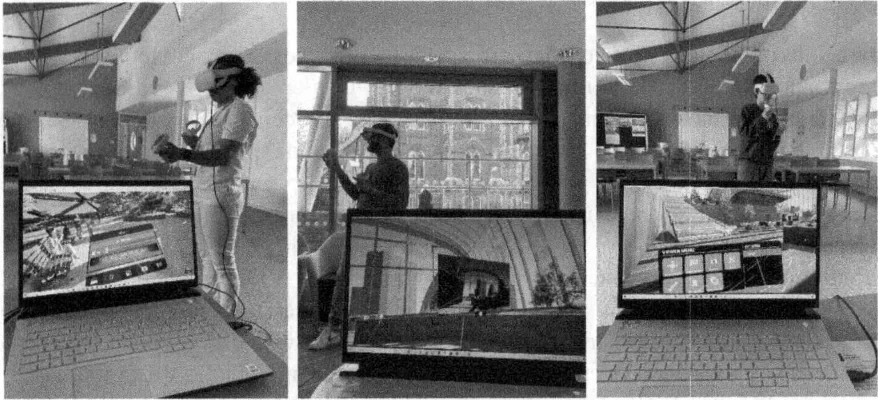

Fig. 2. Participants testing the interactive design features in real-time, source: author.

3.5 Discussion and Conclusion

The present study offers evidence for the potential utilization of virtual reality (VR) technology as a co-design approach in the realm of urban and public spaces design. The combination of walk-along interviews and VR experiments allowed for a comprehensive examination of the physical and virtual experiences, revealing similarities between the two. Participants, both those with prior experience in the spaces and those without, were able to identify design limitations and propose activities and features, with many of their concerns and needs aligning with those of actual space users.

However, the study also sheds light on the limitations of VR technology in achieving a fully immersive virtual environment, such as limitations in physical space and the potential for VR sickness. The development of multimodal haptic devices is deemed crucial for creating a highly immersive VR experience.

In conclusion, the findings of this study provide valuable insights for designers and policymakers in their efforts to create public spaces that are in line with user needs and preferences. Nevertheless, further research is necessary to assess the generalizability and scalability of VR technology in larger and more complex urban design projects.

Funding. The work was supported by the Faculty of Engineering University of Nottingham Research Excellence PhD Scholarship.

References

1. Wilson, A., Tewdwr-Jones, M., Comber, R.: Urban planning, public participation and digital technology: app development as a method of generating citizen involvement in local planning processes. Environ. Plan. B: Urban Anal. City Sci. **46**(2), 286–302 (2019)
2. Bouzguenda, I., Alalouch, C., Fava, N.: Towards smart sustainable cities: a review of the role digital citizen participation could play in advancing social sustainability. Sustain. Cities Soc. **50**, 101627 (2019)
3. Zhang, C., Zeng, W., Liu, L.: UrbanVR: an immersive analytics system for context-aware urban design. Comput. Graph. **99**, 128–138 (2021)
4. Wolf, M., Söbke, H., Wehking, F.: Mixed reality media-enabled public participation in urban planning: a literature review. In: Jung, J., tom Dieck, M.C., Rauschnabel, P.A. (eds.) Augmented Reality and Virtual Reality: Changing Realities in a Dynamic World, pp. 125–138. Springer, Cham (2020). https://doi.org/10.1007/978-3-030-37869-1_11
5. Van Leeuwen, J.P., Hermans, K., Jylhä, A., Quanjer, A.J., Nijman, H.: Effectiveness of virtual reality in participatory urban planning: a case study. In: Proceedings of the 4th Media Architecture Biennale Conference, pp. 128–136 (2018)
6. Safikhani, S., Keller, S., Schweiger, G., Pirker, J.: Immersive virtual reality for extending the potential of building information modeling in architecture, engineering, and construction sector: systematic review. Int. J. Digit. Earth **15**(1), 503–526 (2022)
7. Yu, R., Gu, N., Lee, G., Khan, A.: A systematic review of architectural design collaboration in immersive virtual environments. Designs **6**(5), 93 (2022)
8. Panya, D.S., Kim, T., Choo, S.: An interactive design change methodology using a BIM-based virtual reality and augmented reality. J. Build. Eng. **68**, 106030 (2023)
9. Portman, M.E., Natapov, A., Fisher-Gewirtzman, D.: To go where no man has gone before: virtual reality in architecture, landscape architecture and environmental planning. Comput. Environ. Urban Syst. **54**, 376–384 (2015)
10. Alizadehsalehi, S., Hadavi, A., Huang, J.C.: From BIM to extended reality in AEC industry. Autom. Constr. **116**, 103254 (2020)
11. Zaker, R., Coloma, E.: Virtual reality-integrated workflow in BIM-enabled projects collaboration and design review: a case study. Visual. Eng. **6**(1), 1–15 (2018). https://doi.org/10.1186/s40327-018-0065-6
12. Rubio-Tamayo, J.L., Gertrudix Barrio, M., García García, F.: Immersive environments and virtual reality: systematic review and advances in communication, interaction and simulation. Multimodal Technol. Interact. **1**(4), 21 (2017)
13. Kim, S., Kim, J., Kim, B.: Immersive virtual reality-aided conjoint analysis of urban square preference by living environment. Sustainability **12**(16), 6440 (2020)
14. Meenar, M., Kitson, J.: Using multi-sensory and multi-dimensional immersive virtual reality in participatory planning. Urban Sci. **4**(3), 34 (2020)

15. Huang, Y., Shakya, S., Odeleye, T.: Comparing the functionality between virtual reality and mixed reality for architecture and construction uses. J. Civ. Eng. Archit. **13**(1), 409–414 (2019)
16. Sky-Garden. Sky Garden Visitor Rules & Regulations (2015). https://skygarden.london/terms-conditions/. Accessed 4 May 2020
17. Bosetti, N., Brown, R., Belcher, E., Washington-Ihieme, M.: Public London: The Regulation, Management and Use of Public Spaces. Published by Centre for London, London (2019)
18. Schreier, M.: Varianten qualitativer Inhaltsanalyse: ein wegweiser im dickicht der Begrifflichkeiten. In: Forum Qualitative Sozialforschung/Forum: Qualitative Social Research, vol. 15, no. 1 (2014)
19. Hsieh, H.F., Shannon, S.E.: Three approaches to qualitative content analysis. Qual. Health Res. **15**(9), 1277–1288 (2005)
20. Ehab, A., Burnett, G., Heath, T.: Enhancing public engagement in architectural design: a comparative analysis of advanced virtual reality approaches in building information modeling and gamification techniques. Buildings **13**(5), 1262 (2023). https://doi.org/10.3390/buildings13051262

Designing for Wide Adoption: An Inexpensive and Accessible Extended Reality (XR) Device

Ian Gonsher, Pinyuan Feng, Theo McArn, and Andrew Christenson(✉)

Brown University, Providence, RI 02912, USA
andrew_christenson@brown.edu

Abstract. With the increased adoption of Virtual Reality (VR), Augmented Reality (AR), and Mixed Reality (MR), the question of how to make these technologies more accessible to more people becomes more relevant and urgent [1, 2]. HoloWorld is an Extended Reality (XR) accessory inspired by the illusion of Pepper's Ghost [3]. Our prototype fits onto most tablets and smartphones, providing users with a digital experience that is more spatial and immersive than what a flat screen can provide. In order to find wide adoption, HoloWorld has been developed using a combination of the diegetic [4] and iterative design methods to deliver a few key features. For one, the product is easy to use. HoloWorld is portable and easy to configure with any smartphone. Similar to Google Cardboard [5], it uses a smartphone to provide power, connectivity, and source display. Additionally, the product is inexpensive. Great care has been given to the design of HoloWorld for manufacturability. The materials – corrugated plastic and acetate sheet – can easily be die cut, and produced for pennies on the dollar. Finally, HoloWorld is accessible and designed for broad adoption. The product can be easily branded and is an ideal vehicle for marketing campaigns. Because HoloWorld is inexpensive to produce, and it can be easily branded with content such as logos, QR codes, and demo videos, it presents itself as an ideal vehicle for businesses to reduce their customer acquisition costs.

Keywords: Extended Reality · Three-Dimensional Displays · Telepresence · Prototyping · Design

1 Introduction

With the growing development of VR headsets and AR applications, the boundary between the virtual and the physical is becoming increasingly blurred. Tech companies, such as Meta, Microsoft, etc., are investing heavily in a model of the emerging future internet that brings users into a completely immersive virtual environment [6]. While these devices demonstrate impressive progress for VR applications, the relatively high cost of these devices is still a barrier to entry for many users. If these kinds of XR experiences are to become more ubiquitous in the years ahead, these kinds of devices must become less expensive and more accessible [7].

Recent research projects [8–12] have made these technologies more accessible, giving more people opportunities to experience XR. Products of this type are based on the

C. Stephanidis et al. (Eds.): HCII 2023, CCIS 1836, pp. 185–191, 2023.
https://doi.org/10.1007/978-3-031-36004-6_25

assumption that in order to weave these virtual experiences into the fabric of peoples' daily lives, there needs to be wider adoption. This can only happy if these kinds of systems are inexpensive, accessible, and easy to use. This model is not without its critics. For example, VR headsets are almost completely divorced from physical reality, and serious concerns are emerging about the effects these technologies are having on the mental and physical health of the users [13]. HoloWorld emerged from an investigation into speculative XR models for the next iteration of the internet, in which users are able to live in both worlds simultaneously, so to speak. XR allows users to reference and orient themselves within real and physical spaces and situations while also providing affordances for augmenting that experience with virtual content.

In order for these technologies to find wide adoption, the hardware will need to become accessible, inexpensive, and easy to use. HoloWorld has several features that accomplish this: 1) It is easy to use. HoloWorld is portable and easy to configure with any smartphone. 2) It is inexpensive. Great care has been given to the design or HoloWorld for manufacturability. The materials – corrugated plastic and acetate sheet – can be easily die cut, and produced for pennies on the dollar. Produced in large enough quantities, they could be given away. 3) It is accessible and designed for broad adoption. The product can be easily branded and is an ideal vehicle for marketing campaigns. Along with customized virtual content, such as promotional videos that introduce new products or people to a targeted audience, consumers would be given the hardware itself to develop and discover other applications for HoloWorld.

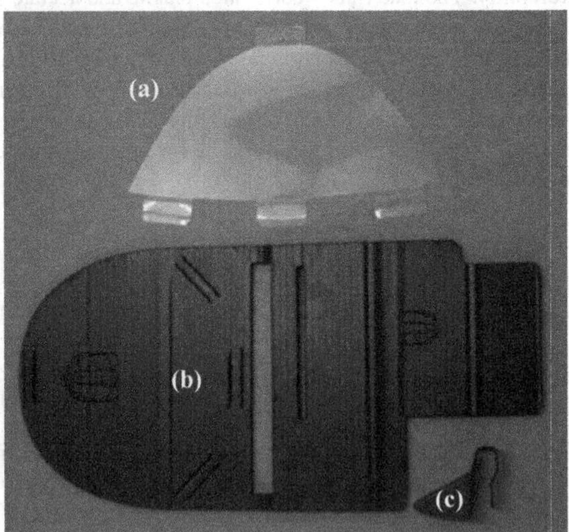

Fig. 1. Aerial view of HoloWorld parts where we have (a) Acetate sheet designed to sit in a slightly curved fashion to create a Pepper's Ghost effect with more depth. (b) Corrugated plastic frame to hold acetate sheet, tablet, and periscope lens. (c) Periscope lens attaches to phone to enable holographic facetime between parties.

2 Prototyping

The team started by debating topics regarding what communication between people might look like 10 years from now and decided a form of XR might be the most promising technology to enhance communication. After a handful of sketches, the team developed user scenarios. By employing the diegetic prototyping method [4], the team was able to develop stories around use cases which further solidified the device's potential utility. With this framework, divergent thinking [14] was employed to develop over 50 prototypes. Most iterations were made and tested using cardboard for the frame and thin acetate for the lens. Through these iterations the team developed three key realizations (see Fig. 2).

It was found that the images exhibit a greater sense of depth when portrayed on a slightly curved surface, as opposed to a flat plane or a conical or tubular shape. A range of view between 110º and 130º on a slightly curved surface was found to be optimal for the desired effect. Images displayed on a dark background are seen as clearer than images on a light background. Additionally, space between the acetate and the background created a small pocket which further enhanced the illusion of a shallow, yet perceivable space. The use of standard video content, as opposed to images that are distorted to enhance their volumetric form, emerged as an important consideration for broader adoption. This allows users to share video conferencing and video links as they normally would. However, the effect is most convincing when this video content is shot on a dark background.

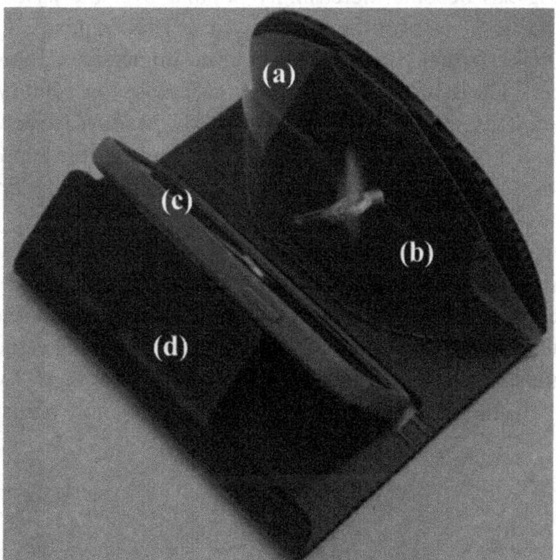

Fig. 2. Photo depicting all elements discovered during prototyping to develop a greater sense of depth and clarity in our image (a) Image portrayed on a curved surface. (b) "Pocket" between acetate sheet and plastic frame that creates a sense of depth. (c) Standard video content on black background appears non-distorted on the acetate and provides a clear image. (d) Frame made of a dark material to improve clarity.

With these three elements in mind, we decided to employ convergent thinking [15] and refined our prototypes until we landed on our most recent design, as shown in Fig. 1. This prototype utilizes laser cutting on black corrugated plastic and thin acetate. For mass production, we envision similar materials to be utilized in conjunction with die cuts. The frame was designed to be portable, lightweight, and flexible such that it may fold into itself to serve as a stand for one's smartphone. The lens was cut in such a way that it can hook onto the base and maintain a slightly curved volumetric shape. This slightly curved surface increases the depth of images and provides a wider range of view with almost no noticeable distortion. Our final prototype is easy to use, can be mass produced at a low cost, and is highly accessible.

3 User Scenarios

HoloWorld, and the adoption of extended reality devices more generally, have the potential to serve many different applications. Throughout the design process we focused on user scenarios that apply extended reality towards reimagining thee future of remotely collaborative work. It was our working assumption throughout the design process that these "gateway scenarios" would help users become more comfortable with the technology, and lead to wider adoption beyond these scenarios.

3.1 Video Conferencing

Video conferencing has become increasingly popular over the past few years and is expected to continue to grow over the coming years. This explosion in popularity will create a push to make virtual communication more immersive. Holographic displays utilizing the Pepper's Ghost effect have been used for close to a century to enhance performance in the arts. This optical illusion is often used nowadays for decorative purposes which lacks practical utility and can be expensive. By applying the Pepper's Ghost effect to an affordable, portable, easy to produce system, we aim to make holographic video conferencing accessible for everyone (see Fig. 3).

Consider a business scenario where you arrive just in time for your video conference with a colleague in another time zone. You grab your phone from your pocket and a flat piece of corrugated plastic from your bag. In just a few seconds you fold the device into shape to hold your phone. A holographic-like image of your colleague appears before you. Given the depth and clarity of the image, it almost feels as though your colleague is in the room with you, allowing for a conversation that feels more realistic and valuable.

Fig. 3. Video conferencing using a HoloWorld device.

3.2 Marketing

An important set of questions the team asked in the development of HoloWorld explored ways to design for wide adoption. If users can benefit from an enhanced XR experience, then how might we give them an example of what this technology is capable of?

Consider a scenario where your company has a brand-new product that they want to introduce to their customers. You send them a thin package with a sheet of information and a HoloWorld. Since they are extremely inexpensive to produce, you are able to give them away to customers for no cost on their end. The frame of the HoloWorld is decorated with the company's branding and a QR code that leads to a product demonstration video to be displayed in a holographic fashion. HoloWorld not only demonstrates new products with a novel and memorable XR experience, but also has minimal or no cost to the customer. Since the cost of the device can be subsidized by the value created for the advertiser or marketer, people will have the opportunity to experiment with XR technology, allowing for free exploration of the product's utility. This could be a viable and important strategy for broad adoption of XR experiences.

3.3 Collaborative Work Environments

Developing ways to improve collaboration in the workplace is becoming increasingly important as companies start to transition to hybrid work-from-home schedules and teams become more global. XR devices have a unique opportunity to make a positive impact in the workplace by enhancing communication in these collaborative work environments [16].

Consider a workplace scenario where a team of engineers from opposite sides of the world are discussing their CAD designs for a unique phone stand. Typically, engineers would discuss the prototype design in 2D, then get a sense of how the prototype might fit in the 3D world by 3D printing. This process can be relatively time-consuming and costly depending on the materials used for 3D printing. With HoloWorld, engineers are able to communicate 2D designs in a 3D space without physically producing the part itself. Quickly and easily, engineers from one part of the world set up their HoloWorld while engineers from the other side of the world prepare their CAD files by making the background black and scaling it so that when it shows up on the HoloWorld the proportions are realistic and accurate. Engineers on the fabrication team examine the part in a holographic-like fashion and notice that certain elements could use some refinement before they 3D print it. By utilizing HoloWorld to check their design before fabrication, the team saves highly valuable time and resources.

4 Conclusion

In this paper, we present our prototype for an XR accessory which is low cost, portable, and easy to use. Further, we present a couple of broad scenarios in which we explore the potential capabilities of the device. Overall, we lay the groundwork for wide adoption and accessibility of XR devices. Because HoloWorld is inexpensive to produce, and it can be easily branded with content such as logos, QR codes, and demo videos, it presents itself as an ideal vehicle for businesses to reduce customer acquisition costs and introduce XR to their customers. In order to understand the true benefits of our product, as well as any technological gaps, more research is needed both in terms of fine-tuning the technology and developing a stronger understanding of the user experience.

References

1. Hillmann, C.: The history and future of XR. In: UX for XR, pp. 17–72. Apress, Berkeley (2021)
2. Görlich, D.: Societal XR—a vision paper. Paradigmplus. **3**, 1–10 (2022). https://doi.org/10.55969/paradigmplus.v3n2a1
3. Senelick, L.: Pepper's ghost faces the camera. Hist. Photogr. **7**, 69–72 (1983). https://doi.org/10.1080/03087298.1983.10442750
4. Harwood, T., Garry, T., Belk, R.: Design fiction diegetic prototyping: a research framework for visualizing service innovations. JSM **34**, 59–73 (2019). https://doi.org/10.1108/JSM-11-2018-0339
5. Fabola, A., Miller, A., Fawcett, R.: Exploring the past with Google Cardboard. In: 2015 Digital Heritage, pp. 277–284. IEEE, Granada (2015)
6. Kraus, S., Kanbach, D.K., Krysta, P.M., Steinhoff, M.M., Tomini, N.: Facebook and the creation of the metaverse: radical business model innovation or incremental transformation? Int. J. Entrep. Behav. Res. **28**, 52–77 (2022). https://doi.org/10.1108/IJEBR-12-2021-0984
7. Coburn, J.Q., Freeman, I., Salmon, J.L.: A review of the capabilities of current low-cost virtual reality technology and its potential to enhance the design process. J. Comput. Inf. Sci. Eng. **17**, 031013 (2017). https://doi.org/10.1115/1.4036921
8. De Angeli, D., O'Neill, E.J.: Development of an inexpensive Augmented Reality (AR) headset. In: Proceedings of the 33rd Annual ACM Conference Extended Abstracts on Human Factors in Computing Systems, pp. 971–976. ACM, Seoul Republic of Korea (2015)
9. Luo, X., Lawrence, J., Seitz, S.M.: Pepper's cone: an inexpensive do-it-yourself 3D display. In: Proceedings of the 30th Annual ACM Symposium on User Interface Software and Technology, pp. 623–633. ACM, Québec City (2017)

10. Herskovitz, J., et al.: Making mobile augmented reality applications accessible. In: The 22nd International ACM SIGACCESS Conference on Computers and Accessibility, pp. 1–14. ACM, Virtual Event Greece (2020)
11. Cardoso, J.C.S.: Accessible tangible user interfaces in extended reality experiences for cultural heritage. In: 2021 IEEE International Symposium on Mixed and Augmented Reality Adjunct (ISMAR-Adjunct), pp. 18–25. IEEE, Bari (2021)
12. Sadler, R., Thrasher, T.: XR: Crossing reality to enhance language learning. CALICO. **40** (2023). https://doi.org/10.1558/cj.25517
13. Nichols, S., Patel, H.: Health and safety implications of virtual reality: a review of empirical evidence. Appl. Ergon. **33**, 251–271 (2002). https://doi.org/10.1016/S0003-6870(02)00020-0
14. Runco, M.A., Acar, S.: Divergent thinking as an indicator of creative potential. Creat. Res. J. **24**, 66–75 (2012). https://doi.org/10.1080/10400419.2012.652929
15. Cropley, A.: In praise of convergent thinking. Creat. Res. J. **18**, 391–404 (2006). https://doi.org/10.1207/s15326934crj1803_13
16. Vichare, P., Cano, M., Dahal, K., Siewierski, T., Gilardi, M.: Incorporating extended reality technology for delivering computer aided design and visualisation modules. In: 2022 14th International Conference on Software, Knowledge, Information Management and Applications (SKIMA). pp. 114–119. IEEE, Phnom Penh (2022)

Mouse-Based Hand Gesture Interaction in Virtual Reality

Adrian H. Hoppe[1], Dominik Klooz[2], Florian van de Camp[1](✉), and Rainer Stiefelhagen[2]

[1] Fraunhofer Institute of Optronics, System Technologies, and Image Exploitation (IOSB), Karlsruhe, Germany
{adrian.hoppe,florian.vandecamp}@iosb.fraunhofer.de
[2] Karlsruhe Institute of Technology (KIT), Karlsruhe, Germany
uwdlg@student.kit.edu, rainer.stiefelhagen@kit.edu

Abstract. Virtual reality requires new forms of interaction and input in three-dimensional environments that isolate the user from the physical world. However, existing input methods, such as handheld controllers or hand gestures, are not yet mature or coherent enough to be easily used by the average user. To address this, a universal set of gestures which are easy to use, remember, and expressive is needed. Based on the observation that the mouse in desktop computing can control different applications adequately, four conceptual input types are proposed: primary and secondary clicks, directional input, and a modifier functionality. These provide flexibility without being overwhelming. To find a promising set of gestures, requirements are formulated based on existing research and observations. Three sets of appropriate gesture combinations are carefully selected and proposed, and a user study is conducted to allow a comparison between them. The study involves a virtual testing environment with tasks to be completed using the gestures. Results show positive responses to all proposed gestures, with one set outperforming the other two in most areas. Based on this and participants' comments, a combination of four top-ranking gestures is proposed as a universal means for virtual reality interaction.

Keywords: Virtual reality · controller interaction

1 Introduction

The maturation of virtual reality (VR) has led to novel ways of human-computer interaction (HCI). However, traditional input devices for two-dimensional (2D) interfaces like mouses and touchscreens do not suffice for a three-dimensional (3D) virtual world. Handheld controllers with buttons and joysticks provide haptic feedback but can be tiring to use and restrict natural hand movements. An alternative approach, using hand gestures with sensor technology and machine learning-powered recognition algorithms, has become viable, allowing users to interact without holding external devices or batteries. However, designing a collection of gestures for different kinds of input is a challenging task. This paper

C. Stephanidis et al. (Eds.): HCII 2023, CCIS 1836, pp. 192–198, 2023.
https://doi.org/10.1007/978-3-031-36004-6_26

aims to find a set of hand gestures that capture a range of input possibilities for interactions in different VR applications. The goal is to design a manageable number of gestures that provide a range of input possibilities, similar to the prevalent computer mouse with a primary click, a secondary click for context-aware actions, and a scroll wheel for directional input. We aim to find a set of gestures that complement each other and are a good fit for a range of input functionalities and each other while respecting boundaries set by hand recognition technology. We present literature on previous work in HCI and gesture interaction, including technical foundations, requirements, and promising gesture candidates. Different types of input needed for general applicability are explord and a set of requirements drawing from literature, experience, and observation is presented. We also present three sets of four gestures each, carefully designed and selected to be useful for different input scenarios, easy to use and test, and suitable for supporting the arms or two-handed interactions. Finally, the paper presents the results of a user study conducted to evaluate the proposed gesture sets.

2 Related Work

Hand gestures as a way for interaction in desktop, augmented and virtual reality environments have been the subject of many scientific papers (e.g., [1–3,6]). However often, the focus of these works doesn't lie on HCI but rather the technical details of detecting and tracking hands using different data like video, depth data or sensor readings processed through machine learning or heuristic approaches. Exploring different—often low-cost—hardware setups or applying hand gestures to fairly specific use cases like controlling robots, launching programs based on static hand poses or navigating Microsoft PowerPoint presentations are other common subjects. Thus, a systematic selection of hand gestures and evaluation thereof are often skipped or only discussed briefly and the proposed interaction concepts are rarely fitting for other use cases. In cases where gesture elicitation is an area of focus, the interplay of gestures is rarely investigated and the gestures are selected with specific applications in mind, not so much general applicability.

Jean-Luc Nespoulous [5] defines gestures as learned movements of body parts conveying meaning that vary across cultures. They can be categorized into arbitrary, mimetic, and deictic gestures. Arbitrary gestures require learning and refer to actors, actions, or objects. Mimetic gestures represent objects or actions through hand movements. Deictic gestures involve pointing and can be specific, generic, or refer to the function of the object. This typology is commonly cited in the context of human-computer interaction. Before the renewed interest in neural networks emerged in recent years, many different techniques and algorithms have been proposed for the detection and tracking of hands and hand gesture recognition. Since these techniques are quite numerous and most have little direct influence on our work, we refer to a survey paper for an overview. Yang et al. [4] provide a good overview over the vast field of gesture interaction, going over different technical modalities (e.g., glove-based tracking and computer

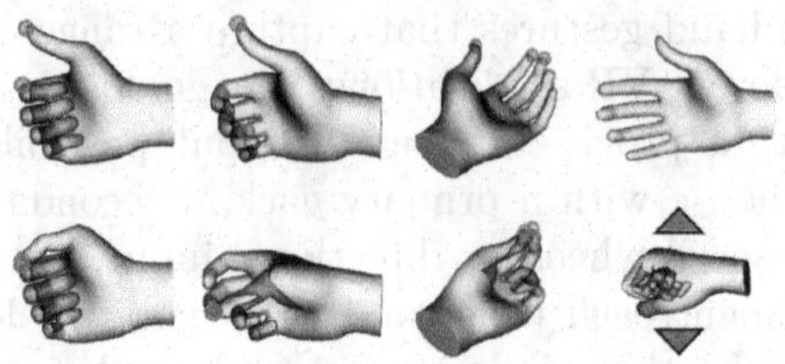

(a) Gestures inspired by a hand-held slideshow presenter device.

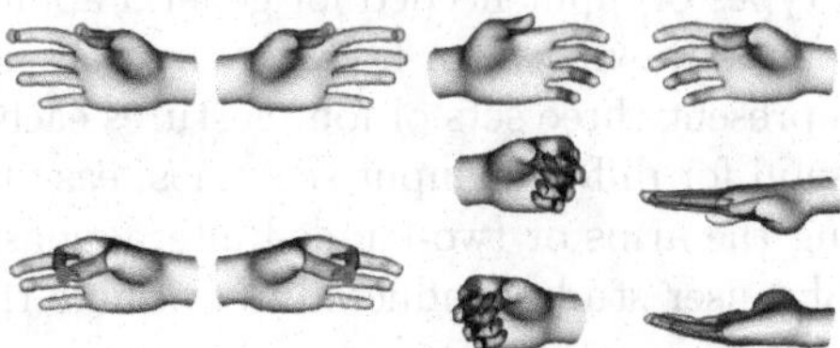

(b) Gestures inspired by the mouse interaction on the surface of a desktop table.

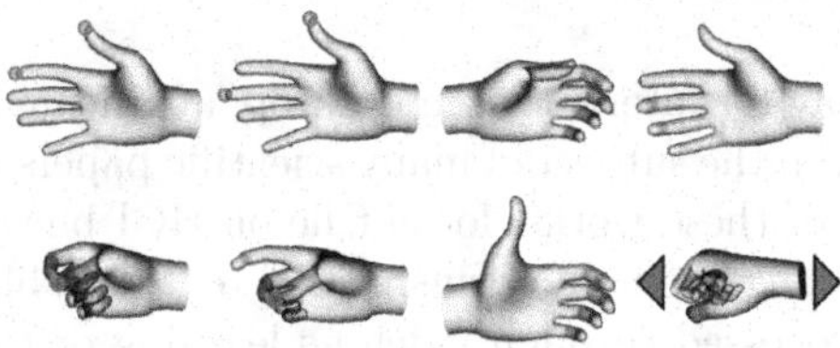

(c) Gestures inspired by bi-manual interactions.

Fig. 1. Three implemented sets of gestures.

vision), different ways of classifying gestures (e.g. static or dynamic gestures) and application areas (e.g. in the operation room, for gaming or virtual education) as well as potential issues in the field (like each application requiring different gestures and thus training time or inadequate point-to-point accuracy compared to a mouse). Regarding the technical aspects, two points worth noting are occlusion problems present with technologies relying on cameras or depth sensors and the moderate precision in detecting a hand posture. Overall, there is a need for a universal set of gestures that is easy to use, remember and expressive enough for use in diverse applications [7].

3 Gesture Set Design

To create a gesture set for a user interface, it is necessary need to strike a balance between having enough gestures to enable expressiveness while avoiding overwhelming users. To ensure this, it is important to consider the types of input that need to be expressed and create a gesture set that is both distinguishable and memorable. Too many gestures may lead to confusion, as they need to be different enough from one another to be recognized by gesture recognition algorithms. A two-button mouse with a scroll wheel is a good example of a traditional HCI input device that provides enough options to control various applications. While specialized input devices may be better suited for specific use cases, a mouse is generally adequate for many applications. In virtual environments, designers can use hand movements to emulate cursor movement, and the mouse's primary click can activate, select, or drag, while the secondary click can open context menus. It is also possible to incorporate directional input through a scroll wheel, which allows users to scroll vertically or horizontally, making it useful for navigating in two dimensions. Adding a modifier button, allows to double the number of inputs available, allowing users to modify the functionality associated with other inputs. To strike a balance between expressiveness and usability, we chose four types of input: primary click, secondary click, modifier button press, and directional input. This collection of input methods enables a wide range of applications while keeping the number and difficulty of gestures manageable. Informed by pre-existing literature dealing with gesture-based input as well as personal observations and the following requirements: intuitiveness, comfort, memorability, recognition Robustness, combined input of multiple gestures, we collected multiple promising gesture candidates and compiled three gesture sets:

This is a description of the first gesture set, named the *Gadgets* set, which uses device metaphors for the primary click and directional gestures. The primary gesture involves holding the dominant hand in a slightly opened fist with the thumb extended and pointing slightly upwards, and then moving the thumb down to make contact with the index finger joint above the knuckle to perform a click. The secondary click gesture involves making contact between the tips of the thumb and middle finger. The modifier gesture involves a pinching motion with the non-dominant hand. The directional gesture involves moving the fist away from a reference point in a vertical direction (see Fig. 1a).

The second gesture set, called *Desktop*, focuses on traditional desktop work environments. The set includes four gestures designed to be performed with hands resting on a surface. The primary and secondary click gestures use pinch-to-click motions with the index and middle fingers, resembling left and right clicks on a mouse. The modifier gesture is executed by extending the thumb of the non-dominant hand and is comfortable and easy to recognize. The directional gesture, made with a fist, resembles operating a throttle control in airplane cockpits and can modulate scrolling speed. The common mouse metaphor ties the set together for easy memorization (see Fig. 1b).

For the third gesture set, named *Bi-manual*, the study tested the use of the non-dominant hand by using two click gestures with the same motion but different hands. The modifier gesture can be performed with either hand to combine it with each of the click gestures. The directional gesture uses hand orientation instead of hand movements. The pinch-to-click gesture was chosen for both primary and secondary clicks, and clenching a fist for the modifier gesture. Combining the modifier gesture with the directional gesture produces directional input (see Fig. 1c).

4 Evaluation

To enable a comparison between the three sets, we conduct a user study (n = 18). We construct a virtual testing environment (see Fig. 2) used to introduce study participants to the gestures as well as tasks to be completed using them. The study was designed as a within-subject study where each of the 18 subjects repeats the main part thrice, once for each set of gestures, with the order of gesture sets randomized between subjects to account for the effects of already being familiar with the tasks and interactions in the second and third rounds. With 18 participants, each gesture set appeared as first, second or third an equal amount of six times in total. The three rounds are framed by two short questionnaires designed to elicit general information about the user upfront and capture general feedback about

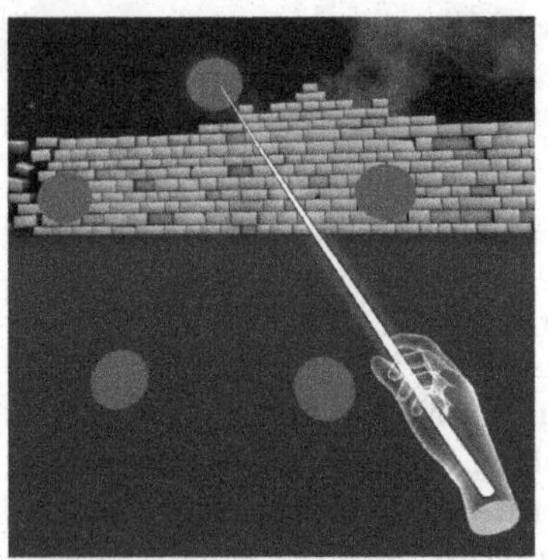

(a) Pointing task.

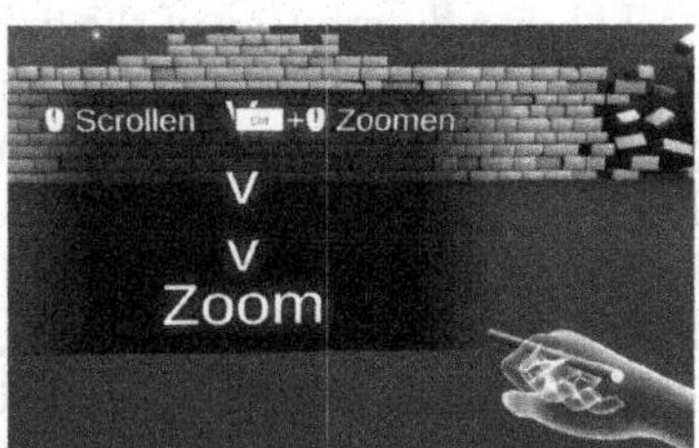

(b) Zooming and scrolling task.

(c) Time-based button press task.

(d) Control of objects in the world.

Fig. 2. Excerpt from the tasks of the user study.

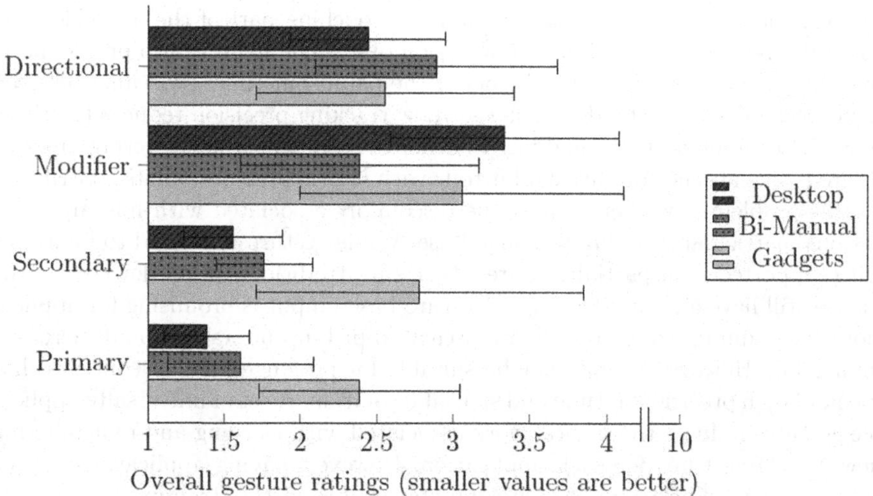

Fig. 3. Gesture type overall ratings. Results as mean values with 95% confidence intervals.

the evaluation and hand gesture interaction in the end. Another set of questions was presented to the users immediately after each round of using a set of hand gestures to collect feedback on that particular set beginning with a NASA-TLX short-form questionnaire to gauge the demand of the set as a whole. Afterwards, four identically structured sections consisting of 10-point Likert scale questions to rate different aspects of each individual gesture as well as text fields to express subjective feedback follow. In order to get a feel for the gestures and form opinions, the gestures were first shown and explained in the real world and afterwards introduced one by one in the virtual testing environment followed by different tasks (see Fig. 2) to test them out. The results show positive responses to all proposed gestures, with one set in particular outperforming the other two in most areas (see Fig. 3). Based on this and study participants' comments, we propose a combination of four top-ranking gestures as a well-composed set providing a universal means for virtual reality interaction.

5 Conclusion and Future Work

The study found that users perceive the proposed hand gestures as natural, intuitive, easy to use and remember, and comfortable when used individually or in combination. The combination of click gestures and directional gestures from the Desktop set, along with the fist modifier gesture from the Bi-Manual set, received the highest ratings and shows promise. The directional gestures were well-received and have potential for three-dimensional input. However, there are still problems affecting the overall performance of gesture-based input, including recognition errors due to occlusion and low tracking precision. Occlusion is a major issue when gestures involve one hand touching part of the other, leading to erratic recognition results. Self-occlusion of a single hand is also problematic, with fingers occluded by other fingers or the palm sometimes switching between being recognized as extended or flexed. Low tracking precision reduces the time-domain accuracy of input, making it harder to start and stop triggering input as desired. The absence of physical buttons with haptic pressure points contributes to this problem. Another issue is the discomfort associated with mid-air interactions, particularly during prolonged use. While gestures designed to be usable with supported arms partially address this issue, traditional input devices like the mouse still have a clear advantage. Gesture-based input is promising for applications like gaming, which benefit from easy-to-pick-up interaction and increased immersion. However, it may not be suitable for prolonged use or contexts that demand high precision in time and spatial resolution. A set of universally applicable gestures reduces the mental work associated with learning and remembering new sets of gestures for each application. However, having application-specific gestures may be better in certain contexts, such as virtual training.

In conclusion, hand gestures are a promising form of input, but there are still challenges that need to be addressed. A set of universally applicable gestures like the proposed Desktop set with modifications may be suitable for use cases where the duration of using hand gestures is not too long or where a mix of gestures and physical input devices is possible.

References

1. Bachmann, D., Weichert, F., Rinkenauer, G.: Review of three-dimensional human-computer interaction with focus on the leap motion controller. Sensors **18**(7), 2194 (2018)
2. Ha, T., Feiner, S.K., Woo, W.: WeARHand: head-worn, RGB-D camera-based, bare-hand user interface with visually enhanced depth perception. In: 2014 IEEE International Symposium on Mixed and Augmented Reality (ISMAR), pp. 219–228 (2014)
3. Lévesque, J.C., Laurendeau, D., Mokhtari, M.: Bimanual gestural interface for virtual environments. In: Proceedings of the 2011 IEEE Virtual Reality Conference, VR 2011, USA, pp. 223–224. IEEE Computer Society (2011). https://doi.org/10.1109/VR.2011.5759479
4. Li, Y., Huang, J., Tian, F., Wang, H.A., Dai, G.Z.: Gesture interaction in virtual reality. Virtual Reality Intell. Hardw. **1**(1), 84–112 (2019). https://doi.org/10.3724/SP.J.2096-5796.2018.0006. https://www.sciencedirect.com/science/article/pii/S2096579619300075
5. Nespoulous, J.L., Villiard, P. (eds.): Morphology, Phonology, and Aphasia. Springer Series in Neuropsychology, 1st edn. Springer, New York (1990). https://doi.org/10.1007/978-1-4613-8969-9
6. Nielsen, M., Moeslund, T.B., Störring, M., Granum, E.: A procedure for developing intuitive and ergonomic gesture interfaces for man-machine interaction (2003)
7. Sampson, H., Kelly, D., Wünsche, B.C., Amor, R.: A hand gesture set for navigating and interacting with 3D virtual environments. In: 2018 International Conference on Image and Vision Computing New Zealand (IVCNZ), pp. 1–6 (2018). https://doi.org/10.1109/IVCNZ.2018.8634656

Full-Face Animation for a Virtual Reality Avatar

Jewoong Hwang(✉) and Kyoungju Park

School of Computer Science and Engineering, Chung-Ang University, Seoul, South Korea
{woong712,kjpark}@cau.ac.kr

Abstract. This research paper proposes a real-time and realistic full facial animation method for virtual reality (VR) applications. Currently, VR applications lack natural upper-face animation, which limits the immersive experiences of self-avatars. Our proposed approach combines existing lip-sync methods for the lower part of the face with a deep-learning method for the upper part. This allows us to achieve natural full-face animation with minimal latency and high computational efficiency. We demonstrate the effectiveness of our approach through experimental results and show that it is suitable for use in VR applications. Our proposed method can help to enhance the realism and immersion of self-avatars in the metaverse.

Keywords: Full-face animation · Virtual Reality · Metaverse

1 Introduction

Natural face animation of self-avatars is essential for immersive experiences in the metaverse. However, achieving this in virtual reality (VR) applications can be challenging due to the need for low latency and high computational efficiency. VR applications typically model the face of avatars with blendshapes, and current VR avatars animate only the lip area using lip-sync methods.

While this approach is suitable for real-time performance in VR, it lacks natural upper-face animation. Existing methods such as MeshTalk [4] can animate the full face but are unsuitable for VR due to their large mesh size and high computational cost. Other lip-sync methods like Oculus Lipsync and VisemeNet [7] or VOCA [1] can be applied in real-time but also lack upper-face animation.

To address these limitations, we propose a real-time and realistic full facial animation method for VR. Our approach combines existing lip-sync methods for the lower part of the face with a deep-learning method for the upper part. This allows us to achieve natural full-face animation with minimal latency, suitable for use in VR applications.

2 Method

Our method reconstructs upper-face prediction from lip sync results. The method's input is a live audio stream; the output is full facial animation. Firstly,

C. Stephanidis et al. (Eds.): HCII 2023, CCIS 1836, pp. 199–206, 2023.
https://doi.org/10.1007/978-3-031-36004-6_27

we gain lower-face animation using a lipsync tool from speech. Next, our DNN model predicts full facial animation from lower-face animation.

Table 1. FPS distribution of collected video clips.

FPS	Number of files	Total length
23.98	37	09:44.237
24.00	22	05:18.625
25.00	276	64:02.600
29.97	138	31:55.582
30.00	23	05:43.967
50.00	6	01:14.000
59.94	16	03:03.166
60.00	1	00:16.050
Total	519	121:18.227

2.1 Data Collection

We collected our dataset by scrolling through online videos and then capturing face blendshapes. We collected files by collecting 1600 videos from the internet. Then we hand-picked 519 files totaling 121 min, which clearly have a single front-facing natural human face. The videos are in 596 × 336 resolution and between 60 23.98 fps as shown on Table 1. The capture rate of the face capture app is set to 24 frames per second, which is approximately the minimum framerate of the video. Our capture scripts play video clips at normal speed and record facial animation using the iPhone 13 mini with the Unity Face Capture app. The result is an 'Apple ARKit' blendshape with 52 blendshapes. We automatically dropped parts of the sequence that failed to record. The resulting dataset size is 153,452 frames which is roughly 106 min.

2.2 Input and Output

Accurate lipsync is crucial when generating facial animation. Lipsync is a task to generate facial animation in sync with speech audio. We used the viseme-based, real-time lipsync solution Oculus Lipsync. This method is lightweight and real-time, so it suits our method. The output of the Oculus lipsync is a 15-dimension viseme vector(range 1 to 100). To use in our model, we convert the 15-dim viseme animation into a 10-dim lower-face blendshape sequence $\mathbf{X_t} = (\mathbf{x_1}, \mathbf{x_2}, ..., \mathbf{x_t})$ using custom mapping.

We made custom mapping based on the JALI viseme sheet (see Table 2). Visemes with no JALI equivalent had to be created from scratch. The activation level of the FACS Action Unit is represented as A to E, A representing trace activation, and E being the maximum intensity. Activation level leading with 'u' notates upper only and is handled accordingly. The activation level is converted to a numeric value, *(A: 0.2, B: 0.4, C: 0.6, D: 0.8, E: 1)* and then is multiplied by the activation level of visemes.

Table 2. Custom blendshape mapping from Oculus Viseme to ARKit blendshapes.

Action Unit	Description	ARKit Equivent	JALI Viseme															
			AAA	AHH	UUU	RRR	TTH	FFF	EHH	OHH	IEE	SSS	SSH	MMM	Schwa			
			Oculus Viseme Equivelent													No Equivents		
			-	aa	U	RR	DD	FF	E	O	I	SS	CH	PP	-	TH	kk	nn
10	Upper Lip Raiser	mouthUpperUp(L/R)	C				C		A		C		B			B		
12	Lip Corner Puller	mouthSmile(L/R)	C						B		C							
14	Dimpler	mouthDimple(L/R)	C															
16	Lower Lip Depressor	mouthLowerDown(L/R)	D	D					B		D	E	B				B	
17	Chin Raiser	mouthShrugUpper	A	A	A	A	A	D	A	A	A	A		E		D	A	
18	Lip Puckerer	mouthPucker			D	C				C			C					
20	Lip stretcher	mouthStertch(L/R)	B						B		B		A				B	
22	Lip Funneler	mouthFunnel	uB			C	uD		B	C	B	C	C			uD	B	
23	Lip Tightener	mouthShrugUpper						uA						uC				uA
27	Mouth Stretch	JawOpen	C	D	A	A	B	A	B	A	A	A	A	A	B	B	B	C
28	Lip Suck	mouthRoll(Lower/Upper)			A			B										

2.3 Our Network

Our deep neural network uses a lower-face blendshape sequence X_t to predict full-facial blendshape sequence $\mathbf{Y_t} = (\mathbf{y_1}, \mathbf{y_2}, ..., \mathbf{y_t})$ recursively. Formally,

$$\hat{\mathbf{y}}_\mathbf{n} = Pred(\mathbf{x_n})$$

Input sequence X_t passes through two layers of unidirectional LSTM[] units. LSTM stands for Long Short-Term Memory and is a type of recurrent neural network (RNN) that can learn long-term dependencies in data. LSTM layers are initiated with a 0-filled state. The first LSTM layer takes 10-dimensional input and outputs 128 dimensions; the next LSTM layer takes 128 dimensions input and outputs 128 dimensions. Four predictor modules predict different sections of the face, namely {brows, mouth, eye, nose}. Each predictor module consists of one multi-head attention (MH-Attention) [6] layer and 3 fully connected layers. The MH-Attention layer has 4 heads, and each head outputs 1-dimensional attended output. The output of the MH-Attention layer is added to the output of the stacked layer, resulting in 132 dimensions. Added result passes into 3 fully-connected layers followed by ReLU functions. We add the resulting variables of each predictor to get the final $\hat{\mathbf{y}}_\mathbf{t}$.

3 Experiments

3.1 Implementation Details

To train our model, we first extracted the relevant blendshapes from the full facial blendshape $\mathbf{Y_t}$ These blendshapes are shown in Table 2. We then averaged the blendshapes that were represented with left and right sides to create a single variable. This was done because our lip-sync animation does not consider the left and right sides of the face separately. The resulting sequence represents the lip-sync animation $\mathbf{X_t}$.

In our training process, we partitioned the data into training and validation sets based on frame length, with approximately 80% of the files reserved for training and the remaining 20% for evaluation. Specifically, the training set comprises 416 files, totaling 122,583 in frame length, while the validation set includes 102 files with a combined length of 30,674.

We trained the model with 40 epochs and a batch size of 10. We used a ADAM [3] optimizer with a learning rate of 0.001 and weight decay of 0.005. Training is done in a Windows PyTorch environment with Nvidia RTX2070 GPU and Intel i9-9900K CPU. Total training time is 2 h 11 min.

3.2 Quantitative Evaluation Measures

We measure Mean per Blendshape Error (MPBE) with our validation set to validate our DNN model.

$$MPBE(\mathbf{X_t}, \mathbf{Y_t}) = \frac{1}{t}\sum_{n=1}^{t} |\mathbf{y_n} - Pred(\mathbf{x_n})|$$

Figure 1 shows the resulting MPBE. The network is better at predicting lip motions but struggles to predict eye motion that is weakly correlated to speech.

Our model was tested in the Unity Barracuda environment to determine its suitability for use in virtual reality applications. The results showed that the model is capable of predicting an entire face in just 6 ms when run in this environment. Furthermore, the entire process - including rendering and lipsyncing - takes an average of only 10 ms. This speed is well within the requirements for VR applications, which typically require a frame rate of at least 90 frames per second (fps), corresponding to a maximum rendering time of 11 ms per frame.

3.3 Qualitative Comparisons

To validate our capture and deep learning methods, we ran our DNN model on the validation set, then rendered the prediction of our method $\hat{\mathbf{Y}}_\mathbf{t}$ and ground truth $\mathbf{Y_t}$. We then compared the renderings accompanied by the original video (Fig. 2). We observed that the brow and mouth moved plausibly. Eye movement was minimal—further research on blinking validated that the activation level of blendshape "EyeBlinkLeft" stays constant, as shown in Fig. 3.

We compare facial animation results produced by our method and previous works by comparing animation results from the same speech audio (see Fig. 4). Compared to other results, our results showed plausible brow movement. Quantitative comparisons with these previous works are impossible because their used test rigs are incompatible with our implementation.

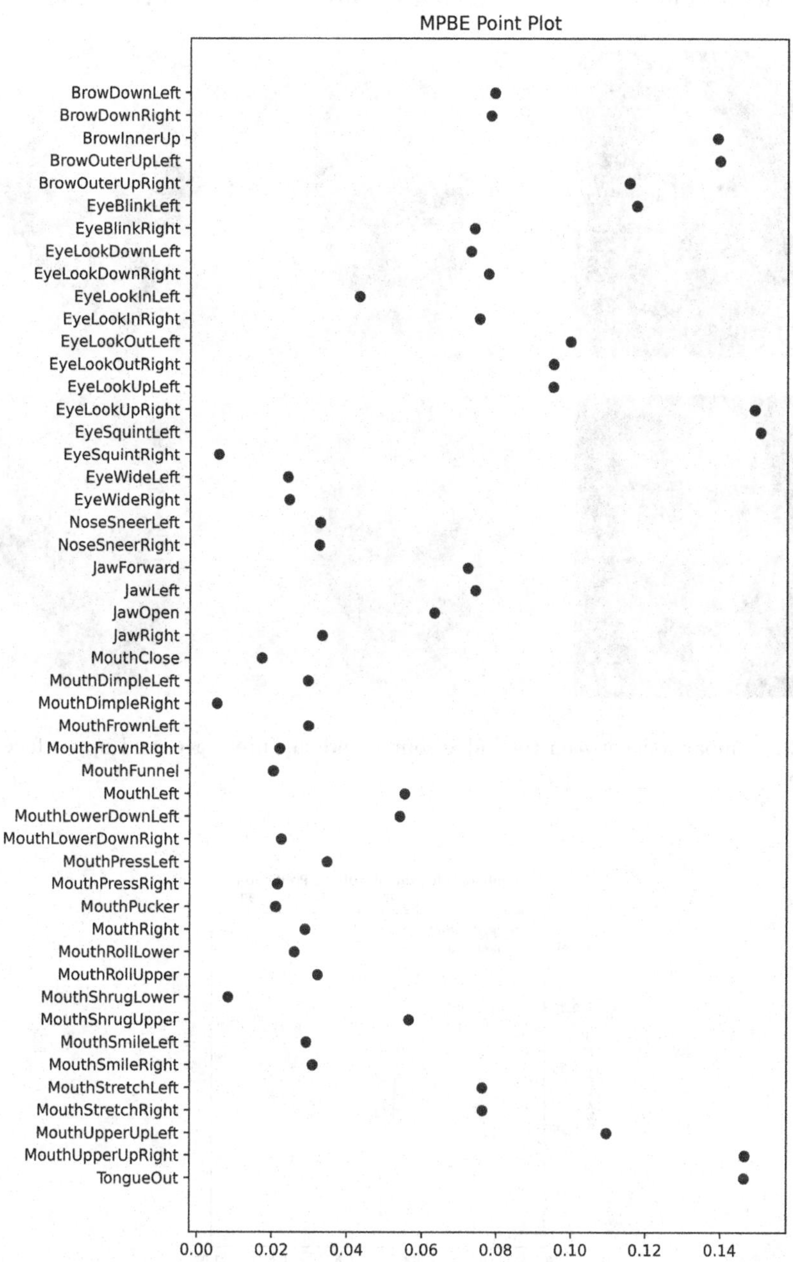

Fig. 1. MPBE Point Plot. Blendshape names are sorted with rough position of the face.

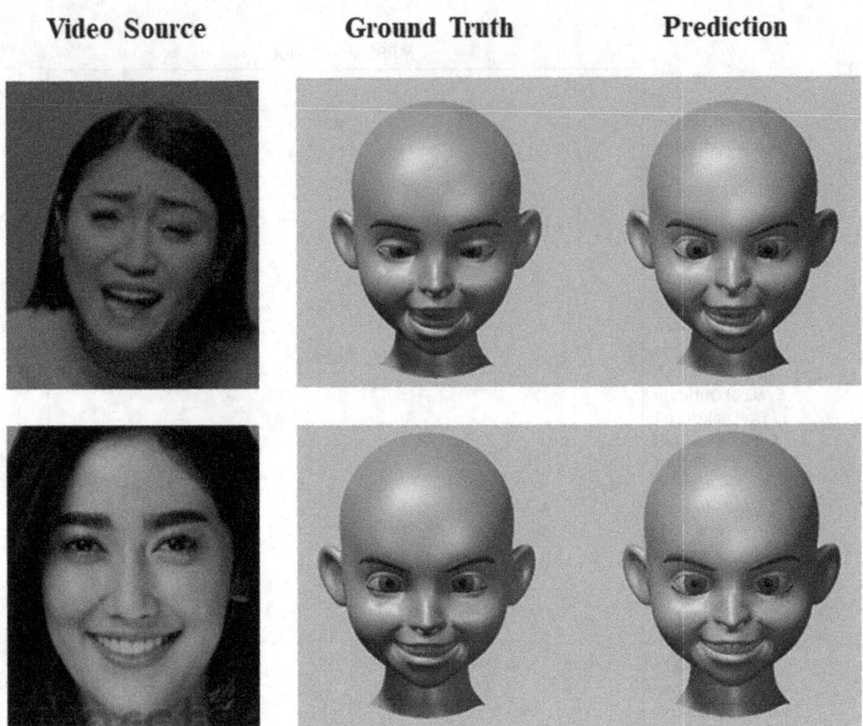

Fig. 2. Comparison between the video source and captured face, and upper face prediction.

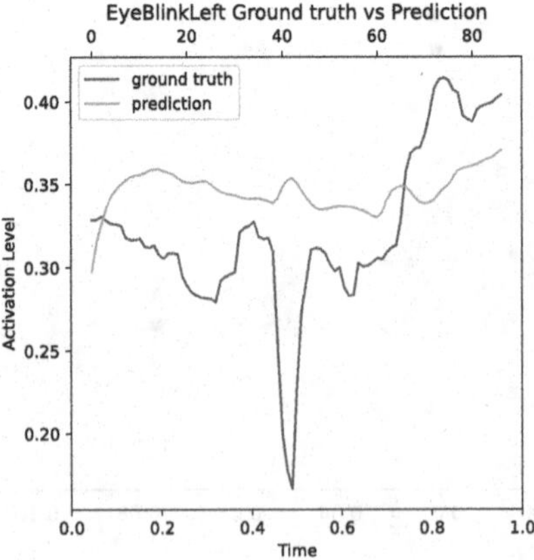

Fig. 3. Comparison between ground truth value and prediction value of blendshape "EyeBlinkLeft"

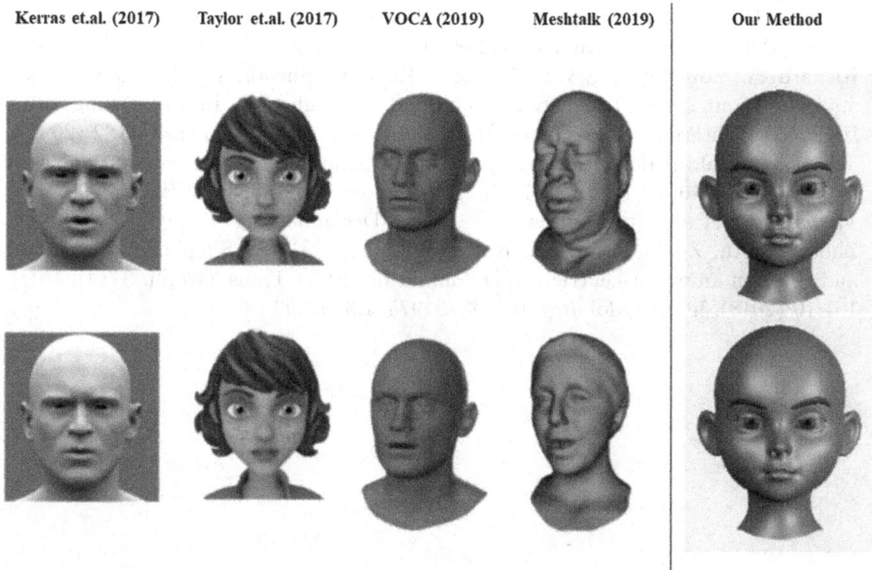

Fig. 4. Comparison between other methods and our methods that is given same audio clip [1,2,4,5]

4 Conclusion

We presented a real-time and realistic full-face animation method for a VR avatar. We evaluated our DNN model by quantitative measures and compared it with previous work. It could generate plausible full-face animation quickly, which is crucial given that short rendering time is crucial in VR use. In future work, we aim to address the issue of eye-blinking in our model to improve the realism of our full-face animation further.

Acknowledgement. This work was supported by the National Research Foundation of Korea (NRF) grant funded by the Korea government (MIST) (No. 2021R1A2C1014210) and by the MSIT (Ministry of Science and ICT), Korea, under the ITRC (Information Technology Research Center) support program (IITP-2023-RS-2022-00156353) supervised by the IITP (Institute for Information & Communications Technology Planning & Evaluation).

References

1. Cudeiro, D., Bolkart, T., Laidlaw, C., Ranjan, A., Black, M.J.: Capture, learning, and synthesis of 3D speaking styles. In: Proceedings of the IEEE/CVF Conference on Computer Vision and Pattern Recognition, pp. 10101–10111. IEEE (2019)
2. Karras, T., Aila, T., Laine, S., Herva, A., Lehtinen, J.: Audio-driven facial animation by joint end-to-end learning of pose and emotion. ACM Trans. Graph. **36**(4), 1–12 (2017). https://doi.org/10.1145/3072959.3073658

3. Kingma, D.P., Ba, J.: Adam: a method for stochastic optimization, January 2017. https://doi.org/10.48550/arXiv.1412.6980
4. Richard, A., Zollhöfer, M., Wen, Y., de la Torre, F., Sheikh, Y.: MeshTalk: 3D face animation from speech using cross-modality disentanglement. In: Proceedings of the IEEE/CVF International Conference on Computer Vision, pp. 1173–1182 (2021)
5. Taylor, S., et al.: A deep learning approach for generalized speech animation. ACM Trans. Graph. **36**(4), 1–11 (2017). https://doi.org/10.1145/3072959.3073699
6. Vaswani, A., et al.: Attention is all you need, December 2017
7. Zhou, Y., Xu, Z., Landreth, C., Kalogerakis, E., Maji, S., Singh, K.: VisemeNet: audio-driven animator-centric speech animation. ACM Trans. Graph. **37**(4), 161:1–161:10 (2018). https://doi.org/10.1145/3197517.3201292

An Interactive Digital Twin of a Composite Manufacturing Process for Training Operators via Immersive Technology

Iman Jalilvand, Jay Jiyoung, Hadi Hosseinionari, Rudolf Seethaler, Bhushan Gopaluni, and Abbas S. Milani(✉)

Materials and Manufacturing Research Institute, The University of British Columbia, Endowment Lands, Canada
{iman.jalilvand,abbas.milani}@ubc.ca

Abstract. Recently, there has been a growing interest in digital learning platforms and immersive technology for teaching, e.g., complex machine operators. This study investigates the use of a Mixed Reality (MR) system for operator training in a thermoforming case study, emphasizing the significance of user interface (UI), user experience (UX), and usability in MR applications. The work proposes a spatial user interface (UI) for MR applications that enables users to interact with virtual objects in the actual environment. Moreover, to enhance the UX, a real-time 3D heat transfer simulation was developed and integrated into the MR application to allow the learner to monitor and control the manufacturing process closely. The proposed framework is validated by an MR headset (Microsoft HoloLens 2). Lastly, a user study with eight participants was conducted, which showed the usability of the app using the System Usability Scale (SUS) questionnaire, scoring an overall usability rate of ~85/100.

Keywords: Mixed Reality · Immersive Training · User Study · User Interface · User Experience

1 Introduction

Recently, a variety of applications, including training, education, and safety, have seen an upsurge in the usage of Extended Reality (XR) systems [1]. The manufacturing industry is a unique instance of this universal trend. Particularly, there is a growing interest in using immersive technologies for complicated machine operators and workforce training. Milgram et al. [2] defined a taxonomy, which is well-known today among various XR platforms, beginning with Mixed Reality (MR) as a technology that brings together 3D content and the physical world; Augmented Reality (AR) as a perspective of the physical world with additional computer-generated features; and Virtual Reality (VR) as a single virtual environment separated from the real world [3]. In recent years, the adaptation of MR applications has particularly evolved owing to the introduction of new enabling equipment.

C. Stephanidis et al. (Eds.): HCII 2023, CCIS 1836, pp. 207–214, 2023.
https://doi.org/10.1007/978-3-031-36004-6_28

To exemplify, Reyes et al. [4] designed and analyzed a MR guiding system for motherboard assembly with 25 participants. Their research indicated that participants with prior experience with AR performed much better at orienting and arranging various motherboard components than those who had merely access to the actual setup. According to the authors, the system provided reasonable dependability and may be preferable for experienced users. In another study, Rokhsaritalemi et al. [5] provided a framework for developing MR applications, including user interaction components. Their suggested approach can help researchers create more effective MR systems for industrial training in harsh situations.

1.1 User Interface (UI), User Experience (UX) and Usability in MR Applications

MR applications feature distinct UIs compared to standard digital training systems, since they use wearable technology to superimpose virtual content on the physical surroundings. MR may not only alter a user's perspective of the actual world, but it also enriches the UX in the actual world instead of replacing it [6]. A significant benefit of adopting MR headsets is that they enable users to move freely inside the MR world [7]. Moreover, vision-based wearable devices allow users to engage with the MR world utilizing hand gesture controls [8]. Since its debut, Microsoft HoloLens has been regularly evaluated by developers and academics from many perspectives [6, 7]. While the current HoloLens offers several advantageous features that distinguish it from other MR HMDs, it also has some technical limitations. For instance, the restricted field of view (FOV) of HoloLens has a negative influence on the system's usability and user experience (UX).

Thus, building a personalized UI for HoloLens applications is a potential way to improve UX [9]. When compared to its predecessor (Microsoft HoloLens 1), Pose-Dez-de-la-Lastra et al. [10] studied the use of Microsoft HoloLens 2 in orthopedic procedures and discovered that it had a nearly 25% increase in AR projection accuracy. Nguyen et al. [11] Developed a MR system for nondestructive evaluation (NDE) training that lets students interact with virtual objects and execute NDE procedures without causing them injury. Their user study favoured the MR-based NDE training method over conventional training methods.

Under the framework of Industry 4.0, Pusch et al. [12] considered the use of MR for operator training. The authors assess the efficacy of three prototypes, including a haptic tablet, a large screen, and a Microsoft HoloLens-based MR version. Feedback indicated that, despite ergonomic limitations, the MR version has the potential to replace existing training techniques and even enable novices to complete the training independently. However, further tests were recommended to generalize these findings. Wu et al. [13] proposed a visual warning system that combines digital twins, deep learning technology, and MR using HoloLens to enhance the safety of construction workers. Testing revealed that the system operates effectively, but more improvement is necessary to solve lens distortion, image-based prediction function, and manual alignment. The applicability of a MR environment for instructing construction engineering students about sensing technologies was also investigated by Ogunseiju et al. [14]. Using eye tracking, usability questionnaires, and verbal feedback, their research assessed the MR environment and discovered that the accuracy of characterized construction activities, the quality of animations, and the ease of access to information and resources are crucial for building effective MR learning environments. Unfortunately, there is still a scarcity of literature on customized UI design for mixed-reality apps employing headsets.

1.2 Objective and Practical Motivation

Here we first designed a spatial UI for the HoloLens application as part of a digital learning prototype enabling user interaction with a combination of virtual content and a real thermoforming set-up. Adhering to UX design principles, the prototype was evaluated via a user study to verify its usability. Thermoforming requires strict adherence to unique sequences of steps to avoid nonuniform thickness distribution (defect) in the final product. Therefore, the present case study is critical to explore MR's potential in such advanced and high-risk manufacturing settings. To simulate the process, the system's 3D heat transfer behaviour amongst digital assets such as heaters and sheets has been simulated (via numerical finite difference method; more details can be found in [15]) and integrated into the MR headset (Microsoft HoloLens 2).

2 Methodology

The proposed XR design workflow is demonstrated in Fig. 1. In the first step, 3D asset and UI elements are designed using the Mixed Reality Toolkit (MRTK), SolidWorks, and ProBuilder feature in Unity. In step 2, objects are imported to Unity 3D scene, and additional visual and audio effects are added. Next, in step 3, the XR development process is accrued out, where all the scenes are designed, and all the virtual elements are added. In steps 4 and 5, objects interactive behaviour, animations, user input systems, and real-time 3D heat transfer simulation among certain elements (heaters and sheet) are developed in C# and deployed to the scene using Visual Studio and Unity.

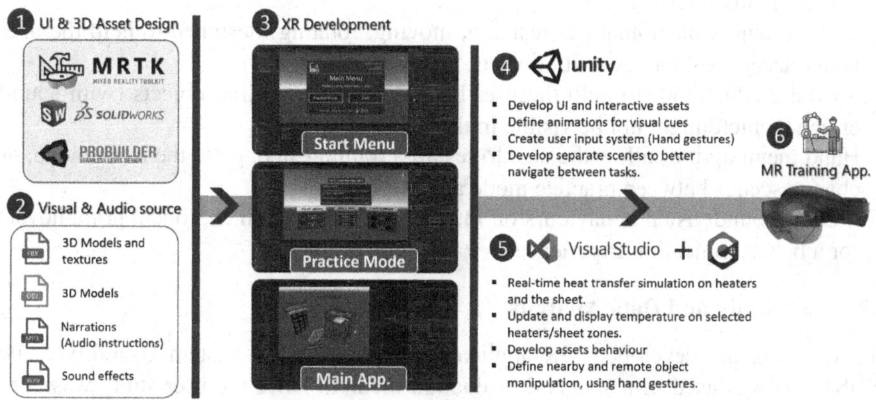

Fig. 1. The present MR application design framework

2.1 UI and UX Design

The methodology for the UI design for HoloLens 2 encompassed a range of UX principles. These included cognitive metrics, physical characteristics, the design of ambient elements, and the provision of visual and auditory instructions. To avoid strain on the user's neck, the spatial UI environment was designed such that the user can grab and move the virtual object to best fit in their comfortable range of height. Since the training procedure involved direct object manipulation, a critical design factor included the size of the object that needed to be manipulated as well as the distance from the viewer's eyes. In terms of system characteristics (hardware and software) of the HoloLens, scenes that are heavily populated with 3D objects or overloaded with scripts that constantly update the objects render may cause lagging and a frame rate drop from 300–320 to 20 frames per second (FPS). Higher frame rates produce more detailed visualizations when observing single virtual objects. Therefore, to avoid a low frame rate in the development stage, some modifications were made to reduce the resolution of the heat transfer simulation to compensate for hardware limitations, which resulted in higher frame rates (up to 85 FPS) even in densely populated scenes.

Visual and audible instructions are crucial for maintaining user engagement and attention in the application. To ensure that the operator clearly understands the virtual environment and its interactive elements, a 'tag-along' methodology [16] was employed to provide the user with visual prompts to complete specific tasks. Audio prompts and instructions were also used to compensate for the lack of visual information within certain unpopulated areas of the virtual space, which led to a higher quality of the UX.

The main features of the UI/UX design in the MR developed app are as follows:

- Practice mode in a separate scene to allow the users to get used to HoloLens 2 input system.
- Voice and visual text instructions (cues) for each training step.
- UI menus constantly follow the user to avoid limited FOV in HoloLens 2 and loss of content in the interface.
- Remote object manipulation (resizing, moving, rotating) designed to help the user better access and interact with objects.
- Spatial Audio (360) to help the user better navigate and find objects (with sound effects) which might not be visible in the user's FOV.
- Hand menu options allow the user to restart a training step, go to the main menu, or change scenes between practice mode and training.
- Various sound/visual behaviours on interactable objects (pinch, touch, grab, hover) for a better immersion experience.

2.2 User Study and Data Analysis

For assessing the developed MR application's usability, the System Usability Scale (SUS) [17] was used as a standard evaluation method. Once the user study was conducted, the correlations between pairs of the SUS questions (using the participants' responses) were statistically analyzed via the Spearman rank-order correlation coefficients. To further analyze the reliability of the SUS and the survey, Cronbach's alpha [18], as a measure of internal (mean) consistency of the data, was also calculated (theoretically, the values can vary between 0 to 1).

3 Results and Discussion

3.1 MR Application

Figure 2 shows the start menu and practice modes of the app., each with various UI features allowing the user to explore and acquaint themselves with the input system of the HoloLens 2. Figure 3 displays the steps of user training within the MR application. The application was simplified by displaying only important interactive features in each phase, and a control panel, which controls power adjustment and on/off switch functions. A screen also displayed the real-time temperature and power usage of each heater.

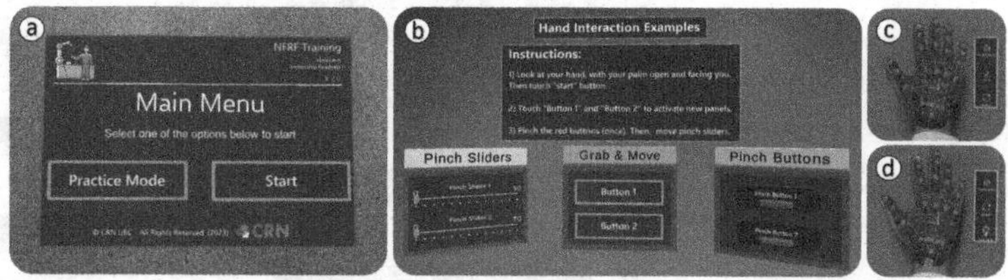

Fig. 2. Screenshots from the "Main Menu" and "Practice Mode" scenes of the MR app. a) shows the available options once the application starts. b) Practice scene options, which allow the user to explore hand interactions (touch, pinch, grab, move, and scale) before testing the Training application. c) Near-Hand menu in Practice Mode. d) Near-Hand menu in Training Application.

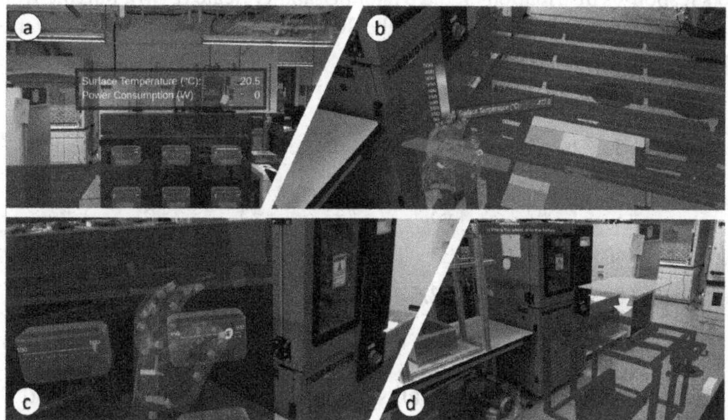

Fig. 3. Features of the developed digital twin for training thermoforming operators. a) Control panel provides the info screen, showing the surface temperature distribution and the power consumption of heaters. b) Visualizing the heater's surface temperature by hovering the hand over a selected heater. Once the heater is pinched, a visual heat bar guide is also shown on the side. c) Adjusting the heater's power range using the slider. d) Text instruction and the guiding arrow are facing the operator.

3.2 User Study

Eight participants with different backgrounds were recruited to test the MR application and provide feedback. Figure 4 depicts their responses on Likert Scale (from strongly disagree to strongly agree). Table 1. Also demonstrates the total score obtained from the SUS questionnaire. With the overall mean of 84.34 (out of 100) and the median of 86.25, the study suggests that the participants have indicated a high usability rate.

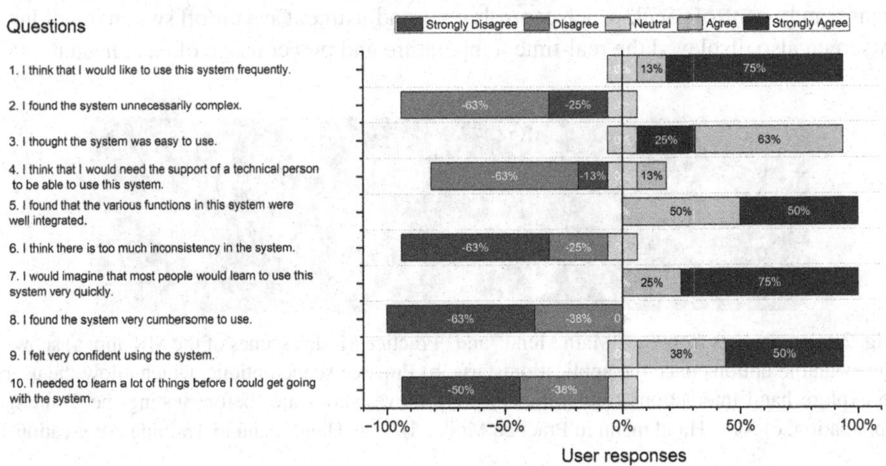

Fig. 4. Users responses distribution on the System Usability Scale (SUS), ranging from strongly disagree to strongly agree. Notice that some of the SUS questions are deliberately (by the standard) set in a negative form (i.e. in these cases'strongly disagree' is the top rate).

Table 1. The SUS score for different users of the MR application

User ID	#1	#2	#3	#4	#5	#6	#7	#8
Survey points	40	23	33	31	35	37	37	34
SUS Score	**100**	**57.5**	**82.5**	**77.5**	**87.5**	**92.5**	**92.5**	**85**

After performing the statistical analysis of the responses, it was found that some questions within SUS were significantly correlated when using a significance (alpha) level of 0.05. Results of the Spearman analysis indicated that there were some significant positive correlations between the following pairs: questions 1 and 9 ($r = 0.717$), questions 3 and 9 ($r = 0.737$). Similar significances were found for some negative-form questions: questions 4 and 8 ($r = 0.71$), questions 4 and 10 ($r = 0.732$), and questions 8 and 10 ($r = 0.802$). Of course, it is possible that the observed correlations might not also be fully logical due to the small sample size. Hence, the Cronbach's alfa mean metric was next calculated to estimate an 'overall internal consistency' measure of the survey, without relying on a particular significance level. The Cronbach's alfa mean was 0.879, indicating that the SUS questions and responses have been relatively consistent.

Of particular note, among the questions, based on Fig. 4, the speed of learning via the MR app (question 7) was highly noted (all participants rated as 'agree' or 'strongly agree').

During the qualitative assessment phase of data collection, participants were also given minimal instructions to operate the HoloLens application. However, some participants required further guidance to use the HoloLens HMD independently. This suggested that developing the necessary skillset through practice is crucial for users to control the virtual environment effectively. With regard to physical aspects and variations in individuals' heights within the test group, potential safety concerns were observed when utilizing the HoloLens HMD. Another issue that emerged during the testing phase concerned the HoloLens2 direct manipulation input model. While general gestures are intuitive, the pinch gesture for grasping augmented objects has been judged non-intuitive because the fingers appear to pass through the objects themselves.

4 Concluding Remarks

This study investigated how a MR system could be developed and used to train thermoforming manufacturing operators. The user study (with 8 participants in a university lab environment) emphasized the significance of UI, UX, and usability in MR applications. A spatial user interface was developed for the MR application, enabling users to interact with virtual items in the physical surroundings. In addition, a real-time 3D simulation of the heat transfer phenomenon in the process was developed and included in the application to enhance the UX. The suggested architecture was tested using a Microsoft HoloLens 2 headset. Participants indicated that the app was usable, with an overall usability score of ~85 out of 100, based on the System Usability Scale (SUS) questionnaire. Internal consistency of the survey data was also evaluated as satisfactory, suggesting that the SUS responses have been useable despite the limited sample size.

Some limitations were observed during the development of the application, including the need for assistance from users to better utilize the HoloLens app, emphasizing the significance of prior practice with the HMD. Additionally, variations in individuals' heights raised potential safety concerns during testing. Moreover, the pinch motion was considered non-intuitive as the fingers appeared to pass through the augmented objects. However, this is directly related to the HoloLens input system and hand gestures, which cannot be modified in the current version. Future research options may also involve targeting participants with other relevant backgrounds, such as industrial technicians. Additionally, incorporating uncertainties into the thermoforming process during training may be beneficial for simulating real-world manufacturing scenarios.

References

1. Doolani, S., et al.: A review of Extended Reality (XR) technologies for manufacturing training. Technologies **8**(4), 77 (2020). https://doi.org/10.3390/technologies8040077
2. Milgram, P., Takemura, H., Utsumi, A., Kishino, F.: Augmented reality: a class of displays on the reality-virtuality continuum. Telemanipulator Telepresence Technol. **2351**, 282–292 (1995). https://doi.org/10.1117/12.197321

3. Azuma, R.T.: A survey of augmented reality. Presence: Teleoper. Virtual Environ. **8**(2–3), 73–272 (1997). https://doi.org/10.1162/pres.1997.6.4.355
4. Reyes, A.C.C., Del Gallego, N.P.A., Deja, J.A.P.: Mixed reality guidance system for motherboard assembly using tangible augmented reality, pp. 1–6 (2020). https://doi.org/10.1145/3385378.3385379
5. Rokhsaritalemi, S., Sadeghi-Niaraki, A., Choi, S.M.: A review on mixed reality: current trends, challenges and prospects. Appl. Sci. **10**, 636 (2020). https://doi.org/10.3390/app10020636
6. Chuah, S.H.-W.: Why and who will adopt extended reality technology? Literature review, synthesis, and future research agenda. SSRN Electron. J. (2019). https://doi.org/10.2139/ssrn.3300469
7. Evans, G., Miller, J., Iglesias Pena, M., MacAllister, A., Winer, E.: Evaluating the microsoft hololens through an augmented reality assembly application. Degrad. Environ. Sensing, Process. **10197**, 101970 (2017). https://doi.org/10.1117/12.2262626
8. Lv, Z., et al.: PreprintTouch-less Interactive Augmented Reality Game on Vision Based Wearable Device. Springer (2015). https://arxiv.org/pdf/1504.06359
9. Hammady, R., Ma, M., Strathern, C., Mohamad, M.: Design and development of a spatial mixed reality touring guide to the Egyptian museum. Multimed. Tools Appl. **79**(5–6), 3465–3494 (2019). https://doi.org/10.1007/s11042-019-08026-w
10. Pose-Díez-De-la-lastra, A., et al.: HoloLens 1 vs. HoloLens 2: improvements in the new model for orthopedic oncological interventions. Sensors **22**(13), 4915 (2022). https://doi.org/10.3390/s22134915
11. Nguyen, T.V., Kamma, S., Adari, V., Lesthaeghe, T., Boehnlein, T., Kramb, V.: Mixed reality system for nondestructive evaluation training. Virtual Reality **25**(3), 709–718 (2020). https://doi.org/10.1007/s10055-020-00483-1
12. Pusch, A., Noël, F.: Augmented reality for operator training on industrial workplaces – comparing the microsoft hololens vs. small and big screen tactile devices. In: Fortin, C., Rivest, L., Bernard, A., Bouras, A. (eds.) PLM 2019. IAICT, vol. 565, pp. 3–13. Springer, Cham (2019). https://doi.org/10.1007/978-3-030-42250-9_1
13. Wu, S., Hou, L., (Kevin) Zhang, G., Chen, H.: Real-time mixed reality-based visual warning for construction workforce safety. Autom. Constr. 139(Dec), 104252 (2022). https://doi.org/10.1016/j.autcon.2022.104252
14. Ogunseiju, O.R., Gonsalves, N., Akanmu, A.A., Bairaktarova, D., Bowman, D.A., Jazizadeh, F.: Mixed reality environment for learning sensing technology applications in construction: a usability study. Adv. Eng. Inform. **53**, 101637 (2022). https://doi.org/10.1016/j.aei.2022.101637
15. Hosseinionari, H., Ramezankhani, M., Seethaler, R., Milani, A.S.: Development of a computationally efficient model of the heating phase in thermoforming process based on the experimental radiation pattern of heaters. Manuf. Mater. Process. **7**, 68 (2023)
16. Fonnet, A., Alves, N., Sousa, N., Guevara, M., Magalhães, L.: Heritage BIM integration with mixed reality for building preventive maintenance. In: EPCGI 2017 - 24th Encontro Port. Comput. Graf. e Interacao, vol. 2017-Janua, pp. 1–7 (2017). https://doi.org/10.1109/EPCGI.2017.8124304
17. Brooke, J.: SUS: a ‘quick and dirty’ usability scale. Usability Eval. Ind. (July), 207–212 (1995). https://doi.org/10.1201/9781498710411-35
18. Cronbach, L.J.: Coefficient alpha and the internal structure of tests. Psychometrika **16**(3), 297–334 (1951). https://doi.org/10.1007/BF02310555

A Study on the Copyright Management Platform for the Virtual Performance Asset Copyright Management and License Contracting in the Metaverse Environment

Won-Bin Kim, ChangHyun Roh, YongJoon Joe, and Dong-Myung Shin(✉)

Lsware Inc, Seoul 08504, Republic of Korea
{wbkim29,rohch,eugene,roland}@lsware.com

Abstract. Metaverse means an environment that transcends the real world. The metaverse environment can be performed without time and space constraints by implanting various activities in the real world. Therefore, it has established itself as an alternative space for not only various tasks and activities in the real world but also cultural contents. Recently, various studies are underway to implement virtual performances that can continue various performances and artistic activities in the real world without being restricted by time and space by utilizing the characteristics of the metaverse. A virtual performance composes a complete content by using various assets such as music, costumes, motions, effects, and locations in a complex way. Each of the various assets used in these virtual performances has separate copyrights, and has separate rights according to the contract with the copyright holder. Therefore, the content provider that provides the virtual performance must obtain the right to license each asset used for the virtual performance. However, since copyright in the metaverse environment has a different form of use from the real world, a different interpretation may be made from copyright contracts in the real world. Therefore, copyright infringement may occur if virtual performance content is constructed using the real-world copyright license contract method. In addition, additional problems such as profit distribution may occur due to duplication, repeated reproduction, and characteristics of digital data that can be reproduced. In addition, due to the characteristics of digital data that can be copied and reproduced, additional problems such as profit distribution may occur. In order to solve this problem, this study designs a platform that can manage copyrights for works used for virtual performances in a metaverse environment, carry out licensing contracts for copyrights, and distribute copyright profits according to contracts.

Keywords: Virtual Performance · Copyright · License · Metaverse

1 Introduction

The metaverse environment is a virtual environment composed of digital data, separated from the real world, but interactive. This metaverse environment is suitable for carrying out virtual activities. Recently, there is a movement to perform performances in the real

C. Stephanidis et al. (Eds.): HCII 2023, CCIS 1836, pp. 215–218, 2023.
https://doi.org/10.1007/978-3-031-36004-6_29

world in the virtual world by utilizing the characteristics of the metaverse. Performing such a performance in a metaverse environment is called a virtual performance, and it can be performed ignoring the time and space constraints of the real world. However, since virtual performances are activities and contents that take place in a digital environment, all elements used in virtual performances are made up of digital data. Representatively, music, costumes, backgrounds, motions, and scenarios are applicable, and digital assets are assets that treat these elements as individual contents. Each of these assets has its own copyright as shown in Fig. 1, and can only be used in a form that meets the terms of the copyright license [1, 2]. Nevertheless, since digital assets are composed of digital data, copying is inevitably easy, and due to this, unauthorized copying, reuse, misuse, abuse, modification, and redistribution may occur. This will adversely affect various content industries based on digital assets, and the virtual performance industry based on the metaverse environment cannot avoid it [3]. Therefore, in order to solve this problem, this study conducts research on a copyright management platform for copyright protection of digital asset contents of virtual performances in the metaverse environment.

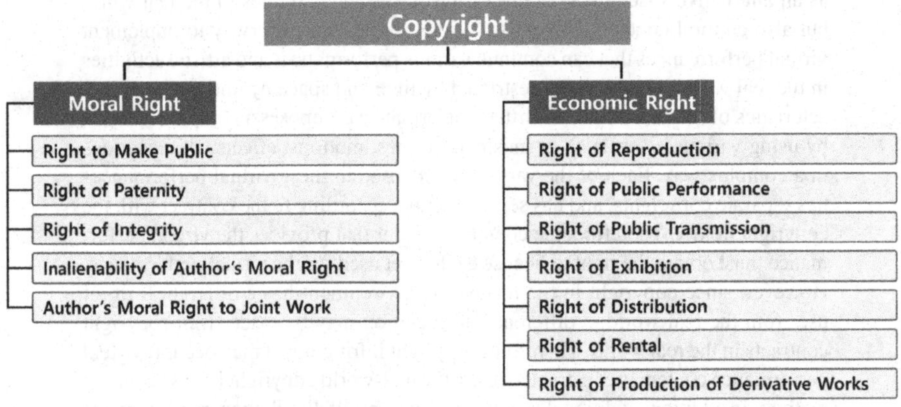

Fig. 1. Detailed structure of copyright

2 Copyright of Contents in Metaverse

Although the metaverse environment lies on the connecting line of the real world, it has a structure that is quite different from the real world. Most notably, there is no space constraint. This is because performances, broadcasts, and exhibitions in the real world are based on physical movements, actions, and forms by people and objects. it becomes impossible Also, even in the case of exhibition, it is impossible to reproduce the exact same thing, so a user who has not obtained a license cannot possess the original of the object according to the due process. However, since data on the metaverse is loaned to a third party and data is copied at the same time, abuse due to duplication of objects can be easily accomplished. In addition, there is a possibility that the limitations of the scope and place of performances, broadcasts and exhibitions may be ignored because the metaverse environment does not have physical space restrictions. Therefore, in order to perform a virtual performance that complies with the copyright law in the metaverse environment, it is necessary to manage and verify the ownership and copyright of content in accordance with the metaverse through a license management tool suitable for the metaverse environment [4–6].

3 Proposed System

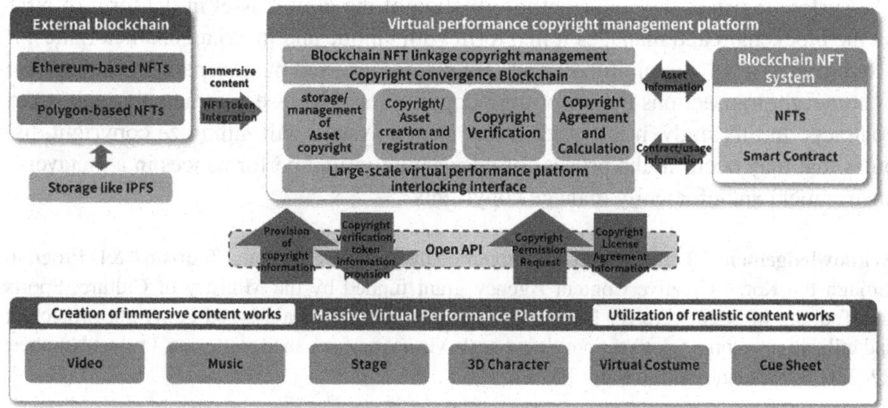

Fig. 2. Proposed virtual performance copyright management platform

In this chapter, we present a system for solving the copyright problem of the digital asset presented above. The proposed system is shown in Fig. 2, which uses blockchain and NFT technology to prevent copyright infringement of digital sets on metaverse. The system provides a virtual performance copyright management platform that can manage the copyrights of digital sets such as videos, music, stages, and 3D characters used in large virtual performance platforms under the premise that a large-scale virtual performance platform exists. The system uses blockchain and blockchain-based NFT technologies to carry out unique information and copyright and license agreements of digital sets. Digital assets registered as NFTs through the blockchain are given irreplaceable properties. Therefore, since integrity is guaranteed through the blockchain, the contents of copyright and license contracts are transparently managed. In addition, through the linkage between the external blockchain and the virtual performance copyright management platform, NFT's copyright information registered on other blockchain platforms can be managed on the virtual performance copyright management platform. This is to expand the data pool available on large-scale virtual performance platforms by securing additional digital sets registered on external blockchain platforms, and to prevent overlapping registration of the same digital sets on internal and external blockchain. This method can manage various digital assets through a virtual performance copyright management platform and provide the basis for legitimate use in a virtual performance platform.

4 Conclusion

This study deals with the problem of copyright management of digital sets used for virtual performances in a metaverse environment. Since the metaverse environment is a virtual environment made of digital data, it is very easy to replicate data. This can cause various copyright problems such as illegal copying, misuse, abuse, unauthorized redistribution, and unauthorized reuse of data. Therefore, copyright management of digital sets requires copyright management in a different way from the real world. To solve this problem, this study proposed a system that can manage copyright information of digital sets and perform transaction contracts using blockchain and NFT technology. The system registers the copyright information of the digital asset in the form of NFT on the blockchain and manages it in a form with unique and invariant characteristics. It also provides a way to minimize copyright disputes caused by transparency and misuse of copyright transactions by performing copyright and license contracts through smart contracts. In this study, it is expected that such a system will minimize copyright disputes that may occur in the process of performing virtual performances in a metaverse environment and efficiently manage copyrights.

Acknowledgement. This research was supported by Culture, Sports and Tourism R&D Program through the Korea Creative Content Agency grant funded by the Ministry of Culture, Sports and Tourism in 2022. (Project Name: Development of blockchain-based copyright protection and utilization technology to support large-scale virtual performance platforms, Project Number: R2022020057, Contribution Rate: 100%).

References

1. Kim, G., Jeon, J.H.: A study on the copyright survey for design protection in Metaverse period. Int. J. Adv. Smart Converg. **10**(3),181–186 (2021)
2. Dionisio, J.D.N., Burns III W.G., Gilbert, R.: 3D virtual worlds and the metaverse: current status and future possibilities. ACM Comput. Surv. (CSUR) **45**(3), 1–38 (2021)
3. Carter, D.: Immersive employee experiences in the Metaverse: virtual work environments, augmented analytics tools, and sensory and tracking technologies. Psychosociol. Issues Hum. Resour. Manag. **10**(1), 35–49 (2022)
4. Chou, C., Chan, P.-S., Huan-Chueh, W.: Using a two-tier test to assess students' understanding and alternative conceptions of cyber copyright laws. Br. J. Edu. Technol. **38**(6), 1072–1084 (2007)
5. Williams, E.: Copyright Law's over-protection of cyber content: digital rights management. Intell. Prop. L. Bull. **12**, 199 (2007)
6. Copyright Law of the United States (Title 17). https://copyright.gov/

Effects of Different Postures on User Experience in Virtual Reality

Eldiaz Salman Koeshandika[1](✉), Hironori Ishikawa[2], and Hiroyuki Manabe[1]

[1] Shibaura Institute of Technology, Tokyo 135-8548, Japan
ma21501@shibaura-it.ac.jp, manabehiroyuki@acm.org
[2] NTT DOCOMO, Kanagawa 239-8536, Japan

Abstract. Virtual reality (VR) applications are normally developed around the assumed body posture that maximizes the immersive experience. Users can, however, assume less optimal postures for reasons such as tiredness or body restrictions. We believe that accommodating such situations would increase the appeal and spread of VR.

We investigated the difference in VR user experience based on body posture by conducting a preliminary study and a user study. Our preliminary study with frequent VR users found that they adopt several postures and prefer to experience VR by sitting first, standing second, lying down third, then other postures. The most popular applications were VRChat, Beat Saber, then others. In our user study, the participants engaged in VR while adopting three different postures: standing upright, sitting on a chair, and lying down on a bean bag. Three VR applications were tested: Beat Saber, VRChat, and Youtube VR. The three postures yielded similar performance with Beat Saber. Lying down offered the slowest performance with VRChat. One reason for this is the difficulty of interacting with in-game objects in VRChat while lying down.

Our research shows the importance of VR application design as the developers must take into consideration extra factors. We suggest several solutions, such as having an adjustable virtual ground to accommodate the user's height and posture in real life or designing a user interface such that users can interact with their VR environment no matter their posture.

Keywords: Virtual Reality · User Experience · Posture

1 Introduction

Virtual Reality (VR) applications provide experiences unlike any other forms of entertainment. Its potential usage has been explored for other fields such as the Metaverse, in which VR and its associated Head Mounted Display (HMD) will likely play an important role [1]. VR applications are usually developed with the user inhabiting a virtual avatar in the virtual world to interact within it and they are designed with certain assumptions as to how the user will position themselves.

C. Stephanidis et al. (Eds.): HCII 2023, CCIS 1836, pp. 219–226, 2023.
https://doi.org/10.1007/978-3-031-36004-6_30

Of course, users still have the freedom to assume any posture they prefer even though it is not the most optimal one. For example, a VR application for communicating with others may be more immersive if the user stands, but the user can instead sit or even lie down if tired. Not only that, VR users who are bedridden can only play VR while lying down, severely restricting their actions in VR applications that assume the standing posture; their field of vision would be restricted while bedridden as they cannot turn their shoulders. To elucidate these issues, we researched how VR users interacted with various applications while taking different postures. We evaluate how each application would perform given different postures and how well their user interface supports the different postures. From our discoveries, we then propose several recommendations for the developer on how they could design VR applications to be more inclusive with regard to the user postures possible. These recommendations will help in developing user VR interfaces that are usable for people who prefer, or must, experience VR while lying down.

2 Related Work

Though posture and user experience for VR have not be researched together extensively, there have been studies on the linkage of cybersickness and user experience [10]. Cybersickness is similar to motion sickness and experienced by people using VR [3]. There are conflicting opinions whether cybersickness negatively affects user experience by reducing their presence in the virtual world [4], or not as cybersickness may be regarded as part of virtual reality [9], but there is a definite link between cybersickness and user experience.

Comparing the effects of different postures in cybersickness in VR has been researched. Zielasko and Riecke [11], for example, grouped several VR research results based on the posture used and the degree of embodiment, how immersive the experience is, during VR, and compared it to several attributes such as long-term comfort and cybersickness. These findings were further researched by them through a survey of VR experts [12]. For example, sitting posture with low and high "degree of embodiment" is more comfortable than standing posture, and that sitting posture with low "degree of embodiment" provides the smallest amount of cybersickness.

Postures other than sitting and standing, such as lying-down, have also been researched,. Marengo et al. noted that people with experience in VR feel more disoriented playing VR while supine, compared to standing upright [5]. Tian et al. found that the disorientation when using VR while lying down can be mitigated by adjusting the orientation of the virtual environment to match the real world, and to have the application feature less virtual acceleration [8], though it may depend on individual resistance [7].

3 Investigations

We conducted two studies for this research: a preliminary study and a user study. The preliminary study investigated what posture VR users would adopt when playing VR applications of their choosing. The user study examines the results of the preliminary study. Drawing on the findings of our user study, we will then offer several recommendations for VR developers to consider when developing applications.

3.1 Preliminary Study

The preliminary study involved filling in a questionnaire created using Google Form. The questionnaire asked the participants to provide demographic information and their experiences of virtual reality. Experiences for this research consisted of the participants' length of time playing VR in a day, most used posture used while playing VR, and their most used VR applications.

The questionnaire was sent by two methods to two groups: a collection of VR players were sent the questionnaire by email, while students in Shibaura Institute of Technology were recruited through dissemination of a QR code. Incentives were given in the form of a 300 JPY Amazon Gift Card for people who answered all questions in the questionnaire. People who answered that they had no experience in VR received no reward.

Preliminary Study Result. 26 respondents answered the questionnaire. Only two answered they had no experience with VR. Figure 1 shows the most popular postures and Fig. 2 shows the most popular applications. The questions were written to be open ended, thus respondents could respond with more than one posture and application. Sitting was the most preferred posture followed by standing. Lying down was the third most preferred posture. With regard to applications, VRChat was the most popular application among the respondents, followed by Beat Saber.

3.2 User Study

The results from the preliminary study formed the basis of the user study.

The user study involved the participants playing VR applications in different postures. The applications and postures were chosen based on the result of the preliminary study. After finishing the experiment, participants were then asked to fill out a questionnaire in which they compared their VR experiences based on the application and the posture.

Three postures, standing, sitting, and lying down, were chosen to be compared. Three different VR applications were chosen for participants to experience in the three postures. The questionnaire after the experiment asked the participants to compare their experiences playing the three applications in the three different postures.

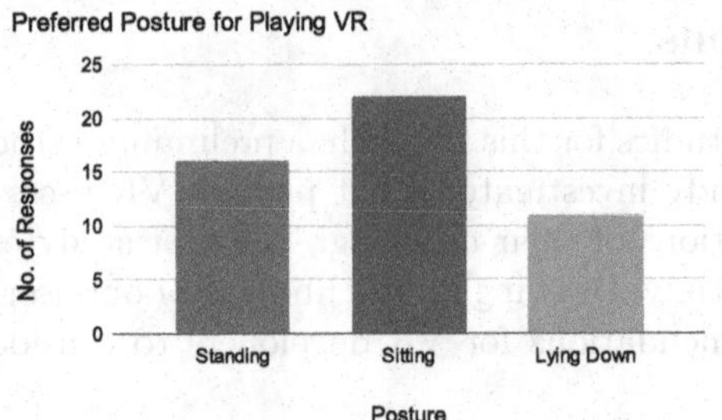

Fig. 1. Preliminary study result for most used posture when playing VR.

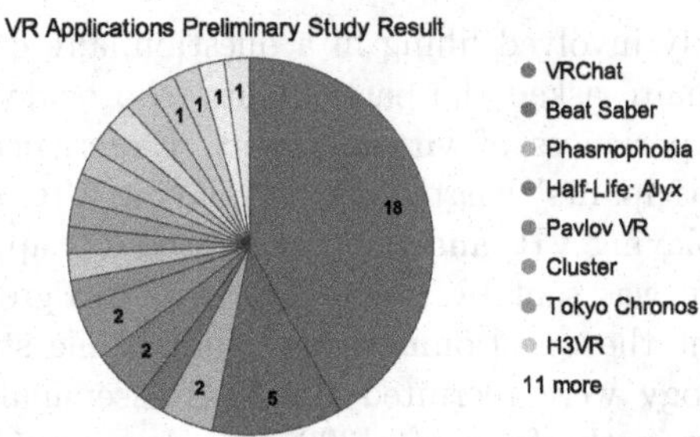

Fig. 2. Preliminary study result for most played VR applications.

Participants. 6 participants were recruited for the experiment, all were students of Shibaura Institute of Technology. 2 participants had experience with VR, 2 had tried VR only once or twice, and the last two had no experience at all. Each participant was given a 1500 JPY Amazon Gift Card for participating and completing the experiment.

Equipment. Three devices were prepared for the participants: Oculus Quest 2, a wheeled chair, and a yogibo bean bag. Participants were to sit on the wheeled for the sitting session, and to lie down on the yogibo bean bag for the supine session. Ample space to support user movement was ensured every time a session was about to begin, by practices such as removing equipment unrelated to the current posture from the experiment area.

Applications. Three VR applications, Beat Saber, VRChat, and Youtube VR, were used in the user study.

Beat Saber is a rhythm game in which the player must cut a series of boxes that approach them in a pattern that follows the music that plays in the game. Participants were instructed to play the same level three times, each in a different posture in the order of standing, sitting, then supine. As only one song is required for this experiment, this experiment used the song provided in the Demo Version of Beat Saber. The performance of the participants was measured using the number of boxes successfully cut for one completed level, which is shown at the end of the level.

VRChat is a massive multiplayer online game with the main purpose of interacting with players all around the world. Due to its nature as a VR application, VRChat also has potential to be used as a platform for VR experiments [6]. For this experiment, participants were instructed to complete several tasks in the VRChat default world for new users. Participant would jump, do a hand gesture, interact with a panel in the VR world, draw a line around their avatar, a circle, a square, and a triangle using a virtual pen, then inputting the text "this is the end of the test" in a message box in the VRChat user profile. Their completion time was measured. The participants undertook the task three times, each time in a different posture: standing, sitting, then supine. Participants were trained on each task before the real test was conducted.

Youtube VR is chosen as the third application to provide a contrast between the more active Beat Saber and VRChat, and also to provide a relaxed experience between the other two applications. Youtube VR was also found to increase interest in subject topics for people who previously had no interest [2]. For this experiment, participants were asked to play three distinct videos, each showing 360°C footage of various cities and locales for around four minutes. Each video was seen in the three different postures: standing, sitting, and lying down. Participants were free to choose which posture they would adopt as long as it was different from the posture they chose before.

Result. Fig. 3 shows the score of each participant. It also shows that, on average, participants attained the highest score while sitting (mean = 189.67/195, s.d. = 4.08), followed by supine (mean = 185.67/195, s.d. = 5.71) then standing (mean = 181.83/195, s.d. = 13.80). The lowest score of standing result could be explained by standing posture as the first posture assumed for Beat Saber. Participants would be unfamiliar with the rhythm of the level in their first session. As they continue to sitting and supine, they would be used to the music and the pattern, resulting in higher score for sitting and supine than standing. Our observations found that participants had an easier time reaching the boxes while sitting as they did not need to move as much compared to standing. In comparison, they had more difficulty reaching the boxes while lying down on the

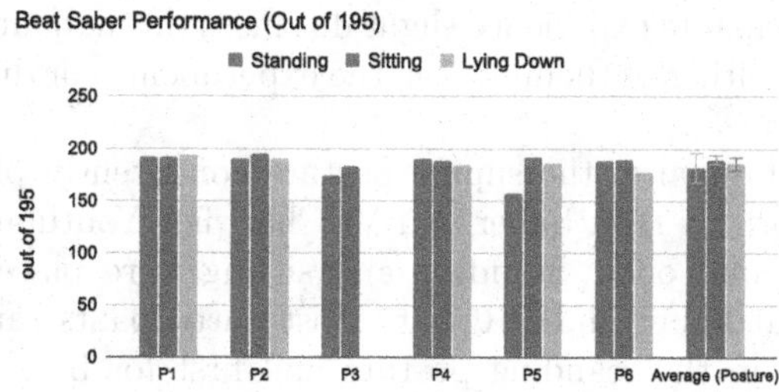

Fig. 3. Beat Saber result for each participant and the average result for each posture

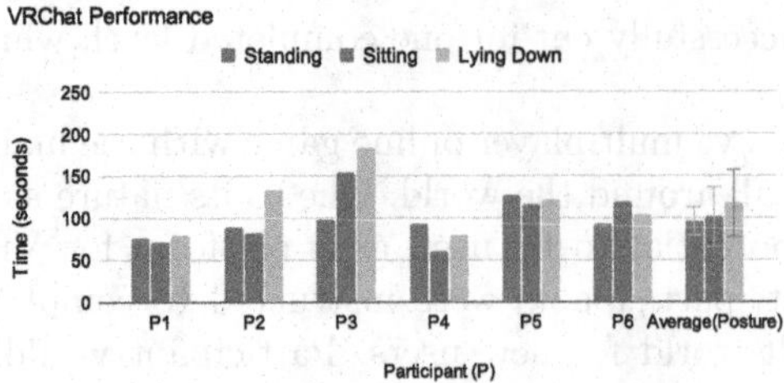

Fig. 4. VRChat result for each participant and the average result for each posture

bean bag, which may explain the lower score. However, these differences do not significantly affect Beat Saber's performance.

For VRChat, participants completed the task the fastest, on average, while standing (mean = 95.67 s, s.d. = 16.60), then sitting (mean = 100.33 s, s.d. = 35.49) with supine last (mean=116.5 s, s.d. = 39.61). Figure 4 shows each participant's performance varies greatly, though performance per posture generally became worse as they changed their posture to sitting, then supine. Participants had trouble rotating their avatar while sitting and supine as they could not rotate their body. One specific issue with the supine posture in VRChat is the difficulty of interacting with in-game objects compared to sitting and standing. When participants were supine, their virtual hands in VRChat were raised to the same height as their shoulder. Those hands are needed to point to the object they would like to interact with, and the unnatural placement of those hands while the participants were supine made it difficult for them to choose the object for the task. Some participants were able to manipulate the selection method to gain similar performance to standing and sitting by positioning themselves awkwardly like their virtual avatar so they could point to the required object correctly. Those who could not performed far worse.

Our observations of the Youtube VR showed that many participants were eager to see the footage of the videos. They also used the panning feature of Youtube VR, which is done by holding the index trigger of the Oculus Quest 2 controller and moving the controller sideways. This allowed the participants to see their surroundings without turning their heads and body. The panning feature was used the most while sitting and supine, but it was also used while standing.

Only two participants experience slight dizziness throughout the experiment, but not enough for either of them to stop the experiment, nor did it visibly affect their performance.

From the questionnaire, the supine posture consistently placed last in the rankings for comfort for Beat Saber and VRChat. For Youtube VR, supine was voted first and second once. Standing and sitting were placed either first or second for the Beat Saber and VRChat. Most participants ranked Beat Saber as most enjoyable in the standing posture and first for best user interface in the sitting and standing postures. Youtube VR received the most first ranking assessments for the best interface while supine.

4 Discussion

Beat Saber and VRChat are VR applications that make the user move, but results between postures show that, on average, participants perform in Beat Saber relatively equal between postures, while they perform the best in VRChat while standing. One reason for this could lie in the scope of each application. Beat Saber may include a lot of action, but the user does not move in the virtual environment. VRChat, on the other hand, allows free movement of the user so they can roam the virtual environment. This shows that the number of postures the user is assumed to adopt in a VR application impacts the complexity of the user interface and so must be considered in application design.

It is possible that the supine posture was favored least by most participants due to the chosen applications not supporting the posture. Many participants commented that they had trouble reaching objects in all applications while supine. One of the causes could be the height at which the participants were lying down. The bean bag was placed close to the ground, thus the participant would also be close to the ground while they were in the virtual world.

4.1 Recommendations for Developer

Based on the findings of our investigation, we propose several recommendations for developers.

The complexity of the application is one of the most important consideration when developing VR application. Beat Saber is a fast-paced game, but its limited field of interaction allows it to be played in various postures with similar results. On the other hand, applications that require/encourage free player movement like VRChat are difficult to play while sitting or standing as both restrict body movement and body movement is simulated in the virtual world. The larger the number of options the user can select from in the VR applications, more methods to access those options must be examined.

One method to increase accessibility in VR is to have a feature that allows the user to look around in the virtual world without having to turn their heads and/or body. This should support users who are unable to turn around to enjoy the VR experience just like the user who is standing or sitting on a rotating chair.

Another method is to make the virtual ground adjustable so that users who are close to the ground can feel as if they were standing. This may come with the risk of sensory conflict due to the difference between the real world height and virtual height.

Overall, to allow people with various needs and limitations to have the same experience in their VR application, developers may choose to either develop a simple but engaging user interface like Beat Saber, or to have a flexible user interface, more than VRChat, that allows a similar degree of freedom no matter the body restrictions of the user.

5 Conclusion

We found that depending on the VR application, different body postures can affect the user experience. Applications which are simplistic and limited in user freedom can be enjoyed relatively equally when standing, sitting, or lying down. Applications that offer realistic movement and environment interaction are not as enjoyable to experience while lying down. We recommend that VR developers should consider including accessibility options for user with various needs and limitations so that they can enjoy the VR application as intended.

References

1. Dincelli, E., Yayla, A.: Immersive virtual reality in the age of the metaverse: a hybrid-narrative review based on the technology affordance perspective. J. Strateg. Inf. Syst. **31**(2), 101717 (2022)
2. Filter, E., Eckes, A., Fiebelkorn, F., Büssing, A.G.: Virtual reality nature experiences involving wolves on youtube: presence, emotions, and attitudes in immersive and nonimmersive settings. Sustainability **12**(9), 3823 (2020)
3. LaViola, J.J., Jr.: A discussion of cybersickness in virtual environments. ACM Sigchi Bull. **32**(1), 47–56 (2000)
4. Lin, J.W., Duh, H.B.L., Parker, D.E., Abi-Rached, H., Furness, T.A.: Effects of field of view on presence, enjoyment, memory, and simulator sickness in a virtual environment. In: Proceedings IEEE Virtual Reality 2002, pp. 164–171. IEEE (2002)
5. Marengo, J., Lopes, P., Boulic, R.: On the influence of the supine posture on simulation sickness in virtual reality. In: 2019 IEEE Conference on Games (CoG), pp. 1–8. IEEE (2019)
6. Saffo, D., Yildirim, C., Di Bartolomeo, S., Dunne, C.: Crowdsourcing virtual reality experiments using vrchat. In: Extended Abstracts of the 2020 Chi Conference on Human Factors in Computing Systems, pp. 1–8 (2020)
7. Terenzi, L., Zaal, P.: Rotational and translational velocity and acceleration thresholds for the onset of cybersickness in virtual reality. In: AIAA Scitech 2020 Forum, p. 0171 (2020)
8. Tian, N., Clément, R., Lopes, P., Boulic, R.: On the effect of the vertical axis alignment on cybersickness and game experience in a supine posture. In: 2020 IEEE Conference on Games (CoG), pp. 359–366. IEEE (2020)
9. Von Mammen, S., Knote, A., Edenhofer, S.: Cyber sick but still having fun. In: Proceedings of the 22nd ACM Conference on Virtual Reality Software and Technology, pp. 325–326 (2016)
10. Wang, G., Suh, A.: User adaptation to cybersickness in virtual reality: a qualitative study. In: 27th European Conference on Information Systems (ECIS 2019): Information Systems for a Sharing Society. Association for Information Systems (AIS) (2019)
11. Zielasko, D., Riecke, B.E.: Sitting vs. standing in VR: towards a systematic classification of challenges and (dis) advantages. In: VR Workshops, pp. 297–298 (2020)
12. Zielasko, D., Riecke, B.E.: To sit or not to sit in VR: Analyzing influences and (dis) advantages of posture and embodied interaction. Computers **10**(6), 73 (2021)

Development of an Immersive Virtual Reality Platform for Innovation in Nursing Education

Knoo Lee[1(✉)], Fang Wang[2], and Blaine Reeder[1,3]

[1] Sinclair School of Nursing, University of Missouri, 915 Hitt Street, Columbia, MO 65211, USA
knooleee@missouri.edu

[2] College of Engineering, University of Missouri, Lafferre Hall, Columbia, MO 65211, USA

[3] Institute for Data Science and Informatics, University of Missouri, 22 Heinkel Building, Columbia, MO 65211, USA

Abstract. The nursing workforce shortage is a pressing global issue that is further exacerbated by the aging nursing education workforce, leading to the retirement of experienced educators who train new nurses. Virtual Reality (VR) training offers potential to improve cognitive experiences and decrease training costs. High Fidelity Simulation (HFS) uses mannequins to simulate clinical experiences but has limited ability to simulate escalating situations, and using hospital resources with trained actors is costly and challenging. Our aim is to develop an open-source, fully-interactive VR training platform that provides a sustainable solution for resource-limited schools of nursing. The first simulation is of a nurse responding to a patient experiencing cardiac arrest in an emergency department scenario. We have completed asset development with less funding compared to off-the-shelf products. Our research describes the clinical aspects of the scenario, challenges of the VR implementation, usability tests, and implications of an open VR training platform for healthcare workers, patients, and caretakers.

Keywords: Virtual Reality · High Fidelity Simulation · Nursing Education

1 Introduction

The shortage of nurses globally has become a significant threat to global health due to the aging nursing workforce and retiring educators [1–4]. This situation is further compounded by the COVID-19 pandemic, which has highlighted the need for adequately trained healthcare professionals to respond to public health emergencies [5]. Immersive virtual reality (VR) technology might be a solution to address this shortage via enhancing nursing education. VR training provides cognitive experiences that decrease training time and lower costs while providing realistic and engaging clinical scenarios [6–8]. The aim of this paper is to describe initial efforts to develop and test a low-cost, sustainable immersive VR training platform for nursing education that can increase capacity to educate new nurses with the current nursing faculty workforce.

C. Stephanidis et al. (Eds.): HCII 2023, CCIS 1836, pp. 227–234, 2023.
https://doi.org/10.1007/978-3-031-36004-6_31

1.1 High Fidelity Simulation in Nursing Education

High Fidelity Simulation (HFS) is a form of education that simulates actual clinical experiences, allowing students to practice and refine their clinical skills. HFS typically uses mannequins that mimic human physiological responses, creating realistic patient scenarios [9]. However, current HFS pedagogical methods have limited ability to simulate escalating situations that nurses may encounter in the real world because using real-world resources such as hospital equipment with trained actors to simulate escalating clinical situations is cost-prohibitive and logistically challenging.

1.2 Virtual Reality (VR) Training

VR training uses computer technology to create a realistic environment that can afford "players" – users of VR systems - the benefit of applied experience, free from the consequences of mistakes in the real-world. VR training has been applied in numerous fields including military and defense [10] aviation and aerospace [11], and healthcare [12, 13]. VR training for nursing education can provide unique opportunities for nursing students to experience realistic and immersive clinical scenarios. As such, VR training for nursing has the potential to revolutionize nursing education by overcoming the challenges inherent to high fidelity simulation. Indeed, there are several current commercial applications in this growing space [14, 15] However, the potential benefits of VR training for nursing education are not without challenges.

1.3 Benefits and Challenges of VR Training for Nursing Education

VR training has numerous potential benefits for nursing education. These including: 1) improved clinical decision-making, 2) increased confidence in clinical skills, 3) reduced training time, 4) flexibility in training schedule, 5) distance education opportunities, and 6) improved efficiency in use of expertise of current nursing faculty workforce. VR provides a safe and controlled environment for students to practice and refine their skills, eliminating the risk of patient harm during training sessions. Additionally, VR training can be used to simulate rare and complex clinical scenarios that may be difficult to recreate using traditional HFS. Thus, VR training can provide an environment where nursing students can gain experience with rare clinical events that is currently unavailable.

There are also several challenges to developing VR training for nursing education. These challenges include: 1) high cost of VR technology, 2) need for specialized software development skills to develop clinical scenarios, and 3) need to create realistic and engaging scenarios that accurately reflect clinical practice, which require software companies to hiring nursing experts, 4) cross-disciplinary collaboration between nursing educators and software developers, 5). Interoperability challenges posed by proprietary technologies available from for-profit companies, which is a barrier to sharing of clinical scenarios between systems and schools. In particular recurring licensing fees for commercial proprietary VR systems are cost-prohibitive. Thus, these systems present a barrier to access, adoption, and sustained use by resource-limited schools of nursing. Therefore, our solution is to develop a cost-feasible and sustainable VR training solution for nursing education that realizes the potential benefits and overcomes current VR challenges and the challenges inherent to HFS.

2 Methods

To address the challenges of developing VR training for nursing education, our approach is to develop an open-source (i.e., available for anyone to use developed VR contents), fully interactive VR training platform that provides a sustainable solution for resource-limited schools of nursing. The long-term vision is a platform that will focus on creating realistic and engaging scenarios that accurately reflect clinical practice. Our initial efforts began with an emergency department scenario involving a patient experiencing cardiac arrest. To date, we have completed assets (i.e., objects required for devising virtual reality such as characters, voice, objects, environments) development for the arrest scenario. Our current list of assets includes all emergency department (ED) equipment and non-playable characters (NPCs), with significantly less funding compared to currently offered, off-the-shelf products. Members of the research team have participated in formative, iterative testing of the VR training platform by navigating the clinical scenario in the player role to verify technical function throughout the process.

2.1 Clinical Scenario Design

Our initial VR training scenario involves a nurse in the emergency department responding to an escalating situation of a patient experiencing cardiac arrest. We have selected this clinical scenario due to two reasons. Firstly, the prevailing pedagogical approach for nursing simulation-based practica, which excels in reproducing the hospital setting, exhibits limited capability in simulating escalating situations, such as cardiac arrest. Secondly, the incidence of cardiac arrest during nursing training is infrequent, potentially hindering the readiness of new graduate nurses for clinical practice. The scenario is designed to simulate a realistic environment and nursing workflow, including patient assessment, initiation of basic life support, defibrillation, and administration of medications. The scenario also includes the interdisciplinary healthcare team, including the physician, respiratory therapist, and registered nurses, who provide collaborative care to the patient. The scenario is based on an evidence-based practice guideline [16] and the Advanced Cardiovascular Life Support (ACLS) manual [17] ensuring that students receive accurate and up-to-date information. In addition, we are designing this initial scenario with the recognition that clinical guidelines change over time and the need to specify a modular approach that enables updates and management of all scenarios with the help of nursing and medicine faculties.

2.2 Team Composition

Developing a VR training platform for nursing education challenge is complex and required that we assemble an interdisciplinary research team with diverse and complementary skill sets. The research team comprises faculty from nursing, medicine, informatics, and engineering. Faculty from the health care disciplines possess a deep understanding of the intricacies of clinical workflows and patient care. They provide domain expertise required to ensure fidelity of the VR clinical scenarios through which nursing and other allied health professionals will receive education. Engineering faculty bring applied VR development experience and a specialized laboratory dedicated to the development of a VR training platform for nursing. As a whole, the team has extensive experience in designing and developing various types of virtual reality applications, with the domain expertise to develop a VR training platform specific to healthcare. The collective skillset of this team enables us to approach the development of the platform from various angles, incorporating the latest technological advancements and the most up-to-date clinical practices. As a result, we are producing an engaging and educational VR simulation that provides nurses, and potentially trainees from other clinical disciplines, with a unique and effective learning experience.

3 Results

We present results of within-team formative testing of our clinical scenario and the outputs that will establish the foundation of our efforts going forward.

Cardiac Arrest Scenario. The initial clinical scenario presented in this study concerned a patient experiencing cardiac arrest (see Fig. 1). This scenario enables the player to accurately assess the patient's condition, specifically ventricular tachycardia, using the attached defibrillator pads. The player was able to effectively collaborate with other medical professionals to implement a series of cardiac pulmonary support techniques, including chest compression and defibrillation, serving as a proof-of-concept for our approach. Notably, the scenario was completed within 5 min without compromising the quality of the hospital settings and non-player characters (NPCs), and without causing any crashes.

Action Sheet. We have made substantial progress towards developing a comprehensive nursing VR simulation scenario of cardiac arrest. The team has created an 'action sheet' that serves as a comprehensive guide for the simulation, ensuring that all necessary components (e.g., NPC voice, animation and specific location list with corresponding time stamps, background noise) are included and accurately reflect real-world scenarios. This has been a valuable tool in guiding the development of the simulation.

Assets Inventory. The current 3D model assets inventory includes patient beds, curtains, poles, infusion pumps, crash carts, syringes, vials, and a defibrillator. Interactive assets are essential for creating a realistic VR simulation, and the team has been able to create them from scratch using 3D modeling software such as Blender; purchased some from the Unity Assets Store, modifying them to make them interactive.

NPC Development Protocol. We have established an NPC protocol to guide design efforts. The team is devising all NPCs (i.e., scribe nurse, medication nurse, student nurse, clinician, respiratory therapist, patients, and caregivers) with corresponding uniforms using the software Reallusion. The character model is then animated using Perception Neuron motion capture with additional open-source animations from Mixamo. These steps help in creating a realistic and engaging VR simulation that can be used to train nursing students and improve their skills.

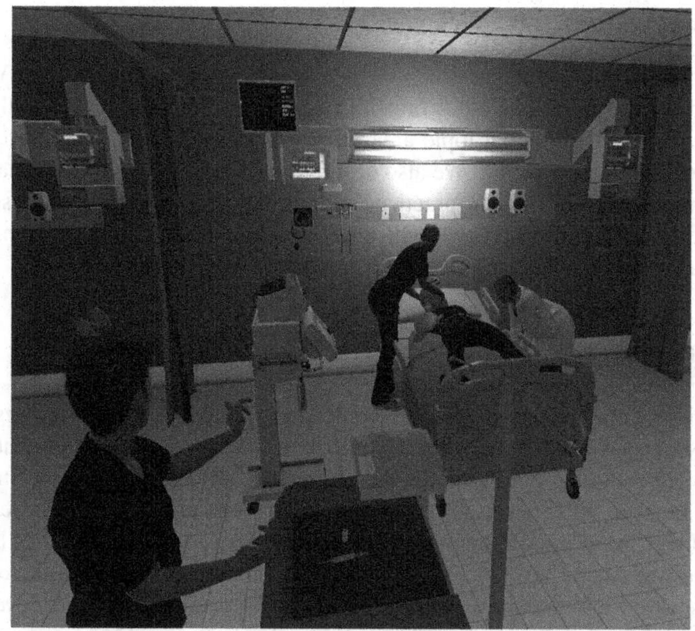

Fig. 1. A proof-of-concept virtual reality training in a cardiac arrest scenario.

4 Next Steps

4.1 Usability and Acceptability Testing with Participants

As next steps, we plan to conduct a pilot study to test the usability and acceptability of the VR with a small group of nursing students as participants. In addition to user perceptions of usability [18] and technology acceptability, [19] we will conduct exploratory measures students' readiness to practice as the future primary outcome of larger studies. The pilot study will inform future design iterations of the VR training platform to the needs of nursing students and educators and real-world clinical practice settings.

Readiness to practice is a concept used in health field literature capturing how prepared a person (e.g., newly graduated nurse or social worker) is to adapt and function as a professional meeting all the expectations from the workplace [20, 21]. It is comprised of four categories (i.e., having a generalist foundation and some job-specific capabilities, providing safe client care, keeping up with the current realities and future possibilities, and possessing a balance of doing, knowing, and thinking) that is captured by the Readiness to Practice Survey [22, 23]. We believe that VR training for nursing education can improve nurses' readiness to practice prior to real-world clinical experiences. Thus, readiness to practice will serve as the primary outcome in future controlled trials of the VR training platform along with other measures (i.e., usability measured with System Usability Scale, technology acceptability measured with Presence – Immersive Tendency Questionnaire) [18, 19].

4.2 Planned Features and Functionality

We plan to build on our initial successes by expanding functionality of the VR training platform. To provide a greater breadth of training experiences, we will develop clinical scenarios in additional topic areas, including obstetric emergencies, pediatric emergencies, and mental health. We also develop functionality to allow for team-based simulations, where students can practice working collaboratively in interdisciplinary healthcare teams. Additionally, we will develop features for remote learning, where students can access the VR training platform from their own devices.

5 Discussion

Overall, the progress made towards developing the nursing VR simulation suggests that the team is on track towards creating a comprehensive and immersive simulation. The results are encouraging and highlight the importance of creating realistic interactive assets and realistic NPCs with corresponding animations and apparel. These findings have important implications for improving nursing education and training. However, several challenges need to be addressed to create a comprehensive and sustainable solution for resource-limited schools of nursing. Cost and specialized software development skills are major barriers for resource-limited schools of nursing. Moreover, proprietary technologies from for-profit companies present interoperability challenges, which act as a barrier to sharing clinical scenarios between systems and schools. The recurring licensing fees for commercial proprietary VR systems are cost-prohibitive, making them inaccessible and challenging to adopt and sustain for resource-limited schools of nursing.

Our solution to these challenges is the development of an open-source VR training platform for nursing education. This platform offers a cost-feasible and sustainable solution for resource-limited schools of nursing to access high-quality nursing education that was previously unattainable. By creating an open-source platform, we can address the interoperability challenges posed by proprietary technologies, enabling easy sharing of clinical scenarios between systems and schools. In addition, an open-source VR training platform offers nursing educators a viable way to gain access to previously inaccessible high-quality nursing education. With the support of this platform, nursing students can refine their skills in a secure setting, lessening the possibility of patient harm. Furthermore, VR training can simulate uncommon and complex clinical scenarios that might be challenging to replicate using conventional HFS, giving nursing students a wider range of clinical experiences that can improve their clinical decision-making, boost their confidence in clinical skills, and shorten training time and costs. Long-term evaluation of the open-source VR training platform's efficacy in enhancing patient outcomes and lowering healthcare costs is planned. Our research will include Comparative Effectiveness Research, Usability and Acceptability Studies, Impact of Patient Outcomes, and Cost-Effectiveness Analysis.

6 Conclusion

The development of immersive VR platforms for nursing education has the potential to revolutionize the way nurses are trained. VR training provides a cost-effective and sustainable solution to the challenges posed by traditional HFS, allowing students to experience realistic and engaging clinical scenarios that improve clinical decision-making and reduce the risk of patient harm. Our approach of developing an open-source, fully interactive VR training platform provides a sustainable solution for resource-limited schools of nursing, ensuring that all students have access to high-quality nursing education.

Acknowledgments. This research was conducted under the financial support of the University of Missouri Postdoctoral Association (MUPA) Research Award and the University of Missouri Graduate Professional Council (GPC) Research Award.

References

1. Drennan, V.M., Ross, F.: Global nurse shortages: the facts, the impact and action for change. Br. Med. Bull. **130**(1), 25–37 (2019)
2. "The greatest threat to global health is the workforce shortage" - International council of nurses international nurses day demands action on investment in nursing, protection and safety of nurses [Internet]. ICN. 2022 https://www.icn.ch/news/greatest-threat-global-health-workforce-shortage-international-council-nurses-international. Accessed 17 Mar 2023
3. Spurlock Jr., D.: The nursing shortage and the future of nursing education is in our hands. J. Nurs. Educ. **59**(6), 303–304 (2020)
4. Jarosinski, J.M., Seldomridge, L., Reid, T.P., Willey, J.: Nurse faculty shortage: voices of nursing program administrators. Nurse Educ. **47**(3), 151–155 (2022)
5. Chan, G.K., Bitton, J.R., Allgeyer, R.L., Elliott, D., Hudson, L.R., Burwell, P.M.: The impact of COVID-19 on the nursing workforce: a national overview. Online J. Iss. Nurs. 26(2), 1–7 (2021). https://doi.org/10.3912/OJIN.Vol26No02Man02
6. Pottle, J.: Virtual reality and the transformation of medical education. Fut. Healthc. J. **6**(3),181. https://doi.org/10.7861/fhj.2019-0036
7. Yavrucuk, I., Kubali, E., Tarimci, O.: A low cost flight simulator using virtual reality tools. IEEE Aerosp. Electron. Syst. Mag. **26**(4), 10–14 (2011). https://doi.org/10.1109/MAES.2011.5763338
8. Parham, G., et al.: Creating a low-cost virtual reality surgical simulation to increase surgical oncology capacity and capability. Ecancermedicalscience **13** (2019). https://doi.org/10.3332/ecancer.2019.910
9. Hanshaw, S.L., Dickerson, S.S.: High fidelity simulation evaluation studies in nursing education: a review of the literature. Nurse Educ. Pract. **46**, 102818 (2020). https://doi.org/10.1016/j.nepr.2020.102818
10. Ahir, K., Govani, K., Gajera, R., Shah, M.: Application on virtual reality for enhanced education learning, military training and sports. Augment. Hum. Res. **5**(1), 1–9 (2019). https://doi.org/10.1007/s41133-019-0025-2
11. Biggs, A.T., Geyer, D.J., Schroeder, V.M., Robinson, F.E., Bradley, J.L.: Adapting virtual reality and augmented reality systems for naval aviation training, Report No.: AD1063175, p. 168. Naval Medical Research Unit Dayton (US) (2018)

12. De Visser, H., Watson, M.O., Salvado, O., Passenger, J.D.: Progress in virtual reality simulators for surgical training and certification. Med. J. Aust. **194**, S38–S40 (2011). https://doi.org/10.5694/j.1326-5377.2011.tb02942.x
13. Elliman, J., Loizou, M., Loizides, F.: Virtual reality simulation training for student nurse education. In: 2016 8th International Conference on Games and Virtual Worlds for Serious Applications (VS-Games) 2016 September 7, pp. 1–2. IEEE (2016). https://doi.org/10.1109/VS-GAMES.2016.7590377
14. Oxford Medical Simulation - Virtual Reality Healthcare Training [Internet]. Oxford Medical Simulation. 2017. https://oxfordmedicalsimulation.com/
15. Virtual Reality Medical Simulation | SimX – The world's best Virtual reality medical training software and nursing simulation training platform. [Internet]. www.simxvr.com. https://www.simxvr.com/
16. Heidenreich, P.A., et al.: 2022 AHA/ACC/HFSA guideline for the management of heart failure: executive summary: a report of the American College of Cardiology/American Heart Association Joint Committee on Clinical Practice Guidelines. J. Am. Coll. Cardiol. **79**(17), 1757–1780 (2022)
17. AHA. Advanced Cardiovascular Life Support: Provider Manual. American Heart Association, Dallas (2020)
18. Brooke, J.: SUS-A quick and dirty usability scale. In: Usability Evaluation in Industry, vol. 189, pp. 4-7. CRC Press (11 June1996)
19. Tcha-Tokey, K., Loup-Escande, E., Christmann, O., Richir, S.: A questionnaire to measure the user experience in immersive virtual environments. In: Proceedings of the 2016 Virtual Reality International Conference 2016 March 23, pp. 1–5. https://doi.org/10.1145/2927929.2927955
20. Joubert, M.: Social work students' perceptions of their readiness for practice and to practise. Soc. Work. Educ. **40**(6), 695–718 (2021)
21. Schmitt, C.A., Lancaster, R.J.: Readiness to practice in generation Z nursing students. J. Nurs. Educ. **58**(10), 604–606 (2019)
22. Wolff, A.C., Regan, S., Pesut, B., Black, J.: Ready for what? An exploration of the meaning of new graduate nurses' readiness for practice. Int. J. Nurs. Educ. Scholar. **7**(1) (2010). https://doi.org/10.3928/01484834-20190923-09
23. Casey, K., Fink, R., Jaynes, C., Campbell, L., Cook, P., Wilson, V.: Readiness for practice: the senior practicum experience. J. Nurs. Educ. **50**, 646–652 (2011)

Developing a Human Behavior Simulation Technology Based on Multiuser Immersive Virtual Reality in an Atypical Architectural Design Process

Jong Woo Lee, Jung Do Kim, Jae Hyoung Go, Yeong Song Jang, and Yun Gil Lee(✉)

Hoseo University, 20, Hoseo-Ro, 79 Beon-Gil, Baebang-Eup Chungcheongnam-do, Asan-Si 31499, Korea
{whddnrpdla,jungdo119,erostar3273}@naver.com, yglee@hoseo.edu

Abstract. The use of immersive virtual reality technology in the field of architectural design is increasing, particularly in commercial settings, where virtual reality technology allows clients to experience the designed building in advance during the architectural design process. The application of multiuse immersive virtual reality provides an environment in which users can directly experience the designed space through their avatars. According to the research results, multiuser immersive virtual reality applications aid creative collaboration and problem-solving in architectural design. The aim of this study was to develop a technology that applies multiuser immersive virtual reality devices and technologies to human behavior simulation in atypical architectural design. By improving ActoViz, a previously developed human behavior simulation technology for atypical spaces, we established a computerized environment in which architects and clients, through their avatars, can experience atypically designed spaces. As the technology described herein uses immersive virtual reality technology, it has the advantage of allowing users to experience the characteristics of an atypical architectural space as if they were in the actual space. In addition, the actions of other users allow participants to experience the "presence" of others, including their behaviors, which is difficult for single agents/avatars to experience. In addition, it aids in creative collaboration.

Keywords: Human Behavior Simulation · Atypical Architectural Design · Multiuser Immersive Virtual Reality · Architectural Design Process

1 Introduction

In the process of designing atypical spaces—that is, spaces with nontraditional or unique shapes—it is easy for architects to overlook the human behavior that takes place in these spaces. Using human behavior simulation technology in architectural design allows human behaviors in atypical spaces to be reviewed in real time during the design process of these spaces [1]. Recent research on human behavior simulation technology in atypical spaces has focused on the responses of human-like agents to these spaces. The inclusion of agents' reactions in these atypical spaces, which may be diverse, enables a more realistic simulation environment [2, 3].

C. Stephanidis et al. (Eds.): HCII 2023, CCIS 1836, pp. 235–240, 2023.
https://doi.org/10.1007/978-3-031-36004-6_32

The development of virtual reality technologies and associated applications provides opportunities to introduce various simulation methods into the architectural design process. Immersive virtual reality technology is now common and can be easily used by anyone. The use of immersive virtual reality technology in the field of architectural design is increasing, particularly in commercial settings, where virtual reality technology allows clients to experience the designed building in advance during the architectural design process. The application of multiuse immersive virtual reality provides an environment in which users can directly experience the designed space through their avatars. According to previous research [4], multiuser immersive virtual reality applications aid creative collaboration and problem-solving in architectural design.

In the process of atypical architectural design, human behavior simulation can inspire architects in aspects related to creativity or suitability [5]. However, the scene of the human behavior simulation transmitted through a computer screen is not a direct experience of the designed space. Immersing oneself in a human behavior simulation using virtual reality technology would allow for more practical inspiration. In addition, it is possible to provide an environment in which multiuser virtual reality technology can enable connection and collaboration with other users at the same time in the design process. This can be a good means of creative collaboration [2].

The aim of this study was to develop a technology that applies multiuser immersive virtual reality devices and technologies to human behavior simulation in atypical architectural design. By improving ActoViz, a previously developed human behavior simulation technology for atypical spaces, we established a computerized environment in which architects and clients, through their avatars, can experience atypically designed spaces [6]. As the technology described herein uses immersive virtual reality technology, it has the advantage of allowing users to experience the characteristics of an atypical architectural space as if they were in the actual space. In addition, through the behaviors of other users, it allows participants to experience the "presence" of others, including their behaviors, which is difficult for single agents/avatars to experience.

2 ActoVizVR: Human Behavior Simulation Technology Based on Multiuser Immersive Virtual Reality

To review the designed atypical space in real time through immersive virtual reality, this technology was developed using Rhino and Grasshopper, which are commercial atypical building design tools. Figure 1 shows the process of using the human behavior simulation technology in an atypical architectural space and the developed multiuser-based immersive virtual reality. After designing the atypical space in Rhino, ActoViz was executed through Grasshopper, and the virtual environment developed in the Unity3D game engine was created in real time.

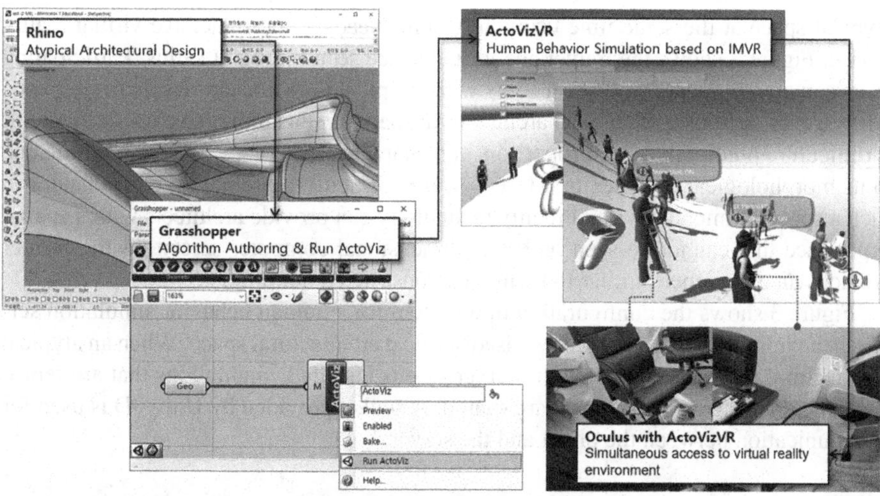

Fig. 1. Multiuser immersive virtual reality–based human behavior simulation in an atypical architectural space using ActoVizVR.

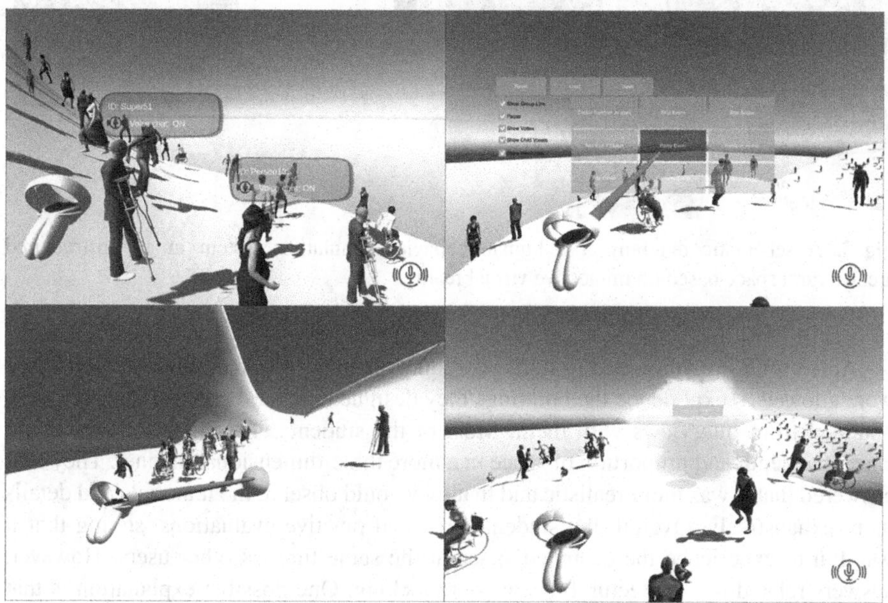

Fig. 2. Scenes of ActoVizVR-based human behavior simulation shown using Oculus.

Various characters capable of autonomous actions were placed in the virtual space that was created based on the atypical space designed by the architect, and these characters acted according to the characteristics of the atypical space and the behavioral characteristics of the other characters. An architect can adopt the identity of one of the avatars and interact with others in this atypical space. Other users can participate in this atypical space at the same time using an Oculus headset, an immersive virtual reality device. Figure 2 shows the immersive virtual space seen through Oculus. Participating users can communicate with other users with simple voices and actions and experience other agents' actions and atypical architectural spaces in this immersive environment. It is difficult to predict the size, proportion, and characteristics of an atypical building due to its morphological complexity. Moreover, it is difficult to predict human behavior in such a space. Immersive virtual reality technology can provide architects with a spatial experience that cannot be seen on a two-dimensional computer screen, as the former provides an experience similar to being in a constructed building.

Figure 3 shows the configuration of a system for a human behavior simulation service in an immersive virtual reality–based atypical architectural space. When an atypical architectural model designed on the server side is installed, simulations that are reproduced by clients based on Quest2 are shared. A socket provided by Unity3D is used for communication between the client and the server.

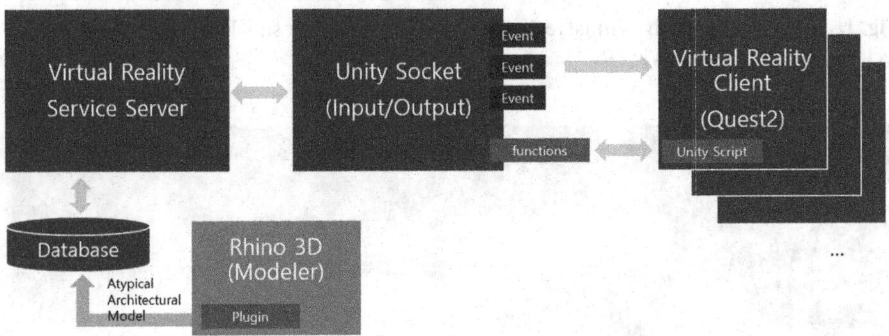

Fig. 3. A schematic diagram of a human behavior simulation system in an unstructured architectural space based on immersive virtual reality.

ActoVizVR was provided to third-year students majoring in architecture, and they were allowed to experience the buildings they designed. Several positive answers were obtained from interviews with them. Most of the students answered that they could check the depth and proportion of space in a more three-dimensional manner. They also answered that it was more realistic and that they could observe the materials and details more exhaustively. Overall, the students provided positive evaluations, stating that it was fun to experience the designed space at the same time as other users. However, answers related to architectural design were lacking. One possible explanation is that the designed building was observed together, and the design work was not carried out. In addition, there was no answer regarding whether agents' behavior or the behavior of other users felt very strange. This may indicate that more appropriate and detailed response actions by agents suitable for the level of visual experience in virtual spaces are needed (Fig. 4).

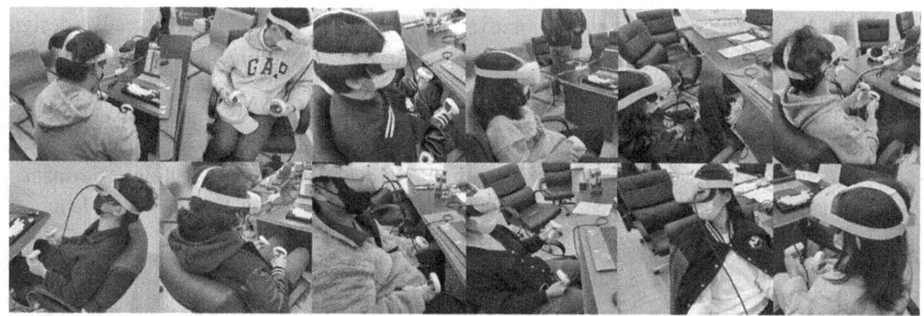

Fig. 4. Students experiencing immersive virtual reality using ActoVizVR.

3 Discussion and Conclusion

The purpose of this study was to develop a technology that applies multiuser immersive virtual reality devices and technologies to human behavior simulation in atypical architectural design. ActoViz, a human behavior simulation technology in an unstructured architectural space that runs on existing computer screens, has been improved to operate on immersive virtual reality technology. ActoVizVR, which was developed through this study, provides architects with an environment in which they can experience more realistic human behavior simulations. In an experiment with architecture students, the possibility of using a human behavior simulation based on immersive virtual reality in the architectural design process was confirmed to some extent. However, it was confirmed that the developed ActoVizVR has functional limitations as a kind of prototype system. In other words, ActoVizVR can provide architects with a more realistic experience of a designed space through virtual reality–based simulation, but there are limitations with regard to functions that are necessary to its role as a creative collaboration tool. Future work must develop a technology that allows multiple users to experience the designed space together and collaborate on design work through additional technology development. In addition, it is necessary to increase immersion by improving the behavior of other users or agents so that they can be reproduced in various ways.

Acknowledgement. This work was supported by the National Research Foundation of Korea (NRF) grant funded by the Korean government (MSIT) (RS-2023-00207964).

References

1. Hong, S.W., Schaumann, D., Kalay, E.: Human behavior simulation in architectural design projects: an observational study in an academic course. Comput. Environ. Urban Syst. **60**(1), 1–11 (2016)
2. Hong, S.W., Lee, Y.G.: Behavioural responsiveness of virtual users for students creative problem finding in architectural design. Archit. Sci. Rev. **62**(3), 238–247 (2019)
3. Anderson, T.A.: On the human figure in architectural representation. J. Architect. Educ. **55**(1), 238–246 (2002)

4. Hong, S.W., Lee, Y.G.: Online collaborative architectural design studio for creative design using online multiuser virtual environment - a case study. J. Archit. Inst. Korea **26**(11), 81–88 (2010)
5. Lee, .G.: A study on the effect of human factor for atypical design in the architectural design studio. Ad. Intell. Syst Comput. 876(1), 130–134 (2018)
6. Lee, Y.G.: ActoViz: A human behavior simulator for the evaluation of the dwelling performance of an atypical architectural space. Commun. Comput. Inf. Sci. **1034**(1), 361–365 (2019)

Searching in Virtual Reality with Teleportation as a Travel Technique

Veasna Ling(✉) and Daniel Cliburn

University of the Pacific, Stockton, CA 95211, USA
v_ling@u.pacific.edu

Abstract. Teleportation is often used as a travel technique in virtual reality (VR) applications when the distance users must travel exceeds the bounds of their real physical space. However, despite the prevalence of teleportation as a travel technique in VR applications, little research has compared multiple teleportation methods for common wayfinding tasks. This paper describes an experiment to compare three teleportation methods (arc, hand selection, and step) for a naïve search task in VR. Results suggest that, while time to complete the task did not differ significantly between the methods, subjects completing the task using the step teleportation method covered significantly less distance than subjects that used the hand selection method. Furthermore, subjects with no prior VR experience took significantly more time and distance, and remembered the locations of significantly fewer objects, than subjects that had several prior VR experiences. This suggests that more research may be necessary to learn to support inexperienced users as they search in VR.

Keywords: Virtual Reality · Teleportation · User Studies

1 Introduction

A common user interaction in virtual reality (VR) applications is to navigate through virtual worlds [6]. Real walking in VR to travel between locations may increase the sense of presence [5], but users are limited to the confines of their real physical space. When compared to traditional controller based techniques, teleportation may increase user ability to estimate distance traveled [2] while decreasing symptoms of motion sickness [3]. Thus, teleportation is often used as a travel technique in VR applications when the distance users need to travel exceeds the bounds of their real physical space. Surprisingly, even though teleportation is utilized frequently for navigation in VR, little research has been conducted to compare multiple teleportation methods for common navigation tasks in VR. In this paper, we describe an experiment to compare three teleportation methods for completing the same search task in VR. The goal of this research is to increase understanding of the utility of multiple teleportation methods as travel techniques to support common navigation tasks in VR.

C. Stephanidis et al. (Eds.): HCII 2023, CCIS 1836, pp. 241–246, 2023.
https://doi.org/10.1007/978-3-031-36004-6_33

1.1 Background

Navigation involves both wayfinding and travel [6]. While travel refers to the mechanism through which a user moves between locations, wayfinding refers to the user's ability to determine a path between locations. Darken and Siebert [1] describe three types of wayfinding tasks: naïve search, primed search, and exploration. In a naïve search, users attempt to find a target location without prior knowledge of the location. In a primed search, users know the location of the target. In an exploration task, users have no specific target location. Previous research suggests that experienced VR users prefer an arc-based teleportation method to complete a primed search task in VR [4]. However, users were able to complete the same task covering significantly less distance when using a step teleportation method, as opposed to arc and hand selection methods, suggesting that users may take more efficient travel paths when using the step method.

This study extends previous research by comparing three teleportation methods (arc, hand selection, and step) for completing a naïve search task in VR. With the arc method, users control a virtual arc to choose the location to which they want to teleport (see Fig. 1). A gray circular object is shown at the end of the arc indicating the location to which users will teleport. Users can manipulate the thumb stick on the controller to choose the direction they want to face at the conclusion of the teleport (indicated by the arrow). With the hand selection method, users teleport to one of a fixed set of locations (the yellow circles shown in Fig. 1, Fig. 2, and Fig. 3). To select a location users point to it with their virtual hand. A gray object will then appear over the location, and users can teleport to the chosen location by pressing a button on the controller. Like the arc method, users can indicate the direction they want to face at the conclusion of the teleport by manipulating the thumb stick on the controller before pressing the button. With the step method, users see no arc or object that indicates the location to which they will teleport. Instead, users simply press a button on the controller to teleport two virtual meters in the direction they face. Users will always be facing the same direction before and after the teleport when using the step method.

Fig. 1. The arc teleportation method.

Fig. 2. The hand selection teleportation method.

2 Experiment

Two virtual environments (VEs) were created to conduct the experiment. Figure 3 (left) shows the training environment where subjects practiced the search task. Figure 3 (right) shows the testing environment in which time and distance traveled were recorded for each visit. In both VEs, subjects began in the area with green walls extending from the VE at the bottom of the map. Subjects searched the VEs until they collected the objects hidden in rooms (two in the training environment and six in the testing environment). The objects were in the same locations for each visit to the VEs.

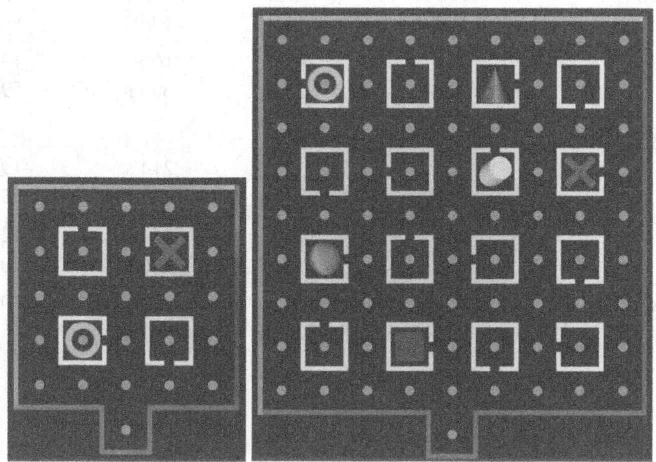

Fig. 3. The virtual training environment is shown on the left, and the virtual testing environment is on the right.

2.1 Subjects

Seventy-eight subjects completed the experiment (50 males, 27 females, and one subject did not specify). The mean age of subjects was 22.4 years (SD = 5.60). Twenty-three subjects indicated no prior VR experience, 33 had experienced VR once or twice, and 22 had experienced VR several times.

2.2 Procedure

Subjects first signed an informed consent and completed a pre-survey, which asked for their age, gender, and amount of prior VR experience. Subjects were then assigned to one of three conditions (arc, hand selection, or step) and completed two trials in the training environment using an Oculus Quest 2. The purpose of the training environment was to allow subjects an opportunity to familiarize themselves with the search task and teleportation method. Subjects then completed four trials in the test environment. After the fourth trial, subjects completed a written assessment that tested their recollection of the locations of the six objects in the testing environment. A total score was calculated as the number of object locations recalled correctly by each subject. The Institutional Review Board at our university approved this procedure.

Table 1. Mean time (in seconds) and distance traveled (in meters)

Method	Trial 1	Trial 2	Trial 3	Trial 4
Arc	246 s 977 m	184 s 830 m	161 s 759 m	163 s 877 m
Hand selection	198 s 1089 m	146 s 916 m	165 s 1058 m	121 s 801 m
Step	244 s 929 m	206 s 828 m	166 s 690 m	137 s 597 m
Prior VR Experience				
No prior VR experience	300 s 1148 m	215 s 922 m	214 s 1024 m	192 s 941 m
Once or twice	208 s 978 m	174 s 834 m	154 s 796 m	126 s 700 m
Several times	187 s 873 m	147 s 826 m	127 s 697 m	108 s 654 m

3 Results

Table 1 shows the results of the experiment. We were interested in answering two research questions. First, is the difference in user performance between methods significant? Second, is the difference in user performance between subjects with different levels of prior VR experience significant? The data analysis reported in this section was conducted using jamovi (jamovi.org). Main effects and interactions are reported only if they are significant.

Repeated measures ANOVAs were conducted for the two dependent variables, **time** and **distance** traveled, with *trial number* as the within-subjects variable and teleportation *method* as the between-subjects variable. With respect to **time**, not surprisingly, there was a main effect of *trial number* ($F(3, 225) = 10.042$, $p < .001$)), suggesting that subjects got faster (took less time) as they progressed through the trials. Tukey post hoc comparisons revealed that subjects took significantly more time on trial 1 than on trial 3 ($t(75) = 3.14, p = .013$) and 4 ($t(75) = 4.36$), $p < .001$). Subjects also took significantly more time on trial 2 ($t(75) = 3.53$, $p = .004$) and 3 ($t(75) = 2.81$, $p = .032$) than on trial 4. With respect to **distance** traveled, again, there was a main effect of *trial number* ($F(3, 225) = 4.68, p = .003$). Tukey post hoc comparisons revealed that subjects covered significantly more distance on trial number 1 than on trial 4 ($t(75) = 3.326, p = .007$). There was also a main effect of teleportation *method* ($F(2, 75) = 3.13, p = .049$). Tukey post hoc comparisons revealed that subjects using the hand selection method covered significantly more distance than subjects using the step method ($t(75) = 2.50, p = .038$). A One-Way ANOVA was conducted with **total score** as the dependent variable and teleportation *method* as the independent variable. The difference between methods was not significant.

It appears the answer to our first research question is "partially." There was a significant difference in distance traveled between the step and hand selection methods. This is likely because hand selection restricts users to moving down only the centers of hallways and to the centers of rooms. Consistent with [4], subjects using the step method could take more efficient paths, allowing them to complete trials in less distance. However, the difference between methods with respect to time and recalling the locations of objects was not significant.

To answer our second research question, repeated measures ANOVAs were conducted for the two dependent variables (**time** and **distance** traveled), with *trial number* as the within-subjects variable and *experience* level as the between-subjects variable. With respect to **time**, there was a main effect of *trial number* ($F(3, 225) = 9.875, p <$ .001)). Tukey post hoc comparisons revealed that subjects took significantly more time on trial 1 than on trial 3 ($t(75) = 3.15, p = .012$) and 4 ($t(75) = 4.33, p < .001$). Subjects also took significantly more time on trial 2 than on trial 4 ($t(75) = 3.28, p = .008$). The difference between trial 3 and trial 4 approached significance ($t(75) = 2.60, p = .053$). There was also a main effect of *experience* ($F(2, 75) = 6.27, p = .003$). Tukey post hoc comparisons revealed that subjects with no prior VR experience took significantly more time to complete trials than those who had experienced VR once or twice ($t(75) = 2.727$, $p = .021$) and several times ($t(75) = 3.370, p = .003$). With respect to **distance** traveled, again, there was a main effect of trial number ($F(3, 225) = 4.221$, $p = .006$). Tukey post hoc comparisons revealed that subjects covered significantly more distance on trial 1 than on trial 4 ($t(75) = 3.157, p = .012$). There was also a main effect of *experience* ($F(2, 75) = 4.48$, $p = .015$). Tukey post hoc comparisons revealed that subjects with no prior VR experience covered significantly more distance than those who had experienced VR several times ($t(75) = 2.848$, $p = .015$). The difference between subjects with no prior VR experience and those that had experienced it once or twice approached significance ($t(75) = 2.307, p = .061$). A One-Way ANOVA was conducted with **total score** as the dependent variable and *experience* as the independent variable ($F(2, 75) =$

3.91, $p = .024$). Tukey post hoc comparisons revealed a significant difference in **total score** ($t(75) = -2.79$, $p = .018$) between subjects with no prior VR experience (M = 2.39) and subjects that had experienced VR several times (M = 3.86).

The answer to our second research question appears to be "yes." There was a significant difference in performance between subjects with different levels of prior VR experience. Subjects with no prior VR experience took significantly more time and distance to complete the trials than subjects with previous VR experience, and recalled the locations of significantly fewer objects than subjects that had experienced VR several times.

4 Conclusion

We described an experiment to compare three teleportation methods for a naïve search task in virtual reality. We found that, not surprisingly, subjects got faster and covered less distance as they progressed through the trials, and the difference between methods with respect to time to complete trials was not significant. However, subjects using the step method covered significantly less distance than subjects that used the hand selection method. Some subjects that used the step method suggested adding a feature to allow rapid teleportation when a button is held down on the controller. This may allow subjects using the step method to complete search tasks faster. We also found that subjects with no prior VR experience took longer, covered more distance, and remembered fewer locations of objects than subjects that had experienced VR several times. This may suggest that more research is necessary to learn how to help inexperienced VR users search more effectively in VR. Future research could also compare teleportation methods with respect to user comfort, as some methods may be more likely than others to induce symptoms of motion sickness.

References

1. Darken, R., Sibert, J.: Wayfinding strategies and behaviors in large virtual worlds. In: Proceedings of the SIGCHI Conference on Human Factors in Computing Systems, pp. 142–149, ACM, Vancouver, Canada (1996)
2. Keil, J., Edler, D., O'Meara, D., Korte, A., Dickmann, F.: Effects of virtual reality locomotion techniques on distance estimations. Int. J. Geo-Inf. **10**(3), 150 (2021)
3. Langbehn, E., Lubos, P., Steinicke, F.: Evaluation of locomotion techniques for room-scale VR: Joystick, teleportation, and redirected walking. In: Proceedings of the Virtual Reality International Conference - Laval Virtual, pp. 1–9, ACM, Laval, France (2018)
4. Lesaca, D., Cheung, H., Jena, T., Cliburn, D.: Comparing teleportation methods for travel in everyday virtual reality. In: Proceedings of the 2022 IEEE Conference on Virtual Reality and 3D User Interfaces Abstracts and Workshops, IEEE, Christchurch, New Zealand (2022)
5. Sayyad, E., Sra, M., Hollerer., T.: Walking and teleportation in wide-area virtual reality experiences. In: Proceedings of the2020 IEEE International Symposium on Mixed and Augmented Reality, pp. 608–617, IEEE, Porto de Galinhas, Brazil (2020)
6. Sherman, W., Craig, A.: Understanding Virtual Reality: Interface, Application, and Design, 2nd edn. Morgan Kaufman, Cambridge (2019)

Guidelines for Designing Mixed Reality Solutions in Remote Scenarios

Bernardo Marques(✉), Samuel Silva, Rafael Maio, Paulo Dias, and Beatriz Sousa Santos

IEETA, DETI, LASI, University of Aveiro, Aveiro, Portugal
bernardo.marques@ua.pt

Abstract. As remote work becomes broadly adopted worldwide due to the recent COVID-19 Pandemic, individuals turn to new digital technologies to address the characteristics of such scenarios. An example is the use of Mixed Reality (MR) to establish a common ground between physically distributed team members. Although existing literature has proposed multiple prototypes, a systematization of the key aspects for guiding newcomers into the field and creating MR solutions has not been addressed. In this vein, this work proposes a set of guidelines for guiding the research community when designing MR tools for remote activities. The guidelines were defined through a participatory process with industry partners (domain experts and target users), as well as considering insights from practitioners and researchers from two workshops conducted at international conferences.

Keywords: Remote Collaboration · Mixed Reality · Guidelines

1 Introduction

An unprecedented impact across the business landscape has been caused by the recent COVID-19 pandemic all over the world. In this context, remote work gained new significance, representing an important artifact to solve various problems in the most effective and fastest way possible when team members cannot be present in the same physical space [3,5,6].

As a consequence, businesses needed to adapt to this new reality by becoming more flexible and agile in embracing new and innovative technologies. An example is the growing interest in using Collaborative Mixed Reality (MR) (Fig. 1) solutions to address the nuances of remote activities [2,4,19].

As reported by Marques et al. (2022), remote team members do not share a common space, being this one of the major reasons for the interest in using MR for such scenarios [14]. In addition, the authors emphasize that MR builds a common ground capable of improving accuracy and efficiency by enhancing the perception of shared information. It may also contribute to better collaboration times, knowledge retention, increased situation understanding and awareness [2,4,18,20].

C. Stephanidis et al. (Eds.): HCII 2023, CCIS 1836, pp. 247–252, 2023.
https://doi.org/10.1007/978-3-031-36004-6_34

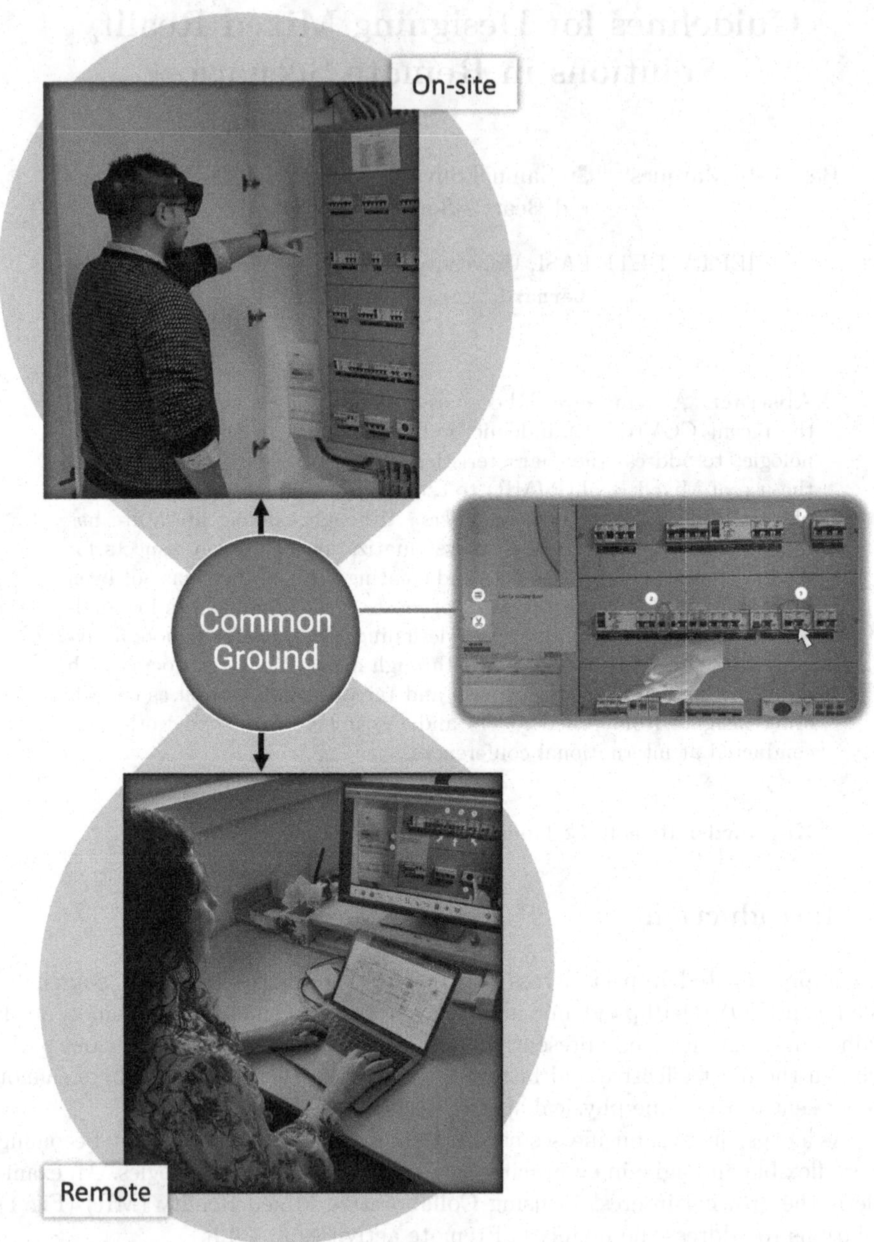

Fig. 1. Scenario of Remote Collaboration supported by Mixed Reality (MR), having an on-site team-member being assisted by a remote expert.

Nevertheless, even though recent surveys provide a detailed overview of the current landscape for Collaborative MR [2,4,7,8,14,15,17,18,20], a concise list of general requirements for designing MR solutions for such contexts has not been proposed yet, as has already happened in other fields like industrial scenarios [16]. This opportunity motivated our research, aiming to provide a starting ground for newcomers and industry practitioners.

In order to foster a more informed and potentially successful adoption of MR, a solution that is being increasingly considered due to the proliferation of remote work, we argue that an effort must be made to guide the creation process of such solutions, thus facilitating its integration on the daily life's of target-users, and in turn, contribute to improving how the collaborative process is conducted on the long run.

2 General Requirements Towards Using MR Technologies in Remote Scenarios

Following the opportunity previously emphasized, next, a first structured overview of general guidelines is proposed. These are the result of a Human-Centered Design (HCD) effort conducted by the authors in the latest years. To elaborate, a participatory process with partners from the industry sector was conducted, involving domain experts and target users in various areas (e.g., Human-Computer Interaction (HCI), User Experience (UX), Virtual, Augmented and Mixed Reality (VR/AR/MR), Information Visualization, Multimodal Interaction, Computer Supported Cooperative Work (CSCW), Industry 4.0).

Furthermore, insights from practitioners and researchers representing a broad spectrum of levels of interest and expertise were also included, taking advantage of the know-how collected from conducting two workshops at international conferences [1,9–13].

Overall, we consider that the following constitute a representative set of fundamental factors that should be taken into consideration, as the basic features, when designing MR solutions for connecting distributed team members during remote activities:

- **support multiple collaboration channels** - establish the common ground and ensure communication, including text, audio, video and image sharing, among others;
- **include authoring features for both on-site and remote members** - according to the collaborator role and devices being used, distinct authoring methods should be possible to better handle the task at hand;
- **encompass different annotation types** - provide features like a pointer, sketch (including different colors), pre-defined shapes (e.g., circles, squares, etc.), notes (including texts, links, others), as well as images, videos or 3D models;

- **supply customization according to the user profile** - adapting the annotation features can help improve collaborators' efficiency by allowing them to define which features they use the most and how they what to visualize the available features;
- **integrate various interaction modalities** - many factors may affect how team members interact with remote tools, hence, it is important to have redundancy and complementary alternatives (e.g., voice, touch, gestures, gaze, etc.);
- **enable visualization of augmented or freeze annotations** - allows selecting if the presented augmented content is aligned on top of the real world or if a freeze image can be positioned according to the collaborator preference;
- **allow temporal ordering and clustering of information during its creation** - providing a guiding order can help others to better understand how to follow a set of annotations;
- **creation of step-by-step annotations** - use sets of simpler annotations when large amounts of information must be exchanged at the same time;
- **reutilization of existing instructions** - cross-referencing similar problems from other collaborative sections, aiming to reuse annotations created to support similar cases;
- **incorporating information regarding different types of relevant events** - ensuring visibility of collaboration status (e.g., creating new annotations, sending new content to be analyzed);
- **consider having an independent view** - certain situations may require that remote members have a different point of view style, providing more freedom to explore the environment and offer guidance on what needs to be done;
- **contemplate multi-user scenarios** - ensure that collaboration is not limited to small teams by taking into account scalability, content synchronicity, as well as ownership;
- **guarantee multi-platform support** - on-site and remote members should be able to use different devices according to the environment context and task needs. It is paramount that the tool can easily be adapted/extended to various platforms.

3 Final Remarks and Future Work

A set of general guidelines for assisting the research community in creating MR solutions for handling remote activities has been proposed. Profiting from this list, we expect to facilitate the design and development of remote solutions, as well as elicit a better systematization of these factors moving forward (which may be further extended through time). We argue that only by having this representative overview can the research community learn from each other's work, thus adding to the existing body of knowledge and providing support for better transferability.

The dynamic advancements of remote work is likely to lead to new requirements as MR technologies evolve. We argue that further work should be put on distilling the plethora of work in this field moving towards a set of heuristics that could drive the principles adopted to design new systems. In turn, these guidelines also pinpoint a first battery of tests that can help improve and evaluate existing systems, a key aspect towards the design of an evaluation framework encompassing the complexity of collaborative MR scenarios.

Acknowledgments. To everyone involved in user studies, and discussion groups, thank for your time and expertise. This research was supported by IEETA, funded through FCT in the context of the project [UIDB/00127/2020].

References

1. Barroso Rego, J.P., Fonseca, L., Marques, B., Dias, P., Sousa-Santos, B.: Remote collaboration using mixed reality: exploring a shared model approach through different interaction methods. In: Proceedings of the European Conference on Computer-Supported Cooperative Work, ECSCW (2020)
2. Belen, R., Nguyen, H., Filonik, D., Favero, D., Bednarz, T.: A systematic review of the current state of collaborative mixed reality technologies: 2013–2018. AIMS Electron. Electr. Eng. **3**, 181 (2019)
3. Biehl, J.T., Farzan, R., Zhou, Y.: Can anybody help me?: Using community help desk call records to examine the impact of digital divides during a global pandemic. In: CHI Conference on Human Factors in Computing Systems, pp. 1–13 (2022)
4. Ens, B., et al.: Revisiting collaboration through mixed reality: the evolution of groupware. Int. J. Hum.-Comput. Stud. **131**, 81–98 (2019)
5. Kerdvibulvech, C., Chen, L.L.: The power of augmented reality and artificial intelligence during the covid-19 outbreak. In: International Conference on Human-Computer Interaction, HCII. pp. 467–476 (2020)
6. Koumaditis, K., Mousas, C., Chinello, F.: XR in the era of covid-19. Behav. Inf. Technol. **40**(12), 1234–1236 (2021)
7. Krauß, V., Boden, A., Oppermann, L., Reiners, R.: Current practices, challenges, and design implications for collaborative ar/vr application development. In: Proceedings of the 2021 CHI Conference on Human Factors in Computing Systems, pp. 1–15 (2021)
8. Marques, B., Silva, S., Alves, J., Araujo, T., Dias, P., Santos, B.S.: A conceptual model and taxonomy for collaborative augmented reality, pp. 1–18. IEEE Transactions on Visualization & Computer Graphics, TVCG, pp (2021)
9. Marques, B., Silva, S., Alves, J., Rocha, A., Dias, P., Santos, B.S.: Remote collaboration in maintenance contexts using augmented reality: insights from a participatory process. Int. J. Interact. Des. Manuf. (IJIDeM) **16**(1), 419–438 (2021). https://doi.org/10.1007/s12008-021-00798-6
10. Marques, B., Silva, S., Dias, P., Santos, B.S.: Do hand-held devices have a future in augmented reality real-life remote tasks? refections on impact/acceptance versus head-mounted displays. In: Proceedings of the European Conference on Computer-Supported Cooperative Work, ECSCW, pp. 1–9 (2022)
11. Marques, B., Silva, S., Dias, P., Santos, B.S.: Remote collaboration using augmented reality: development and evaluation. In: IEEE Conference on Virtual Reality and 3D User Interfaces Abstracts and Workshops (VRW), IEEE VR Tutorials (2022)

12. Marques, B., Silva, S., Dias, P., Santos, B.S.: Remote collaboration using augmented reality: development and evaluation. In: IEEE International Symposium on Mixed and Augmented Reality, ISMAR Tutorials (2022)
13. Marques, B., Silva, S., Dias, P., Sousa-Santos, B.: An ontology for evaluation of remote collaboration using augmented reality. In: Proceedings of the European Conference on Computer-Supported Cooperative Work, ECSCW (2021)
14. Marques, B., Teixeira, A., Silva, S., Alves, J., Dias, P., Santos, B.S.: A critical analysis on remote collaboration mediated by augmented reality: making a case for improved characterization and evaluation of the collaborative process. Comput. Graph. **102**, 619–633 (2022)
15. Merino, L., Schwarzl, M., Kraus, M., Sedlmair, M., Schmalstieg, D., Weiskopf, D.: Evaluating mixed and augmented reality: a systematic literature review (2009–2019). In: IEEE International Symposium on Mixed and Augmented Reality, ISMAR (2020)
16. Quandt, M., Knoke, B., Gorldt, C., Freitag, M., Thoben, K.D.: General requirements for industrial augmented reality applications. Procedia CIRP **72**, 1130–1135 (2018)
17. Ratcliffe, J., Soave, F., Bryan-Kinns, N., Tokarchuk, L., Farkhatdinov, I.: Extended reality (XR) remote research: a survey of drawbacks and opportunities. In: CHI Conference on Human Factors in Computing Systems, pp. 1–13 (2021)
18. Sereno, M., Wang, X., Besancon, L., Mcguffin, M.J., Isenberg, T.: Collaborative work in augmented reality: a survey. IEEE Transactions on Visualization and Computer Graphics, pp. 1–20 (2020)
19. Speicher, M., Hall, B.D., Nebeling, M.: What is mixed reality? In: Proceedings of the CHI Conference on Human Factors in Computing Systems, p. 1–15 (2019)
20. Wang, P., et al.: AR/MR remote collaboration on physical tasks: a review. Robot. Comput.-Integr. Manuf. **72**, 1–32 (2021)

Remote Work Is Here to Stay! Reflecting on the Emerging Benefits of Mixed Reality Solutions in Industry

Bernardo Marques[1(✉)], Samuel Silva[1], Rafael Maio[1], Liliana Vale Costa[2], Paulo Dias[1], and Beatriz Sousa Santos[1]

[1] IEETA, DETI, LASI, University of Aveiro, Aveiro, Portugal
bernardo.marques@ua.pt

[2] DigiMedia, DeCA, University of Aveiro, Aveiro, Portugal

Abstract. Changes experienced in the business landscape over the past years exacerbated by COVID-19 remain unprecedented, e.g., adaptability in the processes, and remote work, among others. One important change that resulted from this, was the accelerated switch from conducting on-site physical activities to more remote scenarios that continued to ensure such activities were maintained, despite the limitations and constraints felt all over the world. This paper discusses these rapid and large-scale changes in various sectors while emphasizing the role of remote work during this period. In particular, reporting the implications of using Mixed Reality (MR) technologies to recreate interpersonal interactions, i.e., support human activities during remote scenarios. Namely, mitigating a number of restrictions, while offering long-term improvements, as well as maintaining distributed team-members connected and motivated. Last, a systematization of current challenges and opportunities is described, providing a guiding list of important topics that must be addressed by the research community in order to create better, more robust solutions to improve how remote collaboration is conducted.

Keywords: Remote Work · Distributed Collaboration · Mixed Reality

1 Introduction

During the recent COVID-19 pandemic, several countries implemented various forms of lockdown, e.g., communities were put into quarantine and were forbidden from traveling and even stepping outside, severely limiting how business was conducted, and in some cases even leading to the full stop of company's activity [1,16,17,21]. Some of the main impacts included the fact that traditional face-to-face interactions were affected by social distancing measures, which limited the size of groups. In addition, the ability to conduct business, manage effective team operations, and share knowledge where it was needed was diminished by the inability to travel and prevalence of expert individuals, working from home. Also important, the organization's ability to continue operations 'as before' was

C. Stephanidis et al. (Eds.): HCII 2023, CCIS 1836, pp. 253–260, 2023.
https://doi.org/10.1007/978-3-031-36004-6_35

limited by fewer on-site workers due to illness, self-isolation, or financial restrictions. In the same way, thousands of experts found it impossible to be physically on the field to address various problems. The training of new or existing workers on products and processes was also affected, creating a challenging endeavor due to the lack of hands-on training. Furthermore, workers avoided surfaces and objects that might have been touched by others due to the potential virus transmission. Besides, supply chains were affected by interruptions in the shop floor, thus requiring more flexible processes to ensure product continuity [10].

Taking into consideration this landscape, businesses needed to adapt to this new reality by becoming more flexible and agile in embracing new and innovative technologies[1]. For example, there was an increase in use cases like remote assistance and training[2] given that employees were less willing to be in close contact with each other. Moreover, travel restrictions prevented the most specialized individuals from being present in the field, while various issues would arise[3]. Hence, remote work gained new significance, representing an important artifact to solve various problems, in the most effective and fastest way possible, when team-members cannot be present in the same physical space [5].

In this context, and to help address the constraints identified, it was important to consider that any lingering transformation of what we do at a distance must rely on convincing and accessible forms of remote collaboration. These circumstances provided a unique opportunity for an upsurge of research and development of new digital technologies to support a variety of activities [15].

2 Mixed Reality Solutions are Gaining Momentum

While Mixed Reality (MR) was already gaining popularity and relevance, being considered as one of the top 10 ranked Information and Communications Technologies (ICT) [18], the unpredictable conditions of the pandemic helped to stimulate an earlier and larger adoption. This situation-changing technology has gained important momentum due to its capacity to mitigate a number of restrictions (e.g., impacts of travel reduction, reduced staffing, as well as physical distancing), while offering opportunities to provide long-term improvements [2,4,6,11]. These solutions combine the advantages of virtual environments and the possibility for seamless interaction with real-world objects and other collaborators (Fig. 1) [3]. Remote MR can be considered a type of collaboration that describes the interaction between physically separated individuals exploring Virtual and Augmented Reality (VR/AR). This concept includes mapping the on-site collaborator environment and juxtaposing digital content over a live

[1] https://www.techtarget.com/searchcio/feature/Use-of-VR-and-AR-in-the-enterprise-increases-during-pandemic [Accessed in Mar. 15, 2023].

[2] https://www.valmet.com/media/articles/services/remote-services-prove-valuable-during-the-covid-19-pandemic/ [Accessed in Mar. 15, 2023].

[3] https://vsight.io/blog/the-covid-19-challenge-ar-in-business-continuity/ [Accessed in Mar. 15, 2023].

view of the physical world using AR, i.e., capturing more dimensional information about the local scene. In turn, this may be reconstructed in a standard display or through VR so remote collaborators can analyze and provide guidance accordingly [14,20]. This approach allows to provide distributed team-members with a common ground environment, i.e., serves as a basis for situation mapping by overlying responsive computer-generated information on top of the real-world environment [9]. It offers unique capabilities to achieve common goals, e.g., improved communication cues for more efficient and easier collaboration, resulting in team-members enhanced perception of the shared content, as well as improved collaboration performance, knowledge retention, and awareness [3,6,19].

Fig. 1. Instructional content creation at a distance: scenario of remote collaboration supported by a Mixed Reality solution, having a remote expert providing assistance to an on-site team-member.

Currently, remote collaboration supported by MR is reaching several areas of applications, including technical support, inspection processes, training and maintenance repairing, which are of extremely usefulness in a wide range of industries[4]. Lessons learned from two years of remote collaboration show that the use of such technologies helped mitigate the impacts of travel reduction, reduced staffing, as well as social distancing. To elaborate, MR elicited a reduction in

[4] https://vsight.io/blog/ar-remote-support-keeping-people-connected-during-covid-19/ [Accessed in Mar. 15, 2023].

errors, downtime, training time, and all other forms of cost and loss, eliminating the need for mass gatherings while keeping the workforce connected[5].

In fact, Sarah Reynolds, Vice President of Marketing at PTC[6]: emphasizes that *"as organizations look to maintain business continuity in this new normal, they are embracing AR to address travel restrictions, social distancing measures, and other challenges impacting their front-line workers' ability to go on-site and operate, maintain, and repair machines of all kinds (...) improve the clarity, precision, and accuracy of their communication and collaboration"*.

Likewise, Scott Montgomerie, cofounder and CEO of Scope AR[7] indicates that *"as people got their feet under them, they realized that our tools are potential lifesavers for their businesses. We had customers that we had lost in previous years because they just weren't quite ready for these innovative tools come back to us and give us a purchase order within five days (...) the response has been tremendous. Particularly in industries like consumer packaged goods where they have to maintain factories and literally can't travel to go maintain them when something goes wrong"*.

To complement, next, some real-life examples of using MR solutions in Industry scenarios are provided to emphasize how this technology was received and used. Stegan Goeris, Process Consulting for Manufacturing Digital Business at Henkel[8] hints that: *"exchange between employees is essential"* and that using MR *"has enabled us to promote virtual collaboration between employees on the production floor and employees working remotely. Despite the current situation, sharing of expertise has not been sacrificed and we can continue to drive knowledge sharing"*. Moreover, Jaume Carreras, Project Manager for the Henkel Digital Transformation team[9] advocates that MR *"has provided us with an efficient alternative to physical meetings at the plants in times of border closures and travels restrictions (...) The direct exchange and immediate feedback made possible via the remote assistance tool ensures efficient virtual collaboration"*.

Furthermore, Maurício Harger, General Director of CMPC[10] highlights the role of MR, stating that this technology *"brought us the comfort of having the assistance of Valmet experts in real time, without them leaving their homes. On the same day, for example, a field service manager, who was providing remote support, attended a CMPC unit in Guaíba and another in Santa Fé, Chile. This*

[5] https://www.forbes.com/sites/forbestechcouncil/2021/09/14/augmented-and-virtual-reality-after-covid-19/ [Accessed in Mar. 15, 2023].

[6] http://thearea.org/covid-19-how-augmented-reality-is-helping-mitigate-business-impact/ [Accessed in Mar. 15, 2023].

[7] https://www.businessinsider.com/coronavirus-pandemic-is-strengthening-enterprise-ar-2020-4 [Accessed in Mar. 15, 2023].

[8] https://www.ptc.com/en/blogs/corporate/henkel-uses-vuforia-chalk-real-time-remote-assistance-covid-19 [Accessed in Mar. 15, 2023].

[9] https://www.imeche.org/news/news-article/augmented-reality-lets-experts-problem-solve-at-a-distance [Accessed in Mar. 15, 2023].

[10] https://www.valmet.com/about-us/references/pulping-and-fiber/valmet-offers-remote-support-with-augmented-reality-in-mill-shutdown-during-pandemic/ [Accessed in Mar. 15, 2023].

was only possible due to the remote support". Harger also adds that he[11] *"fully supports this new way to serve. It makes more sense nowadays, because it avoids time-consuming long-distance journeys and production downtime.*

In another example, David Kleiner, Extended Reality Lab Manager at Toyota[12] reports that *"since people can't come to a classroom anymore because of the pandemic, we're training them remotely using HoloLens through our partnership with Microsoft. Some of the early results are just phenomenal. We found that we could take training from 13 days down to two days. Retention is better and quality is up. It's been great for both new hires and for reskilling existing workers to take on new tasks"*.

On top of that, our research group is also involved in a project with partners from the industry sector, which started by exploring the use of MR for remote scenarios prior to the pandemic. Currently, our partners are introducing MR into logistics's, and assembly lines, having acquire two new Head-Mounted Displays (HMDs) to conduct further studies, aiming to facilitate the workforce daily tasks while also improving productivity, all this having the capacity to remotely connect with off-site experts whenever necessary [7,8,11,13].

In brief, the research described can contribute to several sustainability and development goals proposed by the United Nations (UN)[13], [14] [10], such as: Goal 8 - Promote sustained, inclusive and sustainable economic growth, full and productive employment and decent work for all; Goal 9 - Build resilient infrastructure, promote inclusive and sustainable industrialization and foster innovation; Goal 10 - Reduce inequality within and among countries; Goal 11 - Make cities and human settlements inclusive, safe, resilient and sustainable; Goal 12 - Ensure sustainable consumption and production patterns; Goal 13 - Take urgent action to combat climate change and its impacts.

3 Challenges and Opportunities

Despite the potential reported above, MR solutions are not fully-mature and spread throughout all businesses [14,17]. Most reports encompass synchronous scenarios of one-to-one collaboration, having a remote expert providing guidance to an on-site team-member [12]. Scenarios incorporating multiple team-members or asynchronous situations are not being considered. As for different types of content, exploring 3D shared models is not fully disseminated for wide-use yet. For now, augmented annotations are still the way to go, being simpler to implement and to use, given that they can be applied to most scenarios, with minimal changes. Another limitation is the fact that most features are only available to the remote expert. The on-site worker still lacks identical features to express their

[11] https://www.valmet.com/media/articles/services/the-power-of-remote-tools-in-pulp-mill-shutdowns/ [Accessed in Mar. 15, 2023].

[12] https://thearea.org/david-kleiner-on-how-covid-has-accelerated-ar-at-toyota/ [Accessed in Mar. 15, 2023].

[13] https://sdgs.un.org/goals [Accessed in Mar. 15, 2023].

[14] https://carear.com/sustainability/ [Accessed in Mar. 15, 2023].

thoughts while communicating and requesting assistance. Hence, being limited to capturing the context of the problem and waiting for MR-content to visualize on top of the real-world [10]. Regardless, for MR to evolve and truly be adopted as the designated tool for companies worldwide, further research is still necessary. Next, some important topics are described, representing relevant research opportunities to ensure a larger adoption of such technologies, and, consequently, improving how remote work is conducted:

- **Incorporate team size and dynamics** - Contemplate having various individuals addressing an activity in a collaborative manner, at the same time, as well as their role within the team (e.g., novice, expert, etc.); The increase in team size, its impact on the collaborative process, and how MR technologies may be used represent interesting research opportunities. For example, it is difficult to guarantee that each user clearly understands what others try to communicate, i.e., point at or refer to. It is not unusual to expect that one user's action may interfere with another user's activities. It is paramount to address how information can be shared without cluttering users' fields of view and without interfering with the tasks;
- **Ensure authoring features for all team-members** - Include communication (i.e., contemplate text, audio, video, image or 3D models, etc.), annotations (i.e., encompass different methods (e.g., pointer, sketch, pre-defined shapes, temporal sorting, step-by-step instructions, etc.)) content reutilization (i.e., reuse instructions created to support similar tasks), ownership (i.e., concurrent access and changes to the same artifacts), synchronicity (i.e., changes are shared accordingly among all collaborators), perception (i.e., deliver contextualized content without cluttering the team-member's field of view), awareness (i.e., incorporate different types of notifications), interaction (i.e., explore additional modalities and interaction devices according to task conditions, and environment contexts);
- **Encourage the adoption of the technology** - Involve stakeholders in the design and development process through Human-Centered Design (HCD) methodologies, and promote training sessions for them to learn how to use MR solutions. Hence, listen to team-members, collect feedback/suggestions and adapt what may be necessary for achieving better outcomes. Also, prioritize what the company needs, not what is most popular;
- **Elicit data-driven methods** - Stimulate data collection and analysis, generating a better characterization of the collaborative process. Monitoring can lead to a better understanding of how the collaborative effort unfolds, how MR was used or how group dynamics evolve. Also, what emotions team-members experience or what learning patterns emerge for certain problems;
- **Prompt a larger infrastructure** - Avoid short-term solutions. Team-members must be supported by a well-established infrastructure, capable of including experts, managers, suppliers, and other relevant members of the ecosystem. In other words, invest in a long-term plan capable of supporting company growth accordingly.

4 Final Remarks

Remote work is here to stay. As the world transitions to the 'new normal' after mitigating the effects of the COVID-19 pandemic, scenarios of remote collaboration have become an integral part of the way business is conducted. Thus, now is the time for adopting and investing in new technological solutions that fit each company's needs. The wide potential of MR remote work is quite favorable for this purpose, as collaborative actions incorporate higher flexibility and become more agile moving forward. In this vein, we argue that a new operational model can be achieved through MR solutions, providing more sustainable benefits over the medium/long term. These represent an extremely important role in contributing to addressing multiple limitations faced by distributed team-members on a daily basis, as reported in this work. Thus, recreating interpersonal interactions and disseminating knowledge that challenges physical boundaries while also minimizing the need for expert individuals to travel abroad. It may also have a positive impact on individuals' remuneration, as well as introduce new opportunities in the job market (e.g., individuals with less expertise can conduct tasks, normally not included in their agenda, with the support from off-site experts using MR), which human-resources can capitalize upon.

Acknowledgments. We thank everyone involved in discussion groups and case studies associated with this research line for their time and expertise. We also thank the authors of all studies analyzed for their meaningful insights. This research was developed in the scope of the Augmented Humanity project [POCI-01-0247-FEDER-046103 and LISBOA-01-0247-FEDER-046103], financed by ERDF through POCI. This research was supported by IEETA funded through the Foundation for Science and Technology (FCT), in the context of the project [UIDB/00127/2020].

References

1. Biehl, J.T., Farzan, R., Zhou, Y.: Can anybody help me?: Using community help desk call records to examine the impact of digital divides during a global pandemic. In: Proceedings of CHI Conference on Human Factors in Computing Systems. pp. 1–13 (2022)
2. Bottani, E., Vignali, G.: Augmented reality technology in the manufacturing industry: A review of the last decade. IISE Transactions **51**(3), 284–310 (2019)
3. de Souza Cardoso, L.F., Mariano, F.C.M.Q., Zorzal, E.R.: A survey of industrial augmented reality. Computers & Industrial Engineering 139 (2020)
4. Kerdvibulvech, C., Chen, L.L.: The Power of Augmented Reality and Artificial Intelligence During the Covid-19 Outbreak. In: Stephanidis, C., Kurosu, M., Degen, H., Reinerman-Jones, L. (eds.) HCII 2020. LNCS, vol. 12424, pp. 467–476. Springer, Cham (2020). https://doi.org/10.1007/978-3-030-60117-1_34
5. Koumaditis, K., Mousas, C., Chinello, F.: XR in the era of covid-19. Behaviour & Information Technology **40**(12), 1234–1236 (2021)
6. van Lopik, K., Sinclair, M., Sharpe, R., Conway, P., West, A.: Developing augmented reality capabilities for industry 4.0 small enterprises: Lessons learnt from a content authoring case study. Computers in Industry 117(103208) (2020)

7. Maio, R., Santos, A., Marques, B., Almeida, D., Dias, P., Santos, B.S.: Pervasive Augmented Reality (AR) for Assistive Production: Comparing the use of a Head-Mounted Display (HMD) versus a Hand-Held Device (HHD). In: International Conference on Mobile and Ubiquitous Multimedia, MUM. pp. 1–4 (2022)
8. Maio, R., Santos, A., Marques, B., Almeida, D., Ramalho, P., Baptista, J., Dias, P., Santos, B.S.: Supporting Human Operators in an Industrial Shop Floor through Pervasive Augmented Reality. In: International Conference on Graphics and Interaction, ICGI. pp. 1–4 (2022)
9. Marques, B., Silva, S., Alves, J., Araujo, T., Dias, P., Santos, B.S.: A conceptual model and taxonomy for collaborative augmented reality. IEEE Transactions on Visualization & Computer Graphics pp. 1–21 (2021)
10. Marques, B.: Concepts and methods to support the development and evaluation of remote collaboration using augmented reality. Ph.D. Thesis, Department of Electronics, Telecommunications and Informatics (DETI), University of Aveiro, Aveiro, Portugal pp. 1–178 (2021)
11. Marques, B., Silva, S., Alves, J., Rocha, A., Dias, P., Santos, B.S.: Remote Collaboration in Maintenance Contexts using Augmented Reality: Insights from a Participatory Process, pp. 1–21. International Journal on Interactive Design and Manufacturing, IJIDeM pp (2022)
12. Marques, B., Silva, S., Dias, P., Santos, B.S.: One-to-many remote scenarios: The next step in collaborative extended reality (XR) research. In: Workshop on Analytics, Learning & Collaboration in eXtended Reality (XR-WALC). ACM International Conference on Interactive Media Experiences, IMX. pp. 1–6 (2022)
13. Marques, B., Silva, S., Teixeira, A., Dias, P., Santos, B.S.: A vision for contextualized evaluation of remote collaboration supported by AR. Computers & Graphics **102**, 413–425 (2021)
14. Marques, B., Teixeira, A., Silva, S., Alves, J., Dias, P., Santos, B.S.: A critical analysis on remote collaboration mediated by augmented reality: Making a case for improved characterization and evaluation of the collaborative process. Computers & Graphics **102**, 619–633 (2021)
15. Matthews, B., See, Z.S., Day, J.: Crisis and extended realities: remote presence in the time of COVID-19. Media International Australia **178**(1), 198–209 (2021)
16. Narayanamurthy, G., Tortorella, G.: Impact of covid-19 outbreak on employee performance-moderating role of industry 4.0 base technologies. International Journal of Production Economics 234 (2021)
17. Orlosky, J., Sra, M., Bektaş, K., Peng, H., Kim, J., Kos'myna, N., Höllerer, T., Steed, A., Kiyokawa, K., Akşit, K.: Telelife: the future of remote living. Frontiers in Virtual Reality p. 19 (2021)
18. Rokhsaritalemi, S., Sadeghi-Niaraki, A., Choi, S.M.: A review on mixed reality: Current trends, challenges and prospects. Applied Sciences **10**(2), 636 (2020)
19. Röltgen, D., Dumitrescu, R.: Classification of industrial augmented reality use cases. Procedia CIRP **91**, 93–100 (2020)
20. Speicher, M., Hall, B.D., Nebeling, M.: What is mixed reality? In: Proceedings of CHI Conference on Human Factors in Computing Systems. pp. 1–15 (2019)
21. Steed, A., Ortega, F.R., Williams, A.S., Kruijff, E., Stuerzlinger, W., Batmaz, A.U., Won, A.S., Rosenberg, E.S., Simeone, A.L., Hayes, A.: Evaluating immersive experiences during covid-19 and beyond. Interactions **27**(4), 62–67 (2020)

The Process of Creating Interactive 360-Degree VR with Biofeedback

Asge Matthiesen, Gunver Majgaard(✉), and Marco Scirea

University of Southern Denmark, Odense, Denmark
gum@mmmi.sdu.dk

Abstract. The paper aims to demonstrate the interconnectedness of filmmaking techniques and iterative software design methods during the creation of interactive 360-degree Virtual Reality (VR) scenarios. These scenarios, which were designed to treat social anxiety disorder (SAD), comprised of six distinct simulations. To track patients' biodata, biosensors were integrated with the developed scenarios. In the paper, we provide an overview of the combined development process method and demonstrate how these methods were employed. Our goal is that this combined method for developing interactive 360-degree applications will serve as a useful reference for future designers.

Keywords: Design Methods for VR · VR · Virtual Reality · Social Anxiety Disorder · VR-treatment · 360-degree Videos

1 Introduction

This paper highlights the unique combination of methods used to develop interactive 360-degree Virtual Reality (VR) simulations with biofeedback for treating social anxiety disorders (SAD). The development of 360-degree scenarios required the use film making techniques such as narrative storytelling and manuscript writing methods [1, 2]. The development of the interactive part of the simulation required software development methods in this case a combination of agile iterative methods and game-design methods [3, 4]. Implementation of biofeedback also required agile software development methods. VR was chosen because its ability to provide immersion which was crucial in the therapy [5].

People with social anxiety disorder fear social interactions and may be unwilling to seek treatments involving exposure to social situations [6]. Social exposure conducted in VR, integrated in individual cognitive–behavioural therapy forms the basis for this design case. Virtual Reality Exposure Therapy (VRET) has proven effective for treating social anxiety disorder with similar effects as traditional treatment, and with an effect that has been found to be persistent [6, 7].

People with SAD may experience intense anxiety, self-consciousness, and embarrassment in these situations, and may go to great lengths to avoid them. This can greatly impact the person's life and make it hard to form and maintain relationships, go to work, or school, or participate in other activities. Some common symptoms of SAD include

C. Stephanidis et al. (Eds.): HCII 2023, CCIS 1836, pp. 261–268, 2023.
https://doi.org/10.1007/978-3-031-36004-6_36

the following: Intense fear of being judged or evaluated negatively by others. Worrying for days or weeks in advance of a social event. Experiencing physical symptoms such as a rapid heartbeat, sweating, or nausea in social situations. Avoiding social situations or enduring them with intense distress. Difficulty making friends or maintaining relationships. Difficulty with work or school because of social anxiety. In the scenarios the patients were exposed to their fears in planned and increasing doses. It's important to note that SAD is treatable with therapy, medication, or a combination of both [8].

The VR simulations in this design case is an integral part of a treatment scheme of 10 sessions. All steps of the treatment are guided by a therapist and a standardized manual [9]. In the sessions the patients are provided with knowledge and support to better understand their own illness and triggers for their anxiety. Activities covers an individual set of treatment goals, exposure to the VR scenarios and formative evaluation. The design case consists of six scenarios: the bench, the employee, the shopping, the presentation, the café, and the train. They are developed in the listed order. Each scenario focus on gradually introduction of anxiety triggers such as sitting next to a stranger in the park, making a presentation, ordering food in a café. Interacting with strangers would increase the level for triggers. All the scenarios have integrated biosensors, where an algorithm displays data during the exposure in live feedback.

The simulations developed are currently being applied in a randomized control trial study which evaluates its efficiency as part of exposure therapy in a clinical setting [10]. The design case is part of a bigger research project titled *VR8* which is funded by the Danish Innovation Fund [11].

The novelty in the design case includes the unique combination of design methods, the interactivity for both therapist and patient, the biofeedback, and the number of different scenarios.

2 Technical Platform

The technical platform involved 360-degree recordings using Insta360 [12]. The recordings were imported into Unity 3D [13] where they were made into interactive scenarios. The specific biofeedback sensors also informed the interactive aspects of the scenarios. The scenarios were built on a specific VR headset, an HTC Vive Pro [14], to meet the basic requirements for optimal testing.

2.1 360-Degree Camera

Filming in 360 degrees, also known as *spherical filming* [15], involves capturing footage from all angles, allowing the viewer to look around in any direction. There are a few different ways to film in 360 degrees, including: *Using a 360-degree camera*: There are a variety of 360-degree cameras available on the market, such as the Ricoh Theta, Samsung Gear 360, and Insta360. In this case a 360-degree camera was used in form of the Insta 360 OneX 2 [16]. The reason for choosing this type of camera, was that it came with a software that stitched the two 180-degree recordings together without having to do it manually, and because of the built-in optical stabilization which removes the risk of ending up with a "fisheye" lens perspective. The software provided with Insta

360 was also able to integrate easily with Unity, making it convenient to import all the clips without any further video editing. However, the process of converting the clips and making sure that the resolution fitted the used VR glasses, were a time-consuming activity, and made for a lot of adjusting.

2.2 Biofeedback and Integration

Biofeedback sensors are devices that monitor physiological signals, such as heart rate, skin temperature, and muscle tension. Biofeedback sensors are commonly used in the fields of psychology, sports performance, and rehabilitation, but have also become increasingly used in personal settings (for example, fitness trackers and smartwatches). In the VR8 project, physiological sensors are used to train a machine learning model that has the objective of inform the psychologist about the current anxiety state of the patient and the foreseen changes in this state as the patient navigates the scenario.

Since the focus is on anxiety, two types of sensors have been chosen to be integrated accordingly to the correlation between the physiological signals measured and anxiety: heart rate and galvanic skin response (GSR, also referred to as electrodermal activity). Heart rate is an important physiological indicator of stress and anxiety levels in the body [17]. During times of stress or anxiety, the heart rate usually increases. GSR is a measure of the electrical conductivity of the skin, which can reflect changes in sweat gland activity. GSR has been shown to correlate to psychological arousal and can provide a measure of stress/anxiety [18].

All scenarios have been developed in the Unity 3D game engine [13]; Unity doesn't have any in-built function to communicate with sensors, so we have used an additional software: iMotions [19]. IMotions is a software specialized for recording biofeedback data and store it for scientific analysis. It also provides APIs to pass on information to other programs; we have used these to be able to display and manipulate the sensor data in real time within the Unity scenarios.

3 Methods

The design methods were iterative and inspired by action research and game design [3, 20]. Fullerton's iterative design process is also the backbone for the agile software development in the postproduction phase. The design process is also inspired of filmmaking methods for cinematographic work [1] as well as the traditional narrative method [2]. Other methods such as the development of flowcharts [21], linked the filmmaking and software development processes. The process became rather complicated because it should balance fixed goals based on the psychological angle, a narrative branching structure, film making process and software design. The combination of these methods allowed for a more integrated approach in developing and designing 360-degree scenarios to be used in the treatment of patients with social anxiety disorders.

3.1 Filmmaking Methods

There are some different perspectives on how to create cinematographic work [1], and one of the methods used within this research is *The Traditional Narrative method* [2], which is a method used to create a linear story with a clear beginning, middle, and end. It is based on the three-act structure. The three parts are: *The setup or exposition*: This is the first part, and it introduces the main characters, the setting, and the main conflict or problem. *The rising action:* This is the second part, and it builds on the setup by introducing complications and conflicts that the main characters must overcome. *The resolution or denouement:* This is the final part, and it brings the story to a close by resolving the conflicts and tying up loose ends. In this case the way this method was used was in the development of the flowcharts and initial scene description for each scenario. Each of the six scenarios were built with an opening scene in where the patient is allowed to adjust to being in VR and control their anxiety. Then there is a middle part, in where the patient is allowed to make various actions and interact with the scenario. And finally, an end in where the patient in most of the scenarios end up in the same spot as they began with. This allows both the user and the practitioner to conclude the scenario with a somewhat linear structure.

3.2 Flowcharts Combines Film and Software

The flowcharts combined the software development world and the filmmaking world. Flowcharts are visual representations of a process or algorithm that use different symbols to illustrate the sequence of steps, decision points, and the flow of information or material. Flowcharts are widely used in programming, engineering, business, and other fields to design, analyse, and communicate processes and systems [21]. In this case, the flowcharts, and the development of these, were made for each of the six scenarios and a part of the preproduction phase. The flowcharts illustrated in our case decision points for interactivity and the flow of film clips/scenes.

3.3 Iterative Software Development

Agile software development is an iterative approach to software development that emphasizes flexibility and adaptability [3]. At its core, agile development is focused on delivering working software in short, frequent iterations, typically ranging from one to four weeks in length [4]. These iterations are called sprints, and they are designed to deliver a specific set of features or functionality within a defined time frame. This agile way of developing the software was used in the postproduction phase of the research and were containing the combination of clips shot, the implementation of interactivity within the simulations, the integration of the biofeedback and the software development itself.

3.4 Comparison of Methods

Table 1 below highlights whether the specific elements in the development process originates from software development or film making methods.

Table 1. The table provides an overview of the comparison between methods.

	Software development method	Filmmaking method	Other methods
Ideation + Conceptualization	X	X	X
Preproduction • Narrative/scenes • Flow diagram • Decision making • Planning • Manuscript • Preparations for film shooting	X X	X X X X X	X
Production of Film • Shooting the film		X	
Postproduction • Combining clips • Software development • Interactivity • Integrating with sensors • Testing	X X X X X	X	

4 The Six Scenarios and the Combined Development Process

The six scenarios were built on the premise of real-life scenarios inducing anxiety for patients with SAD. These were selected with clinicians and patients within the project and the chosen themes for the scenarios were confrontations with unknown people, public transport, shopping for groceries, presentations, and the implications of saying no. These themes were condensed into six specific scenarios: "The Bench Scenario", in where the patient practice confronting unknown people. "The Employee Presentation", in where the patient practice to introduce themselves to a new workplace. "The Presentation", in where the patient is exposed to presenting a theme in front of an audience. "The Shopping", in where the patient is to go out and buy groceries. "The Café", where the patient is induced to practice saying no to accepting wrong food they ordered at a café, and at last, "The Train", in where the patient is exposed to public transportation and the challenges, that comes with. The difference within the scenarios consisted of the various ways that both the patient and the clinician can interact with the VR environment. The choices provided to both patient and clinician varies from each theme. The six scenarios were also scalable to either increase or decrease anxiety for the patients.

During the development of the six scenarios a stricter design process gradually emerged. The branching structure was visualized in flowcharts and scene descriptions. The goal was to visualize the manuscript and make visual branches between the anxiety levels. The filmmaking process consisted of both making a manuscript with lines for the actors, planning the film recording, shooting the film clips, and packing them for the software design process. A manuscript writer was hired in to make the language and tone smoother. In each scenario we had two formal formative evaluations mainly conducted with the affiliated psychologists. The first evaluation took place after all the paperwork which included flowcharts, scene descriptions and manuscript. The second after the filmmaking process and software design process. These evaluations assured that the iterative process in which the whole of the scenario was able to be corrected to it with the needs of the main goals for the stakeholders. Based upon these evaluations and in combination with the various methods a new proposal for a model to design this type of scenarios emerged.

Below is a table which provides an overview of the combined development process for all the six scenarios, (see Table 2). The methods combine steps from filmmaking, software development, game design and interaction design. From game design and filmmaking, we have the phases; ideation, conceptualization, preproduction, production, and postproduction [1, 3]. From software development and game design we have the iterative approach which isn't included in the figure below. The steps from iterative design process are testing, evaluating, and revising. All the steps (see the left column in the table below), run through the iterative cycles. The step of formative testing also informs the next scenario which is to be developed.

Table 2. Overview of the combined development process method

Step	Description
Concept - one page	• The psychological angle • Ideation and concept description
Scenes	• Flowcharts with unique labeling • Scene descriptions
Decision making	• Evaluation of scenes • Revision of scenes
Planning	• Deciding location • and finding actors
Manuscript	• Writing detailed manuscript for each scene • Updating flowcharts and making sure no scenes are missing
Shooting the film	• Preparing the film shooting e.g., the order of scenes • Preparing the 360-degree camera and shooting the film
Software development	• Preparing and importing film clips into programming environment • Linking the scenes and programming of the interaction
Hardware	• Building the simulation on to the VR spectacles • Bio sensors
Formative testing	• Testing and refining • Content test, technical and usability test

The formative evaluation provided the developer with feedback and ideas to improve the development method, the psychological angle, planning and the structuring of scenes.

The scenarios became larger and more complex for each new scenario. From the first scenario, the number of triggers and their complexity increased and became more precise and were introduced in greater variation in the later scenarios. Also, the branching in the alternative storylines became more diverse. The locations went from a bench in the park to hiring a train wagon. As the development team became more professional the ambitions rose as did the quality of the resulting scenarios. The increasing awareness of the combined development method has also scaffolded the creation of more intricate content.

5 Summary

The paper highlights were how filmmaking methods and iterative software design methods intertwined in the development of the interactive VR scenarios. During the development of the scenarios a combined iterative development method emerged. The steps of the development method were: conceptualising, making scenes by using flow diagrams, writing the manuscript, shooting the film, software development, hardware integration and formative testing.

From a design perspective the filmmaking process is more deductive, and everything must be planned. Whereas interaction design is more inductive, and the product takes form during the iterative process. In this production we had to balance these opposite design perspectives. Filmmakers want to plan everything ahead whereas game-designers like to be creative also late in the process. Developers must be aware of the contrast in the design approach to make successful products.

The product (the six scenarios) was developed in the most efficient way and these combinations of methods ensured that the product reached its full potential and were a viable option to the standardized treatment. In making this methodological combination we gained a new and innovative approach how to develop this kind of simulation and a new way of looking at development when it comes to 360-degree videos.

We hope that the integrated method (outlined in Table 2) used to create interactive 360 simulations will be a useful point of reference for upcoming VR developers, game designers, educational technology designers, or anyone with similar expertise in their development endeavours.

References

1. Kryeziu, D.: The process of creating a cinematographic work, in pedagogy critical approaches to teaching literature language composition and culture. Anglist. J. **8**(1) (2019). https://doi.org/10.5281/zenodo.2582145. e-ISSN: 1857-8187, p-ISSN: 1857-8179
2. DeGuzman, K.:History & overview of narrative cinema. StudioBinder (2022). https://www.studiobinder.com/blog/what-is-narrative-film-definition/. Accessed 5 Feb 2023
3. Fullerton, T.: Game Design Workshop: A Playcentric Approach to Creating Innovative Games, 4th edn., AK Peters/CRC Press (2018)
4. Džanić, A. et al.: Agile Software Development: Model, Methods, Advantages and Disadvantages. Acta Tech. Corviniensis-Bull. Eng. **15**(4) (2022)
5. Majgaard, G., Stock, C.: Students' development of virtual reality prototypes for training in alcohol-resistance skills. In:12th European Conference on Game-Based Learning ECGBL 2018. SKEMA Business School Sophia Antipolis, France. 4–5 October 2018, pp. 393–401 (2018)
6. Bouchard, S., et al.: Virtual reality compared with in vivo exposure in the treatment of social anxiety disorder: a three-arm randomised controlled trial. Br. J. Psychiatry **210**(4), 276–283 (2017)

7. Matthiesen, A.F., Larsen, L.J.: Facing your fears: Design of a VR tool for usage within exposure therapy for patients with social anxiety disorders combined with selected game-based elements. In: European Conference on Games Based Learning, pp. 844–XIX. Academic Conferences International Limited (2021)
8. Rodebaugh, T.L., Holaway, R.M., Heimberg, R.G.: The treatment of social anxiety disorder. Clin. Psychol. Rev. **24**(7), 883–908 (2004)
9. Clemmensen, L., Torp Ernst, M., Nielsen, C.S., Runge, E., Helweg-Jørgensen, S.: Cognitive Behavioral Therapy for Social Phobia: A Treatment Manual with Exposure in Either in Vivo or Virtual Reality (ed. Translated from Danish). Syddansk Universitet. Telepsykiatrisk center (2021). https://doi.org/10.21996/jc31-kb73
10. Ørskov, P.T., et al.: Cognitive behavioral therapy with adaptive virtual reality exposure vs. cognitive behavioral therapy with in vivo exposure in the treatment of social anxiety disorder: a study protocol for a randomized controlled trial. Front. Psychiatry **13**, 991755 (2022). https://doi.org/10.3389/fpsyt.2022.991755
11. VR8, https://vr8.dk/. Accessed 03 Sept 2023
12. Action cameras: 360 cameras: VR Cameras Insta360. https://www.insta360.com . Accessed 03 Sept 2023
13. Technologies, U. Unity.https://unity.com/. Accessed 03 Sept 2023
14. Vive Pro. VIVE Pro | VIVE United States. https://www.vive.com/us/product/vive-pro/. Accessed 03 Sept 2023
15. Tang, C., Wang, O., Liu, F., Tan, P.: Joint stabilization and direction of 360 videos. ACM Trans. Graphics **38**(2), 1–13 (2019)
16. Insta360 one X2. Insta360. https://www.insta360.com/product/insta360-onex2. Accessed 03 Sept 2023
17. Thayer, J.F., Sternberg, E.: Beyond heart rate variability: vagal regulation of allostatic systems. Ann. N. Y. Acad. Sci. **1088**(1), 361–373 (2006). https://doi.org/10.1196/annals.1376.019
18. Boucsein, W.: Electrodermal Activity. Springer, Cham (2012)
19. Pedersen, M., Bülow, P. iMotions.https://imotions.com/. Accessed 03 Sept 2023
20. Preece, J., Sharp, H., Rogers, Y.: Interaction Design: Beyond Human-Computer Interaction. Wiley (2019)
21. Chapin, N.: Flowchart. In Encyclopedia of Computer Science, pp. 714–716 (2003)

Study of Different Methods to Design and Animate Realistic Objects for Virtual Environments on Modern HMDs

Delrick Nunes De Oliveira[1,2](✉), Agustín Alejandro Ortiz Díaz[1], and Sergio Cleger Tamayo[1,2]

[1] Sidia Institute of Science and Technology, Av. Darcy Vargas, 654, Manaus 69055-035, Brazil
{delrick.oliveira,agustin.diaz,sergio.tamayo}@sidia.com

[2] Universidade Do Estado Do Amazonas, Av. Djalma Batista, 3578 – CEP, Manaus 69050-010, Brazil

Abstract. Head-mounted displays (HMDs) are making virtual environments increasingly viable and real. As of the year 2021, some of the latest HMDs manufactured have incorporated cameras and/or sensors for the recognition and tracking of hands and facial expressions. These new devices include HTC-Vive-Focus-3 manufactured by HTC, HP-Reverb-G2-Omnicept-Edition manufactured by HP, Meta-Quest-Pro, manufactured by Meta, and Pico-4-Pro manufactured by Pico. A human's facial expressions convey emotional and non-verbal information. Transferring these expressions to build more realistic designs is a long-standing problem in computer animation. Recently, the development of facial reconstructions (2D and 3D) has achieved high performance, adjusting to being treatable in real time. There are different types of models for design and animation, more human and realistic models, unrealistic cartoon character models, and non-human models with different facial structures. Regardless of the design, there must be guarantees of a smooth transition between expressions so that the facial animation does not look choppy. This work aims to carry out a study of the main models for the design and animation of objects, which can reflect and support various types of human facial expressions obtained from the complete facial data provided by HMDs that incorporate cameras and/or sensors for face recognition and tracking.

Keywords: Virtual Object Design · Virtual Object Animation · Virtual Environments · Head-mounted displays

1 Introduction

Head-mounted display (HMD) manufacturers are constantly adding new features to their devices to provide users with a richer and more immersive experience in virtual environments. Recently newer devices came with face tracking, and the feature to reproduce with a certain degree of fidelity the same movements of face in a virtual representation of users. Software or virtual environments are considered familiar when they are more attractive and tend to behave like the real world [1].

C. Stephanidis et al. (Eds.): HCII 2023, CCIS 1836, pp. 269–276, 2023.
https://doi.org/10.1007/978-3-031-36004-6_37

The integration of anthropomorphic characters in these environments was a logical advance to facilitate the interactions between the actors, both the users and the software itself. However, imitating the human figure and the interactions between actors pose several challenges. One of the main challenges is replicating the appearance and the feeling of familiarity associated with human actions. Failure to do so can result in the effect known as Uncanny Valley [2]. Recent advances in facial reconstruction have resulted in high-performance models that can be processed in real-time. Various types of models are available for design and animation, including more human and realistic models, unrealistic cartoon character models, and non-human models with different facial structures.

This study aims to investigate the primary models used for designing and animating objects that can reflect and support various types of human facial expressions. The study will use complete facial data obtained from HMDs that incorporate cameras and/or sensors for face recognition and tracking.

For a better organization of the study, it has been divided into these main sessions: "Methods for designing and animating human faces for facial expressions" (Sect. 2); and "Building and animating 3D faces with the use of HMD" (Sect. 3). Section 4 is also included, where the main ideas that were extracted after analyzing each of the referenced articles are presented. We rely on a table that summarizes the main characteristics of the traditional methods. Finally, we present our general conclusions and references.

2 Methods for Designing and Animating Human Faces for Facial Expressions

A realistic and expressive facial animation can bring a character to life and convey emotions and personality to the audience. However, achieving this level of realism requires a thorough understanding of the structure and movement of the face, as well as the use of appropriate tools and techniques. In this section, we will explore the various methods used for designing and animating human faces for facial expressions.

2.1 Traditional Approaches

Blendshapes. The term "blendshapes" describes linear facial models where the basis vectors represent individual facial expressions, rather than being orthogonal. These basis vectors can be referred to as blendshape targets, morph targets, or simple shapes. Additionally, the weights that correspond to each basis vector are often referred to as sliders since they are commonly represented in a user interface as sliders, which are adjusted to change the model appearance. During the animation, the weights associated with each vertex are used to interpolate between the keyframe shapes, creating a smooth transition between the different facial expressions or deformations. The resulting mesh geometry is then deformed based on the current set of parameter values to make the final animated character. Blendshapes can be used to blend segments of the face to provide more granular control over animation and are often combined with other techniques to produce more efficient results [3].

Parameterization. The essential concept for a parameterized model is to build a desired face or facial expression relying on some number of controlling parameter values that can be bound to a set of vertices in the face model, in this way, keyframes are defined with little effort. To make the expression behave as desired, boring manual tuning is required to set values. The limitations of parameterization led to the development of different approaches such as morphing between images and geometry, physically muscle-based animation, and performance-driven animation [4].

Facial Action Coding System (FACS). It is a comprehensive system for describing the movements of the facial muscles, as well as the jaw and tongue, based on an analysis of facial anatomy. FACS is comprised of 44 basic action units (AUs), each of which represents a distinct facial muscle movement. By combining these independent action units, a wide range of facial expressions can be generated. FACS is widely used in research, clinical practice, and the entertainment industry for creating realistic and nuanced facial animations [5].

Physics-Based Muscle Modeling (PBMM). It is a technique that uses physics simulation to achieve more expressive, non-linear facial animation. PBMM involves reproducing facial muscles and their connections in a model and then using physics simulation to do the contraction and relaxation of these muscles. PBMM offers greater control and precision in creating facial expressions, allowing animators to manipulate the underlying model of the muscles and generate corresponding movements automatically, saving time and producing more natural-looking animations. It needs accurate and detailed models of facial muscles and high-performance computing [6].

Performance-Driven Facial Animation (PDFA). It is a method that uses motion capture technology to represent the performance of the character. The process of performance-driven facial animation can be divided into three stages: modeling, capture, and retargeting. The modeling stage has to do with the creation process of the human face model, after being displayed and modified. The capture stage is a phase of feature extraction of input video, so the data can be applied to the model to synthesize the animation. This technique can use approaches that are active or passive. Active approaches include marker-based capture where physical markers are located on the actor's face and tracked throughout the performance. Passive approaches include approaches that utilize video inputs of the actor's face without any markers placed. The Retargeting stage aims to transfer the parameters obtained during the capture step and animate the target model [4].

2.2 Artificial Intelligence Approaches

Generative Adversarial Networks (GAN). It trains two models simultaneously: a generative model that generates data like the training data and a discriminative model that distinguishes between the generated and real data. These models compete in an adversarial process where the generative model tries to generate realistic data to fool the discriminative model, while the discriminative model tries to accurately classify the data. This process is a minimax two-player game because the two models optimize their objectives against each other [7]. Bansal et al. [8] used GAN for video retargeting that enables the transfer of sequential content from one domain to another while preserving the style of the target domain.

Convolutional Neural Networks (CNN). It is a type of deep neural network that excels at processing grid-like data such as images, audio spectrograms, and text sequences. CNNs consist of multiple layers, each with a specific function, including convolutional, pooling, and fully connected layers. During training, the weights of the filters and neurons are adjusted using backpropagation and gradient descent to minimize a loss function. CNNs have achieved state-of-the-art performance in various applications, including image recognition, object detection, segmentation, and natural language processing, due to their ability to learn hierarchical representations of input data [9]. Deng et al. [10] used it for 3D facial reconstruction.

Recurrent Neural Networks (RNN). These connectionist models capture the dynamics of sequences using cycles in the network of nodes. These cycles enable the network to capture temporal and sequential information, making RNNs particularly useful in processing time-series data. Unlike standard feedforward neural networks, RNNs have a recurrent state that allows them to retain information from an arbitrarily long context window, which makes them well-suited for tasks that require the analysis of variable-length sequences of data [11]. Berson et al. [12] used RNN to generate believable facial motions with input constraints such as sparse keyframes, discrete semantic input, or coarse animation.

Variational Autoencoders (VAE). It is a generative model that learns to generate new samples by encoding them into a latent space and then decoding them back into the original space. VAEs have an encoder network and a decoder network. The encoder network maps the input data to a probability distribution in the latent space, while the decoder network maps a sample from the latent distribution back to the original input space. During training, VAEs are optimized to minimize the difference between the distribution generated by the encoder and a predefined prior distribution in the latent space, and the reconstruction loss between the input data and the reconstructed data. Once trained, VAEs can generate new samples by sampling from the distribution in the latent space. VAEs can be used for Generative Modeling, Anomaly Detection, Data Compression, Domain Adaptation, and missing data Imputation [13]. Lombardi et al. [14] use VAE for data compression and to generate with decompression a 3D face model representation for novel view angles.

3D Face Morphable Model (3DMM). It is a generative model that uses two key ideas: First, all faces are in dense correspondence, which allows for meaningful linear combinations of faces to produce realistic morphs. Second, facial shape and color are separated from external factors such as illumination and camera parameters. The model involves a statistical distribution of faces, typically using principal component analysis, and was initially used to generate morphs from 3D scans. However, newer variations use deep learning to directly learn 3DMMs from 2D images [15].

3 Building and Animating 3D Faces with the Use of Head Mounted Display

To **enhance** the immersive experience of XR applications, HMD manufacturers have integrated advanced functionalities in both hardware and software. The latest HMD device of Meta, Meta Quest Pro, is a prime example, featuring sensors that can capture eye and facial movements for applications that support the reproduction of such features in avatars. However, the challenge of generating personalized facial animations that are smooth and lifelike remains due to the limitation of the sensors being within the HMD and the occlusion of the face caused by the device. In this section, we will see some examples of how researchers have addressed these challenges.

Robust Egocentric Photo-Realistic Facial Expression Transfer for Virtual Reality [16]. This work is about facial expression transfer from HMD images to an avatar of previous work. In addition, an end-to-end multi-identity architecture (MIA) and augmentation techniques were proposed to robustify and generalize existing codecs to control Avatars. Below we present some challenges that were faced in this paper. We also show suggested solutions. "Challenge and solution" are shown with the following structure: Challenges— Solution.

- Independence of the face generation from person dynamic attributes and light—Backbone network to extract features.
- Match between avatar data and camera data—use of 3DDM to translate (mesh).
- Account for face angle, slop relative to face, and focus—Data augmentation.
- Generation of mesh and texture in real-time—Use of pre-trained decoder.

Realistic Facial Expression Reconstruction for VR HMD Users [18]. This work proposes a framework that captures advanced activities encoded in action units (AU) through advanced sensing hardware for Electromyography (EMG) [17]. It is called "Faceteq" and can be embedded in an HMD. It also proposes the display of realistic expressions via a closer representation of the user and discovers the connection between basiemotionsns (anger, disgust, fear, happiness, sadness, and surprise) to AU. The challenges and Solutions are shown with the same structure: Challenge—Solution.

Face recognition with occluded parts—usage of EMG in muscles that match AUs.

- Realistic representation of a user in an easy way—3D face reconstruction from 2D image based on 3DMM, non-rigid registration method [19], and usage of FACS-based blendshapes [20].
- Expression recognition—LS-SVM (variation of Support Vector Machine that uses Least Square for optimization) to classify expressions from EMG signals.
- Relationship between AU and six basic emotions—Fern classifier [21].

4 Analysis and Discussion

Table 1 presents a comparison between five methods of facial modeling and 3D animation. Shared methods are: (1) Blendshapes, (2) Parameterization, (3) Facial Action Coding System, (4) Physics-Based Muscle Modeling, and (5) Performance Driven Facial Animation.

Table 1. 3D Facial modeling and animation techniques comparison.

Method	Realism	Efficiency	Flexibility	Ease of use	Expressivity	Accuracy	Interoperability	Cost
(1)	High	High	Low	High	High	Medium	Medium	Medium
(2)	Medium	Medium	High	Medium	Medium	High	Medium	High
(3)	High	Low	Low	Low	High	Medium	Medium	Low
(4)	High	Low	High	Low	High	High	Low	High
(5)	High	High	Medium	Medium	High	High	Medium	High

Overall, the choice of technique depends on the specific needs and constraints of the project or application. Blendshapes are commonly used in gaming and animation due to their high expressivity and ease of use, but they may not be as flexible or accurate as other techniques. Parameterization offers high flexibility and accuracy but requires technical expertise. The FACS is highly expressive but requires extensive training and may not be efficient or flexible. PBMM offers high realism and accuracy but may not be efficient or interoperable. PDFA offers high realism and expressivity while also being efficient and flexible but may require a higher initial investment.

On the other hand, methods based on artificial intelligence techniques, particularly deep learning, have shown promising results in support of the task of designing and animating human faces. Many of these models have been used in a variety of applications such as image synthesis, image rendering, semantic image editing, and so on. However, training using deep learning generally requires a large volume of data, with 3D face images being quite sparse. In addition, they are models that generally consume a lot of space and time resources.

5 Conclusion

The objective of this work was to carry out a study of the main methods of design and animation of real objects that are of interest to our project. We focus on the most widely used methods to work with facial expressions in humans. Both traditional animation methods and those based on artificial intelligence were addressed.

In this first analysis, based on the characteristics of our project, a model based on blendshapes seems promising. This is a very simple, linear, medium-cost approach that is widely used today for realistic facial animation. However, some limitations are highlighted, such as being considered an inflexible approach, that is, presenting a low degree of customization and adaptability to different faces and expressions. Another analyzed idea is to support the limitations of this model with some of the artificial intelligence techniques.

Acknowledgments. This paper was presented as part of the results of the Project "SIDIA-M_AR_Internet_For_Bondi", carried out by the Institute of Science and Technology - SIDIA, in partnership with Samsung Eletrônica da Amazônia LTDA, in accordance with the Information Technology Law n.8387/ 91 and article at the. 39 of Decree 10,521/2020.

References

1. McLeod, R.: Animation Handbook (2019)
2. Mori, M., et al.: The Uncanny Valley [From the Field]. IEEE Robot. Autom. Mag. **19**(2), 98–100 (2012). https://doi.org/10.1109/MRA.2012.2192811
3. Lewis, J., et al.: Practice and theory of Blendshape facial models. In: Eurographics 2014 - State of the Art Reports, p. 20 (2014). https://doi.org/10.2312/EGST.20141042
4. Shakir, S., Al-Azza, A.: Facial modelling and animation: an overview of the state-of-the Art. Iraqi J. Electr. Electron. Eng. **18**(1), 28–37 (2022). https://doi.org/10.37917/ijeee.18.1.4
5. Noh, J.: A survey of facial modeling and animation techniques (2001). https://www.semanticscholar.org/paper/A-Survey-of-Facial-Modeling-and-Animation-Noh/9f1bbb74eb9f808421f46b924d8576bd46eb578a. Accessed 09 Mar 2023
6. Lee, Y., et al.: Realistic modeling for facial animation. In: Proceedings of the ACM SIGGRAPH Conference on Computer Graphics, pp. 55–62 (1995). https://doi.org/10.1145/218380.218407
7. Goodfellow, I., et al.: Generative Adversarial Networks, 10 June 2014. arXiv: https://doi.org/10.48550/arXiv.1406.2661.
8. Bansal, A., et al.: Recycle-GAN: unsupervised video retargeting, 15 August 2018. arXiv: https://doi.org/10.48550/arXiv.1808.05174
9. Montesinos López, O.A., Montesinos López, A., Crossa, J.: Convolutional Neural Networks. In: Montesinos López, O.A., Montesinos López, A., Crossa, J. (eds.) Multivariate Statistical Machine Learning Methods for Genomic Prediction, pp. 533–57710. Springer, Cham (2022). https://doi.org/10.1007/978-3-030-89010-0_13
10. Deng, Y., et al.: Accurate 3D face reconstruction with weakly-supervised learning: from single image to image set, 09 April 2020. arXiv: [Online]. Available:http://arxiv.org/abs/1903.08527. Accessed: Mar. 09, 2023.
11. Lipton, Z., et al.: A critical review of recurrent neural networks for sequence learning, 17 October 2015. arXiv: http://arxiv.org/abs/1506.00019. Accessed 09 Mar 2023
12. Berson, E., et al.: Intuitive facial animation editing based on a generative RNN Framework, 12 October 2020. arXiv: http://arxiv.org/abs/2010.05655. Accessed 09 Mar 2023
13. Kingma, D., Welling, M.: An introduction to variational autoencoders. Found. Trends® Mach. Learn. **12**(4), 307–392 (2019). https://doi.org/10.1561/2200000056
14. Lombardi, S., et al.: Deep appearance models for face rendering. ACM Trans. Graph. **37**(4), 1–13 (2018). https://doi.org/10.1145/3197517.3201401

15. Egger, B., et al.: 3D Morphable face models -- past, present and future, 16 April 2020. arXiv: http://arxiv.org/abs/1909.01815. Accessed 14 Mar 2023
16. Jourabloo, A., et al.: Robust egocentric photo-realistic facial expression transfer for virtual reality. In: Proceedings IEEE Computer Society Conference Computer Vision Pattern Recognition, June 2022, pp. 20291–20300 (2022). https://doi.org/10.1109/CVPR52688.2022.01968
17. "Electromyography (EMG) - Mayo Clinic." https://www.mayoclinic.org/tests-procedures/emg/about/pac-20393913. Accessed 14 Mar 2023
18. Lou, J., et al.: Realistic facial expression reconstruction for VR HMD users. IEEE Trans. Multimed. **22**(3), 730–743 (2020). https://doi.org/10.1109/TMM.2019.2933338
19. Zhang, S., et al.: Automatic 3D face recovery from a single frame of a RGB-D sensor. In: 28th British Machine Vision Conference AFAHBU Workshop," BMVA, August 2017. https://bmvc2017.london/. Accessed 13 Mar 2023
20. Yu, H., et al.: Perception-driven facial expression synthesis. Comput. Graph. **36**(3), 152–162 (2012). https://doi.org/10.1016/j.cag.2011.12.002
21. Ozuysal, M., et al.: Fast keypoint recognition in ten lines of code, June 2007. https://doi.org/10.1109/CVPR.2007.383123

Exploring New Futures in Video See-Through: Experience-es and Scenarios Using XR Technologies

Fernanda Pimentel(✉), Yuri Inhamuns, and Marcos Silbermann

Sidia Instituto de Ciência e Tecnologia, Manaus, AM 69075-830, Brazil
fernanda.pimentel@sidia.com

Abstract. Video-See Through (VST) is a promising tool in the XR (Mixed Reality) market today. VST allows the overlapping of digital elements in a real environment, allowing the user to see in real time the mixture of the virtual and real environment simultaneously, making XR technology more accessible and incorporated into our daily lives. VST is currently in a very experimental phase, but it already shows great promise when used to compose an XR product, gaining great notoriety in the area of security and complementation of the user experience. However, the use of VST is opening up new possibilities for XR to have even more positive impacts in its promising areas such as education, health, industry, entertainment and social. We understand these VST issues, based on research done with benchmarking, analysis of internal documents from Instituto Sidia and analysis of applications that have VST. This article presents the main findings of the exploration so far of VST in the market, presenting different types and uses of VST within an XR experience and how VST can directly influence.

Keywords: Video-see through · Augmented reality · virtual reality · technological innovations

1 Introduction

At SIDIA – Instituto de Ciência e Tecnologia located in the Brazilian city of Manaus, we are exploring scenarios and concepts of experiences using virtual and augmented reality devices. Among our exploratory research interests is the attempt to understand the values and frustrations attributed by users to the daily use of this technology. In this article, we focus on the content produced in the last six months of exploratory research, which involved tools such as benchmarking, user experiments and in-depth interviews, specifically focused on the use of the VST feature applied to different usage scenarios. Such as: productivity, entertainment and games.

While proving to be promising in several areas (Education, healthcare, corporate, entertainment and social), the use of mixed reality HMDs also presents uncertain probabilities, contributing to slower adoption of XR. However, six categories were identified for XR if adopted in the organizational environment:

C. Stephanidis et al. (Eds.): HCII 2023, CCIS 1836, pp. 277–283, 2023.
https://doi.org/10.1007/978-3-031-36004-6_38

Expected cost-effectiveness of XR technology, technology readiness, organizational readiness, security, environment and external pressure, corporate climate (Stephanie Huei-Wen 2018).

The devices launched by Meta in recent years (Meta Quest 2 and Meta Quest Pro), in addition to the device launched by HTC (Pico4) present important advances in the development of VST technology, presenting it as one of the relevant differentials for end consumers. The introduction of color VST technologies with depth sensors in the latest devices to hit the market signals an attempt by these large companies to expand the universe of mixed reality experiences, offering users new ways to use them and apply them in your daily life. Apparently, VST technology is understood as a factor that should boost the expansion of scenarios for the use of XR technologies and bring it closer to end consumers, helping to overcome its niche technology stigma.

In this sense, we structured our research on the use and impacts that the VST has on the evolution of XR technology. It is important to note that our study started from a very specific focus, the implications of the use of VST in user experiences. Through the articulation of exploratory research results carried out in different projects of our institute and a detailed work of surveying references of applications that use VST, their experimentation and critical analysis, we produced this article discussing some important values that VST brings to experiments. -ences of using XR. The purpose of this discussion and compilation of research findings is to expand and consolidate our understanding of the use of VST applied to UX.

2 VST Contexto in XR

Video-See Through (VST) is a tool that has been gaining more and more prominence within the XR market, as it enables the blending of VR and AR realities in the same experience. Currently, the most prominent XR devices on the market are Meta's Oculus Quest, which in turn use the VST technology patented as "Passthrough". It is important to clarify that this is not a new technology, the VST concept emerged in the 1990s and the development of the head mounted display as a mediator of reality in MIT laboratories. These initiatives helped consolidate the field of academic research on HMD (Schmalstieg et al. 2016). The VST allows the user to see the transmission of the real environment around him through an internal screen in the HMD, this procedure happens through the mediation of cameras integrated to the device that capture the real environment (Moreira et al. 2012). VST promises to make the XR a more accessible technology and incorporated into our routine, however the limitation of its cameras, generating low quality images (grainy, distorted) and/or monochrome and/or monoscopic video stream, can end up compromising the overall experience and even performance of the application. (Kern 2023) (Fig. 1).

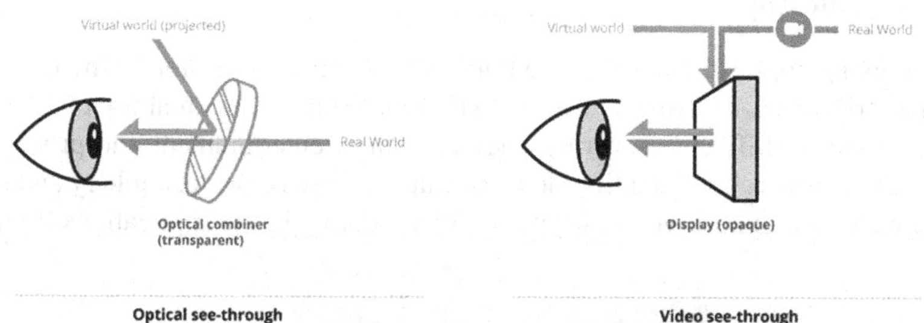

Fig. 1. [3] Left, Optical see-through displays operate based on transparent optics that allow the user to see the surroundings directly along with virtual content. Right: Video see-through displays are opaque; they use a camera to capture the users' surrounding and then displays them on a screen along with computer-generated images. Diagram based on "Breakthroughs in optics that are reshaping augmented reality."

3 Research Methodologies

Methodologically, we carried out three research strategies, at first we performed a benchmarking of applications that use this tool in their experiences, with the objective of analyzing the current use of this technology in the market, and what are its advantages and disadvantages, after the survey of applications, we performed a trial of these applications that were in VST. Followed by the analysis of the documentation produced by our Proof of Concepts (POCs) development projects that explore the capabilities and ways of using the VST, through this we were able to categorize and organize the data in a detailed way.

3.1 Benchmark

At the beginning of the research, we identified the need to carry out an application benchmark, in which we could know which applications on the market already have the Video-See Through technology, in this way, we could understand different experiences of using the technology and see which its potentials and opportunities are related to the user experience. We defined what the analysis metrics would be and took into account some points: Genre, Application context, if it were VR/MR, Inputs.

We separated this benchmark study into two main moments, the first was an internal search, where we were able to raise all the applications that were already known by the institute's teams and that had already been used by them, and in the second moment, we carried out searches on different sites, in order to find out about other applications that have the technology and increase our collection so that the experimentation could be carried out.

Deepening the concept of benchmarking, we can present the formal definition of business application by David T. Kearns, CEO of Xerox, in which "benchmarking is the continuous process of measuring products, services and practices against the strongest competitors, or companies recognized as leaders in their industries" (Camp 1998, p. 8 e10). The same author adds, as a third definition, that the computer industry describes benchmarking as "a standard for comparing other objects or activities" used to measure the performance of hardware and software.

3.2 Testing the Apps

After surveying applications, we carried out experimentation sessions, where we used them in a scripted way, raising specific questions about the contextual use of VST, how it was inserted in different scenarios, such as games, entertainment and productivity scenarios, to that we could identify the main values of use of the technology and in this way, we were able to observe the 4 types of VST existing in the applications (Fig. 2).

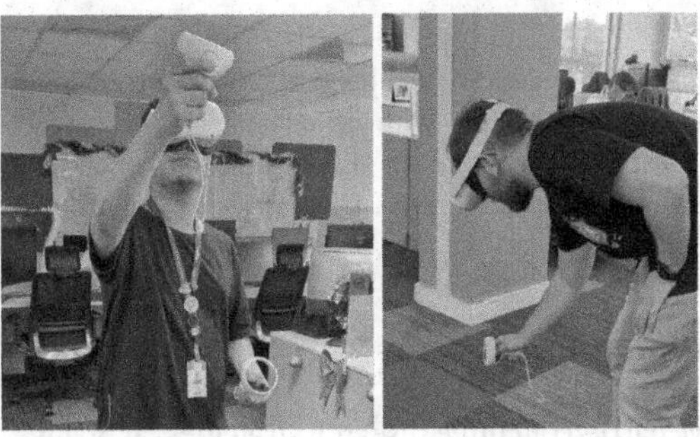

Fig. 2. Experimenting with Applications Using Device Quest 2

3.3 Document Analysis

One of the ways to increase our contextual look in relation to the VST was by using complementary internal works, in this phase of the study, an organization of the material that had studies done on Video-See Through was carried out, when it became essential to look at the set of documents in an analytical way, where the authors of these studies had evaluated technical issues regarding the quality of the see-through video and the user's relationship using the tool, in this third moment it was already possible to understand important issues in the use of VST for work -le, leisure and entertainment.

To A, Pimentel (2001). "Organizing the material means processing the reading according to content analysis criteria, including some techniques, such as filing, quantitative and qualitative survey of recurrent terms and subjects."

4 Results

Such results were obtained through the use of applications that have video-see-through and analyzes made in internal documents. This discovery and exploration phase of the research allowed the identification of a variety of ways to use the built-in VST functionality for different usage scenarios. The main finding of this phase is precisely the mapping of these ways of relating VST and user experiences and deepening the understanding of their mechanisms.

4.1 VST as a Complemente to Experience

From our experiment, we identified that VST can be used as a complement to the experience, adapting to users' needs within a given context of an XR application. We observe this scenario happening in VR productivity applications (Horizon Workrooms, Immersed) where in these scenarios VST is used for reasons of environment spacing configuration or bringing real-world references into the XR application.

We can see VST being used to complement the experience in the Horizon Workrooms application, this is a productivity application that offers to migrate the user's real work environment to a VR environment, aiming at more efficiency and optimization of their work. Before starting the application, the user needs to configure his environment using VST, through which it is possible to define the spacing and height of his work area. By using the VST in this way, it is possible to avoid possible collisions, and you can also get closer to the exact size of the measurements of your real work area.

4.2 Games – VST as Narrative Element

The VST is integrated and helps to enhance the narratives proposed by the studied games, it enriches interaction with elements of the physical world, understanding about the location of colleagues who are present in the same room, it is also possible for the user to be able to insert elements in space, such as objects, characters and dynamics that help to give new meanings to the environment.

We have Dungeon Maker as an example, it is a game in which the user can use the tools in the application and see the physical environment, so that the VST is not out of context and the elements of the virtual and physical scenery intersect, thus, the VST becomes part of the narrative proposed by the game, as the user is no longer the spectator who runs the game to directly participate in the actions, he participates in the game with gestures, postures and actions performed directly with his body.

4.3 Productivity – Recognition and Customizations of Space

The VST is used as a tool to facilitate the performance of work activities through the recognition of space, in productivity activities, the use of the VST has been well used for moments where the user can recognize the table he is working on so that he can be able to integrate other devices into the experience, add other props of your daily life so that it is easily accessible. Thus, the user can organize his space, clearly defining his customization and not being restricted to a fully immersive scenario.

During the COVID-19 pandemic, a study was carried out on how VR can influence learning, a very large rate was observed in the approval of this technology in this scenario, adding that VST can increase user enthusiasm (Xing 2021).

4.4 Interaction with the Real World

With the use of VST users are not completely deprived of the real world and not completely trapped in it. In the course of our research, we analyzed that when users used hybrid experience applications (VR/AR), the use of VST positively influenced application approval, users valued the experience of using an XR application and simultaneously seeing their environment real world and the elements that compose it, allowing you to interact with people and objects in the real world. The same approval was found when a virtual object interacted directly with a real object, that is, the interaction of a virtual object recognizing the surface of a table increased the level of immersion of users within the XR application.

4.5 Reducing the Risk of Accidents

During our research, we identified the use of VST as a prevention for possible accidents, the user can see the physical world while interacting with the virtual environment, in this way, the VST helps to reduce risks, since the user interacts with the physical elements, however, does not prevent accidents from happening, in the same way in the use of VR, where the guardian helps the user with safety, but does not prevent accidents.

When using VST, the physical environment becomes more visible, but as the mix between real and virtual happens, it can clutter the user, causing difficulty in identifying what is real or virtual.

4.6 Seeing Through the Window

The passthrough is like a "window" that connects AR with VR, giving the user the possibility to move between these two realities, an application that makes good use of this transition is The World Beyond that allows the user to move between VR and AR in real-time mapped space using XR.

VST modes in AR/VR:

VST in VR: We see the use of this VST mode in the Immersed application, this application focused on Virtual Reality, which aims to offer a productivity environment, within the application the user can create some "windows" in VR with VST, as well being able to see parts of his environment attention that he wants to migrate into the XR experience, helping him not to be totally alienated from the real world and bringing the real world elements he needs in his work routine into the XR application.

VST in AR: A good example of this use is the SeeSignal application, this application serves to identify the quality of the internet signal in the area, allowing the user to walk identified the quality of the network in each point of his environment. In this way, the user can see the real world, but at the same time see digital elements, showing the quality of the internet signal, in the palm of his hand.

5 Conclusion

Finally, in this article, we point out VST as a promising tool that can be applied in a variety of ways, expanding the horizon from UX to XR. In addition to its usual application in contexts of safety and reduction of risk of user accidents.

However, our compilation of findings points to some important points that must be considered, both specifically in the direct application of VST tools in XR applications, and in a general way in the understanding of UX development for this type of technology. In view of the development of more intuitive experiences for users, we as designers need to think about UX that think about the complementary relationship between immersiveness and the real world. Probably the best question we should ask to develop good XR usage experiences is how to establish this complementarity, so that end users can feel inserted in their everyday life aided by digital elements. VST technology brings important values for us to establish this complementary relationship, but it still needs to offer more quality to end users.

References

Chuah, S.: Why and who will adopt extended reality technology? In: Literature Review, Synthesis, and Future Research Agenda (2018)

Schmalstieg, D., Hollerer, T.: Augmented Reality: Principles and Practice. edn. illustrated. Addison-Wesley Professional (2016)

Meta Quest. https://developer.oculus.com/blog/mixed-reality-with-passthrough/. Accessed 10 Mar 2023

Meta Quest. https://developer.oculus.com/resources/mr-design-guideline/. Accessed 10 Mar 2023

Moreira, L., Amorim, A.: Realidade aumentada e patrimônio cultural: apresentação, tecnologias e aplicações (2012)

Kern, F., Niebling, F., Latoschik, M.: Text input for non-stationary XR workspaces: investigating tap and word-gesture keyboards in virtual and augmented reality. IEEE Trans. Vis. Comput. Graph. (2023)

Xing, Y., et al.: Virtual reality research: design virtual education system for epidemic (COVID-19) knowledge to public (2021)

Camp, R.C.: Benchmarking: the Way to Total Quality. 3rd edn. Pioneira, São Paulo (1998)

Pimentel, A.: The document analysis method: its use in a search historiographic (2001)

Exploring Tertiary Orality in Virtual Reality

Semi Ryu(✉)

Kinetic Imaging, VCU Arts, Richmond, VA, USA
sryu2@vcu.edu

Abstract. This paper will discuss digital orality in my avatar life-review and VR projects, using an emotion AI-sentiment analysis algorithm. Walter Ong wrote about primary orality, which is based on oral cultures, and secondary orality, which depends on literary culture. With the advance of speech technology, tertiary digital orality could be explored, highlighting aspects of emotion, memory, and improvisation in VR media. Orality is an important feature of shamanistic society. Korean shamanism is connected with oral culture with lengthy storytellings, singing and chanting. It is also interesting to see Women attain the opportunity to speak, mediated by a shaman, during the shaman ritual, Kut. Inspired by orality in Korean ritual, I have explored digital orality and have facilitated live speech in my avatar life-review and VR projects for underrepresented populations. In collaboration with a Computer Scientist professor, Dr. Stefano Faralli at University of Rome La Sapienza, Italy, sentiment analysis was implemented for the VoicingElder project, avatar life-review for older adults. Emotion AI- sentiment analysis was used to explore innovative ways of creating empathy, emotional analysis, evaluation, and the overall therapeutic potential in tertiary digital orality. This paper will discuss aspects of digital orality (especially in the VoicingElder avatar life-review session, through the use of sentiment analysis algorithm), and discuss potential emotional communication in VR through speech.

Keywords: Virtual Reality · Orality · Emotion AI

1 Digital Orality

One of my research interests has been oral storytelling which has a spirit of improvisation and emotional communication. Digital orality would bring back some aspects that have been thought absent in digital communication, such as emotion, intuition and improvisation. Water Ong defined three oralities: primary, secondary and third [1]. In traditional nonliterate cultures, the elder's oral storytelling functioned as an intergenerational education process, delivering experiential knowledge, values and passion from generation to generation [2]. The second orality was inspired by literate culture. The third orality is related to digital oraility motivated by the advancement of speech technology. It can bring the aspects of oral culture associated with emotion, memory, intuition, spontaneity and improvisation, in the area of digital communication that have been pre-dominated by texts and visual aspects for a long time.

C. Stephanidis et al. (Eds.): HCII 2023, CCIS 1836, pp. 284–288, 2023.
https://doi.org/10.1007/978-3-031-36004-6_39

Orality is an important feature of shamanistic society. Korean shamanism is connected with oral culture, with lengthy storytellings, singing and chanting. Mudang were illiterate as the lowest social class in the past, and her knowledge was descended from mouth to mouth. Speech is an important modality in communicating with gods, during Kut. It is interesting to see women participants (including Korean shaman "Mudang") attain an opportunity to speak (as gods or a dead person's voice) [3]. Kut worked as a channel for women to speak up, becoming alternative beings. Kut liberates a woman from an oppressive state, empowering her with the position of a god. Lewis similarly notes that possession has always attracted followers among the weak and oppressed, particularly among women in male-dominant societies, like in Korea [4]. By transforming into a god or spirit, the oppressed freely speak about their hidden opinions and emotional states.

Inspired by orality in Korean shaman ritual, speech modality was the first thing to be implemented in the VoicingElder project, as avatar body was a channel for free speech. This speech modality can be personally meaningful for someone who has lived with suppressed speech, for desperate needs for communication shown in Kut. Speech mediated by technology is different from typical speech. For example, the speech amplified by a microphone brings a different perception of speech, allowing the speaker to listen better to what was said, facilitating a self-reflection process. Speech consciousness mediated by an avatar body in my avatar projects is different from normal speech. There are slight delays of lip sync of my avatars which gives different speech perception. This mediated speech gives different aspects of speech- new tempo, new rhythm and tones of speech.

For example, in a session of the VoicingElder project, Mrs.C's story demonstrates new speech perceptions. This is an excerpt from Mrs. C's storytelling:

> "He didn't understand me I was just a li-------ttle girl. He was a strong man, strong and really strong. So the next day we went down to the basement and sat in the recreation room in the basement and I sat on his lap, on his lap, and…he talked to me he talked to me he talked to me. Talk b aba b aba b aba……..I am sorry.. b aba b aba b aba ba ba remember I was a little little girl little little girl. Only four. I did not understand anything about anything, anything, I didn't understand it. I went back upstairs. I have a feeling that, into this left a hole---- in my heart."

Mrs.C made up new expressions such as "b aba b aba b aba…" and have repeated many words such as "strong", "talk to me", " little", " anything", " wanted", etc. She also used dramatic emphasis on certain words (little, strong) with dynamic gestures, which does not usually happen during typical speech modes. Speech behavior changes when we perform as a virtual body, which results in changing the stories.

In shaman rituals and psychodrama, speech is also mediated by the virtual presence of a god, spirit or character which transforms the speech behavior. Once the shaman is transformed into a god and starts behaving as a god, everyone bows on their knees as they clearly experience the shaman as a different being, from voice, gestures, etc. The tone and speed of speech becomes different with altered state of speech consciousness when Mudang speaks the voice of god, depending on different body perception in working with spirit. The use of digital arts media in therapy practice resembles ancient ritual self-experience of cure and release, and digital orality is also a kind of mediated orality that can help people to express their inner feelings by improvisation and performativity.

2 Sentiment Response from Live Speech

Sentiment analysis and response was used in the VoicingElder project, to promote playfulness and an empathetic environment in the life storytelling process. Thus, it helps improve the quality of life of the older adults participants for their perception about their own lived experiences. The VoicingElder system generates a generic idea of the dialogue topic through a combination of speech recognition and simple text classification. This opened the possibilities for appropriate graphic and acoustic feedback, based on sentiment analysis of the speech. 6 emotions were used to be assessed during life storytelling: happy, sad, anger, fear, anxiety and laughter. The VoicingElder system provided audiovisual feedback, based on emotional states of the participant's story (Fig. 1), (Fig. 2), (Fig. 3).

There are 3 different levels of sentiment analysis: document level, sentence level, aspect level [5]. Document level sentiment analysis attempts to classify sentiments in product reviews or news articles, sentence level attempts to classify positive and negative sentiments for each sentence, the aspect level is targeted on capturing multiple sentiments that may be present within a single sentence. VoicingElder project used a sentence level sentiment analysis method [6]. Social media gathers people's information, by collecting behavior, comments, etc. They have used sentiment analysis to analyze thousands of comments, reviews, and survey responses in a short period of time. However, application of sentiment analysis was not much done, especially for live speech used in therapeutic and artistic settings.

The VoicingElder project detects the speaker's current emotional state and polarity continuously during live speech, which further challenges the analysis with written text materials. We used audio wave data containing the participant's speech recorded via microphone, then detected the aforementioned traits through sentiment analysis of textual speech representation via speech recognition.

Fig. 1. Emotional background images: Happiness, Anger.

Fig. 2. Emotional background images: Sadness, Anxiety.

Fig. 3. Emotional background images: Laughter, Fear.

3 Problems in Sentiment Response, and Adaptations

Beta version of sentiment analysis was first time implemented in the VoicingElder, and there were technical problems in this first experiment. During the VoicingElder life-review sessions, we used Google speech API for speech to text feature; however, it was not able to analyze "continuous" speech. The main requirements for the speech recognition to support the nature of live speech sessions is to stream audio and receive the transcription also as a stream with minimum latency. Google cloud speech API has an important for the system development limitation in case of streaming speech recognition - the audio length is limited by 60 s during one session.

It is interesting that the older adults participants were not much impacted by visual feedback. For example, they were not overly distracted when the wrong emotional image was displayed. However, they seemed to pay more attention to sounds. The sound of birds and rain seems to inspire some of the residents' storytelling. This could be due to the older adults' vision issues. Based on beta testing experiences in VoicingElder sessions, Dr. Stefano Faralli, and his Master student Leonid Gunko have updated the SA system for the emotion recognition from live speech, working with Microsoft Cortana, in 2020. The problem addressed was the real-time detection of emotions from live speech.

Another challenge for the VoicingElder sentiment analysis was caused by pronunciation problems from the older adult participants, with their speech having been difficult to detect from speech recognition systems. For optimal performance, sentiment analysis needs to be analyzed using visual data such as gestural and facial, as well as audio from live speech [7]. Gestural and facial information are critical for detecting human emotion. In the future, we will incorporate audiovisual information as well as the textual representation of the speech for a holistic approach in emotional analysis.

4 Future Direction

Recently, we have been working on the SentimentVoice project; VR based talk therapy designed to promote empathy, positive feelings, and mindfulness, using the updated sentiment analysis algorithm developed by Dr. Faralli. It creates immersive virtual environments which allows the participants to vocalize and express one's emotions, and get appropriate audio visual feedback to address feelings and move in more positive directions. The VR program uses algorithms that calculates sentiment, using speech to text, and then analyzes what emotions are presented in the participants' speech, promoting a therapeutic process through storytelling, navigation, and immersion. Tertiary digital orality needs to be continuously discussed with ongoing development of sentiment response systems and discuss how it could be used to express emotion, empathy and therapeutic effects in order to promote spontaneous and improvisational speech platforms in VR.

References

1. Ong, W.: Orality and Literacy: The Technologizing of the Word, 2nd edn. Routledge, New York (2002)
2. Archibald, J.: Indigenous Storywork: Educating The Heart, Mind, Body, and Spirit. UBC Press, Vancouver, p. 93 (2008)
3. Lee, D.H.: Korean shamans: role playing through trance possession. In Richard Schechner, R., Appel, W. (eds.), By Means of Performance: Intercultural Studies of Theatre and Ritual, vol. 164, pp.149–166. Cambridge University Press, Cambridge (1990)
4. Lewis, I.M.: Ecstatic Religion: An Anthropological Study of Spirit Possession and Shamanism. Penguin Books, Middlesex, pp. 112–113 (1971)
5. Liu, B.: Sentiment Analysis: Mining Opinions, Sentiments and Emotions. Cambridge University Press, Cambridge (2015)
6. Gunko, L.: Continuous Emotions Detection From Live Speech [Master's thesis, University of Mannheim, Germany] (2018)
7. Wang, Y., Guan, L.: Recognizing human emotional state from audiovisual signals. IEEE Trans. Multimedia **10**(5), 936–946 (2008)

UX and UI Fundamentals for Mixed Reality: Research and Categorization of Interactions

Alef Santos[(✉)], Hanah Correa, and Marcos Silbermann

Sidia Instituto de Ciência E Tecnologia, Manaus, AM 69055-035, Brazil
alef.santos@sidia.com

Abstract. Conducting interface design research in XR contexts, it was observed the scarcity of studies and documents that compile analyses of interactions in this medium, usually only presenting a brief technical description of its functionality on the platform of the brand or reality device company virtual or augmented. In this way, there was a need to develop a document that would group many interactions in extended reality, describing them technically and presenting an analysis of their visual character and their influence on the user experience. Compiling the main aspects in a single document, with writing that communicates more easily with different professionals who may come to consult such file, in addition, showing positives, negatives, and good practices in scenarios of use of these interactions, valuing the valuing content sharing and democratizing access to a detailed analysis document on a topic that is growing rapidly in technology research today.

Keywords: XR Interactions · Mixed Reality · Interaction Design

1 Introduction

This research was born from a demand built between different projects of our Solutions and UX department of the Sidia research and development center, located in the city of Manaus in northern Brazil. In our department, we develop technological solutions and explore experiences of using emerging technologies. The research presented here is the product of the exploration and cataloging of interactions and interfaces in XR (Mixed reality) applications in the market. The emergence of this demand sought to respond to an initial need for different initiatives for basic and well-structured knowledge on the subject. In this context, the objective of the research was to produce a document to be consumed by designers of different projects involved in the exploration and development of user experiences in the context of XR technologies. This document was initially understood as a transversal legacy to our program for presenting good practices and indications on how interactions and interfaces can be used by designers in the elaboration of specific UX for experiences with XR technologies.

In this sense, in building this very broad document on interactions and interfaces we faced various research challenges, which involved analyzing and categorizing the interactions and structuring the document. A point that should also be emphasized is the importance of exploring a variety of situations in which the interactions are applied,

C. Stephanidis et al. (Eds.): HCII 2023, CCIS 1836, pp. 289–299, 2023.
https://doi.org/10.1007/978-3-031-36004-6_40

generating a broader knowledge about the theme to demonstrate to potential users of the document, that there are several ways to solve problems of XR experiences and that they should be analyzed and pondered in their specific cases.

In this paper, we propose a discussion about the construction of the categorization processes, a description of these interactions, and the best practices used to develop this content aimed at expanding the knowledge delivered to the designers and developers of our research and development center. We believe that the consolidation of the still poorly structured and known knowledge about UX of an emerging technology platform is a relevant and pressing activity, even more so in the field of design and UX (HILLMANN, 2021), for which the proper usage scenarios of these technologies are still unclear and seem decisive for their evolution.

The article is structured in four sessions: in the first we present the methods used in the construction of this research and its final product, contemplating the processes of reference survey of the analyzed applications and their experimentation. In the second session, we discuss the process of categorizing the interactions and interfaces studied about the procedures used to assemble the document, elaborating on the information architecture and the concepts developed during the analysis. Finally, we present some of the solutions found in the elaboration of this document and make a discussion about the knowledge-sharing processes built through this research process.

2 Research Methodology

Our research process was based on three phases: a survey of references to be studied, scripted and collective experimentation of interactions and interfaces, and the final process of analysis and description of the interactions mapped. Considering that the research problem concerned the very categorization of the interactions, we defined their variety and the way to elaborate a basic structure of organization and description of the interactions and interfaces studied. This research process was inserted in a broader process common to Design Thinking (BROWN, 2009), its structuring into a Double Diamond (COUNCIL, 2004) composed of phases of exploration, definition, development, and iteration. This articulation between design thinking processes and experimental research practices was done aiming at our understanding that the overall goal of the research was to build this final product, a kind of "encyclopedia" that should facilitate designers' apprehension of information about interactions and interfaces in experiences of using XR Technologies.

2.1 Double Diamond

As a research methodology, we used the Double Diamond, which is a model already well consolidated by the Design Council (2004). This method consists of four phases: discover, define, develop, and deliver. In the initial exploration phase, we elaborated a basic category system to guide the survey of references to be studied. The selected applications should contain the interactions specified in the previous moment of elaboration of our first version of categorization. In this phase, we downloaded all the experimented applications and structured the experimentation setup. In the next definition phase, we combined the study of the first interactions and the establishment of a basic entry model, the goal of this phase was to establish a kind of minimal set of our experimentation process and basic entry model to compose our document, which at that moment, we called the encyclopedia of XR interactions and interfaces. In the execution phase, we worked extensively on the interactions raised, experimenting, and analyzing collectively each of the selected applications and consolidating the results of our analysis in the construction of the previously structured entries. Finally, in the final phase of validation and iteration of the document, we focused on a thorough process of revision of the document based on critical design practices and discussion between designers and stakeholders about the format and deepening of the existing information in the document.

2.2 Interaction Survey

In this sense, we developed a broad search for benchmarks based on an initial survey of XR applications and their experimentation. This process of experimental study of XR references and applications we call "Immersive benchmarking". First, we conducted extensive Desk research to map the various types of interactions that exist in different XR devices, such as Quest 2, Magic Leap, and HoloLens 2. To do this we studied the official documentation of each device, such as Microsoft and Meta documentation. We mapped about 27 interactions that were categorized and studied during the research. In parallel, we reviewed bibliographic references such as books and UX guidelines published by researchers and the main producers of these devices. After this step, we did our analysis of other interactions not documented or not found in the Desk research. We then decided to survey apps that could have relevant interactions for our research and set out to Experiment with each one to identify these interactions.

2.3 Experimentation: Immersive Benchmarking

After identifying the existing interactions, we decided to set out to find interactions that were not mapped in official documentation or references, for this we put into practice our Immersive Benchmarking. According to David T. Kearns, "Benchmarking is the continuous process of measuring products, services, and practices against the strongest competitors, or against companies recognized as leaders in their industries" (CAMP, 1998, p. 8 and 10), in this sense through Immersive Benchmarking we mapped about 28 applications and games among those available in the XR devices stores and sought to observe through experimentation the behaviors between the user and the entire graphical universe that makes up such XR environments.

For our setup, we reserved an environment where it was possible to define a considerable guardian space to use the applications with more freedom. In this space, there were screens connected to the device so that observers could follow what the researchers were testing. The number of people present per period of application use was three, with one individual for testing the apps, and two others for observation and notes. For note-taking, we used physical notebooks and virtual boards. We determined a study table for each app tested. At the moment that one researcher was testing an app the other two filled in these tables based on the tester's speech and on their observations through the screen that was transmitting the test.

After completing the sessions, we analyzed all the collected notes and began the development of the Interaction categorization document. This document was created in PowerPoint format where we gathered the various interactions studied with analysis of their respective behaviors, graphical interface, and contextual examples.

3 Research Development

3.1 Listing the Interactions and Categorization Process

In this way, we organized more than 27 interactions mapped during the research process into three study themes, general description, behavior, and graphical interface, as well as examples. As we built the structure of the document we categorized the interactions according to their type, arriving at three axes defined based on the user: World-User, Object-User, and User-User.

- **World-User Axis.** The World-User axis encompasses interactions where the user interacts with the World. The interactions categorized in this axis seek to generate immersive experiences for the user so that he can look around and explore the virtual world with freedom. Here concepts such as 6dof and 3dof are explored to provide the user with means to know the world. We can cite among these interactions the Locomotion, Stationary Locomotion, and Movements, being these macro interactions where there are also important sub-interactions, such as Teleport, running, and portals.
- **Object-User Axis.** This axis deals with interactions where the user interacts with objects in the virtual world. These interactions attempt to translate concepts and interactions performed in reality to the XR context. So, the platforms provide this kind of interaction so that the user can interact in several ways with the surrounding virtual objects. Among the most important interactions of this axis, we can mention Direct and Indirect Manipulation and Positioning.
- **User-User Axis.** In this axis, we study interactions that involve users' engagement with other people and their forms of representation in the virtual world. Here we consider the interaction the power of the user to communicate or interact with other users through Multiplayer interactions, for example. Or even the use of 3D Avatars as a way to represent themselves in the XR.

When talking about interactions, we are discussing macro and micro-interactions, the macro-ones are interactions that involve others in their definition, that is, where there are sub-interactions listed. To talk about this difference, we start the research by understanding the types of manipulation that exist. According to Kerawala and Sherer (2022), authors of a part of Microsoft's documentation on interactions, we can exemplify and differentiate these interactions in more detail by relating three types of manipulations in XR devices: direct hand manipulation, indirect manipulation, and motion controllers.

- **Direct manipulation.** Users can touch and manipulate the holograms. Just like every-day life experiences, users can use the same way of manipulating objects in the real world to interact with virtual objects.
- **Indirect manipulation.** This modality allows users to interact with holograms at a distance. Users can place virtual objects anywhere and still access them from any distance through Raycasting.

- **Motion Controllers.** Motion controls extend the user's physical capabilities with precise interactions across a range of distances while using one or both hands. These hardware accessories provide many shortcuts.

According to Kerawala and Sherer (2022) and the Meta Quest Documentation (2022), there are also two modes in the manipulation, Near and Far-field Components. We speak then of Near and Far-field Components:

- **Near-Field Components.** When using direct interactions, this space should be reserved for the most important components or the ones you interact with most frequently.
- **Far-Field Components.** To interact with them, you would need to use a ray cast or locomote closer to the component to bring it into the near field (Fig. 1).

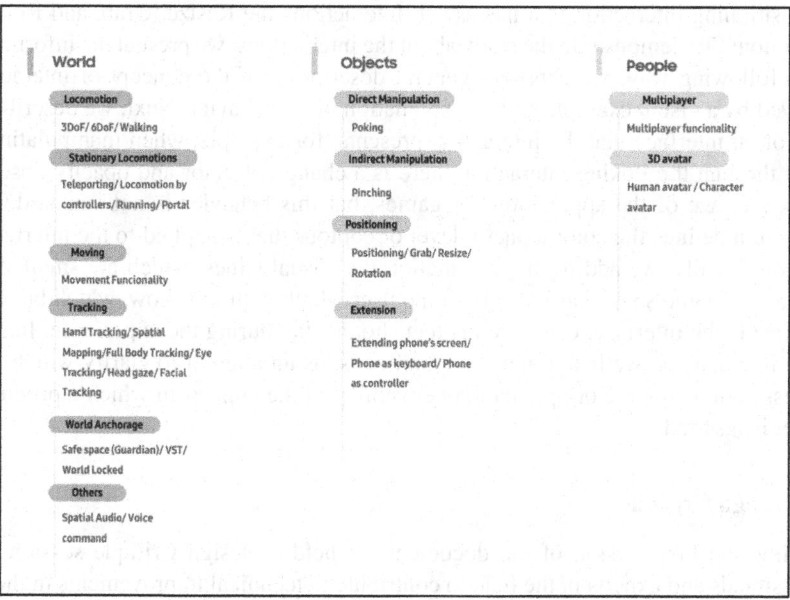

Fig. 1. Diagram showing categorization by axes and themes defined in the list of interactions (Author's Compilation, 2023)

3.2 Practical Test and Analysis of the Interaction

Soon after the listing and categorization phase, we carried out the practical experimentation and analysis of the interactions. To do so, we collected about 28 applications available in the XR devices' stores. We separated a free space to perform the experiments and during the analysis, we sought to observe the context in which the user was inserted when entering the application, which interactions were present, and how the UX and the interface of the interactions were built inside that application or game. Through these experiments we built a vision of how the visual interactions were formed, what were their behaviors, and their pros and cons. For each application or game tested, we created screenshots or gifs to visually demonstrate in the documentation the variations of each behavior. And to faithfully describe the concept of interaction we counted on the support of the official documentation of the large companies that forged them, such as the Meta Quest documentation (2022) and Microsoft Documentation, where we can find a range of content described by Kerawala et al. (2022).

3.3 Entry Construction

Starting from the analysis and experimentation for the construction of the entry, we proceeded to build the document by dividing it into the three already known axes, World, User, and Object. With the subcategories conceptualizing interactions being followed by sub-interactions. We can cite as an example of a subcategory of the Object axis, the Positioning interaction that has as sub-interactions the Resize, Grab, and Rotation interactions. To demonstrate the study about the interactions, we present the information in the following way: we expose a general description of the concept of interaction, followed by a visual example and an explanation of its behavior. Next, we describe the types of an interface that the interaction presents, for example, when manipulating an object through the Poking interaction there is a change of color and opacity observed in the interface of the applications or games, but this behavior is not standard, each application defines the color, opacity level or contour that is applied to the interface in question. Finally, we add to the information the Visual Clues, which are small visual clues as the name says, that indicate to the user which path to follow, which button to click inside the interface, or where his feet should stay during the experience. In some of the interactions, we listed their pros and cons, as an attempt to clarify which were the best options for use or application depending on the context in which a product or project is inserted.

3.4 Design Critique

To refine the first version of the document we held a Design Critique session with professionals and experts in the field to contribute to technical improvements in the XR interaction categorization document. To Gibbons (2016), "A design critique refers to analyzing a design, and giving feedback on whether it meets its objectives." Following this thought through this dynamic we aimed to generate improvements in categorization and content and discover new possibilities for application in other contexts. We contacted four designers from different projects and with different profiles so that they could use and analyze the document for a few days. The profiles we recruited were the following: one focused on UI and information architecture, one XR specialist, one focused on UX, and one generalist. Each participant received a personal copy of the document to be free in suggesting and critically analyzing it, being able to mark comments and add corrections at will. At the end of the predefined days for the dynamic, we held a virtual meeting where the participants could point out their suggestions and corrections.

During the sharing sessions with the designers, we were able to identify some pain points such as poorly structured categorization, confusing or poorly defined terms and concepts, and the need to add more examples for some interactions. Then, with the improvement points mapped out, we started restructuring the document based on the suggestions of the design professionals. We went back to the macro categories previously mentioned, Object, World, and User, and began to redistribute the interactions based on their functionality and interface.

By seeking the opinions of designers from different projects, we also tried to understand in which scenarios interaction research could be applied and used well. Some scenarios emerged, such as being used as a document to assist in the onboarding of project members, or people who are starting their journey in the knowledge of XR devices, as well as being a powerful resource for knowledge sharing about mixed reality.

4 Results

After its elaboration, one can see the practicality of reading a document that compiles several interactions, with their descriptions and critical analyses, helping introductions about the context and facilitating the understanding of this topic in XR. Reaching a beginner as well as an experienced audience. By exposing a thorough description of the interactions, it is possible to share this document with different professionals, helping their understanding of this topic and its translation to different contexts.

The structure developed facilitates the reading of the document, as it presents a summary that displays three major axes that group interactions and can guide the reader to a specific point of interest. Besides the pure description, it is also possible to observe an analysis of each interaction, with its behavior, pros and cons, usage scenarios, and several graphical variations.

Furthermore, the creation of a document that compiles a graphic analysis of several interactions in XR environments democratizes the sharing of knowledge among design professionals, who can access this file as a form of study or consultation on topics related to user interface and user experience in contexts of virtual and augmented reality, a growing theme and in need of new researches and developments, especially related to design. Thus, it is possible to observe the capacity of the contribution that this document has, and it can be a great ally for new projects and works within the universe of extended reality.

4.1 GUI Analysis

To observe the graphical behavior of these interactions, we carried out analysis sessions focusing on their interface, within the XR universe. we consulted the interactions already listed, to filter out those that had graphic elements and from then on, begin to analyze them.

For this step, we consider the same categories used at the beginning, to group the interactions, but at this moment, focusing on those that have graphic elements in their use. For this, we divided the findings of the analysis into three points: description of the interaction; types of interface and visuals used; ideal presentation behavior, and purpose of graphic use. These points aim to describe in detail the visual elements observed and the reason for their use in their respective contexts.

As a criterion, we observe any element of a visual nature that exists when the user performs the interaction in XR. In addition, we seek to observe the same interaction in different applications to identify whether there are patterns, for example in the case of the "Teleport" interaction, where, in different applications, the existing visual feedback is the same, but with different compositions, possible to observe in images x, y and z, where all images show the same teleport action, through different visuals (Fig. 2).

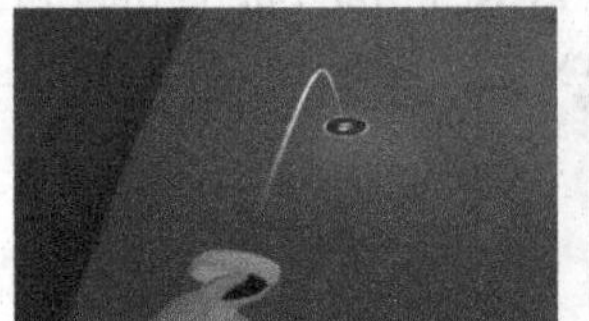

Fig. 2. Example of "Teleport" in VR environment (Author's Compilation, 2023)

In the images, it is possible to observe that the mechanism for carrying out the interaction happens in the same way in different applications–an arc and an indication of the location of the teleportation. However, it is possible to observe different forms of visual representation of the action. In addition to the interactions that have the same mechanism and different visuals, some have different mechanisms to work, but the objective is the same, as is the case of the "object positioning" interaction, in this interaction, it is possible to observe manipulation by the movement of hands–like the "grab" (image x); by finger movement–such as the "pinch" (y image) and even using the device control, in the latter a specific space is shown in the application or game view, the correct place for positioning the manipulated element (Fig. 3).

4.2 Menu Folder–Proposta De Organização

During the development of the document for compiling data and after the critical design session, it was decided that the use of a menu folder for categorization and separation of information description would be the best way to organize the exposure of an extensive amount of information and descriptions, making the document easier to read for those who access it. For this organization, we used three topics–description of the interactions, types of the graphic user interface, visual clues, and best practices on the GUI as seen in images 5 and 6 (Fig. 4).

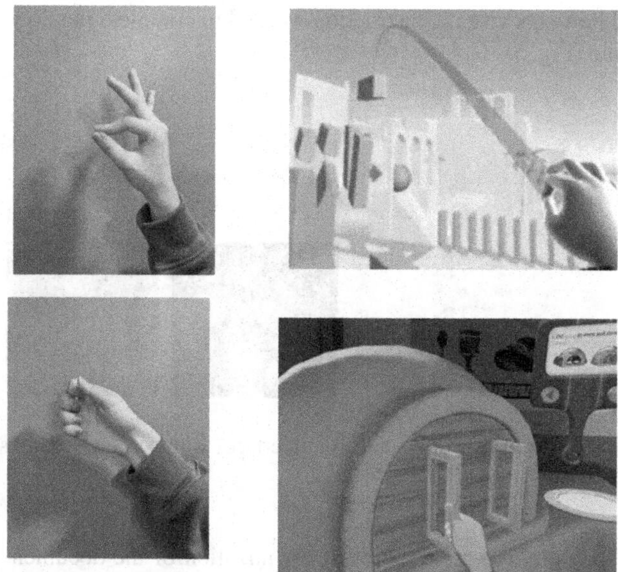

Fig. 3. Examples of "pinch" and "grab" in VR environment (Author's Compilation, 2023)

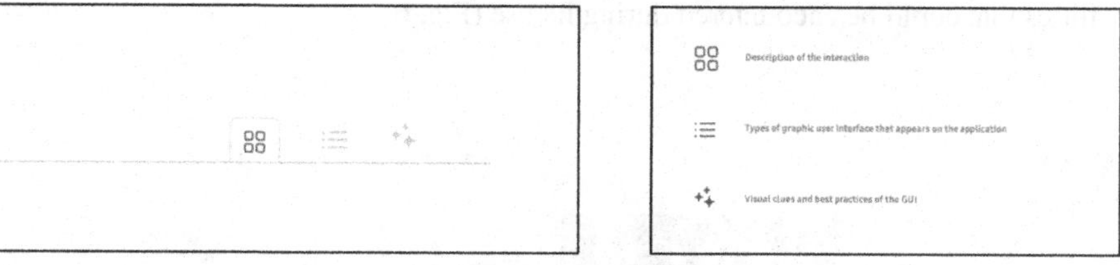

Fig. 4. The Figure. 4 shows the main 3 menus of the document's layout and the 10 shows the description of each menu (Author's compilation, 2023).

Description of Interaction. The first topic was used to insert general descriptions about the interaction, its function, and the experience scenarios in which they are most used, seeking to conceptualize and introduce the reader to a quick reading of understanding about the behaviors and main objective of such interaction.

Types of the Graphic User Interface. At this point, we tried to analyze in detail the varieties of graphical interfaces existing in each interaction, for that, several different applications that contained the same interaction were observed. After a grouping of these interactions and the number of existing variations in its interface, the analysis of the visuals was performed, considering all existing graphic aspects that influenced the experience of this interaction.

Visual Clues and Best Practices. As a last point, we sought to highlight the scenarios for the best use of these interactions, listing the visual aspects that made them a positive experience and how this visual construction worked to complete the flow of use of the software or game (Fig. 5).

Fig. 5. Layout screen for "Types of graphic user interface" with content (Author's Compilation, 2023)

In addition to the three main topics of organization of the document, analyses of pros and cons were also included, using the reading layout of images 15 and 16 about each interaction, scoring positive and negative situations and experiences of each one of them, facilitating the understanding of the reader, about the greatest difficulties or facilities that could be encountered during its use (Fig. 6).

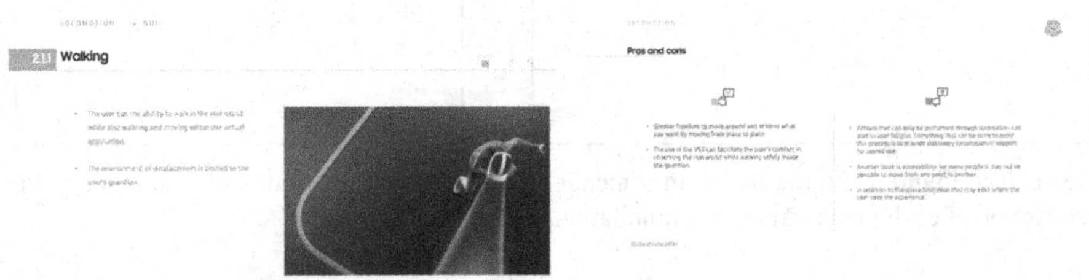

Fig. 6. Layout screens for interaction description" and "pros and cons" (Author's Compilation, 2023)

To complement the analysis of pros and cons, we also sought to point out the visual tips and best practices found in the graphical interfaces and experiences in each of the listed interactions, highlighting in which situations such movements and compositions facilitated the user's flow in the experience.

5 Conclusion

This article chronicled our extensive process of studying and categorizing interactions and user experience interfaces of applications in XR. This study was challenging due to the still limited and immature development of UX for XR applications and aimed at establishing a flow of knowledge sharing between the different teams of our project. The, still, scarce bibliography on the subject presented itself as an opportunity to produce a cross-sectional document and quite in-depth on types, interaction models, good practices related to UX and critical points to be avoided by designers and developers. We believe that the very process of elaborating a way of categorizing interactions and interfaces aimed at expanding the knowledge of professionals has been a relevant experience in advancing our understanding of the establishment of this new technological platform.

References

Brown, T.: Change by Design, 1st edn. HarperCollins, New York (2009)

Camp, Robert C.: Benchmarking: the way to total quality. 3rd ed. Pioneira, São Paulo (1998)

Gibbons, S.: Design Critiques: Encourage a Positive Culture to Improve Products. https://www.nngroup.com/articles/design-critiques/#:~:text=Definition%3A%20A%20design%20critique%20refers,goal%20of%20improvimp%20a%20design. Accessed 13 Mar 2023

Hillmann, C.: UX for XR. 1st end. Apress, Berkeley (2021)

Design, Council.: Framework for innovation: Design Council's evolved Double Diamond. https://www.designcouncil.org.uk/our-work/skills-learning/tools-frameworks/framework-for-innovation-design-councils-evolved-double-diamond/. Accessed 13 Mar 2023

Kewarala, S., Sherer, T.: Hands and motion controllers. https://learn.microsoft.com/en-us/windows/mixed-reality/design/hands-and-tools. Accessed 13 Mar 2023

Sean, K., et al.: Introducing instinctual interactions. https://learn.microsoft.com/en-us/windows/mixed-reality/design/interaction-fundamentals. Access 13 Mar 2023

Microsoft. https://learn.microsoft.com/en-us/windows/mixed-reality/design/point-and-commit. Access 13 Mar 2023

Microsoft. https://learn.microsoft.com/en-us/windows/mixed-reality/design/direct-manipulation. Access 13 Mar 2023

Meta Quest Documentation. https://developer.oculus.com/resources/hands-design-interactions/. Access 13 Mar 2023

User Experience and Immersion in VR and Non-VR Versions of Slime Rancher: A Playtest Evaluation with the ARI Questionnaire and GUESS-18 Scale

Livia Scienza[1,2](✉), Aecio Jorge Macedo Braga[2], Lucia Paloma Freitas da Silva[2], and Mariana Maciel de Maciel[2]

[1] Universidade Federal de São Carlos, Rod. Washington Luiz, - Monjolinho, São Carlos, São Paulo, Brazil
livia.scienza@sidia.com

[2] Sidia Institute of Science and Technology, Colônia Terra Nova, Av. Torquato Tapajós, Manaus, Amazonas 6770, Brazil

Abstract. Many studies have been investigating the use of virtual reality applications and games in therapeutic, educational, rehabilitation and health contexts. Other studies compare VR applications with non-VR applications in terms of how immersive they are but have tested applications and games developed mainly for experimental settings. One of the most prominent points in the use of VR is the supposed greater immersion of the user. Although immersion is a relevant aspect of the VR experience, as far as we know, there are no validated scales to measure immersion in VR applications and games. There is, however, a validated scale for immersion in Augmented Reality contexts: the ARI Scale. The present study aims to use instruments to measure possible differences in the immersion value and user experience of the game Slime Rancher in its VR and non-VR versions. After the playtesting, users had to answer to an adaptation of the Augmented Reality Immersion Questionnaire (ARI) and a validated version of the Game User Experience Satisfaction Scale (GUESS-18). All participants were accompanied by two Game Designers who took notes about each game session and then compared their impressions. Some participants played the VR versions first and others played the non-VR versions first to ensure that the application presentation order would not be an intervening variable. After each version, there was a pause for users to respond to the instruments. Results and limitations of the study are discussed. Design choices of each version are analyzed. This is a work in progress.

Keywords: Virtual Reality · Immersion · Game

1 Introduction

The conceptualization of virtual reality (VR) is not new. The concept of a virtual experience goes back to 1930 with the use of flight simulators. In 1962, Morton Heilig patented the Sensorama, a cabinet with "seat motion, vibration, stereo sound, wind, and aromas,

C. Stephanidis et al. (Eds.): HCII 2023, CCIS 1836, pp. 300–307, 2023.
https://doi.org/10.1007/978-3-031-36004-6_41

which were triggered during the films, intending to fully immerse the individual in the film" [1]. It has been a long journey from Sensorama to today's most modern headsets.

VR devices are being used in the most diverse contexts, from educational [2] and tourism settings [3] to therapy [4] and rehabilitation [5]. One of the most used contexts, however, is gaming experience. These devices have been used mainly for their supposed immersion capabilities and many studies are trying to better understand the mechanisms that allow the VR experience to be fully immersive. However, it is worth mentioning that Immersion itself is still a construct in constant formulation and not many instruments have been developed specifically for extended reality experiences such as VR and Augmented Reality (AR).

In this regard, the Augmented Reality Immersion Questionnaire (ARI Questionnaire) was developed for measuring immersion in AR location-aware settings [6]. Its immersion conceptualization is based on the higher-order model suggested by Cheng et al. (2015) [7]. In this model, immersion is divided into a three-level operationalization and each level (Engagement, Engrossment, Total Immersion) has its sublevels. Total Immersion is divided into Flow and Presence, Engrossment into Emotional Investment and Focus of Attention. Engagement is subdivided into Usability and Interest.

Since gaming is one of the highlights of VR, the use of headsets in this type of experience is subject to a lot of academic studies. But since there are no validated VR Immersion scales and instruments, researchers have been using scales such as the Game User Experience Satisfaction Scale (GUESS) to compare VR games with non-VR games [8–10].

The GUESS Scale [11] is an instrument developed for game designers and researchers to have a validated quality feedback to use in playtesting sessions. It was based on the assessments of over 450 game titles of different genres. Engagement (a player's level of involvement in video games), immersion (being submerged in a digital environment), presence (the feeling of really being in a virtual world), and flow (the balancing of the gamer abilities and the game's mechanics and difficulty levels) are analyzed and each of these areas contain its own factors. The instrument is composed of 55 items and 9 factors: Usability/Playability, Narratives, Play Engrossment, Enjoyment, Creative Freedom, Audio Aesthetics, Personal Gratification, Social Connectivity, and Visual Aesthetics.

To our knowledge, there are no studies using the ARI Questionnaire and the GUESS scale simultaneously to compare two versions of a commercial game. Therefore, the aim of this study is to analyze two versions (VR and non-VR) of the same game (Slime Rancher) using both instruments. Participants think aloud process and game design insights were used to better comprehend the differences between the VR and non-VR versions that could explain possible score variations. There are three hypotheses: 1. The VR version will be more immersive than the non-VR version (ARI Questionnaire); 2. The non-VR version will provide a better user experience overall (GUESS-18); and 3. The presentation order of the game will not influence the scores.

2 Method

Participants.
Participants were workers of a private technology and research institute. So far, 12 participants were recruited (4 female, 8 male). To participate in the study, previous experience with extended reality was required. Only one of the participants had played Slime Rancher (non-VR) before and only one participant had used the HTC Vive device previously.

Instruments and Materials.

Control Questions. Before playing, all the participants had to answer a short questionnaire with the following questions: a) "Have you ever used VR devices?", b) "Have you ever used the HTC Vive?", c) "Have you ever played games in VR?", d) "Have you ever played Slime Rancher?" and e) "Have you ever played Slime Rancher in VR?".

GUESS-18. The scale [12] is a validated short version of the Game User Experience Satisfaction Scale and is composed by the same 9 factors (Usability / Playability, Narratives, Play Engrossment, Enjoyment, Creative Freedom, Audio Aesthetics, Personal Gratification, Social Connectivity and Visual Aesthetics). Since Slime Rancher is a single player game, Social Connectivity was removed from analysis. The 18 items should be answered through a seven-point Likert-type scale (1 = Strongly Disagree to 7 = Strongly Agree). Calculating the subscales scores of the GUESS consists of averaging the items in that subscale and an overall score calculated by summing the subscale scores (Phan et al., 2016). All the 18 items were presented in an online form.

ARI Questionnaire. The questionnaire has 21 items which must be answered based on a seven-point Likert-type scale (1 = Strongly Disagree to 7 = Strongly Agree). The construct is divided into six sublevels: Interest (interest for the application - 4 items), Usability (perceptions about the application's usability - 4 items), Emotional Attachment (emotional connection to the application - 3 items), Focus of Attention (focus during the activity with the application - 3 items), Presence (sense of being in a physical/virtual environment - 4 items) and Flow (being fully absorbed by the application - 3 items). The questionnaire was embedded on an online form and had to be answered right after the participants played one of Slime Rancher's version. The adaptation consisted of using the questionnaire in an online form, replacing the "AR" term by "VR" for the VR version of the game and removing it completely for the non-VR version of the game. These changes are not validated and therefore may give different results than the results of a questionnaire designed specifically for VR experiences in the first place. It would be interesting if there was an instrument to measure immersion in VR in the future.

Slime Rancher. For the non-VR version, participants played Slime Rancher's casual mode. For the VR version, participants played Slime Rancher's VR Playground downloadable content. Both versions contained a short tutorial for the game's controls. Slime Rancher is a game in which the player has a suction gun that can capture and shoot slimes, items, and food. The slimes release items that can be sold in exchange for the game currency: plorts. All the captured items are stored in 4 different slots. When the slots are full, the player cannot store new items. This game was chosen because an already released and consolidated experience was needed. Both the versions of the game should have similar mechanics, controls, and graphics. The game should be casual and provide a quick experience. Considering these factors, Slime Rancher seemed to be a good option.

HTC Vive. Game Designers and Researchers tested the game with an Oculus Pro and an Oculus Quest 2 but chose to use the HTC Vive device for its better compatibility with the Steam software that gave access to both game versions. The headset is connected to the laptop through cables and has two Bluetooth controls. To use the device, two sensors must be placed at similar heights above the user and both sensors must face each other.

3 Procedure

The researcher and game designers explained the premise of the game and explained the procedure regarding the gameplay and scales. Before starting, all the participants answered a short questionnaire with the control questions. Half of the participants played the VR version first and the other half played the non-VR version first. It was suggested that the participant played sitting on a chair positioned between the HTC Vive sensors. After playing the first version for 10 min, the participant answered the online adapted ARI-Questionnaire and the GUESS-18 scale. Shortly thereafter, the participant played the second version of the game for 10 min and answered the questionnaire and scale. After answering it, the researcher and game designers asked if they had any doubts or comments about the session.

During the session, participants were encouraged to think aloud. Their comments were written down. If they had doubts regarding the scale and questionnaire, they could ask the researcher and game designers. Each session with the gameplay and scales took 40 to 50 min to be completed.

4 Results

It is worth noting that these data are partial. For the results to be more robust, more data will need to be collected and statistical analyzes will need to be done to see if differences are statistically significant.

GUESS-18. The sum of means for all the GUESS-18 subscale was 77.3 (SD = 1.9) for the VR version and 90.9 (SD = 1.1) for the non-VR version. Thus, participants found the non-VR version to be superior to the VR version, on average.

All the subscales received higher scores for the non-VR version of the game, except for Play/Engrossment (VR $\overline{x} = 10.7$, SD = 2.6; nVR $\overline{x} = 10.6$, SD = 2.6) and Visual Aesthetics (VR $\overline{x} = 11.8$, SD = 2.4; nVR $\overline{x} = 11.5$, SD = 2.3) subscales, which had similar scores.

ARI Questionnaire. The sum of means for every ARI Questionnaire subscale was 88.6 (SD = 2.1) for the VR version and 104 (SD = 4.7) for the non-VR version. Therefore, participants found that, on average, the non-VR version was superior to the VR version of the game.

All the subscales received higher scores for the non-VR version of the game, except for Presence (VR $\overline{x} = 13.9$, SD = 4.4; nVR $\overline{x} = 11.6$, SD = 5.3) for which the scores were higher for the VR version.

Order of Gameplay. For GUESS-18, regarding the VR version and the order of presentation, the group that played the non-VR first (VR2) tended to give higher scores to Narrative (VR1 $\overline{x} = 5.3$, SD = 2.6; VR2 $\overline{x} = 8$, SD = 3.2), Play / Engrossment (VR1 $\overline{x} = 9.6$, SD = 3.1; VR2 $\overline{x} = 11.8$, SD = 1.3) and Audio Aesthetics (VR1 $\overline{x} = 10.3$, SD = 2.6; VR2 $\overline{x} = 13.5$, SD = 0.5) for the VR version compared to the group that first played the VR game (VR1).

This group also tended to give lower scores for Usability / Playability (VR1 $\overline{x} = 8.5$, SD = 3.6; VR2 $\overline{x} = 7.3$, SD = 4) and Personal Gratification (VR1 $\overline{x} = 10$, SD = 4.1; VR2 $\overline{x} = 7$, SD = 3.2) for the VR version compared to the group that played the VR game first. This can demonstrate that playing the non-VR version first made it easier to understand the mechanics, objectives, and universe in the VR version, but it also provided the possibility to compare the UI and enjoyment of the non-VR with the VR for worse.

For the ARI Questionnaire, in relation to the VR version, the VR2 group tended to give higher scores for Interest (VR1 $\overline{x} = 18$, SD = 4.9; VR2 $\overline{x} = 19.5$, SD = 5.6) and Presence (VR1 $\overline{x} = 13.3$, SD = 5.6; VR2 $\overline{x} = 14.5$, SD = 3.3) for the VR version compared to the VR1 group.

The VR2 group also tended to give lower Flow scores (VR1 $\overline{x} = 16.3$, SD = 3.7; V2R $\overline{x} = 9.3$, SD = 5.5) for the VR version compared to the VR1 group. This data may also point to the fact that first understanding usability in the non-VR version helped participants to situate themselves in the VR version, enabling greater interest in the other functions of the experience. For Flow, having had the most complete experience of the non-VR game may have made it possible to compare it with a less complex version of the game in the VR experience. Therefore, participants would give lower scores.

5 Discussion

Although testing will continue, the thinking aloud process has provided great clues to understanding differences in scale scores for both the GUESS-18 and ARI Questionnaire. Some of the findings are discussed below. The first and third hypothesis of the study were not confirmed, but the second hypothesis seems to be correct. More data and analysis are needed for more certain conclusions.

Motion Sickness. Motion Sickness is common in VR experiences. It happens due to the discrepancy between movement experienced within the application and the absence of movement outside of it. Comparing both experiences (VR and non-VR) with the results, the VR version causes greater discomfort during playtest and this discomfort negatively influences the enjoyment of the game.

The comments made by the participants were insightful and some factors seem to be more impactful. The character movement is made by using a point and walk system and the option to rotate on your own axis is made in a sudden and fast way. Also, there are changes in FPS rate during gameplay, camera motion delay and the size and physics of some objects are not very realistic. It is important that motion sickness is considered when proposing a VR experience. If ignored, the discomfort and nausea might make the player stop playing or avoiding certain in game actions, thus diminishing the designed experience.

A simple way of diminishing nausea within VR experiences is to use a teleportation system [13]. The player does not move continuously, but selects where to go first, clicks and then suddenly appears on the designated place. This system decreases the incongruency of moving inside the game without actually moving on the real world.

One of the participants requested to quit the VR playtest sooner, commenting to be feeling nauseous. There are scales that were designed to measure motion sickness [14] and future studies should consider this variable to better understand immersion in VR settings.

Narrative and Presentation Order. The non-VR game's narrative only provides a basic context for the player to get used to the game's universe and the main gameplay objectives (collecting and feeding slimes, collecting and selling plorts). As the game progresses, new story elements and characters are introduced, but participants don't have enough time within the experience to reach that point.

In the VR game, no introductory text or context about the game universe is presented to the player. Understanding the experience depends on prior contact with the non-VR version, without which there is no contextual understanding when playing on the headset.

In both cases, this absence of explicit narrative can directly affect immersion. Without it, the emotional attachment and the player's general engagement is found to be lacking. However, since there are other activities, mechanics and attractions in the non-VR version, the VR version is even more impaired without a strong narrative.

Graphics. The game's graphics were described by participants as "cute", "captivating", "cartoonish" and "unrealistic". In general, both experiences were received with positive impressions, which can be seen by the similar scores on the Visual Aesthetics subscale of the GUESS-18. However, since the art chosen for the game, as well as its effects, characters (slimes) and sound effects were not based on realism, perhaps the Total Immersion of the experience and the Presence within each version of the game was lower than it could have been if it was more realistic.

Usability. The usability of the game presented some problems in the VR version as it was unable to accurately translate the most important information that exists in the PC version interface. In the VR version, players had difficulty seeing where to select their "slimes" in the virtual weapon when looking at their "hands" in-game, ignoring this element completely. In the PC version, even though it is not visually ideal (UI with too many elements, icons with similar colors, elements on top of each other), it was much faster and simpler to locate the information and to use the controls. It is important that a game provides clear information to the player, as he/she needs it to know what to do or how to react within the experience.

Flow and Controls. The basic game mechanics are the same in both versions (capturing and feeding slimes). However, as the objectives are not clear within the VR version, the experience ends up being more limited and experimental when the participant has not played the PC version first. Players keep trying to understand what to do with the mechanics and controls, and when they do understand the controls, they don't know how to identify the purpose of the activity. Players tended to create their own goals within the VR experience, focused on scenery contemplation and exploration. Since the game does not give any direct reward for any player action, it is to be expected that personal gratification and enjoyment scores (subscales of the GUESS-18) of the game will be lower.

The non-VR version, having a more complete structure of objectives and tutorials, offers everything the player needs to follow the flow of the game and emphasize their activities in overcoming challenges and fulfilling activities. The clearer feedback of correct actions and the achievements of the platform the game is running on (Steam) made players want to continue playing even at the end of the playtest. Many were interested in purchasing the game to play in the future, positively highlighting the game as suitable for people with diverse gaming profiles.

6 Conclusion

This is a work in progress. The playtests will continue to be conducted for more robust results and statistical analysis will be run on SPSS. Limitations should be considered in future studies. Regardless of the ongoing nature, this study shows that VR game design must be well thought for it to be immersive. User interface elements must be accompanied by a good tutorial and motion sickness should be avoided as much as possible. The use of a questionnaire designed for AR experiences is a limitation of this study.

Designing a VR game based on another game is not so simple as the factors that provide fun, good user experience and immersion are beyond a headset. Overall, Slime Rancher VR is just a downloadable content that extends the experience of the non-VR for those who already played the game. It should not be seen as a complete game, but as a fun additional content for short gameplays.

Slime Rancher 2 is on its way and players are eager to know if it will have a VR version as well. If it does, it would be interesting if the experience was designed to be a good game on its own.

References

1. Cruz-Neira, C., Fernandéz, M., Portalés, C.: Virtual reality and games. Multimodal Technol. Interact. **2**(1), 8 (2018)
2. Christian, B., Salvador, C., Christian, G.: Virtual reality (VR) in superior education distance learning: a systematic literature review. Int. J. Inf. Vis. **5**(3), 264 (2021)
3. Melo, M., et al.: Immersive multisensory virtual reality technologies for virtual tourism: a study of the user's sense of presence, satisfaction, emotions, and attitudes. Multimedia Syst. **28**(3), 1027–1037 (2022)
4. Donnelly, M.R., et al.: Virtual reality for the treatment of anxiety disorders: a scoping review. Am. J. Occup. Therapy **75**(6) (2021)

5. Lohse, K.R., et al.: Virtual reality therapy for adults post-stroke: a systematic review and meta-analysis exploring virtual environments and commercial games in therapy. PLoS ONE **9**(3), e93318 (2014)
6. Georgiou, Y., Kyza, E.A.: The development and validation of the ARI questionnaire: an instrument for measuring immersion in location-based augmented reality settings. Int. J. Hum Comput Stud. **98**, 24–37 (2017)
7. Cheng, M.T., She, H.C., Annetta, L.A.: Game immersion experience: its hierarchical structure and impact on game-based science learning. J. Comput. Assist. Learn. **31**, 232–253 (2015)
8. Berkman, M.İ, Çatak, G., Eremektar, M.Ç.: Comparison of VR and desktop game user experience in a puzzle game: "keep talking and nobody explodes." Acad. J. Inf. Technol. **11**(42), 180–204 (2020)
9. Pierce, M.B., Young, P.A., Doherty, S.M.: Engagement and competence in VR and non-VR environments. Proc. Hum. Factors Ergon. Soc. Ann. Meet. **61**(1), 2082–2085 (2017)
10. Shelstad, W.J., Smith, D.C., Chaparro, B.S.: Gaming on the rift: how virtual reality affects game user satisfaction. Proc. Hum. Factors Ergon. Soc. Ann. Meet. **61**(1), 2072–2076 (2017)
11. Phan, M.H., Chaparro, B.S., Keebler, J.R.: The Development and validation of the game user experience satisfaction scale (GUESS). Hum. Factors Ergon. Soc. **58**(8), 1217–1247 (2016)
12. Keebler, J.R., Shelstad, W.J., Smith, D.C., Chaparro, B.S., Phan, M.H.: Validation of the GUESS-18: a short version of the game user experience satisfaction scale (GUESS). J. Usability Stud. **16**(1), 49–62 (2020)
13. Rantala, J., Kangas, J., Koskinen, O., Nukarinen, T., Raisamo, R.: Comparison of controller-based locomotion techniques for visual observation in virtual reality. Multimodal Technol. Interact. **5**(7), 31 (2021)
14. Kim, H.K., Park, J., Choi, Y., Choe, M.: Virtual reality sickness questionnaire (VRSQ): motion sickness measurement index in a virtual reality environment. Appl. Ergon. **69**, 66–73 (2018)

Analysis of Virtual Reality Movies: Focusing on the Effect of Virtual Reality Movie's Distinction on User Experience

Soo-Min Seo and Min-Jae Kimm(✉)

Graduate School of Metaverse, Sogang University, 502 413-12 Nonhyeonro Gangnamgu, Seoul, Korea

alexthedesign@naver.com

Abstract. Virtual Reality movies are changing the Film industry. Virtual Reality Films provide an immersive experience to the audience. However, the study of these advancements of technology in the film industry is lacking. Therefore, this study identified the characteristics of the Virtual Reality movies.

The reason I chose the Virtual Reality movies specifically among other metaverse movies is because it gives the audience the most immersive experience right at this moment.

I further analyzed how the types of Virtual Reality movies differ across diverse factors characterizing the viewing experience of the Virtual Reality movies. The results of the analysis revealed factors that cause different effects on User Experience. This study provides implications for the design direction in which the Virtual Reality movies can provide a higher level of satisfaction to the public. And it's meaning to Human interaction with Virtual Reality Movies.

Keywords: Virtual Reality · Virtual Reality Films · Head Mounted Device

1 Introduction

The film industry has always been open to new technologies, such as 3D or 4D technologies to enhance the viewer experience. The recent emergence of the metaverse and advances of related technologies including Head-Mounted Devices (HMD) has rapidly transformed the film industry, influencing the way producers creates and audiences consume films. This shift has led to an increased interests on how graphical technologies and shooting techniques used in VR movies, shape viewers' experiences on VR movies.

Despite the growing popularity of VR films and distinctive experience viewers have in VR movies, not much research has been conducted on how characteristics VR movies lead to unique experience of VR movies. Viewers' experience of VR movies would be substantially different from that of traditional movies, as film makers harness novel affordance presented by VR technologies. We propose two factors in VR movies, the enlarged Field-of-View (FOV) and social interaction with movie characters, are significant for shaping VR movie experience. By investigating how different components associated

C. Stephanidis et al. (Eds.): HCII 2023, CCIS 1836, pp. 308–312, 2023.
https://doi.org/10.1007/978-3-031-36004-6_42

with these two factors are related to each other, the current study attempts to explore the factors of VR movies and discuss potential experience viewers have within each factor. Our findings may provide insights into the unique characteristics of VR films and their potentials for enhancing the viewer experience.

1.1 Field-of-View (FOV) and Out-of-View Character

FOV refers to how much of the audience's view is available to watch. VR films typically provide a spherical image, enabling audiences to have a 360° FOV. Whereas traditional movies and TV screens provide a flat, front-facing 180° FOV. As a result, audiences watching a 360° VR film must turn their head around to watch the entire scene to check what are around. Many of the 360° scenes do not have significant information back from the viewer, because viewers do not check behind them often.

Yet, film makers often put some props hidden from the viewers' immediate sight, but visible only when the viewers turn their head. Typically, the main story takes place on the front-facing screen, but there are still some films where the audience must turn their heads or even their entire body to check the back of the scene. This is particularly true for horror VR movies, where unpredictability is key to creating an thrilling and unexpected experience for the viewer. By forcing the viewer to move their body and engage with the environment, VR films can create a more visceral and impactful experience that is unique to this medium.

These techniques can lead to heightened experience due to the behavior caused by the user, not by camera move. Because the audience can turn their head or body to change their field of view, characters in the movie are in or out of their view. Audiences are often aware that there exists a character behind them, although the character is invisible to them. These out-of-view characters are also important factors. Since the audience tends to focus on the characters rather than the environment or other elements of the story, They follow them and look around, causing their body to move. According to virtual characters have a significant impact on human emotional responses in virtual environments, as opposed to virtual objects and spaces, and since VR audiences can turn their head or body to change their field of view, out-of-view characters in the movie play an important role. This study reviews the extent to which VR movies employ out-of-view characters and the field of view adapted in such films (Fig. 1).

1.2 Social Interaction

VR films interact with audiences in a way that differentiates them from existing films, mainly through direct eye contact and direct calling out to the audience. This technique, known as 'breaking the fourth wall,' [1] (Brown, Tom, 1950) is rarely used in theater and film to address the audience directly and create a sense of connection between the story and the viewer [2] (Cuddon, 2012). By breaking down the traditional barriers between the story and the viewer, VR films can create a sense of presence and telepresence, making the audience feel as if they are truly part of the story.

In VR films, characters can make direct eye contact with the audience, giving the impression that they are looking right at them. This creates a feeling of intimacy and involvement that cannot be replicated in traditional films. Additionally, characters in VR

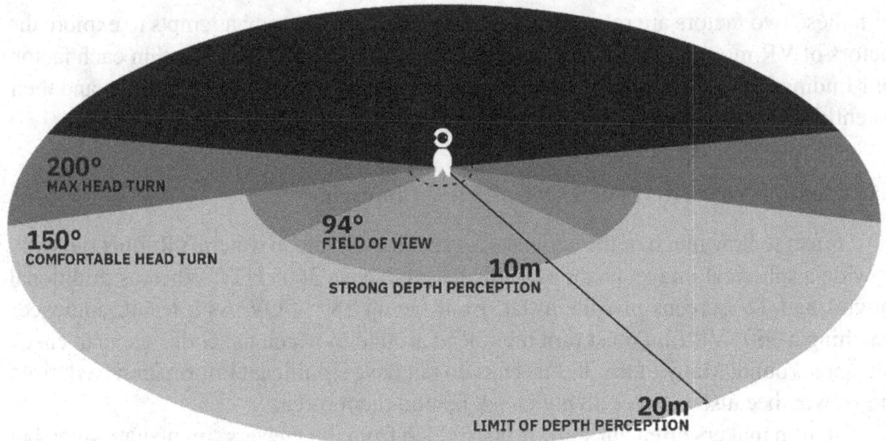

Fig. 1. Field of view of audiences during watching the VR films

films can call out to the audience directly, acknowledging their presence and involving them in the story. This creates a sense of being presence in the movie and makes them an active participant rather than a passive observer.

2 Method

This paper uses a quantitative approach to examine the unique features of VR films and their impact on audience engagement and immersion. To assess the extent to which contemporary VR movies vary in terms of the elements mentioned above, a content analysis was performed. The analysis focuses on VR movies available on platforms such as Steam VR Films, Meta Original Films, Google Original VR Films, and researchable VR films on YouTube. To investigate the impact of specific immersive features on audience engagement and immersion, we conducted a content analysis of 30 VR films. By using a quantitative methodology, we aim to provide empirical evidence that can help inform the development of VR films and enhance the viewer experience.

2.1 Samples

Our analysis examines a sample of 30 VR films, selected based on their availability and popularity on platforms such as Steam VR Films, Meta Original Films, Google Original VR Films, and researchable VR films on YouTube.

Most of the VR Film genres are animation or horror/thriller. Because animated genre is easier to make in VR then a real picture genre. Horror and thriller genre provide immersive implication to audiences. The length of the films was various, as 1 min long to 20 min long, depends on the filmmaker's intention (Table 1).

Table 1. List of the VR films available

	Subject	FOV	Bodily movement	Direct Eye contact	Direct Calling	Body part visuability	Out Of Field characters
1	We live here	360	10	0	0	1	0
2	THE INVISIBLE MAN	360	10	1	1	0	1
3	INVASIONE	360	10	1	1	1	1
4	Avatar 2	360	10	1	1	1	1
5	Tom and Jerry Are Friends	360	10	1	0	1	1
6	THE MISSING FIVE	180	0	1	0	1	1
7	Glace ‡ l'eau	180	0	1	0	0	1
8	But my Grandad Still Sees Gentian	180	0	0	0	0	0
9	Out of the Cave Part 2	180	0	0	0	0	0
10	Henry	360	3	1	0	0	0
11	Moss	180	0	1	1	0	0
12	Dunkerque - 360∞	360	7	0	0	0	1
13	The Martian Trailer	180	0	0	1	1	1
14	IT: FLOAT	360	3	0	1	0	1
15	The Hunger Games	360	3	0	1	0	1
16	Vader Immortal: A Star Wars VR Series	180	0	1	1	1	0
17	Father is gone	360	7	1	0	0	1
18	The monkey wrench gang	360	7	1	0	1	1
19	Oh DeBu	360	3	1	0	0	1
20	The seven story building	360	3	1	1	0	1
21	Pearl	360	7	0	0	1	1
22	Back to the Moon	360	10	1	0	0	1
23	Buggy Night	360	10	0	0	0	1
24	Son of Jaguar	360	10	1	0	0	1
25	Rain or Shine	360	10	1	0	0	1
26	Dear Angelica	360	7	0	0	0	1
27	Always	360	10	0	1	0	1
28	Blade Runner 2049: Memory Lab	180	0	1	1	1	0
29	I PHILIP	360	3	1	1	0	1
30	Wolves in the Walls	360	10	1	1	1	1

2.2 Coding Scheme

This paper utilized a coding scheme to analyze the characteristics of VR films and their impact on audience interaction. The coding process involve distinguishing between 360° VR films, where audiences have a full range of view. 180° VR films, where audiences have a more limited field of view and body-part visibility from the first-person perspective [3] (Slater and Sanchez-Vives 2016). Additionally, the presence or absence of out-of-field characters was coded, as well as the presence of direct eye contact and direct calling. Each film was rated on a 0–1 scale for each independent variable (IV), and inter-coder reliability assessed using Cohen's kappa coefficient. Descriptive statistics calculated to analyze the frequency and distribution of each IV, and cluster analysis used to identify groups of movies based on their combination of IVs. This study aims to inform filmmakers and content creators on how to design and produce VR films that maximize audience engagement, embodiment experience, and provide a novel viewing experience.

3 Result

A significant relationship was found between FOV and bodily movement ($p < 0.05$), while no significant relationship was observed between the other variables ($p > 0.05$).

The correlation coefficients between bodily movement and direct Eye contact, bodily movement and direct Calling, bodily movement and body part visibility, and bodily movement and out of field characters were −0.063, 0.169, 0.192, and −0.075, respectively.

The results of this study suggest that bodily movement in VR environments may have a negative impact on direct Eye contact and out of field characters. This finding is significant because it suggests that the way users interact with their virtual environment may affect their sense of presence and engagement in the experience. The correlation between bodily movement and direct Calling, as well as bodily movement and body part visibility, was found to be negligible. This implies that these variables do not significantly affect users' bodily movements in VR environments.

Furthermore, the chi-squared test results indicated that there was a significant relationship between FOV and bodily movement, which is noteworthy because it suggests that the user's field of view may influence their bodily movement in a VR environment. By taking these findings into account, designers and developers can create VR content that takes into consideration users' bodily movements and gaze direction, thereby enhancing the immersive and satisfying user experience.

4 Conclusion

Based on the findings of this study, when designing VR content, designers and developers should consider the following factors:

Firstly, appropriate interaction design should be applied, considering users' bodily movements and gaze direction. This can enhance users' sense of presence and engagement.

Secondly, visual design should be considered regarding users' field of view. As there was a significant relationship between FOV and bodily movement, designers should consider the user's field of view when designing visual elements.

Thirdly, designers should consider multimodal design such as audio design and touch interaction to enhance users' sense of presence.

Fourthly, designers should provide a variety of VR content to cater to users' preferences and characteristics. By offering diverse themes, difficulty levels, and platforms, users can select content that suits their preferences and characteristics.

In conclusion, this study provides a better understanding of the unique immersive features of VR films and their impact on audience engagement and immersion. The findings of this study can be used to guide the development of VR films that maximize audience engagement and provide a novel viewing experience. Future research may investigate the impact of demographic variables on audience engagement and immersion in VR films, as well as the potential for VR films to impact real-world behavior and attitudes.

References

1. Brown, T.: Breaking the Fourth Wall: Direct Address in the Cinema (1950)
2. Cuddon, J.A.: A Dictionary of Literary Terms and Literary Theory. Wiley, Hoboken (2012)
3. Bucher, J.: Storytelling for Virtual Reality: Methods and Principles for Crafting Immersive Narratives. Routledge, New York (2018)
4. Slater, M., Sanchez-Vives, M.V.: Enhancing our lives with immersive virtual reality. Front. Robot. AI **3**(74), 1–6 (2016)
5. https://mobfish.net/blog/vr-videos/

Effects of Self-avatar Similarity on User Trusting Behavior in Virtual Reality Environment

Liang Tang(✉) and Masooda Bashir

University of Illinois at Urbana Champaign, Champaign, IL 60616, USA
{ltang29,mnb}@illinois.edu

Abstract. The use of avatars, or digital representations of human-like figures, can facilitate embodiment in VR environments by providing a visual representation of the user within the virtual world that enhances their experience of the VR. In this study, we examined the effects of avatar appearance similarity on trusting human behavior toward no-human entities (agents). Our preliminary results revealed avatars with higher similarity has potential to elicit a relatively high level of trust.

Keywords: Human-centered Design · Virtual Reality

1 Introduction

The need to visualize human-like entities increases as virtual reality becomes more interactive. Embodiment is the process of extending humans into the virtual world and experiencing a close resemblance to their actual physical bodies. As a means of facilitating embodiment, avatars are widely used to digitally represent individuals aligned with their physical and psychological identities [1] and allow them to interact with virtual environments in a more natural and immersive way.

The Proteus effect is one of the most significant findings related to self-avatar; it argues both that individuals behave in accordance with their digital self-representation regardless of how others perceive them and that individuals' attitudes and behaviors towards others in the virtual world are influenced by their virtual avatars [2]. This effect can happen in various ways, such as when people's actions are influenced by how they are dressed or how others perceive them. There has subsequently been a growing body of evidence that suggests the embodied experience of inhabiting an avatar different from oneself can generate both emotional and behavioral changes that align with that avatar as well as changes in self-perception, self-compassion, identifiability, and cognitive load [3–5]. Simultaneously, a high similarity avatar could positively impact human levels of immersion and interactivity, resulting in greater engagement, collaboration, and motivation to trust others [6–8].

With the advancement of virtual reality technology, the potential for human-agent interaction in virtual reality is like-wise increasing. This interaction can take many forms—from simple communication to more complex competitive gaming or negotiation scenarios. Human-agent interaction in virtual reality presents several exciting

C. Stephanidis et al. (Eds.): HCII 2023, CCIS 1836, pp. 313–316, 2023.
https://doi.org/10.1007/978-3-031-36004-6_43

possibilities. It remains to be seen, however, how well humans can trust virtual agents in a collaborative environment. When a person trusts someone else, they take a risk by relying on the other person to fulfill their end of the agreement. The person who trusts may therefore experience positive outcomes if the other person follows through on their promises. Yet, they may also experience adverse outcomes if the other person fails to fulfill their agreement. In the context of trust in virtual agents, the Proteus effect may occur when people's behavior is influenced by the way they perceive themselves as trustworthy. For example, if someone perceives themselves as trustworthy, they may be more likely to fulfill their promises and follow through on their commitments. In turn, others may become more trusting of them, and the cycle continues. Past research has discussed how the embodiment of the self-avatar in virtual reality (VR) can induce trusting behavior toward other humans in a shared virtual environment [4]. Even though human-agent interactions elicit similar social effects to human-human interactions, there is no empirical evidence to prove that such an effect can be achieved in human-agent interactions. Based on previous findings, our first hypothesis predicted that avatar similarity would increase people's trusting behavior and willingness to collaborate like human-human interactions. To explore the association between virtual reality (VR) avatar manipulation and trusting behavior in the exercise context, we adopted a variant of the trust game known as the Coin Entrustment Game [7]. We transformed the game into a VR setting to measure participants' trust and collaboration toward virtual agents separately.

2 Experiment

This study investigates the Proteus effect of avatar design on trust from the first-person perspective, with a special focus on how self-avatar similarity moderated trusting behavior. During avatar embodiment in actual exercise, we designed an experiment to compare different self-avatar similarity levels with a face-to-face condition. We used Wolf 3D, Maximo, and Blender to create graphical depictions for avatars and manipulate appearance resemblance experimentally by rendering realistic faces from the picture. It allowed researchers to both modify appearance features later and create animations with erratic body movements.

We adopt Yamagishi's definition of trust as "A voluntary act that exposes one to greater positive and negative externalities." We measured participant trust in agents as "the extent to which [one] voluntarily chooses [their] outcome to be dependent on EA's behavior, or the amount of 'fate control'" [9]. The Coin Entrustment Game is one where players entrust their coins to each other in order to earn more coins. The game typically starts with each player receiving a certain number of coins. The players then take turns entrusting their coins to other players, understanding that the receiving player will return a greater number of coins later. The goal of the game is to earn as many coins as possible by carefully choosing the number of coins to entrust. The trust in this study is therefore the percentage of coins entrusted out of the total number of coins they could entrust (1). A higher entrusted proportion indicated higher trust.

We conducted a pilot lab study and recruited participants (N = 8, 62.5% female and 37.5% male, Age: Mean = 22.9/SD = 1.72). Each participant received 15$ in rewards, and they were incentivized by an additional 20$ amazon gift card if they scored within the top 10%. Participants were invited to the lab and asked to provide facial data by taking a selfie. They were then given instructions on how to use a head-mounted display (Oculus Quest2) and later entered a virtual environment to start playing the game with a pre-designed agent. After the gameplay, participants were asked to complete a post-questionnaire to reflect on their feelings.

Our team created an experimental VR space using the Unity SDK where participants were able to play a coin entrustment game in VR. We also placed a mirror in the VR space that allowed participants to monitor their avatars as they played (Fig. 1).

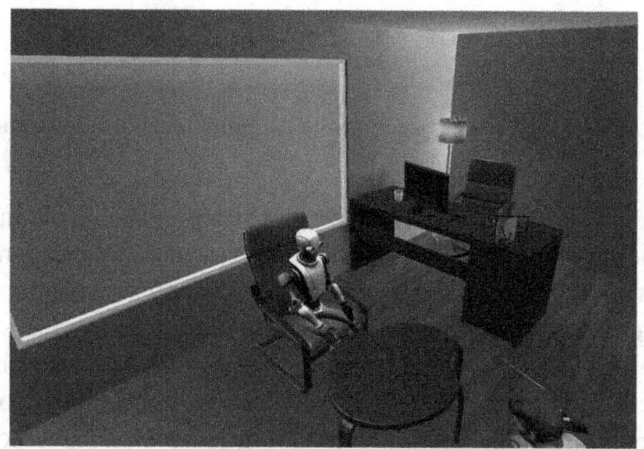

Fig. 1. Scene from the gameplays

The internal review board of the University approved the experimental protocol. All participants provided written informed consent and pre-screening prior to the experiment.

3 Result

In Fig. 2, distributional characteristics of trust for two similarity levels are displayed. This preliminary result might suggest a difference between groups that avatars with higher similarity might elicit a relatively high level of trust. However, the results of the two-sample t-test do not show a statistically significant relationship between the similarity of the avatar to the user and trust in the virtual agent ($p = 0.202$).

Due to the small sample size, meaningful differences in the data may not be detected; therefore, more data is needed to better support our hypothesis. As we are currently only considering similarity at the high and low levels in our pilot study, it is apparent that more levels of similarity will be considered in future research. Furthermore, we will also examine the uncanny valley phenomenon in future research. For example, we will test whether a realistically constructed avatar that differs from a cartoon-like avatar could elicit a lower level of trusting behavior. In this study, we measured trust as behavior that persisted over time during cooperation. Future research could investigate whether similar avatars also facilitate initial trust and cooperation. It is unclear whether people with more similar avatars exhibit more persistent trusting behavior, or if they are more accepting

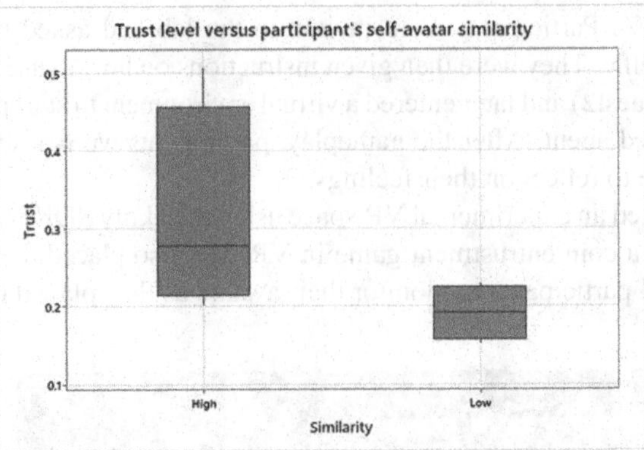

Fig. 2. Participant's trust toward agents with different level of self-avatar similarity

of mistrust and violation and are willing to repair trust after such incidents occur. Lastly, the mechanisms behind the suggested result are unknown. While researchers claim that being embodied with a similar avatar can increase the body's ownership and immersion level, it is not clear whether this is what leads to higher levels of trust.

Our pilot research suggests avatars are more than just a way to bridge the chasm between physical reality and avatar design; specifically, the similarity of the avatar to a person can influence trusting behavior. Overall, our research aims to contribute further evidence of the significance of an accurate self-avatar representation in immersive virtual reality.

References

1. Hepperle, D., Purps, C.F., Deuchler, J., Wölfel, M.: Aspects of visual avatar appearance: self-representation, display type, and uncanny valley. Vis. Comput. **38**, 1227–1244 (2021)
2. Yee, N., Bailenson, J.: The proteus effect: the effect of transformed self-representation on behavior. Hum. Commun. Res. **33**, 271–290 (2007)
3. Waltemate, T., Gall, D., Roth, D., Botsch, M., Latoschik, M.E.: The impact of avatar personalization and immersion on virtual body ownership, presence, and emotional response. IEEE Trans. Vis. Comput. Graph. **24**, 1643–1652 (2018)
4. Steed, A., Pan, Y., Zisch, F., Steptoe, W.: The impact of a self-avatar on cognitive load in immersive virtual reality. In: 2016 IEEE Virtual Reality (VR) (2016)
5. Midha, V., Nandedkar, A.: Impact of similarity between avatar and their users on their perceived identifiability: evidence from virtual teams in second life platform. Comput. Hum. Behav. **28**, 929–932 (2012)
6. Pan, Y., Steed, A.: The impact of self-avatars on trust and collaboration in shared virtual environments. PloS one **12**, e0189078 (2017)
7. van der Land, S.F., Schouten, A.P., Feldberg, F., Huysman, M., van den Hooff, B.: Does avatar appearance matter? How team visual similarity and member-avatar similarity influence virtual team performance. Hum. Commun. Res. 41, 128–153 (2014)
8. Vugt, H.C., Bailenson, J.N., Hoorn, J.F., Konijn, E.A.: Effects of facial similarity on user responses to embodied agents. ACM Trans. Comput. Hum. Interact. **17**, 1–27 (2008)
9. Yamagishi, T., Kanazawa, S., Mashima, R., Terai, S.: Separating trust from cooperation in a dynamic relationship. Ration. Soc. **17**, 275–308 (2005)

An Interactive Drawing Plane for 3-Dimensional Annotation of Geographic Data in Virtual Reality

Gabriel Unmüßig, Adrian H. Hoppe, and Florian van de Camp(✉)

Fraunhofer Institute of Optronics, System Technologies, and Image Exploitation (IOSB), Karlsruhe, Germany
{gabriel.unmuessig,adrian.hoppe,florian.vandecamp}@iosb.fraunhofer.de

Abstract. While three-dimensional environments like in virtual reality are very well suited for the visualization of three-dimensional geographic data, drawing onto such data is much more complex than in 2D. Drawing on geographic data is not trivial due to the terrain and existing solutions for drawing in VR have a mostly artistic focus. This paper presents a novel drawing plane concept that addresses these challenges by enabling the creation of 3D dimensional drawings and annotations of geographic data in VR (Virtual Reality). The drawing plane combines VR interaction and information from Geographic Information Systems (GIS) to allow users to interact with and manipulate annotations on geographic data in a 3D virtual environment. The technique was evaluated in a workshop and received positive feedback for its effectiveness in providing users with a more intuitive and immersive way of interacting with geographic data. Overall, the drawing plane represents a significant advancement, providing users with a powerful new tool for visualizing and annotating geographic data in a 3D virtual environment. This new approach offers a more intuitive and immersive way of interacting with geographic data and has the potential to be used in various real-world applications such as urban planning, natural resource management and others.

Keywords: Virtual reality · digital map · tabletop · controller interaction

1 Introduction

In recent years, virtual reality has become increasingly popular due to the immersive and interactive experiences it offers. One of the applications of virtual reality is in the field of cartography, where it has the potential to revolutionize how we visualize and interact with maps. In a three-dimensional environment, however, drawing on maps is much more complex than on traditional 2D maps. This is because the terrain and elevation of the map need to be taken into consideration when drawing. At the same time, freehand drawing in three-dimensional space presents its own set of challenges. Unlike drawing on a flat surface, it can be difficult to draw with precision and accuracy in a 3D environment. This is why

C. Stephanidis et al. (Eds.): HCII 2023, CCIS 1836, pp. 317–323, 2023.
https://doi.org/10.1007/978-3-031-36004-6_44

it is important to provide suitable tools that enable precise and fast interaction with the virtual environment. To develop such tools, it is necessary to look at existing solutions for 3D drawing and construction and transfer them to the specific application case of 3D annotations in cartography. This paper aims to explore the various challenges involved in drawing on 3D maps and to propose a solution that can make the process more efficient and user-friendly. We propose a drawing method in VR that can lead to the development of more interactive and immersive maps that can provide users with a more intuitive understanding of the environment they are exploring.

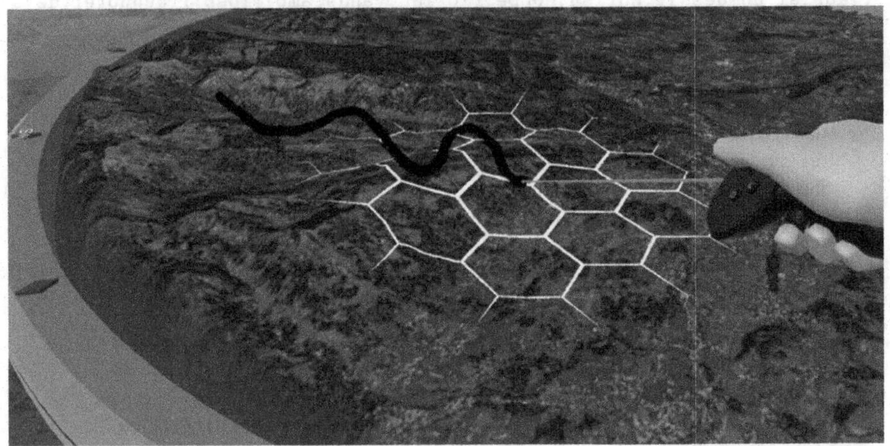

Fig. 1. Hexagon-style visual feedback for the drawing plane.

2 Related Work

VR technology has recently gained popularity for the visualization of geographic data as it provides a more realistic representation of the real world in three dimensions [6,9,10]. However, the process of drawing in a 3D environment like VR is more complex than in 2D, particularly when dealing with terrain properties of maps. Additionally, existing drawing techniques in VR, which are mostly intended for artistic use, are not suitable for this use case [5,7].

Drawing onto or annotating data in three-dimensional space can be divided into several categories. On the one hand, one can distinguish between parametric or planning drawings and artistic drawings. The first one is especially used in the field of CAD (Computer Aided Design) applications, e.g. for the planning of buildings, machines or cities. Here the drawings are defined by parameters such as position, length, width, height. Mostly this is done by text input to have exact values. For artistic drawings, exact positioning is usually not relevant. Instead of using numbers, freehand drawings are used, which, for example, allows faster

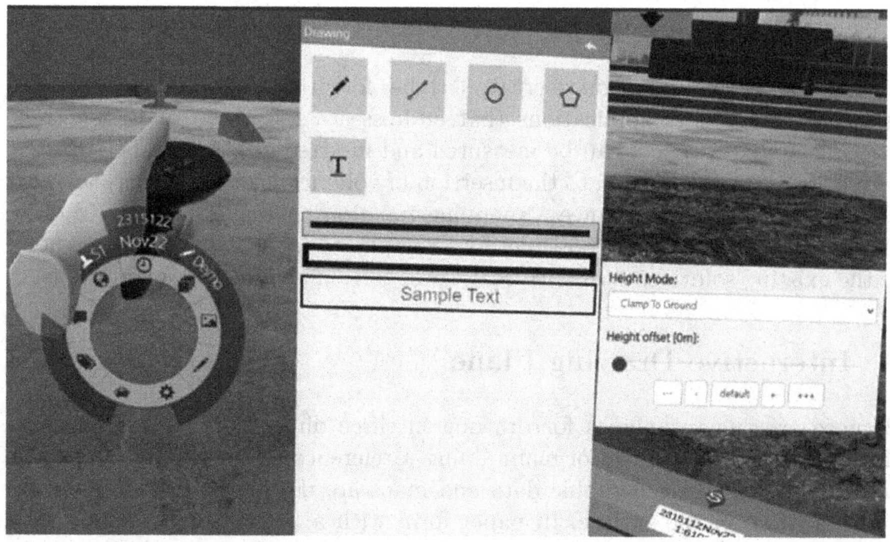

Fig. 2. Annotation menu with dialog for configuring the help layer.

creation of ideas within a design process [8,11]. Another classification can be done by the dimension of the drawn objects. Objects can either have a volume such as cuboids or spheres, or they can consist of surfaces that are indicated by points but have no depth. The last variant is the drawing of lines which have no extension, but are only determined by the distance between two points. As a lot of new concepts in VR are created outside the typical research scope it is important to review existing VR applications that relate to the problem of drawing in three dimensions:

Open Brush (formerly Tilt Brush) [4] is a tool to create 3D paintings. The focus is on drawing lines in various shapes. The controller serves as a brush. In addition to freehand drawings, it is possible to display volumetric and planar auxiliary objects whose surfaces and edges can be painted. All drawings are placed freely. There is no possibility to insert them according to a grid to guarantee fixed lengths.

Gravity Sketch [3] allows for the creation of 3D sketches to quickly create designs in a virtual space. In addition to lines, surfaces and bodies can also be freely inserted. As with Open Brush, there are no auxiliary grids available for the placement of sketches. Gravity Sketch allows for the loading images or 3D models into the scene for reference.

Blocks [2] is also an application to create artistic 3D objects and environments. Unlike Open Brush and Gravity Sketch, the approach here is different. Instead of drawing in three dimensions, simple volumetric bodies can be inserted into a scene. These can then be adjusted by manipulating edges and nodes. In this way, complex objects can be created from the simple solids. Here, too, a planning approach is not possible because there are no grids or options for parameterized objects.

Arkio [1] is an application to create sketches for cities, buildings and interiors. It is one of the only applications that addresses a less the artistic aspect of drawing. Here, distances can be measured and inserted objects can be adjusted to specific sizes. In addition to the insertion of volumetric objects, there are also drawing functions, which have a snapping function making it possible to draw on surfaces. This makes it possible, for example, to label walls. However, none of the existing solutions deal with real world terrain as basis for annotations.

3 Interactive Drawing Plane

Because existing techniques for drawing in three dimensions mostly focus on the artistic aspects instead of maintaining a reference to the earth's surface, it was considered how geographic data and maps are usually used. Users usually add drawings on the surface. In paper form with a pen, in digital maps with the mouse. Elevation information plays only a minor role and is displayed via contour lines, if necessary. However, these require a good imagination to recognize, for example, where a steep slope is. The primary coordinates are the x, y or the latitude, longitude position on the map. Therefore, similar to parametric drawing, the elevation values are assigned to an object or coordinate as a numerical value. This approach would separate visualization from input in a 3D environment. Entering elevation values via a text field is not very intuitive in VR since one has to use an on-screen keyboard to enter the values. In order to make the drawing of georeferenced 3D objects as intuitive as possible for users who are used to working with 2D maps, a dynamic interactive drawing layer in three-dimensional space was created. Free drawing in space as offered by the artistic VR drawing applications is too imprecise as it offers too many degrees of freedom. The interactive drawing plane reduces these by one dimension so that users can draw in a surface as they are used to from a 2D map. The interactive drawing plane is based on the typical work with elevation data in maps, but reverses the interaction order. The user first sets the desired elevation mode and the elevation in meters. Then it is possible to select a drawing mode and the interactive drawing plane is displayed. The drawings on the plane are then inserted at the correct height. This eliminates the need to add a height later. The use of the interactive drawing plane reduces the complexity of the interaction and requires only minimal familiarization, since it is only slightly different from the way one would make annotations on a 2D map. The interactive drawing plane provides support for all annotation types. Points, lines, polygons and circles can be used and of course the list can be extended further. If an annotation is selected for insertion, the interactive drawing plane is activated automatically, depending on the selected height mode. As long as the interactive drawing plane is activated, interaction is restricted the plane instead of the geographic data below. The different plane modes as well as the height in meters can be set in an interactive menu. Figure 2 shows the dialog together with the annotation menu.

Fig. 3. Plotting on auxiliary plane with Absolute height mode.

The dialog offers three different height modes to choose from: With *Clamp To Ground*, drawings are inserted on the surface. Depending on the display format, they may be moved up by a fixed value independent of the zoom level of the geographic data and connected to the ground with a curtain. This makes drawings more visible, but they are still related to the surface. The height value is always set to 0 here. In this mode, the interactive drawing plane is not displayed. With *RelativeToGround*, a height value is set and drawings are added at a distance from the ground. The displayed interactive drawing plane follows the terrain (see Fig. 1), i.e. the lines always have a distance of 100m to the ground, for example. With a height of 0, the drawing lies directly on the terrain. However, a curtain is not displayed here. Among other things, this leads to the fact that lines that are rendered as tubes are only half visible. In this mode, the auxiliary plane follows the terrain at the set height. The *Absolute* option allows the placement of an object above the WGS84 ellipsoid. The altitude indicates the distance between the object and the surface of the ellipsoid in meters. The terrain is not taken into account. Extended objects like lines or surfaces are displayed flat to the surface (see Fig. 3). If the height value is lower than the displayed terrain, objects may lie below the surface. The maximum height value that can be set dynamically adapts to the zoom level of the geographic data. The interactive drawing plane should not rise above the approximate waist height of the user. This ensures that the user can interact with the interactive drawing plane at a sufficiently steep angle. Without this height restriction, the drawing plane may be above the user, causing the user to lose all reference to the surface. A too flat angle additionally reduces the precision of the drawing.

4 Results

In this research study, a user study was conducted to explore the effectiveness of drawing onto the interactive plane. The study involved 7 participants who were asked to use the interactive plane to annotate geographic data. The purpose of the study was to determine whether the use of the interactive plane could provide a quick and effective way to annotate data and whether the participants found the operation of the interactive layer intuitive and easy to learn. During the workshop, the participants were given a brief overview of the interactive plane and how it works. They were then asked to use it to annotate data during a meeting. After the workshop, the participants were asked to provide feedback on their experience using the interactive plane. No formal evaluation was conducted, but the participants were encouraged to provide their honest opinions and suggestions for improvement. The results of the study showed that all participants found the operation of the interactive layer intuitive and easy to learn. They also saw a particular benefit in the quick annotation of geographic data during a meeting. The participants were noted the accuracy and ease of use of the interactive plane and believed that it could be a valuable tool.

Overall, the user study provided valuable insights into the effectiveness of using an interactive plane for annotating data during meetings. The positive feedback from the participants suggests that the use of an interactive plane could be a useful tool in a variety of settings, where quick and accurate annotation of geographic data is required.

5 Conclusion and Future Work

This research paper investigates the different types of three-dimensional drawing techniques available. The techniques were categorized into two groups: artistic and constructive. The focus of this study was on the use of drawings with a geographical reference in virtual reality (VR), which is an area that has not yet been fully explored. To address the challenges of drawing in a 3D environment while maintaining a reference to the earth's surface or map, an interactive plane was implemented. The interactive plane can be adjusted to vary in height, allowing users to draw in three dimensions while still keeping the reference to the map. Additionally, the interactive plane offers several height modes to create annotations at a fixed height or following the terrain. The effectiveness of the proposed technique was evaluated in a workshop, where participants were asked to use the interactive plane to annotate geographic data during a meeting. The participants found the operation of the interactive plane intuitive and easy to learn. They also saw a particular benefit in the quick annotation of geographic data during a meeting. The findings of this study can have significant implications for the field of cartography and VR. The proposed technique could be a valuable tool in a variety of settings, including workshops and meetings, where quick and accurate annotation of data is required. This research contributes to the existing body of knowledge on the use of VR in cartography and provides insights into the potential of three-dimensional drawing techniques with a geographical reference. Further research could be conducted to explore the effectiveness of using the interactive plane in other contexts and to identify any potential limitations or challenges.

References

1. Arkio. https://www.arkio.is. Accessed 17 Mar 2023
2. Blocks. https://arvr.google.com/blocks. Accessed 17 Mar 2023
3. Gravity sketch. https://www.gravitysketch.com. Accessed 17 Mar 2023
4. Open brush. https://openbrush.app. Accessed 17 Mar 2023
5. Banfi, F.: HBIM, 3D drawing and virtual reality for archaeological sites and ancient ruins. **11**, 16–33, July 2020. https://doi.org/10.4995/var.2020.12416, http://polipapers.upv.es/index.php/var/article/view/12416
6. Çöltekin, A., et al.: Geospatial Information Visualization and Extended Reality Displays. Springer, Singapore (2020)
7. Drey, T., Gugenheimer, J., Karlbauer, J., Milo, M., Rukzio, E.: VRSketchin: exploring the design space of pen and tablet interaction for 3D sketching in virtual reality. In: Proceedings of the 2020 CHI Conference on Human Factors in Computing Systems, CHI 2020, pp. 1–14. Association for Computing Machinery, New York (2020). https://doi.org/10.1145/3313831.3376628
8. Dudley, J.J., Schuff, H., Kristensson, P.O.: Bare-handed 3D drawing in augmented reality. In: Proceedings of the 2018 Designing Interactive Systems Conference (2018)
9. Haklay, M.: Virtual reality and GIS: applications. trends and directions, October 2011. https://doi.org/10.1201/9780203305850.ch5
10. Huang, B., Jiang, B., Lin, H.: An integration of GIS, virtual reality and the internet for visualization, analysis and exploration of spatial data, vol. 15, pp. 439–456, July 2001. https://doi.org/10.1080/13658810110046574
11. Joundi, J., Christiaens, Y., Saldien, J., Conradie, P., De Marez, L.: An explorative study towards using VR sketching as a tool for ideation and prototyping in product design. In: Proceedings of the Design Society: DESIGN Conference, vol. 1, pp. 225–234 (2020). https://doi.org/10.1017/dsd.2020.61

Designing User-Centered Simulations of Leadership Situations for Cave Automatic Virtual Environments: Development and Usability Study

Francesco Vona, Miladin Ćeranić, Irma Rybnikova, and Jan-Niklas Voigt-Antons(✉)

Immersive Reality Lab, University of Applied Sciences Hamm-Lippstadt, Hamm, Germany
jan-niklas.voigt-antons@hshl.de

Abstract. Given that experience is a pivotal dimension of learning processes in the field of leadership, the ongoing and unresolved issue is how such experiential moments could be provided when developing leadership skills and competencies. Role-plays and business simulations are widely used in this context as they are said to teach relevant social leadership skills, like those required by everyday communication to followers, by decision-making on compensation, evaluating performance, dealing with conflicts, or terminating contracts. However, the effectiveness of simulations can highly vary depending on the counterpart's ability to act in the given scenarios. In our project, we deal with how immersive media could create experiential learning based on simulations for leadership development. In recent years different variations of extended reality got significant technological improvements. Head-mounted displays are an easy and cost-efficient way to present high-resolution virtual environments. For groups of people that are part of an immersive experience, cave automatic virtual environments offer an excellent trade-off between actual exchange with other humans and interaction with virtual content simultaneously. The work presented is based on developing a user-centered simulation of leadership situations for cave automatic virtual environments and includes the results of a first usability study. In the future, the presented results can help to support the development and evaluation of simulated situations for cave automatic virtual environments with an emphasis on leadership-related scenarios.

Keywords: Leadership Situations · User-Centered Simulations · Cave Automatic Virtual Environments · Usability

1 Introduction

The development of effective leadership skills and competencies has long been recognized as a crucial aspect of organizational success and individual growth

C. Stephanidis et al. (Eds.): HCII 2023, CCIS 1836, pp. 324–331, 2023.
https://doi.org/10.1007/978-3-031-36004-6_45

[19]. However, the process of cultivating these capabilities often hinges on experiential learning, which can be challenging to provide in a controlled and targeted manner [3]. Traditional methods such as role-plays and business simulations have been widely employed to teach essential social leadership skills [16], but their efficacy can be significantly impacted by the performance and adaptability of the individuals involved. As a result, there is an ongoing need to explore novel approaches for delivering experiential learning opportunities in leadership development.

Despite repeated calls and appeals to consider immersive media as a new and potentially fruitful approach to leadership development (e.g. [11]), there is a lack of empirical investigations that aim at developing, testing and evaluating concrete learning tools based on immersive media with the focus of leadership development. With our study, we address this shortcoming.

The rapid advancements in extended reality (XR) technologies, including head-mounted displays and cave automatic virtual environments (CAVEs), offer promising new avenues for enhancing the learning experiences of aspiring leaders [24]. The immersive nature of these technologies enables users to engage in realistic and interactive simulations, providing valuable opportunities for practicing leadership skills in a controlled environment [1]. This paper focuses on the potential application of CAVEs in creating user-centered simulations of leadership situations, addressing the existing gap in experiential learning opportunities.

The motivation behind our research stems from the recognition that immersive media could revolutionize the way leadership skills are developed and practiced. By leveraging the unique capabilities of CAVEs, we aim to provide an effective, interactive, and engaging platform for leadership development, enhancing the overall learning experience [11]. Our work involves the design and implementation of a user-centered simulation tailored for CAVE environments, as well as an initial usability study to assess the effectiveness of our approach.

Ultimately, the findings presented in this paper hold the potential to significantly impact the future of leadership development, providing valuable insights and guidance for the creation and evaluation of simulated scenarios within CAVE environments [2]. By harnessing the power of immersive technologies, we hope to contribute to a more effective, engaging, and accessible approach to leadership education and training, addressing the current lack of empirical investigations in the field [11].

2 Related Work

This section provides an overview of the research landscape relevant to immersive media, tracing its roots from the initial theories of flow to the development of CAVE systems for media presentation.

Flow Theory: The concept of flow, first introduced by [6], refers to a mental state of complete immersion and absorption in an activity. In this state, individuals experience heightened focus, deep involvement, and optimal enjoyment. In the context of media experiences, flow is considered an essential component for achieving immersion and engaging users effectively [10].

Immersion and Presence in Virtual Environments: The concept of presence, or the subjective feeling of being in a virtual environment, has been extensively studied in relation to immersive media. [25] identified three factors that contribute to the sense of presence in virtual environments: vividness, interactivity, and the extent to which the user can control the environment. Lombard et al.[18] proposed six dimensions of presence, including spatial presence, social presence, and self-presence, which have since been used to inform the design of immersive media experiences. High immersive systems can be used to evoke strong emotions [28]. Bio-signals that are related to emotions can be measured in real time and used to adapt content of immersive media systems [20]. Besides technological factors, also social environments can have an influence on user experience and social acceptability of immersive systems [27].

CAVE Systems for Media Presentation: Cave Automatic Virtual Environment (CAVE) systems, introduced by [5], represent a significant advancement in the immersive media presentation. CAVE systems consist of large-scale, room-sized displays that surround users with multiple projection screens, creating an enveloping 3D visual experience [5]. These systems have been widely used in scientific visualization, architectural design, and cultural heritage applications [4]. The inherent advantages of CAVE systems over HMD-based VR, such as the allowance for natural group collaboration and the elimination of motion sickness, have led to their continued relevance and application in various research and industrial contexts [23].

In conclusion, the study of immersive media has evolved from foundational theories of flow and presence to the development of advanced technologies such as VR and CAVE systems. The continued exploration of these technologies will undoubtedly result in novel applications and further insights into the potential of immersive media experiences.

In the field of leadership development, experience, and experience-based tools are considered as the most effective approach to obtaining leadership skills and competencies. In conceptual terms, this idea goes back to the experiential learning theory by [15]. The author states that learning processes could be described as processes of meaning-making from personal experiences. Especially those experiences that are assumed to trigger meaning-making and learning that challenge, irritate, or unsettling. One of the established ways to provide such experiential learning when developing leaders are business games and role-plays. They are widely used in leadership development settings. Leadership students are said to more effectively achieve relevant leadership skills, like those required by everyday interactions with followers, decision-making and decision communicating to followers, or conflict resolution, than using case studies [7]. The main reason is a high level of realism and high involvement of students in business games [14]. Although immersive media is a flourishing field and bear a particularly high potential for experiencing learning, there is barely research on how immersive media could be used in leadership development. Instead, there are several studies that investigate online gaming as a potentially educative tool to develop effective leaders. Reeves et al.[21] argue that multiplayer-online games can teach leadership competencies that are needed in business companies. Some scholars appeal to consider game-based virtual worlds as a "prospective avenue for leadership skill development" since they require a wide array of skills and competencies that are of great value for leadership tasks, like role delegation, member motivation, persuasion, and collaborative work [12]. Virtual reality is also said to hold manifold potential for leadership development since intelligent tutoring tools may be able to adapt situations to the learner's behaviors. Studies argue in favor of the effectiveness of educational tools based on virtual reality and point out that especially avatar-based games provide a psychologically secure environment to test and improve the interactive skills of students in an almost-real way [8].

3 Methods

Participants: Ten people participated in the study (8 self-identified as male and two self-identified as female). The mean age was 30.1 years, with a standard deviation of 5.8. The experiment was approved by the local ethics committee.

Procedure: Participants were invited to a lab room at a different separated time slot to participate alone in the experiment. In the beginning, the participants were welcomed by a moderator and presented with an introduction to the study and its purpose. After signing a consent form, the participants were given a pre-questionnaire asking about demographic information and their affinity for technology interaction [9]. The next step was to introduce participants to the simulated leadership situations. After this introductory part, the participant could start the condition communicated by the moderator. The participants were supposed to play each of the four conditions in randomized order. After each condition, the participant was asked to answer web-based questionnaires encompassing User Experience Questionnaire (UEQ), igroup Presence Questionnaire (IPQ), and Social Presence Questionnaire (SPQ) [13,17,22]. After all the conditions had been played and rated, the participant was asked to rate the overall experience and which condition they liked most. The complete duration of the experiment was around 40 min.

Apparatus: A CAVE (CAVE Automatic Virtual Environment) is a room where the environment is simulated in three dimensions for an observer. The walls in such a room are often made of projection screens on which content can be displayed. CAVE projection systems can consist of up to six projection screens for simulations in a cuboid-shaped room. The CAVE used at the Hamm-Lippstadt University of Applied Science consists of four acrylic glass screens: a front projection, two side projections, and a floor projection screen. Four 3D special projectors are used to project the image, which is redirected onto the projection screens via mirrors due to space limitations in the room. To track the observer's movements, a marker tracking system consists of fixed and mobile infrared cameras. A sound system consisting of subwoofers and passive speakers is also installed.

Virtual Reality Application: The Virtual Reality application was created in Unity and consists of 4 scenarios, and 2 simulated leadership situations, each with animated and non-animated virtual avatars (2×2). All scenarios are composed of at least two people (one real), and the user must impersonate a different character each time (once the boss, and once the employee, for each situation). The 2 simulated leadership situations concern the themes of "giving critical feedback as a supervisor" and "leadership and employee health". In the first scenario, there are 2 people: Tim and Mike. Tim is responsible for the payroll department of human resources. After the introduction of new software that allows for more efficient payroll accounting, Tim is not satisfied with Mike's performance because he is not yet proficient in using the software. Now, in the Human Resources department, the annual staff evaluation is scheduled. In this scenario the user has to play once Tim and the other Mike.

The second scenario concerns workplace health. In German organizations, there are mental risk assessments for every workplace. This is not a measurement of employees' mental health but an analysis to determine whether work activities, the workplace, or the environment in which it takes place are placing employees under stress or could lead to psychological stress or illness. The idea behind this evaluation is to prevent illnesses and inform employees and employers on how to design working conditions so that employees feel well. In this scenario, there are three characters: a manager (Tom) and two employees (Anne and Sören). In this scenario, the user must interpret Tom and Sören once each. All four scenarios take place in the same virtual environment: a very simple office with some furnishings in the background (furniture and plants). Figure 1 shows the experiment with a first person and third person point of view. All avatars have audio that can be played from the moderator's keyboard during the experience. In this way, the experiment moderator can control the entire execution of the experience. Virtual characters will have animations during audio playback in conditions with animated avatars, while in conditions with non-animated avatars, avatars remain in a sitting idle position. Avatars and animations were taken from Mixamo [26].

Fig. 1. On the left: what the user sees in the virtual environment; on the right: a picture taken from outside the CAVE

4 Results

4.1 UEQ-S

The results for the UEQ-S dimensions of the pragmatic and hedonic quality can be found in Fig. 2. For condition 1 (1 virtual user + no animation) hedonic quality was similar to the pragmatic quality (PQ = 1.15, HQ = 1.12). For condition 2 (2 virtual users + no animation) pragmatic quality was rated as being lower compared to the hedonic quality (PQ = 0.15, HQ = 0.92). A similar trend could be observed for condition 3 (1 virtual users + animation) and condition 4 (2 virtual users + animation), for which also pragmatic quality was rated as being lower compared to the hedonic quality (condition 3: PQ = 0.52, HQ = 1.27; condition 4: PQ = 0.6, HQ = 1.15).

4.2 IPQ

For the one virtual user condition (condition 1), the perceived overall presence (G1) was reduced when adding animations from a mean value of 4.4 to 4. Adding animation for the one user condition resulted in a lower experienced spatial presence, from 3.74 to 3.14. In the case of the two-user conditions, adding animation resulted in a higher perceived overall presence (from a mean value of 3.2 to 4.3) and also a higher spatial presence (from 3.14 to 3.42).

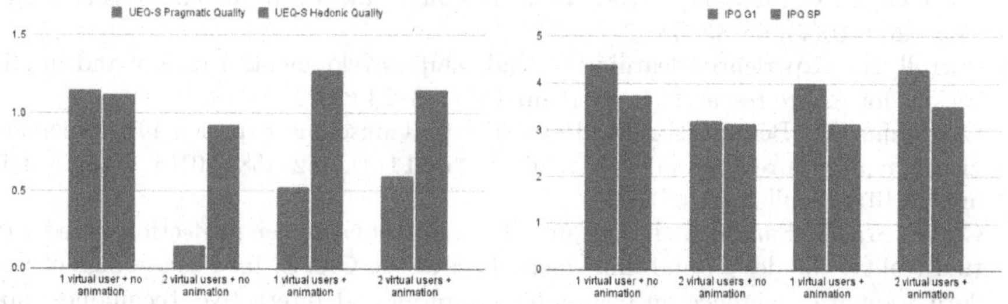

Fig. 2. On the left: Average values over all participants for the two UEQ-S scales pragmatic and hedonic quality. On the right: Average values over all participants for the two IPQ scales general presence (IPQ G1) and spatial presence (IPQ SP).

4.3 After Condition Questions

A 7-value Likert scale was used for the evaluation of the post experiment questions. The results of the questions also show that the first condition, with an avatar and no animation was the one felt most real with a mean value of 4,3. This is probably due to the fact that the avatar in the idle position seemed to maintain eye contact with the user which in the same condition with animation and with two users did not happen. For the second question, in addition to condition 1 (mean = 5.7),also conditions 2 (mean = 5.5) and 4 (mean = 5.6) scored high. This may have to do with the role played during the scenarios.

5 Conclusion

To summarize, it is crucial to exercise prudence in situations involving a single virtual user. Incorporating non-congruent animations may negatively affect both overall and spatial presence perception. As such, it is essential to thoughtfully choose animations and details. In contrast, the presence of two virtual users seems to enhance the experience, as the addition of animation appears to have a generally positive influence on presence.

The vast potential of immersive media for experiential learning and training in leadership cannot be understated. Nonetheless, educational institutions must recognize the significant time and effort necessary for the development, testing, and evaluation of such tools. Furthermore, forging a more robust connection between leadership theories and innovative leadership development tools presents an opportunity for future research and practical applications.

References

1. Blascovich, J., Bailenson, J.: Infinite Reality: Avatars, Eternal Life, New Worlds, and the Dawn Of The Virtual Revolution. Harper Collins, New York (2011)
2. Bowman, D.A., McMahan, R.P.: Virtual reality: how much immersion is enough? Computer **40**(7), 36–43 (2007)
3. Carroll, B.: Experiential learning in leadership development: a review and implications for future research. Leadership **18**(1), 3–23 (2022)
4. Carrozzino, M., Bergamasco, M.: Beyond virtual museums: experiencing immersive virtual reality in real museums. J. Cult. Herit. **11**(4), 452–458 (2010). https://doi.org/10.1016/j.culher.2010.04.001
5. Cruz-Neira, C., Sandin, D.J., DeFanti, T.A.: Surround-screen projection-based virtual reality: the design and implementation of the CAVE. In: Proceedings of the 20th Annual Conference on Computer Graphics and Interactive Techniques, pp. 135–142 (1992). https://doi.org/10.1145/133994.134045
6. Csikszentmihalyi, M.: Beyond Boredom and Anxiety: Experiencing Flow in Work and Play. Jossey-Bass, Hoboken (1975)
7. Dentico, P.: LeadSimm: collaborative leadership development for the knowledge society. Dev. Bus. Simul. Experiential Learn. **26**, 98–106 (1999)
8. Fecke, J., Müller, L.: Simulationen in virtuellen lernumgebungen: Welche vor- und nachteile haben avatarbasierte und videokamerabasierte formate bei der durchführung von rollenspielen? Zeitschrift für Hochschulentwicklung **17**(1), 215–232 (2022)
9. Franke, T., Attig, C., Wessel, D.: A personal resource for technology interaction: development and validation of the affinity for technology interaction (ATI) scale. Int. J. Hum.-Comput. Interact. **35**(6), 456–467 (2019)
10. Ghani, J.A., Deshpande, S.P.: Task characteristics and the experience of optimal flow in human-computer interaction. J. Psychol. **128**(4), 381–391 (1994). https://doi.org/10.1080/00223980.1994.9712742

11. Guthrie, K.L., Jones, T.B., Osteen, L., Hu, S.: Developing leadership education through virtual simulations. J. Leadersh. Educ. **10**(1), 54–68 (2011)
12. Guthrie, K.L., Phelps, K., Downey, S.: Virtual worlds. a developmental tool for leadership education. J. Leadersh. Stud. **5**(2), 6–13 (2011). https://doi.org/10.1002/jls
13. Heim, J., Brooks, P., Følstad, A., Schliemann, T.: Fitness for purpose evaluation methodology. Technical report, University of Nottingham
14. Hunsaker, P.L.: Leadership evaluation and training through behavioral simulations: Method, results, and future directions. In: New Horizons in Simulation Game and Experiential Learning, vol. 4, pp. 40–47 (1977)
15. Kolb, D.: Experiential learning: Experience as the source of learning and development. Prentice Hall, Englewood Cliffs (1984)
16. Kolb, D.A.: Experiential learning: Experience as the Source of Learning and Development. FT Press, Upper Saddle River (2014)
17. Laugwitz, B., Held, T., Schrepp, M.: Construction and evaluation of a user experience questionnaire. In: Holzinger, A. (ed.) USAB 2008. LNCS, vol. 5298, pp. 63–76. Springer, Heidelberg (2008). https://doi.org/10.1007/978-3-540-89350-9_6
18. Lombard, M., Ditton, T.: At the heart of it all: The concept of presence. J. Comput.-Mediated Commun. **3**(2) (1997). https://doi.org/10.1111/j.1083-6101.1997.tb00072.x
19. Northouse, P.G.: Leadership: Theory and Practice. Sage Publications, Thousand Oaks (2018)
20. Pinilla, A., Voigt-Antons, J.N., Garcia, J., Raffe, W., Moller, S.: Real-time affect detection in virtual reality: a technique based on a three-dimensional model of affect and EEG signals. Front. Virtual Reality **3**, 964754 (2023). https://doi.org/10.3389/frvir.2022.964754
21. Reeves, B., Malone, T.W., O'Driscoll, T.: Leadership's online labs. Harv. Bus. Rev. **86**(5), 58–66 (2008)
22. Schubert, T.W.: The sense of presence in virtual environments: a three-component scale measuring spatial presence, involvement, and realness. Z. für Medienpsychologie (2003)
23. Shaw, C.D., Green, M.: Beyond the head-mounted display: toward immersive multi-display systems. IEEE Comput. Graphics Appl. **34**(6), 6–10 (2014). 964754 https://doi.org/10.1109/MCG.2014.117
24. Slater, M.: Place illusion and plausibility can lead to realistic behaviour in immersive virtual environments. Philos. Trans. R. Soc. B: Biol. Sci. **364**(1535), 3549–3557 (2009). 964754
25. Steuer, J.: Defining virtual reality: Dimensions determining telepresence. J. Commun. **42**(4), 73–93 (1992). https://doi.org/10.1111/j.1460-2466.1992.tb00812.x
26. Systems, A.: Mixamo.com. https://www.mixamo.com/#/
27. Vergari, M., Kojić, T., Vona, F., Garzotto, F., Möller, S., Voigt-Antons, J.N.: Influence of interactivity and social environments on user experience and social acceptability in virtual reality. In: 2021 IEEE Virtual Reality and 3D User Interfaces (VR), pp. 695–704. IEEE (2021)
28. Voigt-Antons, J.N., Spang, R., Kojić, T., Meier, L., Vergari, M., Möller, S.: Don't worry be happy-using virtual environments to induce emotional states measured by subjective scales and heart rate parameters. In: 2021 IEEE Virtual Reality and 3D User Interfaces (VR), pp. 679–686. IEEE (2021)

An Evaluation of Virtual Reality for Terrain Assessment

Boris Wagner(✉), Adrian H. Hoppe, Florian van de Camp, and Sebastian Maier

Fraunhofer Institute of Optronics, System Technologies and Image Exploitation IOSB, 76131 Karlsruhe, Germany

boris.wagner@iosb.fraunhofer.de

Abstract. With the availability of quickly created and inexpensive 3D representations of the real world, it is important to investigate whether users can derive additional value from them, particularly when combined with the possibilities of Virtual Reality (VR) visualization.

To evaluate possible benefits, a study was conducted which focused on the specific tasks of aerial image analysts and covered the use of 3D geodata in terrain assessment.

The study compared the use of 3D geodata in VR with 2D displays, using a digital orthophoto with 20 cm resolution and digital terrain models from the ASTER system. The task for the user was to find a route with minimal gradient between a start and destination point while avoiding steep gradients. The base map used was a digital orthophoto in 20 cm resolution (DOP20). In 2D, the height information was conveyed by isohypses. In VR, the digital terrain model (DTM) from the ASTER system was used.

The results of the evaluation showed that the actual task goal, the lowest maximum gradient, was best achieved in VR. However, the subjects needed considerably more time to complete the tasks in VR. In VR, the test persons were also more cautious, they planned the routes considerably longer, but as already mentioned, they achieved the objective better.

Overall, the results of this study suggest that while VR may offer added value in terrain assessment, it may not be as efficient as 2D planning for those trained in map reading. However, for new users or those who are less familiar with the terrain, VR may offer a more intuitive and immersive experience, allowing them to better understand and interpret the data. Further research is needed to fully understand the potential benefits and limitations of using VR for terrain assessment and to identify the most appropriate use cases for this technology.

Keywords: Aerial image analysis · terrain analysis · maps · geo data · Virtual Reality · user study

1 Introduction

Now that 3D representations of the real world are available quickly, inexpensively and up-to-date, the question arises as to whether a user can derive added value from them. In addition, this geo data can be combined with the new possibilities of VR (Virtual

C. Stephanidis et al. (Eds.): HCII 2023, CCIS 1836, pp. 332–339, 2023.
https://doi.org/10.1007/978-3-031-36004-6_46

Reality) representation. For the special tasks of an aerial image interpreter, the following considerations and a complete evaluation of the use of 3D geodata by aerial photo interpreters both on desktop PCs and in a VR environment was executed.

Many studies (i.e. [1]) and research projects note the growing need for immersive environments, which users increasingly demand to visualize geospatial data. AR (Augmented Reality) and VR technology are becoming more and more widespread and thus reaching new users. However, it must be considered that this new technical possibility does not always allow a 1:1 use of the data as before, but an adaptation of the (geo)data (and the interaction) is necessary [2]. It should now be noted that the adaptation of geodata still receives a great deal of potential for improvement and has not yet been optimally researched and implemented.

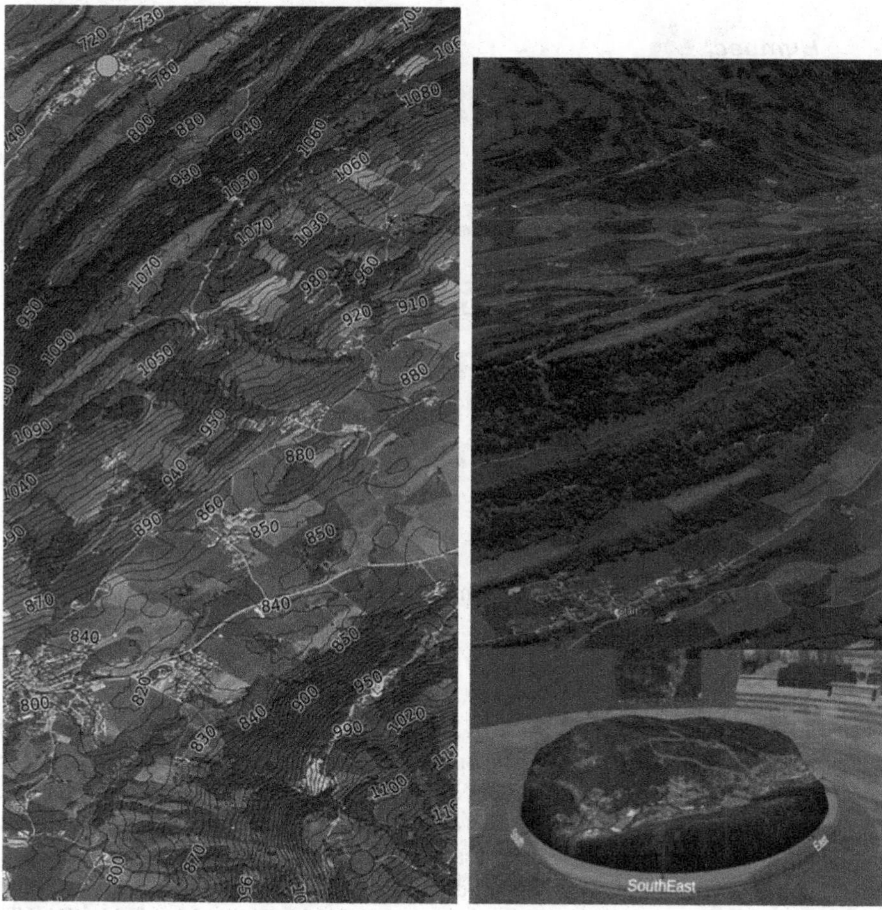

Fig. 1. 2D-View with isohypses and start/stop point

Fig. 2. 3D-VR view with DTM

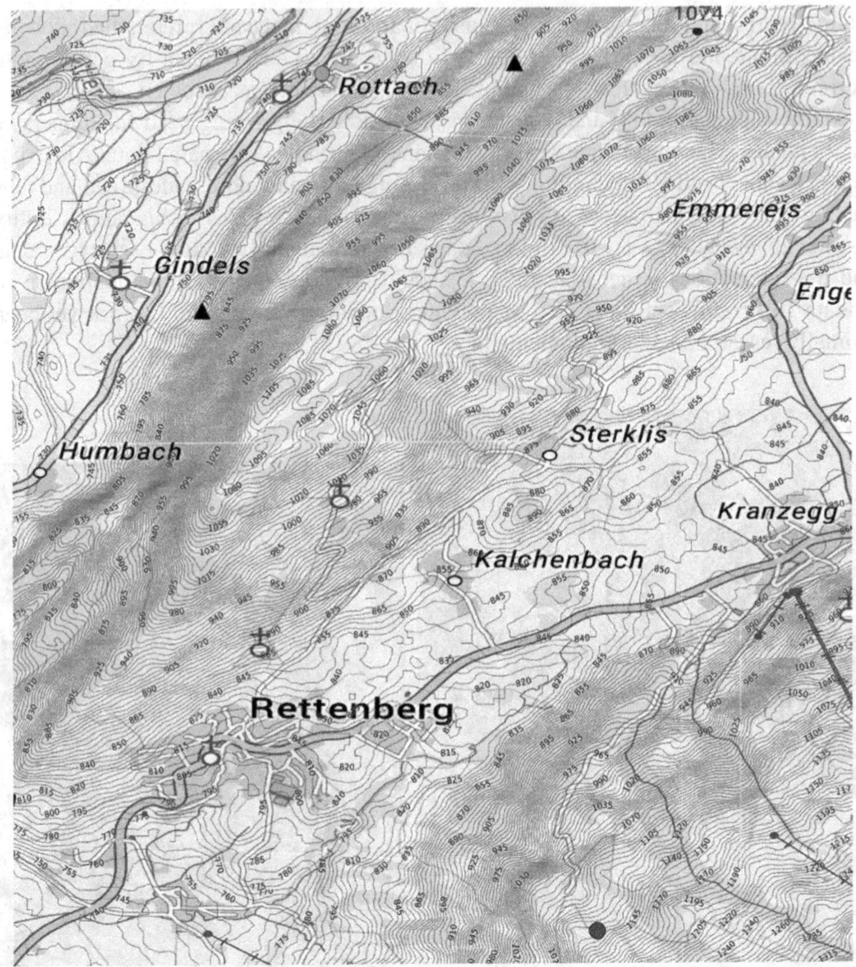

Fig. 3. Area 1 – southern mountainous region in Germany

1.1 Evaluation

Abstract. The evaluation covers the use of 3D geodata in a terrain assessment task by the user. Topographic maps are given in 2D on the PC screen and as a 3D model in VR (see Fig. 1 and Fig. 2). The task is to quickly capture and evaluate the shape of the terrain. The user has to find a route with the lowest possible gradient between the given start and destination, as well as avoid steep gradients. The length of the route is secondary. This terrain section is evaluated as a product of the task and compared with the other map display types. The evaluation was carried out with the Digital Map Table (DigLT) and DigLT^{VR} from the Fraunhofer IOSB [3].

1.2 Procedure and General Conditions

The 10 test persons are confronted with two areas. Each half of the test persons alternately receive area 1 in 2D and area 2 in VR and vice versa (see Fig. 3 and Fig. 6).

The base map is a digital orthophoto in 20 cm resolution (DOP20). In 2D, the height information is conveyed by means of isohypses. In VR, the digital terrain model (DTM) from ASTER [4] is used.

The test persons start in a view in which the start and finish as well as a sufficiently large environment can be seen directly without having to pan or zoom the maps.

The test persons are between 37 and 72 years old, two female and eight males.

Three test persons have very good cartographic knowledge, the rest have little knowledge.

None of the test persons have any in-depth experience with VR.

The following graphics Fig. 4 and Fig. 5 as well as Fig. 7 and Fig. 8 show the respective plans of the subjects. For ease of visibility in the report, it is always backed up with the DTM from black (lower terrain) to white (higher terrain).

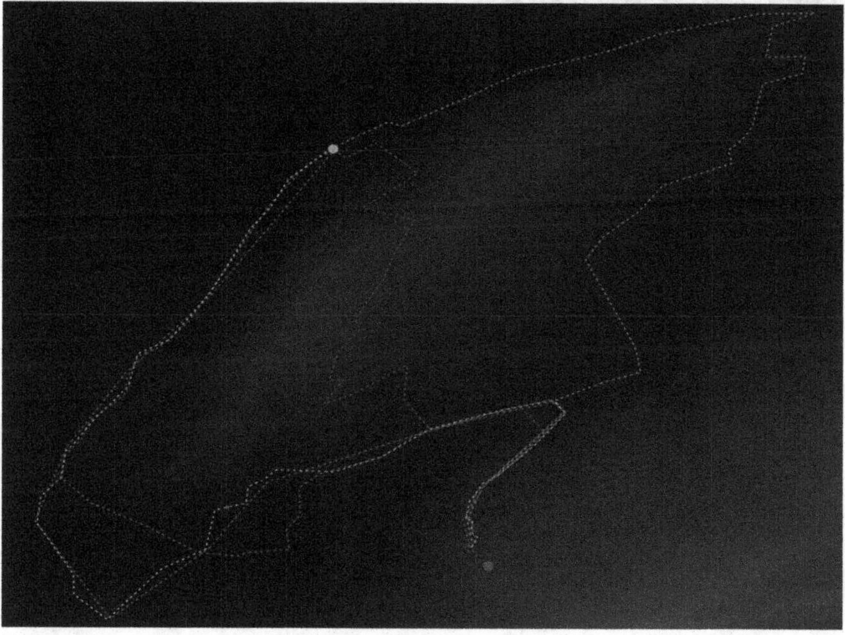

Fig. 4. Planning done in 2D – Area 1

Fig. 5. Planning done in VR – Area 1

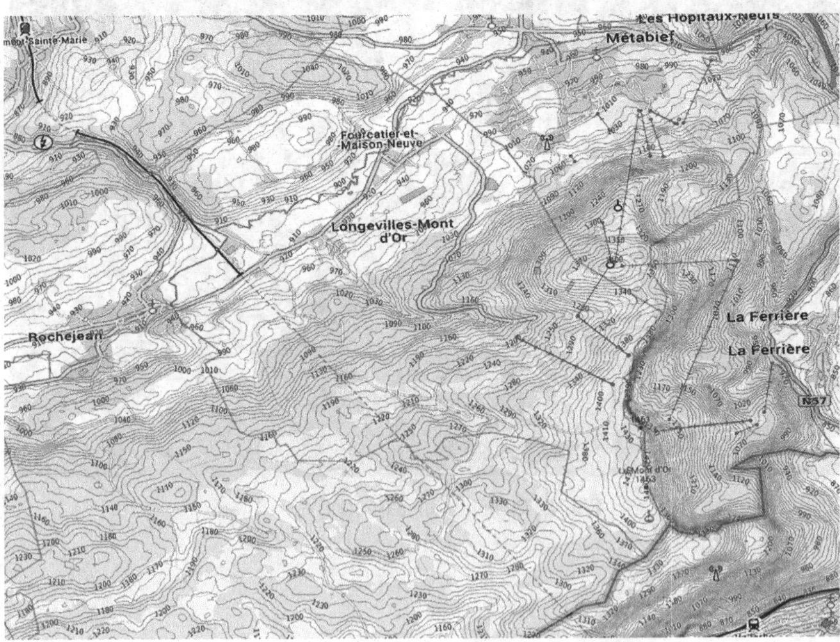

Fig. 6. Area 2- mountainous area at the France-Swiss boarder

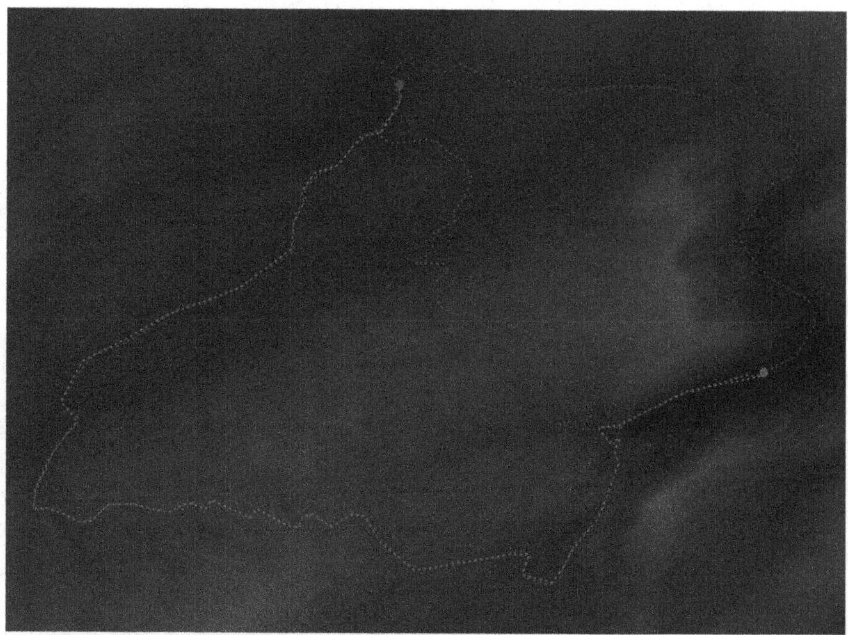

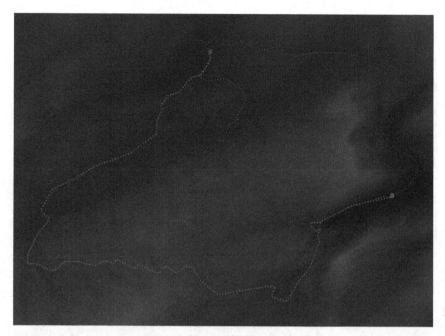

Fig. 7. Planning done in 2D – Area 2

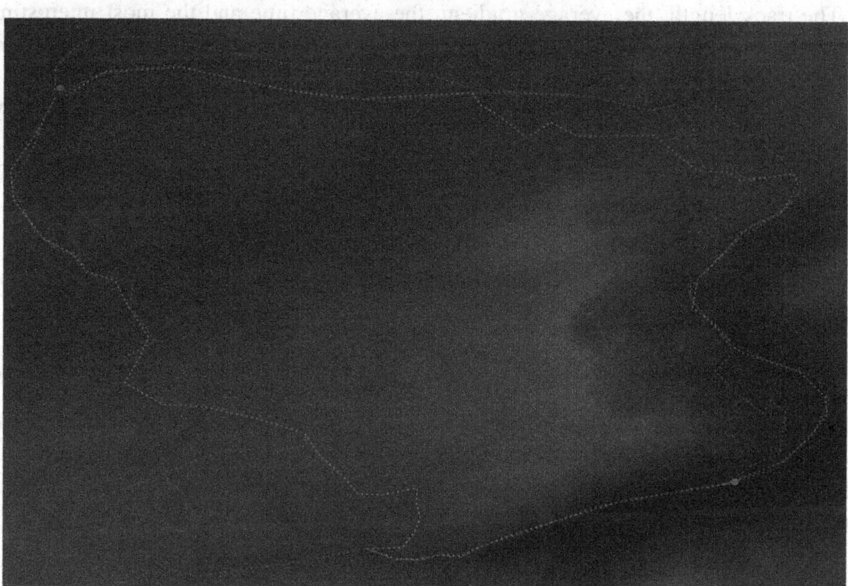

Fig. 8. Planning done in VR – Area 2

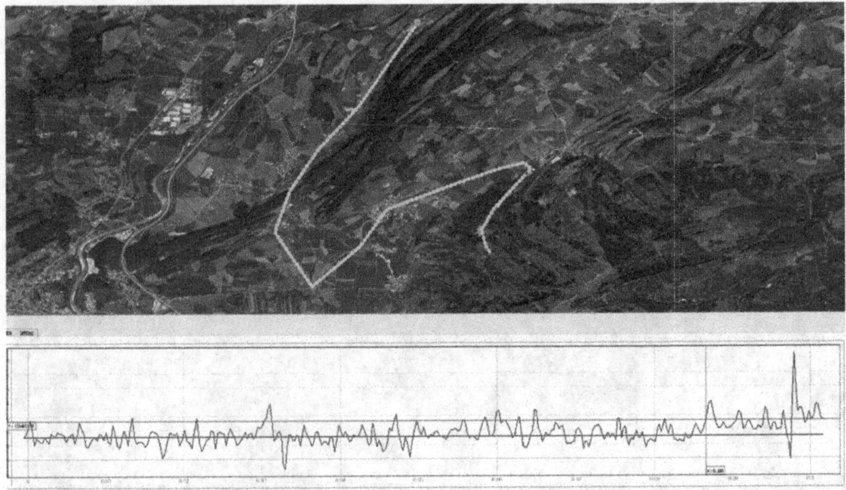

Fig. 9. Example evaluation of the route - graph shows gradient in percent

2 Results

The evaluation of the plans is done in QGIS in which the tracks are calculated with the DEM to a terrain section (see exemplary Fig. 9).

The track length, the average gradient, the average time and the most interesting aspect, the maximum gradient, were determined. This is done separately for 2D and VR, as well as for the respective area.

In the following, the results are listed separately according to the area and the type of presentation:

	Area 1-2D	Area 1-VR	Area 2-2D	Area 2-VR
Maximum gradient in percent	71%	61%	85%	46%
Average route lengths	11.0 km	12.6 km	27.5 km	17,4 km
Average planning time	0:51 s	1:37 s	1:30 s	2:41 s
Average gradient in percent	10.8%	10,6%	8.7%	9%

The average gradient is to be understood as a control value as to whether the results are plausible. If the start/finish is the same, the gradient should be identical across all routes. The results are approximately the same, the slight deviation is due to rounding errors over the several thousand data points along the route.

3 Conclusion

The actual task goal, the lowest maximum slope, is best achieved in VR. However, the test persons need considerably more time to complete the tasks in VR. In VR, the subjects are also more cautious, they plan the routes considerably longer in some cases, but as already mentioned, they achieve a better objective.

It is therefore questionable whether planning in VR offers much added value. The route lengths and planning times are considerably longer than with 2D planning. In addition, it can be assumed that staff trained in map reading can plan even more efficiently in 2D.

References

1. Marriott, K., et al. (eds.): Immersive Analytics, p. 1. Springer Nature Switzerland AG (2018)
2. Edler, D., Keil, J., Wiedenlübbert, T., et al.: Immersive VR experience of redeveloped post-industrial sites: the example of "Zeche Holland" in Bochum-Wattenscheid. KN – J. Cartograp. Geograph. Inform. 267–284 (2019)
3. Fraunhofer IOSB – DigLT. https://diglt.de/en/. Accessed 23 March 2023
4. Wikipedia ASTER. https://en.wikipedia.org/wiki/Advanced_Spaceborne_Thermal_Emission_and_Reflection_Radiometer. Accessed 23 March 2023

Toward a Gesture System Architecture in Extended Reality Based on a Multi-dimensional Taxonomy of Gestures

Powen Yao(✉), Tian Yang, and Michael Zyda

University of Southern California, Los Angeles, CA 90007, USA
{powenyao,tyang863,zyda}@usc.edu
https://viterbischool.usc.edu/

Abstract. Gesture-based interactions have been widely applied in Human-Computer Interaction areas. As Extended Reality technology (XR) has grown rapidly, gesture has also grown in importance as a way of interaction in XR. Although there have been many efforts on gesture taxonomy in HCI, there is a lack of works that classify gestures focusing on their applications and roles in XR domains. We have been working on a taxonomy that incorporates important previous works on gesture taxonomies, modifies, and injects new dimensions for the taxonomy to better reflect the wide variety of contexts and scenarios in XR. This paper presents a gesture system architecture for Extended Reality based on our ongoing work on a multi-dimensional taxonomy of gesture in XR applications. This gesture system architecture can be used to build general-purpose gesture systems that will be easy for both designers and users to choose the right gesture for the situation at hand.

Keywords: Multi-Dimensional Taxonomy · Gesture System Architecture · Hyperphysicality

1 Introduction

Extended Reality (XR) is an umbrella term that covers the different realities in the Reality-virtuality continuum [4]. XR brings users into an environment very similar to the real world. The virtual aspects of XR allow many interactions to become easily accessible in XR when they were not before. XR technologies bring unique qualities, such as the user's body and the environment, which greatly influence Human-Computer Interaction (HCI) in XR.

Gesture Taxonomies. Gestures can be seen as a user's willful intention for a certain effect as exhibited by their action and interpreted in a certain context. Given that the contexts in XR can change dramatically, so can the relationship between a user action (or gesture) and its associated effect. We found that the existing gesture taxonomies we have examined have not reflected the unique

C. Stephanidis et al. (Eds.): HCII 2023, CCIS 1836, pp. 340–347, 2023.
https://doi.org/10.1007/978-3-031-36004-6_47

qualities of XR. This encouraged us to propose a new gesture taxonomy that is better suited to gestures applied in XR environments.

There are also more specific taxonomies that deal with different classes of gestures, such as taxonomies for Surface Gestures [8], taxonomies for Motion Gestures [5], and recently, many taxonomies of Mid-Air Gestures [1,2,7]. Given that these different classes of gestures can be utilized in XR, the proposed taxonomies should unify and include dimensions in these specific taxonomies when possible. This provides designers with a taxonomy that includes important considerations for XR as a starting point.

Gesture System Architecture. We propose a new architecture for a gesture system in XR based on our gesture taxonomy. Generally, this architecture detects gestures performed by XR users based on their physical characteristics, handles them by the gesture mapping related to the context, and creates the associated effects for the users. It is a highly customizable system, allowing designers and users to easily create new gestures or customize the gesture's effect based on different contexts. These different contexts also help users to learn and differentiate how the same actions can lead to different effects, allowing for a greater interaction space.

2 XR Qualities

XR brings several qualities that distinguish XR from other computing paradigms. We'll briefly take a look at some of the qualities, how they impact XR, and how they need to be considered in a gesture taxonomy for XR.

User. The most important quality of XR is perhaps the relationship between users and the computing environment. In XR, users are able to interact in an environment directly. Interaction is directly translated to their digital counterparts in the form of heads, hands, and other body parts. With the presence of users' body, users can make use of their kinaesthetic senses; they can also take advantage of their personal, peripersonal, and extrapersonal space for spatial interactions.

Hyperphysical Environment. The environment in XR can also be structured differently to follow different laws of physics. This can be useful for entertainment, necessities to overcome real-world restrictions, or simply helpful for making a more convenient XR experience. Teleportation as a locomotion method is an example of hyperphysical interaction. It does not follow the laws of physics in the real world; however, its usefulness in fulfilling the above needs makes it one of the most common locomotion options in VR.

Region. 6DOF XR is inherently spatial, which increases the need to consider the spatial context of gestures. The environmental context can change rapidly as the user traverses the environment. For example, when the user comes home from a grocery trip and moves from the car into the kitchen. The user has gone from a public space into a private space while traveling through several regions, each intended for different purposes. User interactions in XR should thus take into account these spatial contexts.

Object as an Interactor. XR systems can generate and track virtual objects, which allows any objects the user picks up to be turned into interactors. Any object can become an interactor and thus be used to perform gestures. For example, you can shake an apple, be it a virtual apple or a real apple, and the XR system will produce the associated effect of the gesture, which may be an information popup about the apple.

Multiple Interactors. Given that any object can be an interactor and the user's body parts can also serve as interactors, multiple interactors are common in XR. Compared to Surface Gestures on mobile devices, which also deal with multiple interactors, surface Gestures in XR may have access to additional information about the interactors themselves. For example, the exact position and rotation of the surface within the world space and the orientation of the finger, and which exact finger is used. The additional context can reframe the way we think about what constitutes surface gestures and other interactions in XR.

3 Taxonomy

We have based our proposed taxonomy primarily on works of Taxonomy of Gestures in Human-Computer Interaction by Vafaei[6], which is in turn based on the prior taxonomy work of Wobbrock et al. and Ruiz et al.[5,8]. We also incorporate elements of design space from works by Ens et al.[3].

Ruiz et al., followed by Vafaei, divided the dimensions of a gesture into two classes - Physical Characteristics and Gesture Mapping. We continue to use these same classes in our taxonomy. We will briefly discuss our taxonomy in the following section, especially on the dimensions that we modified substantially or proposed.

3.1 Physical Characteristics

We broaden the scope of the Physical Characteristics (PC) class to include any interactor and, in doing so, convert dimensions based on hands in Vafaei's work to more general dimensions based on the broader concept of interactors. Physical Characteristics, then, can be viewed as **"physical characteristics of the interactor and the action performed by the interactor."**. Our taxonomy of Physical Characteristics is listed in Table 1.

Position and Rotation. Object movement of objects in 3D space can be defined as translation (the change of position) and rotation (the change of self-orientation). Therefore, these two aspects are essential for defining a spatial gesture. Our taxonomy defines two dimensions of Position and Rotation, each containing three sub-dimensions: x, y, and z, denoting the three axes in Cartesian coordinates. Each of these sub-dimensions includes two categories: Relevant or Irrelevant. Relevant means that this axis is used in the gesture, and Irrelevant means that this gesture does not care about this axis, i.e., the movement of this gesture involved does not matter.

Table 1. Gesture taxonomy in the class Physical Characteristics.

Dimensions	Sub-dimensions	Categories	Sub-categories	Description
Position	*x*	*Relevant*		Gesture involves the x-axis of position
		Irrelevant		Gesture ignores the x-axis of position
	y	*Relevant*		Gesture involves the y-axis of position
		Irrelevant		Gesture ignores the y-axis of position
	z	*Relevant*		Gesture involves the z-axis of position
		Irrelevant		Gesture ignores the z-axis of position
Rotation	*x*	*Relevant*		Gesture involves the roll-axis of rotation
		Irrelevant		Gesture ignores the roll-axis of rotation
	y	*Relevant*		Gesture involves the pitch-axis of rotation
		Irrelevant		Gesture ignores the pitch-axis of rotation
	z	*Relevant*		Gesture involves the yaw-axis of rotation
		Irrelevant		Gesture ignores the yaw-axis of rotation
Form		*Static*		No motion/change is in gesture
		Dynamic		Motion/change occurs in gesture
Interactor		*User Body*	*Hand*	Arm is fixed, but palm or fingers move
			Arm	Arm moves (hand moves as well)
			Head	Gesture is performed by head movement
			Shoulder	Gesture is performed by shoulder movement
			Foot	Gesture is performed by foot movement
			Eyes	Gesture is performed by pupil movement
			Mouth	Gesture is performed by lip movement
			Other body parts	Gesture is performed by other body part
		Input Device		Gesture utilizes Input Device as an interactor
		In-Environment Object		Gesture utilizes In-Environment Object as an interactor
Multiplicity		*Simple*		Gesture utilizes only one interactor
		Multiple		Gesture utilizes multiple interactors
Action Symmetry		*Symmetric*		Gesture utilizes multiple interactors performing similar motion
		Asymmetric		Gesture utilizes multiple interactors doing performing different motion
Interactor Homogeniety		*High*		Interactors are very similar in its form and function
		Medium		Interactors are only somewhat similar in its form and function
		Low		Interactors are not similar in its form and function
Complexity		*Simple*		Gesture involves an atomic gesture
		Compound		Gesture involves multiple atomic gestures
Motion Threshold		*None*		Gesture does not involve changes in position or rotation
		Position / Angle		Gesture involves changes in position/angle
		Velocity		Gesture involves changes in velocity/angular velocity
		Acceleration		Gesture involves changes in acceleration/angular acceleration
		Jerk		Gesture involves changes in jerk/angular jerk

Motion Threshold. This taxonomy focuses on the different ways position or rotation changes over time. This ranges from distance, velocity, acceleration, and jerk, as well as the angular equivalents. Some gestures may involve a simple change in distance to trigger the effects, while another may require a sudden forceful jerk.

Interactor. The interactor dimension specifies whether the interactor is a part of the user's body, an input device (such as a motion controller), or an in-environment object. The User Body is considered a category in our work that includes subcategories such as heads, hands, eyes, mouths, legs, and so on. Input Device includes headsets, motion controllers, 6DOF trackers, and so on. In-environment objects are any tracked objects, be they virtual or physical, that the user can interact with.

3.2 Gesture Mapping

We view any dimensions within the Gesture Mapping class as providing context from different perspectives and define the Gesture Mapping class as **"any quality that can be used as context to map an action to a different effect"**. Our taxonomy of Gesture Mapping is listed in Table 2.

Source of Meaning. The Source of Meaning dimension is the pool of knowledge and experience that the user and the audience draw upon to make sense of the gesture. The source could be based on understanding the laws of physics in the real world. Alternatively, the Hyperphysical category refers to the user understanding the gesture based on some alternate set of laws of physics that explain how objects and the world would work. Although very few things are truly universal, the Universal category refers to knowledge that is commonly known. In contrast, the Cultural category refers to knowledge that is limited to a specific group. Lastly, Arbitrary/None refers to gestures where there is no real-world source of meaning to draw upon.

Action Mapping and Effect Mapping. A gesture has a direct relationship in Action Mapping if the performed action matches the utilized meaning, such as the user running with legs as the interactor trying to convey the meaning of running. It would have an indirect relationship if the user mimics running with other body parts, such as fingers or arms.

A gesture has a direct relationship in Effect Mapping if the resulting effect matches the utilized meaning, such as the user's character running in response to the user's action conveying the meaning of running. If the same action and meaning lead to a different character running or a machine operating, then there is an indirect relationship.

Coordinate System. The Coordinate System dimension is critical in providing the audience with reference to make sense of most gestures. For this dimension, we propose the following categories: Object, Region, World, User, Interactor, Independent, and Mixed Dependencies.

Environment/Region. In XR, the user may travel between different environments, whether virtually or physically in real life. The user performing a finger-snapping gesture may open the garage door in the garage, play smooth jazz in the bedroom, and flush the toilet in the restroom.

Target. The Target dimension deals with whether or not the gesture is applied to specific targets. The target can be designated by prior actions such as a voice command or another gesture. It may also be designated in other ways and may not immediately change after the completion of the gesture. It can also be designated as part of a compound gesture using a simple gesture.

Table 2. Gesture taxonomy in the class Gesture Mapping.

Dimensions	Sub-dimensions	Categories	Description
Source of Meaning		*Physical*	Gesture derives its meaning from laws of physics
		Hyperphysical	Gesture derives its meaning from an alternate laws of physics
		Universal	Gesture derives its meaning from a generally universal set of values
		Cultural	Gesture derives its meaning from shared cultural values
		None	Gesture does not derives its meaning from any particular source; its arbitrary
Target		*Has Target*	Gesture has at least a target to interact with
		No Target	Gesture has no target to interact with
Action Mapping		*Direct*	Direct Relationship between Intent and Action
		Indirect	Indirect Relationship to Gesture between Intent and Action
Effect Mapping		*Direct*	Direct Relationship between Intent and Effect
		Indirect	Indirect Relationship to Gesture between Intent and Effect
Coordinate System		*Object / Interactable*	Coordinate system to process the gesture is based on an object
		Region	Coordinate system to process the gesture is based on a region
		World	Coordinate system to process the gesture is based on the world
		User	Coordinate system to process the gesture is based on the user
		Interactor	Coordinate system to process the gesture is based on the interactors
		Independent	No particular coordinate system is needed to process the gesture
		Mixed Dependencies	Use combination of coordinate system
Interaction Context		*Object*	Gestures require interaction with specific objects
		Region	Gestures require interaction with region-specific context
		World	Gesture require interaction with the world
		User	Gestures require interaction with the user
		Mixed Interaction Context	Gestures require interaction with multiple kinds of above components
		No Context	Gestures do not require interaction within any context
Temporal		*Continuous*	Action/task is performed during gesture
		Discrete	Action/task is performed after completion of gesture
Environment	*Region*	*Region-Associated*	Effect of gesture is relevant to which region it is performed in
		Region-Independent	Effect of gesture is independent from region
Social Context		*Private*	Only me
		Personal	My friends
		Social Groups	My teammates
		Public	Anyone else
User	*Proximity*	*Personal Space*	Gesture is performed in user's Personal Space
		Peripersonal Space	Gesture is performed in user's Peripersonal Space
		Extrapersonal Space	Gesture is performed in user's Extrapersonal Space
		Not Relevant	Gesture is performed in any space
	Posture	*Standing*	Gesture is based on User in the standing posture
		Sitting	Gesture is based on User in the sitting posture
		Lying Down	Gesture is based on User in the lying posture
		Other postures	Gesture is based on User in other postures not listed above
	Mobility	*Stationary*	Gesture is based on if the User is stationary
		Mobile	Gesture is based on if the User is travelling
		Mobile/Transportation Method	Gesture is based on the User's transportation method, e.g. bicycle, bus, car
Audience		*Human*	Gesture has human as the audience
		Rigid System	Gesture has a rule-based program as the audience
		Intelligent Agent	Gesture has an intelligent agent similar to human

4 Gesture System Architecture

We propose the following gesture system architecture for XR based on the gesture taxonomy discussed above. Our Gesture System Architecture is shown in Fig. 1. This architecture has two responsibilities based on the two classes in the gesture taxonomy. The first is responsible for detecting gestures based on

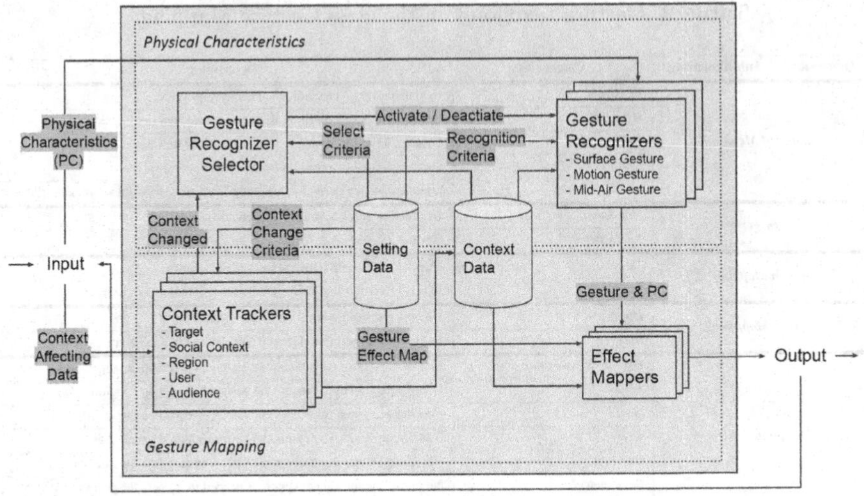

Fig. 1. Our proposed Gesture System Architecture

physical characteristics. The other responsibility is gesture mapping, which requires the system to track all the different factors and contexts.

A dotted region indicates whether a module contributes to Physical Characteristics or Gesture Mapping. Rectangular shapes indicate modules that are responsible for processing data. Stacked Rectangular shapes indicate multiple modules are available for processing data, depending on the provided data. Further, modules can be added and removed based on the developer's needs. Lastly, the cylinder shape indicates Data/Database used by the Gesture System.

Information about the world comes into this Gesture System as Input to the Context Trackers. Context Trackers use these Context Affecting Data to determine the current contexts, which are then stored in Context Data. It then sends an event to Gesture Recognizer Selector to inform which contexts have changed.

Upon receiving the event, Gesture Recognizer Selector uses the Context Data and Setting Data to determine and set the states of different Gesture Recognizers to be active or inactive.

If a Gesture Recognizer has been set active by the Selector, it will process PC Data along with Setting Data and Context Data to determine whether a gesture has been performed. Once it has recognized a gesture, it will send an event containing Gesture Data and relevant PC Data to the Effect Mappers.

The Effect Mapper will look at Gesture, PC, Setting, and Context Data to determine the effects. Each Effect Mapper would be associated with other systems that are capable of producing the desired effects.

Setting Data are used by each of the modules in the architecture. It is used by Context Trackers to determine the condition when a context would switch, the Gesture Recognizer Selector for selection, Gesture Recognizer to adjust its recognition criteria, and Effect Mapper to determine which effect a gesture would cause. While there is no explicit arrow going into the Setting Data, as a typical gesture recognition process would not change the Setting Data. However, developers can modify the Setting Data at compile time to suit their needs. Similarly, users can modify the Setting Data at run-time while in Gesture Edit Mode.

5 Conclusion

In this paper, We propose a new Gesture System Architecture in Extended Reality. It is based on our ongoing work of a multi-dimensional taxonomy of gestures in Extended Reality. Our Gesture System Architecture incorporates the two classes of dimension in the taxonomy - physical characteristics and gesture context mapping. The resulting Gesture System Architecture can easily incorporate any new dimensions proposed by future researchers by adding new modules to handle new contexts as well as new classes of gestures. The Gesture System Architecture is highly-customizable by both XR developers and users. We hope that our work can help improve efficiency and usability for gesture-based XR application design and user experience.

References

1. Aigner, R., et al.: Understanding mid-air hand gestures: a study of human preferences in usage of gesture types for HCI. Microsoft Res. TechReport MSR-TR-2012-111 **2**, 30 (2012)
2. Carfì, A., Mastrogiovanni, F.: Gesture-based human-machine interaction: taxonomy, problem definition, and analysis. IEEE Trans. Cybern. (2021)
3. Ens, B., Quigley, A., Yeo, H.S., Irani, P., Piumsomboon, T., Billinghurst, M.: Counterpoint: exploring mixed-scale gesture interaction for AR applications. In: Extended Abstracts of the 2018 CHI Conference on Human Factors in Computing Systems, pp. 1–6. ACM, Montreal QC Canada, April 2018. https://doi.org/10.1145/3170427.3188513, https://dl.acm.org/doi/10.1145/3170427.3188513
4. Milgram, P., Kishino, F.: A taxonomy of mixed reality visual displays. IEICE Trans. Inf. Syst. **77**(12), 1321–1329 (1994)
5. Ruiz, J., Li, Y., Lank, E.: User-defined motion gestures for mobile interaction. In: Proceedings of the SIGCHI Conference on Human Factors in Computing Systems, pp. 197–206 (2011)
6. Vafaei, F.: Taxonomy of Gestures in Human Computer Interaction. North Dakota State University, Fargo (2013)
7. Vuletic, T., Duffy, A., Hay, L., McTeague, C., Campbell, G., Grealy, M.: Systematic literature review of hand gestures used in human computer interaction interfaces. Int. J. Hum Comput Stud. **129**, 74–94 (2019)
8. Wobbrock, J.O., Morris, M.R., Wilson, A.D.: User-defined gestures for surface computing. In: Proceedings of the SIGCHI Conference on Human Factors in Computing Systems, pp. 1083–1092 (2009)

Change of Users' Eye Height Based on Their Moving Speed

Takuya Yoshimura and Yukio Ishihara(✉)

Shimane University, 1060 Nishikawatsu-cho, Matsue-shi, Shimane 690-8504, Japan
iyukio@ipc.shimane-u.ac.jp

Abstract. This research will seek an intuitive way of changing a user's eye level from 170 cm to 17 m, ten times higher than human eye levels, during moving fast in a virtual environment. Users' eye level was reportedly preferred at a high position as if being a giant, though it is still unclear how their eye level should transition from low to high positions when starting to move fast. We conduct an experiment in that users perform a simple task involving high-speed moving under two transition methods. Then we examine which method is appropriate and intuitive concerning the psychological burden the users feel. Finally, we show it is preferred that the eye level rises linearly rather than it teleports immediately, but no significant difference in the psychological burden.

Keywords: eye level change · high-speed moving · desktop-based virtual environment

1 Introduction

Imagine yourself in a town or city built in a virtual environment and going to some destination. Walking and running are the main means of locomotion because you would get similar visual experiences to those in the real environment. On the other hand, other ways of moving faster would be appropriate rather than walking and running when going far in a huge city.

In the research [1], Abtahi et al. reported that a user's eyes at a high level were preferred when moving at high speed in a virtual environment as if being a giant, which also reduced motion sickness. However, it remains to be seen how the user should transition between a human-sized person and a giant to change their eye level. Although the user could manually trigger the transition between the two whenever they want, this research will seek a more intuitive method that relates to and triggers the transition by the user's natural locomotion. Also, it creates inherently expected experiences.

Let's consider a simple method: a user's eye level changes between low and high when a predefined time passes after they start moving at 50 km/h, approximately ten times faster than the human walking speed (hereinafter called high-speed moving). What is the problem with this? The user might feel dizzy and disoriented because their eye level rises or lowers in the blink of an eye, leading

C. Stephanidis et al. (Eds.): HCII 2023, CCIS 1836, pp. 348–354, 2023.
https://doi.org/10.1007/978-3-031-36004-6_48

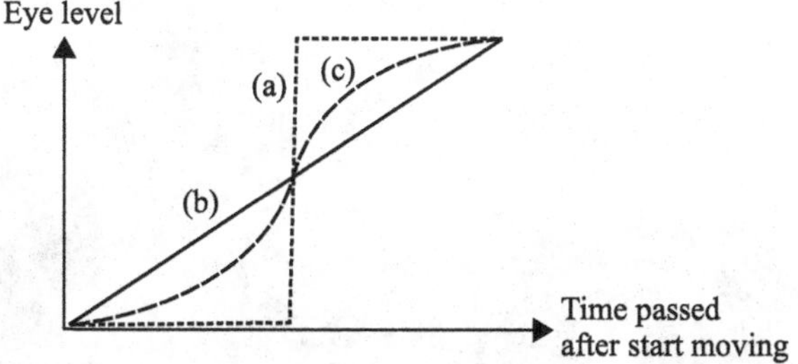

Fig. 1. Possible transition methods to change a user's eye level when transitioning from stationary to high-speed moving states, or 50 km/h. (a) shows a discrete transition, while (b) and (c) show continuous transitions.

Fig. 2. An overview of Shimane University.

to a significant change in their view. Thus, intuitive methods need to conduct continuous and gradual transitions, as shown in Fig. 1. (a) shows the discrete transition mentioned above. (b) and (c) shows continuous transitions in linear and nonlinear ways, respectively. As a first step, this research will compare (a) and (b) concerning how much psychological burden users feel.

2 Shimane University Built on Unity

We build the Shimane University campus in a virtual environment on the Unity platform(2021.3.9f1) provided by Unity Technologies, where users manipulate the mouse to walk freely and explore the campus. Figure 2 shows the main entrance of Shimane University, both on Unity(a) and site(b). As seen in (a), it renders buildings and streets using real photos, which follows the result of the research [2]. They reported that when creating objects in a virtual environment: buildings, entrances, windows, pillars, streets, or any objects, they should be as simple as possible to reduce motion sickness, and the texture of those objects should be realistic to create a sense of presence.

Figure 3 shows a user's view on the ground. The user can go forward by left-click of the mouse and backward by right-click. The user also can look around by

Fig. 3. A user's view from the main entrance.

sliding the mouse. To choose walking, running, or high-speed moving, the user needs to press predefined keys to turn into the corresponding mode. However, this research does not focus on walking or running. Thus, we do not change the mode but set it to high-speed moving.

Figure 4 compares the change of a user's view while high-speed moving under the two transition methods. First, the user stands at rest in front of the main gate, corresponding to the bottom row. Their eye level is 170 cm. After they start high-speed moving, the eye level is held for a while, then it will rise immediately to 17 m, ten times higher than the previous eye level. On the other hand, for the linear transition (b), the eye level will rise linearly as time passes.

3 Examination of Two Transition Methods

We built the Shimane University campus and recruited 12 subjects from our university. We asked them to complete a simple task. In the task, the subjects aim to get as many poles as possible for 60 s, which appear one after another on the campus. Figure 5 shows a set of poles that appear in ascending order. To get a pole, the subject needs to stop in the vicinity of two meters from each pole. Then, the pole disappears, and the next one will appear at the same time. The position of each pole was predefined and common among the subjects. Figure 6 shows an experimental setup where a subject sat one meter from the 50-inch display and performed the task. (b) shows a user's view when they started the task. Each subject was given a couple of minutes to get used to manipulating the mouse to move around in the virtual environment. Then, they performed two trials of the same task, one in the discrete transition and the other in the linear transition. Half of the subjects completed the discrete transition first, then the linear followed. The other half did vice versa to eliminate order effects. After each trial, they answered the questionnaire shown in Fig. 7. Although it shows the English version, we used the Japanese version and asked the subjects to answer it on a Likert-Scale from 1(I strongly disagree) to 5(I strongly agree).

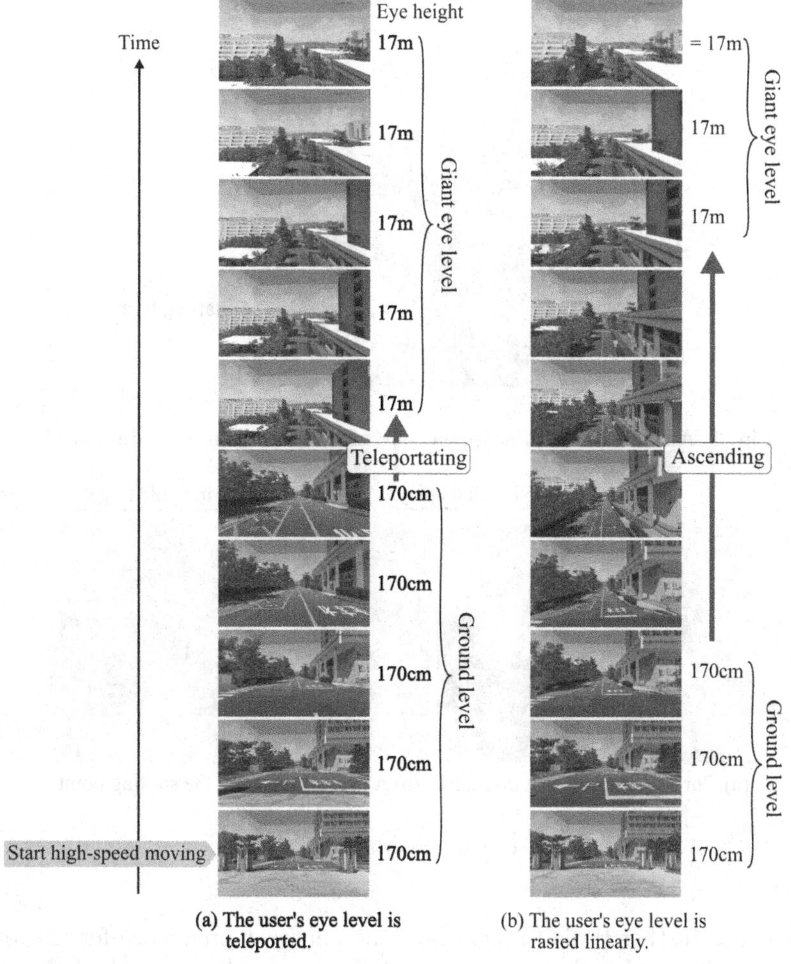

Fig. 4. Comparison of a user's view between the two transition methods.

After completing all subjects' trials, we analyzed the questionnaire results using the Wilcoxon signed-rank sum test. Figure 8 shows the result. None of the questions was found significant between the discrete and linear transitions. However, Q1 (I liked walking(moving) around in this mode) tends to be significant with $p < 0.1$.

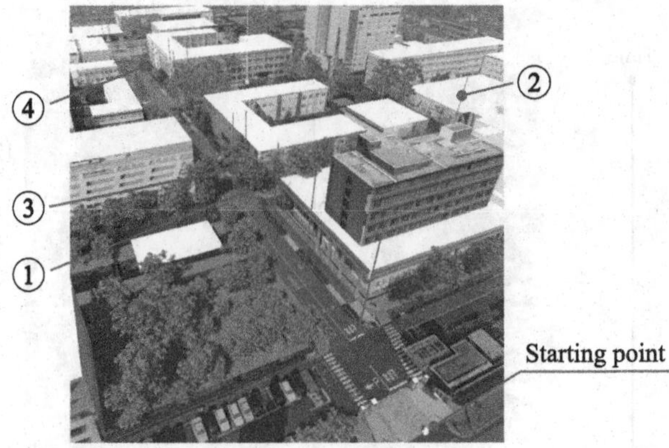

Fig. 5. A set of poles that appear one after another in ascending order.

(a) Our experimental environment (b) A user's view from the starting point

Fig. 6. Our experimental setup.

We need further trials to determine the apparent preference for discrete or linear transitions. In addition, we plan to seek a nonlinear method that more naturally fits our experience so that we would feel as if we were taking off and flying in mid-air during high-speed moving.

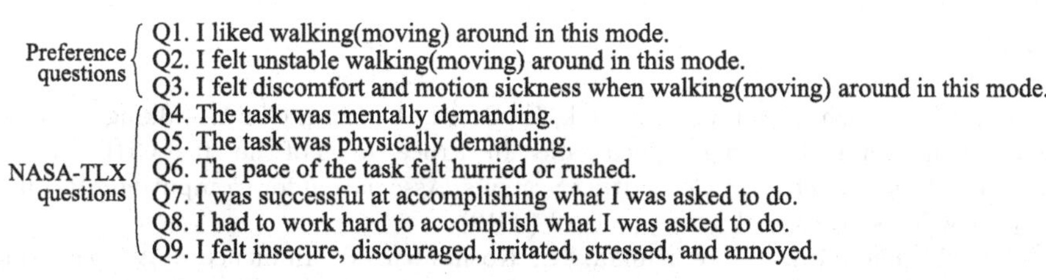

Preference questions
Q1. I liked walking(moving) around in this mode.
Q2. I felt unstable walking(moving) around in this mode.
Q3. I felt discomfort and motion sickness when walking(moving) around in this mode.
NASA-TLX questions
Q4. The task was mentally demanding.
Q5. The task was physically demanding.
Q6. The pace of the task felt hurried or rushed.
Q7. I was successful at accomplishing what I was asked to do.
Q8. I had to work hard to accomplish what I was asked to do.
Q9. I felt insecure, discouraged, irritated, stressed, and annoyed.

Q1. この環境で歩行（移動）することが好きですか？
Q2. この環境で歩行（移動）する際に不安定さを感じましたか？
Q3. この環境で歩行（移動）する際に不快さや車酔いを感じましたか？
Q4. どの程度の知的・知覚的活動（考える，決める，計算する，記憶する，見るなど）を必要としましたか？
Q5. どの程度の身体的活動（押す，引く，回す，制御する，動き回るなど）を必要としましたか？
Q6. 仕事のペースや課題が発生する頻度のために感じる時間的切迫感はどの程度でしたか？
Q7. 作業指示者によって設定された課題の目標をどの程度達成できたと思いますか？
Q8. 作業成績のレベルを達成・維持するために，精神的・身体的にどの程度いっしょうけんめいに作業をしなければなりませんでしたか？
Q9. 作業中に，不安感，落胆，いらいら，ストレス，悩みをどの程度感じましたか？

Fig. 7. Questionnaire.

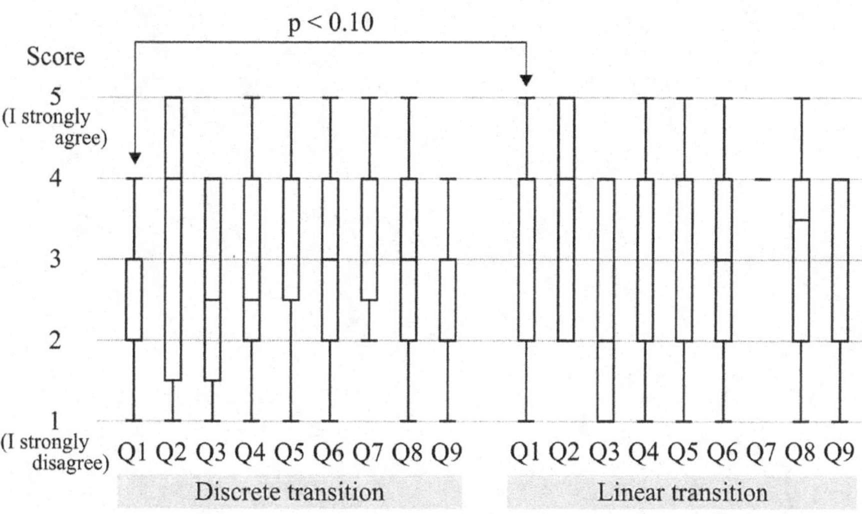

Fig. 8. Statistical analysis of the questionnaire results.

4 Conclusions

In this work, we built Shimane University on the Unity platform and examined which transition method: discrete or linear, was suitable during high-speed moving with respect to the psychological burden users feel. The result shows that the linear transition tends to be preferred but insignificant.

References

1. Abtahi, P., Gonzalez-Franco, M., Ofek, E., Steed, A.: I'm a Giant: walking in large virtual environments at high speed gains, In: Proceedings of the 2019 CHI Conference on Human Factors in Computing Systems. Association for Computing Machinery, New York, USA, vol. 522, pp. 1–13 (2019)
2. Fujiki, T., Ichimura, S., Terashima, K., Koshimizu, T.: Influence of VR content accuracy about reality and motion sickness with walk-through. Jpn. Soc. Educ. Technol. **36**, 73–76 (2012)

The Design Strategy of AR-Based Travel Experience in the Post-pandemic Era – An Exploratory Case Study in China

Yani Zhang and Han Han(✉)

Shenzhen University, Shenzhen, China
han.han@szu.edu.cn

Abstract. The Chinese tourism industry is transforming digitization and customization, and the COVID-19 pandemic has accelerated this trend. Tourists are increasingly seeking experiential tourism and this shift has made experiential tourism a vital focus of the industry. Augmented Reality (AR) technology has emerged as a promising tool to enhance the tourism experience. This study combines AR with experiential marketing and experience design to provide possible design strategies that utilize AR tools to promote a more comprehensive tourism experience. Adopting a case study-based qualitative research strategy with theoretical and empirical support, the study summarizes the advantages of AR in the tourism industry. It provides a design-driven approach that outlines design focuses from the five dimensions of the strategic experience module (SENSE, FEEL, THINK, ACT, and RELATE), effectively connecting marketing communication and AR-based tourism service experience. It lays the foundation for future research in two aspects: operational tools for design practices (user experience design, interface design, and service design in the tourism industry) and theoretical exploration in interdisciplinary subjects such as marketing communication, tourism management, and service design.

Keywords: Experience Design · Cultural Tourism · Augmented Reality

1 Introduction

1.1 Research Background

China's Tourism Industry is Shifting to Digitalization and Personalization. The prevalence of the Internet, artificial intelligence, 5G, and other technologies has influenced the structure of the tourism industry, driving it towards digitalization and customization. The emergence of the COVID-19 pandemic has accelerated this transformation. Domestic research suggests that the pandemic will have long-term and potential impacts on the tourism industry, changing its development pattern and intensifying competition among tourism enterprises [1]. In the post-pandemic era, all stakeholders in the tourism industry are actively seeking innovative changes, providing a rare opportunity

C. Stephanidis et al. (Eds.): HCII 2023, CCIS 1836, pp. 355–363, 2023.
https://doi.org/10.1007/978-3-031-36004-6_49

for the development and transformation of the tourism industry [2]. Against this backdrop, it is necessary to accelerate the innovation, upgrading, and optimization of the tourism product system. Through industry integration and cross-border cooperation, the tourism product system can be innovated and enriched, and a diverse and integrated development pattern of tourism products can be created. Furthermore, it is crucial to accelerate the digital transformation of tourism enterprises, enhance their management, service, and marketing operations with digital and intelligent technologies, and promote the innovation of digital tourism enterprises [3].

Tourists are Increasingly Seeking Immersive and High-Quality Experiences. The rapid economic growth has resulted in a marked increase in citizens' income and an optimization of travel consumption needs, shifting from mass tourism to a more personalized form [4]. The COVID-19 pandemic has impacted travelers' destination and product choices, prompting researchers to study tourist demand and enhance the attractiveness of tourism products to improve destinations' competitiveness. Following the pandemic, a greater number of people are expected to opt for short-distance local trips [5], and temporary adaptations to travel such as solo travel, small-scale group travel, luxury private tours, and health-oriented tourism are anticipated to gain popularity in China. The preference for slow-paced, immersive, and experience-focused high-quality travel is anticipated to rise [6]. To increase tourist satisfaction, smart tourism solutions and comprehensive tourism complexes can be developed [7]. Additionally, the Z-generation, whose consumption preferences are driven by experiences, shows a trend of relying on AR tools for both travel and entertainment, becoming a driving force in the growth of tourism consumption in the Chinese market [8].

1.2 Literature Review

Customer Experience in Tourism. In the tourism industry, customer experience is of great importance, comprising four elements: cognitive, affective, sensory, and conative. It is influenced by all stimuli encountered during the three stages of pre-consumption, during consumption, and post-consumption, including contextual and brand-related factors, and affected by individual differences, ultimately resulting in different outcomes related to the brand for consumers [9]. As economist Abbott mentioned in Quality and Competition, people desire satisfying experiences rather than products, which are achieved through activities. By providing an excellent customer experience, the tourism industry attracts and retains tourists, increases customer loyalty and satisfaction, and enhances word-of-mouth and repeat purchase rates. Excellent customer experience can be achieved through various means, such as providing personalized and customized tourism products, optimizing service processes, providing convenient booking and payment experiences, and offering a clean, safe, and comfortable tourism environment. With the development of digital and intelligent technology, the tourism industry is increasingly emphasizing the use of digital means to provide personalized, convenient, and all-around customer experiences.

Experiential Marketing. Schmitt proposed the concept of experiential marketing, which focuses on customer experience, in contrast to the narrow focus on functional features and benefits. According to Schmitt, experiences result from encountering, undergoing, or living through things and provide sensory, emotional, cognitive, behavioral, and relational values that replace functional values [10]. Additionally, Schmitt proposed the Strategic Experiential Modules (SEMs), which include sensory (SENSE), affective (FEEL), cognitive (THINK), physical, behavioral (ACT), and social-identity experiences (RELACT). Each SEM has its own objectives, internal structure, and principles, providing managers with a framework for creating and managing user experiences [10].

AR Technology. AR is a methodology for integrating virtual information into the physical world, utilizing tools such as multimedia, 3D modeling, real-time tracking, intelligent interaction, and sensing [11]. AR interaction can be executed through various channels, including mobile terminal-based AR interaction modes, head-mounted displays, mirrors, desktops, and holographic projections [12]. This unrestricted and immersive mode of information presentation offers a clearer and more engaging information display. In recent years, a growing number of research institutions, academic institutions, and businesses have invested in AR research, producing substantial scholarly articles and research outcomes, which demonstrate the viability and innovative aspects of AR technology [11]. The impact of AR technology on the tourism experience is reflected in its influence on people's perception of tourist destinations and consumption behaviors, thereby providing technical support for the continued improvement and enhancement of the tourism experience through experiential marketing.

2 Research Objectives and Research Method

The prior discussion highlights the substantial interest that AR technology has garnered in both the Chinese tourism industry and academic spheres. AR has been utilized in diverse domains, including digital tour guiding, heritage reconstruction, mobile tour guidance, and commercial promotion. This study endeavors to investigate how to improve the overall tourist experience through the adoption of rational strategies and methods via an interdisciplinary approach that encompasses marketing communication, tourism management, and service design.

This study adopts a qualitative approach and primarily utilizes case studies as its investigation method to provide theoretical and practical support. Theoretically, the literature on tourism experience strategy [10, 13–15] and the research on AR-based marketing [16–19] provides a foundation for the selection and analysis of cases. Empirically, 59 representative cases from 2020 to 2022 in China were selected and analyzed (such as the Mogao Caves, the Forbidden City, the Shanghai Museum, etc.). These cases were sourced from online searches and literature research, with the online search platforms being well-known Chinese Internet platforms such as WeChat, Zhihu, Weibo, Baidu, etc., and the literature materials were sourced from China National Knowledge Infrastructure.

3 Case Study of Tourism Based on AR

This study utilizes theoretical foundations to classify empirical cases of augmented reality (AR) marketing into three types based on the marketing functions of AR: ① AR for advertising, ② AR for product management, and ③ AR for customer service. These cases typically involve distinct content and utilize different AR tools to achieve specific AR marketing objectives (Fig. 1).

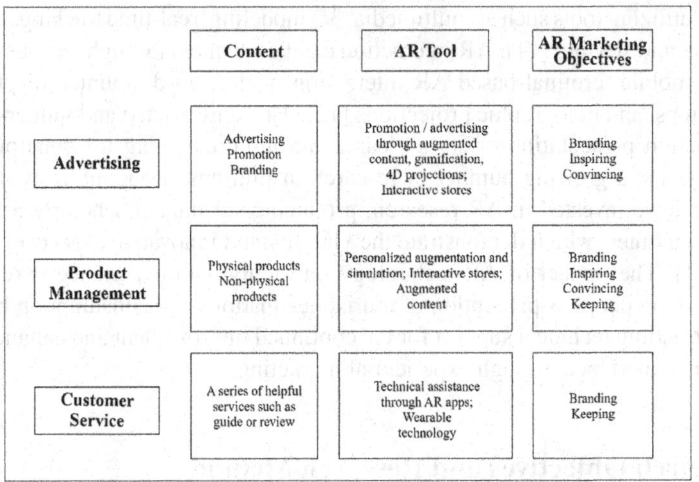

Fig. 1. Classification of AR Based on Marketing Functions.

The first type of AR (AR for advertising) encompasses advertisements, promotion and branding campaigns. The approach and focus of the usage of AR during the pre-journey and mid-journey phases are different. In the pre-journey phase, marketing efforts are typically centered around SENSE and ACT marketing, utilizing mobile device scanning for AR enhancement to stimulate potential travelers' senses and pique their interest. For example, cooperating merchants and hotels near a places/museum can display additional information through AR features in a mobile app to inform travelers and elicit consumer desire. For instance, the AR ticket (Fig. 2) at Ayi River scenic spot presents a scene of two people wearing traditional ethnic costumes rowing a boat, making it entertaining. Additionally, places/museums can offer AR tickets to travelers, allowing them to have a more realistic and dynamic audio-visual interaction with the site, thereby enhancing the travelers' pleasure during the journey. In the mid-journey phase, the focus of experience design shifts to sensory, cognitive, and associative marketing. Immersive experiences, storytelling, social interactions, and other designs become increasingly crucial for enhancing the tourists' experience, and technologies such as personal mobile devices, public interactive screens, AR glasses, and 4D projection are frequently utilized. The design of AR filters, for example, must consider the context of the scene, and allow for customization by travelers. Travelers taking photos with virtual characters or settings (Fig. 3) and sharing them on social software can promote the place.

Fig. 2. AR ticket

Fig. 3. AR character

Fig. 4. Palace Museum Calendar

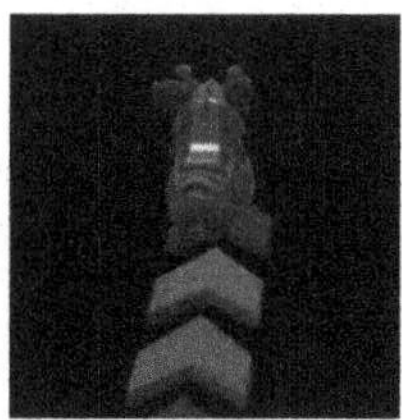

Fig. 5. Virtual guide

The second type of AR (AR product management) application, known as AR product management, involves both tangible and intangible products. The design focus of AR product management typically centers on the SENSE, FEEL, and THINK marketing. The challenge for AR product management is to enable travelers to experience personalized service, good interactivity, and knowledge acquisition. For example, AR product customization can be used to provide travelers with physical photos based on AR technology, allowing them to better recall their previous travel experiences. AR social media has emerged as a new focus, which goes beyond using AR filters to take photos or videos, and instead presents a completely new way of social interaction. The "Buwu Space" app enables users to record and share their feelings by placing AR time capsules in the space, which can also be effectively applied in places of prayer. AR cultural and creative products can be regarded as an upgraded version of traditional cultural and creative products, by adding AR technology to the foundation of tangible products, the product content is enriched. For example, the "Palace Museum Calendar" (Fig. 4) in Beijing allows buyers to scan through an AR mini program on WeChat and carefully observe the objects in the calendar, adding to the product's interest and attracting consumers to visit the Palace Museum. These types of AR cultural and creative products can serve as travel souvenirs or promotional materials.

The third type of AR (AR for customer service) refers to a series of activities and processes that provide support and assistance, such as guidance or review. The design focus is typically on SENSE, FEEL, THINK, and RELATE marketing, aiming to create immersive and user-friendly interactive experiences for travelers. For instance, AR guides and explanations need to be contextualized and sufficiently interactive, with external designs, adhering to principles of design. At tourist places/museums, interactive virtual guides can be created, that is strongly associated with the places and offer visitors a fun experience. For example, the Shanghai Museum designed a personal guide named "Xiaotong," (Fig. 5) which uses AR glasses to interact with visitors, including voice and gesture interactions with artifacts, enhancing the visitor's exhibition experience. AR narrative games combine immersive scene experiences, AR scene reproductions, and other interactive methods, to provide visitors with a more immersive and enjoyable tourism experience. Visitors can experience traditional culture and historical stories while following the game rules, such as the "Play and Travel in Southern Song Memory" activity in West Lake Scenic Area, which uses the above methods to make the visitors' travel experience more interesting.

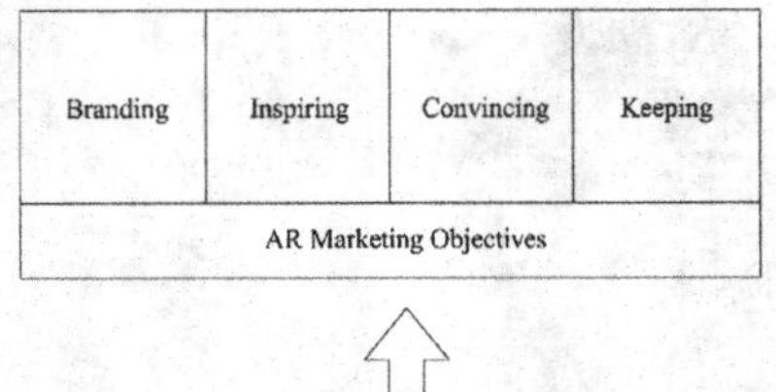

Strategic Experiential Modules	Design Focus Based On Experience Design	AR Tools
SENSE Marketing	Immersive Experience (e.g: Immersion, Presence, Aboutness)	Personalized augmentation and simulation; Augmented content; 4D projections
	Multimodal Interaction (e.g: Vision, Hearing, smell, Touch, Taste)	
FEEL Marketing	Narrative (e.g: Storytelling, Aboutness)	Personalized augmentation and simulation; Augmented content; 4D projections; Gamification
	Personized Service (e.g: Customized products, Customized experience)	
	Social Interaction (e.g: Social needs, Collaboration)	
	Gamification (e.g: Engagement, Happiness, Loyalty)	
	Interactivity (e.g: Guide, Feedback, Participation)	
THINK Marketing	Perceived Novelty (e.g: Learning, Satisfaction)	Personalized augmentation and simulation; Augmented content; 4D projections; Gamification
	Effective Cognition (e.g:Provide clear goals, Match skills with tasks)	
ACT Marketing	Endorsement (e.g: Celebrity, Idol)	Promotion / advertising through augmented content
	Co-branded (e.g: Famous brand, Idol,Celebrity)	
RELATE Marketing	Social-identity Experiences (e.g: Ace/Ethnicity, Gender, Social class)	Promotion / advertising through augmented content; 4D projections; Gamification
	Holistic Experiences (e.g: SENSE, FEEL, THINK, ACT, RELATE)	

Fig. 6. Strategy of AR-based Travel Experience

4 Results and Discussion

4.1 The Advantages of Applying AR Technology in Tourism Destinations

For tourists, AR technology can expand the perceptual dimensions and increase the cognitive depth. With its immersive and interactive features, AR technology can overlay digital information onto the real world, providing tourists with more comprehensive and entertaining information about the history, cultural background, and other relevant details of the scenic spots or museums. This enhances tourists' experience and engagement, making their perception and cognition more comprehensive.

For tourist places/museums, AR technology has strong flexibility. Through AR technology, the same scenic spot can present different scenes or characters. For example, the scenic places/museum can quickly change the scene according to different festivals or special events, bringing a fresh experience to tourists. This encourages short-distance travelers to revisit the place, providing support for the sustainable operation of tourist places/museums. Furthermore, AR technology can provide customized experiences for different tourist groups, meeting different travel purposes by changing the sensory and interactive aspects. For example, more interaction for family travelers and more explanations for educational tourists.

For businesses and hotels near tourist places/museums, AR technology provides a more convenient advertising channel. Businesses can cooperate with tourist places/museums to integrate advertisements or promotional information into AR scenes, allowing tourists to naturally understand the relevant information of the business and hotel in AR scenes. This enhances the businesses' and hotels' exposure, increases customer flow and sales, and also provides more information for tourists' choices.

4.2 Strategy of AR-Based Travel Experience

Figure 6 presents a strategic framework for creating AR-based travel experiences. This framework can be utilized by planners or organizers of attractions/museums to achieve their AR marketing objectives by employing suitable strategic modules at various stages of the customer journey. The framework is designed to enhance the overall customer experience by utilizing AR technology to provide multi-dimensional value, including sensory, emotional, cognitive, behavioral, and relational values, and create an immersive and memorable customer experience. This approach enables a comprehensive and holistic approach to designing and implementing AR-based travel experiences, promoting a customer-centric approach to experience design and marketing.

AR-Based SENSE Marketing in Tourism. SENSE marketing creates experiences that attract tourists' senses through visual, auditory, olfactory, tactile, and gustatory methods. Perception marketing is the focus of overall marketing in various stages of tourism and requires attention to multimodal interactions and immersion when designing experiences. AR tools typically include personalized augmentation and simulation, augmented content, and 4D projections. Showcasing the characteristics of a tourist place/museum through tickets or personal devices before the trip can easily capture customers' hearts and leave them with a good impression, increasing the likelihood of them visiting. Sensory marketing can enhance immersion and increase tourists' happiness during travel. For example, an interesting AR guide during the journey from one place to another can achieve this goal.

AR-Based FEEL Marketing in Tourism. FEEL marketing is a marketing method that aims to create positive emotional experiences, ranging from mild to intense, such as joy and pride. This stage requires narrative, personalized services, social interaction, gamification, and interactive design. The AR tools used typically include personalized augmentation and simulation, augmented content, 4D projections, and gamification. Storytelling through AR in experience design can bring tourists into the scenario and evoke their emotions. When designing interactions or games, it is necessary to consider the type of tourist and the difficulty of the interaction, and avoid giving tourists too much frustration, as few tourists enjoy negative emotions.

AR-Based THINK Marketing in Tourism. THINK marketing aims to attract tourists by stimulating their cognition and problem-solving abilities. This stage requires creating novelty and providing clear goals, matching skills with tasks. The AR tools used typically include personalized augmentation and simulation, augmented content, 4D projections, and gamification.

AR-Based ACT Marketing in Tourism. ACT marketing is a marketing method that stimulates tourists' motivation, inspiration, and emotions by displaying different lifestyles and interactive methods. This type of marketing can be achieved through celebrity endorsements or brand collaboration. The AR tools used typically include promotion/advertising through augmented content. The celebrity in the place/museum does not necessarily have to be a living person; it can also be a historical figure. For example, through AR, tourists can interact with historical figures to achieve the goal of ACT marketing.

AR-Based RELATE Marketing in Tourism. RELATE marketing is a holistic approach to marketing that encompasses the SENSE, FEEL, THINK, and ACT aspects of customer experience design. However, RELATE marketing goes beyond individual, personal experiences by linking individuals to something beyond their personal status, which may include ideals of the future self, group identification, or cultural affinity. AR tools, such as 4D projections and gamification, are commonly used in RELATE marketing, which aims to create connections between individuals and entities beyond themselves. To achieve the goals of RELATE marketing, attention must be given to travelers' social-identity experiences and the overall travel experience.

5 Conclusion

AR provides more possibilities for enhancing tourism experiences. This study categorizes AR into three types based on its marketing functions and identifies five key areas of AR-based experience design based on the strategic experience module, offering a reference framework for enhancing tourism experiences. This study lays the foundation for future research, not only in terms of manipulable tools for design practices (such as user experience design, interface design, and service design in the tourism industry) but also for theoretical exploration across the disciplines of marketing communication, tourism management, and service design.

References

1. Ma, C., Zhang, Y.: Exploration of the upgrading path of intelligentization for tourism passenger transport enterprises under normalized prevention and control of COVID-19. Price Theory Pract. **445**, 155–158 (2021)
2. Xia, J., Feng, X.: The impact of COVID-19 on tourism industry and its countermeasures. China Bus. Market **34**, 3–10 (2020)
3. Chen, Y., Xie, C.: Tourism development under normalized epidemic prevention and control: transformational opportunities and strategic optimization. Tourism Tribune **36**, 5–6 (2021)
4. Shu, B., Xu, Q.: Evolution of China's tourism industry and transformation of development in the post-epidemic era. J. South-Central Univ. National. (Hum. Soc. Sci.) **42**, 73–80+184 (2022)
5. Wang, R., Tang, X., Liu, Z., Wu, C.: Impact of COVID-19 on the homestay industry: An empirical study based on the four-quadrant model. China Market 1071, 59–62 (2021)
6. Wang, R., Song, R., Xu, Y.: New trends in tourism demand under the background of COVID-19: Based on a review of domestic and foreign literature. Resource Develop. Market, 1–16
7. Xiang, H., Hu, H.: The influence of ticket price perception on tourism satisfaction: a case study of Zhangjiajie Scenic Area. Price Theory Pract. **429**, 139–142 (2020)
8. Lai, Y., Zhou, H., Li, J.: Understanding China's "Z Generation" and embracing the new wave of consumption. Develop. Res. **39**, 44–55 (2022)

9. Grimaldi, S., Fokkinga, S., Ocnarescu, I.: Narratives in design: a study of the types, applications and functions of narratives in design practice. In: Proceedings of the 6th International Conference on Designing Pleasurable Products and Interfaces, pp. 201–210. (2013)
10. Schmitt, B.: Experiential marketing. J. Mark. Manage. **15**, 53–67 (1999)
11. Chen, Y., Wang, Q., Chen, H., Song, X., Tang, H., Tian, M.: An overview of augmented reality technology. In: Journal of Physics: Conference Series, p. 022082. IOP Publishing (2019)
12. Shi, J., Hao, J., Nie, Q.: Research on qiang culture redesign based on AR technology. In: HCI International 2022 Posters: 24th International Conference on Human-Computer Interaction, HCII 2022, Virtual Event, June 26–July 1, 2022, Proceedings, Part III, pp. 271–279. Springer (2022). https://doi.org/10.1007/978-3-031-06417-3
13. Godovykh, M., Tasci, A.D.: Customer experience in tourism: a review of definitions, components, and measurements. Tourism Manage. Perspect. **35**, 100694 (2020)
14. Lv, M., Wang, L., Yan, K.: Research on cultural tourism experience design based on augmented reality. In: Rauterberg, M. (ed.) HCII 2020. LNCS, vol. 12215, pp. 172–183. Springer, Cham (2020). https://doi.org/10.1007/978-3-030-50267-6_14
15. Han, D.-I., tom Dieck, M.C., Jung, T.: User experience model for augmented reality applications in urban heritage tourism. J. Heritage Tour. **13**, 46–61 (2018)
16. Rauschnabel, P.A., Felix, R., Hinsch, C.: Augmented reality marketing: how mobile AR-apps can improve brands through inspiration. J. Retail. Consum. Serv. **49**, 43–53 (2019)
17. Cranmer, E.E., tom Dieck, M.C., Fountoulaki, P.: Exploring the value of augmented reality for tourism. Tourism Manage. Perspect. **35**, 100672 (2020)
18. Javornik, A.: [Poster] classifications of augmented reality uses in marketing. In: 2014 IEEE International Symposium on Mixed and Augmented Reality-Media, Art, Social Science, Humanities and Design (ISMAR-MASH'D), pp. 67–68. IEEE (2014)
19. Rauschnabel, P.A., Babin, B.J., tom Dieck, M.C., Krey, N., Jung, T.: What is Augmented Reality Marketing? Its Definition, Complexity, and Future. vol. 142, pp. 1140–1150. Elsevier (2022)

Applications of AI Technologies in HCI

Artificially Intelligent and Interactive 3D Hologram

Sarah AlShaghroud[1,2], Amal AlShuwaier[1,2], and Lama AlRakaf[1,2(✉)]

[1] Software Engineering Department, Alfaisal University, Riyadh, Kingdom of Saudi Arabia
lsalrakaf@alfaisal.edu

[2] Human-Computer Interaction (HCI) Lab, Alfaisal University, Riyadh, Kingdom of Saudi Arabia

Abstract. An artificially intelligent and interactive 3D holographic assistant is a cutting-edge technology that aims to provide users with an immersive and engaging experience that will revolutionize the way humans interact with machines. The system utilizes holographic technology to display a virtual assistant that can interact with users through voice commands. The holographic assistant is designed to guide users through entertaining and enriching conversations, providing them with responses to questions as a conversational agent and assistance. The system is powered by artificial intelligence algorithms that enable the holographic assistant to understand and respond to user queries in real-time. The system's 3D display technology creates a lifelike image of the assistant, making the interaction feel more natural and intuitive. The proposed system utilizes a Multi-Model system in conjunction with a Holographic view, which leverages advancements in computer graphics and multimedia technologies to enhance the way people view and interact with the virtual world. This includes incorporating technologies like augmented reality (AR) and hologram display.

Keywords: Artificially Intelligent · Interactive · Hologram · Volumetric Projection · Humanoid · Holography

1 Introduction

Holographic spaces and volumetric objects have been designed for a wide range of applied domains such as telepresence [1], civil engineering [2] and education [3] just to name a few. Recent advances in graphics and visualization have contributed towards the rapid advances in the creation and deployment of holographic displays such as the systems described in [4] and [5].

1.1 Background

Holograms, natural language processing, and human-computer interaction (HCI) are three distinct areas of research that have become increasingly important in recent years. Each technology has its own unique characteristics and applications, but they are all

C. Stephanidis et al. (Eds.): HCII 2023, CCIS 1836, pp. 367–373, 2023.
https://doi.org/10.1007/978-3-031-36004-6_50

related in their ability to enhance communication and interaction between humans and machines.

Holograms are three-dimensional images that are created using optical technology. They can be used to create realistic representations of objects or people, and they have a wide range of applications in fields such as entertainment, medicine, and engineering. Holograms can be used to create immersive experiences that allow users to interact with virtual objects in a more natural way than traditional 2D interfaces.

The relationship between holograms, NLP, and HCI lies in their ability to facilitate communication between humans and machines. Research has shown that holograms can provide a more immersive experience for users by allowing them to interact with virtual objects in a more natural way than traditional 2D interfaces [6]. NLP enables computers to understand human language better, which makes it easier for users to communicate with machines using natural language instead of complex commands or programming languages. HCI focuses on creating interfaces that are intuitive and easy to use for humans so that they can interact with machines more effectively.

2 Natural Language Processing

2.1 Overview of NLP

Natural Language Processing (NLP) is a subfield of Artificial Intelligence (AI) that focuses on the interaction between human language and computers [7, 8]. In the context of holography, NLP involves the development of algorithms and computational models that enable computers to understand, interpret, and generate human language by the conversational agents in the holographic display [9].

2.2 Utilized NLP Techniques

The first step is to recognize the user's speech and understand the meaning behind it. This involves several processes, including speech recognition, syntactic analysis, and semantic analysis.

Speech Recognition. The holographic assistant uses automatic speech recognition (ASR) technology to convert the user's spoken words into text. This process involves analyzing the sound waves of the user's speech and matching them with pre-defined speech patterns to identify individual words.

Syntactic Analysis. Once the spoken words are converted into text, the holographic assistant applies syntactic analysis to understand the grammatical structure of the sentence. This involves identifying parts of speech such as nouns, verbs, and adjectives and analyzing how they are organized within the sentence.

Semantic Analysis. After analyzing the grammatical structure of the sentence, the holographic assistant applies semantic analysis to understand the meaning behind the words. This involves analyzing the context in which the words are used to determine their intended meaning.

Speech Synthesis. Once the holographic assistant has understood the user's speech, it generates a response. The response can be in the form of text or speech. If the response is in the form of speech, the holographic assistant uses speech synthesis technology to convert the text into spoken words.

Speech synthesis involves converting the text into phonemes, which are the smallest units of sound in a language. The holographic assistant then applies rules to generate the appropriate intonation, stress, and rhythm for the spoken words.

Interaction. The final step in the NLP process is interaction. The holographic assistant must be able to interact with the user in a natural way, using appropriate responses and prompts. This involves applying knowledge of natural language generation, dialog management, and context-awareness.

Natural Language Generation. The holographic assistant generates responses that are natural-sounding and appropriate for the context of the conversation. This involves selecting appropriate words and phrases, organizing them into grammatically correct sentences, and applying appropriate intonation and stress.

Dialog Management. The holographic assistant manages the flow of the conversation, ensuring that the user's requests are fulfilled, and any necessary clarifications are made. This involves keeping track of the context of the conversation and using appropriate prompts and responses to keep the conversation flowing smoothly.

Context-Awareness. The holographic assistant must be aware of the context of the conversation, including the user's previous requests and the current state of the system. This allows it to provide appropriate responses and suggestions based on the user's needs and preferences.

2.3 The Relationship Between NLP and HCI in the Hologram's Design Process

The hologram's structured interfaces, being they visual or oral, are designed to supply a partial solution to many difficulties of natural communication with virtual agents as noted in [10]. By utilizing NLP techniques, the conversational agent was designed to detect voice commands and produce a suitable response. Through natural language processing, the conversational agent can analyze the context of a conversation, identify the intent behind a user's message, and provide relevant information or assistance. With advanced NLP capabilities, user experience is enhanced due to the manner of interaction. Being able to interact with our system in a seamless and intuitive way results in more meaningful and personalized interactions with users.

3 Conversational Agents in Holographic Interactions

3.1 Conversational Agent's Conceptual Design

As shown on the state diagram in Fig. 1, the model undergoes several states during operation, starting with the listening state. This state is activated when the model actively awaits a voice command or query from the user to initiate a conversation, for example, "Hello Sydney." Once speech is detected and captured, the model transitions into the speech detected state. At this point, two options are available based on the clarity of the captured voice. If the voice command is unclear, the model will disregard it and return to the listening state for new commands. Conversely, if the voice is clear, the model proceeds to the processing state where speech is translated into text for the chatbot on the server to analyze. In the analyzed state, the chatbot composes a reply into an API response for Unity. This API response includes various data, such as the audio reply, animations (e.g. waving, explaining), phoneme data for the model to lip-sync the audio reply, and emotions. All this data is transmitted to Unity for visualization on the hologram. Once the streaming is complete, the model returns to the listening state to await new commands and continue the conversation.

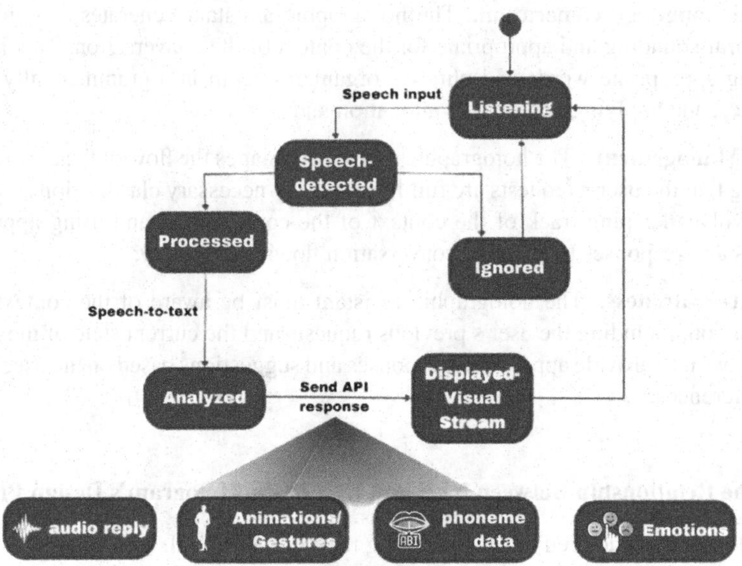

Fig. 1. State Diagram of an Interactive Hologram

3.2 The 3D Model of the Hologram's Visual Design

The 3D model was designed using the Unity reality engine which is a software platform that provides a range of tools that aid in the creation of objects in the virtual realm. As an audio response form, the 3D model is lip synced and has several gestures that align with the response, this adds a level of realism which contributes toward an immersive experience for users. The visual and auditory design aims to provide a seamless integration of sound and visuals that enhances the user's overall experience.

4 Hologram Gauze

4.1 Overview of the Materials Used in the Hologram Gauze

Hologram Gauze is a specialized textile material that is utilized for generating holographic displays. This fabric functions by reflecting light in a manner that gives rise to the impression of a three-dimensional image that appears to be suspended in mid-air. Hologram Gauze exhibits diverse applicability, particularly in fields such as entertainment, advertising, and performing arts. This methodology is often preferred due to its various advantages, such as ease of transportation. Projection gauze is lightweight and foldable, thus facilitating its transportability. The assembly time is minimal, as the apparatus can be promptly put together. It can be affixed to a truss, lighting bar, or frame, rendering it operational without delay. Moreover, this design occupies less space, as it is vertically oriented and obviates the necessity for a 45° mirror and a stage pit that accommodates a projection screen.

4.2 Design and Implementation

The creation of hologram gauze involves the use of a highly transparent metallic scrim composed of polyester or cotton with silver coating, which is affixed to a circular truss. The technique requires four high-lumens projectors which are installed on the ceiling, each placed at a 45-degree angle towards the gauze to project the 3D model from four different angles, including the front, back, left, and right views. Providing an immersive experience for the viewer (Fig. 2).

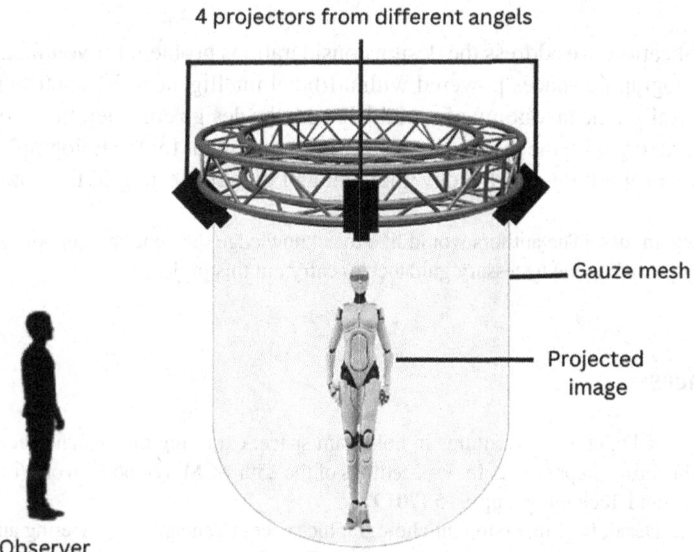

Fig. 2. Artificially Intelligent and Interactive 3D Model Integrated with Hologram Technology.

4.3 Interaction Design Considerations for Holograms

In this section, we present an overview of design considerations that are aligned with the taxonomy of social VR that was presented in [11]. The experience that a given feature in the hologram interaction is intended to augment varies as it pertains to the experience of the user (i.e. the self), interaction with others, or interacting with the physical and digital environment in the holographic experience.

Within the category of "Self" the design features include the avatar representation, customization, manipulation and traversal. The trade-offs between full-body vs partial-body avatars need to be considered in such designs. The tracking element of individuals in close proximity to the hologram space as well as gaze tracking of users interacting with the conversational agent would require detailed avatar manipulation and/or traversal.

Within the category of "Interacting with Others," the design considerations include communication types, communication privileges and activities for scaffolding the interaction. The aspects of designing interactions with voice, physical expressions such as gestures and the visualized bio-adaptive feedback collectively contribute towards a seamless user experience in interacting with the hologram.

Within the category of the "Environment," the design considerations include user manipulation of the environment such as altering the hybrid virtual-physical space which includes the avatar along with the hologram's design space, in addition to the spawning area. One additional aspect in the design is the context of interaction in public spaces which entails specific design considerations for auditory perception, visual perception and privacy considerations.

5 Conclusion

In this publication, we address the design considerations problem for volumetric projections in holographic spaces powered with artificial intelligence. We contribute with an approach to align the taxonomy of social VR with the design considerations for the user, others interacting with the avatar as well as the environment for the holographic display. Future lines of work involve the development and iterative testing of the hologram.

Acknowledgements. The authors would like to acknowledge the generous support of Dr. Areej AlWabil for providing the necessary guidance to carry out this project.

References

1. Anjos, R.K.D., et al.: Adventures in hologram space: exploring the design space of eye-to-eye volumetric telepresence. In: Proceedings of the 25th ACM Symposium on Virtual Reality Software and Technology, pp. 1–5 (2019)
2. Mutis, I., Desai, R.: Immersion into holographic spaces to enhance engineering and architecture design interpretations. In: Computing in Civil Engineering 2019: Visualization, Information Modeling, and Simulation, pp. 63–70. American Society of Civil Engineers, Reston, VA (2019)

3. Huang, H., Chen, C.W., Hsieh, Y.W.: Factors affecting usability of interactive 3D holographic projection system for experiential learning. In: Learning and Collaboration Technologies. Design, Development and Technological Innovation: 5th International Conference, LCT 2018, Held as Part of HCI International 2018, Las Vegas, NV, USA, July 15–20, 2018, Proceedings, Part I 5, pp. 104–116 (2018). Springer. https://doi.org/10.1007/978-3-319-91743-6_7
4. Nakamura, K., Yamamoto, K., Ochiai, Y.: Computer generated hologram optimization for lens aberration. In: SIGGRAPH Asia 2022 Posters, pp. 1–2 (2022)
5. Sahin, E., Stoykova, E., Mäkinen, J., Gotchev, A.: Computer-generated holograms for 3D imaging: a survey. ACM Comput. Surv. **53**(2), 1–35 (2020)
6. Huang, H., Chen, C.W., Hsieh, Y.-W.: How does a holographic AR display work? and what are its applications?, Holographic AR Display: A Cutting-Edge Technology Allowing Individuals to Interact Better with Digital Content. Research Dive (2023). https://www.researchdive.com/blog/how-does-a-holographic-ar-display-work-and-what-are-its-applications#:~:text=Holographic%20AR%20displays%20provide%20a,%2Ddimensional%20(3D)%20objects. Accessed 23 March 2023
7. Manaris, B.: Natural language processing: a human-computer interaction perspective. In: Advances in Computers, vol. 47, pp. 1–66. Elsevier (1998)
8. Karamanis, N., Schneider, A., Van Der Sluis, I., Schlogl, S., Doherty, G., Luz, S.: Do HCI and NLP interact?. CHI 2009 Extended Abstracts on Human Factors in Computing Systems, pp. 4333–4338 (2009)
9. Girish, P., Omkar, P., Shweta, D., Munot, S.: Holographic artificial intelligence assistance. JournalNX - A Multidiscipl. Peer Rev. J. 230–233 (2021). Retrieved from https://repo.journalnx.com/index.php/nx/article/view/1928
10. De Angeli, A., Petrelli, D.: Bridging the gap between NLP and HCI: a new synergy in the name of the user. In: Proceedings of the CHI 2000 Workshop on Natural Language Interfaces, vol. 4 (2000)
11. Jonas, M., Said, S., Yu, D., Aiello, C., Furlo, N., Zytko, D.: Towards a taxonomy of social vr application design. In: Extended Abstracts of the Annual Symposium on Computer-Human Interaction in Play Companion Extended Abstracts, pp. 437–444 (2019)

Toward an AI-Collaborated Authoring Tool for Writing Flash Fiction

Byung-Chull Bae[1(✉)], Yeji Kim[2], Mingyeong Yu[3], Seyoung Park[3], Youngjune Kim[3], and Yun-Gyung Cheong[4]

[1] School of Games, Hongik University, Sejong, South Korea
byuc@hongik.ac.kr

[2] School of Design Convergence, Hongik University, Sejong, South Korea

[3] NCSoft, Seongnam, South Korea
{yuminkyeong8,park30,youngjune}@ncsoft.com

[4] Department of AI, SKKU, South Korea The Social Innovation Convergence Program, SKKU, Suwon, South Korea
aimecca@skku.edu

Abstract. Flash fiction refers to short stories, usually around 1,000 words, featuring characteristics such as criticism, satire, and twists at the climax. This paper describes the design of an authoring tool prototype that leverages artificial intelligence technology to help novice writers easily create flash fiction. With our prototype, users can develop a plot outline by selecting a sequence of appropriate story units, then complete a story by filling in the text description. In addition, users can manually enter keywords as hashtags, or relevant hashtags can be automatically generated based on the user's writing. Hashtags thus act as a means of communication between the user and AI during the story-writing process. After the completion of the prototype, we plan to conduct a pilot study with amateur/professional writers to investigate the prototype's usability.

Keywords: Authoring tool · Flash fiction · Prototype

1 Introduction

Various AI authoring tools are emerging with rapid advances in neural language models [4,6]. While these tools provide compelling features with language generation and story coherence, they often need more narrative aspects. This paper proposes an authoring tool prototype to co-write with AI, mainly to write flash fiction with a twist ending. To this end, we focus on two issues. One is to clarify story units similar to the narrative functions defined by Vladimir Propp [5]. The other is to provide an overall outline and procedure of the prototype.

Propp's 31 "narratemes" or "narrative units" explain a plot structure commonly appearing in traditional Russian folktales. Inspired by Propp's work, we defined 17 story units (Proposal, Constraints, Prohibition, Dilemma, Acceptance, Acquisition, Utilization, Qualm, Confession, Accident, Penance, Attempt,

C. Stephanidis et al. (Eds.): HCII 2023, CCIS 1836, pp. 374–379, 2023.
https://doi.org/10.1007/978-3-031-36004-6_51

Success or Failure, Discovery, Twist, Price, and Hidden Truth) based on the selected flash fiction written by Kim Dong-sik (see Fig. 1). Kim is a well-known novelist in South Korea, publishing more than 300 flash fiction since 2018. We also build a dataset for story units by annotating selected story samples.

In our prototype, users can develop a plot outline by selecting a sequence of appropriate story units, then complete a story by filling in the text cell. The user can manually enter keywords as hashtags in the "Text Description" cell, or relevant hashtags are automatically generated based on the user's writing. Hashtags thus act as a tool for communication between the user and AI.

Act	No.	Story Unit	Description
Act I	1	Proposal	A protagonist is given a proposal that is hard to refuse - a basic description of a story idea.
	2	Constraints	Rules or constraints accompany the proposal that the protagonist should follow.
	3	Prohibition	A specific rule or behavior is not allowed by the protagonist. (It can be combined with the Constraints unit.)
	4	Dilemma	The protagonist faces a dilemma of whether to accept or reject the proposal. The protagonist's needs or desires are also described.
	5	Acceptance	The protagonist accepts the proposal.
	6	Acquisition	The protagonist acquires a special gift or tool through which the protagonist's desires are fulfilled.
Act II	7	Utilization	The protagonist utilizes the acquired gift or tool to satisfy their needs/desires.
	8	Qualm	The protagonist comes to have qualms about utilizing the acquired gift or tool as it accompanies immoral or unethical results.
	9	Confession/ Disclosure	Some facts unknown to the reader are revealed by the protagonist's confession (or by other characters' disclosure).
	10	Accident/ Violation	An accident happens so that the prohibition is violated.
	11	Penance	The protagonist regrets the misbehaved acts that he did.
	12	Attempt	The protagonist tries to correct the situation.
	13	Success or Failure	The protagonist's attempt is succeeded or failed.
Act III	14	Discovery	The protagonist recognizes a new fact that they did not know.
	15	Twist	An unexpected event happens, or new information is revealed.
	16	Price	The protagonist pays the price for their behavior.
	17	Hidden Truth/ Explanation	An untold hidden truth is revealed, and the surprise is resolved.

Fig. 1. 17 story units based on Kim Dong-sik's selected short stories

2 Prototype Design

2.1 Design Consideration

Our ultimate goal is to build a creative platform for beginners who want to write flash fiction with ease. The target user also includes novice authors who wish to get help from AI during the story-writing process. The primary design considerations are as follows:

- Design as simple as possible and to be similar to familiar text writing formats, considering users who are unfamiliar with authoring tools.
- Consider various situations during writing to avoid disrupting the user's writing flow.
- Improve writing speed by deleting and modifying the text paragraphs with ease.

We consider a web-based platform as the final implementation. As for design references, we refer to web-based text writing and creative forms such as Google Colab and other blogging sites. The initial screen of our prototype is shown in Fig. 2.

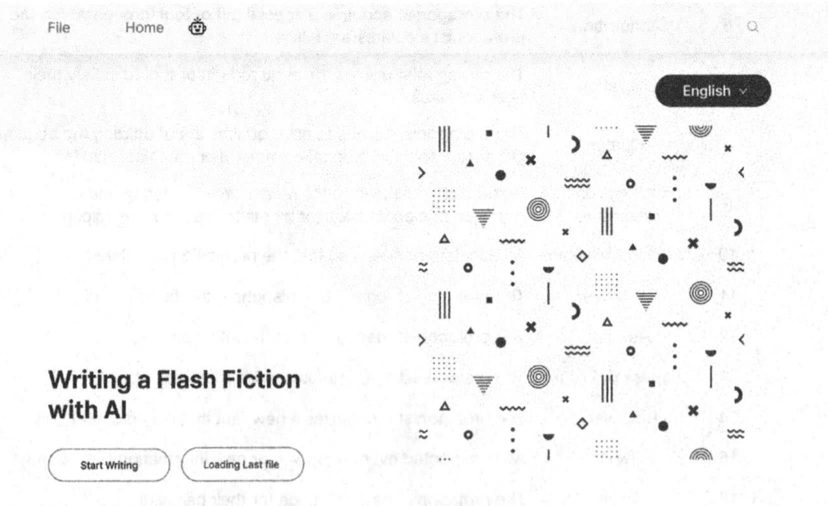

Fig. 2. Initial screen of the authoring tool prototype

2.2 Features

One of the primary features of this authoring tool is that users can select predefined story units. Users can develop their stories based on the 17 story units defined from Kim Dong-sik's collection of selected short stories.

We posit that the users generally conceive the plot outline first and then flesh out the text description. Based on this assumption, the main screen consists of two parts - Plot Outline and Text Description - as shown in Fig. 3.

The proposed authoring tool prototype is based on a text cell. When a text cell is selected, an editing bar appears to adjust the text cell so that the users can modify the location of the text cell and delete or add it. The prototype includes the features as follows:

- **Basic Text Editing**: The tool supports the basic functions of text editing - write, delete, and modify.
- **Story Unit Selection**: Users can select the most appropriate story unit based on their writings. It is also possible for AI to recommend candidate story units based on the text written by the user.
- **Hashtag Selection or Automatic Generation**: Users can manually add appropriate hashtags under the text cell, and it is also possible that AI can automatically generate proper hashtags. Each hashtag can be deleted with a single click, and the AI-made hashtags are distinguished from the user-made ones by using different colors.
- **Automatic Text Completion**: Users can click the robot-shaped AI button on the top bar to create appropriate text descriptions based on the plot outline and the hashtags.
- **Re-recommendation**: If the user does not like the AI's recommendation text, they can click the re-recommend button in the upper right corner of the text cell. Then the AI will recommend another text description.
- **View The Whole Story**: The tool provides writing and reading modes. In the writing mode, users can freely write and modify what they write with the collaboration of AI, moving the plot outline and the text description cell up and down. In the reading mode, users can view the whole story without modifying it by clicking the view button at the bottom of the screen.

2.3 Collaboration with AI

Recent applications for story generation actively utilize story data collection and composition by various approaches - such as crowdsourcing, common sense-based inference models [2] - by exploiting large-language models such as GPT-3 [1] or the new GPT-4. This paper adopts the following two tasks based on state-of-the-art natural language generation technologies.

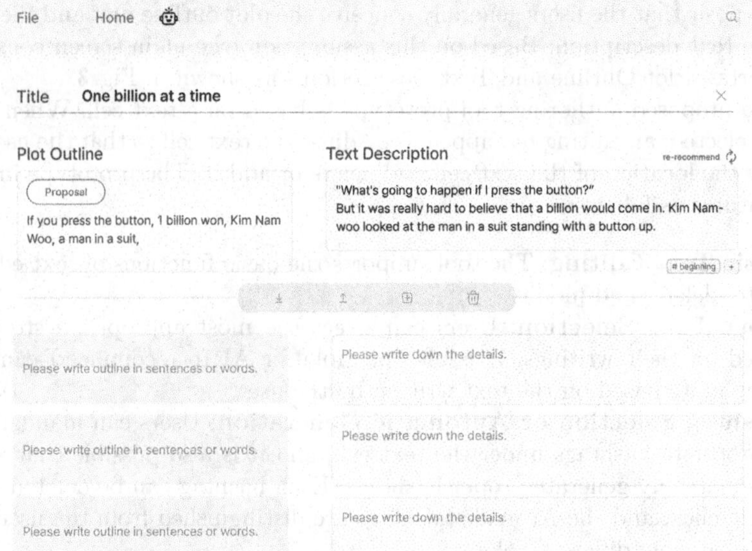

Fig. 3. Main screen of the authoring tool prototype

- **Hashtag generation**: The tool generates appropriate hashtags to represent user-generated text in real-time. The properly generated hashtags can serve as a means of communication between users and the AI. We adopt text summarization techniques [3] for generating hashtags.
- **Text generation**: The tool can generate text (or paragraphs per particular story unit) with the help of large language models, such as GPT-3/GPT-4. The model will need additional training data to generate text descriptions properly. Currently, we are making annotated dataset with the defined 17-story units. After the annotation completes, we will fine-tune the language model fitting for generating flash fiction with a twist ending.

3 Conclusion

This paper proposes an AI-collaborated authoring tool prototype that helps users write flash fiction easily. The proposed prototype was designed based on story units after analyzing Kim Dong-sik's selected short stories. In addition, the tool employs hashtags to communicate between the user and the AI with the help of generative language models such as GPT-3 and the new GPT-4. In future work, after the completion of the prototype, we plan to conduct a pilot study with amateur/professional writers to investigate the prototype's usability.

Acknowledgements. This work was supported by the National Research Foundation of Korea (NRF) grant (2021R1A2C1012377, 2019R1A2C1006316).

References

1. Dale, R.: Gpt-3: What's it good for? Nat. Lang. Eng. **27**(1), 113–118 (2021). https://doi.org/10.1017/S1351324920000601
2. Emelin, D., Le Bras, R., Hwang, J.D., Forbes, M., Choi, Y.: Moral stories: situated reasoning about norms, intents, actions, and their consequences. In: Proceedings of the 2021 Conference on Empirical Methods in Natural Language Processing. pp. 698–718. Association for Computational Linguistics, Online and Punta Cana, Dominican Republic (November 2021). https://doi.org/10.18653/v1/2021.emnlp-main.54, https://aclanthology.org/2021.emnlp-main.54
3. Kim, E., Yoo, T., Cho, G., Bae, S., Cheong, Y.G.: The CreativeSumm 2022 shared task: A two-stage summarization model using scene attributes. In: Proceedings of The Workshop on Automatic Summarization for Creative Writing. pp. 51–56. Association for Computational Linguistics, Gyeongju, Republic of Korea (October 2022), https://aclanthology.org/2022.creativesumm-1.8
4. Mirowski, P., Mathewson, K.W., Pittman, J., Evans, R.: Co-writing screenplays and theatre scripts with language models: an evaluation by industry professionals (2022). https://doi.org/10.48550/ARXIV.2209.14958, https://arxiv.org/abs/2209.14958
5. Propp, V.: Morphology of the Folktale. University of Texas (1968)
6. Yuan, A., Coenen, A., Reif, E., Ippolito, D.: Wordcraft: story writing with large language models. In: 27th International Conference on Intelligent User Interfaces. pp. 841–852. IUI 2022, Association for Computing Machinery, New York, NY, USA (2022). https://doi.org/10.1145/3490099.3511105

Generative AI for Immersive Experiences: Integrating Text-to-Image Models in VR-Mediated Co-design Workflows

Chris Bussell, Ahmed Ehab, Daniel Hartle-Ryan, and Timo Kapsalis(✉)

Derby Urban Sustainable Transition (DUST), University of Derby, Derby, UK
{c.bussell,t.kapsalis}@derby.ac.uk

Abstract. Text-to-image AI models can generate novel images for design inspiration. Yet, their applications for collaborative design (co-design) purposes and interoperability within simulation-based, immersive settings have been scarcely explored. In this paper, we propose a novel, multi-modal approach for interactive public participation in urban design projects. The main objectives of our research are (a) to describe a methodological workflow of integrating text-to-image AI models into VR-mediated co-design workshops, and (b) to investigate the applicability of the proposed workflow through a set of completed and prospective case studies. Both studies are parts of a broader research project, which aims to revitalize the city of Derby, UK through producing a series of sustainable design visions. Through these case studies, we discuss some preliminary results and introduce our future work.

Keywords: Virtual Reality (VR) · Text-to-Image · Generative AI · Co-design · Urban Design

1 Introduction

Public participation is a process that involves engaging members of the public in decision-making processes that affect their lives, communities, and environment [11]. In an urban design context, the goal of public participation is to foster greater transparency, accountability, and democratic governance, by ensuring that the voices and perspectives of all stakeholders are taken into account [12]. Collaborative design (or, *co-design*) workshops have been regularly applied by city officials as well as design professionals and researchers to effectively engage local stakeholders in urban processes, such as neighborhood regeneration schemes [13]. A co-design workshop typically involves a series of structured activities to facilitate a shared understanding of the challenge being addressed and generate ideas for potential design solutions that better reflect the needs and preferences of the local population [14]. In many cases, designers have employed tools and techniques from the field of Human Computer Interaction (HCI) – for instance, visual representation in digital forms – to facilitate stakeholders' participation in the process of designing the built environment, thus resulting in participatory and interactive paradigms of urban dialogue [15, 16].

C. Stephanidis et al. (Eds.): HCII 2023, CCIS 1836, pp. 380–388, 2023.
https://doi.org/10.1007/978-3-031-36004-6_52

1.1 Theoretical Background

Virtual Reality (VR) is a computer-generated immersive experience that simulates a three-dimensional environment in which users can interact with digital content in real-time [1]. VR is being increasingly applied in the built environment industry for various purposes, such as design collaboration, design review, performance analysis, and facility management. Specifically, VR enables designers, clients, and other stakeholders to experience and evaluate a building project before construction, facilitating design decision-making and problem-solving [2]. Moreover, VR provides a more efficient and effective way of reviewing design elements than traditional methods, and allows for interactive and immersive training and simulation of building operations and maintenance. Additionally, VR can enhance user experience and engagement in a building project, contributing to greater user satisfaction and ultimately improving the success of the project [5].

VR has emerged as a promising technology for urban design collaboration. It offers immersive and interactive experiences to urban design stakeholders, including citizens, planners, designers, and policymakers, by creating a 3D virtual environment that can be navigated in real-time [3, 4]. In recent years, several studies have explored the potential of VR in urban design collaboration, covering a range of topics, such as public participation, decision-making, and stakeholder engagement [5, 6, 9]. VR has been used for visualizing urban design scenarios, assessing the impact of design decisions on the environment and the quality of life, and enhancing collaboration among stakeholders [33]. These studies have shown that VR can facilitate a more effective and inclusive urban design process, leading to better outcomes in terms of design quality, social equity, and environmental sustainability [6, 7].

The creation of an immersive VR model for collaborative urban design poses several challenges that must be addressed in order to ensure its success. These challenges include the design of a VR model that accurately represents the complexities of real-world urban environments, which requires a high level of detail and precision and the integration of a diversity of data sources such as Geographic Information Systems (GIS) and Building Information Models (BIM) [8]. Additionally, the development of a framework that supports multi-user collaboration in a user-friendly and effective manner is crucial and requires careful consideration of the user interface and interaction design. The system must provide the necessary tools for users to manipulate and interact with the VR model, while also being intuitive and straightforward to use. Furthermore, ensuring the accessibility of the VR model to all collaborators, regardless of their technical expertise or equipment, requires the creation of a scalable and flexible system that can accommodate a wide range of hardware and software configurations [4, 9, 10]. In conclusion, overcoming these challenges is critical for the success of VR-based collaborative urban design initiatives, as it enables urban designers to collaborate effectively and create innovative designs that accurately reflect the complexities of real-world urban environments.

Recent advancements in the field of artificial intelligence (AI), especially with respect to image generation and natural language processing tasks, have led to the increasing application of machine learning to domain-specific aspects of the built environment [17, 18]. The proliferation of AI generative models, such as Variational Autoencoders [19] and Generative Adversarial Networks [20], have allowed design professionals and researchers to recreate images of buildings, districts, and cities in a bid to explore design alternative options, integrate contextual data, and improve communication of design proposals. More recently, diffusion models have been developed as a more powerful technique for image generation. Some popular generative models include DALL-E 2 [21], Stable Diffusion [22], Imagen [23], and Make-a-Scene [24], which all utilize natural language processing algorithms to generate images from textual descriptions given by the user. Text-to-image diffusion models simulate the distribution of the corresponding image using a diffusion process that iteratively refines the image over multiple steps [25]. This process enables the model to capture complex visual details and synthesize images that are both diverse and realistic [26, 27]. It has been observed that images generated through diffusion processes are more accurate to what humans would perceive to be real, when compared to those produced by other generative models [28–30].

Despite the emergence of generative AI, remarkably little research has hitherto focused specifically on possible uses of text-to-image models for urban design purposes [18]. A recent study, which delved into this topic, evaluated the potential for text-to-image models to design realistic images and scenes with a view to supporting urban design processes [31]. After a series of software experiments, researchers concluded that AI-generated imagery could reflect the human perception on various aspects of the built environment, such as design qualities [31]. They thereby suggested that text-to-image models might have the potential to substitute population surveys as a tool for gathering human feedback on urban design matters [31]. Drawing on this claim, researchers from Toretei and SPIN Unit have developed *Urbanist AI*, a generative AI platform for participatory planning [32]. The platform leverages natural language processing tools to enable community members with limited design experience communicate their ideas on urban revitalization schemes and create urban design scenarios using textual prompts [32]. Urbanist AI was recently employed by the City of Helsinki as the main tool for a series of co-design workshops, which intended to study local community's preferences with respect to redesigning certain streets of the city [32]. Workshop participants produced numerous alternative visions, which were later collated and discussed with city officials and planning consultants [32]. Whilst both pieces of research are regarded as encouraging steps towards validating the potentiality of generative AI for co-creating urban design scenarios, neither have dealt with (a) communicating the AI-generated concepts in various formats other than images (e.g., VR environments), and (b) subsequently exploring users' interactions with neoteric and multi-modal visualization techniques. By addressing both aspects, the present research provides a significant opportunity to advance the understanding of text-to-image models, from an HCI perspective.

1.2 Purpose

In this paper, we propose a novel, multi-modal approach for interactive public participation in urban design projects. The main objectives of our research are (a) to describe a methodological workflow of integrating text-to-image AI models into VR-mediated co-design workshops, and (b) to investigate the applicability of the proposed workflow through a series of completed and prospective case studies.

2 Methodology

We propose a workflow of integrating text-to-image AI models into VR-mediated co-design workshops to support urban design interventions. For the prospective co-design workshops, we assume that at least one study participant and one investigator will partake in a co-design session. In an urban design context, members of the community (e.g., residents, local entrepreneurs, and action groups) as well as planning authorities will comprise the group of participants. The proposed workflow consists of five steps, which are analyzed below:

- *Step 1 – simulation of the current urban settings.* Firstly, the investigators create a virtual 3D model of the real-world environment, such as a city street or region, whose design they intend to revision. For our experiments, we have created the models using the Rhino 3D software. The simulated model is typically a three-dimensional mesh of polygons that defines the surface geometry of the object or objects included, such as buildings, landscape elements, and street infrastructure. The model should precisely represent the physical attributes and characteristics of the actual urban environment. As soon as the investigators create the digital replica for the area-of-interest, they need to export a two-dimensional representation (i.e., base image) of the model along with a depth map of the exported image. Investigators can choose among top, side, or axonometric views of the model to export as a base image for the next steps. They can also select multiple base images corresponding to different perspectives of the model to better inform the design ideation process.
- *Step 2 – generation of participants' visual input.* Base images along with their depth maps are then imported into a platform for text-to-image generation. For our experiments, we have selected Stable Diffusion, a pre-trained text-to-image model, as the basic component of the generative platform, which we then custom-built using the Grasshopper3D component of Rhino3D software. The platform will enable workshop participants to generate images from textual descriptions of their alternative visions for the study area. For example, if an instance of a residential building block is presented as a base image, participants can provide prompts of their preference, such as "a building with a brick façade", to recreate a visualization of the initial building coated in a brick-made frontage. The pre-trained, text-to-image model that underpins the platform will then return a recreated image according to the given prompt. The integration of the base-image depth localizes the generation of alternative scenes for the base image based on participants' prompts. This step can be repeated multiple times until the output image satisfies participant's requirements. In the case that more than one base image has been selected, the step is also repeated for as many times as appropriate.
- *Step 3 – selection of design scenarios.* Next, the investigators collate all images generated by participants' text prompts to identify the most prevalent features on images. Those can refer to natural elements (e.g., trees), built elements (e.g., curb ramps), or design qualities (e.g., cycle infrastructure). The collation process is achieved through an integrative method, which combines recognition of similar patterns in the generated images and counting the frequency of specific words or phrases used by participants to construct their prompts. For instance, if the word "trees" has been found multiple times among participants' prompts and tree-like patterns have been repeatedly

detected by the visual analysis, it is very possible that most participants would prioritize trees for the reimagined area. As soon as the investigators identify the most significant elements based on participant generations, they should be able to synthesize appropriate design scenarios for the area of study. The exact number of scenarios produced as well as level of design intervention applied depend on investigators' intentions and requirements of different projects.

- *Step 4 – 3D modelling and animation of the selected scenarios.* Once a design scenario is selected, the first step is to model the design of the scene using 3D modelling software. Autodesk Maya and Houdini were chosen for this task due to their high capabilities in creating a detailed and high-fidelity model. Following the modelling stage, the models are then exported to real-time rendering software such as Unreal Engine 5. This software is utilized to refine the model's lighting, materials, and textures in preparation for the animation phase. The animation phase in Unreal Engine 5 plays a critical role in the development of an immersive virtual reality (VR) model for collaborative urban design projects. The purpose of this phase is to enliven the three-dimensional (3D) representation of the urban environment, thereby creating a realistic and interactive experience for stakeholders. The animation phase involves the integration of interactive elements and animations into the 3D model, including dynamic elements such as traffic, people, and other factors that contribute to the immersive experience.
- *Step 5 – functionality of an interactive VR platform.* The final stage in this workflow involves creating an interactive virtual reality (VR) platform using the Unreal Engine 5 game engine to project the animated scenes and models into an immersive environment. Building an interactive immersive model for VR requires advanced coding skills from investigators and the use of visual scripting languages such as Blueprints or C++. Through this process, investigators can add interactivity to the VR model by incorporating elements such as user-controlled movements, object interactions, and animations. This stage represents a crucial step in the development of an immersive VR experience, as it determines the extent to which users can engage with and explore the virtual environment. However, it is also a complex and challenging step that requires a high degree of technical expertise and attention to detail to ensure the VR experience is seamless and immersive.

3 Case Study

To validate the proposed workflow, we have selected a case study that was implemented as part of a wider research project conducted in the University of Derby, UK. The project for Derby's Urban Sustainable Transition (DUST) is a co-creation initiative that aims to develop innovative design solutions and strategies for the homonymous city. The DUST research team, which comprises of all four co-authors of this paper, collaborates with local stakeholders to reconceptualize Derby as a more sustainable, prosperous, and resilient urban environment, while improving the quality of life for residents. Specifically, we have been preparing design proposals for public realm enhancements across the city and will invite local stakeholders to contribute to the discussion on how certain interventions may affect the cityscape. Through utilizing the workflow proposed in the Methodology section of this paper, we intend to co-create multiple intervention scenarios for various sites in the city to better inform the placemaking process (Fig. 1). We provide some preliminary results from the application of the proposed workflow for co-design workshops in the context of DUST in the following subsection.

Fig. 1. 3D digital model of the city of Derby created using Unreal Engine 5, source: Author.

3.1 Open Workshop

In order to evaluate the effectiveness of the workflow, participants were invited to test the Virtual Reality (VR) platform in open showcase events prior to launching the experiment. These events served as an opportunity for participants to provide feedback and preferences on the VR model, which were then used to fine-tune and optimize the VR platform to meet the needs and requirements of stakeholders. The open showcase events also provided a means to demonstrate the potential of the VR model to a wider audience and generate interest in the urban design project. To meet the hardware requirements, the Oculus Quest 2 was utilized for virtual interactions and connected with a PC and two big screens, one of which showed the participants' real-time interaction in the virtual world, while the other displayed a video animation of the city model. The investigators recorded and analyzed the participants' interactions during the showcase.

The showcase event was hosted at the Derby City Lab, which is based on the concept of Urban Rooms and houses the City Living Room. It features a rolling program of dynamic exhibitions and discussion groups focused on ideas to regenerate Derby. The DUST event took place over three weeks in September 2022, during which both the public and stakeholders, including policy makers and organizations such as Derby City Council, Canal River Trust, Marketing Derby, Down to Earth, Environment Agency, and transportation agencies such as Toyota and Trent Barton, were invited to test the VR model and share their ideas. The feedback gathered during these showcase events contributed to the success of the urban design project and ensured that the VR model met the needs and requirements of stakeholders (Fig. 2).

Fig. 2. Participants interactions during the DUST showcase event, Derby City Lab, source: Author.

4 Discussion and Future Work

The application of the proposed workflow helped us identify three key themes resulting from participants' interaction with virtual models: sustainability, accessibility, and place making. Participants expressed their ideas and concerns related to humanizing the streets and increasing pedestrianization, the lack of vibrant spaces in the city center, new ideas and means of public and clean transportation, the need for more green spaces and gardens along the river side, and the implementation of 15-min mixed-use neighborhoods. We conducted a coding analysis to organize and highlight these discussions into themes and subthemes, which required a micro-scale focus on different case studies and areas in Derby. This approach allowed for a comprehensive and detailed understanding of the needs and preferences of the stakeholders, which informed the optimization of the VR platform. Specifically, the feedback gathered during the showcase event facilitated the creation of an interactive environment and different design scenarios that participants could interact with and test during the subsequent stages of the VR experiment.

In the near future, we plan to employ the workflow proposed in the Methodology section of this paper into a co-creation study, which investigates the potentiality of low-traffic, shared streets at Derby's neighborhoods. The overall study design has recently received ethical approval by the College Research Ethics Committee, University of Derby. For this research, the goal is to design a more pedestrian-friendly environment that encourages community engagement and improves the quality of life for residents. To achieve this, we plan to introduce a series of design interventions that encourage social interaction, enhance livability, and help build a stronger sense of community in the area, such as nature-based parklets, outdoor exercising spaces, and cycle infrastructure. Utilizing the proposed workflow, we will be inviting locals to test different design scenarios and solicit their ideas in a series of open workshops. We expect that participants' text-to-image-generated input as well as their interaction with the simulated environments in VR will help us recreate the streetscape and contribute to local planning policies.

Funding. This project has been generously supported by the Osborne Legacy. The financial assistance provided by the legacy has been instrumental in the successful completion of this research effort.

References

1. Portman, M.E., Natapov, A., Fisher-Gewirtzman, D.: To go where no man has gone before: virtual reality in architecture, landscape architecture and environmental planning. Comput. Environ. Urban Syst. **54**, 376–384 (2015)
2. Meenar, M., Kitson, J.: Using multi-sensory and multi-dimensional immersive virtual reality in participatory planning. Urban Sci. **4**(3), 34 (2020)
3. Zhang, C., Zeng, W., Liu, L.: UrbanVR: an immersive analytics system for context-aware urban design. Comput. Graph. **99**, 128–138 (2021)
4. Safikhani, S., Keller, S., Schweiger, G., Pirker, J.: Immersive virtual reality for extending the potential of building information modeling in architecture, engineering, and construction sector: systematic review. Int. J. Dig. Earth **15**(1), 503–526 (2022)
5. Liu, X.: Three-dimensional visualized urban landscape planning and design based on virtual reality technology. IEEE Access **8**, 149510–149521 (2020)
6. Schrom-Feiertag, H., Stubenschrott, M., Regal, G., Matyus, T., Seer, S.: An interactive and responsive virtual reality environment for participatory urban planning. In: Proceedings of the 11th Annual Symposium on Simulation for Architecture and Urban Design pp. 1–7 (2020)
7. Kim, S., Kim, J., Kim, B.: Immersive virtual reality-aided conjoint analysis of urban square preference by living environment. Sustainability **12**(16), 6440 (2020)
8. Yu, R., Gu, N., Lee, G., Khan, A.: A systematic review of architectural design collaboration in immersive virtual environments. Designs **6**(5), 93 (2022)
9. Panya, D.S., Kim, T., Choo, S.: An interactive design change methodology using a BIM-based Virtual Reality and Augmented Reality. J. Build. Eng. 106030 (2023)
10. Delgado, J.M.D., Oyedele, L., Demian, P., Beach, T.: A research agenda for augmented and virtual reality in architecture, engineering and construction. Adv. Eng. Inform. **45**, 101122 (2020)
11. Michels, A.: Citizen participation in local policy making: design and democracy. Int. J. Public Adm. **35**(4), 285–292 (2012)
12. Binder, T., Brandt, E.: The design: lab as platform in participatory design research. CoDesign **4**(2), 115–129 (2008)
13. Nabatchi, T., Leighninger, M.: Citizenship, outside the public square. In: Public Participation for 21st Century Democracy, pp. 1–12 (2015)
14. Sanders, E.B.-N., Stappers, P.J.: Co-creation and the new landscapes of design. CoDesign **4**(1), 5–18 (2008)
15. Pillai, A.G., et al.: Communicate, Critique and Co-create (CCC) future technologies through design fictions in VR environment. In: Companion Publication of the 2020 ACM Designing Interactive Systems Conference, pp. 413–416 (2020)
16. Paasch Knudsen, S., Husted Hansen, H., Ørngreen, R.: Exploring the Learning Potentials of Augmented Reality Through Speculative Design, pp. 156–163 (2022)

17. Gu, N., Amini Behbahani, P.: A critical review of computational creativity in built environment design. Buildings **11**(1), 29 (2021)
18. Yildirim, E.: Text-to-image generation - AI in architecture. Art Archit. Theory Pract. Exper. **97** (2022)
19. Kingma, D.P., Welling, M.: Auto-Encoding Variational Bayes. CoRR, abs/1312.6114 (2013)
20. Goodfellow, I., et al.: Generative adversarial networks. Commun. ACM **63**(11), 139–144 (2020)
21. Open AI: DALL·E 2 (2002). https://openai.com/product/dall-e-2
22. Stability AI: Stable Diffusion Public Release (2023). https://stability.ai/blog/stable-diffusion-public-release
23. Google Research: Imagen: Text-to-Image Diffusion Models (2022). https://imagen.research.google/
24. Gafni, O., Polyak, A., Ashual, O., Sheynin, S., Parikh, D., Taigman, Y.: Make-a-scene: scene-based text-to-image generation with human priors. In: Avidan, S., Brostow, G., Cissé, M., Farinella, G.M., Hassner, Tal (eds.) Computer Vision – ECCV 2022: 17th European Conference, Tel Aviv, Israel, October 23–27, 2022, Proceedings, Part XV, pp. 89–106. Springer Nature Switzerland, Cham (2022). https://doi.org/10.1007/978-3-031-19784-0_6
25. Rombach, R., Blattmann, A., Lorenz, D., Esser, P., Ommer, B.: High-resolution image synthesis with latent diffusion models. In: Proceedings of the IEEE Computer Society Conference on Computer Vision and Pattern Recognition, 2022-June, pp. 10674–10685 (2022)
26. Saharia, C., et al.: Photorealistic Text-to-Image Diffusion Models with Deep Language Understanding (2022)
27. Ruiz, N., Li, Y., Jampani, V., Pritch, Y., Rubinstein, M., Aberman, K.: DreamBooth: Fine Tuning Text-to-Image Diffusion Models for Subject-Driven Generation (2022)
28. Ho, J., Jain, A., Abbeel, P.: Denoising diffusion probabilistic models. Adv. Neural. Inf. Process. Syst. **33**, 6840–6851 (2020)
29. Dhariwal, P., Nichol, A.: Diffusion models beat GANs on image synthesis. Adv. Neural. Inf. Process. Syst. **11**, 8780–8794 (2021)
30. Gu, S., et al.: Vector quantized diffusion model for text-to-image synthesis. In: Proceedings of the IEEE Computer Society Conference on Computer Vision and Pattern Recognition, 2022-June, pp. 10686–10696 (2022)
31. Seneviratne, S., Senanayake, D., Rasnayaka, S., Vidanaarachchi, R., Thompson, J.: DALLE-URBAN: capturing the urban design expertise of large text to image transformers (2022)
32. UrbanistAI: UrbanistAI (2023). https://www.urbanistai.com/
33. Ehab, A., Heath, T.: Exploring immersive co-design: comparing human interaction in real and virtual elevated urban spaces in london. Sustain. **15**(12), 9184 (2023). https://doi.org/10.3390/su15129184

Patent Litigation Prediction Using Machine Learning Approaches

Sheng-Hui Chen and Chia-Yu Lai(✉)

National Pingtung University of Science and Technology, Pingtung 91201, Taiwan
chiayulai@mail.npust.edu.tw

Abstract. Over the past few years, there has been a great deal of interest in patent litigation. However, in prior studies, patent litigation prediction mainly relied on bibliographic information, while other useful data was largely neglected. To fill this research gap, this study proposes an ensemble machine learning classifier to predict patent litigation. The research datasets come from the recently released United States Patent and Trademark Office (USPTO) research datasets, including patent examination and patent assignment data. Patent litigation features are trained to build machine learning models to predict patent litigation. According to our experimental results, the litigation prediction model is capable of predicting litigation with an accuracy of 79%, significantly higher than previous studies. The patent litigation prediction model can assist firms in identifying potential lawsuits, reducing lawsuit costly damage, and developing future R&D strategies.

Keywords: Patent Litigation · Machine Learning · Patent Analysis · Prediction Model

1 Introduction

Patents contain information about technology development, and many companies apply for patents to make the technology protected by patent rights. The number of patent applications has been increasing rapidly in recent decades [1, 2]. Patent litigation is a legal process for the patent owner to exercise patent rights. In general, patent litigation occurs when production or development activities infringe on patent rights.

Patent litigation imposes a significant financial and time burden on the patent owner. Litigation is expensive and potentially burdens innovation activities [3]. Moreover, patent litigation can cause difficulties in allocating research and development resources. Therefore, being able to predict which patents will be litigated can be very valuable.

Over the past few years, there has been a great deal of interest in patent litigation in both the legal and economic literature. Most of the prior studies discuss the factors that influence patent litigation and the differences between litigation patents and non-litigation patents from some perspectives, such as economics and law [4–7]. Prior studies found that in the past, there were few reliable, comprehensive, free, and publicly accessible sources of patent litigation data [8]. So far, there are a few research works

C. Stephanidis et al. (Eds.): HCII 2023, CCIS 1836, pp. 389–395, 2023.
https://doi.org/10.1007/978-3-031-36004-6_53

on predicting patent litigation. For example, logistic regression analysis predicts the likelihood of patent litigation [9].

To comprehensively understand the difference between a litigated patent and a non-litigated patent, we collected the basic information from the patent to predict litigation key features. In addition, patent examination and assignment information as predictive litigation features are also considered in this study. To solve the financial and innovation difficulties caused by the uncertainty and unpredictability of patent litigation. The main objective of this study is to predict the likelihood of patent litigation.

The results of the model analysis show that our prediction model can accurately predict patent litigation, and this model is helpful in eliminating the uncertainty of patent litigation. This study uses complex machine learning algorithms and constructs a model from a more comprehensive perspective to fill the research gap in predicting patent litigation. The model can help companies analyze whether patents will be litigated and develop financial and R&D strategies in advance.

2 Literature Review

Several previous studies have focused on the differences between litigated patents and non-litigated patents, identifying patent litigation based on patent value [4, 6, 10]. Drawing upon previous patent litigation studies, the results and insights are ripe for further research and evaluation [5].

2.1 Patent Litigation Indicators

Lanjouw and Schankerman [11] found that domestic patent owners are more likely to be litigated than foreign ones, while patents owned by individuals are more likely to be litigated than patents owned by companies. Furthermore, this study indicated that those litigation patents have more claims and forward citations. Allison *et al.* [10] pointed out that litigation patents are valuable patents, where this relationship is quite strong and bidirectional. The results of the research show that litigation patents are often more valuable than others, and valuable patents are often more likely to be litigated than others. Allison *et al.* [10] found three predictors of patent litigation: patent claims, forward citations, and backward citations. Specifically, the more patent scope, the more technology is cited, and the more citations received, the more likely it is to be litigated. Marco and Miller [12] demonstrated that the relationship between specific features of patent examination and patent infringement litigation, finding family size (defined as the number of jurisdictions seeking patent protection) had a strong positive relationship with litigation likelihood. Similarly, patents with more independent claims are more likely to be litigated. The number of CPC classifications is positively correlated with litigation. Patents that pass the USPTO appeal process during examination have a 50% increased chance of being litigated.

2.2 Predicting Patent Litigation

In this section, several studies are considered to examine patent characteristics and patent litigation likelihood through statistical analysis methods.

Su *et al.* [9] proposed a method to predict patent litigation and measure patent value. There are two research purposes: 1). Examine whether there are significant differences between litigation and non-litigation patents. 2). Examine whether patent characteristics are related to litigation probability. The research uses descriptive statistics, two-sample, T-test, and ANOVA to understand the characteristics of litigation patents and the difference between litigation and non-litigation patents. A logistic function was used to curve fit 3,910,844 patents to calculate the probability of patent litigation.

Chien [13] also proposed a method to predict patent litigation based on regression analysis. The results of regression analysis found that litigation patents are more likely to go through re-examination, while litigation patents are more likely to be transferred, and litigation patents are more likely to pay maintenance fees.

3 Methodology

3.1 Research Process

This study collects four patent-related datasets: Utility Patent, Patent Litigation Dataset, Patent Examination Dataset, and Patent Assignment Dataset, all provided by the USPTO. Figure 1 shows the research process.

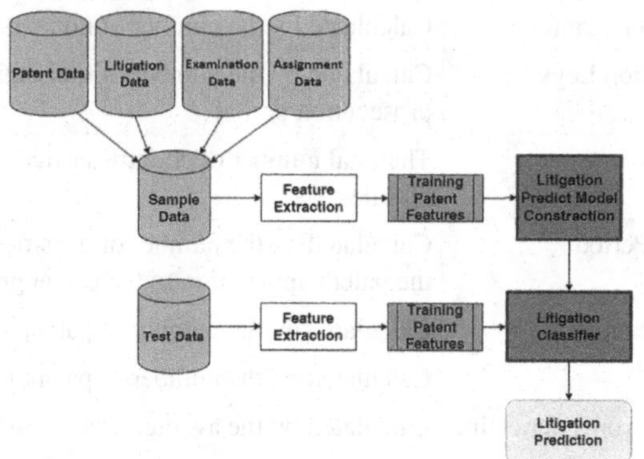

Fig. 1. Research Process.

This search has four steps: First, sample patent litigation data is selected to integrate with the other three datasets. Second, patent features are extracted from four patent-related datasets, and the feature values are calculated. Third, we build our prediction models by using feature values as model inputs with litigation outcomes as binary classification tasks for training. Fourth, as a result, the models are evaluated using a confusion matrix and receiver operating characteristic curve (ROC).

3.2 Feature Extraction

In this section, several patent features significantly relevant to patent litigation are summarized, and patent features are mainly divided into three parts: patent features, patent examination features, and patent assignment features. Table 1 summarizes all patent features considered in this study.

Table 1. All patent features considered.

Variables	Description
Number of Appeal	Calculated by the number of appeal submissions during the prosecution period
Number of Assignees	Calculated by the total number of assignees
Number of Backward Citations	Calculated by the number of patent citations
Number of Classifications	Calculated by the number of Cooperative Patent Classification (CPC)
Number of Dependent Claims	Calculated by the number of dependent claims
Number of Final Reject	Calculated by the number of final rejections received during the prosecution period
Number of Forward Citations	Calculated by the number of citations the patent received
Number of Independent Claims	Calculated by the number of Independent claims
Number of Inventors	Calculated by the total number of inventors
Number of Non-Patent Citations	Calculated by the number of non-patent citations
Number of Transaction Logs	Calculated by the number of transactions during the prosecution period
Patent Family Size	The total number of countries calculated as patent families
Patent Prosecution Period	Calculated by the number of days from the filing date of the patent application to the patent grant date
Recorded Assignments	Calculated by the number of patent assignments
Recorded Mortgage	Calculated by the number of patent mortgage
Average number of words per claim	Calculated by the average word count per claim

4 Results

4.1 Data

Litigation data from the USPTO Litigation Dataset. This study first obtained utility patents that participated in infringement lawsuits between 2010 and 2016 and screened out the patents in the CPC, including G and H sections (Physics and Electricity). These patents may have been involved in infringement lawsuits before 2010. Second, the 11,153 patents may include prior granted patents. To avoid training on older patents, litigation patents were filtered between 2001 and 2016. Finally, non-litigation patents are randomly selected based on the number of litigation patents granted each year, and the CPC include G and H section.

4.2 Model Evaluation

In order to test whether the model is overfitting, this study divides the data set into the training set and test set according to the ratio of 80:20. It uses 10-fold cross-validation to avoid the bias of the model to the data. In addition, ROC is often used as an evaluation method for classification models. Since predicting patent litigation is a binary classification task, this study uses the ROC curve method to evaluate the performance of litigation prediction models.

Table 2 shows the accuracy of the litigation prediction model. This study divides the model into three types to verify whether assignment and examination data can help the model predict more accurately. The first column reports the results of the analysis using baseline and assignment variables, the second column reports the results of the analysis using baseline and examination variables, and the third column reports the results of the analysis using all variables described in the Methodology.

Table 2. Performance for Prediction Model

Train	Model 1		Model 2		Model 3	
	RF	XGB	RF	XGB	RF	XGB
Accuracy	0.778	0.7718	0.792	0.7826	0.7955	0.7888
Precision	0.7862	0.7729	0.7912	0.7787	0.7958	0.7853
Recall	0.765	0.7711	0.7939	0.7909	0.7961	0.796
F1-Score	0.7755	0.772	0.7925	0.7848	0.796	0.7906
Test	Model 1		Model 2		Model 3	
	RF	XGB	RF	XGB	RF	XGB
Accuracy	0.7767	0.7674	0.7835	0.7801	0.7858	0.7858
Precision	0.7811	0.7636	0.7808	0.7719	0.7854	0.7851
Recall	0.7637	0.7688	0.7831	0.79	0.7814	0.782
F1-Score	0.7723	0.7662	0.782	0.7808	0.7834	0.7835

Model 1 and Model 2 show that removing some important patent features will bring great losses to the prediction model, which shows that assignment and examination greatly impact patent litigation. As a result, the Model 3 trained by assignment and examination shows a strong predictive capability, with an accuracy rate of 0.79.

Figure 2 shows the results of the 10-fold cross-validation ROC analysis using the RF classifier and the XGB classifier. The two classifiers showed powerful predictive performance, with the AUC reaching 0.87.

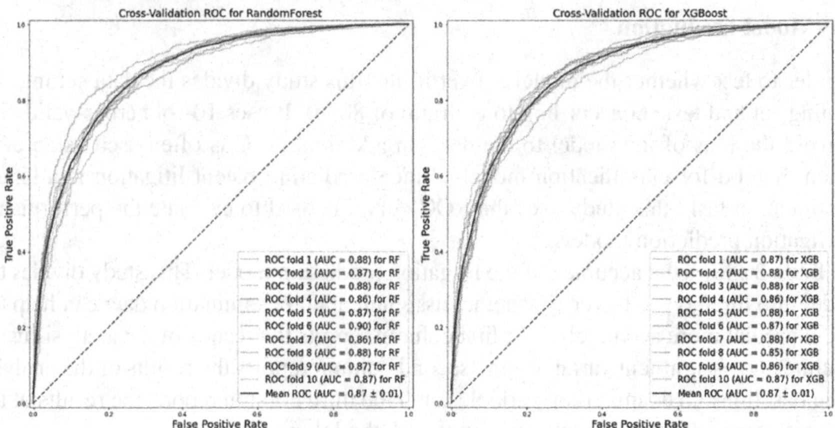

Fig. 2. Receiver Operating Characteristic Curve for RandomForest and XGBoost

5 Conclusion

This study proposes a model for predicting patent litigation using an advanced machine learning classifier, which can accurately predict patent litigation by patent features, assignment, and examination features. In addition, the model also shows that patent citation and prosecution period have high feature importance for the litigation prediction task. This study uses machine learning to build models from three different perspectives, namely patent feature, patent assignment, and patent examination, to fill the research gaps in predicting patent litigation. Moreover, patent litigation is an extremely costly and lengthy process, so predicting patent litigation is useful. For example, the company can analyze the likelihood of future patent litigation using the model and develop financial or R&D strategies in advance.

Finally, this study has the following limitations. First, the USPTO patent litigation data set only includes all litigation cases submitted to the court before 2016. If future research can add more samples, the prediction model will be more powerful. Second, most of the patent data is composed of unstructured text. If future research can use text mining tools to extract patent features for training, it can help the model to make better predictions. Finally, as mentioned earlier, patent litigation is expensive and time-consuming. Predicting the duration of patent litigation is undoubtedly a future research direction.

References

1. Kortum, S., Lerner, J.: What is behind the recent surge in patenting? Res. Policy **28**, 1–22 (1999)
2. Hall, B.H.: Exploring the patent explosion. J. Technol. Transf. **30**, 35–48 (2004)
3. Juranek, S., Otneim, H.: Using machine learning to predict patent lawsuits. NHH Department of Business and Management Science Discussion Paper (2021)
4. Lanjouw, J., Schankerman, M.: Stylized facts of patent litigation: value, scope and ownership. National Bureau of Economic Research Cambridge, Mass., USA (1997)

5. Allison, J.R., Lemley, M.A., Walker, J.: Extreme value or trolls on top-the characteristics of the most-litigated patents. U. Pa. L. Rev. **158**, 1 (2009)
6. Lerner, J.: The litigation of financial innovations. J. Law Econ. **53**, 807–831 (2010)
7. Bessen, J., Meurer, M.J.: The patent litigation explosion. Loy. U. Chi. LJ **45**, 401 (2013)
8. Marco, A.C., Tesfayesus, A., Toole, A.A.: Patent litigation data from US district court electronic records (1963–2015) (2017)
9. Su, H.-N., Chen, C.M.-L., Lee, P.-C.: Patent litigation precaution method: analyzing characteristics of US litigated and non-litigated patents from 1976 to 2010. Scientometrics **92**, 181–195 (2012)
10. Allison, J.R., Lemley, M.A., Moore, K.A., Trunkey, R.D.: Valuable patents. Geo. Lj **92**, 435 (2003)
11. Lanjouw, J.O., Schankerman, M.: Characteristics of patent litigation: a window on competition. RAND J. Econ. 129–151 (2001)
12. Marco, A.C., Miller, R.D.: Patent examination quality and litigation: is there a link? Int. J. Econ. Bus. **26**, 65–91 (2019)
13. Chien, C.V.: Predicting patent litigation. Tex. L. Rev. **90**, 283 (2011)

A Systematic Literature Review on Image Captioning

Yi Ding(✉)

Tongji University, Shanghai 200092, China
alyyya2022@gmail.com

Abstract. Image captioning is a technology that generates textual descriptions of images by integrating computer vision and natural language processing. This review aims to provide a comprehensive overview of current state-of-the-art image captioning models and techniques, summarize the critical approaches, evaluate their performance on benchmark datasets, highlight main challenges and limitations, and provide insights into future research directions. The systematic literature review followed a PRISMA-based approach and formulated three research questions (RQs) to construct the review. The study extracted and synthesized data from 49 eligible papers on visual and language models, datasets employed, and evaluation mechanisms used to measure performance. We found that it is evident that large-scale models and pre-training strategies have significantly advanced the field of image captioning. Specific sub-tasks for image captioning in certain applications have also contributed to the development of unique datasets. Future research directions in image captioning can be focused on solving the issues of expensive and scarce paired datasets, as well as shifting towards user-centric sub-tasks from generalization. This review can serve as a valuable resource for researchers, practitioners, and enthusiasts interested in image captioning.

Keywords: Image Captioning · Systematic Literature Review · SLR · Deep Learning

1 Introduction

Image captioning is a subfield of computer vision and natural language processing that aims to generate a textual description of an image. This technology has attracted significant attention from researchers due to its potential applications in various fields, such as image retrieval, image understanding, and assistive technology for visually impaired individuals. In recent years, significant progress has been made in this area, thanks to the development of deep learning techniques and the availability of large-scale annotated image datasets.

This review aims to provide a comprehensive overview of the current state-of-the-art image captioning models and techniques. Specifically, this review aims to summarize the critical approaches used for image captioning, evaluate their performance on benchmark datasets, highlight the main challenges and limitations, and provide insights into future research directions.

C. Stephanidis et al. (Eds.): HCII 2023, CCIS 1836, pp. 396–404, 2023.
https://doi.org/10.1007/978-3-031-36004-6_54

2 Methods

In this systematic literature review, we follow a systematic approach to investigate state-of-the-art image captioning research. We use a PRISMA-based[1] approach to guide the review process, as Fig. 1 shows.

2.1 Research Questions

Firstly, we formulate three research questions (RQs) to construct the review:

RQ1: What deep learning models are used for visual encoding and language modeling in image captioning tasks?

RQ2: What are the datasets used for image captioning?

RQ3: What evaluation metrics are commonly used in the literature to evaluate the performance of image captioning models?

2.2 Primary Search

To answer these questions, we conducted a preliminary search of two widely used databases, Web of Science and Scopus, using the following query string:

("image caption*" OR "image description*") AND "deep learning".

We limited the search to journal and conference papers published between 2018 and 2022. The preliminary search yielded 863 records and was reduced to 580 after removing duplicate records from both databases.

2.3 Screening

We then screened the records, removing those unrelated to the image captioning topic to ensure relevance and completeness. A total of 277 records were retained for full-text eligibility assessment.

2.4 Eligibility

Finally, we selected papers that met our inclusion criteria, including using deep learning techniques for image captioning tasks, reporting experimental results on benchmark datasets, and using standard evaluation mechanisms to measure performance. Based on quality assessment, 66 eligible papers were selected.

2.5 Extraction and Synthesis

After selecting the 66 studies, we extracted and synthesized data, including the visual and language models, the datasets employed, and the evaluation mechanisms used to measure performance. The synthesis aims to summarize the facts in the literature and describe past work and new research directions.

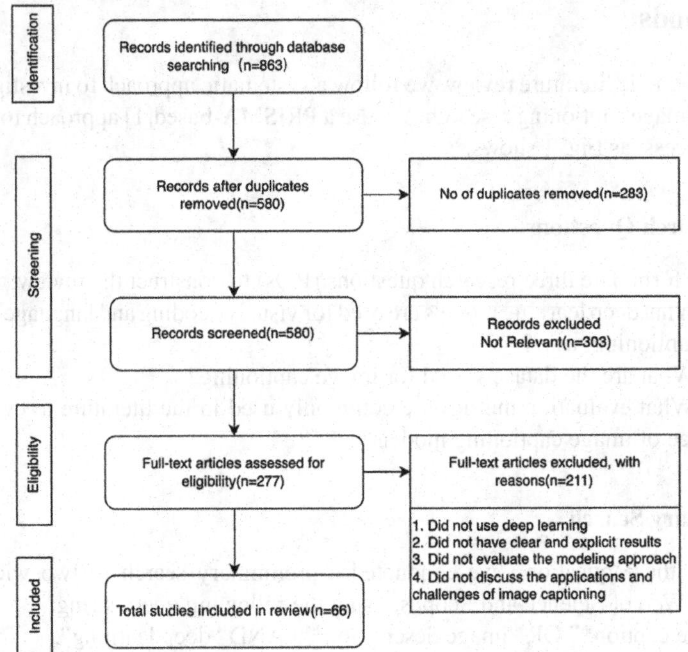

Fig. 1. Synthesis of the SLR flow based on the PRISMA model.

3 Results

The task of image captioning is achieved by performing the following key tasks in sequence. First, features are extracted from the image, detecting different objects in the image, followed by recognizing the relationships between the objects. Once objects are detected and relationships recognized, the text description is generated, an ordered sequence of words that forms a grammatically correct and natural sentence based on the relationships between the image objects. In abstract terms, this is a problem of mapping images to word sequences, with the input being pixels, which are encoded into feature vectors through the first step of visual encoding. These feature vectors then serve as input to the second step of language modeling and output as a sequence of words decoded from the given vocabulary.

3.1 RQ1 Result

From the collected literature, we can answer RQ1 (*What deep learning models are used for visual encoding and language modeling in image captioning tasks?*), and the results are presented in Table 1.

Table 1. Overview of deep learning models used in image captioning tasks.

Visual Encoding			**Language Models**		
-	Non-Attentive	Global CNN Features	-	LSTM-based	Single-layer LSTM
-	Additive Attention:	Grid-based			Two-layer LSTM
		Region-based			Boosting LSTM With Self-Attention
-	Graph-based Attention		-	CNN-based	
-	Self-Attention:	Region-based	-	Transformer-based	
		Patch-based	-	Image-Text Early Fusion	BERT-like
		Image-Text Early Fusion	-	Non-Autoregressive	

3.2 RQ2 Result

The summarized answers to RQ2 (*What are the datasets used for image captioning?*) can be accessed in Table 2. Three types of datasets appear in the literature related to image captioning.

The first type is standard captioning datasets, which contain a large number of general-domain images, each associated with multiple captions, such as *Flickr30K* [2], *Flickr8K* [3], and *Microsoft COCO* [4].

The second type is pre-training datasets, which can be image captioning datasets with low-quality captions or datasets collected for other tasks. For instance, the *Conceptual Captions* [5, 6] dataset is a collection of approximately 3.3 million (CC3M) and 12 million (CC12M) images with weakly-related descriptions collected from the web using loose filtering procedures. Additionally, pre-training such datasets requires substantial computational resources and performance costs. Hence, some pre-training datasets are not currently publicly available, such as those containing 2.5 billion and 4 billion image-text pairs used to train DALL-E [7] and CLIP [8].

The third type is domain-specific datasets. These datasets may involve visual domains (e.g., types and styles of images) and semantic domains. The distribution of terms used to describe images in a specific domain may be significantly different from those used for general-domain images. This aspect will be discussed in more detail in the following sections.

3.3 RQ3 Result

Based on the collected literature, we can briefly answer RQ3(What evaluation metrics are commonly used in the literature to evaluate the performance of image captioning models?).

Evaluating the quality of generated captions is a challenging and subjective task, as captions not only need to comply with grammar and fluency but also need to correctly reference the input image, making it complex. The most common evaluation mechanisms

Table 2. Overview of main image captioning datasets.

Datasets	Nb. Images	Nb. Captions (per Image)	Nb. Words (per Caption)
Flickr30K [2]	31 K	5	12.4
Flickr8K [3]	8 K	5	10.9
Microsoft COCO [4]	132 K	5	10.5
CC3M [5]	3.3 M	1	10.3
CC12M [6]	12.4 M	1	20.0

found in the literature include the BLEU score [9], METEOR score [10], ROUGE score [11], CIDEr score [12], and SPICE score [13]. Of course, besides these standard evaluation metrics, there may be other diverse indicators to measure model performance depending on the specific requirements of the image captioning task.

4 Discussion

4.1 Large-Scale Models and Pre-training Strategies

Recent years have seen significant advancements in image captioning thanks to the emergence of large-scale models and pre-training strategies.

Regarding visual encoding, region-based features have delivered compelling performances and have been the state-of-the-art choice for years. However, the development of better-trained grid features, self-attentive visual encoders, and large-scale multi-modal models like CLIP have re-opened discussions on which feature model is most appropriate for image captioning. Additionally, training better object detectors on large-scale data and employing end-to-end visual models trained from scratch have become popular strategies. The success of BERT-like [14] solutions performing image and text early-fusion suggests that visual representations integrating textual information are suitable.

As for language modeling, recurrent models have been the standard. However, their slow training and struggle to maintain long-term dependencies have prompted the adoption of autoregressive and Transformer-based solutions. Massive pre-training on large, unsupervised corpora using encoder-decoder or BERT-like architectures, often in conjunction with textual tags, has also led to impressive performance. It suggests that visual and textual semantic relations can be learned from not well-curated data. Finally, exploring massive pre-training on generative-oriented architectures is a promising direction for further research, as it has already demonstrated at least comparable performance to early-fusion counterparts.

4.2 Application-Specific Image Captioning

Image captioning can simplify and automate activities involving generating text from images. Research on image captioning tailored to specific applications often comes with the collection of relevant small-scale datasets, providing convenience to subsequent researchers in the respective domains.

Captioning systems can be applied to medical report generation, for which they need to predict disease labels and attempt to emulate the style of medical reports [15]. In addition to healthcare, image captioning has been applied to other fields involving personal safety, such as describing traffic accidents [16], analyzing crime scenes [17], and identifying drug paraphernalia [18]. Another important application of image captioning is in assistive technologies for the visually impaired, where image captioning methods must be able to provide descriptive information even with low-quality visual input [19].

Another interesting application is generating art descriptions, which enables visually impaired individuals to appreciate works of art. It requires not only the description of the factual aspects of the artwork but also its background and style and conveys the message of the art description [20]. For this purpose, captioning systems can also rely on external knowledge, such as metadata. For the cultural tourism industry, captioning can be generated based on tourism site images and visitor review metadata [21]. A similar application is automatic headline generation for news articles [22, 23], which should describe named entities in the article [24] and maintain the rich news style [25, 26]. Similarly, besides accurately describing image content, describing meme images used on social media often requires consideration of abstract features behind the images, such as humor, sarcasm, and reference [27].

5 Conclusion

This systematic literature review investigated the deep learning models, databases, and evaluation metrics used in the last five years of image captioning research. To conduct this study, we searched articles from two academic databases, selected 66 primary studies for literature review after applying inclusion and exclusion criteria to all articles, extracted data using a data extraction mechanism, and conducted an in-depth analysis.

Generating captions for images is a challenging task for artificial intelligence as it combines the difficulties of computer vision and natural language processing. In addition, the task itself lacks a clear definition, and captions can be generated in various styles and goals. Although recent literature and experiments have shown performance improvements on standard datasets, many challenges remain in terms of accuracy and generalization results, as well as requirements for fidelity, naturalness, and diversity. Future research can focus on the following two directions.

5.1 Solutions for Expensive and Scarce Paired Datasets

Solutions for Expensive and Scarce Paired Datasets Image captioning models are data greedy and heavily rely on paired datasets where visual and textual data are aligned. Although such datasets are available, this approach is not scalable as constructing large-scale image/description datasets is extremely costly, as it requires manual annotation. Methods utilizing unpaired datasets, such as weakly supervised learning, have been proposed to address this issue. While these methods show promise, much work is still needed to improve their results. On the other hand, pre-training on large-scale datasets is becoming a reliable strategy even if not very precise. In this regard, facilitating the public release of these datasets will be the foundation for fostering reproducibility and enabling fair comparisons. The continuously increasing scale of pre-training models is also a concern, requiring research on alternative solutions with lower computational intensity to promote equality within the community.

5.2 From Generalization to User-Centric Sub-tasks

While pre-training on large-scale datasets provides a promising direction to improve generalization performance, generating captions focused on specific domains and producing captions with different styles and purposes remains one of the primary open challenges in image captioning. Conventional image captioning models generate factual captions with a neutral tone that does not interact with end-users. Instead, some image captioning sub-tasks are specifically designed to address user requests and may help address this issue. For instance, personalized image captioning aims to attract user interest by generating descriptions that consider the user's existing knowledge, active vocabulary, and writing style, avoiding stating the obvious. Controllable captioning places users in a loop by requiring them to choose and prioritize what should be described in the image, enhancing human-machine interaction. Similarly, multilingual captioning aims to extend the applicability of captioning systems to other languages, promoting fairness across regions. These sub-tasks will all be promising directions for future development.

References

1. Page, M.J., et al.: The PRISMA 2020 statement: an updated guideline for reporting systematic reviews. Int. J. Surg. **88**, 105906 (2021). https://doi.org/10.1016/j.ijsu.2021.105906
2. Young, P., Lai, A., Hodosh, M., Hockenmaier, J.: From image descriptions to visual denotations: new similarity metrics for semantic inference over event descriptions. TACL **2**, 67–78 (2014). https://doi.org/10.1162/tacl_a_00166
3. Hodosh, M., Young, P., Hockenmaier, J.: Framing image description as a ranking task: data, models and evaluation metrics. J. Artific. Intell. Res. **47**, 853–899 (2013). https://doi.org/10.1613/jair.3994
4. Lin, T.-Y., et al.: Microsoft COCO: common objects in context. In: Fleet, D., Pajdla, T., Schiele, B., Tuytelaars, T. (eds.) ECCV 2014. LNCS, vol. 8693, pp. 740–755. Springer, Cham (2014). https://doi.org/10.1007/978-3-319-10602-1_48
5. Sharma P., Ding N., Goodman S., Soricut R.: Conceptual captions: a cleaned, hypernymed, image alt-text dataset for automatic image captioning. Presented at the Proceedings of the 56th Annual Meeting of the Association for Computational Linguistics (Volume 1: Long Papers) July (2018). https://doi.org/10.18653/v1/P18-1238
6. Changpinyo S., Sharma P., Ding N., Soricut R.: Conceptual 12M: pushing web-scale image-text pre-training to recognize long-tail visual concepts. Presented at the Proceedings of the IEEE/CVF Conference on Computer Vision and Pattern Recognition (2021)
7. Ramesh, A., et al.: Zero-shot text-to-image generation. In: Proceedings of the 38th International Conference on Machine Learning, pp. 8821–8831. PMLR (2021)
8. Radford, A., et al.: Learning transferable visual models from natural language supervision. In: Proceedings of the 38th International Conference on Machine Learning, pp. 8748–8763. PMLR (2021)

9. Papineni, K., Roukos, S., Ward, T., Zhu, W.-J.: Bleu: a method for automatic evaluation of machine translation. In: Proceedings of the 40th Annual Meeting of the Association for Computational Linguistics, pp. 311–318. Association for Computational Linguistics, Philadelphia, Pennsylvania, USA (2002). https://doi.org/10.3115/1073083.1073135
10. Banerjee, S., Lavie, A.: METEOR: an automatic metric for MT evaluation with improved correlation with human judgments. In: Proceedings of the ACL Workshop on Intrinsic and Extrinsic Evaluation Measures for Machine Translation and/or Summarization, pp. 65–72. Association for Computational Linguistics, Ann Arbor, Michigan (2005)
11. Lin, C.-Y.: ROUGE: a package for automatic evaluation of summaries. In: Text Summarization Branches Out, pp. 74–81. Association for Computational Linguistics, Barcelona, Spain (2004)
12. Vedantam, R., Lawrence Zitnick, C., Parikh, D.: CIDEr: consensus-based image description evaluation. Presented at the Proceedings of the IEEE Conference on Computer Vision and Pattern Recognition (2015)
13. Anderson, P., Fernando, B., Johnson, M., Gould, S.: SPICE: semantic propositional image caption evaluation. In: Leibe, B., Matas, J., Sebe, N., Welling, M. (eds.) ECCV 2016. LNCS, vol. 9909, pp. 382–398. Springer, Cham (2016). https://doi.org/10.1007/978-3-319-46454-1_24
14. Devlin, J., Chang, M.-W., Lee, K., Toutanova, K.: BERT: Pre-training of Deep Bidirectional Transformers for Language Understanding (2019). http://arxiv.org/abs/1810.04805. https://doi.org/10.48550/arXiv.1810.04805
15. Jing, B., Xie, P., Xing, E.: On the automatic generation of medical imaging reports. In: Proceedings of the 56th Annual Meeting of the Association for Computational Linguistics (Volume 1: Long Papers), pp. 2577–2586 (2018). https://doi.org/10.18653/v1/P18-1240
16. Rochel, S.N.S., Luc, R.J., Thomas, M., Victor, M.: Deep learning: traffic accident captioning model in madagascar mother language. In: 2022 8th International Conference on Control, Decision and Information Technologies (CoDIT), pp. 996–1001 (2022). https://doi.org/10.1109/CoDIT55151.2022.9804080
17. Mahesha, P., Royina, K.J., Lal, S., Anoop Krishna, Y., Thrupthi, M.P.: Crime scene analysis using deep learning. In: 2021 6th International Conference on Signal Processing, Computing and Control (ISPCC), pp. 760–764 (2021). https://doi.org/10.1109/ISPCC53510.2021.9609350
18. Zhao, B.: DrunaliaCap: image captioning for drug-related paraphernalia with deep learning. IEEE Access **8**, 161326–161336 (2020). https://doi.org/10.1109/ACCESS.2020.3021312
19. Captioning Images Taken by People Who Are Blind | SpringerLink. https://link.springer.com/chapter/10.1007/978-3-030-58520-4_25. Accessed 17 March 2023
20. Bai, Z., Nakashima, Y., Garcia, N.: Explain me the painting: multi-topic knowledgeable art description generation. In: 2021 IEEE/CVF International Conference on Computer Vision (ICCV), pp. 5402–5412. IEEE, Montreal, QC, Canada (2021). https://doi.org/10.1109/ICCV48922.2021.00537
21. Bounab, Y., Oussalah, M., Ferdenache, A.: Reconciling image captioning and user's comments for urban tourism. In: 2020 Tenth International Conference on Image Processing Theory, Tools and Applications (IPTA), pp. 1–6 (2020). https://doi.org/10.1109/IPTA50016.2020.9286602
22. Ramisa, A., Yan, F., Moreno-Noguer, F., Mikolajczyk, K.: BreakingNews: article annotation by image and text processing. IEEE Trans. Pattern Anal. Mach. Intell. **40**, 1072–1085 (2018). https://doi.org/10.1109/TPAMI.2017.2721945
23. Biten, A.F., Gomez, L., Rusinol, M., Karatzas, D.: Good News, Everyone! context driven entity-aware captioning for news images. Presented at the Proceedings of the IEEE/CVF Conference on Computer Vision and Pattern Recognition (2019)

24. Tran, A., Mathews, A., Xie, L.: Transform and tell: entity-aware news image captioning. Presented at the Proceedings of the IEEE/CVF Conference on Computer Vision and Pattern Recognition (2020)
25. Liu, F., Wang, Y., Wang, T., Ordonez, V.: Visual News: Benchmark and Challenges in News Image Captioning (2021). http://arxiv.org/abs/2010.03743. https://doi.org/10.48550/arXiv.2010.03743
26. Yang, X., Karaman, S., Tetreault, J., Jaimes, A.: Journalistic Guidelines Aware News Image Captioning (2021). http://arxiv.org/abs/2109.02865. https://doi.org/10.48550/arXiv.2109.02865
27. Wang, L., et al.: Automatic Chinese meme generation using deep neural networks. IEEE Access. **9**, 152657–152667 (2021). https://doi.org/10.1109/ACCESS.2021.3127324

Towards an Automatic Prompt Optimization Framework for AI Image Generation

Ling Fan[1,4(✉)], Harry Jiannan Wang[2], Kunpeng Zhang[3], Zilong Pei[4], and Anjun Li[4,1]

[1] Tongji University, Shanghai 200092, China
lfan@tongji.edu.cn
[2] University of Delaware, Newark, DE 19716, USA
[3] University of Maryland, College Park, MD 20742, USA
[4] Tezign, Shanghai, China

Abstract. Generative AI experienced a boom in 2022 with highlights such as the releases of Stable Diffusion for image generation and ChatGPT for conversational text generation. Although millions of images have been generated using products such as DALL-E 2, DreamStudio, and Midjourney, the learning curve for developing good text prompts that can lead to high-quality images remains steep, especially for inexperienced and less-technical users. Although various prompt engineering guides and tutorials have been developed to provide tips and guidance on prompt writing, there has been scant research on automatic prompt improvement algorithms and methods. In this paper, we present an automatic prompt optimization framework based on NLP analysis of a large prompt database and various machine learning models. A product based on our framework was developed and deployed for two months and real data were collected to evaluate our framework.

Keywords: Generative AI · NLP · Prompt Engineering · Text-to-Image

1 Introduction

Recently, the burgeoning development of generative AI makes the whole world excited. As one of the most natural interfaces for human beings, text-to-image generation products like DALL-E, DreamStudio and Midjourney give a promising future for people to boost their creativity and fulfill their imagination with minimal learning cost and effort. However, as the sole input to the models in the context of text-to-image generation, prompt has a great impact on the quality of the generated results. Millions of trials have been done by community numbers comprised of artists and researchers, and some of the prompts produce astonishing artworks. By systematic analysis, we detect great differences between these prompts and human natural expression. Although there are tutorials which help people manually conduct a machine-preferred prompt, it still costs a lot for people to learn and try.

In order to bridge the gap, a few work has been done. Promptomania prompt-builder [1] provides modifiers for users to choose from. When users enter the original prompt, it shows a list of modifiers such as artist's style for them to choose. These modifiers serve

C. Stephanidis et al. (Eds.): HCII 2023, CCIS 1836, pp. 405–410, 2023.
https://doi.org/10.1007/978-3-031-36004-6_55

as an in-time dictionary for users to look up. However, it requires tons of manual labor and domain knowledge to collect and organize the modifiers and users still have to try intensively to get a desirable result. Some websites, such as Lexcia and PromptHero, collect prompts of generated images from open-source communities, and allow users to search for great prompts or images according to their intentions as their initial inputs. But there isn't always a prepared prompt exactly fit user intention. MagicPrompt [3] is a series of GPT-2 models intended to generate prompts, which automatically complements user's input to generate better images. However, due to their uneven training dataset, these models tend to add extra objects and mismatch between objects and modifiers, thus misguide imaging AIs to twist user intention (Fig. 1).

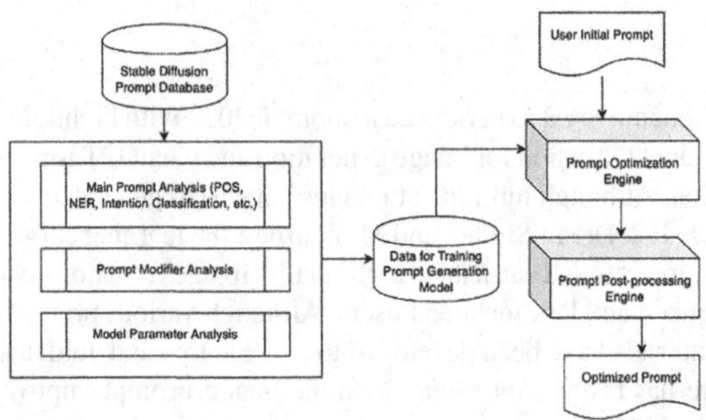

Fig. 1. Automatic Prompt Optimization Framework

In our work, we introduce an automatic prompt optimization framework for AI image generation. Firstly, we extract subjects, objects and modifiers from our collected prompt database with the help of systematic NLP analysis like POS, NER, Intention Classification, etc. For subjects, we use zero-shot text classification model to distinguish the classification of the main subject of the prompt [4]. As for modifiers, we apply decision-tree to stimulate the tendency of whether a modifier prefers a certain subject. Then we keep the training datasets balanced via undersampling technique [9]. We use their different combinations as the input text while using the entire prompt as the target text. We then use these input-target text pairs to finetune a T5 model [7] to automatically generate longer prompt to use as our prompt optimized engine. A post-processing engine is used to retain original prompt intention.

2 Methods

2.1 Data Collection and Pre-processing

We collected 140,000 high quality prompts from Lexica [2] as our prompt database. A prompt can be considered to have three components: the main prompt which indicates the user's intention, the modifiers such as styles, perspective, and artists which enrich the details and dominate the style of images, and model parameters, such as seed, step, and guidance. We use spaCy [6], an open-source library for Natural Language Processing in Python to extract the user intention of the prompts. Then we use zero-shot text classification model to distinguish the classification of the intention of the prompt. Target 13 categories are as follows: *human, portrait, comics animation movie characters, goods, food, fruit, electronic product, product, traffic, city, natural, animal, tools.* When the model predicts an intention belongs to one of *human, portrait, comics animation movie characters* categories, we decide it to be *with-character* type, while others to be *no-character*. Then we use undersampling technique to keep a 1:1 ratio between *with-character* and *no-character* types to construct a balanced and high-quality training dataset. We only take the prompts with user intention at the beginning of the prompt, in order to avoid the generative model from adding more subject words during the training and learning process. After cleaning and balancing, 30,000 high-quality, balanced prompt data can be obtained and will be used to train our model in prompt optimized engine. Through experiments, we found that even if the main prompts do not contain subjects of characters, as long as the prompts include the name of an artist who draws people often, the generated result will have a high probability of being an image of human characters. Therefore, it is necessary to analyze the artists' tendency to draw human characters.

Firstly, we use decision tree classification algorithm [5] to fit the artists and intention types (*with-character* or *no-character*) in the prompt so that we can obtain the feature importance of each artist, which indicates the tendency of containing the artist's name in the prompt to draw characters in generated results.

$$Y(\text{with or no character}) = F(X(\text{artists list of per prompt}))$$

Then we calculate the frequency of the artist drawing characters f, that is:

$$f = \frac{\text{occurrences of artist name as modifier and generating characters}}{\text{occurrences of artist name as modifier}}$$

We filter out the less mentioned artists and predict that an artist name with feature importance above the mean and f greater than 50% in the prompt will generate an image with characters. By using this algorithm, we can get a list of artists who have the tendency to generate an image with characters.

2.2 Prompt Optimization Process

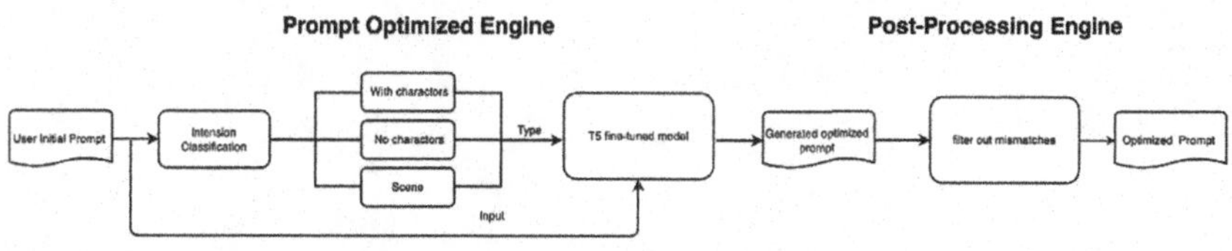

Fig. 2. Prompt Optimization Process

Figure 2 shows the workflow of prompt optimization. We use the 30,000 preprocessed text pairs to fine-tune a special T5 model [10], which powers our Prompt

Optimized Engine. First, we classify user's original intention into one of the 13 categories aforementioned. If the classified category is among *human, portrait, comics animation movie characters*, we further predict whether the intention may want to have character or not. Secondly, we use the find-tuned T5 model to optimize the user input with controlled generated prompt length according to the following heuristics:

- *human, portrait, comics animation movie characters* categories with characters: 70 tokens to get as much modifier as possible.
- *food, fruit, electronic product, product, tools* categories: 30 in order to get a more accurate result and lower the risk of twisting user intention.
- *city, natural, animals, traffic*: 50 tokens to get a balanced number of modifiers.

The Prompt Post-Processing Engine further optimize the prompt by conducting two tasks. First, if the category is *no-character type*, we filter out the names in the list of artists who have the tendency to generate an image with characters. Second, we add commonly used negative prompts, such as "amateur, poorly drawn, ugly, flat" to improve the generation quality.

3 Evaluation

A product based on our framework was developed and deployed for two months and real user data entries were collected to evaluate our framework, including the user's prompts, the optimized prompts, model parameters, and the generated images. We only selected the images generated using the same model and parameters, which are 4617 in total. We used stratified sampling based on *with-character* or *no-character* type of the prompts and manually selected 200 images for the human evaluation. For each prompt, we generate two images, one with the user's original prompt and another one with our optimized prompt and then ask three human evaluators to judge which image has better quality given the original prompt. Majority voting is used to rank the results. 75% of optimized images are considered to have higher quality than images without prompt optimization, which illustrates the effectiveness of our proposed framework. Table 1 shows some sample generation results.

Table 1. Sample generation results

User Input	Optimized prompt
Mars World Cup Peppa Pig	Mars World Cup Peppa Pig, ethereal, highly detailed, digital painting, artstation, concept art, smooth, sharp focus, illustration, Art by Artgerm and Greg Rutkowski and Alphonse Mucha, Unreal Engine 5, 8K, unreal engine 5, cinematic lighting, trending on ArtStation, 8k, HD

Bali	Bali, a city, tropical, beautiful, highly detailed, digital painting, artstation, concept art, smooth, sharp focus, illustration, Art trending on Artstation

Mobius strip	Mobius strip, intricate, elegant, highly detailed, digital painting, artstation, concept art, smooth, sharp focus, illustration, Art by Artgerm and Greg Rutkowski and Alphonse Mucha, octane render, 8k, unreal engine. art by artem demura

4 Conclusion

Based on systematic analysis of a large prompt database, we proposed an automatic prompt optimization framework for AI image generation, which contains a Prompt Optimization Engine whose model is fine-tuned from the state-of-art text generation language model, and a Post-Processing Engine to enhance the prompt generation results. We conduct a preliminary evaluation with human experts on real user data from a product developed based on our framework, whose result shows the prominent improvement of quality on the image generated from our optimized prompt. For our future research, we are working on several improvements such analyzing a much large dataset based on the DiffusionDB project [8] and developing algorithms to select high quality prompts based on image aesthetics scores.

References

1. Stable Diffusion prompt Generator-promptoMANIA. https://promptomania.com/stable-diffusion-prompt-builder/. Accessed 03 Mar 2023
2. Lexica. https://lexica.art/. Accessed 03 Mar 2023
3. MagicPrompt-Stable-Diffusion. https://huggingface.co/Gustavosta/MagicPrompt-Stable-Diffusion. Accessed 03 Mar 2023
4. Pushp, P.K., Srivastava, M.M.: Train Once, Test Anywhere: Zero-Shot Learning for Text Classification (2017). http://arxiv.org/abs/1712.05972
5. Priyam, A., Gupta, R., Rathee, A., Srivastava, S.: Comparative analysis of decision tree classification algorithms. Int. J. Curr. Eng. Technol. **2**, 334–337 (2013)
6. spaCy. https://spacy.io/. Accessed 03 Mar 2023
7. Raffel, C., et al.: Exploring the limits of transfer learning with a unified text-to-text transformer. J. Mach. Learn. Res. **21**(1), 5485–5551 (2020)
8. Wang, Z.J., Montoya, E., Munechika, D., Yang, H., Hoover, B., Chau, D.H.: DiffusionDB: A Large-scale Prompt Gallery Dataset for Text-to-Image Generative Models (2022). http://arxiv.org/abs/2210.14896
9. Liu, X.Y., Wu, J., Zhou, Z.H.: Exploratory undersampling for class-imbalance learning. IEEE Trans. Syst. Man Cybern. B. **39**, 539–550 (2009)
10. t5-base. https://huggingface.co/t5-base. Accessed 03 Mar 2023

Creating a Positive Reframing Dictionary Using Machine Learning

Hiroyuki Fukasawa, Kentaro Go(✉), Fumiyo Fukumoto, Jiyi Li, and Yuichiro Kinoshita

University of Yamanashi, Takeda, Kofu 400-8511, Japan
{g22tk018,go,fukumoto,jiyi,ykinoshita}@yamanashi.ac.jp

Abstract. Positive reframing is a cognitive process that involves giving negative events a new positive interpretation, leading to positive behavioral options and perceptions. Our research project aims to promote positive emotions by presenting positive reframing sentences to the negative ones the user has entered using a keyboard. To achieve this, we propose using GPT-3, a natural language processing model, to generate a large number of reframing dictionary entries in a short time. We trained GPT-3 on manually generated reframing pairs and tested it on new negative sentences. Our results show that, with three or more pairs of training data, GPT-3 can generally reframe negative sentences as expected. Our technique can be used to construct a high-quality reframing dictionary, which can help promote positive emotions and well-being.

Keywords: Positive reframing · Reframing keyboard · Reframing dictionary · Sentiment analysis · GPT-3

1 Introduction

Technological advancements have enhanced efficiency and productivity in our daily lives. Recently, there has been an increasing focus on how technology influences people's emotions and behaviors. As a result, the study of "positive computing" [1] has developed, creating a framework for designing technologies that boost psychological well-being and human potential. Positive computing aims to improve users' mental health and the surrounding environment by using technology to support their well-being. One way to enhance psychological well-being is through reframing [2]. Reframing is a cognitive process in which an alternative view of a situation replaces the original one. Reframing dictionaries have also been created to transform negative words into positive expressions through reframing. Cavanaugh et al. [3] showed that stress management training with reframing techniques for high-stress administrators led to more positive thinking and stress reduction among participants. Seligman [4] suggests that providing positive feedback on negative thoughts can improve a child's self-esteem. This

This work is supported by JSPS KAKENHI Grant Number JP20K11904.

C. Stephanidis et al. (Eds.): HCII 2023, CCIS 1836, pp. 411–417, 2023.
https://doi.org/10.1007/978-3-031-36004-6_56

reframing is expected to promote positive feelings by presenting an optimistic interpretation to people who initially had a negative viewpoint, and by informing them about different choices and new behaviors.

In this study, we incorporate positive reframing into the process of word prediction using a smartphone's software keyboard. A detailed explanation is shown in Fig. 1. When a user enters a phrase with negative connotations, the system offers a positively reframed phrase as a conversion option, along with a predictive conversion candidate, promoting the user's positive emotional state during software keyboard use. In the Go et al. [5] research, a Japanese reframing dictionary was developed through a workshop. Reframing was performed manually by multiple people, creating one to four possible options for each of the 396 negative terms. While manual reframing can produce high-quality conversion candidates, it is a time-consuming process that may lead to a reduction in the overall number of candidate patterns generated. To overcome this issue, this study uses GPT-3, a natural language processing model, to generate positive expressions for negative words and phrases, automatically creating a reframing pair. GPT-3 is trained on vast amounts of text, allowing it to adapt to the specified task with minimal training data requirements. In this study, we additionally trained GPT-3 by adding a small number of manually created reframing pairs. Then, new negative sentences were input into the learned model to obtain output results.

2 Related Work

2.1 Reframing Keyboard

The Reframing Keyboard, developed by Go et al. [5], displays positive impressions when a user types a negative Japanese word, in addition to the usual conversion candidates. The aim is to enhance users' positive emotions by presenting them with reframed expressions. Reframing transformation candidates were derived from a pre-existing Japanese corpus. Initially, lexemes with emotional polarity values between –0.80 and –1.00 were culled from the word emotional polarity correspondence chart, regarded as possessing potent negative connotations. From these, 4,202 terms were extracted, less likely to be erroneously perceived as negative. The prevalence of these words was subsequently examined, and 2,164 negative terms were extracted from the 4,202 most recurrent words on the Web. Four individuals manually assessed the extracted negative words, and those deemed negative by three or more people were extracted from the 2,164 words previously culled. Consequently, 926 words were ultimately designated as possessing negative impressions. Subsequently, the chosen negative words underwent manual reframing. The top 480 most frequently occurring negative words were extracted, and 8 participants generated 1 to 4 candidates for each word. For instance, for the term "idiot," one might enumerate positive candidates such as "much to learn," "sincere," "witty," and the like. This process yielded 695 positive conversion candidates for 396 words through manual reframing.

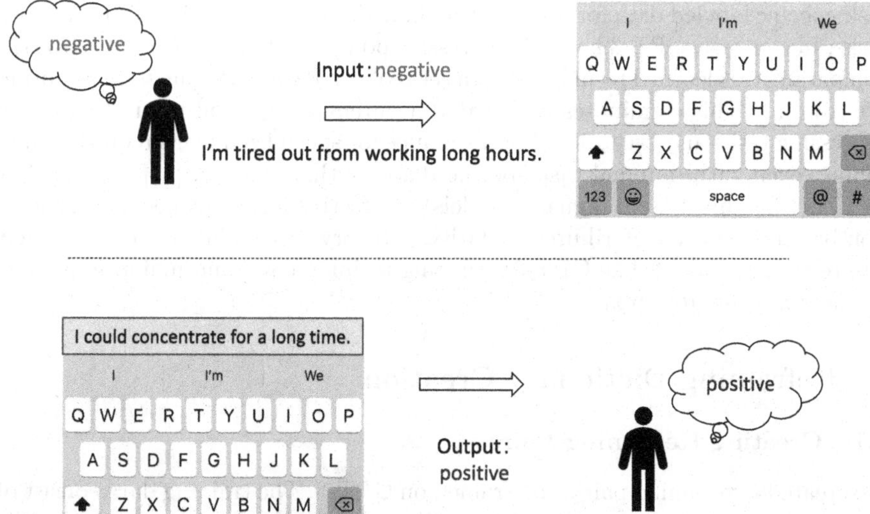

Fig. 1. The concept of reframing keyboards

2.2 Sentiment Analysis

Sentiment analysis constitutes the prediction of human emotions derived from textual, auditory, and facial cues. In the methodology delineated by Turkey [6], sentiment expressions within the input text are extracted utilizing a polarity lexicon, facilitating text-based emotional analysis. Mohammad et al. [7,8] executed a large-scale crowdsourcing survey to ascertain human emotional responses to specific words, demonstrating the feasibility of quantifying emotional associations evoked by lexemes and created a polarity dictionary suitable for machine learning. Saif et al. [9] revealed that traditional polarity dictionaries frequently encompass simplistic expressions encapsulating positive or negative word connotations, proving inadequate for handling context-dependent meaning shifts. The Twitter dataset was employed to train Word2Vec, with the resultant word vectors utilized to update the polarity dictionary. Preotiuc-Pietro et al. [10] explored the influence of personal attributes, such as personality, age, and gender, on negative tweets on Twitter. Muhammad et al. [11] considered that the polarity of a word depends on the context in which it is included. Based on evaluative findings across various social media platforms, they proposed SmartSA, a system that amalgamates a general polarity dictionary with category-specific vocabulary and sentiment, accounting for both local and global contexts.

2.3 GPT-3

GPT-3 is a natural language processing model introduced by OpenAI [12]. Conventional natural language processing models require fine-tuning with abundant task-specific labeled data for accuracy, making data collection difficult for certain tasks. In contrast, GPT-3 has rich expressive power because it has up to 1.75 trillion parameters learned from large data sets collected from various sources during pre-training. This culminates in elevated accuracy for general natural language processing tasks and exceptional performance for specialized tasks requiring fine-tuning, even with minimal task-specific data. Dathathri et al. [13] showed that PPLM (Plug and Play Language Models) is effective for controlled text generation based on specific attributes (polarity, category), by training smaller models on pre-trained models like GPT-3, reducing training costs and maintaining naturalness in generated text.

3 Reframing Dictionary Creation

3.1 Creating Reframing Pairs

We created a reframing pair to be trained on GPT-3. The training data consist of reframing pairs, which comprise phrases that employ negative expressions, paired with phrases that have been restructured into positive interpretations of those expressions. Initially, five negative sentences were devised for different situations. In this case, the situation represents the object of the negative emotion: self, others, or other events or occurrences. After crafting negative sentences, we developed sentences that could be construed positively in response to each negative statement. In this study, we generated positive phrases with brief sentence lengths that facilitate reframing output on a software keyboard. One of the authors generated the reframing pairs, which were then reviewed by another researcher and revised to enhance their naturalness. Although the number of reframing pairs created is extremely limited, it is sufficient to have fewer training data for a specific task because GPT-3 has been pre-trained with larger datasets and hyperparameters than other pre-trained models, and it already possesses substantial expressive power in sentence generation. The created reframing pairs are shown in Table 1.

Table 1. The created reframing pairs with pair ID

Pair ID	Negative phrase	Positive phrase
P1	I'm not good with people	I can think uniquely
P2	He's stubborn	He's consistent in his thinking
P3	I was fired from work	It gave me time to look at myself
P4	I took the criticism	I got valuable input
P5	I had a big injury	I'm not dead

3.2 Learning with Reframing Pairs

The created reframing pairs are utilized to adjust the negative sentences input into GPT-3, allowing them to be reframed and transformed. In this study, we employ Elicit [14], a tool developed by Ought [15], for training GPT-3. To observe the differences in output based on the number of reframing pairs used for training, we divide the number of reframing pairs trained on GPT-3 from one to four and examine the output for each. The negative sentence selected as a test input pertains to a daily life event: "I took the criticism." Reframing pairs, excluding the selected ones, are added as training data one by one, starting from the top of Table 1. Additionally, to evaluate the output for other negative sentences, we input "I am tired of studying hard." as another negative sentence.

4 Reframing Results with GPT-3

Table 2 and 3 show the respective results generated by GPT-3 after inputting the two sentences. Among the outputs obtained, when only one pair of training data was present, the outputs either contained the same sentences as the input or were not properly reframed. In the case of two pairs of training data, some of the anticipated reframing transformations occurred, while others yielded inadequate sentences. With three or more pairs of training data, the output generally exhibited the expected reframing. Additionally, the sentence lengths varied, as no restrictions were imposed on the output sentence length. Since this study aims to produce sentences on a software keyboard, it will be necessary to constrain sentence length in the future. As no evaluation has been conducted on the output sentences at this time, a quantitative assessment of the impact of reframed expressions on humans and the polarity values within the sentences is warranted.

Table 2. Result of reframing "I took the criticism."

Training data (Pair ID of Table 1)	Reframed phrases
P1	I can't be criticized I didn't give in to criticism I listen, understand and contribute to the collective spirit
P1, P2	I can decide to ignore the criticism I'm learning from the criticism criticism is informative
P1, P2, P3	I am stronger than I look I listened to the criticism and then I took actionfrom what I learned The discussion and criticism helps my understanding
P1, P2, P3, P5	It helped me do better It made me realize my flaw I was able to use it for my own benefit

Table 3. Result of reframing "I am tired of studying hard."

Training data (Pair ID of Table 1)	Reframed phrases
P1	I am passionate of studying I'm glad that I have experienced so many things I listen, understand and contribute to the collective spirit
P1, P2	I can decide to ignore the criticism I'm learning from the criticism I can do better if I work hard
P1, P2, P3	It will pay off in the future I have a beautiful future ahead of me I am not afraid of life
P1, P2, P3, P5	I have never learned so much in my life Working hard requires self-control I can give myself a rest

5 Conclusion

In this study, we have developed a reframing dictionary to automatically generate reframing expressions for negative statements. Future work involves adjusting the output sentence length, conducting human evaluations of the output sentences, and quantitatively assessing the polarity values within the sentences. After creating the reframing dictionary, we plan to implement it on a software keyboard and have users evaluate any emotional changes experienced during its use.

References

1. Calvo, R.A., Peters, D.: Positive Computing: Technology for Wellbeing and Human Potential. MIT Press, Cambridge (2014)
2. Lambert, N.M., Fincham, F.D., Stillman, T.F.: Gratitude and depressive symptoms: the role of positive reframing and positive emotion. Cogn. Emot. **26**(4), 615–633 (2012)
3. Cavanaugh, M.A., Boswell, W.R., Roehling, M.V., Boudreau, J.W.: An empirical examination of self-reported work stress among U.S. managers. J. Appl. Psychol. **85**(1), 65–74 (2000)
4. Seligman, M.E.P.: The Optimistic Child: A Proven Program to Safeguard Children Against Depression and Build Lifelong Resilience. HarperOne, California (2007)
5. Go, K., Moriya, Y., Kinoshita, Y., Li, J., Fukumoto, F.: Happy text entering: promoting subjective well-being using an input method for presenting positive words and phrases. In: Proceedings of the 2022 Conference, pp. 153–158. ACM (2022). https://doi.org/10.1145/3520495.3520521

6. Turney, P.D.: Thumbs up or thumbs down? semantic orientation applied to unsupervised classification of reviews. In: Proceedings of the 40th Annual Meeting on Association for Computational Linguistics (ACL 2002), pp. 417–424. Association for Computational Linguistics, USA (2002). https://doi.org/10.3115/1073083.1073153
7. Mohammad, S.M., Turney, P.D.: Crowdsourcing a Word-Emotion Association Lexicon. Comput. Intell. **29**(3), 436–465 (2013). https://doi.org/10.1111/j.1467-8640.2012.00460.x
8. Mohammad, S.M., Turney, P.D.: Emotions evoked by common words and phrases: using mechanical turk to create an emotion lexicon. In: Proceedings of the NAACL HLT 2010 Workshop on Computational Approaches to Analysis and Generation of Emotion in Text, pp. 26–34. Association for Computational Linguistics, Los Angeles, CA (2010)
9. Saif, H., He, Y., Fernandez, M., Alani, H.: Adapting sentiment lexicons using contextual semantics for sentiment analysis of Twitter. In: Presutti, V., Blomqvist, E., Troncy, R., Sack, H., Papadakis, I., Tordai, A. (eds.) ESWC 2014. LNCS, vol. 8798, pp. 54–63. Springer, Cham (2014). https://doi.org/10.1007/978-3-319-11955-7_5
10. Preoţiuc-Pietro, D., et al.: The role of personality, age, and gender in tweeting about mental illness. In: 2nd Workshop on Computational Linguistics and Clinical Psychology: From Linguistic Signal to Clinical Reality, pp. 21–30. Association for Computational Linguistics, Denver, Colorado (2015). https://doi.org/10.3115/v1/W15-1203
11. Muhammad, A., Wiratunga, N., Lothian, R.: Contextual sentiment analysis for social media genres. Knowl.-Based Syst. **108**, 92–101 (2016). https://doi.org/10.1016/j.knosys.2016.05.032
12. OpenAI: GPT-3. https://openai.com/. Accessed 15 Mar 2023
13. Dathathri, S., et al.: Plug and play language models: a simple approach to controlled text generation. arXiv preprint https://arxiv.org/abs/1912.02164 (2019)
14. Elicit. https://elicit.org/. Accessed 15 Mar 2023
15. Ought. https://ought.org/. Accessed 15 Mar 2023

Exploratory Analysis of the News in Easy Language (NiEL) Corpus to Identify Characteristic Patterns for Natural Language Processing

Claudia Hösel(✉), Matthias Baumgart, Benny Platte, Christian Roschke, and Marc Ritter

Hochschule Mittweida - University of Applied Sciences, 09648 Mittweida, Germany
{hoesel,baumgart,platte,roschke,ritter}@hs-mittweida.de

Abstract. While comprehensive corpora are available for resource-rich languages such as English in different domains, which can be made usable for natural language processing (NLP) applications, this is not the case for resource-poor languages. Parallel or monolingual corpora must first be created and adequately processed in order to make them usable for later NLP applications. In the past, selected variants of a standard language were increasingly identified as resource-poor languages and corresponding resources were created. The German Easy Language, as a highly simplified variant of the Standard German language, can be defined as a resource-poor language, since here, too, hardly any NLP-suitable corpora are available. In this paper, we present the News in Easy Language (NiEL) corpus, a monolingual text resource for German Easy Language. By means of exploratory analysis using selected NLP tools, characteristic patterns for Easy Language can be derived at both word and sentence level. The identified patterns of Easy Language can be compared in perspective with patterns from standard language texts. Our results show that multiple tools from the NLP domain are suitable for German Easy Language as well as for German Standard Language. Features like word variance, sentence depth but also average word and sentence length can be distinguished. The features extracted in this way are suitable for the development of models, whereby initial implications for the natural language processing of Easy Language can be derived. The results form an important basis for further research in the domain of Easy Language. As a low-resource language that has been primarily analyzed intellectually, another added value of our work also lies in the implications for natural processing of plain language derived from the exploratory analysis of the corpus.

Keywords: Natural Language Processing · Low Resource Language · Easy-to-Read · Corpus · Pattern Recognition

C. Stephanidis et al. (Eds.): HCII 2023, CCIS 1836, pp. 418–425, 2023.
https://doi.org/10.1007/978-3-031-36004-6_57

1 Introduction

Easy Language (also: Easy-To-Read) is a variant of standard language that is reduced on all linguistic levels and aims to enable people with cognitive impairments to access information [1].

The creation of Easy Language texts can be seen as a translation process, which takes place within a single language between different levels of complexity. This so-called intralingual translation is based on rules that were developed with the participation of people with intellectual disabilities. Two sets of rules are currently used in practice for the creation of texts in Easy Language: The set of rules from Inclusion Europe [2] and the set of rules from the Netzwerk Leichte Sprache [3]. The two sets of rules are largely comparable in terms of language and typography. Easy Language texts that conform to the rules are characterized, among other things, by the use of short words, the extensive avoidance of foreign and technical words, and a simple sentence structure. On the linguistic level, the recommendations indicate a reduction of the morphological, lexical and syntactic means of standard language. A further specification of the rules can be found, for example, in Maaß [4] and Bredel/Maaß [1]. Among other things, they advocate the use of the mediopoint for compound words. The process of intralingual translation into Easy Language takes place mostly intellectually. The goal of existing research is to identify approaches to automate this process (e.g. [5, 6]). For this purpose, texts from the Easy Language domain have to be analyzed using extensive data corpora. Such corpora are only available to a limited extent, since Easy Language is a resource-poor language. While comprehensive textual resources exist for resource-rich languages, such as English, this is not the case for resource-poor languages or language varieties [7].

This paper focuses on the construction of a monolingual Easy Language corpus for the news text type. Different NLP tools are applied to this corpus and analyzed to what extent these tools are suitable for natural language processing of Easy Language.

2 Overview

For German Easy Language, there are only a few text resources that are suitable for natural language processing. Klaper et al. [8] present a monolingual parallel corpus for German, which contains a simplified equivalent of the texts in addition to the standard language text. The parallel corpus includes 7,000 sentences and 70,000 tokens. Säuberli et al. [9] create a parallel corpus from news articles published by the Austria Presse Agentur, using news texts simplified intellectually to B1 level of the Common European Framework of Reference for Languages (CEFR) as a second resource. Based on this corpus, Spring et al. [10] generate a new text corpus with diverse text types for German, which contains simplified equivalents at levels A1, A2, B1. Hansen-Schirra et al. [11] present with the Geasy corpus a parallel corpus for the German language, which contains as a second corpus resource exclusively equivalents in Easy Language. The corpus, which is still under construction, contains standard language texts with a volume of 1,087,643 words and Easy Language texts with a volume of 292,552 words. None of these corpora can be used for our research project. Existing corpora with simplified variants of the German standard language are either not text type-pure or do not contain texts simplified exclusively at the Easy Language level. However, both aspects in combination are relevant for the development of suitable semi-automated solutions in the translation process. In terms of text type purity, the challenges of designing appropriate applications for narrative text types are different from those for informative text types. This applies, for example, to metaphor recognition, which is more relevant for narrative text types such as fairy tales than for news, due to the characteristics of the text type.

For selected natural language processing tools, various challenges have been identified in the past that are already the subject of existing research. For example, ambiguities in the use of punctuation marks could be identified as a central challenge for the segmentation of standard language texts and thus for tokenizers [12].

In syntactic sentence analysis, ambiguities arising from prepositional phrase or coordination ambiguity have been identified as a challenge for parsers and addressed in various research papers (e.g. [13, 14]). In named entity recognition (NER), ambiguity can also pose a challenge for NE recognizers (e.g. [15, 16]). While the suitability of existing NLP tools in the context of standard language texts has been the subject of much research, an analysis of the suitability of these tools within Easy Language has yet to be conducted.

3 Methods

The methodological procedure consists of two steps. In the first step, a monolingual data corpus consisting of news texts was created for German Easy Language. In the second step, different NLP tools were applied to this corpus as well as to an additionally created standard language corpus and the outputs were analyzed accordingly. The methodological procedure of the individual steps is presented in detail below.

3.1 Creation of a Corpus with Texts in Easy Language

The construction of the corpus can be divided into two basic processes, data acquisition and annotation, within which different process steps were carried out. For the construction of the corpus, the text type message was selected, since a sufficient amount of comparable texts in Easy Language exist for this type of text. Characteristic for the text type message is the information function with simultaneously missing thematic restrictions [17]. The focus on the text type News (News in Easy Language) gave the corpus its name (NiEL-Corpus).

As part of the data acquisition process, 959 news texts in Easy Language were collected from a German online platform and stored in different formats, such as text document and screenshot. To collect the text data, a web crawler was created and configured so that all Easy Language news texts retrievable at the time were downloaded one by one and persistently stored as XML. The resulting text collection was then semi-automatically annotated, with header information such as title, publication date, author, and body information stored for each news article. The semantic classes, i.e. the formal meaning of the sentence for the text, were identified and stored as body information. In the intellectual annotation process, it was decided for each sentence whether it was a statement, a part of speech, an enumeration, etc. In addition, text structural elements such as headings, subheadings, and paragraphs were annotated.

3.2 Application of the NLP-Tools

NLP tools were then applied to the NiEL corpus thus generated and the outputs were analyzed. In order to better classify outputs, a corpus of standard language news texts in German was created according to the scheme mentioned in 3.1. The corpus in German standard language contains approximately the same number of texts as the NiEL corpus. The tools were applied to both corpora and outputs were analyzed intellectually in each case. This procedure allowed us to draw first conclusions regarding the suitability of certain procedures within each tool.

For the NLP tools, we focused on tokenizers, parsers, and named-entity recognizers (NER), sometimes researching different procedures and applying concrete implementations to both corpora as examples in order to compare the outputs. For the tokenizers, we were particularly interested in any differences in output between rule-based and statistical methods. For the rule-based tokenizers, we focused on those that use only word boundaries (implementation: NLTK word tokenizer) for segmentation and those that use word boundaries and punctuation marks as separators (implementation: NLTK word-punct tokenizer) [18]. For the statistical methods we took a closer look at a tokenizer that uses the maximum entropy principle and works with a supervised model (implementation: OpenNLP Tokenizer ME [19]). For parsers, we focused on dependency parsers, using neural network-based architectures. In our exploratory study, we implemented the dependency parser of the Stanza toolkit [20]. For named entity (NE) recognition, we use a rule-based approach (Implementation: SpaCy NER - German Large [21]) and an approach based on deep learning technologies and word embeddings (Implementations: Flair Framework NER - German Large, Flair Framework NER German Legal). The latter differs in terms of the datasets used and the number of named entities (German Large: 4 NE; German Legal: 19 NE) [22].

4 Results

Overall, our results show that the applied tools from the NLP field are suitable in principle for German Easy Language as well as for German Standard Language. Nevertheless, some specifics of Easy Language, especially the mediopoint, require special attention when choosing concrete procedures. In the analysis of the output, characteristic patterns for Easy Language also emerged at the word and sentence level.

For tokenizers, visual separators in particular, such as the mediopoint or hyphens, can pose a challenge, as they are sometimes interpreted as segment boundaries depending on the concrete procedure. In our study, we implemented tokenizers based on both rule-based and statistical methods. The output of both methods does not allow for generalizations regarding their suitability for Easy Language, especially for the rule-based methods. In our explorative analysis it became apparent that rule-based tokenizers, which use word boundaries as separators, are quite suitable for Easy Language, since, for example, words separated with mediopoints remained as a unit. Similar results were also obtained with the statistically based tokenizer. In contrast, our results suggest that rule-based tokenizers, which use word and sentence boundaries as separators, seem less suitable for tokenizing Easy Language texts. In our study, for example, words separated with mediopoints were not recognized as a unit (e.g., 'South', '·', 'America'). Figure 1 presents the intellectual comparison of the outputs exemplarily for Easy Language (translation: "And samba comes from South·America.").

Method	Implementation	Output
Rule-Based	NLTK word tokenizer	'Und', 'Samba', 'kommt', 'aus', 'Süd·amerika', '.'
Rule-Based	NLTK wordpunct tokenizer	'Und', 'Samba', 'kommt', 'aus', 'Süd', '·', 'amerika', '.'
Statistical	OpenNLP Tokenizer ME	'Und', 'Samba', 'kommt', 'aus', 'Süd·amerika', '.'

Fig. 1. Comparison of the results of applying different tokenization methods to Easy Language texts.

For parsers, the sentence depth is relevant, which tends to be low in Easy Language due to the extensive absence of subordinate clauses and thus does not pose a challenge for parsers. This result also emerged when applied to the NiEL corpus. In contrast, sentence depth is somewhat higher for the standard language corpus due to the use of subordinate clauses. Overall, our results suggest that when parsers are applied to Easy Language texts, specific sentence structure is not an explicit source of error. Our results suggest that using parsers on Easy Language texts, as opposed to using them on standard language, is less prone to errors due to the shorter sentences.

The dependency parser we used from the Stanza toolkit is suitable for Easy Language and did not show any problems with the modified syntax compared to application to standard language. Overall, the parser outputs suggest that Easy Language is characterized by short sentences with clear relationships between subject, object, and verb, while standard language does use more complex sentence structures with subordinate clause constructions. For some grammatical categories based on Universal Dependency Relations, differences between Easy Language and Standard Language are noticeable. For example, the category "root", which refers to the root of the sentence, occurs more frequently in Easy Language than in Standard Language. In addition to any variations in the corpus, this result could also be attributed to the fact that Easy Language tends to use shorter sentences, but uses only one sentence for each statement and thus uses more sentences overall to represent facts. The category "det" expresses the relation between nominal head and its determiner [23] and is more common in Easy Language. This could be attributed to the fact that facts are taken up several times in Easy Language and the same designations or phrases are also used. The same applies to the category "nsubj" (nominal subject). The category "punc" (puctuation), in which the differences between Easy Language and standard language are not too great, is also striking. This could be due to the fact that shorter sentences in Easy Language tend to balance out longer subordinate clause constructions in standard language.

For named entity recognition, it can be concluded based on the exploratory analysis that the NE recognizers investigated are suitable for both Standard Language and Easy Language. With regard to the number of identified entities, more unique entities could be found for texts in Standard Language than for texts in Easy Language. The reason for this could be the tendency of higher word variance in standard language texts. While Easy Language texts describe facts with the same words or phrases, standard language aims at variability. Regarding the distribution of entities in individual categories, Easy Language and Standard Language show similarities. Deep-learning-based approaches recognized entities more reliably than rule-based approaches. No differences were found between Easy Language and Standard Language in the assignment of ambiguous named entities to different categories. Problems with ambiguity occurred in both Standard Language and Easy Language texts. However, differences in both procedures used suggest themselves. An entity was assigned a term more frequently to multiple categories in rule-based procedures. This might indicate a better context sensitivity and thus a better handling of ambiguities than in deep learning-based approaches, while at the same time showing a need for possibly more differentiated entity classes. Figure 2 shows the number of multiply assigned entities for Easy Language and Standard Language. It becomes clear that the rule-based NER implementation of the SpaCy framework assigns a comparable number of entities multiple times for Easy Language and for Standard Language. What is striking about the NE-Recognizer of the Flair framework is the different assignment of the two implementations used. While multiple assignments occur more frequently with Flair German Large for the standard language, they could be assigned more clearly with Flair German Legal. The reason for this could be the differentiated entity classes in Flair German Legal. With Easy Language, the situation is exactly the opposite.

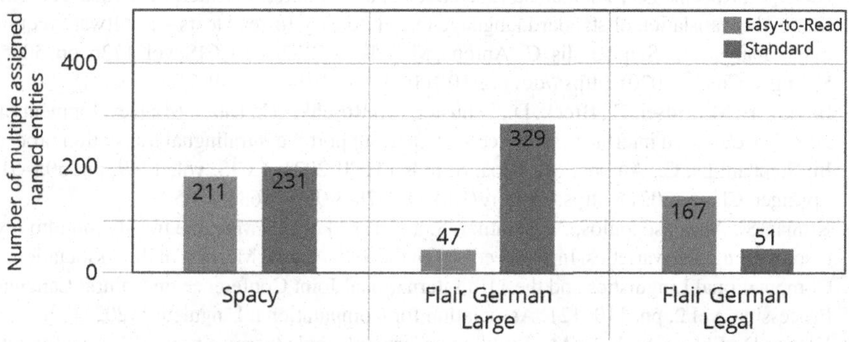

Fig. 2. Number of multiply assigned entities for Easy Language and Standard Language.

5 Conclusion

The NiEL corpus we created allowed us to apply various NLP tools and assess their suitability for Easy Language. Our results show that all the tools we investigated can be applied to Easy Language texts. Both rule-based and statistical tokenizers are suitable for tokenizing texts in Easy Language. Among the methods studied, rule-based methods that use word and sentence boundaries as separators showed problems in dealing with mediapoints. With regard to syntactic sentence analysis, our explorative analysis suggests that Easy Language tends to be easier to parse than standard German texts due to its shallow sentence depth. In this context, further characteristic patterns of Easy Language could be derived, which also coincide with patterns named in the literature. With regard to the recognition of named entities, the results suggest that the investigated recognizers are suitable for both Standard Language and Easy Language. To what extent the mediapoints used in Easy Language influence the results positively or negatively cannot be conclusively stated. Further research is needed in this regard. Our results form an important basis for further research in the domain of Easy Language and contribute to supporting translators in the intellectual translation process by means of (semi-)automated assistance systems.

References

1. Bredel, U., Maaß, C.: Leichte Sprache: Theoretische Grundlagen. Orientierung für die Praxis. Dudenverlag, Berlin (2016)
2. Inclusion Europe: Information for all. European standards for making information easy to read and understand. https://easy-to-read.inclusion-europe.eu/wp-content/uploads/2014/12/DE_Information_for_all.pdf. Accessed 02 Mar 2023
3. Netzwerk Leichte Sprache: Die Regeln für Leichte Sprache (2013): https://www.leichte-sprache.org/wp-content/uploads/2017/11/Regeln_Leichte_Sprache.pdf, last accessed 2023/03/02
4. Maaß, C.: Leichte Sprache Das Regelbuch. Lit-Verlag, Münster (2015)
5. Hösel, C., Roschke, C., Thomanek, R., Rolletschke, T., Platte, B., Ritter, M.: Process automation in the translation of standard language texts into easy-to-read texts – a software requirements analysis. In: Stephanidis, C., Antona, M. (eds.) HCII 2020. CCIS, vol. 1226, pp. 50–57. Springer, Cham (2020). https://doi.org/10.1007/978-3-030-50732-9_7
6. Baumgart, M., Hösel, C., Breck, D., Schuster, M., Roschke, C., Ritter, M.: Development of a holistic web-based interface assistance system to support the intralingual translation process. In: Stephanidis, C., Antona, M., Ntoa, S. (eds.) HCII 2021. CCIS, vol. 1419, pp. 505–511. Springer, Cham (2021). https://doi.org/10.1007/978-3-030-78635-9_65
7. Kumar, S., Anastasopoulos, A., Wintner, S. and Tsvetkov, Y.: Machine translation into low-resource language varieties. In: Proceedings of the 59th Annual Meeting of the Association for Computational Linguistics and the 11th International Joint Conference on Natural Language Processing, vol 2, pp. 110–121. Association for Computational Linguistics (2021)
8. Klaper, D., Ebling, S., Volk, M.: Building a German/simple German parallel corpus for automatic text simplification. In: Proceedings of the Second Workshop on Predicting and Improving Text Readability for Target Reader Populations, pp. 11–19. Association for Computational Linguistics, Sofia, Bulgaria (2013)
9. Säuberli, A., Ebling, S., Volk, M.: Benchmarking data-driven automatic text simplification for German. In: Proceedings of the 1st Workshop on Tools and Resources to Empower People with Reading DIfficulties (READI), pp 41–48. European Language Resources Association, Marseille, France (2020)
10. Spring, N., Rios, A., Ebling, S.: Exploring German multi-level text simplification. In: Proceedings of the International Conference on Recent Advances in Natural Language Processing (RANLP 2021), pp. 1339–1349. INCOMA Ltd. (2021)

11. Hansen-Schirra, S., Nitzke, J., Gutermuth, S.: An intralingual parallel corpus of translations into German easy language (geasy corpus): what sentence alignments can tell us about translation strategies in intralingual translation. In: Wang, V.X., Lim, L., Li, D. (eds.) New Perspectives on Corpus Translation Studies. NFTS, pp. 281–298. Springer, Singapore (2021). https://doi.org/10.1007/978-981-16-4918-9_11
12. Palmer, D.D.: Tokenisation and Sentence Segmentation. CRC Press, Boca Raton (2000)
13. Olteanu, M., Moldovan, D.: Pp-attachment disambiguation using large context. In: Proceedings of the Conference on Human Language Technology and Empirical Methods in Natural Language Processing, pp. 273–280. Association for Computational Linguistics, Vancouver (2005)
14. Osama, M., Zaki-Ismail, A., Abdelrazek, M., Grundy, J., Ibrahim, A.: Score-based automatic detection and resolution of syntactic ambiguity in natural language requirements. In: IEEE International Conference on Software Maintenance and Evolution (ICSME), Adelaide, SA, Australia, pp. 651–661 (2020)
15. Bhandari, N., Chowdri, R., Singh, H., Qureshi, S.R.: Resolving ambiguities in named entity recognition using machine learning. In: International Conference on Next Generation Computing and Information Systems (ICNGCIS), Jammu, India, pp. 159–163 (2017)
16. Stoffel, F., Jentner, W., Behrisch, M., Fuchs, J., Keim, D.: Interactive Ambiguity Resolution of Named Entities in Fictional Literature. In: Computer Graphics Forum, vol. 36, no. 7, pp. 189–200. John Wiley & Sons Ltd. (2017)
17. Brinker, K., Cölfen, H., Pappert, S.: Linguistische Textanalyse. Eine Einführung in die Grundbegriffe und Methoden, 9th edn. Erich Schmidt Verlag, Berlin (2018)
18. NLTK Tokenizer. https://www.nltk.org/api/nltk.tokenize.regexp.html. Accessed 20 Jan 2023
19. OpenNLP Tokenizer ME. https://opennlp.apache.org/docs/1.8.1/apidocs/opennlp-tools/opennlp/tools/tokenize/TokenizerME.html. Accessed 20 Jan 2023
20. Qi, P., Zhang, Y., Bolton, J., Manning, C.D.: Stanza: a python natural language processing toolkit for many human languages. In Proceedings of the 58th Annual Meeting of the Association for Computational Linguistics: System Demonstrations, pp. 101–108. Association for Computational Linguistics (2020)
21. SpaCy NER. https://spacy.io/usage/linguistic-features#named-entities. Accessed 20 Jan 2023
22. Flair NER. https://github.com/flairNLP/flair. Accessed 20 Jan 2023
23. Universal Dependencies. https://universaldependencies.org/u/dep/det.html. Accessed 02 Mar 2023

Artificial Intelligence Applied to Trees "Fingerprints" Identification in the Amazon Rainforest

Paulo Hermida[1(✉)], Mauro Teófilo[1], Barbara Formoso[1], and André Vianna[2]

[1] Mobile Innovation Lab, Sidia Institute of Science and Technology, Manaus, AM, Brazil
{paulo.hermida,mauro.teofilo,barbara.formoso}@sidia.com

[2] Idesam - Conservation and Sustainable Development, Manaus, AM, Brazil
andre.vianna@idesam.org

Abstract. In the Amazon rainforest, trees are often given the same name because they share similar external characteristics such as color, smell, texture, and durability. Scientists face difficulty in identifying the unique features of these trees using a magnifying glass due to the similarity in their traits. To overcome this challenge, we propose using image classification models embedded in smartphones that can identify trees without requiring an internet connection. These models were trained on a dataset of 30 tree species using images that were obtained through macroscopic analysis of the tree's structure, enabling precise identification. The accuracy rate of this approach was over 95%, demonstrating its effectiveness.

Keywords: trees identification · forest management · wood trade frauds

1 Introduction

The primary focus of this work is to identify different types of wood botanically. This is an essential step to detect errors and fraudulent practices. When plants are alive, their reproductive and morphological parts are analyzed to identify them. However, during processing, these characteristics are often lost, making it challenging to identify the wood accurately. In the Amazon, different species may have the same popular name because they look similar, making it difficult to differentiate between them based on properties such as color, smell, texture, and durability. This, combined with the difficulty of identifying structures with the naked eye, often leads to mistakes in the timber trade. For sawn wood, macroscopic identification techniques are useful, as they require simple instruments and no magnification to analyze the wood's anatomical characteristics. There are various methods for identifying forest species in the Amazon,

Supported by Sidia Institute of Science and Technology http://www.sidia.com Idesam - Conservation and Sustainable Development https://www.idesam.org.

C. Stephanidis et al. (Eds.): HCII 2023, CCIS 1836, pp. 426–432, 2023.
https://doi.org/10.1007/978-3-031-36004-6_58

based on anatomical and organoleptic characteristics such as color, brightness, taste, smell, density, grain, and texture. Although widely used by field agents, macroscopic analysis can also be inconclusive because many species have similar anatomical characteristics. In this context, it's important to create tools that can aid field agents in their identification work. Existing literature suggests that artificial intelligence, machine learning, and computer vision can be effective in reducing subjectivity when identifying wood specimens. However, many of these AI-based methods only work for a small number of species that aren't found in the Amazon biome, which has thousands of different species, with only a few that can be sustainably managed. This study aims to address this gap by developing technology that focuses on identifying commercially viable wood species from the Amazon biome. This technology will be accessible through a smartphone app that uses AI models to identify species from sawn wood images captured on the device, even in areas with limited or no internet connectivity. Therefore, identifying the botanical species of wood becomes a more challenging task. This work contributes to solving this problem considering the following aspects:

1. Developing and implementing a process to capture images of wood samples from the Wood Laboratory of the Forest Engineering Course at the State University of Amazonas, Itacoatiara-AM.
2. Compiling a dataset featuring species from the Amazon, which can be accessed by the scientific community, thereby facilitating new research opportunities in this field.
3. Constructing and training a model to classify the various species included in the aforementioned dataset.
4. Designing an application that utilizes the previously trained model embedded, to provide a technological solution to a wide range of issues across various industries.

2 Methodology

The methodology used is divided into three phases; the first is related to the sample preparation process for the collection of images for the dataset. The images follow the specification of the Wood Macroscopic Analysis [2]. The second phase is related to the creation and training of a deep learning model for image classification. The third and last phase was the creation of an application that, using the model created in the previous item, makes the prediction of the species.

Macroscopic wood analysis refers to the study of the physical characteristics of wood that can be seen without using a microscope. To prepare a sample for this type of analysis, the wood is collected from a tree trunk, branch, or log, and then cut to a size suitable for examination. The sample is dried to remove any moisture, sanded to create a smooth surface, and may be stained to improve the visibility of different structures. Finally, the sample is mounted on a slide or cardboard for further examination or measurement. Overall, the preparation of wood for macroscopic analysis involves several steps to ensure that the sample is properly dried, sanded, and stained to provide accurate information about the structure and characteristics of the wood. The Fig. 1shows an example of a magnifying glass used to identify wood in the final phase of the macroscopic analysis process.

Fig. 1. Gathering pictures to form a dataset, using a smartphone equipped with a magnifying glass that has a 10× zoom.

The dataset creation process involves sample preparation, capture and post-processing on the images. Figure 1 shows the capture made using a smartphone and a 10× magnifying glass. In Fig. 2 some images that are part of the dataset.

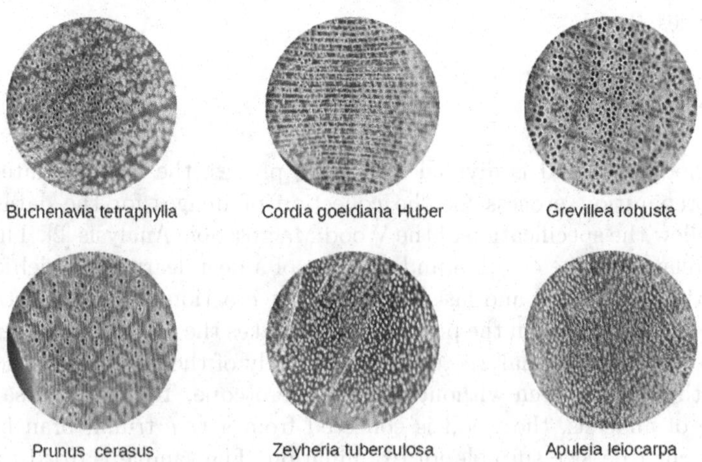

Fig. 2. Dataset images samples.

3 Image Classification Model

The training of the deep learning model that will classify the images was carried out, using the transfer learning technique. In this method, a model trained in one task is reused in a second task, in our case, wood classification. By applying transfer learning to a new task, significantly higher performance can be achieved considering that the amount of data in our dataset is not enough to train a complete model. Transfer learning is so common that it is rare to train a model for an image classification task or tasks related to natural language processing from scratch. Instead, researchers and data scientists prefer to start with a pre-trained model that already knows how to classify objects and has learned general features like edges, shapes in images, etc. MobileNet [4], ImageNet [3], AlexNet [1] and Inception [5] are typical examples of models that serve as a basis for transfer of learning.

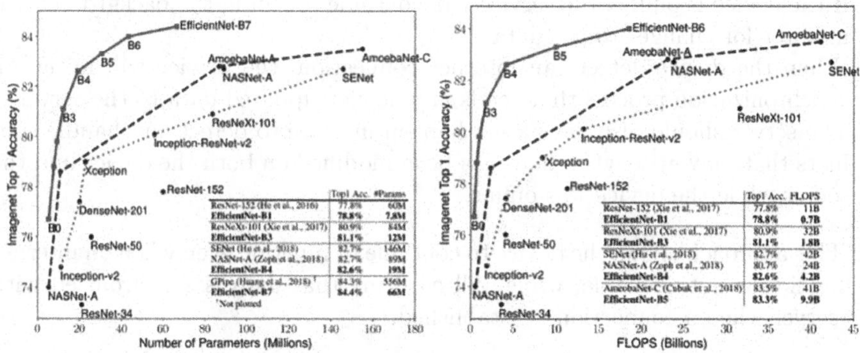

Fig. 3. EfficientNet is the actual State of the Art in the image classification task.

The model chosen was EfficientNet that is a family of neural network models developed by Google Brain Team in 2019, with the aim of achieving high accuracy with significantly fewer parameters and computations than existing state-of-the-art models such as ResNet and Inception. The main innovation behind EfficientNet is the use of a compound scaling technique that uniformly scales the depth, width, and resolution of the network. Specifically, the network is first scaled in depth (number of layers), width (number of channels), and then resolution (image size). This scaling approach ensures that the network is well-suited for a broad range of image classification tasks and achieves high accuracy with fewer parameters. EfficientNet uses a combination of convolutional layers, depthwise separable convolutions, and squeeze-and-excitation (SE) modules to capture and represent the important features of an image. Depthwise separable convolutions are used in place of regular convolutions, as they are more computationally efficient, and SE modules are used to selectively emphasize important features. EfficientNet models have achieved state-of-the-art performance on several image classification benchmarks, as seen in the Fig. 3, including the ImageNet dataset. Moreover, due to their small size and efficient architecture, they can be easily deployed on mobile devices and embedded systems. The final version of the model had an accuracy of the 95% with minor of 10 Mb of size.

4 Architecture Proposed

The proposed solution to this scenario is to implement a local caching system that stores the predictions while the smartphone is offline and then synchronizes it with the server when an internet connection is available. Here's a general outline of how this could work:

- Set up a local database on the device where the predictions can be stored.
- Was implemented a service or background process that periodically checks for an internet connection.
- If the device is offline, the service will continue to run in the background and monitor for changes to the data.
- When the device detects an internet connection, the service will initiate a synchronization process that sends any new or updated data to the server.
- The server should also have a mechanism in place to detect and handle conflicts that may arise when data has been modified on both the device and the server while the device was offline.

This approach allows the device to continue to function even when an internet connection is not available, while still ensuring that data is synchronized with the server when a connection is established.

5 The Final Solution Interfaces

In this section, we will display the screens of the Android app that employ the built-in model, along with the online interface that consolidates all the predictions produced by different users of the app. The primary screens of the app are presented in Fig. 4.

In the (a) the camera is taking pictures non-stop and transmitting them to the model. When the model recognizes a certain species, the application changes to another screen (b) which displays the top three possible species in descending order of how confident the model is in its identification. If there is a connection to the internet available, the prediction data will be transmitted instantly to the server. However, in the absence of an internet connection, the data will be stored locally and will be transmitted automatically to the server as soon as a connection is re-established.

Figure 5 displays the prediction query screen on the web platform, which allows users to view all the predictions made. The screen includes a map indicating the precise location of each prediction.

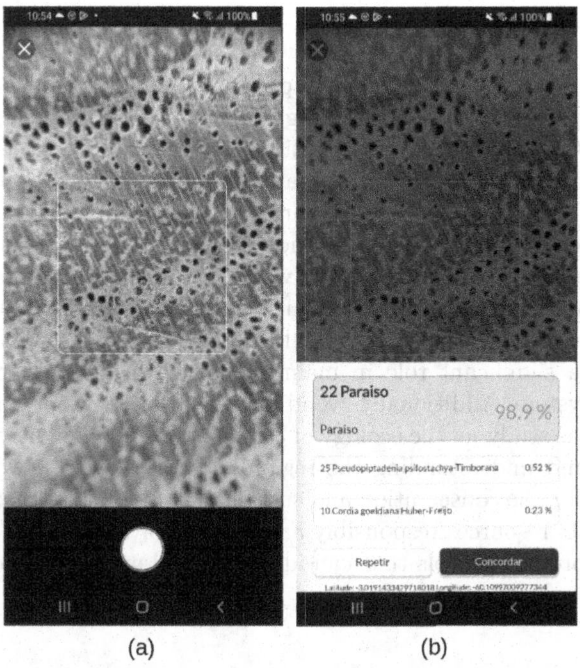

Fig. 4. WEB environment for consulting the predictions made.

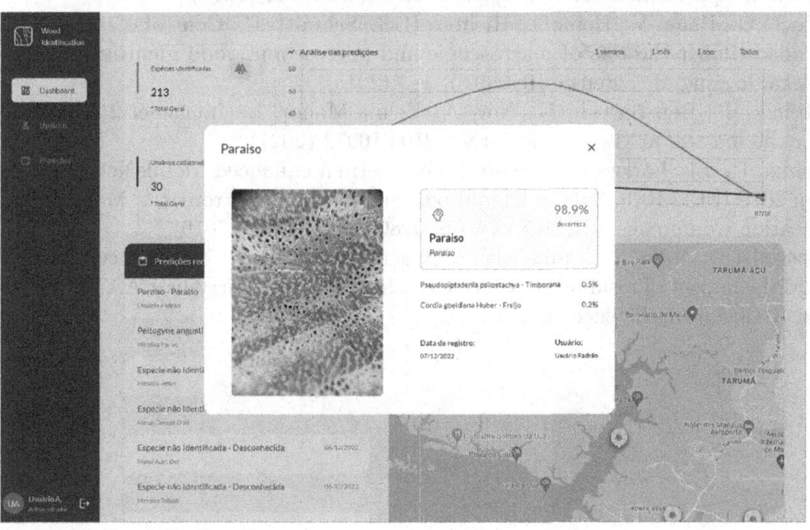

Fig. 5. WEB environment for consulting the predictions made.

6 Conclusion

In the Amazon forest, identifying the type of wood being harvested is extremely important for various reasons. Illegal logging is causing deforestation and biodiversity loss in the Amazon, and by identifying the type of wood being harvested, authorities can determine if it was obtained legally and take necessary action. The Amazon forest is an essential resource for local communities and the world at large, providing timber, fuelwood, and other valuable products. Understanding the properties of different types of wood can aid in developing sustainable management practices for the forest's long-term viability. Identifying endangered or threatened tree species is also critical for developing conservation strategies, as trees play a significant role in maintaining the health and biodiversity of the forest ecosystem. Additionally, wood identification is important for scientific research, such as studying the ecology of the forest, developing new products and technologies, and understanding the region's history. Overall, wood identification is crucial for the conservation and sustainable use of the Amazon forest and for managing its resources responsibly and sustainably. Our work contributes to this effort by providing tools that can identify wood with 95% accuracy.

References

1. Alom, M.Z., et al.: The history began from alexNet: a comprehensive survey on deep learning approaches. arXiv preprint arXiv:1803.01164 (2018)
2. Koch, G., Haag, V., Heinz, I., Richter, H.G., Schmitt, U.: Control of internationally traded timber-the role of macroscopic and microscopic wood identification against illegal logging. J. Forensic Res. **6**(6), 1–4 (2015)
3. Ridnik, T., Ben-Baruch, E., Noy, A., Zelnik-Manor, L.: Imagenet-21k pretraining for the masses. arXiv preprint arXiv:2104.10972 (2021)
4. Sinha, D., El-Sharkawy, M.: Thin MobileNet: an enhanced MobileNet architecture. In: 2019 IEEE 10th Annual Ubiquitous Computing, Electronics & Mobile Communication Conference (UEMCON), pp. 0280–0285. IEEE (2019)
5. Szegedy, C., Ioffe, S., Vanhoucke, V., Alemi, A.A.: Inception-v4, inception-ResNet and the impact of residual connections on learning. In: Thirty-first AAAI Conference on Artificial Intelligence (2017)

Automated Ontology Generation

Christianne Izumigawa(✉), Bethany Taylor, and Jonathan Sato

Naval Information Warfare Center Pacific, San Diego, CA, USA
{christianne.g.izumigawa.civ,bethany.j.taylor3.civ,
jonathan.k.sato.civ}@us.navy.mil

Abstract. Ontologies are human- and machine-readable conceptualizations that define domain concepts and their relationships. The context provided by these representations are essential for advanced reasoning applications and explainable artificial intelligence efforts. Despite their advantages, however, automating ontology generation from text is difficult due to a number of challenges. To bring greater awareness to those challenges and to initiate discussion on possible solutions, we provide a definition of ontologies, the motivation behind our work, a set of key challenges, and an overview of adjacent solutions in recent work.

Keywords: Ontology Learning · Natural Language Processing

1 Introduction

Sowa and Biemann define ontologies as "shared conceptualizations" of a domain [7,9]. Similar to dictionaries, ontologies outline a set of terms and their respective meanings. Surpassing dictionaries, however, ontologies also serve the purpose of defining relationships between terms. If the defined relationships are purely hierarchical, they are called taxonomies. Otherwise, they are generally referred to as ontologies. Based on Sowa and Biemann's definition, ontologies can be classified into one of three categories: formal, terminological, or prototype-based [7,9]. In this work, we will focus on the first two categories.

1.1 Formal Ontologies

Formal ontologies are logic-based conceptualizations that provide domain knowledge in the form of axioms. Axioms are statements that are considered true for the given domain [10] and can include hierarchical as well as property-related information. While axioms can be simple, the *combination* of axioms can describe complex relationships and interactions.

To better illustrate a formal ontology, we introduce a simple example with 3 axioms: a Beagle is a type of dog, a Maine Coon is a type of cat, and a thing cannot be both a cat and dog at the same time. From these 3 axioms, we are able to easily derive 2 more axioms: a Beagle cannot be a type of cat, and a Maine Coon cannot be a type of dog. Furthermore, every new type of dog or cat

C. Stephanidis et al. (Eds.): HCII 2023, CCIS 1836, pp. 433–438, 2023.
https://doi.org/10.1007/978-3-031-36004-6_59

Axioms	Meaning
subClassOf(Beagle, Dog)	"Beagle is a type of dog"
subClassOf(Maine Coon, Cat)	"Maine Coon is a type of cat"
disjointWith(Dog, Cat)	"Dog cannot be a cat; cat cannot be a dog"

Derived Axioms	Meaning
disjointWith(Beagle, Cat)	"Beagle cannot be a type of cat"
disjointWith(Maine Coon, Dog)	"Maine Coon cannot be a type of dog"

Fig. 1. A formal ontology example with 3 specified axioms. This example shows that 3 specified axioms can easily produce 2 other derived axioms without the need to explicitly state them.

added to the ontology will have the same property that it cannot be both a dog and cat at the same time, so it will also produce a derived axiom.

While formal ontologies are easy to reason about, they are the most difficult type of ontology to infer from natural language text. In most text documents, simple axioms are assumed to be known by the reader and are not explicitly stated. Even in cases with explicit statements, it can be difficult to automatically generate truthful and consistent axioms from text. Because of these setbacks, formal ontologies are typically made by human experts rather than automated processes.

1.2 Terminological Ontologies

Terminological ontologies (term ontologies) are term-based conceptualizations that provide domain knowledge through associations of terms (i.e. hypernyms, hyponyms, synonyms, and antonyms). While they can hierarchically represent the same information as formal ontologies, they lack the other critical axioms and logic that formal ontologies provide.

Following our previous example of cats and dogs, we form a term ontology (shown in Fig. 1) that contains the following information: Beagle is a type of dog, Maine Coon is a type of cat, a dog is a type of animal, a cat is a type of animal, and the words "dog" and "cat" are antonyms. Because the information presented is given by semantic associations, term ontologies are easier to automatically generate from text than formal ontologies. The applications that can be built on this type of ontology are limited though.

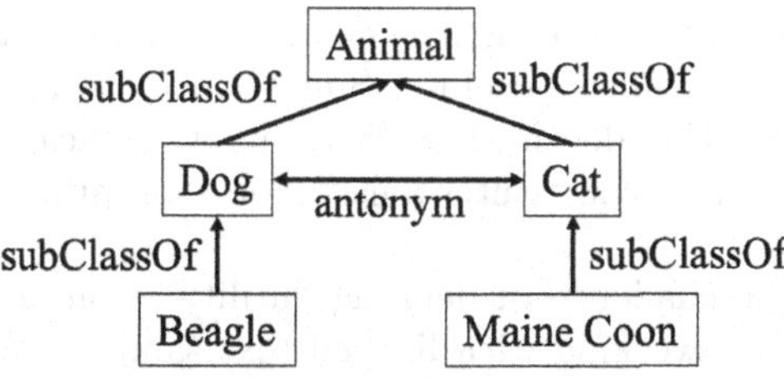

Fig. 2. A term ontology example showing the relationships of each term to another.

2 Motivation

In the field of explainable artificial intelligence (XAI), ontologies bridge the gap between human insight and efficient machine processing by providing human-machine teams a shared medium to communicate and draw understanding from [13]. By constraining domain terminology, ontologies enable contextually appropriate explanations and have been shown to help humans understand black-box classification predictions in the medical domain [3]. In natural language processing (NLP), ontologies help to generate better predictions for document classification, co-reference resolution, question answering, and entity disambiguation [7].

Aside from machine learning applications, ontologies are beneficial to other fields as well. Experts across various industries have contributed to the development of well-known ontologies such as the Financial Industry Business Ontology (FIBO) [11] and the Chemical Entities of Biological Interest (ChEBI) ontology [12]. In these fields, ontologies document and define industry standards with the added benefit of future utility towards automation efforts.

Despite their importance, however, ontologies are often hand-crafted by a subset of domain experts in a way that is difficult to scale and upkeep. While organizations may not have the personnel necessary to curate an ontology, many organizations have an abundance of documentation on their domain of interest. To capitalize on the available data and to resolve the problem of hand-generating ontologies, we seek a solution that is able to automatically generate domain ontologies from a text corpus in lieu of human experts.

3 Key Challenges in Ontology Learning from Text

In this work, automated ontology generation refers to the following idea: given a text corpus and target domain, produce a formal ontology that gleans as much ontological information from the corpus as possible. While this working definition invites a wide variety of solutions, it also highlights a wide variety of challenges.

3.1 Limitations by Input Text

Similar to other NLP problems, an immediate limitation of this problem setup is the content and quality of the input text. The text corpus must have enough information in it, as well as the right type of information in it, to produce an ontology that can be deemed "useful." Since the working definition of automated ontology generation doesn't specify a target application, there is a need to determine what content constitutes a useful or appropriate corpus apart from a specific use-case.

In addition to the challenge of defining "utility" from a text corpus, there is also the challenge of working with limited text samples. While it is common practice to use existing knowledge bases and ontologies to supplement missing information [5,6], niche internal processes rarely align with supplementing resources and thereby limit the advantage of using existing ontologies.

3.2 Multiple Correct Ontologies

In recent works, it has been shown that it is possible to complete a version of an ontology from a text corpus without having a specific application in mind [5,6]. However, in those cases, an ontology was being extended (and therefore already had a structure and training samples in place), or supplemental references provided a structure that aligned with the desired ontology.

The issue of multiple correct ontologies is that there isn't a metric to compare whether one ontology representation is better than another without an application in mind. For example, in Fig. 2, a formal ontology with the axiom "disjointWith(Dog, Bear)" instead of "disjointWith(Dog, Cat)," would still be a valid formal ontology. There would be a loss in the amount of derived terms, but the ontology is still correct.

Similar to the previous limitation by input text, there is a need to define the application of the domain in order to produce meaningful hierarchies of terms and domain concepts.

3.3 Deriving Axioms from Text

Masked language models interpret the meaning of words by their statistical significance to their neighbors [4]. While this is extremely useful for question answering and chat capabilities, there is still the issue that it is difficult to derive axioms and logic from text [7,14]. It is even harder to do so when the text corpus on a given domain is limited to a couple hundred instances rather than the millions that might exist in other domains.

Moreover, while logic-based consistency checkers can catch inconsistent and error-inducing axioms [1], they are unable to check whether the information presented in the ontology is inaccurate. In this situation, there is a need to generate accuracy metrics between the corpus and the inferred axioms.

4 Adjacent Solutions in Recent Work

While there are still unanswered questions in the automated ontology generation problem space (e.g. whether or not a "usefulness" metric can be defined apart from a use-case or user feedback), recent work from adjacent domains have provided insight into how to solve parts of the previously mentioned key challenges.

4.1 Metrics for Automated Ontology Generation

Hohenecker et al. proposed ontology reasoning with the use of deep neural networks (DNNs) [14]. By providing the DNN with facts and rules about the domain, the DNN was able to learn the derived statements necessary to answer logic-based queries. Figure 3 presents a modified version of an example ontology given in Hohenecker et al. While the method requires a formal ontology to reason over, their work demonstrates that it is possible to solve reasoning tasks with an appropriate ontology. Working backwards, we could use similar models to find the form of ontologies that do and do not solve reasoning tasks. This could be one way to create metrics that alleviate the problem of multiple correct ontologies.

Axioms	Meaning
holds(Mary, apple)	"Mary holds an apple"
isAt(Y, Z) ← holds(X,Y) ∧ isAt(X,Z)	"Objects are at the same location as the one holding them"
isAt(Mary, kitchen)	"Mary is in the kitchen"
Derived Reasoning	**Meaning**
isAt(apple, kitchen)	"The apple is in the kitchen"

Fig. 3. A modified formal ontology example from [14] that describes an ontology reasoning task.

4.2 Ontology Extensions

Memariani et al. proposes an automated way to extend ontologies in the chemical structures domain. Though their work is based on a transformer architecture trained on strings that represent chemical entities as a linear sequence of characters, their method has implications of ontology extension in any domain. By training the model on the ontology that is already available, they are able to learn the ontology's structure through multi-label prediction and successfully extend the ChEBI ontology.

While this may not solve the challenge of automatically generating an ontology from scratch, once a sufficiently large ontology is generated, this work proves that there exists a way to automatically extend the ontology by utilizing its existing structure.

5 Conclusion

To highlight the importance of ontologies, we provided the motivation behind our work and noted the beneficial implications that ontologies can have on XAI, NLP, medical and financial domains. We also brought to attention the challenges faced by automated ontology generating pipelines in the hope of adding interest and new solutions to the field.

References

1. Musen, M.A.: The Protégé project: a look back and a look forward. AI Matters **1**(4) (2015). Association of Computing Machinery Specific Interest Group in Artificial Intelligence https://www.ncbi.nlm.nih.gov/pmc/articles/PMC4883684/
2. Weston, J., Bordes, A., Chopra, S., Mikolov, T., Rush, A.M., van Merriënboer, B.: Towards AI-complete question answering: a set of prerequisite toy tasks, arXiv:1502.05698
3. Panigutti, C., Perotti, A., Pedreschi, D.: Doctor XAI: an ontology-based approach to black-box sequential data classification explanations. In: Proceedings of the 2020 Conference on Fairness, Accountability, and Transparency, FAT2020, pp. 629–639, New York, NY, USA, 2020. Association for Computing Machinery. ISBN: 9781450369367. https://doi.org/10.1145/3351095.3372855
4. Devlin, J., Chang, M.-W., Lee, K., Toutanova, K.: BERT: pre-training of deep bidirectional transformers for language understanding. https://doi.org/10.48550/arXiv.1810.04805
5. Memariani, A., Glauer, M., Neuhaus, F., Mossakowski, T., Hastings, J.: Automated and explainable ontology extension based on deep learning: a case study in the chemical domain. (2021). https://doi.org/10.48550/arXiv.2109.09202
6. Elnagar, S., Yoon, V., Thomas, M.: An automatic ontology generation framework with an organizational perspective. In: Proceedings of the 53rd Hawaii International Conference on System Sciences (2020). https://doi.org/10.48550/arXiv.2112.02682
7. Biemann, C., Ontology learning from text: a survey of methods. In: LDV Forum, vol. 20, pp. 75–93. (2005)
8. Xu, Y., Rajpathak, D., Gibbs, I., Klabjan, D.: Automatic ontology learning from domain-specific short unstructured text data. https://doi.org/10.48550/arXiv.1903.04360
9. Sowa, J. F. (2003). Ontology. http://www.jfsowa.com/ontology/ (last modified 2010)
10. World Wide Web Consortium (W3C). OWL 2 Web Ontology Language (2012). https://www.w3.org/TR/owl2-syntax/#Axioms. Accessed 2012
11. FIBO Members. Financial Industry Business Ontology (FIBO) (2023). EDM Council. https://spec.edmcouncil.org/fibo/
12. Hastings, J., et al.: ChEBI in 2016: improved services and an expanding collection of metabolites. Nucleic Acids Res. **44**, D1214–D1219 (2016). https://doi.org/10.1093/nar/gkv1031
13. Saeed, W., Omlin, C.W.: Explainable AI (XAI): a systematic meta-survey of current challenges and future opportunities. Knowl.-Based Syst. **263** (2021). https://doi.org/10.48550/arXiv.2111.06420
14. Hohenecker, P., Lukasiewicz, T.: Ontology reasoning with deep neural networks. J. Arti. Intell. Res. **68**, 503–540 (2020)

Knowledge-Grounded and Self-extending NER

Sudarshan Kamath Barkur[1(✉)], Sigurd Schacht[1], and Carsten Lanquillon[2]

[1] University of Applied Sciences, Ansbach, Germany
{s.kamath-barkur,sigurd.schacht}@hs-ansbach.de
[2] University of Applied Sciences, Heilbronn, Germany
carsten.lanquillon@hs-heilbronn.de

Abstract. The wave of digitization has begun. Organizations deal with huge amounts of data, such as logs, websites, and documents. A common way to make the information contained in these sources machine-accessible for automated processing is to first extract the information and then store it in a knowledge graph. A key task in this approach is to recognize entities. While common named entity recognition (NER) models work well for common entity types, they typically fail to recognize custom entities. Custom entity recognition requires data to be manually annotated and custom NER models to be trained. To efficiently extract the information, this paper proposes an innovative solution: Our *Gazetteer* approach uses a knowledge graph to create a coarse and fast NER component, reducing the need for manual annotation and saving human effort. Focusing on a university use case, our Gazetteer is integrated into a chatbot for entity recognition. In addition, data can be annotated using the Gazetteer and an NER model can be trained. Subsequently, the NER model can be used to recognize unseen custom entities, which are then added to the knowledge graph. This will improve the knowledge graph and make it self-extending.

Keywords: Large Language Models · Knowledge Graphs · Named Entity Recognition (NER) · Chatbots

1 Introduction

The digitization of data is emerging at a fast pace. Information resides in structured, semi-structured, or unstructured data. Structured data refer to well-defined data that typically appear in tables, for example, relational databases and spreadsheets. Semi-structured data do not have a fixed or full definition, but still have some structure, such as JSON data. Unstructured data does not have a fixed structure, like text from Internet websites or audio files.

To extract information from unstructured data, language models can be used to convert the data into so-called triples. Triples consist of information fragments relating a *subject* to an *object* by means of a *predicate*. For structured and semi-structured data, triple extraction depends on the format of the data. The format of certain tables allows for easy triple extraction. For example, consider the

C. Stephanidis et al. (Eds.): HCII 2023, CCIS 1836, pp. 439–446, 2023.
https://doi.org/10.1007/978-3-031-36004-6_60

semi-structured HTML tables from a website with detailed data about a person. The person is the subject, the attributes mentioned in the table header (or the first row, depending on the orientation of the table) are the predicates, and the values mentioned for the corresponding attributes are the objects. Once the data is in the form of triples, it can be stored in a knowledge graph as nodes and edges. Subjects and objects are represented as nodes, and the predicate, which relates a subject and an object, is represented by an edge between the nodes.

The knowledge graph makes it possible to organize and store information. It allows the addition of metadata and linking elements. Patterns and relationships can also be identified, providing a better understanding of the data. The knowledge graph can be linked to other applications such as chatbots.

In order to effectively extract the information from the knowledge graph, the entity needs to be looked up in the knowledge graph to find the corresponding node. Then the required information should be extracted from the corresponding nodes and given back to the user. In use cases such as a chatbot, where information is retrieved by asking questions in natural language, it is necessary to recognize both the intent and entities in order to look up the corresponding information in the knowledge graph.

Frameworks like Flair [6], libraries like SpaCy [5] and HuggingFace transformers [8] offer pre-trained models for the NER task. Given some text, these models can recognize entities and their spans, as these models are already trained to accomplish the same task. If the pre-trained models cannot recognize the entities, the model needs to be trained again. For example, in legal, medical, or custom datasets, texts need to be annotated for the entities and then be provided as training data to the model. This requires manual effort to clean and annotate the text.

This paper introduces the Gazetteer, which offers entity recognition, with the source being the knowledge graph. The Gazetteer matches the text given as input, to the entities existing in the knowledge graph. Since the data to be annotated is already present in the knowledge graph, it can be used:

- to pre-annotate training data which saves time for human annotation.
- as a standalone NER model which requires no training.

2 Problem Statement

As discussed above, the knowledge graph can be a good source of information. A chatbot acts as an interface between the user and the data, replacing conventional search. The chatbot can be connected to the knowledge graph so that user queries can be answered with the help of the information present in the knowledge graph. The information related to the university is extracted from the university's web pages and then processed and stored in the knowledge graph. For the university use case, we have developed a chatbot called DIAS [7], which enables students to search for information, answers commonly asked questions, and searches for information related to people or study programs. The bot is built using the Rasa Framework [10], which has the DIET classifier (dual intent and entity transformer) for joint training of intents and entities. In addition, the framework also offers regex and conditional random rields (CRF) for entity recognition, with the possibility to integrate a pre-trained SpaCy model or any other custom model of choice. For entity recognition and intent classification, the examples must be annotated and provided to the framework, which can then train the DIET classifier.

Named entity recognition (NER) is an important component of a chatbot. NER is necessary to understand the entities referred to in the chat, which can be used to fill up slots used for internal processing or to query the database or the knowledge graph. For example, common questions are asked about a person working at the university or any study program. In this case, it is necessary to identify the entities (i.e. the name of the person or the study program) that are being referred to by the user in the chat.

Many entities are specific to the university domain. There are even differences among universities. Furthermore, the chatbot may have to deal with languages that are not widely spoken or for which the available models can only recognize few entities. For example, popular frameworks for NER such as Flair [6] and libraries such as SpaCy [5] have NER models trained in the German language. These models are typically trained on the CoNLL-2003 dataset [11] and can recognize only four entity types: persons (PER), locations (LOC), organizations (ORG), and miscellaneous (MISC). On the contrary, the English model trained on the OntoNotes 5.0 dataset can recognize 18 entity types.

Additionally, if the domains are very specific, there are two scenarios:

- There are additional data present, but it needs to be annotated manually.
- There is not enough data to train the model, but the entities need to be recognized.

Data annotation requires human effort. This effort can be reduced by pre-annotation. Additionally, it is beneficial to build components that can be reused. In the chatbot scenario, it makes sense to import the trained NER model with custom code within the Rasa Framework for better reusability rather than training the entity recognition with Rasa. The Gazetteer can do entity recognition directly from the knowledge graph. No additional annotations need to be done in the text that is being provided to the Rasa Framework for intent classification. This saves human effort.

3 Related Work

Pasupat and Liang [9] mention an approach of zero-shot extraction by giving a natural language query and a single web page. Here, the emphasis is on the layout and the placement of the entities extracted and the linguistic features of the entities being extracted [9]. The DOM tree elements with less than 140 characters are extracted. This approach gets around 40.5% accuracy on the test set in a zero-shot setting.

Another similar approach uses conditional random fields (CRF), which are trained on the partially annotated data, to use it to tag the dataset. The token sequence is encoded using a pre-trained transformer encoder. Each tag is scored and the distribution of the scores is learned by the CRF. This approach was used by Effland and Collins [4]. Their model "EER-BERT-all" reports an F1 score of 73.6 % on the CoNLL dataset.

4 Gazetteer Implementation

4.1 Data Preparation for the Knowledge Graph

To prepare the knowledge graph for the chatbot, the website of the university was crawled. The structure of the page was studied manually to understand the parts of the website that contain the required data, excluding other parts of a website such as a header or navigation links. All tables related to the people and the study programs were converted into a JSON object. The first column of the table served as the JSON key, and the second column contained the JSON value. The topic of the page and the URL were also stored, which was then used to correlate to the person being referred. The same procedure was used to extract the data associated with the study programs.

The JSON data can be transformed into a triple, where the subject (i.e. a person or a study program) is linked via a relation/predicate (i.e. the JSON key) to an object (i.e. the JSON value). Subjects and objects are stored as nodes. The predicates or relations are stored as edges. Therefore, in the knowledge graph, each person is represented as a node, and all values such as the telephone number, address, email, and roles are also represented as a node. The connections between the nodes are the edges, which highlight that a given person has the given address, and so on. Furthermore, in the data for the study program, it can be seen that the study program manager and the academic councellors are people. These were linked to their corresponding nodes using edges. The JSON data is input into the ArangoDB [2] using the Python connector Python-Arango [3]. Before the data are inserted, a graph is defined. Each vertex collection and edge collection is defined (Tables 1 and 2).

Table 1. List of attributes for a person

Attribute name in ArangoDB	Meaning	Corresponding Pre-trained Entity
person	Name of the person	PER
telefon	Telephone number	
sprechzeiten	Availability	
email	Email	
anschrift	Address	LOC
funktionen	Roles	
lehrgebiete	Teaching Areas	
titel	Title	

Table 2. List of attributes for a study program

Attribute name in ArangoDB	Meaning	Corresponding Pre-trained Entity
studiengang	Study Program	
kurzform	Abbreviation	
studienart	Study type (Full-time or Part-time)	
abschluss	Degree at completion	
studienstart	Start semester of a Study	
zulassungsbeschränkung	Admission Restrictions	
vorlesungsort	Location	LOC
sprache	Language	
studiengangleitung(person)	Study Program Manager	PER
studienfachberatung(person)	Academic Councellor	PER
url	URL	

4.2 Connection to FlashText

The knowledge graph contains all the entities in the form of nodes. The information from the nodes is fed directly into the module called FlashText [12]. FlashText is faster than Regex, as the complexity depends on the size of the document, whereas the complexity of Regex depends on the product of the document size and the keywords to be identified [12]. FlashText is connected to the knowledge graph in ArangoDB using Python-Arango [3].

In addition, if parts of an address are separated by commas, the address is broken down into more components to facilitate identification, even if there are prepositions in the text. Similarly, names are divided into first and last names, enabling the annotation of individuals even if they are referred to only by their last name.

4.3 Data Preparation for the Model

The paragraphs are created by providing the JSON object to ChatGPT [1] and prompting it to generate a paragraph in German. This was done for the persons and the study program JSON objects. As our Gazetteer can already identify these elements with 100% probability, this annotates the data that the SpaCy model has to learn. Therefore, the process of dataset creation and training is automated.

5 Training and Evaluation

5.1 Training

The complete dataset was split into train and test set with ratio of 80:20. The training was done for 80 epochs for the model *de_core_news_lg*, which is a pre-trained model offered by SpaCy.

5.2 Evaluation

For the evaluation of entity recognition, the metrics precision, recall and F1-score are used:

Precision This measure is the ratio of the positives that are correctly predicted to the total positive predictions made by the model.

Recall This measure is the ratio of the positives that are correctly predicted to the total positives present in the dataset.

F1-score This measure is a harmonic mean of precision and recall, in order to combine the precision and recall to give a balanced evaluation.

The results of the evaluation are mentioned in Table 3. It can be observed that the model performs well overall, with difficulties in predicting the "Lehrgebiet" of a person.

Table 3. NER Evaluation Metrics - overall and per entity

Entity Type	Precision	Recall	F1-Score
Overall	91.55	92.44	91.99
PER	93.92	92.67	93.29
FUNKTION	92.90	96.00	94.43
STUDY	94.29	98.51	96.35
LEHRGEBIET	57.69	53.57	55.56
EMAIL	98.77	97.56	98.16
TELEFON	96.05	98.65	97.33
ZEIT	100.00	100.00	100.00
LOC	96.04	95.10	95.57
URL	98.78	98.78	98.78
TITLE	97.96	96.00	96.97
ORT	97.33	96.05	96.69
KURZFORM_STUDY	89.16	98.67	93.67
ABSCHLUSS_STUDY	88.89	100.00	94.12
SPRACHE	80.95	100.00	89.47
ZULASSUNGSBESCHRAENKUNG	100.00	100.00	100.00
STUDIENART_STUDY	75.00	100.00	85.71
ZEIT_STUDY	66.67	100.00	80.00
SEMESTER	100.00	100.00	100.00

5.3 Self-Extension Aspect

In order to achieve self-extension of the Named Entity Recognition (NER), it is essential to ensure that any new information identified by the NER system is integrated back into the knowledge graph. To facilitate this process, the Gazetteer is employed in three distinct modes.

Firstly, the Standalone mode leverages the knowledge graph as the primary source for entities. This mode is particularly useful in situations where all possible entities are already present in the knowledge graph, allowing for efficient and accurate identification of entities.

Secondly, the Tandem mode involves the Gazetteer working in conjunction with a pretrained model, enabling the detection of previously unseen entities within text. Both the model and the knowledge graph are frozen.

Finally, the Extension mode involves a collaborative approach between the Gazetteer and the model. Here, unseen entities are recognized by the model and integrated back into the knowledge graph. If the model fails to identify an entity, this is marked for future training, enhancing the performance of the model, and ultimately leading to a self-extending NER system.

In summary, the Gazetteer plays a critical role in facilitating the self-extension of NER models by enabling the seamless integration of new entities back into the knowledge graph, with each of the three modes providing unique benefits depending on the specific scenario.

6 Conclusion

The following summarizes our observations:

Self Extending NER In the Extension mode, the Gazetteer becomes a self extending NER, with the knowledge graph extending itself with the help of the model and model becomes better trained with the help of the Gazetteer.

Speed Gazetteer does not have a restriction on the context size like a Large Language Model. Therefore, even when preparing the data for training, the Gazetteer could annotate 300 paragraphs in 0.5 s. This means faster NER in a chatbot scenario and also quicker annotations to annotate the dataset for retraining.

Standalone Component Gazetteer can be integrated as a standalone component into the chatbot, especially in the cases where the domain in restricted or small.

Always up to date As the component is synced to the knowledge graph, the entities it can recognize / tag is up-to-date. The websites can be crawled at regular intervals and the knowledge graph can always contain recent data. Adding new data and new entity types is not a problem.

7 Future Work

To further advance the work conducted thus far, several ideas can be proposed for future research. Firstly, efforts should be focused on the recognition of relationships between new entities that are added to the knowledge graph. This would enable the development of more advanced models that can understand the context of entities and their connections to each other.

Furthermore, we need to improve our method to identify potential entities in sparsely annotated data, where some of the entities are labeled but not all. In the existing scenario, the model learns to mark a potential entity as not an entity, as there is no annotation present. One possible solution to address this issue is through the use of embeddings from pre-trained language models, which could be used to generate confidence scores and perform clustering based on a sliding window over the text.

Finally, the use of GPT-3 with few-shot prompting is recommended as a means of reducing the need for extensive human effort in data annotation. However, challenges related to hallucinations and incorrect spans generated by the model must be addressed to ensure its effectiveness.

References

1. AI, O.: ChatGPT - a sibling of InstructGPT which is trained to follow an instruction (2023). https://chat.openai.com/chat
2. ArangoDB: ArangoDB - a native multi-model database with flexible data models for documents, graphs, and key-values (2023). https://www.arangodb.com/
3. Community, A.: Python Arango - Python driver for Arango (2023), https://github.com/ArangoDB-Community/python-arango
4. Effland, T., Collins, M.: Partially supervised named entity recognition via the expected entity ratio loss (2021). https://doi.org/10.48550/ARXIV.2108.07216, https://arxiv.org/abs/2108.07216
5. Explosion: SpaCy - Industrial-strength Natural Language Processing (NLP) in Python (2023). https://spacy.io/
6. Flair: Flair - a very simple framework for state-of-the-art Natural Language Processing (NLP) (2023). https://github.com/flairNLP/flair
7. Henne, S., Mehlin, V., Schmid, E., Schacht, S.: The DIAS project. development of an intelligent digital assistant in higher education. In: Proceedings of the 4th International Conference Business Meets Technology (BMT22). Editorial Universitat Politècnica de València (2023)
8. HuggingFace: HuggingFace Transformers - State-of-the-art Machine Learning for Pytorch, TensorFlow, and JAX (2023), https://github.com/huggingface/transformers
9. Pasupat, P., Liang, P.: Zero-shot entity extraction from web pages. In: Proceedings of the 52nd Annual Meeting of the Association for Computational Linguistics (Volume 1: Long Papers). pp. 391–401 (2014)
10. Rasa: Rasa - an open source machine learning framework to automate text and voice-based conversations (2023). https://rasa.com/
11. Sang, E.F., De Meulder, F.: Introduction to the CoNLL-2003 shared task: language-independent named entity recognition. arXiv preprint cs/0306050 (2003)
12. Singh, V.: Replace or retrieve keywords in documents at scale. arXiv preprint arXiv:1711.00046 (2017)

Assessment of Emotional and Social Intelligence Using Artificial Intellegent

Akif Khilmiyah[1(✉)] and Giri Wiyono[2]

[1] Universitas Muhammadiyah, Yogyakarta, Indonesia
akif.khilmiyah@umy.ac.id
[2] Universitas Negeri, Yogyakarta, Indonesia

Abstract. Artificial Intelligence (AI) is a branch of computer science that emphasizes the development of machine intelligence, thinking patterns, and working like humans. In the field of education, there is often a problem with learning patterns that include learning methods and strategies that are not comprehensive. The purpose of the Artificial Intelligence theory movement is to understand what intelligence is and make machines more useful in education to facilitate students learning according to their experiences. Creating a better quality of student learning and efforts to implement value formation along with the character of students and students. This aims to test the effectiveness of an android-based emotional and social intelligence assessment instrument (PKES) designed to measure student character achievement from learning outcomes. The research used a quantitative method with an experimental, descriptive approach. The trial was conducted at four primary schools in Bantul with 150 grade IV and V students in proportional random sampling. Data collection techniques through questionnaires using the P-KES-SD application. Data analysis using descriptive statistics. The results of this study show that (1) The design of character assessment applications in online learning consists of user flowcharts, admin flowcharts, data flow diagrams, entity relationship data, (2) Character achievements from online learning aspects of emotional intelligence aspects are highest affective aspects in the character of responsibility, peace-loving, hard work, honesty, and the highest in cognitive aspects is only tolerance. Meanwhile, social intelligence is highest in cognitive aspects in the character of tolerance, love of the homeland, hard work, care for the environment, and the lowest character of caring for others. This proves that Artificial Intelligence has facilitated the task of teachers in assessing student character and making it easier for students to find out the level of emotional and social intelligence that has been achieved from learning.

Keywords: Artificial Intellegent · Emotional and Social Intelligence · Primary School First Section

1 Introduction

Artificial Intelligence (AI) is a branch of digital literacy systems that has a large role in the process of developing intelligence [1]. Digital literacy is more associated with the technical skills of accessing, stringing, understanding, and disseminating information.

C. Stephanidis et al. (Eds.): HCII 2023, CCIS 1836, pp. 447–453, 2023.
https://doi.org/10.1007/978-3-031-36004-6_61

According to Paul Gilster, [2] digital literacy is defined as the ability to understand and use information from a very wide range of sources accessed through computer devices. Bawden in Chanda Halim [3] offers a new understanding of digital literacy rooted in computer literacy and information literacy. Digital literacy is more associated with the technical skills of accessing, stringing, understanding, and disseminating information.

In the field of education, there are often problems with learning patterns that include learning methods and strategies that are not comprehensive. Students often misinterpret the material given, which is not an absolute mistake for their educators or their students. However, there is a need for an innovation system that can improve the quality of mindset and competence so as to minimize these events. Thus, innovation is needed to improve the quality of education in the form of a system that supports the field of education, such as artificial intelligence.

The purpose of the Artificial Intelligence theory movement is to correctly understand what artificial intelligence is and how to make this machine more useful in education to facilitate students in learning according to their experience. Creating a better quality of student learning and efforts to implement the formation of values and student character. Education is not only related to students' quantitative competence but also related to the values and character obtained during their education.

Therefore, this research was conducted in order to help make it easier for teachers to assess the character of students in aspects of emotional and social intelligence by using the PKES.SD application (Emotional and Social Intelligence Assessment for Primary School children). This study focused on introducing the design of android-based emotional and social intelligence assessments and knowing the empirical test of the effectiveness of this application to measure student character achievement aspects of emotional and social intelligence that students have achieved.

2 Literature Review

2.1 Emotional Intelligence

Emotional intelligence is a person's cognitive ability to regulate emotions, express emotions, and understand and assess emotions in oneself and others [4]. This opinion is reinforced by Triana Indrawati [5], Salovey [6], Cuéllar-Molina, García-Cabrera, Déniz [7], Hillary Anger Elfenbien and Carolyn MacCann [8], and Bar-On in Diana Amado Alonso et al. [9] Emotional intelligence is a set of skills, and interconnected emotional and social behaviors such as understanding others, expressing oneself, interacting with others, overcoming everyday problems, challenges, and pressure.

Meanwhile, according to Akif Khilmiyah and Giri Wiyono [10], Ilmi Al Idrus and Damayanti [11], Bryan Forsyth [12], and Goleman [13], Emotional intelligence is divided into five aspects, namely: 1). Recognizing one's own emotions or self-awareness, 2). Managing self-emotions, 3). Self-motivating, 4). Recognizing the emotions of others, 5). Fostering relationships with others.

2.2 Social Intelligence

As for the notion of social intelligence as explained by Mochamad Ilham Akbar [14], Akif Khilmiyah [15], Katarzyna Knopp A.[16], Mojca Kukanja Gabrijelčič [17], Eko

Purwanti and Pipit Diah Noviana [18], Phan Trong Ngo [19], Goleman [20], and Febi Junaidi [21] Social intelligence is a person's ability to understand their environment, have a high ability to communicate with others, and understand and listen to and process social information and awareness social.

3 Research Method

The research method used is experimental, and the research approach is carried out in a quantitative descriptive manner. The trial was conducted in 4 elementary schools in Bantul with participants of 150 students in grades IV and V by proportional random sampling. Data collection techniques used questionnaires in the P-KES-SD application. Data analysis using descriptive statistics. Utilization of Artificial Intelligence for educational character assessment using experimental methods. This method is tailored to student interests, student abilities, and student learning experiences, especially in the operation of e-learning-based technology and to student responses related to character values. AI can be simplified when preparing data for analytics and developing algorithmic models that are then integrated and integrated into android-based PKES.SD application system products.

4 Findings and Discussion

4.1 Application System Design.PKES.SD

The design of the android-based PKES.The SD application system is made in the form of a flowchart as follows (Fig. 1):

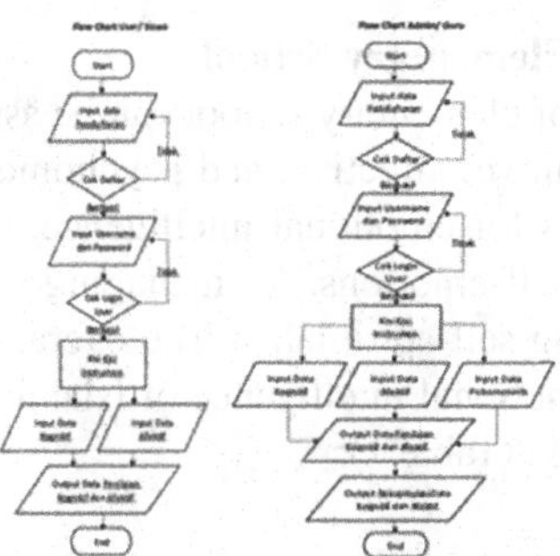

Fig. 1. Student Flowchart and Teacher Flowchart

The two flowchart images above show that teachers and students alike have access to fill out this application. The PKES. SD program is divided into 2 main menus, namely: Student menu, only accessible to students who already have an account as a student. Teacher Menu, accessible only to teachers, principals, and school employees who already have a teacher account. The student menu facility contains instruments for the assessment of cognitive and affective aspects. The teacher's menu contains psychomotor aspect assessment instruments. See a recap of all student assessment results. Print the results of the assessment. Remove incorrect or already unnecessary assessments. Enroll new users/students, schools, and teachers. The Data Flow Diagram is as follows (Fig. 2):

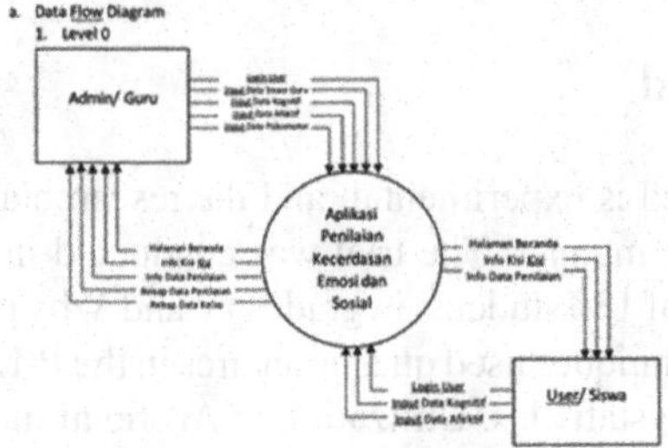

Fig. 2. Emotional and Social Intelligence Assessment Application

At this level. The teacher, as the admin, is in charge of user login, student and teacher data input, and cognitive, affective, and psychomotor data input. On the home page, there is already instrument grid info, assessment data info, assessment data recapitulation info, and class data recapitulation. On the login user or student, there is also input cognitive and affective data from the student. Sample Heading (Forth Level). The contribution should contain no more than four levels of headings. The following Table 2. Summary of Emotional Intelligence Indicator Assessment gives a summary of all heading levels.

4.2 Results of the Assessment of Emotional and Social Intelligence of Elementary School

Emotional Intelligence of Elementary School.

The emotional intelligence of elementary school can be assessed through three aspects of assessment, namely cognitive, affective, and psychomotor. In this aspect, there are five main indicators or areas for emotional intelligence, namely (a) recognizing self-emotions, (b) appreciating self-emotions, (c) managing self-emotions, (d) controlling self-emotions, and (e) feeling self-spirituality. The overall results of all indicators and these three aspects of the emotional intelligence of Islamic elementary school students can be seen in the table below (Table 1):

Table 1. Categorization of indicators

Aspects	Low	Currently	Tall
Affective	1–4	5–8	9–1
Cognitive	1–2	3–4	5–6
psychomotor	1–4	5–8	9–1

Table 2. Summary of Emotional Intelligence Indicator Assessment

Indikator	Cognitive	Affective	psychomotor
Recognizing Your Emotions	C	T	T
Appreciating Your Emotions	C	T	T
Managing Your Emotions	C	T	T
Controlling your own emotions	C	L	T
Feel your spirituality	C	T	T

Noted: C: Currently, T: Tall, T: Tall

Based on the table above, it is seen that the cognitive aspects in elementary school students are still in the moderate category. As for the affective aspect in general, it is included in the high category. Thus, it can be interpreted that the emotional intelligence of elementary school in the cognitive aspect can be said to be good, although the indicators of controlling emotions still fall into the low category. As for the psychomotor aspect in all domains, it falls into a high category.

Social Intelligence of Elementary School.

In the social intelligence of elementary school, there are three aspects of assessment. There are five main indicators or areas for social intelligence, namely (a) respect for others, (b) social responsibility, (c) social cooperation, (d) tolerance for others, and (e) effective communication with others. The overall results of all these indicators and three aspects of the social intelligence of elementary school students can be seen in the table below (Tables 3 and 4):

Table 3. Categorization of indicators

Aspects	Low	Currently	Tall
Affective	1–4	5–8	9–12
Cognitive	1–2	3–4	5–6
psychomotor	1–4	5–8	9–1

Based on the data above, it can be seen that the social intelligence of elementary school in carrying out good behavior or good deeds towards others, such as socializing, empathizing is only because of the habituation that has been taught, then for the affective aspect also falls into the high category, it then encourages students to have a high sense of empathy to always interact with others, socialize well, communicate well. In the results of the assessment above, the cognitive aspect is still in the moderate category. This needs to be improved because, basically, when the student is doing social good and other good deeds, they do not know the reason why it is recommended to behave well like that, which is evidenced by the smaller number of scores on the cognitive aspect.

Table 4. Summary of Social Intelligence Indicator Assessment

Indicator	Cognitive	Affective	psychomotor
Respect others	C	T	T
Social responsibility	C	T	T
Social cooperation	C	L	T
Be considerate of others	C	L	T
Effective communication with others	C	L	T

C = Currently L = Law T = Tall

5 Conclusions

Based on the results of the analysis of this study shows that: (1) The design of character assessment applications in online learning consists of user flowcharts, admin flowcharts, data flow diagrams, and entity relationship data, (2) Character achievements from online learning aspects of emotional intelligence aspects are highest affective aspects in the character of responsibility, peace-loving, hard work, honesty, and the highest in cognitive aspects is only tolerance. Meanwhile, social intelligence is highest in cognitive aspects in the character of tolerance, love of the homeland, hard work, care for the environment, and the lowest character of caring for others. This proves that Artificial Intelligent has facilitated the task of teachers in assessing student character and making it easier for students to find out the level of emotional and social intelligence that has been achieved from learning.

References

1. Ahmad, A.: "Mengenal artificial intelligence, machine learning, neural network, dan deep learning." no (2017)
2. Billy, I.K., Khotimah, W.N.: Implementasi aritificial intellegence pada game defender of metal city dengan menggunakan finite state machine. J. Tek. Pomits **6**(2), 2017 (2017)
3. Halim, C., Prasetyo, H.: Penerapan artificial intellegence dalam computer aided instructure (CAI). J. Sist. Cerdas 1(1), 50–57 (2018). ISSN: 2622–825
4. Costa, A.C.F., Faria, L.: Implicit theories of emotional intelligence, ability and trait-emotional intelligence and academic achievement. Psychol. Top. **29**, 43–61 (2020). https://doi.org/10.31820/PT.29.1.3
5. Indrawati, T.: Peranan kecerdasan emosi dan dukungan sosial terhadap kesejahteraan psikologis siswa SMP terbuka di cirebon. Edukasia Islamik **2**(1), 70–88 (2017). https://doi.org/10.28918/JEI.V2I1.1630
6. Abdo, M., Feghali, K., Zgheib, M.A.: The role of emotional intelligence and personality on the overall internal control effectiveness: applied on internal audit team member's behavior in Lebanese companies. Asian J. Account. Res. **7**(2), 195–207 (2022). https://doi.org/10.1108/AJAR-04-2021-0048/FULL/PDF
7. Cuéllar-Molina, D., García-Cabrera, A.M., M. de la C. Déniz-Déniz.: Emotional intelligence of the HR decision-maker and high-performance HR practices in SMEs. Eur. J. Manage. Bus. Econ. **28**(1), 52–89 (2019). https://doi.org/10.1108/EJMBE-10-2017-0033/FULL/PDF

8. Elfenbein, H.A., MacCann, C.: A closer look at ability emotional intelligence (EI): what are its component parts, and how do they relate to each other? Soc. Pers. Psychol. Compass **11**(7), 1–13 (2017). https://doi.org/10.1111/SPC3.12324
9. Alonso, D.A., León-Del-barco, B., Mendo-Lázaro, S., Gallego, D.I.: Examining body satisfaction and emotional-social intelligence among school children: educational implications. Int. J. Environ. Res. Public Health **17**(6), 2120 (2020). https://doi.org/10.3390/IJERPH17062120
10. Khilmiyah, A., Wiyono, G.: Emotional and social intelligence assessment model for student character reinforcement. Int. J. Educ. Manage. **35**(4), 789–802 (2021). https://doi.org/10.1108/IJEM-02-2020-0046/FULL/XML
11. Al, S.F.I., Damayanti, I.P.S.: Pengembangan Kecerdasan Emosional Peserta Didik Di Sekolah Dasar Melalui Pendidikan Karakter. PENDASI: J. Pendidik. Dasar Indonesia, 4(1), 137–146 (2020). https://doi.org/10.23887/JPDI.V4I1.3120
12. Forsyth, B., Davis, H.C., Maranga, K., Fryer, R.A.: Emotional intelligence related to university students and managers: a qualitative study. J. High. Educ. Theory Pract. **20**(8), 11–19 (2020). https://doi.org/10.33423/JHETP.V20I8.3226
13. Yulika, R.: Pengaruh Kecerdasan Emosi dan Motivasi Belajar Terhadap Prestasi Belajar Siswa Di Smp Negeri 1 Sengkang. J. Inspiratif Pendidikan **8**(2), 252–270 (2019). https://doi.org/10.24252/ip.v8i2.7838
14. Akbar, M.I., Chandra, T.K., Setyowati, R.A., Isnaeni, F., Zahro, S.L., Yuniar, A.D.: Interelasi kecerdasan sosial dengan interaksi sosial mahasiswa luar Jawa Fakultas Ilmu Sosial Universitas Negeri Malang. J. Integrasi dan Harm. Inovatif Ilmu-Ilmu Sos. **1**(5), 598–604 (2021). https://doi.org/10.17977/UM063V1I5P598-604
15. Khilmiyah, A.: Penilaian Pendidikan Karakter (Aspek Kecerdasan Emosional dan Sosial), I. Yogyakarta: Penerbit Samudra Biru (Anggota IKAPI) (2021)
16. Knopp, K.A.: The children's social comprehension scale (CSCS): construct validity of a new social intelligence measure for elementary school children. Int. J. Behav. Dev. **43**(1), 90–96 (2018). https://doi.org/10.1177/0165025418787923
17. Gabrijelčič, M.K., Antolin, U., Istenič, A.: Teacher's social and emotional competencies: a study among student teachers and students in education science in Slovenia. Eur. J. Educ. Res. **10**(4), 2033–2044 (2021). https://doi.org/10.12973/EU-JER.10.4.2033
18. Purwanti, E., Noviana, P.D.: Social intelligence contribution in perspective learning outcomes of elementary school social science subject. Int. J. Instr. **15**(3), 337–340 (2019). https://doi.org/10.2991/ICET-19.2019.84
19. Ngo, P.T., Nguyet, L.M., Hoa, H.Q., Ha, T.T., Trang, N.T.T.: Social intelligence of secondary school students in Vietnam. Elementary Educ. Online **20**(5), 4740 (2021). https://doi.org/10.17051/ILKONLINE.2021.05.525
20. Goleman, D.: Kecerdasan Emosi Untuk Mencapai Puncak Prestasi. PT Gramedia Pustaka Utama (1999)
21. Junaidi, F., Suwandi, S., Saddhono, K., Wardhani, N.E.: The value of social intelligence in the textbooks for elementary school students. In: International Conference of Humanities and Social Science (ICHSS), vol. 1, no. 1, pp. 60–68 (2022). https://doi.org/10.1234/ICHSS.V1I1.9

Active Noise Control of Airborne Road Noise Based on Artificial Intelligent Computed Road Classification and Adaptive Digital Filter

Sang-Kwon Lee(✉), Orhun Okcu, and Kanghyun An

Acoustics and Vibration Signal Processing Laboratory, Inha University, Incheon 22212, South Korea

sangkwon@inha.ac.kr

Abstract. The study presents a new method for real time noise control based on road surface classification technology using deep learning and active noise cancellation technology using digital adaptive filter. Recently active noise control (ANC) method for structure vibration induced road noise is developed and applied to real car for road noise control. This method is effective for ANC of road noise due to structural vibration of car body but is not effective for ANC of road noise due to air borne noise source such as interaction noise between tire and road surface. Acceleration signals measured on the car body have been used for ANC of structure borne noise. However, a new reference signal is required for ANC of air borne noise. Interaction noise between tire and road surface is severe on the concrete road than the other road such as asphalt. The reference signal should be correlated to interaction noise between tire and road surface. In the paper, the type of road surface is classified in real time throughout deep learning of the measured interaction noise based on convolutional neural network (CNN). The reference signal of interaction noise on concrete road was obtained by calculating instantaneous frequency of interaction noise and was successfully applied to ANC of airborne induced road noise.

Keywords: Road Noise · Road Classification · Convolutional Neural Network · Active Noise Control

1 Introduction

In this study, a new road surface classification method that includes snow load is presented based on a tire pavement interaction noise (TPIN) signal and a deep learn-ing train using a CNN architecture. Two tires made by two different companies and two road surfaces were used for this method. Thus, four classes were classified. The TPIN signal is obtained using a rugged microphone installed on the wheel cover, and it is transformed into 2-dimensional (2D) image data using continuous wavelet transform (CWT). The image signal is used as the input to the CNN architecture. A new CNN architecture was constructed for the classification of two road surface types and two tires.

C. Stephanidis et al. (Eds.): HCII 2023, CCIS 1836, pp. 454–459, 2023.
https://doi.org/10.1007/978-3-031-36004-6_62

2 Tire Pavement Interaction Noise

Tire-pavement interaction Noise (TPJN) is noise caused by interactions between rolling tires and road surfaces. After measuring the TPIN using a microphone, transform TPIN to images using continuous wavelet transform (CWT). The transformed images are used to classify the driving road and tire using convolutional neural network (CNN). The road and tire classification network using CNN is required for braking systems in autonomous vehicle. The CNN in this paper can classify snow road, asphalt road, and two types of tires with over 97% accuracy. In concrete road, the periodic impulse noise is generated due to the periodic groove on the concrete road. This is loudness sound and air-bone noise. The periodic noise can be cancelled by the ANC. This is air-borne road noise active noise cancellation (ARANC). In this case, the reference signal is the periodic signal, and its instantaneous frequency can be used for the generation of reference signal.

3 Theory

3.1 CNN Architecture

CNN is a type of artificial neural network that optimizes weights based on an in-put image feature map. The feature map is extracted through a convolution operation between the input data and a predefined convolution kernel. CNN is widely known for its excellent performance in various image-recognition tasks. Recently, CNN techniques have been applied in various fields of mechanical engineering. Defect classification of power driving systems, prediction of tire-transmitted noise, and vehicle structure defect classification are successful applications in mechanical engineering [1–3]. The modem concept of CNN was first suggested by LeCun et al. [4]. In that paper, Yann LeCun introduced LeNet-5 to recognize letter patterns. LeNet-5 uses a convolution operation on a 32 × 32-pixel input image to achieve this goal. The feature map is then compressed using a pooling operation. After repeating the above process twice, the final feature map was unfolded to flatten and connected to a fully connected layer. The number of nodes in the last fully connected layer was equal to the number of classes. The values at each node were normalized between O and 1 using the Softmax layer. Using this normalized score, LeNet-5 can determine the class of an input letter. These suggested procedures, from convolution, pooling, and fully connected layers to softmax layers, have become the basic architecture of CNN.

3.2 Active Noise Cancellation

The target of the LMS algorithm is to compute optimum filter coefficients that minimize the mean square error. Thus, the iterative steepest descent method is used to determine these filter coefficients. Each iteration is carried out in the direction of the gradient of the error surface [5].

$$\mathbf{W}_{n+1}=\mathbf{W}_n+\mu(-\nabla_n) \tag{1}$$

The error signal can be expressed as

$$e(n) = d(n) - x(n)\mathbf{W}_n \tag{2}$$

Consequently, the gradient of squared error becomes.

$$\nabla e^2(n) = -2e(n)x(n) \tag{3}$$

If Eq. 4 is substituted in Eq. 2, the final LMS algorithm becomes as follows.

$$\mathbf{W}_{n+1}=\mathbf{W}_n+\mu e(n)x(n) \tag{4}$$

where μ is a convergence factor (step size) that controls stability. To avoid divergence which occurs from insufficient spectral excitation, the leaking mechanism is used during the weight update calculation. The leaky LMS algorithm can be written as

$$\mathbf{W}(n+1) = n\mathbf{W}(n) + \mu x(n)e(n) \tag{5}$$

where ν is the leakage factor with $0 < \nu \leqslant 1$. There is a trade-off between robustness and the loss of performance while adjusting the leakage factor [6].

4 Test

4.1 Classification of Road Type

Table 1 lists the total number of images generated for each test case. The number of images is equal regardless of the tire position if the tire type and road type are un-changed. This is because the front-wheel data and rear-wheel data are measured sim-mutinously and controlled by the same digital signal processor mentioned. Consequently, the length of the acquired data was the same for every measurement. The procedures used to create the final dataset were as follows. First, randomly extract approximately 4000 images from one case. Second, it was divided into three subsets: one for training, another for validation, and the other for testing. The training set uses approximately 60% of the total image, validation set uses approximately 20%, and test set takes the remaining. Third, the first two steps are repeated for all test cases. Finally, the created datasets of the same type are merged. Accuracy of classification was 98.1% for test set. Figure 1 shows the confusion matrix for the classification of two road types.

Table 1. Total number of generated images for each test case.

Rear Wheel	Tire-A	Tire-B
Asphalt	4718	6322
Concrete	11157	7785

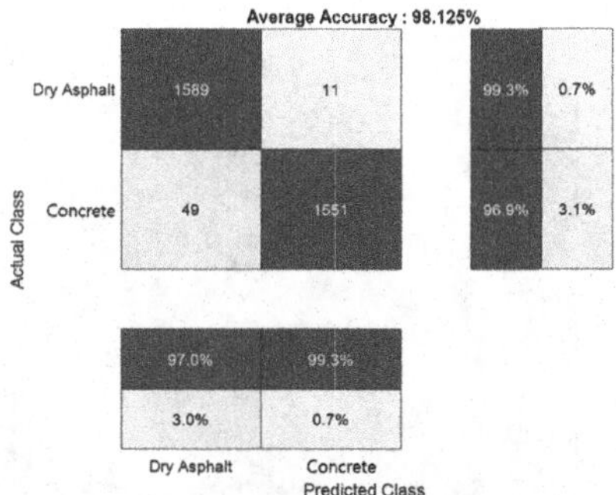

Fig. 1. Train results for TPIN signals using CNN architecture for classification of road sur-faces and tires.

4.2 Air-Borne Road Noise Active Noise Cancellation (ARANC)

The ARANC test is proceed while driving on the highway with acceleration speed. The road type has been changed from concrete type to asphalt type. The noise is measured inside cabin of test car. The airborne noise is occurred and disappear on the asphalt road inside cabin as shown in Fig. 2 (a).

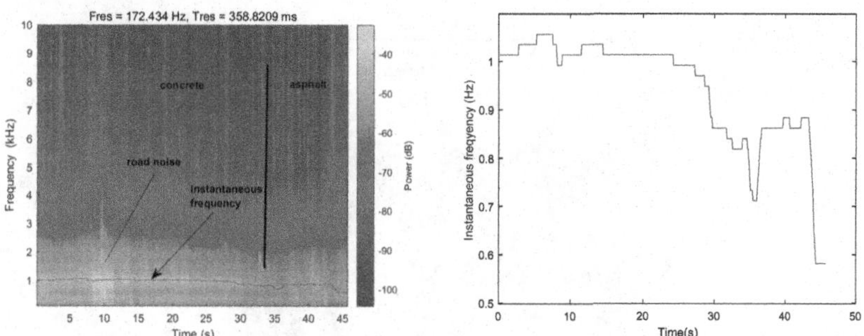

Fig. 2. Airborne road noise measured on the concrete road and asphalt road. (a) spectrogram (b) instantaneous frequency (f_i)

Airborne road noise should be suppressed by ARANC method. In the first test, the instantaneous frequency is calculated as shown in Fig. 2(b), and it is used for the generation of the frequency modulated signal. The frequency modulation signal is used for reference signal of ARANC. Before applying the method on the real time control, the simulation is performed by using Matlab Simulink (Mathwork, USA). For the feasibility test of ARANC, the FXLMS algorithm is applied to interior noise measured on the only concrete road. Figure 3 shows the results of ARANC for the interior noise.

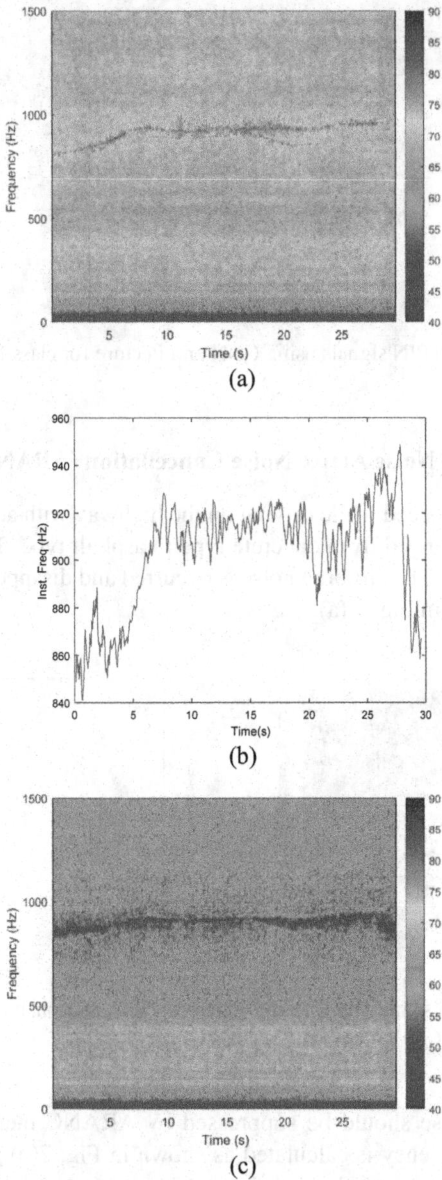

Fig. 3. Airborne road noise measured on the concrete road and asphalt road. (a) Before ARANC (b) instantaneous frequency (f_i) (c) After ARANC.

5 Conclusions

Interior noise caused by TPIN noise is airborne noise. ARANC method is proposed to suppress the airborne tire TPIN. This method is based on classification of road type and ANC technology. The CNN architecture is used for the classification of road type while driving on concrete road and asphalt road. Accuracy of the proposed CNN architecture is achieved to 98.1%. ARANC method is applied to interior noise caused by TPIN on concrete road. This work is simulated using Simulink. The key work for this application is to find the instantaneous frequency for the reference signal. After applying ARNAC to the suppression of interior noise, the airborne TPIN is suppressed completely. In the future work, the proposed method is going to be applied to suppress the interior noise in real vehicle.

Acknowledgements. . This work was supported by the grant funded by the Korea evaluation institute of industrial technology (KEIT) (No. 20018706). This work was supported by the National Research Foundation of Korea (NRF) grant funded by the Korea government (MSIT) (No. 2022R1F1A1062889).

References

1. Lee, S.-Y., Lee, S.-K.: Deep convolutional neural network with new training method and transfer learning for structural fault classification of vehicle instrument panel structure. J. Mech. Sci. Technol. **34**(11), 4489–4498 (2020). https://doi.org/10.1007/s12206-020-1009-3
2. Kim, S., An, K., Back, J., Lee, S.-K., Lee, C., Kim, P.: Health monitoring of power driving system using sound signal based on deep leaming. Korean Soc. Noise Vibr. Eng. **31**, 47–56 (2021)
3. Lee, S.-K., et al.: Prediction oftire pattern noise in early design stage based on convolutional neural network. Appl. Acoust. **172**, 107617 (2021)
4. LeCun, Y., Bottou, L., Bengio, Y., Haffner, P.: Gradient-based learning applied to document recognition. Proceedings of the IEEE **86**, 2278–2324 (1998)
5. Bernard, W., Samuel, D.S.: Adaptive signal processing. Englewood Cliffs, NJ: Prentice Hall (1985)
6. Kuo, S.M., Morgan, D.R.: Active Noise Control Systems, vol. 4. Wiley, New York (1996)

A Model of Computational Creativity Based on Engram Cell Theory

Qinhan Li[1] and Bin Li[2(✉)]

[1] Washington Institute for Health Sciences, Arlington, VA 22203, USA
[2] Georgetown University, Washington, DC, USA

Abstract. Artificial Intelligence technology has made remarkable progress in machine learning, but it is still in its infancy in creative thinking or computational creativity. In 2018, Yang and Li proposed that the physiological basis for the formation of memories and concepts in the human brain is engram cells (interneuron), and creative thinking is the process of forming new engram cells to connect previously seemingly unrelated concepts. During this process, association and prediction play a key role. In this study, a computational model based on engram cell theory was coded in Python to mimic the process of creative thinking. The validity of the model was tested by simulating the phenomenon of language generation and summarizing the artificial food-set regularity in the plus maze. The results show that, given 29 initial words and certain grammatical rules, the language generation program generates 25,405 sentences after 130,000 calculations, and these generated sentences can be combined into various short paragraphs. After 50 times of training in the cross-maze puzzle solving program, the model can master 100% of the rules of artificial food settings. In conclusion, a computational model of creative thinking based on engram cell theory can creatively and automatically generate sentences and paragraphs and can learn and summarize laws to solve simple puzzles. We plan to further use this model to address complex real-world problems, such as the study of cancer therapeutic targets.

Keywords: creative thinking · engram cell theory · computational model · language generation · puzzle solution

1 Introduction

With the continuous advancement of science and technology, human beings are more and more confident to solve complex natural and social problems, such as cancer treatment, COVID-19 prevention, and even war, economic recession, etc. The reason why these problems are complex is that they contain a huge amount of content, such as the interaction of billions of biomolecules in cells, and the thought activities of billions of people in society. When this information is extracted, they appear as huge amounts of data. Such a huge amount of data and knowledge is far from being able to be processed by an individual's brain alone, so computer systems must be used to help scientists analyze it [1].

C. Stephanidis et al. (Eds.): HCII 2023, CCIS 1836, pp. 460–464, 2023.
https://doi.org/10.1007/978-3-031-36004-6_63

However, the current artificial intelligence algorithm is still in a very preliminary stage, and cannot replace human beings in advanced thinking, such as creating new theories and new products. Computational creativity (CC) is an emerging research field that brings together psychology, cognitive science, linguistics, anthropology, and other anthropocentric sciences. As an engineering endeavor, the research explores getting computers to build an autonomous system that produces novel and useful outputs worthy of the label "creative" [2].

On average, the human brain contains about 100 billion neurons, and each neuron may be connected to as many as 10,000 other neurons, forming about 1,000 trillion synapses [3]. This extremely complex interconnected circuit of neurons is the physiological basis for perception, memory, motor control, emotion and higher cognition [4]. In 2018, Yang and Li proposed that the physiological basis of creative thinking is the process of forming new engram cells (interneurons), which connect previously formed engram cells representing existing memories and concepts at a higher level. This association and prediction of new connections is the process of creative thinking [5].

Based on the theory of engram cells of creative thinking, this study uses the Python language to build two model programs that simulate the process of creative thinking. The first is a language generation model, and the second is a puzzle-solving model. We expect to use these two simple models to verify the ability to achieve a certain computational creativity based on the theory of engram cells of creative thinking.

2 Materials and Method

These two programs were coded with Python 3.10. The flowcharts are shown in Fig. 1. The language generation program consists of 2 parts: the first part is the sentence generation program that performs the following functions: setting basic vocabulary (7 adjectives, 4 nouns, 9 adverbs, 5 intransitive verbs, 4 transitive verbs, a total of 29 words), defining the grammatical role of basic vocabulary, randomly associating vocabulary and sentences generated based on grammatical rules. After removing duplicates, these generated sentences are saved in a file. The second part is the paragraph generation program, which randomly executes to generate paragraph topics (time, place, person, etc.), selects all sentences that meet the topic from the sentence file and saves them as a file, and then randomly selects sentences that meet the requirements from the file and generate a paragraph.

The puzzle-solving mode program simulates a common animal experiment in cognitive science, which is to train mice/rats to learn the pattern of artificially placed food positions in the cross maze. The program performs the following functions: input the food placement and prompt rules in the plus maze, training (the program randomly generates puzzle solutions and check answers), testing (test the puzzle solutions obtained through training) and output the testing results and rules summarized by the program.

In the program's test, the sentence generation program performed 130,000 random sentence-making operations, during which the number of new sentences generated was recorded. The paragraph generation program was run 20 times, and the generated text paragraphs were printed. For the puzzle-solving program, the training times were set as 5 times, 10 times, 20 times, 50 times and 100 times, and then the test success rates were recorded respectively.

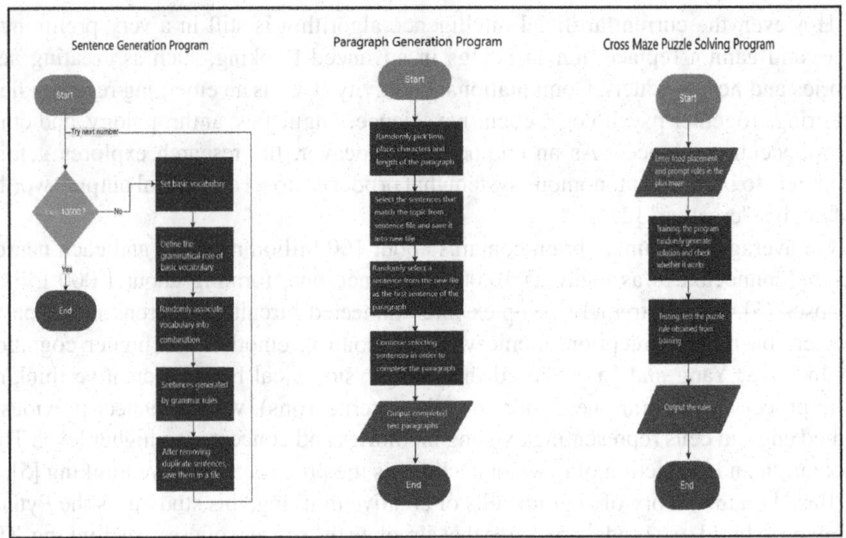

Fig. 1. Flowcharts of the sentence generation, paragraph generation and puzzle-solving programs.

3 Results

For the sentence generation program, we performed 130,000 random sentence generation operations, and recorded the process of generating new sentences, and the results showed that a total of 25,000 unique sentences were generated (Fig. 2).

For the paragraph generation program, we ran it 20 times and recorded the generated text paragraphs. A typical text paragraph is shown in the screenshot below (Fig. 3).

For the puzzle-solving program, the results show that the success rate of learning is not very stable at low training times. But when the number of training reaches 50 times, the success rate of learning reaches 100% (Fig. 4).

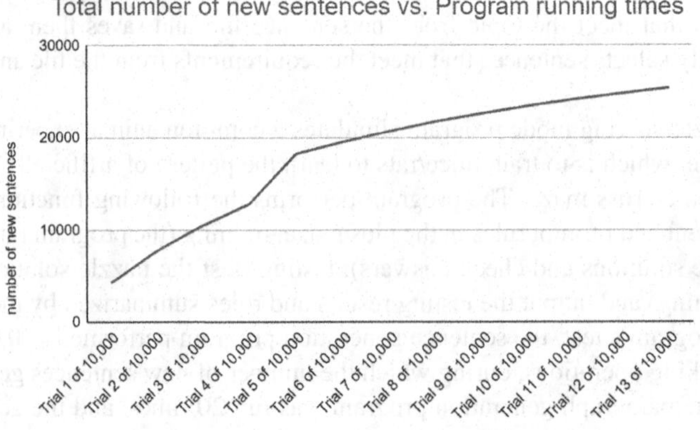

Fig. 2. Number of runs of the sentence generator and number of new sentences generated.

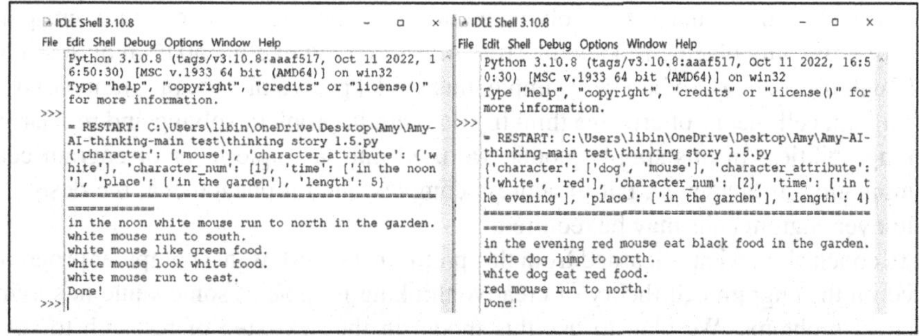

Fig. 3. The typical text paragraphs generated by the paragraph generation program.

Fig. 4. Training times versus test success rate in the puzzle-solving program.

4 Discussions

Human beings have the ability to think, not only to grasp the laws of nature, but also to use these laws to create things that are useful for human survival. Computer and artificial intelligence technology are a tool to enhance human thinking ability, and the development of this technology will further accelerate the progress of human civilization. At present, machine learning algorithms have been widely used in various fields, but "machine creation" or "computational creativity" is still in its infancy. The purpose of this study is to establish a program model based on the engram cell theory of creative thinking. In this study, two simple models for simulating creative thinking have been completed, one is language generation model and the other is puzzle-solving model.

In the language generation model, we chose an initial vocabulary of 29, and it was shown that after 130,000 runs, the program produced 25,405 distinct sentences. On the basis of these sentences, paragraphs of text that meet the predetermined requirements can be generated. Although due to time constraints, the program did not produce vivid stories because we could only choose a limited initial vocabulary and screening rules for grammar and storyline, this result shows that this simple model has a certain ability of language creativity.

The test results of the puzzle-solving model show that the model can fully grasp the rules of artificially placing food in the cross maze after completing 50 training sessions. Although the rules we set are very simple, this model proves that the program based on the engram cell theory of creative thinking has certain problem-solving and regularity-seeking abilities. In this simple model, we used only a single layer of engram cells (combination of elements), but to address complex natural phenomena, the design of multilayer engram cells may be required.

In conclusion, what is learned from this preliminary work is that computer programs based on the engram cell theory of creative thinking may be of some value in solving practical problems. We plan to use this model in the next step of research to solve some complex real-world problems, such as finding therapeutic targets for cancer and designing targeted drugs for cancer treatment.

References

1. Mazzocchi, F.: Complexity in biology: Exceeding the limits of reductionism and determinism using complexity theory. EMBO Rep. **9**(1), 10–14 (2008)
2. Veale, T., Cardoso, F.A.: Computational Creativity the Philosophy and Engineering of Autonomously Creative Systems, 1st edn. Springer, New York (2019)
3. Zhang, J.: Basic Neural Units of the Brain: Neurons, Synapses and Action Potential. arXiv.org (2019)
4. Bermúdez, J.L.: Cognitive Science: An Introduction to the Science of the Mind, 3rd edn. Cambridge University Press, Cambridge (2022)
5. Yang, D., Li, B.: Association, prediction, and engram cells in creative thinking. Cogent Psychol. **5**(1), 1493806 (2018)

Animal Hunt: AI-Based Animal Sound Recognition Application

Yi Heng Lin(✉) and Owen Noel Newton Fernando(✉)

Nanyang Technological University, 50 Nanyang Avenue, Singapore 639798, Singapore
LINY0103@e.ntu.edu.sg, ofernando@ntu.edu.sg

Abstract. This paper describes the development of an A.I. application for animal sound classification using pre-trained and custom-trained machine-learning models deployed on mobile devices. The research aims to address the challenges of traditional animal acoustic sound signal analysis, which is computationally intensive, requires a strong network connection, and is challenging to implement on low-cost microcontroller-based systems. By using Yet Another Mobile Network (YAMNet), a pre-trained model, and a custom-trained model, animal sounds and noises can be identified in real time, and the animal making the sound can be determined. The accuracy of the predictions is evaluated using a mobile device's trained model against test datasets in three different modes. Although the animal scope is currently limited to birds found in Singapore due to dataset constraints, the system can be expanded to other animals and species as long as sufficient datasets are available, making it a promising solution for continuous real-time biodiversity monitoring.

Keywords: Sound Recognition · TensorFlow Lite · YAMNet · Audio Event Classification · Edge Device Audio Classification

1 Introduction

Audio classification is the process of listening to and analyzing audio recordings. Categorizing animal cries for wildlife observation and preservation is just one of many applications at the core of a broad spectrum of contemporary A.I. technology. Audio classification projects, like those mentioned above, begin with annotated audio data from wild animals. These data are necessary for machines to learn the nuance between each audio sample. With the aid of these data, the machine will be able to develop the ability to distinguish between different animal sounds to carry out discrete tasks. Measuring acoustically distinct features is one of the most critical aspects of sound animal analysis. These features are used in bioacoustics analysis, and classifications are manually extracted from spectrogram plots [1]. Manual acoustic species identification takes a long time, and analysis time can take up to ten times as long as the recording time [1] due to numerous noise pollution in the recording. To speed up the process, the majority of animal acoustic sound signal analysis and identification systems employ short-time Fourier transform, wavelets, and spectral energy distributions. However, this analysis

C. Stephanidis et al. (Eds.): HCII 2023, CCIS 1836, pp. 465–474, 2023.
https://doi.org/10.1007/978-3-031-36004-6_64

has several drawbacks; these techniques are computationally intensive, require a strong network connection for data loading and unloading, and are challenging to implement on low-cost microcontroller-based systems [2]. These drawbacks show that a new system is needed to accelerate and ease the process of continuous real-time biodiversity monitoring.

As such, the goal of this project is to present a new system for animal sound classification by implementing a pre-trained machine model, Yet Another Mobile Network (YAMNet) [3], that will be used to perform audio classification in real-time to detect noises and animal sounds followed by a custom trained machine model that uses Keras [4], a deep learning-based neural networks that employ TensorFlow (T.F.) an open-source library for numerical computation and large-scale machine learning [5] to create a machine model that identifies which animal is present in real-time. Both models will be converted into Tensor Flow Lite (TFL) using TensorFlow Lite Converter (TFLC) as TFL is designed for on-device machine learning, which compresses our models into a more compact and efficient machine learning model format [6]. The models will then be deployed into mobile, microcontrollers, and other edge devices. Consequently, by deploying the TFL model into our devices, it solves the five significant constraints that previous systems had met, which are: latency - no round-trip to a server; privacy - no personal data leaves the device, connectivity - no internet connectivity is required, size - reduced model and binary size, power consumption - efficient inference and a lack of network connections [6]. Lastly, the accuracy of prediction and identification will be evaluated using a mobile device's trained model against test datasets.

2 Literature Review

2.1 General Overview on Sound Analysis for Wildlife

Accurate knowledge of wildlife identity, geographic distribution, and evolution is crucial for sustainable development and biodiversity conservation. Monitoring wildlife populations is an essential approach for assessing ecosystems in terms of conservation priority, particularly in regions with high overall biological diversity that often face extinction. Autonomous Recording Units (ARUs) have become a widely used sampling tool in ecological research and monitoring over the past decade, allowing researchers to conduct point counts in almost any densely vegetated habitat over longer periods of time [7]. While automated assessment of soundscapes in the hyper-diverse tropics presents significant challenges relative to less diverse systems, it also presents a higher upside [8]. The tropics harbor a hugely disproportionate percentage of Earth's biodiversity, more than three-quarters of all species and over 90% of the planet's terrestrial birds, and international biodiversity targets will be impossible to meet if these systems are not conserved. However, the tropics are widely neglected in biodiversity and ecosystem function literature [9], and conclusions from studies in temperate regions are often wrongly used as the basis for assumptions about tropical systems where they do not apply [10]. Biased research priorities and difficulties with field surveys in the tropics have led to overlooked biodiversity losses [11] and flawed baseline species occurrence data [12]. As a result, ARUs are well-suited to address these issues by generating detailed data that can be recorded simultaneously, stored permanently, and reviewed by multiple observers, which can lead to the relative overestimation of species richness and abundance at sites with more favorable viewing conditions [13].

2.2 Reviewing Existing Sound Analysis

The high amount of effort required to analyse recorded soundscapes manually means that comprehensively analyzing large datasets is prohibitively time-intensive, neutralizing many of the advantages provided by continuous. Recent advancements in bioacoustics research have focused on utilizing deep neural networks for sound event recognition [14, 15]. One approach that has been attempted is the use of convolutional neural network (CNN) classifiers to identify bird calls based on visual representations of these sounds, such as spectrograms [16–18]. While this method has shown success for bird sound recognition in focal recordings, it has proven less effective for continuous, omnidirectional soundscapes. Passive acoustic monitoring has become an increasingly valuable tool for habitat assessments and observing environmental niches. However, the manual processing of extensive collections of soundscape data is time-consuming and not ideal. This has led to automated attempts to advance the process [19]. Despite these efforts, the lack of suitable validation and test data has prevented the development of reliable acoustic event detection and identification techniques. The BirdCLEF competition in 2021 attempted to tackle this challenging task. Despite achieving remarkable results using deep artificial neural networks with spectrograms as input data, generating analysis outputs with high precision and recall, particularly when targeting a high number of species simultaneously, remains a challenge. Post-processing of detections and the use of additional metadata were essential in achieving top results. The competition also set up a high vocal activity in some test recordings and segments without audible bird vocalizations dominating the count. Because of this, threshold tuning (especially for' no-call segments) had a significant impact, often masking the actual performance of the algorithms. As a result, many participants relied on separate' no call' detection systems to improve their overall scores. [20] Thus, bridging the gap between high-quality training samples (focal recordings) and noisy test samples (soundscape recordings) is still one of the most challenging tasks in the field of audio event recognition.

2.3 Urban Biodiversity in Singapore

Urban biodiversity has become a prominent topic in recent years as cities around the world experience unprecedented levels of urbanization. Like many other cities, Singapore has experienced a rapid increase in urbanization, yet its fauna remains surprisingly diverse. The majority of the island's remaining species are housed in nature reserves such as Bukit Timah Nature Reserve, Sungei Buloh Wetland Reserve, Singapore Bird Park, and The Singapore Zoo. This is due to the "garden city" and "city in a garden" initiatives introduced by then-Prime Minister Lee Kuan Yew in 1967 and 1998, respectively, to create Singapore a clean, green city with abundant lush greenery to improve the quality of life of its residents. [21] and to incorporate greenery not only into the physical environment but also into the daily life of Singaporeans. [22] In the grand scheme of things, biodiversity was not only a "nice-to-have" but a "must-have" for Singaporeans who wished to remain on their land and continue to create their own nation from the bottom up. As a result, Singaporeans who remained are accustomed to seeing and hearing wild animals while going about their everyday activities. Despite this, the majority of Singaporeans are unable to identify local animals, particularly by the sound they make, as fundamental knowledge of local animals is not included in the Singapore Education System due to the topic's diversity, making it impractical to teach, leading many to turn to the Internet for solutions.

2.4 Reviewing Existing Software Applications

The creation of animal audio analysis software is not new, and there are several noteworthy applications in the market. These applications function on various platforms, but for our specific scenario, we will only focus on mobile platforms as wild animal sounds are frequently heard in everyday life. As a result, we will prioritize mobile devices over personal computers for using the application due to their convenience and portability. As we are creating an application for identifying animals found in Singapore, it is crucial to compare existing animal sound identification applications to understand their features and functionalities. Table 1 was created to compare these applications and identify the most useful functionalities for our AnimalHunt application. The functionalities that we considered for analysis include the ability to record and identify animal sounds, the availability of additional information such as pictures, descriptions, and habitat information, offline recognition capability, search and filter feature, the ability to detect other animal species and whether the application is able to recognize Singapore Wildlife. This analysis will also help us determine which functionalities to include in our application to provide the most comprehensive tool for identifying animals in Singapore.

The table above highlights Merlin Bird ID as a highly featured app. However, it does have certain limitations, such as its incapability to recognize animals other than birds and most of the birds found in Singapore. Nonetheless, it can be considered one of the best animal sound recognition applications available in the market and will serve as a benchmark for our AnimalHunt application. As a result, AnimalHunt will primarily focus on identifying animals in Singapore, with an emphasis on birds, while also considering the possibility of including other animal species if sufficient data is available. In addition, the application will integrate all identified functionalities to create a user-friendly and comprehensive tool for identifying birds in Singapore that is accessible to anyone with a mobile device.

Table 1. Comparison of features between different animal sound recognition apps in Appstore

Application	Record & identify	Bioinformation	Offline Recognition	Search & Filter feature	Detect other animal species	Recognizes Singapore Wildlife
BirdNET	Yes	Yes	No	By location and bird name	Birds Only	No
ChirpOMatic	Yes	Yes	Yes	By bird name	Birds Only	No
Song Sleuth	Yes	Yes	Yes	By bird name	Birds only	No
Smart Bird ID	Yes	Yes	Yes	By bird name	Birds only	No
BirdGenie	Yes	Yes	No	By bird name	Birds only	No
Merlin Bird ID	Yes	Yes	Yes	By location and bird name	Birds only	Yes (support 5–10 + species)

3 Data Collection and Preparation

To identify and display bio information for birds unique to Singapore through our application, we have collaborated with the Singapore Birds Project, a community-driven initiative dedicated to documenting all wild bird species in the country through individual accounts. The audio files used in the machine training process are sourced from the community-based website Xeno-canto, which provides wildlife sounds from around the world. However, due to the community-driven nature of the audio datasets, the format and quality of the files can vary. As a result, we need to perform standardization and pre-processing of the audio dataset to ensure accurate identification.

3.1 Audio Dataset Standardization

Audio Dataset Quality. The Xeno-Canto website employs its own audio quality rating system. Therefore, for our training audio set, we will use their ratings. The following are the general recommendations for the quality of Xeno-Canto audio files:

A: Loud and clear
B: Clear, but the animal is a bit distant or there is some interference with other sound sources
C: Moderately clear, or there is considerable interference
D: Faint recording or a lot of interference

E: Barely audible

For this project, we will primarily use Grade A and B audio datasets as our training set and Grade A to D as our testing set.

Audio Dataset Quantity and Limitation. Having a large dataset can reduce estimation variance and improve prediction accuracy, as the likelihood of having more data containing meaningful information increases, which is beneficial for prediction. As a result, we have established a minimum dataset size of 90 audio files and a maximum of 150 audio files for each bird species for this project. This is due to the scarcity of audio datasets for Singapore wildlife and to prevent an imbalanced dataset in our machine model. The dataset may comprise only Grade A audio files, or a combination of Grades A and B, owing to the limited number of audio files available on the website.

Audio Dataset Pre-processing. To train a network using audio signals, pre-processing of the audio dataset is necessary. Typically, a short-time Fourier transform (.stft) is applied to the audio signal and converted to spectrograms or Mel spectrograms using a logarithmic scale [19]. However, in this project, we are utilizing the YAMNet model for transfer learning, so all audio datasets must be pre-processed according to the YAMNet specification. This involves resampling the audio dataset to 16000 Hz with single-channel audio to feed into the YAMNet model. This will then be fed into the model, and it will generate Mel spectrograms that will be passed into the MobileNet, producing embeddings for training the new model [20].

4 System Design and Implementation

4.1 System Overview

The process depicted in Fig. 1 involves loading AnimalHunt onto a mobile device and utilizing the Tensorflow Lite interpreter for making inferences. It begins with collecting and extracting datasets of animals and audio clip features during the Feature Preparation phase (Step 1). The extracted data is then used to train a custom TF model that includes the YAMNet Model as a noise detector and filter, as our custom data pertains only to animals (Step 2). This model is then converted into a TFLite model that can be embedded into a mobile phone (Steps 3, 4, & 5). During deployment, audio is loaded in real-time (Step 6), and its features are extracted and classified using the YAMNet Model as the first inference, followed by our custom classifier for a second inference to identify the animal producing the sound (Step 7).

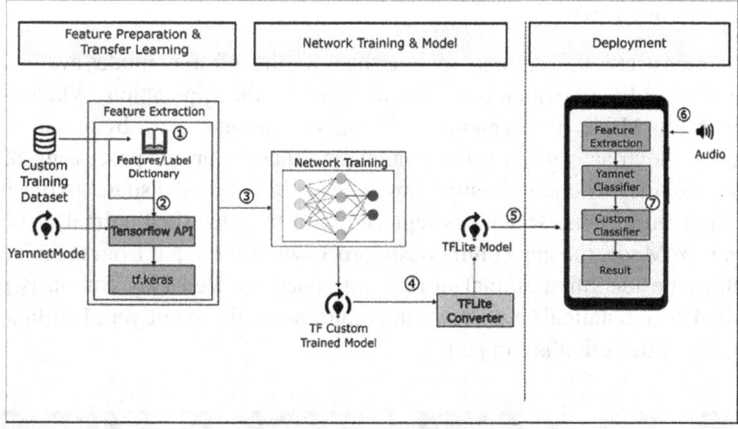

Fig. 1. System Overview

4.2 AnimalHunt Sound Identification

Figure 2 outlines the process of animal identification in the application. First, the audio data is sent to the TFL custom model, which comprises the YAMNet Classifier and our Custom Classifier. YAMNet is used to identify whether the sound is made by an animal, followed by the Custom Classifier to determine the specific animal. The application calculates the species probability and identification quantity, obtaining the highest average. Based on this, the application provides the user with the final prediction.

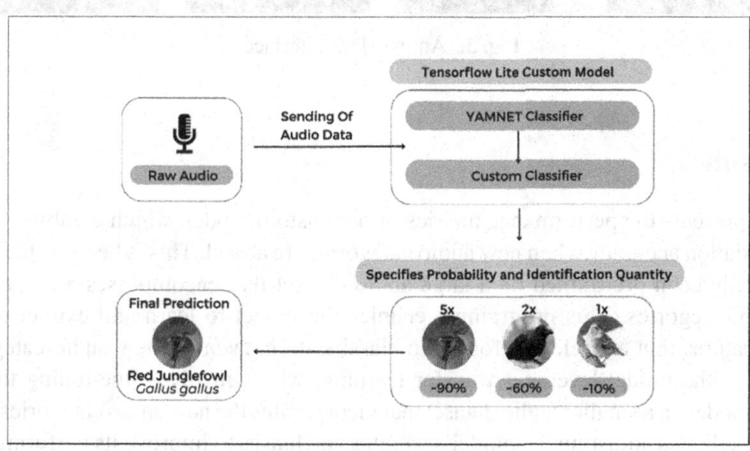

Fig. 2. AnimalHunt Sound Identification

4.3 AnimalHunt Interface

Figure 3 demonstrates the various user interfaces for the different modes available in the 2 × 2 Grid View List when an animal is detected by the application. When using the Single and Multi-Mode, users can initiate the identification process by pressing the Red Play Button, which activates a spinner indicating that the app is processing the audio input from the microphone to identify any animals based on the sound. After pressing the Red Stop Button, the spinner is replaced with the identified animal displayed in colour. In Live Mode, the app continuously processes audio input from the microphone and displays the identified animal in real time once the Red Play Button is pressed. Previously detected animals are shown in colour, while those not yet identified remain greyed out until detection is stopped.

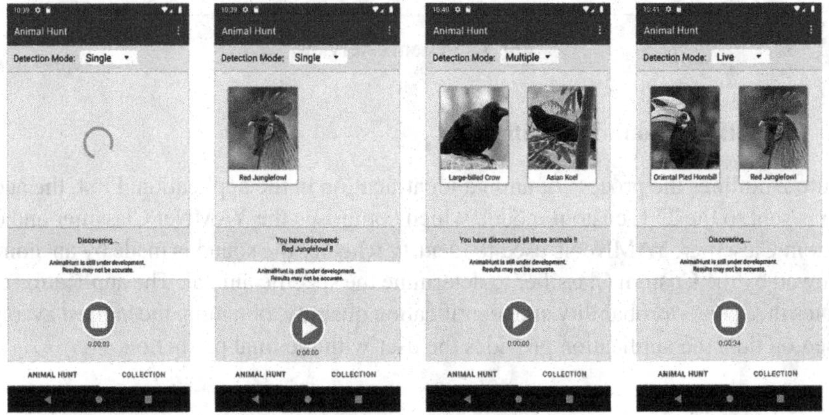

Fig. 3. AnimalHunt Interface

5 Result

Table 2 presents the performance metrics of our custom model, which exhibit low train and validation accuracy when new audio categories are added. This is because the model has already been pre-trained on a large audio dataset that encompasses a broad range of audio categories. This pre-training enables the model to learn and extract general audio features that are relevant for audio classification, even for new audio categories. Moreover, the model leverages transfer learning, which involves fine-tuning the pre-trained model on a smaller audio dataset that incorporates the new audio categories. Fine-tuning facilitates adjusting the model's weights and biases to improve its performance in the new audio categories. By starting with the pre-trained weights, the training process is expedited and overfitting is minimized. As a result, the pre-training on a large audio dataset and the fine-tuning on a smaller audio dataset that contains new audio categories lead to lower train and validation accuracy. Nonetheless, this limitation can be addressed by providing more audio datasets for the new audio categories, allowing the model to enhance its accuracy in classifying audio signals into their respective categories.

Table 2. Network Training Result

Training Accuracy	Validation Accuracy	Epoch	Batch Size
0.4422	0.4405	200	256

6 Conclusion

In conclusion, AnimalHunt is an innovative tool that employs deep neural networks to monitor animal activity, holding immense potential for the study and conservation of wildlife. By utilizing sound recordings from mobile phone microphones, the application enables users to analyze the behavior of a focal animal alongside the environment around it, offering a unique approach to animal activity monitoring. Furthermore, AnimalHunt places great emphasis on public participation in the data acquisition process, sparking the interest of many users eager to submit their observations. Thus, the application serves as a starting point for public services that allow users to record, analyze, and learn about the animals in their environment, making a significant contribution to the study and conservation of Singapore's rich biodiversity.

References

1. Riede, T., Zuberbühler, K.: The relationship between acoustic structure and semantic information in Diana monkey alarm vocalizations. J. Acoust. Soc. Am. **114**(2), 1132–1142 (2003)
2. Chesmore, E.D.: Automated bioacoustic identification of species. An. Acad. Bras. Ciênc. **76**(2), 435–440 (2004)
3. Plakal, M., Ellis, D.: Yamnet, January 2020. https://github.com/tensorflow/models/tree/master/research/audioset/yamnet. Accessed 18 Sept 2022
4. Moolayil, J.: Learn Keras for Deep Neural Networks: A Fast-Track Approach to Modern Deep Learning with Python. Apress, Berkeley (2019)
5. Abadi, M., et al.: TensorFlow: a system for large-scale machine learning. In: TensorFlow, Savannah, GA, USA (2016)
6. "Tensorflow Lite," TensorFlow. https://www.tensorflow.org/lite/guide#:~:text=Optimized%20for%20on%2Ddevice%20machine,inference%20and%20a%20lack%20of. Accessed 21 Jan 2023
7. Shonfield, J., Bayne, E.: Autonomous recording units in avian ecological research: current use and future applications. Avian Conserv. Ecol. **12**(1) (2017)
8. Barlow, J., et al.: The future of hyperdiverse tropical ecosystems. Nature **559**(7715), 517–526 (2018)
9. Wilson, K.A., et al.: Conservation research is not happening where it is most needed. PLoS Biol. **14**(3), e1002413 (2016)
10. Clarke, D.A., York, P.H., Rasheed, M.A., Northfield, T.D.: Does biodiversity– ecosystem function literature neglect tropical ecosystems? Trends Ecol. Evolut. **32**(5), 320–323 (2017)
11. Socolar, J.B., Valderrama Sandoval, E.H., Wilcove, D.S.: Overlooked biodiversity loss in tropical smallholder agriculture. Conserv. Biol. **33**(6), 1338–1349 (2019)
12. Boakes, E.H., et al.: Distorted views of biodiversity: spatial and temporal bias in species occurrence data. PLoS Biol. **8**(6), e1000385 (2010)

13. Darras, K., et al.: Comparing the sampling performance of sound recorders versus point counts in bird surveys: a meta-analysis. J. Appl. Ecol. **55**(6), 2575–2586 (2018)
14. Kahl, S., Wood, C.M., Eibl, M., Klinck, H.: BirdNET: a deep learning solution for avian diversity monitoring. Ecol. Inform. **61**, 101236 (2021)
15. Shiu, Y., et al.: Deep neural networks for automated detection of marine mammal species. Sci. Rep. **10**(1), 1–12 (2020)
16. Grill, T., Schlüter, J.: Two convolutional neural networks for bird detection in audio signals. In: 2017 25th European Signal Processing Conference (EUSIPCO)
17. Lasseck, M.: Audio-based bird species identification with deep convolutional neural networks. In: CLEF working notes 2018, CLEF: Conference and Labs of the Evaluation Forum, Avignon, France, September 2018 (2018)
18. Mühling, M., Franz, J., Korfhage, N., Freisleben, B.: Bird species recognition via neural architecture search. In: CLEF working notes 2020, CLEF: Conference and Labs of the Evaluation Forum, Thessaloniki, Greece, September 2020 (2020)
19. Wood, C.M., Kahl, S., Chaon, P., Peery, M.Z., Klinck, H.: Survey coverage, recording duration and community composition affect observed species richness in passive acoustic surveys. Methods Ecol. Evol. **12**(5), 885–896 (2021)
20. Joly, A., et al.: Overview of LifeCLEF 2021: an evaluation of machine-learning based species identification and species distribution prediction. In: Selçuk Candan, K., et al. (eds.) CLEF 2021. LNCS, vol. 12880. Springer, Cham (2021). https://doi.org/10.1007/978-3-030-85251-1_24
21. S'pore to become beautiful, clean city within three years (1967, May 12). The Straits Times, p. 4. Retrieved from NewspaperSG; Lee, K. Y. (2000). From third world to first: The Singapore story: 1965–2000: Memoirs of Lee Kuan Yew (p. 188). Singapore: Times Editions: Singapore Press Holdings. Call no.: RSING 959.57092 LEE-[HIS]
22. Lee, J. (1998, December 11) 'City in a garden' plan set out for Singapore. The Straits Times, p. 3. Retrieved from NewspaperSG; Prime Minister's Office. (2014, November 6) Speech by Prime Minister Lee Hsien Loong at the opening of Bishan Park – ABC Waters, 17 Mar 2012. Prime Minister's Office website. http://www.pmo.gov.sg/mediacentre/speech-prime-minister-lee-hsien-loong-opening-bishan-park-abc-waters-17-mar-2012. Accessed 23 Jan 2023

Prediction of Human Color Emotion on the Images Using Convolutional Neural Network

Akira Masuda and Yoshihisa Shinozawa(✉)

Faculty of Science and Technology, Keio University, Yokohama, Japan
shino@ae.keio.ac.jp

Abstract. In this study, we propose a method for predicting color emotion in real images using the mutual effect of color schemes. Features that take into account color interactions (synergy, contrast, area concentration, visual saliency, and perspective effects) are extracted from the image. For example, synergy is the effect that the more warm colors contains in the image, the warmer it feels. On the other hand, the contrast is the effect that both the warm and cold colors contain in the image, the warmer it feels. These features are then used to predict the color emotion of the color scheme by a convolutional neural network. Then, we collect color emotion data for brightness and warmth through pairwise comparison experiments. We evaluate the effectiveness of the proposed method on the collected pairwise comparison data.

Keywords: Color emotion · Color scheme · Color emotion prediction formula · Convolutional neural network

1 Introduction

Everything has color information. The consumer receives the color as a design. On the other hand, the producer decides on the color scheme, taking into account the effect of the color on human emotions. Colors contain a variety of information and influence human emotions. For example, red is associated with passion and caution, and yellow with brightness and hope. If we can understand the relationship between these colors and emotions (color emotions), it will be possible to induce people's emotions through colors.

Therefore, attempts have been made to index the emotions expressed by color schemes. In particular, a color emotion prediction formula has been proposed to index color emotions such as heartiness, conspicuousness, brightness, and warmth from a single color [1]. A method is proposed to index color emotion even when multiple colors are combined, by introducing area effect that extends the color emotion prediction formula [2]. Furthermore, a method is proposed to automatically select a color scheme for the intended color emotion [3].

In this study, we attempt to devise a method for predicting people's color emotion caused by color schemes for images. In particular, we propose a method for predicting

C. Stephanidis et al. (Eds.): HCII 2023, CCIS 1836, pp. 475–482, 2023.
https://doi.org/10.1007/978-3-031-36004-6_65

color emotion using the mutual effects of color schemes. Features that take into account color interactions (synergy, contrast, area concentration, visual prominence, and perspective effects) are extracted from the image. These features are then used to predict the color emotion of the color scheme by a convolutional neural network. We collect color emotion data for brightness and warmth through pairwise comparison experiments, evaluate the proposed method.

2 Related Work

2.1 Color Emotion Prediction Formula

Color emotion prediction formula is an expression that estimates the quantitative value of the emotion of heartiness, conspicuousness, brightness, and warmth from a color [1]. In this study, brightness and warmth are the subjects. The physical quantity of brightness (predicted color emotion value) $x_{b,A}$ for a single color A is calculated from Eq. (1).

$$x_{b,A} = b_0 + \sum_{v=1}^{9} b_v x_v \tag{1}$$

$$Z_{1A} = C cos\theta, Z_{2A} = C sin\theta, Z_{3A} = 8.33V \tag{2}$$

$$x_1 = Z_{1A}, x_2 = Z_{2A}, x_3 = Z_{3A}, x_4 = Z_{1A}^2, x_5 = Z_{2A}^2, x_6 = Z_{3A}^2, x_7 = Z_{1A}Z_{2A}, x_8 = Z_{1A}Z_{3A}, x_9 = Z_{2A}Z_{3A}$$

In Eq. (1), the coefficients $b_v (v = 0, 1, \cdots, 9)$ are constants. In Eq. (2), C denotes the saturation of a single color A in the Munsell color system, θ denotes hue, and V denotes lightness. The same procedure is used for the warmth estimator. The physical quantity of warmth $x_{w,A}$ for a single color A is calculated from Eq. (4).

$$x_{w,A} = w_0 + \sum_{v=1}^{9} w_v x_v \tag{4}$$

In Eq. (4), the coefficients $w_v (v = 0, 1, \cdots, 9)$ are constants.

2.2 Prediction of Color Emotion Using Area Effect

In the previous study [2], a method was proposed to consider the effect of area on the feelings of brightness and warmth (area effect). Let $\alpha : \beta : \gamma$ be the area ratio of the component colors A, B, and C in the three-color scheme j. If the estimated amount of color A's brightness is $x_{b,A}$, color B's brightness is $x_{b,B}$, and color C's brightness is $x_{b,C}$, the estimated amount of the three-color scheme j's brightness, $x_{b,j}$ is calculated from Eq. (5).

$$x_{b,j} = \alpha x_{b,A} + \beta x_{b,B} + \gamma x_{b,C} \tag{5}$$

$$\alpha + \beta + \gamma = 1$$

The same procedure is used to calculate the warmth estimator $x_{w,j}$ for the three-color scheme j.

3 Proposed Method

3.1 Pairwise Comparison Experiment

In this study, the following pairwise comparison experiments are conducted to collect data on color emotion. As shown in Fig. 1, two images that assume the coordination of a room by color scheme are displayed on the browser and presented to the subject. Pairwise comparison experiments are conducted in which subjects are asked to select images that they perceive as bright or warm. As for the images presented to the subjects, they consist of five types of furniture: "sofa and pillars," "table," "wall," "window," and "floor," as shown in Fig. 1. In Fig. 1, the color scheme was changed by three colors for "sofa and pillars" and "wall", and by four colors for "table" ($3 \times 3 \times 4 = 36$ images). These three types of furniture are of equal area.

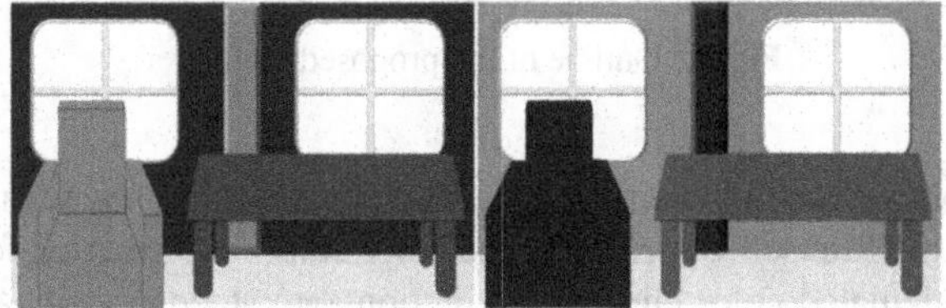

Fig. 1. Pairwise comparison experiments

The subjects are 20 people with normal color vision. The number of pairwise comparison experiments per subject is 630 (There are ${}_{36}C_2$ combinations of two images) $\times 2$ items (brightness, warmth), which is 1,260. In the experiments, the lighting and display conditions in the room are the same. Thurston's pairwise comparison method is then applied to the data collected in pairwise comparison experiments. For each image, we calculate the pairwise comparison scores for brightness and warmth, and rank the 36 images in order of brightest or warmest. We conduct three types of pairwise comparison experiments from Experiment (1) to Experiment (3). In each of the three experiments, the color scheme of the "sofa and pillars," "table," and "walls" is set to be different, and 36 images are created. The same color is used for the "window" and "floor" as shown in Fig. 1. The number of subjects in each of the three pairwise comparison experiments is 20 (60 subjects in total).

3.2 Outline of the Proposed Method

In this study, we aim to reproduce a pairwise comparison experiment in which images are ranked based on the color emotion of brightness and warmth. An outline of the proposed method is shown in Fig. 2.

3.3 Calculation of Color Emotion Predictions

The size of the image is $X \times Y$ (the size of the image used is 512×288). Let $M(x, y) = (\theta, C, V)$ be the Munsell value at coordinates $(x, y)(x = 1, 2, \cdots, X, y = 1, 2, \cdots, Y)$

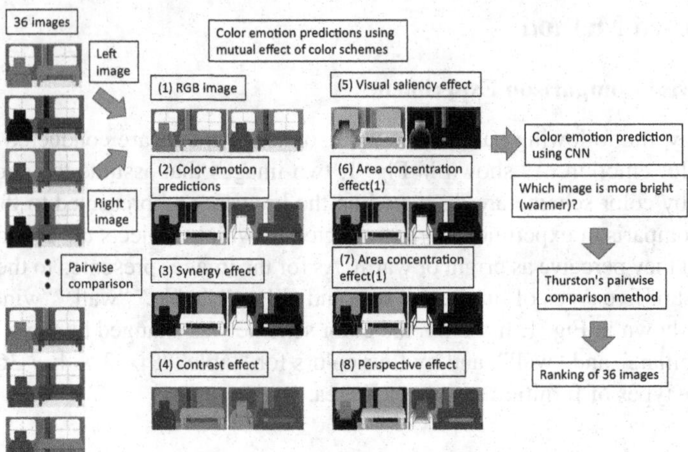

Fig. 2. Outline of the proposed method

in the image. For each coordinate (x, y), the brightness $f_b(x, y)$ and warmth $f_w(x, y)$ are calculated from the Munsell values using the color emotion prediction formula (Eq. (1) and (4)). The calculated color emotion predictions are standardized. A positive standardized color emotion predictions represents brighter or warmer, while a negative value represents more subdued or cooler.

Figure 2(2) shows an image of the color emotion predictions calculated for a RGB image Fig. 2(1). In Fig. 2(2), white (bright) indicates a higher value for color emotion prediction, and black (dark) indicates a lower value.

3.4 Color Emotion Predictions Based on Mutual Effects of Color Schemes

In this study, color emotion predictions are calculated using the mutual effects of color schemes, and these are used as feature values.

- Area Effect

To realize the area effect, the brightness $f_b(x, y)$ and warmth $f_w(x, y)$ for each coordinate (x, y) are added over the entire image. If the image's brightness and warmth are I_{b1} and I_{w1}, respectively, taking the area effect into account, they are obtained from Eq. (6) and (7).

$$I_{b1} = \sum\nolimits_{x=1}^{X} \sum\nolimits_{y=1}^{Y} f_b(x, y) \tag{6}$$

$$I_{w1} = \sum\nolimits_{x=1}^{X} \sum\nolimits_{y=1}^{Y} f_w(x, y) \tag{7}$$

In the area effect, the image with larger I_{b1} (I_{w1}) values are predicted to be brighter (warmer).

- Synergy effect

Synergy effect is an effect in which a color is affected by brightness or warmth of the surrounding area of a certain color. A warmer color is perceived as warmer when it is surrounded by warmer colors. From brightness $f_b(x, y)$ for each coordinate (x, y), brightness $f_{b2}(x, y)$ by synergy effect can be calculated from Eq. (8).

$$f_{b2}(x, y) = \sum_{j=-K/2}^{K/2} \sum_{i=-K/2}^{K/2} f_b(x+i, y+j)G(i, j) \tag{8}$$

In Eq. (8), G is the Gaussian filter and K is the size of the Gaussian filter. Warmth $f_{w2}(x, y)$ by synergy effect is calculated in the same way.

- Contrast effect

Contrast effect is an effect that affects a color when there is a difference in brightness or warmth between a certain color and the surrounding area. The effect is that when a bright color is surrounded by subdued colors, the brighter color stands out. From brightness $f_b(x, y)$ for each coordinate (x, y), brightness $f_{b3}(x, y)$ by the contrast effect can be calculated from Eq. (9).

$$f_{b3}(x, y) = \sum_{j=-K/2}^{K/2} \sum_{i=-K/2}^{K/2} f_b(x+i, y+j)H(i, j) \tag{9}$$

In Eq. (9), H is the Mexican hat filter and K is the size of the Mexican hat filter. Warmth $f_{w3}(x, y)$ by contrast effect is calculated in the same way.

- Visual saliency effect

Visual saliency effect is an effect that the brightness or warmth of colors in areas that easily attract people's attention have on other areas. It is an effect in which the color emotion of a highly salient area becomes more prominent. In this study, saliency maps are created from RGB images. Let $\mathrm{S}(x, y)$ be the saliency value of the coordinate (x, y) on the created saliency map (in this study, the value is from 0 to 255). The higher the value of $\mathrm{S}(x, y)$, the more likely a region is to attract attention. From brightness $f_b(x, y)$ and saliency value $\mathrm{S}(x, y)$ for each coordinate (x, y), brightness $f_{b4}(x, y)$ by visual saliency effect is calculated from Eq. (10).

$$f_{b4}(x, y) = f_b(x, y) \times \mathrm{S}(x, y) / \sum_{i=1}^{X} \sum_{j=1}^{Y} S(i, j) \tag{10}$$

Warmth $f_{w4}(x, y)$ by contrast effect is calculated in the same way.

- Area concentration effect

Area concentration effect is an area effect that takes into account the degree of color concentration in the same area. It is an effect in which the color emotion in a concentrated area is more prominent than in a scattered area. The following two methods are used for area concentration effects.

- Area concentration effect (1): If the proportion of the same color as the coordinate (x, y) in the $\mathrm{N} \times \mathrm{N}$ area centered on the coordinate (x, y) is R or more, brightness

$f_{b5}(x, y)$ and warmth $f_{w5}(x, y)$ by area concentration effect (1) are r times of $f_b(x, y)$ and $f_w(x, y)$.

- Area concentration effect (2): Area concentration effect (2) is calculated by considering the variation of predicted color emotion values within an N × N region centered at the coordinates (x, y). Brightness $f_{b6}(x, y)$ by area concentration effect (2) is calculated by Eq. (11). Warmth $f_{w6}(x, y)$ by area concentration effect (2) is calculated in the same way.

$$f_{b6}(x, y) = f_b(x, y) / \sqrt{\sum_{i=-N/2}^{N/2} \sum_{j=-N/2}^{N/2} \left((f_b(x, y) - f_b(x+i, y+j) \right)^2} \quad (11)$$

- Perspective effect

Perspective effect is the effect of enhancing the color emotion of objects that are close and weakening the color emotion of objects that are far away. For the distance images, disparity maps are created from RGB images. Let D(x, y) be the value of the coordinate (x, y) on the created disparity map (in this study, the value is from 0 to 255). From brightness $f_b(x, y)$ and the value of the disparity map S(x, y) for each coordinate (x, y), brightness $f_{b7}(x, y)$ by perspective effect can be calculated from Eq. (12). Warmth $f_{w7}(x, y)$ by perspective effect is calculated in the same way.

$$f_{b7}(x, y) = \begin{cases} f_b(x, y) \times \mathrm{D}(x, y) & \mathrm{D}(x, y) \geq T \\ f_b(x, y) \times \alpha & \mathrm{D}(x, y) < T \end{cases} \quad (12)$$

3.5 Training with Convolutional Neural Network

To replicate a pairwise comparison experiment, we input two images and train convolutional neural network (CNN) that can predict which image is brighter or warmer. The structure of proposed CNN is shown in Fig. 3.

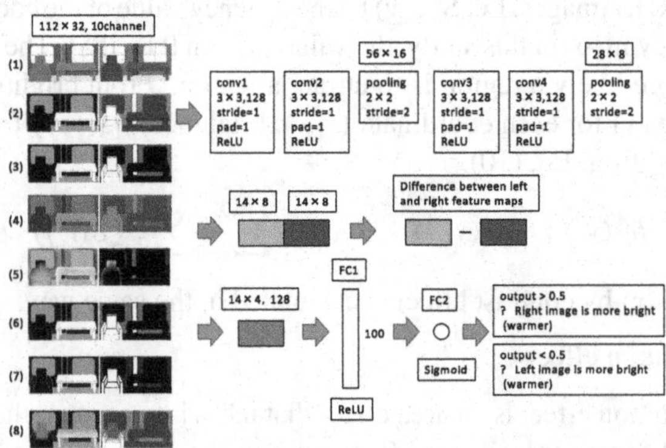

Fig. 3. Structure of proposed convolutional neural network

As shown in Fig. 3, RGB image and 7 types of feature images are input to CNN. Since the image size is 512 × 288, the size of two images side by side becomes 1024 × 288. This is reduced to 112×32 and input to the input layer of CNN. The number of channels is 3 for RGB image and 1 for the others, for a total of 10 channels. Since three types of pairwise comparison experiments are conducted, CNN trains the results of two experiments and predicts the results of the remaining experiments (for example, training the results of Experiments (1) and (2) (1,260 times) and predicting the results of Experiment (3) (630 times)). The above is repeated three times with different training and prediction data.

3.6 Prediction Using Trained CNN

For each experiment, 36 images are combined bilaterally (630 times ($_{36}C_2$)). After training, CNN is used to predict 630 times which of the two images is brighter or warmer. If the output value from CNN is greater than a threshold value (0.5 in this study), the right image is judged brighter (warmer), and if it is less than the threshold value, the left image is judged brighter (warmer). Then, Thurston's pairwise comparison method is applied to the 630 predictions to rank the 36 images.

4 Evaluation

For the evaluation method, we rank brightness and warmth of 36 images for three type of pairwise comparison experiments. The results are then compared with the ranking results of the actual pairwise comparison experiments. When the rank of the experiment for $i(i = 1, 2, \cdots, 36)$ images is p_i and the rank of the prediction result by the proposed method is t_i, the sum of squared error U is calculated from Eq. (13).

$$\mathrm{U} = \sum\nolimits_{i=1}^{36} (p_i - t_i)^2 \tag{13}$$

Also, the agreement rate between the results of 630 pairwise comparison experiments and the results of the pairwise comparison predicted by the proposed method is calculated. In order to evaluate color emotion predictions using the mutual effect between color schemes, a pairwise comparison is conducted based on the sum of the color emotion predictions calculated for each of the two images, and the results are ranked by Thurston's pairwise comparison method. The results are then compared with those of the actual pairwise comparison experiment. We compare these results with those from CNN. Results are shown in Table 1.

Table 1 shows the averaged results of three different experiments. In the case of CNN, since the prediction accuracy varies from training to training, we repeat 10 times and calculate the average of the 10 iterations. Table 1 shows that the CNN improved the agreement rate by about 4% in the case of brightness, and by about 8% in the case of warmth. The sum of the squares of the errors also improved for both brightness and warmth. We are able to demonstrate the effectiveness of the proposed method, which calculates color emotion predictions based on the mutual effects of color schemes and ranks images using CNN.

Table 1. Results with mutual effects of color schemes and CNN

Mutual effect	Brightness		Warmth	
	Agreement rate	Sum of squared error	Agreement rate	Sum of squared error
Color emotion predictions	82.3%	1280	80.0%	2645
Synergy	82.2%	1284	80.1%	2645
Contrast	82.2%	1288	79.9%	2621
Visual saliency	79.7%	1796	79.8%	2636
Area concentration (1)	82.1%	1302	79.9%	2652
Area concentration (2)	82.0%	1289	79.9%	2630
Perspective	82.9%	1255	79.9%	2486
Proposed CNN	86.4%	844	87.9%	700

5 Conclusion

In this study, we attempted to devise a method for predicting color emotion corresponding to real images. We proposed a method for calculating color emotion predictions based on the mutual effects of color schemes (synergy, contrast, visual saliency, area concentration, and perspective), and for ranking images using a convolutional neural network. We then evaluated the proposed method by collecting data on brightness and warmth through pairwise comparison experiments. The results showed that the proposed method significantly improved the accuracy. In the future, we will conduct pairwise comparison experiments on images with a larger number of color schemes and collect data. In addition, we will improve CNN and the prediction method.

References

1. The Color Science Association of Japan: Handbook of Color Science. 2nd edn. University of Tokyo Press, pp. 311–316 (2011)
2. Sakai, H., Doi, M.: Prediction formulas of color feelings taking into account the emotional scale and area effect for three-color combinations. J. Color Sci. Assoc. Jpn. **37**(6), 616–617 (2013)
3. Sakai, H., Urabe, N., Nayatani, Y.: A method for selecting two-color combinations with various affections. J. Color Sci. Assoc. Jpn. **31**(Suppl.), 36–37 (2007)

Semi-automatic Basketball Jump Shot Annotation Using Multi-view Activity Recognition and Deep Learning

Samuel E Matos Flores(✉)

Polytechnic University of Puerto Rico, 00918 San Juan, Puerto Rico
matos_130418@students.pupr.edu

Abstract. Statisticians introduce subjectivity while recording game statistics. This research aims to reduce this problem using a multi-view pose classification model, starting with the jump shot location event annotation. Basketball simulations will be conducted to determine if the proposed model can be more objective than a human statistician recording the same jump shot event. To this end, the Exhaustive Basketball System (EBS) was developed. EBS is a web application that allows customizable courts and game rules variations, enabling storing in-game event data. Allowing the extraction of the necessary jump shot coordinates data recorded by the statistician during the simulations for analyses. By controlling the number of players, game time duration, and an agility index grouping technique proposed for the basketball simulations, their impact on the coordinates data will be analyzed in an ANOVA 3*2*3 factorial design with three repetitions. The response variable is the average distance of the jump shot attempts event annotation regarding the ground truth location. While other researchers have worked on jump shot recognition using a single view of the court, our research attempts to contribute to this concept but with multiple synchronized viewing angles in addition to subjectivity reduction. We expect to prove an ideal game statistics generation technique to register objective statistics. Moreover, be a pathway for objective game statistics and present recommendations for future work related to other sports or fields that could benefit from the proposed technique.

Keywords: machine learning · basketball · subjectivity

1 Introduction

Statistical techniques have become essential to modern sports with the growing field. Sports statistics have continuously grown and provide enriched information in the decision-making of play strategies and player scouting [2, 12, 17, 18, 27]. It has also been used in sports media and broadcasting with tools to increase fan engagement and customer satisfaction. Sports betting, ticket sales, player enhancement, and player training are a few things that statistics in sports benefit. Thanks to data science and statistical modeling, statistics and analytical data continue evolving for better accuracy and precision. Nevertheless, statistics in modern sports are generated and recorded by statisticians.

C. Stephanidis et al. (Eds.): HCII 2023, CCIS 1836, pp. 483–490, 2023.
https://doi.org/10.1007/978-3-031-36004-6_66

Non-professional leagues register a limited number of statistics on a sheet of paper from the total actions that can be recorded in a game [21]. Thus, not recording valuable data for further analysis can be wearisome.

"Human activity recognition (HAR) aims to recognize activities from a series of observations on the actions of subjects and the environmental conditions." [30]. The National Basketball Association (NBA) has been one of these professional sports leagues to welcome this type of research. Currently, SportVU is the official tracking partner of the NBA. SportVU is a costly camera system, $100,000, that tracks each player's coordinates and the ball [23, 24, 27]. Still, this system does not record all statistics generated during an NBA game. Each home team has its scorekeeper lineup that usually consists of four statisticians. Such an approach creates the potential for inconsistency, errors, and bias in data [23, 24]. A human interprets these statistics, and each can interpret an action during a game with different details. Subjectivity can be found in the statistics recorded by a statistician [7, 11, 23–25]. A clear example of this subjectivity was the case of an NBA scorekeeper who awarded a player with twenty-three assists, including several that were "comically bad." [24]. Subjectivity has also been found in recreational, lower-level professional, high-level, college, and K-12 leagues [21]. This research aims to reduce this problem by using a multi-view pose classification model to study if it can reduce subjectivity in the jump shot location data annotated by a scorekeeper or a statistician. Determining if the proposed approach can lead to entirely objective statistics generation.

2 Literature Review

Current techniques utilized to recognize players, the ball, and in-game events are presented. First, using Bluetooth devices to track the players and ball movement [6, 14]. Despite the results presented in both investigations, a suggestion that inertial sensors are "not conducive to popularization and application" is a concern [9]. Thus, allowing to indicate that Bluetooth tracking systems face the same situation since both technologies require the player to wear the device. In a series of publications, a scoring system was developed for amateur boxing matches [1, 7]. They wanted to reduce the "scoring controversies" of these matches created by the judges during the event scoring [1, 7]. Thus, deciding who was deemed victorious by objectively evaluating their performance. Next, machine learning and deep learning models with a single view are presented. Firstly, the study of jump shot event recognition. The study of recognizing the jump shot event from a single viewing angle has been accomplished [8, 9, 19, 22]. Detection of the jump shot event, the attempt's success, and from where in the court it was attempted by the player [22]. Secondly, the broadcast imagery from the basketball game has been used as the primary data source for models to analyze [5, 10, 29]. Though these proposed models work with the data transmitted from the sporting broadcast channels, they are susceptible to unexpected viewing angle changes from the transmission. Medium. This situation is a possible limitation that some models are unprepared to handle [29].

Furthermore, having a single view from the sporting event may generate occlusions events that may affect the model's estimations. Thus, the third technique to be presented is the utilization of multiple stationary viewing angles. With the suggested approach, researchers have been able to track the ball and trajectory of players [12, 13, 16]. Presenting how using multiple stationary angles eliminates unpredicted changes in viewing angles and reduces occlusion events. Moreover, this approach does not require subjects to wear a device to be tracked.

3 Materials and Methodology

3.1 Exhaustive Basketball System (EBS)

EBS was designed and developed to capture the jump shot data the statisticians will record and consequently used to analyze the subjectivity reduction the proposed model may achieve. It has five main modules that allow multiple levels of customization for each game scenario taught during the design process. Customizable courts from color, size, dimensions, and court line placement. Players and teams with particular case use. Users can create standard (regular games) or special games (mixed genders, different courts to the one assigned to the team, custom number of players per team, among many other options). Finally, live statistics generated by the statistician recording the in-game events can be viewed. The most crucial section of this system and why it was developed were the precision of the court displayed on the screen and the data the statisticians would generate. For example, each court area is painted with figures; it's not a generic image for all courts. Every twelve pixels represent one foot in real life; therefore, if we take the NBA's basketball court dimensions 94 feet long by 50 feet wide, the system will display 1128 by 600 court on the screen. Allowing the display of precise dimensions. Therefore, the statisticians expect to capture more accurate jump shot location data. Finally, the statisticians can record all in-game events statistics like assists, blocks, rebounds, and fouls while using this system section (see Fig. 1).

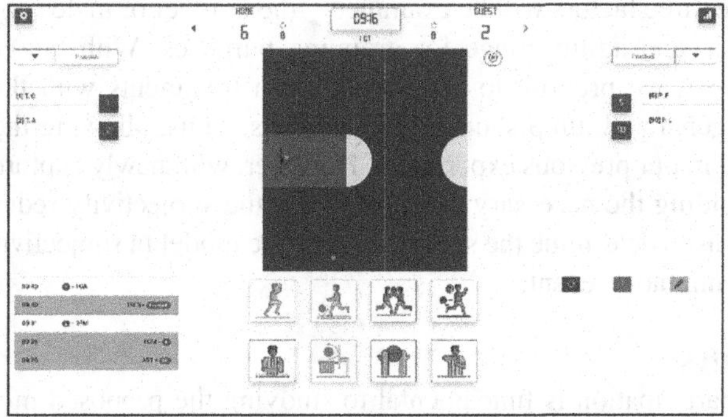

Fig. 1. EBS in-game event recording section.

3.2 Proposed Procedure

This research aims to study the significance of using a multi-view pose classification model to recognize the jump shot attempt and determine how objective the proposed model can be compared to a statistician. First, determine the model's structure for analyzing the sensor data captured by GoPro cameras [9, 22]. The model will be developed and trained with multiple angles of the in-game events using a dataset known as APIDIS [17, 26]. Additionally, our own captured data. For each viewing angle, the pose estimation of the players will be detected using OpenPose [3, 4, 15, 28]. After discarding the detected poses that do not belong to the players on the court, the two-dimensional features will be fed into a Bayesian neural network to classify the players' actions [8, 9]. When the network classifies the action as a jump shot event, a transformation will be applied to establish the coordinates of the event's location [22] (see Fig. 2).

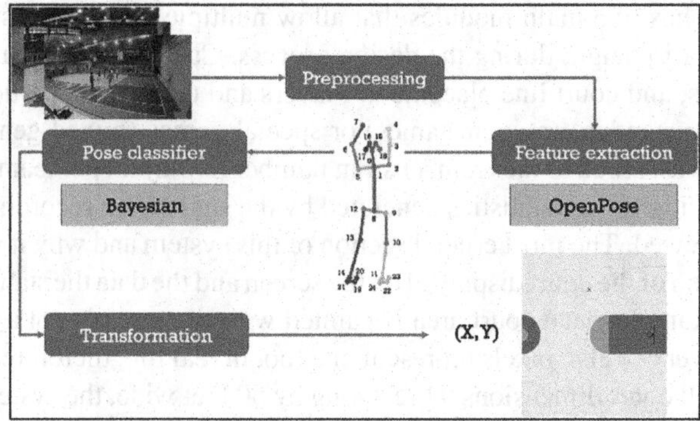

Fig. 2. Proposed model visualization.

After the model training, different treatments regarding the model's capacity will be studied. Three GoPro Hero 9 cameras in a basketball half-court record different scenarios where three factors will be examined—the number of male subjects per team, the game length, and agility range for grouping purposes. With the combination of the factors' levels, we propose to capture eighteen treatments with three repetitions to analyze the generated jump shots by the subjects. Thus, allowing the validation of results obtained in our previous experiment. However, with newly captured sensor data. Moreover, providing the necessary sensor data for the subjectivity reduction analysis. Thus, allowing us to determine the significance of the model in subjectivity reduction in the jump shot annotation event.

Statistical Analysis

The subjects' participation is fundamental to studying the proposed model's behavior in different basketball scenarios. Approval of the Inter-American University of Puerto Rico (IAUPR) Institutional Review Board has been granted. By controlling the number of players, game time duration, and an agility index grouping technique proposed for the basketball simulations, their impact on the coordinates data will be analyzed in an ANOVA 3*2*3 factorial design with three repetitions.

Factors

Three factors will be studied during the simulations of basketball games to generate the sensor and jump shot data. These are the following:

1. The number of male subjects per team that are older than 21 years old and younger than 31 years with a height of 5′ 4″ up to 6′ 4″ with a minimum of 6 months of experience.
2. Game length (game clock).
3. Agility range grouping as a result of the T-Test agility evaluation metric.

Levels

1. The number of subjects participating per team will be one, two, or three players. Therefore, this factor will have three levels.
2. The time the participants play will be ten or twenty minutes. Thus, this factor will have two levels.
3. The T-Test agility drill will provide the ability to examine the subjects. The only purpose of the exercise will be to establish a grouping mechanism for the subjects participating in the treatments. The critical interval values proposed are 11.69 and 10.22 s [20]. Therefore, this final factor has three levels.
   (1) AI-1 agility index, subjects that score s > 11.69 s.
   (2) AI-2 agility index, subjects that score is 11.69 ≥ s ≥ 10.22 s.
   (3) AI-3 agility index, subjects that score is s < 10.22 s.

Treatments

This experimental phase is considered a 3 * 2 * 3 factorial design (Table 1).

Table 1. Tabular visualization of the proposed treatments.

		Game length					
		Ten (10) minutes			Twenty (20) minutes		
Agility interval (AI)		1	2	3	1	2	3
Subjects (per team)	1	jad_1	jad_{18}	jad_7	jad_4	jad_{15}	jad_{10}
	2	jad_2	jad_{17}	jad_8	jad_5	jad_{14}	jad_{11}
	3	jad_3	jad_{16}	jad_9	jad_6	jad_{13}	jad_{12}

jad_w The average distance of the jump shot attempts event annotation regarding the ground truth location of the same event.

Therefore, jad_w for each treatment will be calculated with the following equation:

$$jad_w = \left(\sum_{i=1}^{n}\sqrt{\left(R_{i_x} - A_{i_x}\right)^2 + \left(R_{i_y} - A_{i_y}\right)^2}\right)/n \quad (1)$$

Where:

w = treatment number.
i = jump shot attempt index.
n = total number of jump shot attempts per treatment.
R_i = absolute coordinates (ground truth) of the jump shot attempt i.
A_i = coordinates of i generated by the studied source (statistician or model).

Answer
The average distance of jump shot attempts event annotation regarding the ground truth location of the same event is presented in Eq. 1. Allowing to test the capability of the model to work with the sensor data captured of the treatments above and comparing it with the statistician generating the same location registration on EBS. Where the most objective and precise source of the annotation should be closer or equal to zero.

4 Hypothesis

With the utilization of the proposed model, we expect to study if it's capable of reducing the naturally generated subjectivity by the statisticians who annotate the in-game events in basketball games, starting with the jump shot. The central hypothesis is that the model will have more objective and precise estimations of the location where the player attempted the jump shot. Having the average distance per treatment closer to zero than the statistician, the answer per treatment in our ANOVA design. However, at what cost? Is the model going to miss more jump-shot events than the statistician? The proposed approach may generate more objective data when it can detect the event compared to a statistician that may miss fewer jump shots compared to the model and register the event but with subjectivity. The possible trade-off will also be analyzed.

5 Significance of Study

The significance of this proposed study is to provide a minimum risk of statistician's susceptibility at a low cost and accurate statistics of the location of each attempt to score the basketball. Offer insight into the time factor for statisticians and how it negatively affects the objectivity of the statistics. Present possible future implementations of the proposed model in the sport and how teams may benefit from the information the model provides. We expect that, with the two proposed experiments, we can demonstrate that the multi-view pose classification model could help with subjectivity reduction created by statisticians in basketball—a possible pathway for accurate sports statistics shortly.

References

1. Bruch, H., Hahn, A.G., Helmer, R.J., MacKintosh, C., Blanchonette, I., McKenna, M.J.: Evaluation of an automated scoring system in a modified form of competitive boxing. Proc. Eng. **13**, 445–450 (2011). https://doi.org/10.1016/j.proeng.2011.05.112
2. Cao, C.: Sports data mining technology used in basketball outcome prediction (Doctoral dissertation) (2012)

3. Cao, Z., Hidalgo Martinez, G., Simon, T., Wei, S., Sheikh, Y.A.: Openpose: realtime multi-person 2d pose estimation using part affinity fields. IEEE Trans. Patt. Anal. Mach. Intell. (2019)
4. Cao, Z., Simon, T., Wei, S.-E., Sheikh, Y.: Realtime multi-person 2d pose estimation using part affinity fields. In: Cvpr (2017)
5. Chen, L. H., Chang, H.W., Hsiao, H.A.: Player trajectory reconstruction from broadcast basketball video. In: ACM International Conference Proceeding Series, pp. 72–76 (2017). https://doi.org/10.1145/3133793.3133801
6. Figueira, B., Gonçalves, B., Folgado, H., Masiulis, N., Calleja-González, J., Sampaio, J.: Accuracy of a basketball indoor tracking system based on standard bluetooth low energy channels (NBN23®). Sensors (Switzerland) **18**(6), 2–9 (2018). https://doi.org/10.3390/s18061940
7. Hahn, A.G., et al.: Development of an automated scoring system for amateur boxing. Proc. Eng. **2**(2), 3095–3101 (2010). https://doi.org/10.1016/j.proeng.2010.04.117
8. Huang, C.-L., Shih, H.-C., Chen, C.-L.: Shot and scoring events identification of basketball videos. In: 2006 IEEE International Conference on Multimedia and Expo, pp. 9–12, July 2006. https://doi.org/10.1109/ICME.2006.262923
9. Ji, R.: Research on basketball shooting action based on image feature extraction and machine. Learning **8**, 138743–138751 (2020). https://doi.org/10.1109/ACCESS.2020.3012456
10. Johnson, N.: Extracting player tracking data from video using non-stationary cameras and a combination of computer vision techniques. In: MIT Sloan Sports Analytics Conference, pp. 1–14 (2020)
11. Lin, T., Yang, Y., Beyer, J., Pfister, H.: SportsXR - immersive analytics in sports. In: CHI 2020: CHI Conference on Human Factors in Computing Systems, pp. 25–30 (2020). https://doi.org/10.1145/3334480. arXiv 2004.08010
12. Meng, W., Xu, S., Li, E., Zeng, X., Zhang, X.: Accurate 3D locating and tracking of basketball players from multiple videos. In: SIGGRAPH Asia 2018 Technical Briefs, SA 2018 (2018). https://doi.org/10.1145/3283254.3283265
13. Monier, E., Wilhelm, P., Rückert, U.: A Computer vision based tracking system for indoor team sports. In: The fourth International Conference on Intelligent Computing and Information Systems (2009)
14. Nguyen, L.N.N., Rodríguez-Martín, D., Català, A., Pérez-López, C., Samà, A., Cavallaro, A.: Basketball activity recognition using wearable inertial measurement units. In: ACM International Conference Proceeding Series, 07–09 September (2015). https://doi.org/10.1145/2829875.2829930
15. Simon, T., Joo, H., Matthews, I., Sheikh, Y.: Hand keypoint detection in single images using multiview bootstrapping. In: Cvpr (2017)
16. Tanikawa, S., Tagawa, N.: Player Tracking using Multi-viewpoint Images in Basketball Analysis. In: Proceedings of the 15th International Joint Conference on Computer Vision, Imaging and Computer Graphics Theory and Applications, (VISI-GRAPP), pp. 813–820 (2020). https://doi.org/10.5220/0009097408130820
17. Thomas, G., Gade, R., Moeslund, T.B., Carr, P., Hilton, A.: Computer vision for sports: current applications and research topics. Comput. Vis. Image Underst. **159**, 3–18 (2017). https://doi.org/10.1016/j.cviu.2017.04.011
18. Tichy, W.: Changing the game: "Dr. Dave" Schrader on sports analytics. Ubiquity 2016, Article 1, pp. 1–10, May 2016. https://doi.org/10.1145/2933230
19. Tien, M.-c., Chen, H.-t., Chen, Y.-w., Hsiao, M.-h., Lee, S.-y.: Shot classification of basketball videos and its application in shooting position extraction. In: IEEE International Conference on Acoustics, Speech and Signal Processing – ICASSP 2007 (2007). https://doi.org/10.1109/ICASSP.2007.366100

20. Pauole, K., Madole, K., Garhammer, J., Lacourse, M., Rozenek, R.: Reliability and validity of the T-Test as a measure of agility, leg power, and leg speed in college-aged men and women. J. Strength Cond. Res. **14**(4), 443–450 (2000)
21. Perin, C., Vuillemot, R., Stolper, C.D., Stasko, J.T., Wood, J., Carpendale, S.: State of the art of sports data visualization. Comput. Graph. Forum **37**(3), 663–686 (2018). https://doi.org/10.1111/cgf.13447
22. Ratgeber, L., Ivankovic, Z., Gojkovic, Z., Milosevic, Z., Markoski, B., Kostic-Zobenica, A.: Video mining in basketball shot and game analysis. In: Acta Polytechnica Hungarica, vol. 16, no. 1, pp. 7–27 (2019). https://doi.org/10.12700/APH.16.1.2019.1.1
23. van Bommel, M., Bornn, L.: The van excel effect: adjusting for scorekeeper bias in NBA box scores. In: MIT Sloan Sports Analytics Conference, pp. 1–15 (2016)
24. van Bommel, M., Bornn, L.: Adjusting for scorekeeper bias in NBA box scores. Data Min. Knowl. Disc. **31**(6), 1622–1642 (2017). https://doi.org/10.1007/s10618-017-0497-y
25. van Bommel, M., Bornn, L., Chow-White, P., Gao, C.: Home sweet home: quantifying home court advantages for NCAA basketball statistics, pp. 1–13 (2019). https://doi.org/10.48550/arXiv.1909.04817. arXiv 1909.04817
26. Vleeschouwer, C., et al.: Distributed video acquisition and annotation for sport-event summarization (2008)
27. Wang, K.-C., & Zemel, R.: Classifying NBA Offensive Plays Using Neural Networks. MIT Sloan Sports Analytics Conference, 1–9. (2016),
28. Wei, S.-E., Ramakrishna, V., Kanade, T., Sheikh, Y.: Convolutional pose machines. In: Cvpr (2016)
29. Wen, P.-C., Cheng, W.-C., Wang, Y.-S., Chu, H.-K., Tang, N.C., Liao, H.-Y.M.: Court reconstruction for camera calibration in broadcast basketball videos. IEEE Trans. Visual Comput. Graphics **22**(5), 1517–1526 (2015). https://doi.org/10.1109/TVCG.2015.2440236
30. Zhang, S., Wei, Z., Nie, J., Huang, L., Wang, S., Li, Z.: A review on human activity recognition using vision-based method. J. Healthc. Eng. (2017). https://doi.org/10.1155/2017/3090343

Detecting Minors According to South African Law Using Computer Vision Methods

Tevin Moodley and Siphesihle Sithungu(✉)

University of Johannesburg, Kingsway Avenue and, University Rd, Auckland Park, Johannesburg 2092, South Africa
{tevin,siphesihles}@uj.ac.za

Abstract. Age estimation is one of the areas of interest in computer vision, which is evident from the increased amount of related research over the last few years. This is largely due to the exceptional levels of classification accuracy demonstrated by Convolutional Neural Networks (CNNs) in computer vision tasks. One of the main challenges faced when training age detection models are accounting for people's diversity, which raises the importance of using datasets with as much diversity as possible. Another important factor to consider is the reason behind performing age estimation, which can either classify people's age or detect if someone's age exceeds (or is below) a specific threshold. This paper presents work done to detect minors according to South African law (which is under 18 years of age). South Africa is a very diverse country. As such, the UTK-Face dataset, containing face images with a wide range of ethnicities, was used to train the Inception Resnet V2 to detect minors according to South African Law. The dataset was reduced to only include relevant images with the aim of obtaining an equal distribution of gender and ethnicity to ensure relevance to the South African context. A model accuracy of 99.73% was achieved, demonstrating the model's ability to distinguish between underage and legal age classes. It was also noted that class imbalance and the reduced number of samples were inhibiting factors to the model's performance in terms of precision and recall.

Keywords: Age detection · Deep learning · Computer vision · Inception Resnet V2

1 Introduction

One of the most significant challenges South Africans face is dependence on addictive substances, which can lead to cases of overdose. Apart from the risk of overdose, substance abuse generally leads to negative adolescent behaviour, such as crime, antisocial activities and poor academic performance. Long-term consequences can lead to suicide, psychological distress, the contraction of contagious diseases and accidents [13]. The prevalence of underage drinking in South

C. Stephanidis et al. (Eds.): HCII 2023, CCIS 1836, pp. 491–497, 2023.
https://doi.org/10.1007/978-3-031-36004-6_67

Africa cannot be ignored, and some of the responsibility can be attributed to negligence by owners of establishments that sell alcohol, resulting in underage teenagers becoming frequent customers [14].

The legal drinking age is the same as the driving age (among other things, such as voting) in South Africa, and it is considered the age of majority (the threshold of adulthood as recognised by law) according to the *Age of Majority* Act [11]. With the increasing trend in the global use of technology and the drive towards automation, it is reasonable to predict that the task of automating age detection, especially with respect to detecting minors, will be of paramount importance in the foreseeable future. An example of a practical application is embedding age estimation systems in cigarette vending machines to better supervise or manage cigarette sales [6].

Convolutional Neural Networks (CNNs) are one of the most widely used deep learning models in computer vision and other fields, such as natural language processing. The increased application of CNNs to various tasks is due to their impressive performance on a wide range of datasets. This resulted in computer vision tasks that were significantly difficult in the past, such as autonomous vehicles and reliable face recognition becoming possible to accomplish [9].

Traditional methods require explicit feature extraction, meaning it must be performed manually. This approach makes it difficult to obtain the most optimal features in order to train a deep-learning model. On the other hand, the modern feature extraction process provided by CNNs is efficient at identifying optimal features and has a robust capability to adapt to noise in images [10].

Transfer learning and *data augmentation* are useful in cases where the dataset being used is relatively small. One of the widely used pre-trained CNNs is the Inception Resnet V2, which uses transfer learning and is pre-trained on the ImageNet database [7].

2 Problem Background

Age estimation is a method for automatically labelling a subject's face with a real number representing their age. The assigned age could be interpreted as perceived, actual or estimated. Perceived age can only be estimated according to visual age information from the subject's face. Whereas estimated age is the subject's age as predicted by a machine from their visual appearance. It is worth noting that appearance age is not always consistent with actual age due to the variable nature in which individuals age [1].

There is not a significant amount of age estimation research in the literature [8], which could result from age estimation not being viewed as a classical classification problem. This is because age estimation can also be viewed as a regression problem or even as both classification and regression in a hierarchical manner. Moreover, it is difficult to obtain images of a single subject across different ages and the diverse information provided by faces can result in attributes specific to ageing not being properly captured [1].

Recent work has shown that the use of Convolutional Neural Networks (CNNs) has introduced new levels of accuracy with regard to age estimation from faces [10]. As such, there has been an increase in the number of works proposing the use of (CNNs) for age estimation from faces. Some of the most relevant works are discussed in the following subsection.

2.1 Related Works

In [10], the authors proposed the MA-SFV2: Mixed Attention-ShuffleNetV2 model, which combined the known ShuffleNetV2 CNN with a mixed-attention mechanism. The model was tested on the FG-NET and MORPH2 datasets and produced a mean absolute error better than some of the state-of-the-art models (although it did not surpass them on the overall task of age estimation).

The Ranking-CNN [5], a model that contains a series of conventional CNNs trained on ordinal age labels, was applied to the task of age estimation and was shown to statistically outperform state-of-the-art models on benchmark datasets. In [4], the *COnsistent RAnk Logits (CORAL)* framework was applied to facial age estimation and showed a promising reduction in prediction error when compared to a conventional ordinal regression CNN.

In [12], the authors proposed the mean-variance loss function for age estimation through distribution learning. The mean-variance loss was used in conjunction with softmax loss and mutually embedded into CNNs for facial age estimation. Experimental results showed improved performance compared to the state-of-the-art on the MORPH2, FG-NET and CLAP2016 datasets. Deep Regression Forests (DRFs) [15] (where the split nodes of regression trees are connected to the fully connected layer of a CNN) were also applied to age estimation and produced promising results in comparison to the state-of-the-art.

Even though the similar works mentioned above were on age estimation, their focus was not on detecting if a sample was below or above a specified threshold, which is the aim of the work proposed in this paper: recognising samples that fall below the age of majority (18 years) according to South African law. In addition, the work presented in this paper aims to perform such detection using a dataset containing samples with as much diversity as possible.

3 Proposed Model

This research paper aims to detect minors according to South African law by drawing distinctions between *Underage*, and *Legal age* faces using the *UTKFace* dataset. Figure 1 illustrates the proposed model used to achieve age detection of minors according to South African law using the *Inception Resnet V2* architecture. From Fig. 1, the *UTKFace* dataset is fed into the Inception Resnet V2 architecture, and those images are subsequently trained to derive distinctive features that are used to make distinctions within the dataset.

3.1 Dataset Setup

The *UTKFace* dataset is a large-scale face dataset with a long age span ranging from 0 to 116 years. The dataset consists of over *20 000* face images with

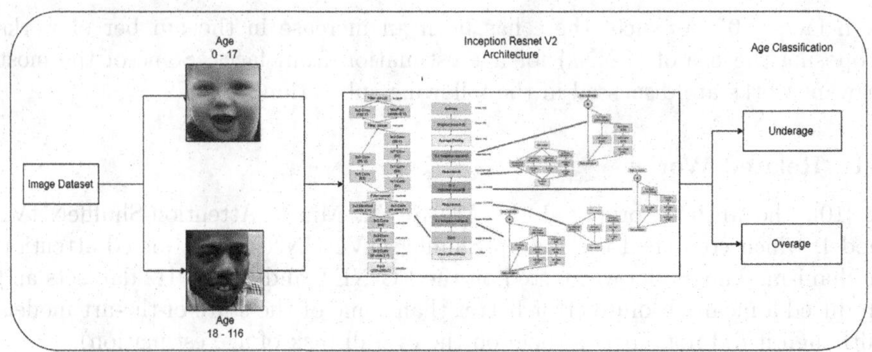

Fig. 1. The proposed model to achieve Age Detection according to South African Law using the Inception Resnet V2 Architecture.

annotations of age, gender, and ethnicity [16]. To prepare the dataset, the data is split into two categories *Underage*, which includes all ages from 0–17 years and *Legal age*, which includes ages 18–116. There is a total of 10 000 images used. The original dataset is reduced to ensure that only the relevant images are chosen, whereby an equal distribution of gender and ethnicity is catered to ensure the study is applicable within the South African context. The dataset is split using a 70:30 rule, where 7000 images belong to the training set, and 3000 images belong to the testing set. The image size of 128 × 128 pixels is chosen through testing and validation.

3.2 Model for Implementation

Resnet and Inception have been central to the largest advances in image recognition performance in recent years while maintaining promising results at a relatively low computational cost. Using transfer learning, the Inception Resnet V2 model achieves Age classification. *Inception Resnet V2* is a convolutional neural network that is trained on more than a million images from the *ImageNet* database. The network consists of 164 layers deep and can classify images into 1000 object categories. The architecture is formulated based on a combination of the Inception structure and the Residual connection, as seen in Fig. 2. Multiple-sized convolutional filters are combined with residual connections within the Inception-Resnet block [2].

Using residual connections avoids the degradation problem caused by deep structures and reduces the training time, resulting in less overhead related to computational complexity. Using transfer learning, the architecture is formed. The following parameters are applied, *include top* is set to *false*, *weights* is set to *imagenet*, which will result in the weights being initialised randomly, the *input tensor* is set to *none* and the image size used is 128 × 128. The specified parameters were set to establish a baseline which may allow existing architectures

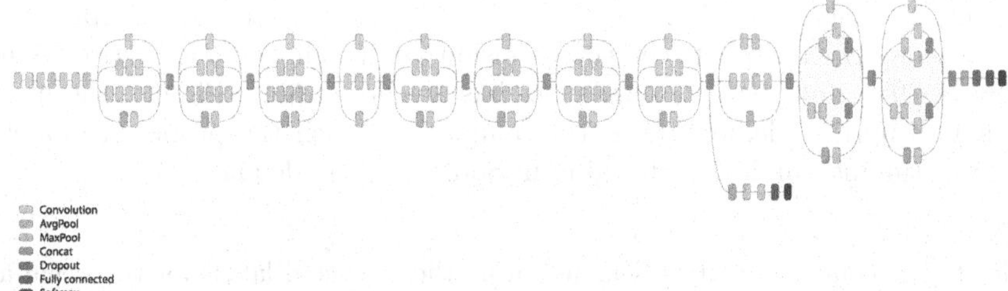

Fig. 2. A figure illustrating the architecture of the Inception Resnet V2 network [3].

to be compared and analysed fairly for future works. The model was run on 50 epochs, and the batch size was set to 32.

4 Results and Findings

The results achieved illustrates the manner in which the *Inception Resnet V2* architecture is able to detect minors within a South African context. The Inception Resnet V2 architecture achieved a training accuracy of **99.73%**. Table 1 illustrates the precision, recall, f1-score and support for the proposed model for the respective classes on the test set. From Table 1, the *Underage* class exhibits a precision score of 66%, whereas the *Legal age* class has a precision score of *90%*. The precision score demonstrates the manner in which the model does not label positive predictions as negative corrections. The Legal age class performs exceptionally well in this regard, which is supported using Table 2, where the Legal age class correctly predicted a *90%* ratio of positive observations to the total predicted positive observations. The Underage class precision score is *66%*, which may be a result of the Legal age class incorrectly predicting 809 samples as *Underage*.

Table 1. The precision, recall and f1-score for the proposed Inception Resnet V2 architecture on 50 epochs.

Class	Precision	Recall	F1-score	Support
underage	66%	97%	79%	1652
Legal age	90%	40%	55%	1348

The recall score determines the ratio of correctly predicted positive observations to the total predicted positive observations. From Table 1 and 2, the *Underage* class performs well with a 97% recall score which is supported by 1595 samples out of 1652 samples being correctly predicted. The Legal age class struggles to correctly predict the positive observations, whereas 809 samples are incorrectly predicted as Underage, which is the majority of the samples. The f1-score shows the ratio between the precision and recall, the underage class has a score of 79%, and the Legal age class has a score of 55%. Finally, the model accuracy of 99.73% demonstrates the manner in which the proposed model is able to distinguish underage drinking in South Africa adequately.

Table 2. The confusion matrix demonstrating the predicted labels for the Legal age and underage classes.

Class	Underage	Legal age
Underage	1595	57
Legal age	809	539

From the results obtained in Table 1 and 2, there seems to be a trade-off between the two classes where each class either suffers in terms of precision or recall score. A possible reason for this may be due to *class imbalance*, the underage class has 1652, and the Legal age class has 1348 samples, respectively. The class imbalance may seem insignificant. However, the dataset was manually edited in an attempt to make it more relevant from a South African context, and subsequently, the edited dataset was reduced to a smaller size which may be a cause of the poor precision and recall scores for the respective classes. Adding more data while ensuring that the relevancy is kept intact may allow the model to produce even better results on the test set.

5 Conclusion

This research paper demonstrated the manner in which the Inception Resnet V2 model is able to draw features to distinguish between underage and Legal age citizens in South Africa to detect minors with a model accuracy of 99.73%. The ability to perform such detection could aid in the prevention of illegal acts that could arise where the age of majority is concerned, such as the purchase of alcohol or cigarettes by minors. The results presented in this paper were not compared to the works cited in the literature study due to our work not based on a generic application of a deep learning model to a benchmark dataset. Moreover, our work is not based on predicting the specific age of a person but on predicting whether their age falls beneath (or above) the legal age in South Africa.

References

1. Angulu, R., Tapamo, J.R., Adewumi, A.O.: Age estimation via face images: a survey. EURASIP J. Image Video Process. **2018**(1), 1–35 (2018). https://doi.org/10.1186/s13640-018-0278-6

2. Baldassarre, F., Morín, D.G., Rodés-Guirao, L.: Deep koalarization: image colorization using CNNs and Inception-ResNet-v2. arXiv preprint arXiv:1712.03400 (2017)
3. Bhatia, Y., Bajpayee, A., Raghuvanshi, D., Mittal, H.: Image captioning using Google's Inception-ResNet-v2 and recurrent neural network. In: 2019 Twelfth International Conference on Contemporary Computing (IC3), pp. 1–6. IEEE (2019)
4. Cao, W., Mirjalili, V., Raschka, S.: Rank consistent ordinal regression for neural networks with application to age estimation. Pattern Recogn. Lett. **140**, 325–331 (2020). https://doi.org/10.1016/j.patrec.2020.11.008. https://www.sciencedirect.com/science/article/pii/S016786552030413X
5. Chen, S., Zhang, C., Dong, M., Le, J., Rao, M.: Using ranking-CNN for age estimation. In: Proceedings of the IEEE Conference on Computer Vision and Pattern Recognition (CVPR), July 2017
6. Farazdaghi, E., Eslahi, M., El Meouche, R.: An overview of the use of biometric techniques in smart cities. In: International Archives of the Photogrammetry, Remote Sensing & Spatial Information Sciences (2021)
7. Ferreira, C.A., et al.: Classification of breast cancer histology images through transfer learning using a pre-trained Inception ResNet V2. In: Campilho, A., Karray, F., ter Haar Romeny, B. (eds.) ICIAR 2018. LNCS, vol. 10882, pp. 763–770. Springer, Cham (2018). https://doi.org/10.1007/978-3-319-93000-8_86
8. Fu, Y., Guo, G., Huang, T.S.: Age synthesis and estimation via faces: a survey. IEEE Trans. Pattern Anal. Mach. Intell. **32**(11), 1955–1976 (2010)
9. Li, Z., Liu, F., Yang, W., Peng, S., Zhou, J.: A survey of convolutional neural networks: analysis, applications, and prospects. IEEE Trans. Neural Netw. Learn. Syst. **33**(12), 6999–7019 (2022). https://doi.org/10.1109/TNNLS.2021.3084827
10. Liu, X., Zou, Y., Kuang, H., Ma, X.: Face image age estimation based on data augmentation and lightweight convolutional neural network. Symmetry **12**(1) (2020). https://doi.org/10.3390/sym12010146. https://www.mdpi.com/2073-8994/12/1/146
11. Mahery, P., Proudlock, P.: Legal guide to age thresholds for children and young people. Children's Institute, University of Cape Town: University of Western Cape (2011)
12. Pan, H., Han, H., Shan, S., Chen, X.: Mean-variance loss for deep age estimation from a face. In: Proceedings of the IEEE Conference on Computer Vision and Pattern Recognition (CVPR), June 2018
13. Prinsloo, J., Ladikos, A., Neser, J.: Attitudes of public school learners to under-age drinking and illegal substance abuse: a threat to social stability? Child Abuse Res. S. Afr. **6**(1), 28–40 (2005)
14. Semosa, A.: Underage drinking among the youth in South Africa (2022)
15. Shen, W., Guo, Y., Wang, Y., Zhao, K., Wang, B., Yuille, A.L.: Deep regression forests for age estimation. In: Proceedings of the IEEE Conference on Computer Vision and Pattern Recognition (CVPR), June 2018
16. Zhang, Z., Song, Y., Qi, H.: Age progression/regression by conditional adversarial autoencoder. In: IEEE Conference on Computer Vision and Pattern Recognition (CVPR). IEEE (2017)

Autonomous Behavior of Biped Robot by Learning Camera Images

Manabu Motegi(✉)

Takushoku University, 815-1 Tatemachi, Hachioji-shi, Tokyo 193-0985, Japan
mmotegi@ms.takushoku-u.ac.jp

Abstract. COVID-19 infection has been prevalent worldwide from the end of 2019, and people have spent more time at home avoiding contact with others. In such an environment, it is expected that avatars with physicality will act in the real world. This makes it possible to promote social life and economic activities through the avatars of each person, even if humans do not engage in face-to-face activities. In such a world, it is desirable for humans to remotely control avatar robots, and for robots to learn from those logs and behave autonomously. Therefore, in this paper, we investigated a method for robots to learn from human operation logs and continue autonomous behavior without colliding with the environment. The method proposed in this paper is divided into the following three steps. First, a human operates a bipedal walking robot via a GUI, and records the image of the robot-mounted camera and the selection behavior at that time. Next, machine learning is performed from the recorded images and selection behavior. Finally, the robot is autonomously behaved using the learned results. As a result, it was confirmed that the robot continues to behave autonomously for a relatively long time without colliding with the environment.

Keywords: Machine Learning · Camera Image · Autonomous Behavior

1 Introduction

We conducted a basic study for a small bipedal walking robot to learn from human operation logs and behave autonomously.

Since the end of 2019, COVID-19 has spread rapidly, limiting the activities of people around the world. In order to prevent infection, we need a way for people to continue their daily activities without contacting each other. However, there are problems that are difficult to solve with the teleconferencing system. This is an area that requires interaction with the real world, such as work related to nursing care and logistics, and daily activities such as travel. It is very difficult to use when the robot does not have autonomy and has only a remote control function. This is because it is a heavy burden for the operator to always remotely control the robot. However, it is impossible with the current technology to enable a robot to behave autonomously in any environment without remote control by humans. Therefore, in this paper, we will examine how the robot behave autonomously by learning from human operation logs.

C. Stephanidis et al. (Eds.): HCII 2023, CCIS 1836, pp. 498–506, 2023.
https://doi.org/10.1007/978-3-031-36004-6_68

2 Conventional Research

In recent years, research on autonomous behavior related to robots, drones, and automobiles has been conducted. However, many of these methods use many types of sensors in addition to camera images, which is costly. Also, the algorithm for autonomous behavior tends to be complicated [1]. Traditional image-based navigation require a multi-step process. For example, first, features are extracted from a camera image [2]. Next, a map is created using these results [3]. Finally, the behavior is determined according to the rules, which were set in advance [4]. The above is the general method [5]. However, in these multi-step processes, readjustment is required at each step when the environment changes. In addition, there is a problem that errors occur at each stage and accumulate. Therefore, research using deep learning that takes a camera image as an input and generates an output directly from it is also being conducted [5,6]. This is the so-called end-to-end method. However, these are premised on using a large number of images as learning data. Therefore, it seems that the case where the learning data is small is not taken into consideration.

From the above, we decided to carry out an initial study to reflect the human operation logs in the robot autonomous behavior.

3 System Requirements for Realization

As mentioned above, camera images and human operation logs are used for the robot to behave autonomously. For this reason, the system needs to understand when and how humans are operating robots. In addition, it is a burden for humans to remotely control the robot for a long time. Therefore, if there is a certain amount of operation logs, it is desirable that the robot can behave autonomously by learning it. Therefore, we have organized the requirements of this system as follows.

(1) It is possible to acquire camera image and human operation logs (logs acquisition).
(2) It is possible to learn from a small number of camera image and human operation logs (learning from a small number of data).
(3) When a robot behave autonomously, it is possible to behave autonomously without colliding with the environment (determination of autonomous behavior).

4 System Implementation and Experiment

Figure 1 shows the system architecture, the robot used in the experiment, and the GUI for the user to operate the robot. Figure 2 shows the experimental environment. Table 1 shows the structure of the convolutional neural network used in the experiment. Then, Fig. 3 shows the structure of the learning part in which SVM is added to the convolutional neural network. Table 2 shows the confusion matrix for the evaluation data.

4.1 Implementation for Requirements (1) (Logs Acquisition)

First, in the constructed system, the part related to log acquisition of the above-mentioned requirement (1) is described. As shown in Fig. 1(a), the robot used in the experiment is NAO6 (manufactured by Softbank Robotics). The primitive behavior of this robot is set to forward, right turn, left turn, and backward. The parameters of each behavior are 10 cm for each of forward and backward, and 10° for each of the right and left turns. The NAO6 has a total of two cameras on the forehead and mouth, but in this experiment only the forehead camera was used. A notebook PC (FUJITSU LIFEBOOK WA3/D3, CPU: Intel Core i7-9750H, memory: 8 GB) was used as the PC for sending operation commands to NAO6 and learning. In addition, the notebook PC and NAO6 are configured to communicate via Wi-Fi AP. In addition, the system was constructed using python as the software language.

The GUI shown in Fig. 1(b) was constructed. In the experiment, first of all, a human operated a robot using this GUI. In the system, when a human clicks each behavior button on the GUI, the selected behavior and the robot camera image before the behavior are recorded. The experimental environment shown in Fig. 2 is the laboratory of the author's university. In this environment, the robot was operated using Fig. 1(b). The selection behavior and image were saved as learning data. We made three round trips from the front of Fig. 2(a) to the refrigerator of Fig. 2(b), and acquired a total of 624 images, including 22 images for backward behavior, 310 images for forward behavior, 77 images for left turn, and 215 images for right turn. Of these, about 80% of the data was used as learning data, and the remaining 20% was used as evaluation data.

4.2 Implementation for Requirements (2) (Learning from a Small Number of Data)

Next, we describe the system-implemented method for learning with a small number of data in the above-mentioned requirement (2). Regarding the above learning data, the input was the robot camera image and the output was the behavior selected by human. Then, fine tuning was performed on the convolutional neural network that had already been learned. Here, the convolutional neural network used this time is MobileNet V2 [7] that has been trained for 1000 types of image classification using ImageNet [8], which is a data set for image recognition. MobileNetV2 has the structure shown in Table 1. In the system,

Keras [9], which is a deep learning library of python, is imported and used. As shown in Table 1, the inputs to MobileNetV2 are camera images of size 192×192 in consideration of learning time, and the outputs are the four primitive behavior described above: forward, right turn, left turn, and backward.

In fine tuning, it is necessary to make trial and error as to which blocks of MobileNetV2 is best to be trained. Therefore, learning was performed while shifting the mobileNetV2 from after the 9th block to after the 16th block each by one block. Here, the MobileNetV2 block corresponds to the bottleneck part in Table 1. It exists from the 1st block to the 16th block. In each learning, the batch size was 32, the learning rate was 0.00001, and 100 epochs were performed. However, when the above fine tuning was performed, the accuracy of the training data and the evaluation data did not improve. Therefore, as shown in Fig. 3, the fully connected layer for selecting each behavior was deleted from MobileNetV2 after fine tuning, and the output of the average pooling layer was used as the input of the SVM. The output of the SVM is four: forward, right turn, left turn, and backward, and these are used during the autonomous behavior of the robot.

The highest accuracy for the evaluation data was when SVM was applied to the fine-tuned version of MobileNetV2 from the 13th block onward. Therefore, in this experiment, we fine-tuned the 13th block and later of MobileNetV2 and used the output as the input of SVM. In this experiment, python's scikit-learn library was used to use SVM, and the SVM parameters were determined using the GridSearchCV function.

Table 2 shows the SVM confusion matrix for the evaluation data at this time. The rows in Table 2 show the correct answer data, and the columns show the prediction results. The predicted result of the backward behavior was about 53%, and 47% of the cases were mistakenly recognized as a right turn. This is because the experimental environment does not require much backward behavior, so the operator rarely used backward behavior. On the other hand, for the forward behavior, the prediction result was correct at a high rate of 99%. This is because, there are relatively many data when moving forward, which is 310 when the robot is operated. For the left turn, the correct answer for the prediction result was 69%. It was 25% when it was mistakenly recognized as a right turn. It is considered that this is because the data of 3 round trips was acquired in the experimental environment, and the behavior was instructed such as right turn on the outward route and left turn on the return route in the similar camera image.

For the right turn, the correct answer for the prediction result was 75%. In this case, 23% mistakenly recognized as forward. This is because there are many obstacles on the left side in the experimental environment, and the operator often instructed the right turn in advance even in a situation where robot could move forward.

5 System Evaluation

5.1 Evaluation of Requirement (3) (Determination of Autonomous Behavior)

Figure 4 shows a photograph of an autonomous behavior experiment. Regarding the above-mentioned requirement (3), the robot was made to behave autonomously using the learned system. For comparison, the time until the robot collides with the environment was measured in each of the following cases.

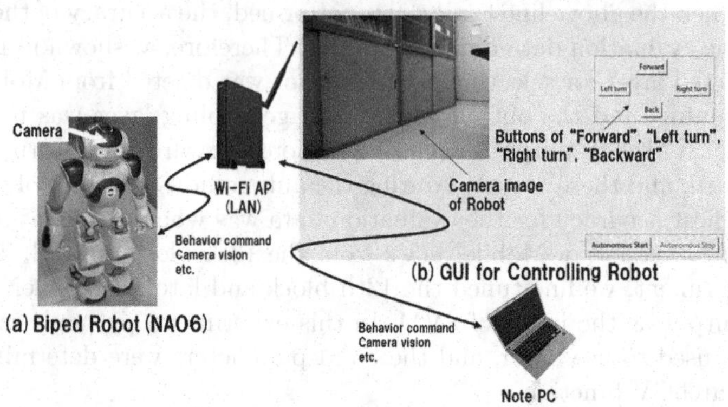

Fig. 1. System architecture: Robot (NAO6) and GUI used in the experiment

Fig. 2. Experimental environment

(1) When the robot is autonomously behaved only by fine-tuning the 13th block onward of MobileNetV2.
(2) When the final layer of MobileNetV2 that has been fine-tuned from the 13th block onward is deleted as described above, and the robot is autonomously behaved using the result of classifying the output of the MobileNetV2 by SVM.

Table 1. Convolutional Neural Network (MobileNetV2) used in the experiment [7]

Input	Operator	t	c	n	s	
$192^2 \times 3$	conv2d	-	32	1	2	
$96^2 \times 32$	bottleneck	1	16	1	1	
$96^2 \times 16$	bottleneck	6	24	2	2	1~16 block
$48^2 \times 24$	bottleneck	6	32	3	2	1~16 block
$24^2 \times 32$	bottleneck	6	64	4	2	1~16 block
$12^2 \times 64$	bottleneck	6	96	3	1	1~16 block
$12^2 \times 96$	bottleneck	6	160	3	2	Fine-tuning after 13 block
$6^2 \times 160$	bottleneck	6	320	1	1	Fine-tuning after 13 block
$6^2 \times 320$	conv2d 1×1	-	1280	1	1	Fine-tuning after 13 block
$6^2 \times 1280$	avgpool 6×6	-	-	1	-	Fine-tuning after 13 block
$1 \times 1 \times 1280$	dense	-	4	-	-	Fine-tuning after 13 block

t:expantion rate, c:output channel,
n:repeat number of same layer, s:stride

Table 2. SVM's confusion matrix on the evaluation data

		Predicted behavior			
		Backward	Forward	Left turn	Right turn
Correct behavior	Backward	53%	0	0	47%
	Forward	0	99%	0	1%
	Left turn	0	6%	69%	25%
	Right turn	1%	23%	1%	75%

Figure 4 are experimental images when autonomous behavior is performed according to (1) and (2) above. The left column is the image of the camera mounted on the robot. The right column is an external camera image taken for recording. In both cases, the robot was autonomously behaved from almost the same position in front of Fig. 2(a). As mentioned above, learning was performed using the data when a human reciprocates the robot from the front of Fig. 2(a) to the refrigerator of Fig. 2(b) three times. Therefore, it is expected that the robot will reach the refrigerator and then return to the starting point of autonomous behavior.

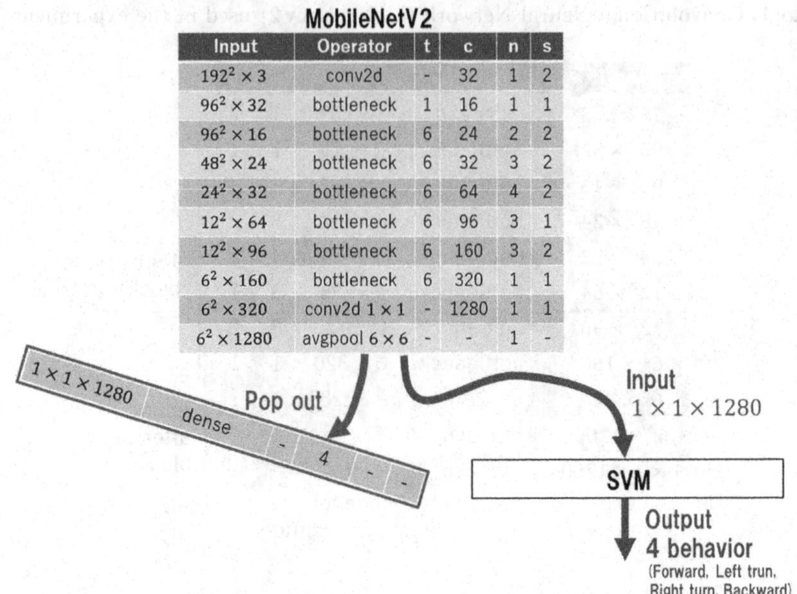

Input	Operator	t	c	n	s
$192^2 \times 3$	conv2d	-	32	1	2
$96^2 \times 32$	bottleneck	1	16	1	1
$96^2 \times 16$	bottleneck	6	24	2	2
$48^2 \times 24$	bottleneck	6	32	3	2
$24^2 \times 32$	bottleneck	6	64	4	2
$12^2 \times 64$	bottleneck	6	96	3	1
$12^2 \times 96$	bottleneck	6	160	3	2
$6^2 \times 160$	bottleneck	6	320	1	1
$6^2 \times 320$	conv2d 1 × 1	-	1280	1	1
$6^2 \times 1280$	avgpool 6 × 6	-	-	1	-

Fig. 3. Structure of the learning system part

However, in the case of (1) above, it did not reach the refrigerator. In about 5 min and 30 s, it moved in the direction of collision with the cabinet on the left side of Fig. 2(a), and the left arm collided. This is because the camera image that should normally make a right turn is misrecognized and is moving forward.

On the other hand, in the case of (2) above, it behaved autonomously for about 9 min and 30 s, which was longer than in the case of (1) above. In addition, compared to the case of (1) above, the robot autonomously behaved to a distant refrigerator without collision. However, the experiment was canceled because the left arm collided with the refrigerator when making a right turn in front of the refrigerator. At that time, a vibration phenomenon was observed in which a right turn and a left turn were repeated near the cabinet with a towel, near the refrigerator. This is because this method only reflexively selects primitive behavior from the robot-mounted camera image, and does not consider the time-series context of the behavior. Avoiding this vibration phenomenon and selecting the behavior to return to the start point from the refrigerator are future issues.

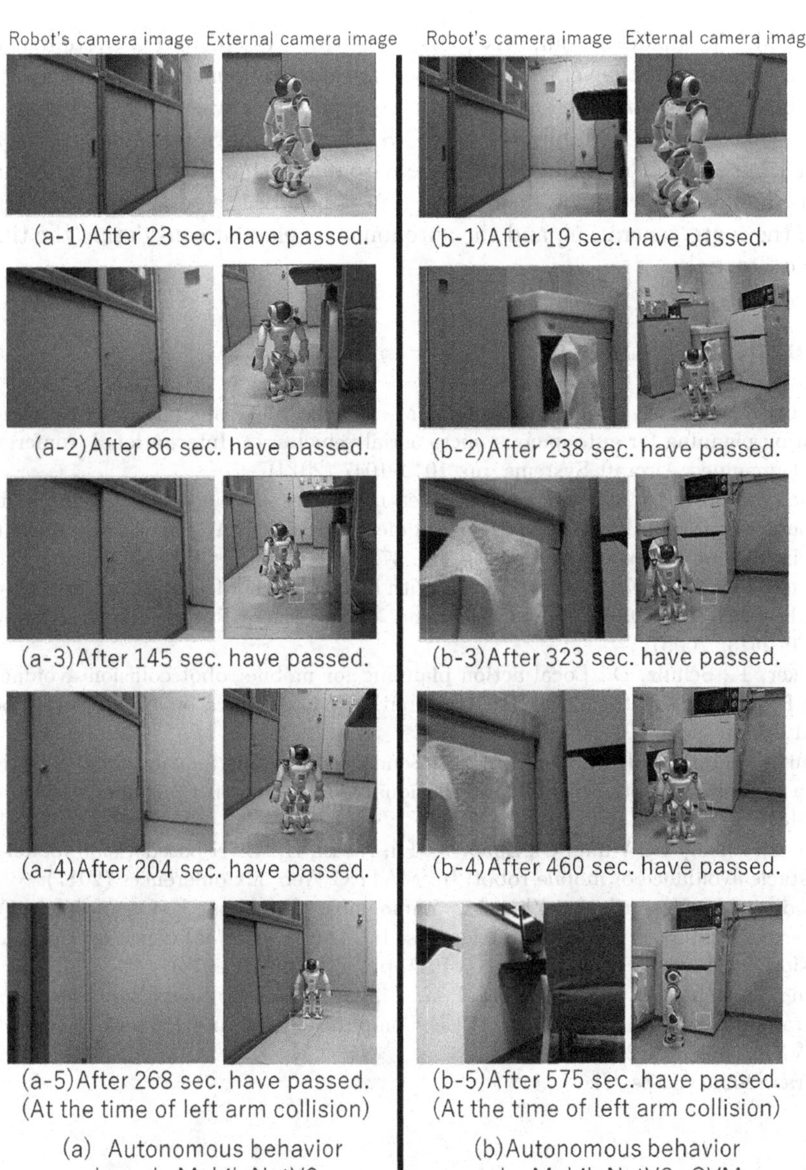

Fig. 4. Picture of autonomous behaving

6 Conclusions

As a basic study for realizing an avatar in the real world, we examined a system that selects autonomous behavior by learning from the camera images and the human operation logs. The system was a combination of fine-tuned MobileNetV2 and SVM. We made a comparison between this system and a system using only fine-tuned MobileNetV2, regarding the autonomous behavior time until the robot collides with the environment. As a result, it was confirmed that the system that combines MobileNetV2 and SVM can behave autonomously for a longer time without colliding with the environment than the case of only fine-tuned MobileNetV2. In the future, we plan to study the setting of the target point, the route generation, and the autonomous behavior considering the time-series context.

References

1. Nieuwenhuisen, M., Droeschel, D., Beul, M., Behnke, S.: Obstacle detection and navigation planning for autonomous micro aerial vehicles. In: International Conference on Unmanned Aircraft Systems, pp. 1040–1047 (2014)
2. Vale, A., Lucas, J.M., Ribeiro, M.I.: Feature extraction and selection for mobile robot navigation in unstructured environments. In: 5th IFAC/EURON Symposium on Intelligent Autonomous Vehicles, vol. 37, no. 8, pp. 102–107 (2004)
3. Jeong, W.Y., Lee, K.M.: Visual SLAM with line and corner features. In: Proceedings of the IEEE/RSJ International Conference on Intelligent Robots and Systems, pp. 2570–2575 (2006)
4. Belker, T., Schulz, D.: Local action planning for mobile robot collision avoidance. In: Proceedings of the IEEE/RSJ International Conference on Intelligent Robots and Systems, pp. 601–606 (2002)
5. Kim, Y.-H., Jang, J.-I., Yun, S.: End-to-end deep learning for autonomous navigation of mobile robot. In: IEEE International Conference on Consumer Electronics (2018)
6. Liu, C., Zheng, B., Wang, C., Zhao, Y., Fu, A., Li, H.: CNN-based vision model for obstacle avoidance of mobile robot. In: MATEC Web of Conferences (2017)
7. Sandler, M., Howard, A., Zhu, M., Zhmoginov, A., Chen, L.-C.: MobileNetV2: inverted residuals and linear bottlenecks. In: The IEEE Conference on Computer Vision and Pattern Recognition (CVPR), pp. 4510–4520 (2018)
8. Deng, J., Dong, W., Socher, R., Li, L.-J., Li, K., Fei-Fei, L.: ImageNet: a large-scale hierarchical image database. In: IEEE Computer Vision and Pattern Recognition (CVPR), pp. 2–9 (2009)
9. Keras (2021). https://keras.io

PromptIE - Information Extraction with Prompt-Engineering and Large Language Models

Sigurd Schacht[1(✉)], Sudarshan Kamath Barkur[1], and Carsten Lanquillon[2]

[1] University of Applied Sciences Ansbach, Ansbach, Germany
sigurd.schacht@hs-ansbach.de
[2] University of Applied Sciences Heilbronn, Heilbronn, Germany

Abstract. Extracting triples of subjects, objects, and predicates from text to populate knowledge bases traditionally involves several intermediate steps such as co-reference resolution, named entity recognition, and relationship extraction. Treating triple extraction as translation task from source sentences to sets of triples, we present an end-to-end solution for information extraction that uses task prefixes to prompts a fine-tuned large language model to extract triples from text. Thus, the need for data labeling and training multiple models is reduced.

Keywords: OpenIE · Large Language Models · Triple Extraction · Prompt Engineering

1 Introduction

In today's digital age, vast amounts of unstructured data are being generated daily, making it challenging to automatically extract meaningful insights. Information extraction (IE) supports populating knowledge bases by automatically extracting relationships between entities from unstructured or semi-structured text stored as triples of subjects, objects, predicates. However, IE models are mostly trained using supervised learning [17], which is costly and lacks labeled datasets, especially in languages other than English. By contrast, open information extraction (OpenIE) differs from classical IE in that it focuses on extracting all possible relation triples from a given input text without predefined entity or relation types [11]. Yet, OpenIE faces challenges in identifying multiple and unknown triples in the input, which could be irrelevant, incorrect, or incomplete.

To address these challenges, we propose a new approach to OpenIE based on a translation model optimized through prompt engineering. Our approach involves creating a specific dataset for the German language to train an OpenIE system and fine-tuning a pre-trained language model on a specific translation task mapping German text to triples. Consequently, the language model can be adapted to extract triples from German language text more effectively, improving the precision and recall rates of OpenIE.

C. Stephanidis et al. (Eds.): HCII 2023, CCIS 1836, pp. 507–514, 2023.
https://doi.org/10.1007/978-3-031-36004-6_69

1.1 Problem Statement and Contribution

Populating organization-specific knowledge graphs in several projects, we were faced with the issue that there are hardly any datasets for end-to-end OpenIE in specific languages other than English. In addition, there were issues regarding classical extraction approaches as they were not able to identify all relevant relations and entities, in particular if they where absent in the training data. For example, in the OntoNotes dataset for German only four entity types exist, whereas the English version contains 18 different entity types. Hence, there is a need for a model that allows to identify unknown entities without creating huge datasets for them.

Our main contributions in the paper are as follows:

1. A process description for generating a high-quality dataset in a language of choice that can be used to fine-tune a LLM for OpenIE treating triple extraction as a translation task.
2. The PromptIE model as a valuable tool for OpenIE in various applications as it can efficiently extract multiple triples from input sentences or paragraphs. It is based on a translation approach, uses a pre-trained MT5 model, and is optimized for speed and efficiency, making it suitable for use on commodity hardware. Moreover, the model is capable of extracting previously unseen and unknown relations that are not present in the training data or predefined classes. The model can be integrated into other named entity recognition (NER) systems. Specifically, it can predict relations given the head and tail entities, predict the head given the relation and tail, or predict the tail given the head and relation.

2 Dataset German Re-TACRED

One of the major issues is the lack of a high-quality German dataset for the relation extraction task. By using existing English datasets, however, and reformatting them to ensure that they meet the required standards, we can create a reliable German dataset.

We use the "TAC Relation Extraction Dataset" (TACRED), which is a large-scale relation extraction dataset that contains 106,264 examples [21,22]. It consists of newswire and web text from the corpus "TAC KBP Comprehensive English Source Corpora 2009–2014", which was used in the yearly "TAC Knowledge Base Population" (TAC KBP) challenges. The original data set contains 41 relation types, such as `per:cause_of_death` or `per:employee_of`. In addition, even if there were no relationships present in the data, it would still be labeled with a special token called `no_relation` [5,12,21]. We apply the transformations suggested in the study "ReTACRED: Addressing Shortcomings of the Tacred Dataset" [18] to fix some majors flaws in the dataset.

To create our German dataset, first we reformat the Re-TACRED dataset by joining individual tokens to form complete sentences. When using machine translation, named entities are likely to be translated as well. This results in a loss of knowledge about them. To address this issue, we replace all labeled entities with special entity tokens. This allows us to preserve the identities of the original entities during the translation process. After machine translation step, the entity tokens are to be resubstituted with their original names.

We translate each of the 106,264 paragraphs into German using the AI-based translation service *DeepL* [3]. Next, the translated paragraphs are reviewed by German-speaking professionals to ensure that they are of high quality and meet the required standards. To ensure that the relationships in the dataset are consistent, we keep the relationships in English and translate only entities to German, except for names (see above). This approach allows us to maintain the original relationships in the dataset and avoid any potential confusion or errors that may arise from machine translation. In addition, we perform co-reference resolution by using regex search and replace through clearly identified patterns, such as search and replace with common identifiers like *he*, *she*, *it*, or *first*. This step is crucial in ensuring that the entities in the dataset are accurate and can be used for reliable relation extraction.

Based on these steps, we transform the Re-TACRED dataset into a German variant while preserving the 41 relation types of the original dataset. Thus, we obtain a reliable dataset for OpenIE training suitable for German text. Our process can be easily applied to any other language, since all steps are automated using Python scripts, except for the quality assurance of the translation. DeepL proved to be an effective tool producing high-quality translations that only require minor manual corrections.

3 PromptIE

Our approach to OpenIE, referred to as *PromptIE*, uses translation approaches from one language to another language to extract triples. We treat triples as their own language and, thus, are able to use standard translation approaches. Specifically, PromptIE translates from German to German triples using the MT5 multi-lingual transformer architecture.

3.1 Approach

The main idea behind PromptIE is inspired by the milIE approach [8], which uses the BERT architecture, has multiple parallel downstream heads for identifying head, relation, or tail entities and performs the extraction process as an iterative call to the model. Yet, PromptIE simplifies this approach by using only one downstream head and eliminating the iterative approach to identify multiple triples that exist in a given text.

3.2 Input and Output Format

The input format is a sentence in German. The output consist of at least one head entity, a relation, and a tail entity. In our case, the model produces triples for each request.

Input: 'KUALA LUMPUR, Malaysia -LRB- AP -RRB- Inspector-General of Police Abdul Rahim Noor Sein Rücktritt wurde am Freitag wirksam.'
Output: '[Abdul Rahim Noor] [per:title] [Inspector-General of Police]'

3.3 Generation and Decoding

We employ the MT5 model as a state-of-the-art pre-trained language model for various natural language processing tasks. In particular, we use a fine-tuned MT5 model for doc2query, a method that predicts queries for a given document and expands it with those predictions using a sequence-to-sequence model trained on pairs of queries and relevant documents [13,20]. We use the doc2quey model *svalabs/mt5-large-german-query-gen-v1* from Huggingface, which is pre-trained on German data.

We observe that models that extract queries from given documents perform well on the triple translation task. Our system inputs not only the document but also a prompt consisting of three elements: an instruction (e.g., "translate the given text to triples") and the document (in our case, a paragraph or sentence) and a suffix consisting of an element of the triple where the focus should be (head, relation, or entity). The model is used as is, with a specific head for query/triple generation as the downstream task.

Furthermore, our system incorporates beam search, a heuristic search algorithm that generates a sequence of outputs. By extracting the top ten examples of addition using beam search, our system provides multiple possible translations or relations between entities. This feature enhances the accuracy and reliability of our system, making it a robust solution for various applications.

To ensure that the outputs generated by our system are logically consistent with the given input text, our system is evaluated using a NLI model. This model evaluates whether the outputs generated by our system include entities from the input text, which is essential for accurate translations and relations between entities. Overall, our system's architecture and model design enable it to provide accurate and efficient translations and relations between entities, making it a valuable tool for various natural language processing tasks.

3.4 Training PromptIE

During the training phase, each data point is transformed into different outputs to ensure that each element of the triple–head, relation, and tail–has to be predicted. We achieve this by transforming each data point into three data points for training. Specifically, a training point consisted of an input sentence, which included a prompt instruction, the sentence, and a suffix indicating which elements of the triple has to be predicted (e.g., head). The head or tail of the triple is then masked, and the model is trained to predict it.

The training process is run on two A40 Nvidia cards with 40 GB of video memory based on the using the Huggingface transformer library. We fine-tune the model for six epochs with a batch size of ten. To calculate the loss, we use the bleu score [15], a commonly used metric for machine translation tasks. The suffix used during training ensures that the model can later be triggered to focus on a specific relation. This procedure allows our system to be versatile and effective in various use cases.

4 Evaluation

We evaluate the performance of our model in extracting triples from German language text. To ensure an unbiased evaluation, we use a subset of the dataset that is not used during training or testing. The model is prompted with [instruction] [sentence] [suffix], which indicates the starting element of the triple. We generate ten output triples for each sentence using beam search decoding, and compare them with the expected prediction using Levenshtein distance. Out of the 2000 sentences evaluated, 1664 have a total match, resulting in an accuracy of 83.2%.

One strength of our model is its ability to extract unseen relations. To determine their validity, we use ChatGPT from openAI as an NLI model and evaluate unseen triples from our PromptIE model by checking if they can be extracted from the given sentences. We remove direct matches and duplicates from the predicted results yielding 10,788 triples.

We generate a prompt enabling ChatGPT to act as an NLI model checking if a triple can be extracted from given sentences. By definition in the prompt, the output is returned as a JSON object, including *extraction_possible* and a *confidence score*. For the 10,788 requests, the ChatGPT-NLI model predicts that 9,208 triples can be extracted from the given text and, thus, are assumed to be valid. The remaining 1,580 triples are rated as not possible to extract. Hence, we determine a 85.3% accuracy score, which is similar to the result of direct matches.

Evaluating unseen triple generation is a challenging task. To verify that the ChatGPT model does not have major evaluation flaws, we sample 100 random data points and validate the decision of the ChatGPT-NLI model manually. In 67 out of 100 cases, the model is correct according to our judgement. To account for the potential errors of the model, we estimate the accuracy of the model to be about 57% (0.85 * 0.67) for extracting unseen triples.

5 Related Work

The development of information extraction systems has gone through several stages, including rule-based approaches, automatic rule learning, and statistical learning. The emergence of unstructured text data from the Internet and social networks has made rule-based systems too inflexible to handle the necessary information [1].

Thus, newer methods such as deep learning have been incorporated into the information extraction process, with the advantages of increased speed and reduced processing steps. The development of OpenIE systems has aimed to create a more open and generalized approach to extracting relationships between entities from unstructured text. The first generation of OpenIE systems relied on shallow syntactic features [6,7], while the second generation combined syntactic features with deep learning techniques [4,10].

Current state-of-the-art OpenIE systems are dominated by neural networks, especially attention-based models, with a focus on pre-training and fine-tuning and using large datasets and are focused on generative task [9]. Notable among these systems are Multi^{2}OIE, which leverages BERT as a bidirectional transformer model for multi-lingual triple extraction through multihead attention [16]. Further, milIE employs a multi-lingual BERT model with multiple downstream heads in an iterative extraction process [8]. Another system which uses transformer models to extract triples and utilizes translation models as a basis for triple extraction is DeepEx. DeepEx uses the capability of generative models as zero-shot translation and ranks generative triples with a separate BERT model trained on a large corpus of Wikipedia data and corresponding triples called T-REx [19]. To restrict the generation of relations, DeepEx employs a constrained beam search [2], which only decodes defined linked tokens.

Our PromptIE is an OpenIE system that draws mainly from DeepEx and milIE. However, the focus is not only to extract triples from predefined categories, but also to extract unknown and unseen triples. In addition, we aim to simplify the system while still maintaining its effectiveness. To achieve this, we eliminated the ranking model, the constrained beam search, and employed standard beam search. We also transform the data during training to shift the focus of generation through beam search, discard iterative generation processes, and reduce the number of downstream heads to only one. In addition, we use special prompts to initiate the generation and evaluation processes.

6 Conclusion and Future Work

PromptIE, our OpenIE model based on prompting, shows verify promising results. The model is able to extract a significant number of direct gold triples with an accuracy of 83.2%. Moreover, it matches unseen triples with an accuracy of 85%, which is quite impressive. According to manual validation based on a sample of 100 data points, 67% of the triples are assumed to be correct, yielding a correct accuracy of about 57%. Nevertheless, this approach helps to showcase the method's potential. Further improvements could be made by altering the prompt.

Although we did not compare our model's performance with other OpenIE models, it is worth noting that those models are not trained on German language and our model is not trained on English. Still, our model's ability to extract unseen relations and generate valid triples has promising applications in various natural language processing tasks.

Even though our model performs well, we need to improve its output by filtering out erroneous triples and hallucinations before presenting them to end users. We use ChatGPT-NLI to verify the top ten elements, which could also be used as a filter. To improve the ChatGPT-NLI output quality, we need to explore further ways for improvement.

We believe that reinforcement learning based on human feedback (RFHF) is a promising approach. To identify the correct elements, we propose using the RFHF method, which involves manually labeling the data to determine which output is better. This involves training a reward model and then applying reinforcement learning to further improve the approach [14]. Additionally, a ranking model, similar to the one described in [19], can also be trained at the end of this process to improve prediction accuracy.

Retraining the model with English data is another potential improvement in our study. This would enable us to compare our model's performance directly to existing OpenIE models and identify its strengths and weaknesses. We believe that our model has potential for various natural language processing tasks and expect that our approach will also enhance accuracy and reliability of other models.

References

1. Adnan, K., Akbar, R.: Limitations of information extraction methods and techniques for heterogeneous unstructured big data. Int. J. Eng. Bus. Manag. **11**, 1847979019890771 (2019)
2. De Cao, N., Izacard, G., Riedel, S., Petroni, F.: Autoregressive entity retrieval. arXiv preprint arXiv:2010.00904 (2020)
3. DeepL: DeepL translate - the most accurate translator in the world. https://www.DeepL.com/translator
4. Del Corro, L., Gemulla, R.: ClausIE: clause-based open information extraction. In: Proceedings of the 22nd International Conference on World Wide Web, pp. 355–366 (2013)
5. Ellis, J., Getman, J., Graff, D., Strassel, S.: TAC KBP comprehensive English source corpora 2009–2014. https://doi.org/10.35111/3RXW-5114. https://catalog.ldc.upenn.edu/LDC2018T03
6. Etzioni, O., Banko, M., Soderland, S., Weld, D.S.: Open information extraction from the web. Commun. ACM **51**(12), 68–74 (2008)
7. Fader, A., Soderland, S., Etzioni, O.: Identifying relations for open information extraction. In: Proceedings of the 2011 Conference on Empirical Methods in Natural Language Processing, pp. 1535–1545. Association for Computational Linguistics (2011). https://aclanthology.org/D11-1142
8. Kotnis, B., et al.: milIE: modular & iterative multilingual open information extraction. http://arxiv.org/abs/2110.08144
9. Liu, P., Gao, W., Dong, W., Huang, S., Zhang, Y.: Open information extraction from 2007 to 2022 - a survey. http://arxiv.org/abs/2208.08690
10. Mausam, M.: Open information extraction systems and downstream applications. In: Proceedings of the Twenty-Fifth International Joint Conference on Artificial Intelligence, pp. 4074–4077 (2016)
11. Niklaus, C., Cetto, M., Freitas, A., Handschuh, S.: A survey on open information extraction. In: Proceedings of the 27th International Conference on Computational Linguistics, pp. 3866–3878. Association for Computational Linguistics (2018). https://aclanthology.org/C18-1326
12. NIST: text analysis conference (TAC) KBP 2017 tracks. https://tac.nist.gov/2017/KBP/index.html

13. Nogueira, R., Yang, W., Lin, J., Cho, K.: Document expansion by query prediction. http://arxiv.org/abs/1904.08375
14. Ouyang, L., et al.: Training language models to follow instructions with human feedback. arXiv preprint arXiv:2203.02155 (2022)
15. Papineni, K., Roukos, S., Ward, T., Zhu, W.J.: BLEU: a method for automatic evaluation of machine translation. In: Proceedings of the 40th Annual Meeting of the Association for Computational Linguistics, pp. 311–318 (2002)
16. Ro, Y., Lee, Y., Kang, P.: Multi^{2}OIE: multilingual open information extraction based on multi-head attention with BERT. In: Findings of the Association for Computational Linguistics: EMNLP 2020, pp. 1107–1117 (2020). http://arxiv.org/abs/2009.08128
17. Stanovsky, G., Michael, J., Zettlemoyer, L., Dagan, I.: Supervised open information extraction. In: Proceedings of the 2018 Conference of the North American Chapter of the Association for Computational Linguistics: Human Language Technologies, Volume 1 (Long Papers), pp. 885–895. Association for Computational Linguistics (2018). http://aclweb.org/anthology/N18-1081
18. Stoica, G., Platanios, E.A., Póczos, B.: Re-TACRED: addressing shortcomings of the TACRED dataset. http://arxiv.org/abs/2104.08398
19. Wang, C., Liu, X., Chen, Z., Hong, H., Tang, J., Song, D.: Zero-shot information extraction as a unified text-to-triple translation. In: Proceedings of the 2021 Conference on Empirical Methods in Natural Language Processing, pp. 1225–1238. Association for Computational Linguistics (2021). https://aclanthology.org/2021.emnlp-main.94
20. Xue, L., et al.: mT5: a massively multilingual pre-trained text-to-text transformer. arXiv preprint arXiv:2010.11934 (2020)
21. Zhang, Y.: Stanford TACRED homepage. https://nlp.stanford.edu/projects/tacred/
22. Zhang, Y., Zhong, V., Chen, D., Angeli, G., Manning, C.D.: Position-aware attention and supervised data improve slot filling. In: Proceedings of the 2017 Conference on Empirical Methods in Natural Language Processing, pp. 35–45. Association for Computational Linguistics (2017). http://aclweb.org/anthology/D17-1004

Designing an AI-Powered Journalism Advisor: A User-Centered Approach

Catherine Sotirakou(✉), Theodoros Paraskevas, Irene Konstanta, and Constantinos Mourlas

Faculty of Communication and Media Studies, National and Kapodistrian University of Athens, Athens, Greece
{katerinasot,tsparaskevas,irkonsta,mourlas}@media.uoa.gr

Abstract. This paper delineates the preliminary outcomes of the "IQ Journalism" project, which endeavors to develop an intelligent agent tailored for journalistic articles. By harnessing the capabilities of Artificial Intelligence methodologies, the proposed advisor is designed to provide journalists and editors with real-time suggestions to enhance audience engagement and improve the quality of the written text. As the advisor's content and functionality have been previously determined through the model, the interface's graphical design remained the principal factor in optimizing its usability. Recognizing that the AI advisor's service ought to be specifically tailored to the requirements of the journalists using it, a user-centered design was adopted, and an Iterative Design approach was employed. Firstly, we reviewed existing systems of online text editors and AI assistants, which led to the creation of visual prototypes. Secondly, the prototypes were presented to a group of 10 professional journalists and MSc students in a focus group, where the participants discussed their preferences regarding the prototypes and what adjustments they would like. In total four design phases were conducted, resulting in the creation of a functional prototype with an improved user experience.

Keywords: Usability · User Centered Design · AI Assistant · Journalism · Audience Engagement

1 Introduction

Incorporating AI in newsrooms, can help identify important features in complex data, save time and effort, and recognize trends by grouping similar data (Hansen et al. 2017). Audience engagement has become increasingly important in today's news cycle, where readers act as evaluators and distributors (Singer 2014, Boylan 2001) in a network that ultimately enhances and extends the original publication. As a result, engagement serves as a new concept bridging the gap between news creation and reception. AI technologies can lead the way in producing engaging and quality content by assisting journalists in news production. Specific media elements that impact the audience's cognitive and emotional responses (Broersma 2019, Batsell 2015) can be improved using AI technologies. IQ Journalism builds upon these ideas by applying AI technologies in the Greek media

C. Stephanidis et al. (Eds.): HCII 2023, CCIS 1836, pp. 515–522, 2023.
https://doi.org/10.1007/978-3-031-36004-6_70

context. Journalists are already familiar with text editors and AI assistants for their daily tasks, so an intelligent advisor specifically aimed at creating more engaging content could be quite beneficial.

2 Methodology

Acknowledging the importance of customizing the AI advisor's service to cater to the specific needs of the end users, namely journalists, a user-centered design (UCD) was followed, and an Iterative Design methodology was implemented (Hartson 2012). Considering that journalists are already familiar with existing similar applications, we gathered and examined eight popular online editors/writing assistants, culminating in the development of visual prototypes. Subsequently, these prototypes were showcased to a focus group comprising 10 professional journalists and editors, where participants deliberated on their preferences concerning the screens and suggested desired modifications. Ultimately, four steps of iterative design were followed, namely Requirements Analysis, Prototype, Evaluation and Redesign, leading to the construction of a functional prototype featuring enhanced user experience properties.

3 Review of Existing Tools

In the initial phase of the design process for the IQ Journalism platform, a study of eight existing online text editors and AI assistants was conducted to incorporate best practices in the development of our visual prototypes. The outcomes of this review are outlined in Table 1.

Most of the text editors and AI assistants reviewed demonstrated similar characteristics, including:

Minimalistic style, "distraction free" writing: Text editors should cater to the primary objective of users, which is undisturbed writing and editing of their content.

Menu bars and AI support: Menus can be found in a left-hand sidebar, while AI-generated feedback and recommendations are displayed to the right of the text.

Color utilization: Most of the evaluated text editors employ a gentle color scheme, using various hues to signify distinct types of suggestions.

Table 1. Existing text editors and AI assistants review findings.

Text editor	Findings
Grammarly[1]	Within the dashboard, users can access all their documents, and it provides suggested words and phrases which are highlighted in color and underlined in the text. Suggestions appear on the right side and the dashboard presents a score number in relation to the user's objectives at the top right corner
Sapling[2]	Suggestions are on the ride side of the text, with the corresponding words and phrases being emphasized
ProWritingAid[3]	Corresponding words are directly indicated within the text with suggestions on the ride side
Wordture[4]	Suggestions are provided directly in the text, with problematic text chunks being indicated by underlining. Users can select the highlighted segments to accept recommended changes
Hemingway editor[5]	Various colors are used for different kinds of issues (adverbs, passive voice, phrase complexity, readability)
Calmly writer Online[6]	The menu for the document is located on the left-hand side, with the right-hand side providing commentary and guidance. Color-coding, underlining and informational pop-ups are employed to indicate various aspects of the suggestions made
Wordcounter[7]	Minimal interface design. Details are provided on the right side
Ginger[8]	The "rephrase" feature of this tool provides users with alternative phrasings based on the context of each sentence, which are indicated by color-coding and underlining of the respective words

4 The Iterative Design Process Steps Followed in the Development of the IQ Journalism Platform

4.1 User Requirements Analysis

There are two primary tasks that journalists must undertake. The first involves composing and revising text based on AI-generated recommendations. The second encompasses the management of text files and folders. The capacity to organize files and store them in folders, could be useful for journalists who write news stories intended for various media

[1] https://www.grammarly.com/writing.
[2] https://sapling.ai/grammar-check.
[3] https://prowritingaid.com/.
[4] https://www.wordtune.com/.
[5] https://hemingwayapp.com/.
[6] https://www.calmlywriter.com/online/.
[7] https://wordcounter.net/.
[8] https://www.gingersoftware.com/.

outlets and social media networks. The use-case diagram presented in Fig. 1 illustrates the tasks to be accomplished within the framework of IQ Journalism.

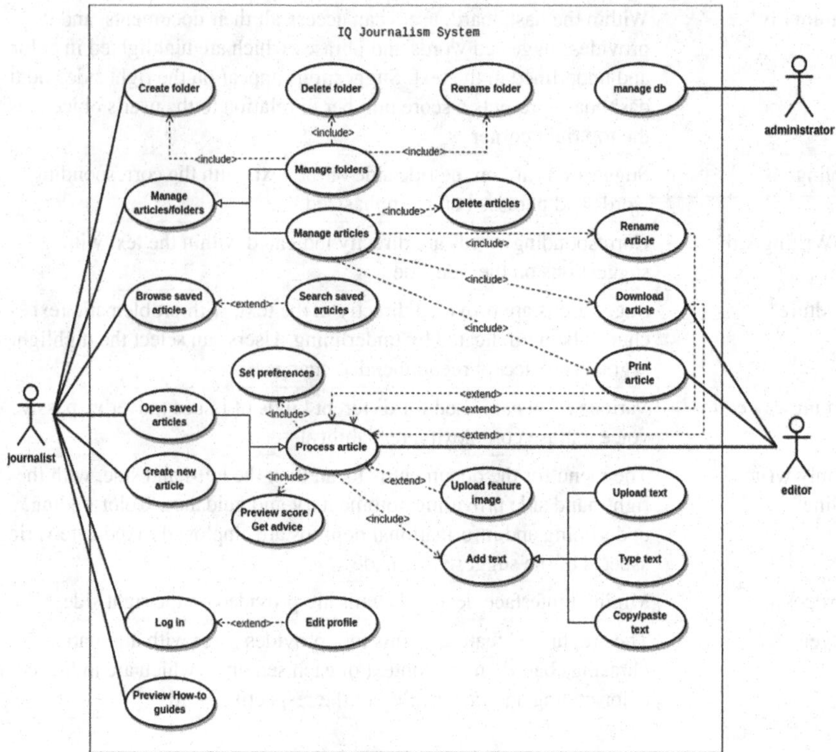

Fig. 1. Use Case Diagram

In the context of text editing, it is crucial for the AI advisor to offer precise recommendations, which requires journalists to define their preferences beforehand, i.e., article intended for social media, genre, length, multimedia elements and so on. For instance, the featured image of a news article intended for Facebook will be analyzed, along with the accompanying text. The following activity diagram (Fig. 2), shows the writing/editing process using the AI suggestions provided in IQ Journalism.

4.2 Prototyping

Based on the findings of the requirements analysis phase, we designed a set of screens using Drawio[9] acting as the first preliminary edition of our product to visualize, verify, validate and improve the idea behind the product (Fig. 3 presents the Homepage screen). Utilizing the menu items positioned at the top of the screen and a button accompanied by a brief description at the center of the page, a new user can obtain information about the application (Demo, About, Help) and can initiate its use (My Dashboard, Start Writing).

[9] https://github.com/jgraph/drawio-desktop/releases/tag/v16.5.1.

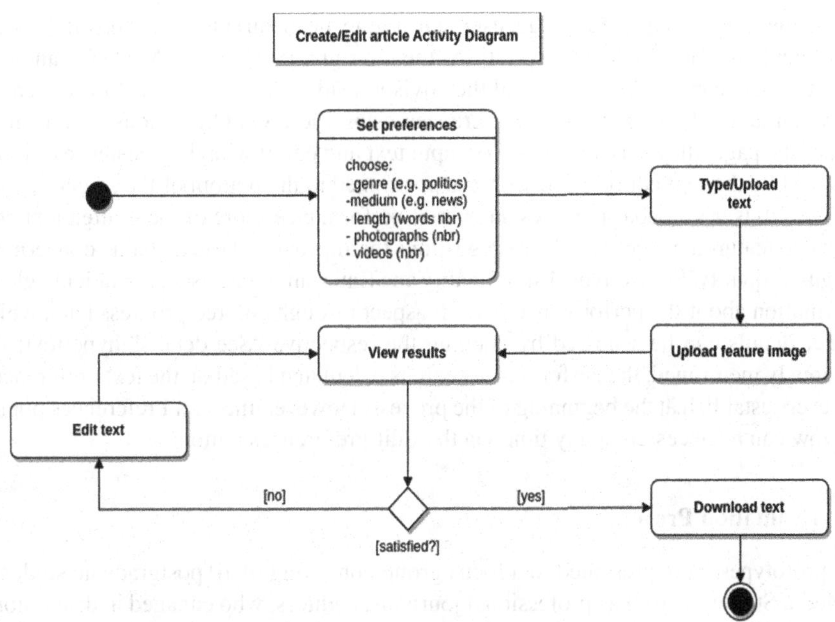

Fig. 2. Create/Edit text Activity Diagram

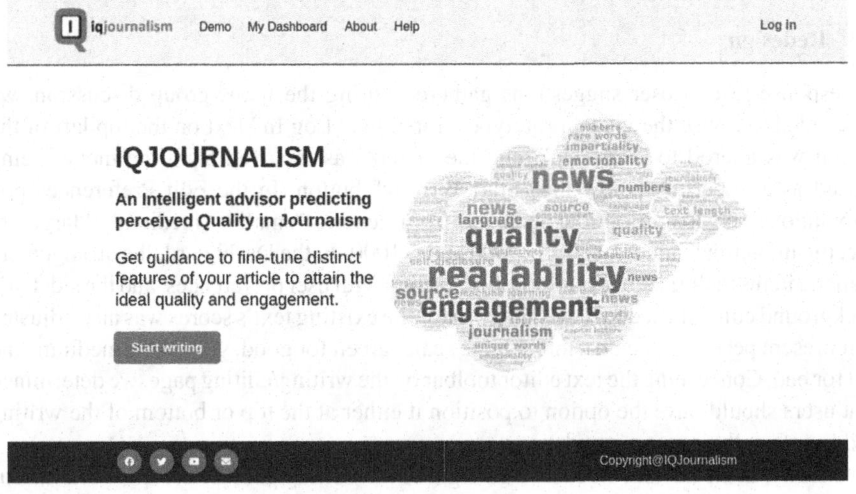

Fig. 3. IQ Journalism Home page

The dashboard for registered users is divided into two sections: on the left, users can manage folders containing text files, access their profile page, and obtain assistance, while through the graphical representations of texts situated in the main area of the page, they can opt to open existing texts or create new ones.

On the text writing/editing page, users can toggle the menu sidebar on and off through the Menu button located at the top left. At the top right, using the IQ Mode On and Off buttons, users can display or conceal the advisor's sidebar, respectively. Consequently, users can tailor the page to their preferences using these On/Off options. The central area of the page allows users to paste or input text and edit it with the assistance of tools provided by the text editor's bar, which is positioned at the bottom of the screen.

The advisor's sidebar provides an overall performance score of the written text and uploaded featured image, as well as suggestions for improving the text quality concerning Language quality, Subjectivity, Emotionality and Entertainment. Users can quickly glean information about the performance in each aspect through colored progress bars, while further details can be accessed by clicking the respective "See details" hypertext. As previously mentioned, the performance score is calculated based on the text preferences that users establish at the beginning of the process. However, the Text Preferences popup window can be accessed at any time via the Edit Preferences button.

4.3 Evaluation Process

The prototypes were presented to a focus group consisting of 10 postgraduate students in Media Studies as well as professional journalists/editors, who engaged in discussions about their preferences pertaining to the prototypes and the alterations they desired.

Their primary observations, delineated in Table 2, were predominantly shaped by their specific familiarity with analogous text editors and writing assistants.

4.4 Redesign

In response to end user suggestions gathered during the focus group discussion, we proceeded to revise the visual prototypes. First, the "Log In" text on the top left of the screen was altered to "Sign Up", and the Demo was removed from the menu, being placed as a hyperlink below the "Start Writing" button. In the Edit Preferences pop up window, text length options changed from generic "small", "medium", "large" to specific numerical values: <300, <1000 and >1000. In the Dashboard, the arrangement of menu items in the sidebar was modified to align with user preferences, and the sidebar's background color shifted to dark. The color of the existing text's scores was also adjusted to represent performance on a three-value scale: green for good, yellow for medium, and red for bad. Concerning the text editor toolbar on the writing/editing page, we determined that users should have the option to position it either at the top or bottom of the writing pad based on their recommendations.

Finally, in the advisor sidebar to the right of the writing pad, the colors of the various factors' progress bars will undergo further review in the upcoming evaluation phase of the working prototype.

Table 2. Focus group results.

Page	Issue	Preferences
Homepage	Header menu > Menu items	The order of the menu items should be: The Demo should be relocated from the menu to below the "Start Writing" button, and the My Dashboard, About, and Help items should remain in the menu
Dashboard	Background color of the left sidebar	The consensus among all participants was that they had a preference for the dark theme
Dashboard	Text's score	The participants indicated a preference for a color scheme (e.g., red-yellow-green) to represent the scores of the documents
Writing/editing page	IQ mode buttons	Most users expressed that the IQ mode ON/OFF option was beneficial, as it could accommodate the individual needs of each user
Writing/editing page	Text editing toolbar	Most participants indicated a preference for the text editing toolbar to be situated above the text pad

5 Discussion

An intelligent agent offering real-time suggestions for crafting high-quality journalistic texts that bolster audience engagement necessitates a precise, clean, and minimalistic design. The application's interface must be both comprehensive and intuitive.

In this paper, we discussed the methodology underlying the application's design, the analysis of user requirements, and the stages of designing, evaluating, and revising the visual prototypes. Adhering to the principles of user-centered and iterative design and incorporating the target end-users' input into the IQ Journalism interface, we ensured the development of an intuitive task workflow. Our objective is to establish a user-friendly and easy-to-navigate platform that allows users to customize it according to their specific authoring needs, ultimately generating quality content that captivates readers.

Acknowledgments. This research has been co-financed by the European Regional Development Fund of the European Union and Greek national funds through the Operational Program Competitiveness, Entrepreneurship and Innovation, under the call RESEARCH – CREATE – INNOVATE (project code: T2EDK-04616).

References

Batsell, J.: Engaged Journalism: Connecting with Digitally Empowered News Audiences. Columbia University Press, New York (2015)

Boylan, J.: The elements of journalism: what Newspeople should know and the public should expect. Columbia Journalism Rev. **39**(6), 70 (2001)

Broersma, M.: Audience engagement. In: Vos, T.P., Hanusch, F., Dimitrakopoulou, D., et al. (eds.) The International Encyclopedia of Journalism Studies. Wiley, Hoboken (2019)

Hansen, M., Roca-Sales, M., Keegan, J.M., King, G.: Artificial intelligence: practice and implications for journalism. Columbia Journalism School (2017). https://doi.org/10.7916/D8X92PRD

Hartson, R., Pyla, P.S.: The UX Book: Process and Guidelines for Ensuring a Quality User Experience. Elsevier, Amsterdam (2012)

Singer, J.: User-generated visibility: secondary gatekeeping in a shared media space. New Media Soc. **16**(1), 55–73 (2014)

Automatic Virtual Makeup System Using User-Preference Information

Hiroshi Takenouchi[1(✉)], Shion Isayama[1], and Masataka Tokumaru[2]

[1] Fukuoka Institute of Technology, Fukuoka 811-0295, Japan
h-takenouchi@fit.ac.jp
[2] Kansai University, Osaka 565-0842, Japan

Abstract. We present an automatic virtual makeup system with an interactive evolutionary computation (IEC) method using user preference information. While purchasing cosmetic items, users try each cosmetic item and check their appearance. Consequently, users feel burdened to try numerous cosmetic products before making a choice. To avoid this burden, some companies have developed virtual makeup applications for cosmetic displays using tablet devices. However, users who try numerous cosmetic items to choose from become confused and burdened with making the correct selection. Therefore, we propose an automatic virtual makeup system to generate users' favorite makeup patterns using their preferences. The system employs the IEC method to generate a user preferred makeup. The IEC method is a probability retrieval technique adopted to generate designs that satisfy user preference. Moreover, the proposed system contains direct manipulation operations for choosing a user's favorite makeup part design. We performed evaluation experiments to investigate the effectiveness of the proposed system from the viewpoints of the IEC with paired comparison applications. The subjects were female students in their twenties. From the results, we confirmed that the proposed system was useful from the viewpoint of applying the IEC method to a virtual makeup system.

Keywords: Virtual makeup · Interactive evolutionary computation · Paired comparison evaluation

1 Introduction

Artificial intelligence (AI) and information technology (IT)-based applications has been developed for applying cosmetics virtually, such as YouCam make. However, it is difficult for makeup beginners to apply each cosmetic and check the appearance and coordination because makeup combinations are numerous.

To solve the above, we employ an interactive evolutionary computation (IEC) method that generates user-preferred objects by an evolutionary computation (EC) technique dynamically based on user-preference information [1]. The IEC method has been employed for robot movement generation [2], face image generation [3], etc.

In this study, we propose an automatic makeup generation system using the IEC method. Users evaluate various makeup patterns presented by the proposed system based

C. Stephanidis et al. (Eds.): HCII 2023, CCIS 1836, pp. 523–529, 2023.
https://doi.org/10.1007/978-3-031-36004-6_71

on their preferences. When evaluating makeup patterns, users hard to decide with n-stage evaluation because the appearance difference of color or shape of makeup is slight. Therefore, we employ the winner-based paired comparison (WPC) method [4] to evaluate various makeup patterns. Users only evaluate the superiority and inferiority of two makeup patterns and easy to evaluate makeup patterns. The proposed system uses a general genetic algorithm (GA) as an EC method.

The proposed system manifests a direct manipulation operation in user evaluation for realizing makeup itself. Users can select their preferred makeup part while evaluating makeup patterns. After selecting the preferred makeup part, the proposed system always uses the selected makeup part design in all makeup patterns.

Some researchers have proposed automatic makeup systems using various techniques. For example, Park et al. [5] proposed an automatic makeup generation system based on the user personal color. This system extracted iris, hair, and skin colors as personal colors from a user's face image and applied makeup patterns, however, it does not use user-preference for makeup patterns. Our proposed system generates user-preference makeup patterns dynamically based on user-preference information.

We perform an evaluation experiment with real users and investigate the usefulness of the proposed system from the viewpoint of a real application. We consider three cases in purchasing cosmetics (for job hunting, going out, and casual) and measure satisfaction levels for generated makeup patterns and times spent on evaluating the generated makeup patterns.

2 Proposed System

2.1 Schematic of the Proposed System

Figure 1 shows a schematic of the proposed system. First, the proposed system generates initial gene candidates at random and creates makeup patterns corresponding to each candidate. Then, it presents two makeup patterns. The user chooses their favorite makeup pattern or decides whether he/she likes both makeups or dislikes both. After the makeup evaluation for each generation, users can fix their favorite cosmetic design part. Then, the proposed system performs the GA processing and generates new candidates. The user evaluates the generated candidates again. These processes are repeated until the user's favorite makeup pattern is generated.

2.2 Evaluation Method by WPC

Figure 2 shows a schematic of the evaluation of the WPC method. First, the system allocates one point for each created design. The number of evaluations is 3 (= n–1), when n is the number of candidates. Here, Makeup A beats Makeup B in the first round. Hence, the system adds the evaluation value of Makeup B to that of Makeup A. The evaluation value of Makeup A will now become 2 points. If Makeup A beats Makeup C in the second round, the system adds the evaluation value of Makeup C to that of Makeup A, which makes it 3 points. Assuming Makeup D beats Makeup A in the third round, the system then adds the evaluation value of Makeup A to that of Makeup D. Hence, the evaluation value score of Makeup D is 4 points. With these, the final evaluation values of Makeups, A, B, C, and D, are 3, 1, 1, and 4 points, respectively. Then, the system uses these evaluation values for GA operations.

The proposed system allows users to judge both makeup patterns as like and dislike. When judging both likes (dislikes), the lower (higher) evaluation value becomes the same as the higher (lower) evaluation value. If two makeups have the same evaluation values, both evaluation values are added (subtract) to one. For the next match, the proposed system changes either one to new makeup pattern.

2.3 Design Parts of Makeup

Figure 3 shows the design parts of makeup. We used seven makeup parts: foundation, eyebrow, eyeshadow, cheek, lip, mascara, and eyeliner. Each part has four to sixteen designs. The proposed system generated approximately two million ($\cong 2^{21}$) makeup patterns. We assigned a bit pattern to each design by considering the similarity between the design appearance of each part and gene rows.

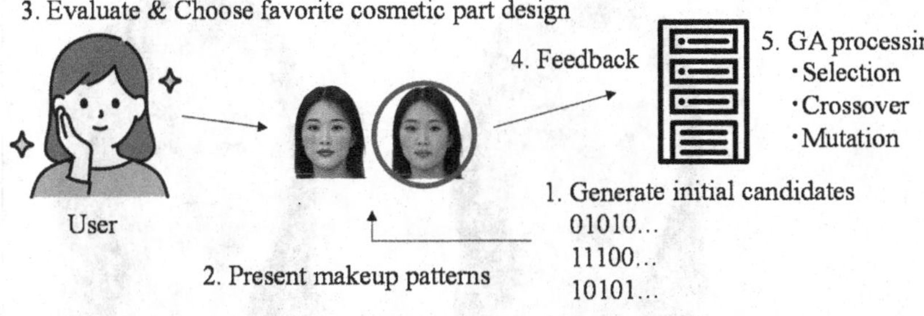

Fig. 1. Schematic of the proposed system[1]

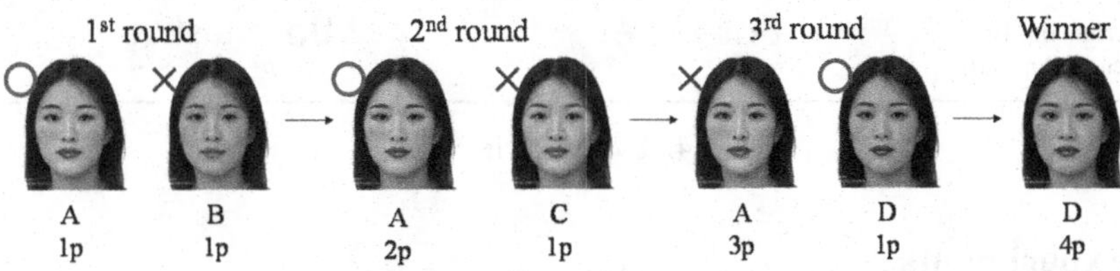

Fig. 2. Evaluation of the WPC method

2.4 Evaluation Interface

Figure 4 shows the evaluation interface. The user clicks the preferred makeup pattern image between two images. When the options are given as "likes" or "dislikes," the user clicks the "Both like!" or "Both dislike!" button. After finishing each evaluation, the proposed system moves to the next competition.

[1] The lady's face image generated by the generative adversarial network method is an imaginary. Nevertheless, we use the subject's face in the experiment.

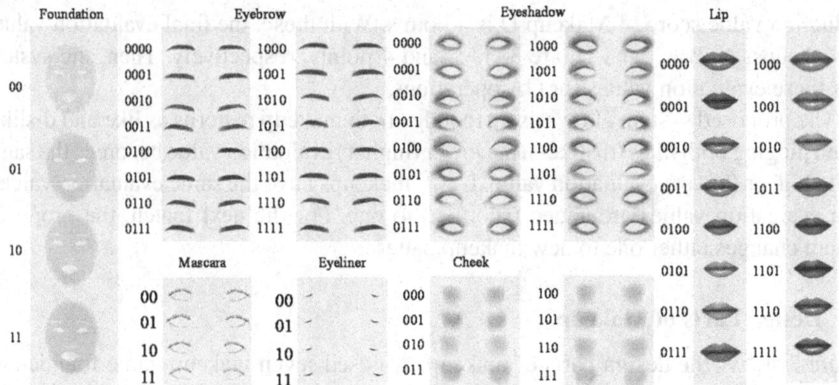

Fig. 3. Design parts of makeup

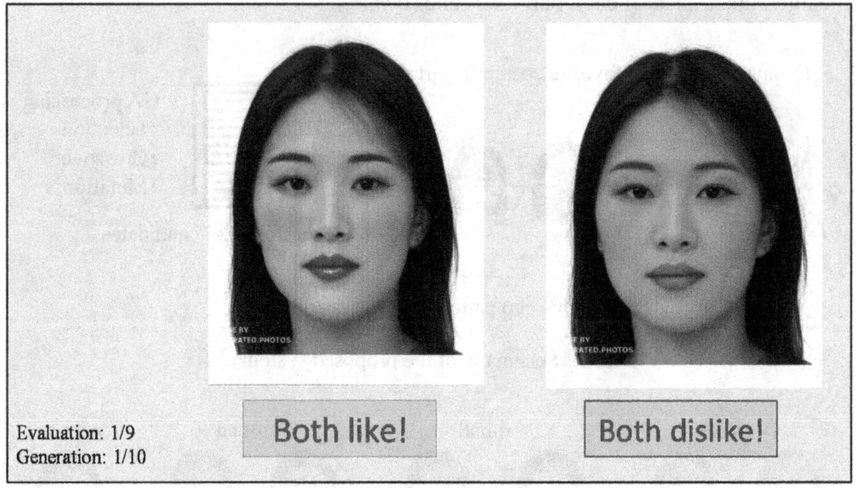

Fig. 4. Evaluation interface

3 Experiments

3.1 Outline of the Experiment

We performed evaluation experiments with real users to investigate the effectiveness of the proposed system. We employed six female university students in their twenties. Each subject used the proposed system and the compared system (without direct manipulation) for three patterns: to make herself up for job hunting, going out, and casual. The experiment was performed after the subjects had been adequately informed about the procedures and we obtained their informed consent.

Table 1 shows the experimental parameters. We set the GA parameters to common values. Each subject uses each system in each situation to finish the 10th generation (= 9 paired comparisons × 10 generations).

Table 1. Experimental parameters

Candidates	10	Selection	Roulette selection + Elite preservation
Gene length	21 bits	Crossover	Uniform crossover
Generations	10	Mutation rate	15%

3.2 Results

Table 2 shows the results of the direct manipulation frequency. Each subject used a direct manipulation operation at least once. We confirmed a similar tendency in other situations. Some subjects commented that the proposed system was better than the compared system because it can select their favorite cosmetic design. Therefore, the direct manipulation operation of the proposed system was useful for making up.

Figure 5 shows the results of the average satisfaction levels at the 1st and 10th generations and evaluation times spent from starting makeup evaluation to ending 10th generation evaluation. Notably, the evaluation times of the proposed system did not include the time of direct manipulation operation.

In all situations, the satisfaction levels of both systems in the 10th generation were higher than those in the 1st generation (initial makeups generated randomly). Therefore, the makeup patterns of both systems can evolve to match user preferences.

The evaluation times of the proposed system in all cases were longer than that of the compared system. This was because the proposed system allowed subjects to select their favorite cosmetic part design, and each subject spent time evaluating the presented makeup patterns carefully in the proposed system.

From the questionnaire results, all subjects answered that the proposed system was easier to evaluate makeup than the compared system. However, the proposed system may not reduce user evaluation loads. We will improve the proposed system in terms of reducing user evaluation loads.

Table 2. Direct manipulation frequency (Job hunting).

		Subject A							Subject B							Subject C							Subject D							Subject E							SubjectF						
		F	C	Eb	Es	L	M	El	F	C	Eb	Es	L	M	El	F	C	Eb	Es	L	M	El	F	C	Eb	Es	L	M	El	F	C	Eb	Es	L	M	El	F	C	Eb	Es	L	M	El
Generation	1																																										
	2																																										
	3																																										
	4																																										
	5																																										
	6																																										
	7																																										
	8																																										
	9																																										

*F: Foundation ,C: Cheek, Eb: Eyebrow ,Es: Eyeshadow ,L: Lip ,M: Mascara ,El: Eyeliner

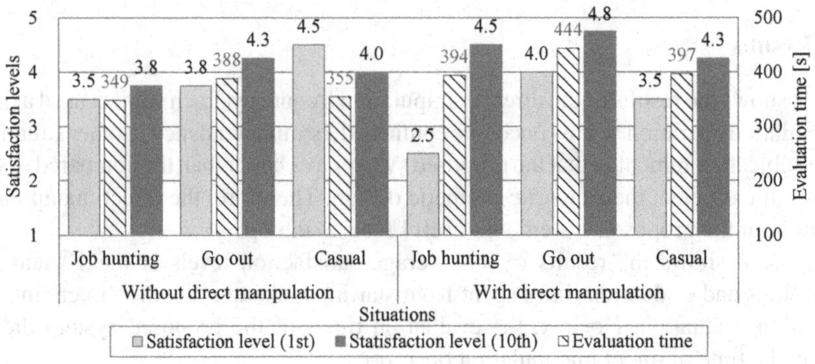

Fig. 5. Results of the satisfaction levels and evaluation times

4 Conclusion

We proposed an automatic makeup system with an IEC method based on user-preference information. Our experimental results showed that the direct manipulation operation of the proposed system was useful for makeup. Moreover, the proposed system can generate user preferred makeup in various cases. In the future, we will focus on the application of the proposed system for general people's use.

References

1. Takagi, H.: Interactive evolutionary computation: fusion of the capabilities of EC optimization and human evaluation. Proc. IEEE **89**(9), 1275–1296 (2001)
2. Liu, J., Ono, S., Zhu, B.: Three-dimensional robot motion design by combining inter-active and non-interactive evolutionary computation for an intelligent transformable phone robot: BaBi. In: Proceedings of 2021 IEEE Congress on Evolutionary Computation (CEC), pp. 1012–1019. IEEE, Poland (2021)
3. Zaltron, N., Zurlo, L., Risi, S.: CG-GAN: an interactive evolutionary GAN-based approach for facial composite generation. In: Proceedings of the Thirty-Fourth AAAI Conference on Arti-ficial Intelligence, pp. 2544–2551 (2020)

4. Takenouchi, H., Tokumaru, M.: Character design generation system using multiple users' gaze information. IEICE Trans. Inf. Syst. **E104-D**(9), 1459–1466 (2021)
5. Park, J., Kim, H., Ji, S., Hwang, E.: An automatic virtual makeup scheme based on personal color analysis. In: Proceedings of the 12th International Conference on Ubiquitous Information Management and Communication, pp. 1–7. Association for Computing Machinery, Malaysia (2018)

Method to Detect Movement in the Eyes Using Neural Networks. Peru Case

Eduardo Alfonso Torres Luna[1], Ana Maria Guerrero Millones[2], Moises David Reyes-Perez[3], Alberto Gomez Fuertes[2], and Jhoselit Lisset Facho-Cornejo[4](✉)

[1] Señor de Sipan University, Pimentel, Peru
[2] Cesar Vallejo University, Pimentel, Peru
[3] General Studies Academic Unit, Norbert Wiener University Private S.A, Lima, Peru
[4] San Martin de Porres University, Pimentel, Peru
jhoselitlfachocornejo@gmail.com

Abstract. The detection of eye movements is a promising technology for the management and control of devices, which offers innumerable possibilities to people with certain physical limitations. In today's society there is a gap that needs to be overcome and obstacles that need to be removed in favor of people with certain physical disabilities, in order to allow them to carry out activities in conditions of equality with others. There are many people with problems of paralysis in the upper and lower extremities which prevent them from being able to carry out their most basic activities by their own means, depending for this purpose on the help of third parties. The purpose of this research was to develop a method, which allowed the detection of eye movement, making use of artificial neural networks. This method consists of four stages, which are: Cataloging of the physical movements of the eyes; Image processing; neural network design and training; and finally the implementation of a prototype and performance measurement of the neural network. This research is considered very important in trying to achieve a method that is economical and efficient, the same that allows the detection of eye movements, which serve for further research that aims to guide mobile vehicles or control of devices with organs other than the extremities, to be more exact with the movement of the eyes, that is, through the gaze. An environment has been developed in PHP as a prototype or test environment, the evaluation of the performance of the neural network, as well as for obtaining the characteristic matrices of the dataset, which are taken from photographic images of the human eye, detecting the position of the iris, and according to this the movement will be determined. The training of the artificial neural networks was carried out in the Joone framework.

Keywords: Eye movement method · neural network · measurement of neural network performance · Image processing

C. Stephanidis et al. (Eds.): HCII 2023, CCIS 1836, pp. 530–537, 2023.
https://doi.org/10.1007/978-3-031-36004-6_72

1 Introduction

1.1 Problematic Reality

ONU (2021). In his publication presented on his web portal, which he titles; "Disability and health". Based in Geneva, Switzerland, the World Organization Health, mentions that more than 1,000 million people, which borders approximately 15% of the population worldwide, presents some type of of disability. And this number is increasing drastically due to demographic trends, also to the population and its aging and to the incidence of chronic diseases. There is a chance that some disability, whether temporary or permanent, is experienced by nearly everyone at some point in their life.

1.2 Literature Review

Development of a Method. It is defined as the path or via, in other words, the means used to achieve an objective or end. (Perez and Gardey 2008). A method is defined by other authors as a specific procedure that It is used to achieve consistent results in reaching an objective. Is a series of ordered and successive steps that lead to reaching a goal. Is an organized and systematic way to reach an objective, which can be applied in various areas of study. The method developed in the present work oriented in the detection ocular movement, basically consists of four phases or stages, which are:

First stage: Cataloging of images of the physical movements of the eyes to shape the dataset.

Second stage: Image processing to obtain the vector matrix of features.

Third stage: Design and Training of the artificial neural network.

Fourth stage: Implementation of the prototype and evaluation of the performance of the neural network.

Eye movements are movements that are made individually each eye. Through these movements it is possible to observe static objects or in motion. In the eyes there are two types of musculature; the muscles intrinsics which deal with the focus and variation in the diameter of the pupil, and the extrinsic muscles which allow movement of the globe ocular, these are controlled by three pairs of extraocular muscles; the what are the medial and lateral rectus muscles; the superior rectus muscles and lower; and the superior and inferior oblique muscles.

For the present study, the definition of the movements is considered conjugated binoculars in the same sense and direction, which are called versions, in these you can define nine positions of the gaze, such as: Primary position which is equivalent to the gaze in the center, supraversion the same thing that is equivalent to looking up, infraversion which is equivalent to looking down, levosupraversion this is equivalent to looking up and to the left, levoversion which is equivalent to looking to the left, levoinfraversion that is equivalent to the gaze down and to the left, dextroinfraversion the same as equivalent to the look down and to the right, dextroversion which is the look towards the right, dextrosupraversion as gaze up and to the right. (GMA Clinic 2012).

Five gaze positions are considered as a stimulus for the variable dependent, that is, the response of the neural network to movements that will be detected, which they are; Primary position, gaze in the center, supraversion, looking up, infraversion, looking down, levoversion, gaze to the left, dextroversion, gaze to the right.

Types of Eye Movements. There are three types of eye movements, although they are different, they are correlated. These are:

Fixation Movements. Which consist of keeping the eyes stable at one point. Barreña optics (2019), Spain, on its web portal mentions that; each jerk or jerk of the eye is preceded by an ocular fixation, the eyes remaining almost static for approximately 250 thousandths of a second. This is when the information is extracted. Eyes constantly need to go refixing the objects by performing these fixing movements.

Convergence Movements. They happen once the object has been fixed. These movements maintain focus, whether he is moving same object or the observer. They are coordinated movements of the eyes, where there is a simultaneous deviation of their axes towards the point of vision.

Saccadic Movements. They are jumping movements from one point to another.

Spain, on its web portal it publishes that they are quick movements that allow you to follow the line you want to read and allow each word to be focused in the area with greater vision on the retina.

Ocular Motility. It is a property, which allows the increase of the field effective visual, both monocular and binocular. Allows you to maintain focus of the image in the fovea and the alignment of the eyes, avoiding diplopia or vision double. It mentions (Martínez de Carneros) on its website. The motor system in ocular motility is responsible for carrying out the following actions.

Detection of Eye Movements Using Neural Networks. The Motion detection is performed by analyzing the matrix of motion characteristics. The images of the movements of the eyes, which previously classified and subjected to the training process, are processed by a fully connected artificial neural network of the multilayer perceptron type, the which detects the pattern of gaze position.

Artificial Intelligence. I quote definitions from different researchers.

Mention that artificial intelligence involves the study of mental abilities using computer models. Conceptualizes artificial intelligence as the study made to the calculations by which a computer can perceive, reason and Act.

Artificial Intelligence Models. At present, artificial intelligence It covers a wide space, among the models we can mention: To the analysis linear discriminant, decision trees, logistic regression, regression linear, Naive Bayes, k-nearest neighbors algorithm, learning vector quantization, the support of vector machines, the technique of Bagging and Random forest, fuzzy logic, artificial neural networks.

Types of Artificial Neural Networks.

Regarding their topology according to the pattern of connections, they can be:

Monolayer. They have a single layer, there are no cycles or feedback, all the signs go from the entrance to the exit. Among these there are the perceptron, Adaline.

Multilayer. It has several layers, there are no cycles or feedback.

All signs have a direction from the entrance to the exit. He multilayer perceptron.

Recurrent. At least presents a closed cycle of activation neural (feedback). Boltzman, Elman, Hopfield machine.

Regarding their learning, they can basically be:

Supervised Learning. Requires a set of samples of solution patterns for your training.

Unsupervised or Self-organized Learning. Does not require a sample set of solution patterns for your training.

Multilayer Perceptron. This manages to evolve from the simple perceptron incorporating layers with hidden neurons, thanks to which it manages to process nonlinear functions. In the multilayer perceptron the output of a neuron is the entrance of the following, this has an architecture made up of a input layer which receives data from outside the network, an input layer output which is the one that emits the results, and one or more hidden layers in which which the weighting and activation functions are executed.

Two phases can be seen in the multilayer perceptron:

Propagation: Phase where the results of the output of the network are calculated following an order from the input values forward.

Learning: Phase in which the errors that are obtained at the output of the network.

are propagated backwards (backpropagation), through this process achieves the modification of the weights of the connections with the purpose from, that by means of the error gradient function, the estimated value of the network is getting closer and closer to the real.

Confusion Matrix. Also called error matrix, it is a tool which is used to visualize the performance of a learning algorithm supervised type, applied in machine learning in the field of artificial intelligence.

Objectives. Carry out the development of a method to detect movement in the eyes using neural networks.

Catalog images of the physical movements of the eyes for the conformation of the dataset.

Carry out the image treatment process to obtain the array of feature vectors.

Carry out the design and training process of the neural network.

Implement a prototype to measure network performance neural.

2 Method

The present project is inclined to make use of the type of research Applied according to its purpose, according to its design it is Experimental, in terms of its approach is Quantitative, with respect to its scope it is exploratory and according to your data source it is Field Research. Regarding the research design, it is Quasi-experimental, within the experimental design. Quasi-experimental design is often investigates with duly formed experimental and control groups, and the subjects are not randomly assigned to one or the other group. (Cook and Campbell 1986), mention that quasi-experiments should be considered as an alternative to experiments, when these they do not have random assignment.

The sample is 385 captures of images of said movements, the The confidence level is 95% and the margin of error is 5%.

For the first specific objective: "Catalog images of the physical movements of the eyes for the conformation of the dataset".

For the second specific objective: "Carry out the treatment process of images to obtain the matrix of feature vectors".

Observation was also applied for the collection of the vectors of dataset characteristics obtained from the "generate dataset" module of the prototype.

For the third specific objective: "Carry out the design and process of neural network training. The observation guide was applied neural network training.

For the fourth specific objective: "Implement a prototype to measure the performance of the neural network. The observation guide was used results of the classification of eye movements detected by the prototype application based on the sample.

The sample is made up of 385 photos of eye movement taken from a person under a controlled environment. The images are distributed in 77 by each kind of eye movement. The number of transaction types of the eye are 5.

This instrument allowed collecting the results of the detection of eye movement to subsequently apply the measures statistics such as the Kappa index and the confusion matrix. Screening Results Summary Observation Guidance Applied movement of the eyes depending on the sample. Also the observation guide of calculation operations of the Matrix accuracy, precision, sensitivity, and specificity metrics of confusion for each class.

3 Results

It has been possible to develop a method that allows detecting the eye movements using artificial neural networks. Said method, through expert judgment, was qualified as ADEQUATE unanimously.

It has been possible to satisfactorily catalog the images of the movements of the eyes, which was essential to determine the neural network architecture. The cataloging of movements physical data of the eyes also allowed the conformation of the dataset for the training of said network, as well as for the execution of the itself in the process of detecting eye movement. Bliss cataloging covers five basic movements defined as position primary which is equivalent to looking straight ahead, superversion which is equivalent to looking up, infraversion which is equivalent to the gaze down, levoversion equivalent to gaze to the left, and dextroversion which is equivalent to looking to the right. With this definition, the direction of the basic movements is achieved with the that a device should have.

It has been satisfactorily achieved to carry out the process of image processing, which is necessary to obtain the matrix of feature vectors, the same thing that is vital for training and execution of the neural network. Image processing consists of six processes which are: Image capture, resizing, scale grayscale, histogram equalization, color inversion, and binarization. These processes were applied in an orderly manner to an image of true color of eye movement, each process produces a transformation in the image successively until it becomes in a 200-digit binary array, with values of 0 for the pixels black and 1 for white pixels. It is important to mention that for the image histogram equalization process, the values of the parameter that modifies the brightness were different for the training of neural networks, as for the execution of the same; being the values of 210 for training and 160 for execution in the case of the first neural network; And 210 for the training and 174 for the execution in the case of the second neural network. The setting of the parameters that modify the brightness for the execution of the networks, allowed perform better on the movement classification task ocular.

The design of the neural network has been achieved, as well as its training process satisfactorily. Neural network used is of the multilayer perceptron type and the activation function is sigmoid. It was concluded that there is no clear rule that allows to design the architecture of a neural network in a way preset. However, the convergence of the networks was reached neuronal factors in a short time, modifying on the basis of tests, the factors of its architecture, as well as modifying in the same way, the training hyper-parameters. The first neural network for detection of eye movements consists of an input layer made up of 200 neurons, which is equivalent to the number of pixels represented by their binary values that have the image of the eye movement; it also has two hidden layers of 25 and 14 neurons; and finally an output layer of 5 neurons, each of which represents each of the eye movement classifications. The second neural network for eye movement detection It consists of an input layer also made up of 200 neurons, which which is equivalent to the number of pixels represented by its binary values that the image has; this second neural network counts with a hidden layer of 70 neurons; and finally also a layer of output of 5 neurons, each of which also represents each one of the classifications of eye movement. For the training of For the neural network, a computer with an Intel Core i3 processor of 2.3GHz. And 4Gb of RAM, it was not necessary to do without hardware 107 specialized for processes with a high computational load.

It has been successfully implemented in the Php language, a prototype to measure the performance of neural networks. This prototype It consists of 3 modules which allow generating the dataset, executing a simulation and process sampling. The main part or core of the prototype is made up of matrices of synaptic weights, as well as matrices of the bias values, in addition to the summation processes weighted and sigmoid activation functions. In the module that allows you to run the simulation, there are two repositories of images of eye movements, a repository that houses the 385 images that make up the sample, and another repository containing other images made up of 35 photographs of eyes of different colors belonging to to various people of different sexes and ages, these images serve to run the simulation of eye movement detection. He prototype is a web application and can be accessed using from any web browser by accessing the following url address: https://visiondirection.sistemasdegestion.site/ According to the metrics used, in the first neural network and based on to the sample, an accuracy, precision, sensitivity and specificity were achieved 100%. The first neural network was also made a measurement of its performance using the Kappa index, in which a coefficient of 1, which ranks it with a strength of agreement Almost perfect. Then, according to these results, it was observed that the Neural network performance is almost perfect when subjected to the detection of eye movements of the same person as provided the eye movement images for the network training. On the other hand in the second neural network which was trained with a dataset made up of 175 photographs of the eyes of different colors belonging to different people of different sexes, traits and ages, was obtained based on the sample and according to the metrics used, an accuracy of 99.38%, precision of 98.55%, 98% sensitivity and 99.61% specificity. Regarding the coefficient 108 The kappa index obtained for the second neural network was 0.98. It can be concluded that using the method developed in the present investigation it is feasible to satisfactorily build a network artificial neural to achieve eye movement detection (Fig. 1).

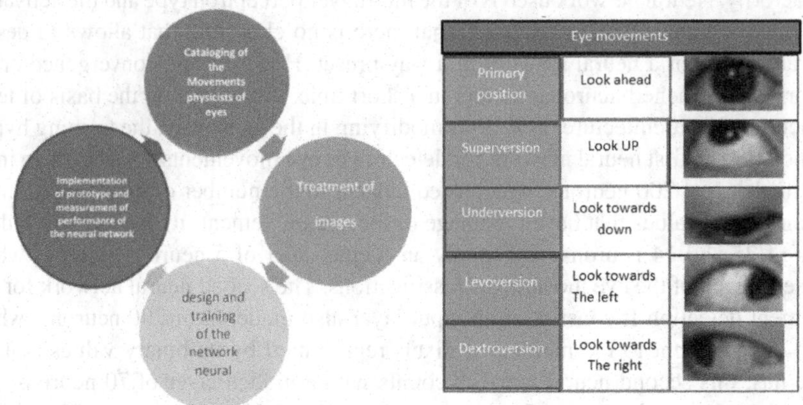

Fig. 1. Stages of the method developed to detect eye movement Source: Self Made

4 Conclusions

An environment has been developed in PHP as a prototype or development environment. Tests, the evaluation of the performance of the neural network, as well as to obtain the matrices of characteristics of the dataset, which are taken from photographic images of the human eye, detecting the position of the iris, and according to this the movement will be determined. He training of artificial neural networks was carried out in the framework Joone.

The second step of the developed method is to treat the image until decompose it to its binary values, which make up the feature vector matrix. The treatment of the images of the ocular movement to be able to obtain the matrix of characteristics, was carried out by means of a application created in PHP and was carried out by performing the following processes from a true color image of the right eye of a person.

The artificial neural network used to detect the movement of eyes, is of the Multilayer Perceptron type, which is made up of multiple layers, the same thing that manages to solve problems that they are not linearly separable, which the perceptron cannot do simple.

Training a neural network involves adjusting the weights of each one of the neurons that integrate it, that is to say, an attempt is made to assign to the neurons the weights that offer the best results, this with the purpose of, that the output layer provides responses as as close as possible to the desired answer.

References

Optical barrier: The importance of eye movements (2019). Recovered from: https://xn--opticabarrea-khb.es/la-importancia-los-movimientosoculares/

GMA Clinic: Versions and Ductions (2012). Accessed https://www.clinicagma.com/blog/versiones-y-ducciones/

Cook and Campbell: Quasi-experimental and longitudinal designs (1986). Accessed http://diposit.ub.edu/dspace/bitstream/2445/30783/1/D.%20cuasi%20y%20longitudinales.pdf

De Carneros, M.: ocular motility (2020). Recovered from: https://www.martinezdecarneros.com/motilidad-ocular/

Perez, J., Gardey, A.: Method definition (2008). Accessed https://definicion.de/metodo/

Torwards Trustworthy Machine Learning based systems: Evaluating breast cancer predictions interpretability using Human Centered Machine Learning and UX Techniques

Jonathan Ugalde[1,2](✉), Eduardo Godoy[1,2], Diego Mellado[2,3,4], Eduardo Cavieres[2,3], Bastian Carvajal[3], Carlos Fernández[3], Pamela Illescas[5,6], Rodrigo H. Avaria[7], Claudia Díaz[3,8], Rodrigo Ferreira[8], Marvin Querales[9], Scarlett Lever[3], Julio Sotelo[2,3], Steren Chabert[2,3], and Rodrigo Salas[2,3]

[1] Escuela de Ingeniería Informática, Universidad de Valparaíso, Valparaíso, Chile
jonathan.ugalde@postgrado.uv.cl

[2] Millennium Institute for Intelligent Healthcare Engineering (iHealth), Santiago, Chile

[3] Escuela de Ingeniería C. Biomédica, Universidad de Valparaíso, Valparaíso, Chile

[4] Doctorado en Ciencias e Ingeniería para la Salud, Facultad de Medicina, Universidad de Valparaíso, Valparaíso, Chile

[5] Doctorado en Ciencias mención Biofísica y Biología Computacional, Facultad de Ciencias, Universidad de Valparaíso, Valparaíso, Chile

[6] Centro Interdisciplinario de Neurociencia de Universidad de Valparaíso, Universidad de Valparaíso, Valparaíso, Chile

[7] Doctorado en Estadística, Instituto de Estadística, Facultad de Ciencias, Universidad de Valparaíso, Valparaíso, Chile

[8] Centro Metropolitano de Imagenología Mamaria (CMIM), Servicio de Salud Metropolitano Sur (SSMS), San Miguel, Chile

[9] Escuela de Tecnología Médica, Facultad de Medicina, Universidad de Valparaíso, Viña del Mar, Chile

Abstract. Although the use of Machine Learning techniques has been widely used in the literature in order to predict breast cancer. The focus of these works has been to improve the performance of classification algorithms for greater diagnostic accuracy. However, for these classification models to be used in a real environment, such as a cancer diagnosis assistance system in an oncology institution, in addition to high performance, models must also offer predictions that are easy to understand by radiologists who make the final diagnosis. In this work, we evaluate the level of trust from users in an AI-based system for breast cancer identification. This system uses computer vision and Deep Learning (DL) techniques to classify breast mammography and identify abnormalities associated with lumps or cancer tumors. The evaluation performed in this work focuses on the interpretability of the system and the explanations that are shown to users. To evaluate the interpretability of the model's predictions, AI-based

C. Stephanidis et al. (Eds.): HCII 2023, CCIS 1836, pp. 538–545, 2023.
https://doi.org/10.1007/978-3-031-36004-6_73

systems evaluation techniques from the Human-Centered Machine Learning (HCML) field were used, as well as classic usability and user experience (UX) techniques.

The results obtained show that users' trust is related to the presentation of the explanations, that is, to how the system UI displays the predictions and shows the zones of the images used to calculate the predictions. In this sense, it was also possible to observe that the classic techniques of usability and UX have a relationship with the level of trust perceived by the users, which was measured with HCML evaluation techniques.

Keywords: Trusworthy · Human-Centered Machine Learning · User Experience

1 Introduction

Currently, mammography is the best examination for detecting breast cancer preventively [12,15]. However, the accuracy of the diagnosis can be affected by the experience of the radiologist. According to some studies [6], the average error rate in radiological interpretations can reach 30%, which is mainly due to inherent limitations in human perception. Biopsy, which is the method used to reduce errors (false positives and false negatives), is an invasive and painful procedure for the patient [19], as well as being costly for the institution that performs it. Additionally, only between 15% and 30% of biopsies are malignant [20], generating a large number of unnecessary procedures that cost time and resources and can be uncomfortable for patients. To address this problem, techniques are being developed to assist the clinical professional in their diagnosis [8,11,21], and in recent years, advances in Machine Learning (ML) have enabled the development of AI technologies. In this regard, several studies based on Deep Learning (DL) applied to mammography have shown very promising results [5,9,11,16,21]. These technologies not only show performance similar to that of humans but can also increase productivity and efficiency in detection by radiologists.

In this study, the level of trust perceived by users of an Artificial Intelligence (AI)-based tool is analyzed. This tool is an AI-based platform for providing automatic diagnostic assistance for breast cancer through mammography analysis, combined with a module for prioritizing potentially positive cases for evaluation by radiologists to reduce diagnosis time. To do so, we will use a Human-Centered Machine Learning (HCML) approach, supported by user experience (UX) techniques, to analyze the interpretability and perceived confidence of system users. The aim is to assess the usefulness of employing UX techniques in the AI model development cycle under the HCML approach.

The rise of machine learning and artificial intelligence has brought about a new era of product design, where the focus is not only on accuracy but also on user satisfaction [7,8,13,18]. Human-centered machine learning and user experience (UX) testing are two important approaches in this new paradigm that aim to create tools and products that are intuitive, effective, and satisfying for users

[7,14]. HCML is an approach to machine learning that is centered on human needs, behaviors, and preferences. This approach involves collecting and analyzing data about users, their contexts, and their goals in order to design machine learning models that are accurate and trustworthy [13]. It is a human-centered approach that aims to make machine-learning models more accessible and usable for non-expert users.

HCML is gaining popularity due to the concerns raised by influential technology firms and research labs about the human context [7]. A workshop in conjunction with the Conference on Human Factors in Computing Systems in 2016 [4] explained that HCML should explicitly recognize the human aspect when developing ML models, re-frame machine learning workflows based on situated human working practices and explore the co-adaptation of humans and systems. In this sense, HCML can be considered as the User Experience (UX) of AI [3].

UX testing, on the other hand, is a process of evaluating how users interact with a product or system in order to identify usability issues, areas for improvement, and opportunities for innovation. UX can be used in HCML approach as an instance for evaluating the results and trustworthiness of an AI-based system, using final user perceptions about predictions made by an AI model [13]. In this sense, the relationship between human-centered machine learning and UX testing is one of mutual support, with each approach informing and enhancing the other. By incorporating user feedback into the design and development process, human-centered machine learning can create models that are not only accurate but also trustworthy.

2 Methods

In order to evaluate the level of trust perceived by users of the selected AI-based system, the user experience evaluation stage of the software development process was adapted to collect data on users' perception of the underlying Deep Learning model predictions interpretability and trustworthiness of the system.

The approach used for conducting user experience tests was an adaptation of the cognitive walkthrough approach. Cognitive walkthroughs derive from cognitive analyses and are named as such because the specialist conducting the session navigates through a predetermined task scenario as a typical user would [2]. However, in order to evaluate system usability, tests will be conducted with inexperienced end users. In this way, the aim is to verify the confidence that the use of the system and the underlying artificial intelligence can inspire users.

Regarding to UX classic techniques, usability is an information system quality attribute that assesses how comfortable user interfaces are [1]. This attribute is guided by five basic quality attributes [10]: Learnability, Efficiency, Memorability, Errors, and Subjective satisfaction. Learnability refers to the ease with which users can learn the essential functions and features of a system. It is a measure of how quickly users can learn to use the system effectively without any prior experience. Efficiency is a measure of how quickly a user can complete tasks or transactions using a system once they become familiar with it.

It is essential to mention that the unit of time selected for calculating usability metrics is minute. In this sense, both Learnability and Efficiency metric will be calculated as the number of minutes required to learn a task and tasks performed per minute, respectively, as shown in Table 1.

Table 1. User Experience Metrics

Attribute	Definition	Metric
Learnability	Rate of Minutes required to perform a task by an inexpert user (M_{in}) and an expert user (M_{ex})	$L = \frac{M_{in}}{M_{ex}}$
Efficiency	Number of task performed in a minute by an user	$E = \frac{totaltasks}{totalminutes}$
Errors	Number of errors in a task execution	$Errors$

Memorability is a measure of how easy it is for a user to remember how to use a system after a prolonged period without using it. This attribute is not evaluated because the tool analyzed is being launched in its first version during the performed UX test. The Errors attribute is related to the number of errors made by the user while performing a specific task.

And Subjective satisfaction is associated with user perception of system usability aspects. In order to assess the user perception regarding different usability characteristics of the system, at the end of the tests, the user will be asked to answer a brief survey based on an adaptation of a questionnaire called User Experience Questionnaire (UEQ-S), proposed in [17]. This survey has a long and a short version. Due to the time limitation of testing users, the short version of this questionnaire will be used, which consists of 8 perception questions, each answered on a 7-point Likert scale. Each question allows users to provide their perception about a usability attribute of the evaluated system, which represents important feedback for future improvements. In addition to 3 questions of UEQ-S that could be used to measure trustworthiness, a question to collect user perception about AI model predictions of trustworthiness was added. The UEQ-S adaptation with its nine questions is shown in Table 2.

3 Results

The adapted usability tests were performed by four users (2 radiologists and two medical Technologists), each executing five different tasks in the system. Selected users consist of medical staff from an oncological institution in Santiago, Chile. Usability tests were conducted to evaluate the performance of an analyzed system. To ensure a controlled and distraction-free environment for the users, one of the researchers visited a medical institution to prepare the experimental setup. The experiment was conducted using a computer with an internet connection and a private office within the institution's premises. User testing was conducted over five days, from March 13th to March 17th, 2023. One test was executed each day

Table 2. User Experience Questionnaire (UEQ-S) Adaptation

	Likert Scale 1 2 3 4 5 6 7	
UX Perception		
inefficient	O O O O O O O	efficient
boring	O O O O O O O	exiting
not interesting	O O O O O O O	interesting
conventional	O O O O O O O	inventive
usual	O O O O O O O	leading edge
Trustworthiness Perception		
obstructive	O O O O O O O	supportive
complicated	O O O O O O O	easy
clear	O O O O O O O	confusing
Uncertain	O O O O O O O	Trustworthy

to minimize the risk of fatigue or loss of concentration among the participants. Table 3 shows the average metrics values by the user and global metrics mean values.

Table 3. User UX-HCML Test Results

Metric	User 1	User 2	User 3	User 4	Mean
Learnability	0.92	0.78	0.84	0.83	0.84
Efficiency	23.14	1.207	0.777	0.907	6.51
Error	0.00	0.00	0.00	0.00	0.00

The results obtained indicate that the system has good usability indicators. Regarding Learnability, it achieved a global average of 0.84, indicating that new users of the system can learn and perform tasks with some ease, with a quick learning curve. On the other hand, while the Efficiency indicator has good values, they are very disparate for each task, mainly because the tasks were unbalanced in terms of complexity. It is also important to mention that users are experts in the underlying logic of the system, so they are familiar with the technical language used in the system and can follow instructions intuitively. This explains why the Error metric obtained a score of 0 and why the values of Learnability and Efficiency also had good results.

As shown in Table 4, the system was generally well evaluated by the users, both in terms of usability and the trustworthiness of the predictions made. The responses related to UX perceptions obtained an overall score of 4.69, and particularly positive responses were obtained for UX Perceptions. However, it is

Table 4. UEQ-S Adaptation results

Metric	User 1	User 2	User 3	User 4	mean
UX Perception					6.05
Efficient	5	3	5	5	4.50
Exiting	6	6	7	7	6.50
Interesting	7	6	7	7	6.75
Inventive	6	6	7	6	6.25
Leading	6	6	7	6	6.25
Trustworthiness Perception					4.69
Supportive	5	4	5	5	4.75
Easy	6	5	7	6	6.00
Clear	3	3	7	4	4.25
Trustworthy	3	3	4	5	3.75

observed that the questions related to Trustworthiness Perceptions present a clear difference compared to the responses of UX Perceptions, with a difference of 1.36 points on the Likert scale. These results indicate that although the system design is user-friendly or easy to use, this does not guarantee that the user will trust the predictions offered, potentially perceiving the system as less reliable. Nevertheless, this difference is not alarming given that both aspects evaluated show an evaluation above user indifference (value 3 on the 7-point Likert scale).

4 Conclusions

For AI-based systems, this type of end-user evaluation helps researchers and practitioners diagnose the level of trust perceived by users regarding their AI models. With respect to the experiments conducted in this research, it can be concluded that classical usability tests serve as a valuable tool for obtaining feedback from users of AI-based systems, both in terms of their interpretability and trustworthiness. The difference found in the values of UX perceptions and trustworthiness perceptions raises questions for future work, especially in investigating the factors that influence users' perception of the interpretability and trustworthiness of predictions made by an AI-based system. In addition, this type of experiment also opens up avenues for evaluating other dimensions of trustworthiness, such as fairness, to evaluate whether there is any relationship between the usability of the system and the fairness perceived by users.

Acknowledgments. This research was partially founded by the Chilean ANID FONDEF 20i10332 Project and ANID-Millennium Science Initiative Program ICN2021-004. Also, J. Ugalde was partially funded by the Escuela de Ingeniería Informática, Universidad de Valparaíso, Chile, through grant No. 101.016/2020.

References

1. Usability heuristics for user interface design. https://www.nngroup.com/articles/ten-usability-heuristics/. Accessed 27 Feb 2023
2. Hom, J.: http://www.sidar.org/recur/desdi/traduc/es/visitable/Herramientas.htm (1996). Accessed 27 Feb 2023
3. Lovejoy, J.: Google. https://design.google/library/ux-ai/ (2018). Accessed 27 Feb 2023
4. CHI 2016: Proceedings of the 2016 CHI Conference on Human Factors in Computing Systems. Association for Computing Machinery, New York, NY, USA (2016)
5. Allugunti, V.R.: Breast cancer detection based on thermographic images using machine learning and deep learning algorithms. Int. J. Eng. Comput. Sci. **4**(1), 49–56 (2022)
6. Berlin, L.: Radiologic errors and malpractice: a blurry distinction. Am. J. Roentgenol. **189**(3), 517–522 (2007)
7. Bond, R.R., et al.: Human centered artificial intelligence: weaving UX into algorithmic decision making. In: RoCHI, pp. 2–9 (2019)
8. Chen, H., Gomez, C., Huang, C.M., Unberath, M.: Explainable medical imaging AI needs human-centered design: guidelines and evidence from a systematic review. npj Digital Medicine **5**(1), 156 (2022)
9. Godoy, E., et al.: A named entity recognition framework using transformers to identify relevant clinical findings from mammographic radiological reports. In: 18th International Symposium on Medical Information Processing and Analysis, vol. 12567, pp. 286–295. SPIE (2023)
10. Grau, X.F.: Principios básicos de usabilidad para ingenieros software. In: JISBD, pp. 39–46 (2000)
11. Hamed, G., Marey, M.A.E.-R., Amin, S.E.-S., Tolba, M.F.: Deep learning in breast cancer detection and classification. In: Hassanien, A.-E., Azar, A.T., Gaber, T., Oliva, D., Tolba, F.M. (eds.) AICV 2020. AISC, vol. 1153, pp. 322–333. Springer, Cham (2020). https://doi.org/10.1007/978-3-030-44289-7_30
12. Humphrey, L.L., Helfand, M., Chan, B.K., Woolf, S.H.: Breast cancer screening: a summary of the evidence for the us preventive services task force. Ann. Internal Med. **137**(5_Part_1), 347–360 (2002)
13. Kaluarachchi, T., Reis, A., Nanayakkara, S.: A review of recent deep learning approaches in human-centered machine learning. Sensors **21**(7) (2021). https://doi.org/10.3390/s21072514, https://www.mdpi.com/1424-8220/21/7/2514
14. Lindvall, M., Molin, J., Löwgren, J.: From machine learning to machine teaching: the importance of UX. Interactions **25**(6), 52–57 (2018)
15. Luo, C., et al.: Advances in breast cancer screening modalities and status of global screening programs. Chronic Dis. Transl. Med. **8**(02), 112–123 (2022)
16. Rautela, K., Kumar, D., Kumar, V.: A systematic review on breast cancer detection using deep learning techniques. Arch. Comput. Methods Eng. **29**(7), 4599–4629 (2022)
17. Schrepp, M., Hinderks, A., Thomaschewski, J.: Design and evaluation of a short version of the user experience questionnaire (UEQ-S). Int. J. Interact. Multimedia Artif. Intell. **4**(6), 103–108 (2017)
18. Shin, D.: User perceptions of algorithmic decisions in the personalized AI system: perceptual evaluation of fairness, accountability, transparency, and explainability. J. Broadcasting Electron. Media **64**(4), 541–565 (2020). https://doi.org/10.1080/08838151.2020.1843357

19. Szynglarewicz, B., Matkowski, R., Kasprzak, P., Forgacz, J., Zolnierek, A., Halon, A., Kornafel, J.: Pain experienced by patients during minimal-invasive ultrasound-guided breast biopsy: vacuum-assisted vs core-needle procedure. Eur. J. Surgical Oncol. (EJSO) **37**(5), 398–403 (2011). https://doi.org/10.1016/j.ejso.2011.02.002, https://www.sciencedirect.com/science/article/pii/S0748798311000618
20. Uchida, S., Fernández, G., T, M., Durán, M., Gálvez, T.: Characterization of lesions associated with microcalcifcations bi-rads 4a over a 11-year period of stereotactic breast biopsies. Revista Chilena de Radiologia **18**, 30–35 (2012)
21. Ueda, D., Yamamoto, A., Onoda, N., Takashima, T., Noda, S., Kashiwagi, S., Morisaki, T., Fukumoto, S., Shiba, M., Morimura, M., et al.: Development and validation of a deep learning model for detection of breast cancers in mammography from multi-institutional datasets. PLOS ONE **17**(3), e0265751 (2022)

Humanoid Robot as a Debate Partner

Hae Seon Yun[1(✉)], Heiko Hübert[2], Abdullah Sardogan[2], Niels Pinkwart[1], Verena V. Hafner[1], and Rebecca Lazarides[3]

[1] Department of Computer Science, Humboldt University of Berlin, Berlin, Germany
yunhaese@informatik.hu-berlin.de, pinkwart@hu-berlin.de, hafner@inforamatik.hu-berlin.de

[2] HTW Berlin - University of Applied Sciences, Berlin, Germany
heiko.huebert@htw-berlin.de, abdullah.sardogan@student.htw-berlin.de

[3] University of Potsam, Potsdam, Germany
rebecca.lazarides@uni-potsdam.de

Abstract. In this paper, we describe our design and development process of a humanoid robot, Pepper, as a debate partner by integrating open-source, offline Generative Pre-trained Transformer models, namely GPT-J 6B and BLOOM. We used our tool flow, which integrates open-source offline tools to animate a robotic agent to listen, speak and gesture in a human-like manner, to create a debate partner in a humanoid robot. This paper provides a technical description of the integration of GPT models into our tool flow. The first implementation was presented to a group of teachers and as a second prototype, several questioning schemes and post filtering were implemented to attain better responses from a robotic agents. The developed second prototype will be used for a pilot study with prospective users.

Keywords: GPT-J · Robotic Learning Companion · Pepper

1 Introduction

Upon the introduction of Generative Pre-trained Transformer (GPT), ethical concerns of plagiarism and endorsed cheating have been surfaced, especially in education [1]. Despite these concerns, GPT can help fill knowledge and experience gaps. For example, GPT can provide synonyms and paraphrased sentences similar to an editing service for a publication. As such, the use of GPT can add a value to an educational practice in the area of critical thinking which requires reflection and discussion. In a school setting, students are encouraged to gather information and express their opinions on the topics of political and social issues. However, as debate encompasses different sources of information and the discussion of information from different perspectives, it can be daunting for students who have not been introduced to it or given sufficient opportunity to practice it. A teacher at a vocational school in Germany suggested using GPT to introduce a robot as a debate partner, as students struggle with debating, especially those who need to make a tremendous commitment to acquiring advanced language skills. As a research shows that, a pedagogical agent can provide a safe net for

C. Stephanidis et al. (Eds.): HCII 2023, CCIS 1836, pp. 546–552, 2023.
https://doi.org/10.1007/978-3-031-36004-6_74

learners to try out their ideas without giving them the impression of being judged or evaluated [2], a robot with GPT can act as a debate partner for students to practice in debating.

2 Background

2.1 Debate to Facilitate Critical Thinking Skill

Debate involves an argument through the discussion of opposing views which develops critical thinking skills and through debate, students retain information better as they are challenged with conflicting ideas and engaged in a verbal discussion with others [3]. Debating involves more than just expressing one's ideas; it involves gathering information, assessing the credibility of the gathered information, checking for logical consistency, eliminating assumptions, choosing effective ways of communicating and listening attentively to the opposition, including gauging the non-verbal communication [3]. In [4], experiences and examples of teaching critical thinking through debating are delineated and the importance of the auditory shield where people can experiment with expressing their opinions without fear of being judged by others, is emphasized in order to promote their critical thinking skills.

2.2 Large Language Model, GPT

GPT models are designed to produce text including translation and Q & A among all, Chat GPT has been the center of the spotlight in year 2023. ChatGPT is trained with enormous data from Common Crawl [5] using Large Language Model (LLM) and its benefits and controversy in usage in an academic context are fervently discussed. GPT can assist researchers in producing well-written, structured academic papers, which could relieve the burden of linguistic revision and effort that many would otherwise have to devote. In addition to LLM bringing the publication editing service closer to researchers, for statistical analysis, LLM can also narrow the gap between statistics guru and the novice. In the same way that the internet reduces the knowledge gap between academically and socially privileged and non-privileged people, LLM can also reduce the knowledge gap. Unlike ChatGPT which is a commercial product, open-source GPT models such as GPT-J 6B and BLOOM offer more flexibility for integration, e.g. with respect to data privacy and setting up self-hosted, offline GPT services. These models are trained on the large-scaled data set to generate texts on a prompt [6]. Both BLOOM and GPT-J 6B have configuration parameters that can be modified. In this study, we have adopted the BLOOM model (bloom-7b1) to implement a robot as a debate partner.

2.3 Social Robot as a Debate Partner

The presence of pedagogical agents shows a promising effect on the learning experience in addition to motivation and social skills [2,7,8]. When pedagogical agents are physical robots rather than a screen-based avatar interacting with learners, the benefits the pedagogical agents on learning are enhanced [9–12].

Studies on the attribution of robot appearance to roles claim that a humanoid robot is suitable as a teacher or an instructor, whereas a non-humanoid robot is suitable as a learning companion and a peer [13]. However, regardless of the type of a robot used to design a partner, the benefits of having a physical being for a user to speak out their mind is prominent [14]. Therefore, in our study, we use a humanoid robot, Pepper to design a debate partner.

3 Method

In our previous work [15,16], we introduced a tool flow that integrates open-source offline tools to animate a robotic agent to speak and gesture similarly to humans. Following this work and observing some standards to ensure the sustainability of the tool in user scenarios and the data privacy of the users, we adopted open source GPT models to implement a robotic debate partner. We examined two GPT models (GPT-J 6B and BLOOM) for their usage as a debate partner and selected the BLOOM model to implement the first robotic debate parnter. We used several questioning schemes to elicit better responses from a robotic agent such as using Q&A, keywords or phrase patterns. We also developed a post-filtering approach to derive more accurate responses. For users to interact verbally with the robotic agent and ask questions, we integrated VOSK, an offline speech to text system.

3.1 Questioning Scheme

Initially, we have used Q and A format to inquire response from the GPT models. For example, "Q: What are the benefits of wearing school uniforms? A:". The robotic debate partner with Q& A questioning scheme was presented to a group of teachers at the vocational school in Germany in January 2023. As the output response include opinions, personal story and narratives, responses were not deemed always suitable as debate reasoning. To acquire the response that corresponds to debate context, the opinion statement with follow-up filling word was inserted to the GPT model. In our case, "OPINION STATEMENT" + "BECAUSE" was entered to the GPT model (e.g., "Living in the city is better than living in the countryside because") as shown in the Fig. 1). Compared to the first Q and A approach, "OPINION STATEMENT" + "BECAUSE" generated more debate appropriate reasoning. Yet, many times, unexpected responses were presented, which included various personal anecdotes and advertisement. Therefore, we have proceeded in implementing post processing and filtering of the GPT responses.

3.2 Post-filtering

Within a few seconds, the robotic debate partner replied to the debate topic, yet responses contained some non-constructive, subjective statements. Therefore, we

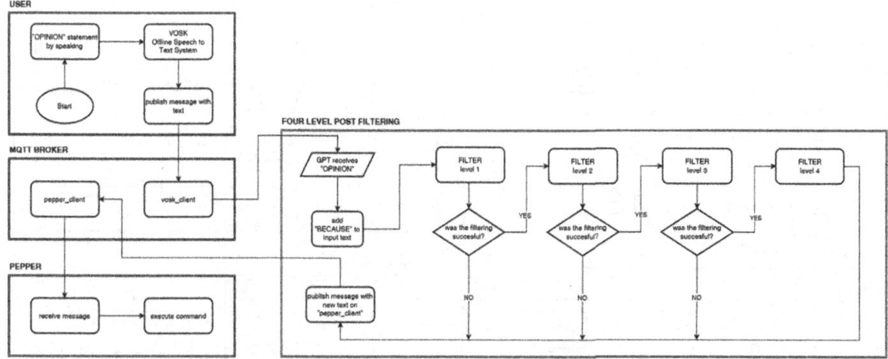

Fig. 1. User's Opinion Statement inserted as "OPINION" + "BECAUSE" into GPT model and the statement filters through 4 level post filtering to generate better debate reasoning response

have created stages of post-filtering including validation check, forbidden word groups check and four level iterative questioning to extract relevant responses as shown in Fig. 2.

First in our validation check, we utilized the python library, Enchant [1], to filter out responses that were not in English dictionary. We then created the forbidden words group to filter out subjective opinions. In particular, the forbidden words group includes personal pronouns such as 'i ', 'our ', 'we ', 'me ', 'my ', and 'myself ', as most factual and objective publications do not contain personal pronouns. Secondly, we noticed that the advertisement of certain websites were promoted using the phrase "for further". Therefore, this phrase was also added to the group of prohibited words.

Four-level filtering was implemented including validation, error handling and iterative questioning. When an opinion sentence was entered (first input), "BECAUSE" was appended to the end of the sentence and fed to the GPT model. The GPT model generates output sentences that complete the first input sentence with "because". These sentences are then run through the validation test. If it passes the validation test successfully, the output sentence (OUTPUT 1) is appended with "SUCH AS" and inserted back to the GPT model. If the validation fails, the error handling process takes over and publishes the message such as "Please rephrase your opinion". Through error handling and iterative questioning process, the previous output sentence is inserted as an input with the filling word and the corresponding responses are spoken out by a robotic debate partner.

[1] http://pyenchant.github.io/pyenchant/.

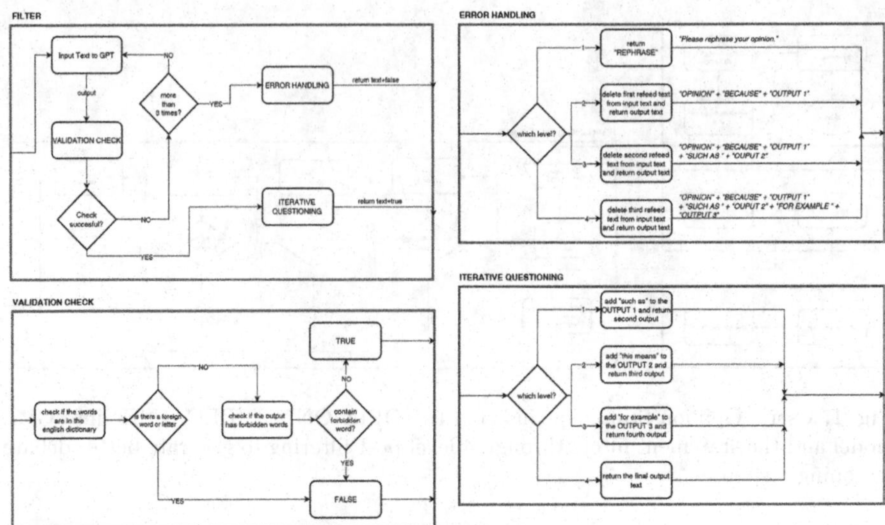

Fig. 2. Each filter includes validation check, error handling and iterative questioning

4 Result

One of the debate questions from [3] (e.g. Is the future of shopping malls threatened by e-commerce?) was transposed to a statement and spoken to our robotic debate partner to retrieve reasoning response. GPT receives the opinion sentences as, "The future of shopping malls is threatened by e-commerce" appended with "because" and go through the post filtering process as follows:

```
process query: The future of shopping malls is threatened by
e-commerce because
 finished in 3.957 secs
Answer:
The future of shopping malls is threatened by e-commerce because
consumers can buy things they want within a few hours
of putting an order. And because they have this
type of instant gratification,
Attempt number:  1
START VALIDATION CHECK
START CHECKING SPELLING
START CHECKING FORBIDDEN WORDS
START PROCESSING TEXT
LEVEL  1
ADDING  SUCH AS
START FILTERING
LEVEL  2
process query: The future of shopping malls is threatened by
e-commerce  because consumers can buy things they want within
a few hours of putting an order such as
```

```
finished in 2.829 secs
Answer:
The future of shopping malls is threatened by e-commerce because
consumers can buy things they want within a few hours of putting
an order such as clothes, perfumes, makeup and cosmetics and others.
People are able to
```

After going through the four level post filtering which includes error handling and iterative questioning, the final response that the robotic debate partner speaks out was as follows:

```
The future of shopping malls is threatened by e-commerce because
consumers can buy things they want within a few hours of putting
an order such as clothes, perfumes, makeup and cosmetics and others.
This means that they could be more inclined to buy from online shops.
For example, in 2008 about 70 percent of the sales in department
stores in America were online.
```

We reviewed the appropriateness of the responses by inserting the same input 10 times. The answers varied yet all answers were neutral with valid reasons which may fit in a debate context. For a robotic debate partner to retrieve the response, maximum of 25 s with 10 iterations were needed and each input took average 2.32 s (min: 0.74 s, max: 3.48 s).

To enhance the human robot interaction, we added greetings, introduction phrases, feedback in the design of a robotic debate partner.

5 Discussion and Outlook

In this work, we have implemented a humanoid robot, Pepper, as a debate partner. Our motivation for creating a humanoid robot as a debate partner is to support a human debate partner to have a safe environment to practice in forming an argument and also to listen to the argument of the counterpart. To achieve this, we have utilized open source, offline tools in conjunction with the open source GPT model. Using GPT out of the box produced unexpected results, so we developed post-filtering schemes so that the a robotic debate partner could present appropriate reasons for the argument. In our follow-up study, we will introduce the robotic debate partner and conduct a pilot study to design an appropriate debate scenario between a human and a robotic debate partner.

Acknowlegements. This project was primarily funded by the Deutsche Forschungsgemeinschaft (DFG, German Research Foundation) under Germany's Excellence Strategy - EXC 2002/1 "Science of Intelligence" - project number 390523135

References

1. Sharples, M.: Automated essay writing: an AIED opinion. Int. J. Artif. Intell. Educ. **32**(4), 1119–1126 (2022)
2. Johnson, W.L., Rickel, J.W., Lester, J.C., et al.: Animated pedagogical agents: face-to-face interaction in interactive learning environments. Int. J. Artif. Intell. Educ. **11**(1), 47–78 (2000)
3. Roy, A., Macchiette, B.: Debating the issues: a tool for augmenting critical thinking skills of marketing students. J. Mark. Educ. **27**(3), 264–276 (2005)
4. Mitchell, G.R.: Debating with robots: IBM project debater and the advent of augmentive automated argumentation (2020)
5. Wikipedia, "Gpt-3." Accessed 27 Feb 2023
6. Wang, B., Komatsuzaki, A.: GPT-J-6B: a 6 billion parameter autoregressive language model, May 2021. https://github.com/kingoflolz/mesh-transformer-jax
7. Johnson, W.L., Lester, J.C.: Pedagogical agents: back to the future. AI Mag. **39**(2), 33–44 (2018)
8. Kim, Y., Baylor, A.L.: based design of pedagogical agent roles: a review, progress, and recommendations. Int. J. Artif. Intell. Educ. **26**, 160–169 (2016)
9. Van den Berghe, R., Petersen, H., Hellendoorn, A., van Keulen, H.: Programming a robot or an avatar: a study on learning outcomes, motivation, and cooperation. In: Companion of the 2020 ACM/IEEE International Conference on Human-Robot Interaction, pp. 496–498 (2020)
10. Leyzberg, D., Spaulding, S., Toneva, M., Scassellati, B.: The physical presence of a robot tutor increases cognitive learning gains. In: Proceedings of the Annual Meeting of the Cognitive Science Society, vol. 34, no. 34 (2012)
11. Robins, B., Dautenhahn, K., Boekhorst, R.T., Billard, A.: Robotic assistants in therapy and education of children with autism: can a small humanoid robot help encourage social interaction skills? Univ. Access Inf. Soc. **4**, 105–120 (2005)
12. Tapus, A., Tapus, C., Mataric, M.: The role of physical embodiment of a therapist robot for individuals with cognitive impairments. In: RO-MAN 2009-The 18th IEEE International Symposium on Robot and Human Interactive Communication, pp. 103–107. IEEE (2009)
13. Hegel, F., Lohse, M., Wrede, B.: Effects of visual appearance on the attribution of applications in social robotics. In: RO-MAN 2009-The 18th IEEE International Symposium on Robot and Human Interactive Communication, pp. 64–71. IEEE (2009)
14. Robots can help improve mental wellbeing at work - as long as they look right. https://www.cam.ac.uk/research/news/robots-can-help-improve-mental-wellbeing-at-work-as-long-as-they-look-right. Accessed 17 Mar 2023
15. Yun, H.S., et al.: AI-based open-source gesture retargeting to a humanoid teaching robot. In: International Conference on Artificial Intelligence in Education, pp. 276–279. Springer (2022)
16. Hübert, H., Taliaronak, V., Yun, H.: AI based gesture and speech recognition tool flow for educators. In: ICERI2022 Proceedings, pp. 6395–6400. IATED (2022)

Author Index

C. Stephanidis et al. (Eds.): HCII 2023, CCIS 1836, pp. 553–556, 2023.
https://doi.org/10.1007/978-3-031-36004-6